Russia
a country study

Federal Research Division
Library of Congress
Edited by
Glenn E. Curtis
Research Completed
July 1996

On the cover: "The Bronze Horseman," statue of Peter the Great in St. Petersburg, symbol of Russian autocracy and subject of a fantasy short story by Aleksandr Pushkin

First Edition, First Printing, 1998.

Library of Congress Cataloging-in-Publication Data

Russia: a country study / Federal Research Division, Library of Congress ; edited by Glenn E. Curtis.—1st ed.

p. cm. — (Area handbook series, ISSN 1057–5294) (DA Pam ; 550–115)

"Research completed July 1996."

Includes bibliographical references (pp. 621–665) and index.

ISBN 0–8444-0866–2 (hc : alk. paper)

1. Russia (Federation). I. Curtis, Glenn E. (Glenn Eldon), 1946– . II. Library of Congress. Federal Research Division. III. Series. IV. Series: DA Pam ; 550–115.

DK510.23.R883 1997   97–7563
947.086–dc21   CIP

Headquarters, Department of the Army
DA Pam 550–115

For sale by the Superintendent of Documents, U.S. Government Printing Office
Washington, D.C. 20402

Dedicated to the memory of Ray Zickel, with deep appreciation for his painstaking work on *Soviet Union: A Country Study,* the predecessor to the current volume.

Foreword

This volume is one in a continuing series of books prepared by the Federal Research Division of the Library of Congress under the Country Studies/Area Handbook Program sponsored by the Department of the Army. The last two pages of this book list the other published studies.

Most books in the series deal with a particular foreign country, describing and analyzing its political, economic, social, and national security systems and institutions, and examining the interrelationships of those systems and the ways they are shaped by historical and cultural factors. Each study is written by a multidisciplinary team of social scientists. The authors seek to provide a basic understanding of the observed society, striving for a dynamic rather than a static portrayal. Particular attention is devoted to the people who make up the society, their origins, dominant beliefs and values, their common interests and the issues on which they are divided, the nature and extent of their involvement with national institutions, and their attitudes toward each other and toward their social system and political order.

The books represent the analysis of the authors and should not be construed as an expression of an official United States government position, policy, or decision. The authors have sought to adhere to accepted standards of scholarly objectivity. Corrections, additions, and suggestions for changes from readers will be welcomed for use in future editions.

Robert L. Worden
Acting Chief
Federal Research Division
Library of Congress
Washington, DC 20540–4840
E-mail frds@loc.gov

Acknowledgments

The authors are indebted to numerous individuals and organizations who gave their time, research materials, and expertise on affairs in the Russian Federation to provide data, perspective, and material support for this volume. Thanks go to Raymond Zickel, who organized the early stages of the book's preparation, including the selection of chapter authors, and who contributed the lacquer-box chapter illustrations. The research process was supported by the work of Joseph Rowe and David Osborne, who identified numerous valuable sources. The publications office of the Organisation for Economic Co-operation and Development in Washington, D.C., and Charles Yost of the International Trade Commission also contributed useful material. Ray Brandon lent invaluable research, editorial, and writing assistance as intern to the book editor.

Thanks also go to Ralph K. Benesch, former monitor of the Country Studies/Area Handbook Program for the Department of the Army, under whose guidance the plan for the six volumes on the post-Soviet states was formulated. In addition, the authors appreciate the advice and guidance of Sandra W. Meditz, Federal Research Division coordinator of the handbook series. Special thanks go to Marilyn L. Majeska, who supervised editing; to Andrea T. Merrill, who performed the final prepublication editorial review and managed production; to Wayne Horne, who designed the book cover and the title page illustrations for the ten chapters; and to David P. Cabitto, who provided graphics support and, together with the firm of Maryland Mapping and Graphics, prepared the maps and charts. Vincent Ercolano and Janet Willen edited the chapters, and Helen Fedor was responsible for assembling and organizing the book's photographs. The numerous individuals who contributed photographs are acknowledged by name in the photograph captions.

The contributions of the following individuals are gratefully acknowledged as well: Barbara Edgerton and Izella Watson, who did the word processing and initial typesetting; Janie L. Gilchrist and Stephen C. Cranton, who prepared the camera-ready copy; and Joan C. Cook, who prepared the Index.

Contents

List of Figures

Preface

At the end of 1991, the formal dissolution of the Soviet Union was the surprisingly swift result of decrepitude within that empire. The Russian Federation was one of the fifteen "new" nations that emerged from that process; in this form, Russians retained much of the domination over nearby minority groups that they had exercised in the days of the Russian Empire and the Soviet Union. But the major changes that have occurred since 1991 fully justify the new subseries of Country Studies describing all fifteen of the former Soviet republics in their past and present circumstances. The present volume is the fifth in the six-volume series, which is the successor to the one-volume *Soviet Union: A Country Study*, published in 1991.

The marked relaxation of Soviet-era information restrictions, which began in Russia in the late 1980s and accelerated after 1991, allows the presentation of reliable, complete information on most aspects of life in the Russian Federation—including many of the negative aspects such as corruption, environmental degradation, and deterioration of the military that were reported only incompletely in earlier volumes. Scholarly articles and periodical reports have been especially helpful in accounting for the years of independence in the 1990s and in evaluating the earlier times that form the backdrop for the most recent period. The authors have described the historical, political, economic, and social background of Russia as the context for their current portraits. In each case, the author's goal was to provide a compact, accessible, and objective treatment of five main topics: historical background, the society and its environment, the economy, government and politics, and national security. Military insignia, a standard feature of the Country Studies series, have not been included in this volume because, at the time of preparation, the Ministry of Defense of the Russian Federation was in the process of changing insignia, and budget shortages delayed its publication of a comprehensive chart. Brief comments on some of the more useful, readily accessible sources used in preparing this volume appear at the end of each chapter. Full references to these and other sources used by the authors are listed in the Bibliography.

In most cases, personal names have been transliterated from Russian according to the system approved by the United States

Board on Geographic Names (BGN). In the case of widely known individuals whose names appear frequently in Latin alphabets, such as Joseph V. Stalin and Boris N. Yeltsin, the widely used conventional form of the name has been chosen. Geographical names are treated in the same way: places such as Moscow and St. Petersburg and geographical names such as Siberia and Lake Baikal are rendered in conventional form, but all other geographical names appear in the transliteration of the BGN system. Some Soviet-era place-names such as the cities of Gor'kiy and Sverdlovsk have been changed in the 1990s (to Nizhniy Novgorod and Yekaterinburg, respectively, in the case of these two examples), and the newest forms are used in this book.

Organizations commonly known by their acronyms (such as IMF—the International Monetary Fund, and KGB—the Committee for State Security) are introduced in full form, supplemented with the vernacular form where appropriate. Autonomous republics such as the Republic of Chechnya are introduced in full form in the detailed description of those regions in Chapter 4, but short forms (in the case of this example, Chechnya) are used elsewhere.

Measurements are given in the metric system; a conversion table is provided in the Appendix. The Chronology at the beginning of the book lists major historical events in Russia from the founding of Kievan Rus' to the significant events of the first nine months of 1997. To amplify points in the chapters, tables in the Appendix provide statistics on the environment, the population, economic conditions, political events, and the military establishment.

The body of the text reflects information available as of July 31, 1996. Certain other portions of the text, however, have been updated. The Introduction and Chronology include events and trends that have occurred since the completion of research, the Country Profile includes updated information as available, the Bibliography lists recently published sources thought to be particularly helpful to the reader, and Table 23 includes newly available statistics.

Table A. Chronology of Important Events

Period	Description
NINTH CENTURY	
ca. 860	Rurik, a Varangian, according to earliest chronicle of Kievan Rus', rules Novgorod and founds Rurik Dynasty.
ca. 880	Prince Oleg, a Varangian, first historically verified ruler of Kievan Rus'.
TENTH CENTURY	
911	Prince Oleg, after attacking Constantinople, concludes treaty with Byzantine Empire favorable to Kievan Rus'.
944	Prince Igor' compelled by Constantinople to sign treaty adverse to Kievan Rus'.
ca. 955	Princess Olga, while regent of Kievan Rus', converts to Christianity.
971	Prince Svyatoslav makes peace with Byzantine Empire.
988	Prince Vladimir converts Kievan Rus' to Christianity.
ELEVENTH CENTURY	
1015	Prince Vladimir's death leads Rurik princes into fratricidal war that continues until 1036.
1019	Prince Yaroslav (the Wise) of Novgorod assumes throne of Kievan Rus'.
1036	Prince Yaroslav the Wise ends fratricidal war and later codifies laws of Kievan Rus' into *Rus'ka pravda* (Justice of Rus').
1037	Prince Yaroslav defeats Pechenegs; construction begins on St. Sofia Cathedral in Kiev.
1051	Ilarion becomes first native metropolitan of Orthodox Church in Kievan Rus'.
TWELFTH CENTURY	
1113–25	Kievan Rus' experiences revival under Grand Prince Vladimir Monomakh.
1136	Republic of Novgorod gains independence from Kievan Rus'.
1147	Moscow first mentioned in chronicles.
1156	Novgorod acquires its own archbishop.
1169	Armies of Prince Andrey Bogolyubskiy of Vladimir-Suzdal' sack Kiev; Andrey assumes title "Grand Prince of Kiev and all Rus'" but chooses to reside in Suzdal'.
THIRTEENTH CENTURY	
1219–41	Mongols invade: Kiev falls in 1240; Novgorod and Moscow submit to Mongol "yoke" without resisting.
1242	Aleksandr Nevskiy successfully defends Novgorod against attack by Teutenic Knights.
1253	Prince Daniil (Danylo) of Galicia-Volhynia accepts crown of Kievan Rus' from pope.
FOURTEENTH CENTURY	
1327	Ivan I, prince of Moscow, nicknamed Ivan Kalita ("Money Bags"), affirmed as "Grand Prince of Vladimir" by Mongols; Moscow becomes seat of metropolitan of Russian Orthodox Church.

Table A. (Continued) Chronology of Important Events

Period	Description
1380	Dmitriy Donskoy defeats Golden Horde at Battle of Kulikovo, but Mongol domination continues until 1480.
FIFTEENTH CENTURY	
1462	Ivan III (the Great) becomes grand prince of Muscovy and first Muscovite ruler to use titles of tsar and "Ruler of all Rus'."
1478	Muscovy defeats Novgorod.
1485	Muscovy conquers Tver'.
SIXTEENTH CENTURY	
1505	Vasiliy III becomes grand prince of Muscovy.
1510	Muscovy conquers Pskov.
1533	Grand Prince Ivan IV named ruler of Muscovy at age three.
1547	Ivan IV (the Terrible) crowned tsar of Muscovy.
1552	Ivan IV conquers Kazan' Khanate.
1556	Ivan IV conquers Astrakhan' Khanate.
1565	*Oprichnina* of Ivan IV creates a state within the state.
1571	Tatars raid Moscow.
1581	Yermak begins conquest of Siberia.
1584	Fedor I crowned tsar.
1589	Patriarchate of Moscow established.
1596	Union of Brest establishes Uniate Church.
1598	Rurik Dynasty ends with death of Fedor; Boris Godunov named tsar; Time of Troubles begins.
SEVENTEENTH CENTURY	
1601	Three years of famine begin.
1605	Fedor II crowned tsar; first False Dmitriy subsequently named tsar after Fedor II's murder.
1606	Vasiliy Shuyskiy named tsar.
1610	Second False Dmitriy proclaimed tsar.
1610–13	Poles occupy Moscow.
1611–12	Forces from northern cities and Cossacks organize counterattack against Poles.
1613	Mikhail Romanov crowned tsar, founding Romanov Dynasty.
1631	Metropolitan Mogila (Mohyla) founds academy in Kiev.
1645	Aleksey crowned tsar.
1648	Ukrainian Cossacks, led by Bogdan Khmel'nitskiy (Bohdan Khmel'nyts'kyy), revolt against Polish landowners and gentry.
1649	Serfdom fully established by law.
1654	Treaty of Pereyaslavl' places Ukraine under tsarist rule.
1667	Church council in Moscow anathemizes Old Belief but removes Patriarch Nikon; Treaty of Andrusovo ends war with Poland.
1670–71	Stenka Razin leads revolt.
1676	Fedor III crowned tsar.

Table A. (Continued) Chronology of Important Events

Period	Description
1682	Half brothers Ivan V and Peter I named co-tsars; Peter's half sister, Sofia, becomes regent.
1689	Peter I (the Great) forces Sofia to resign regency; Treaty of Nerchinsk ends period of conflict with China.
1696	Ivan V dies, leaving Peter the Great sole tsar; port of Azov captured from Ottoman Empire.
EIGHTEENTH CENTURY	
1700	Calendar reformed; war with Sweden begins.
1703	St. Petersburg founded; becomes capital of Russia in 1713.
1705–11	Bashkirs revolt.
1708	First Russian newspaper published.
1709	Swedes defeated at Battle of Poltava.
1710	Cyrillic alphabet reformed.
1721	Treaty of Nystad ends Great Northern War with Sweden and establishes Russian presence on Baltic Sea; Peter the Great proclaims Muscovy the Russian Empire; Holy Synod replaces patriarchate.
1722	Table of Ranks established.
1723–32	Russia gains control of southern shore of Caspian Sea.
1725	Catherine I crowned empress of Russia.
1727	Peter II crowned emperor of Russia.
1730	Anna crowned empress of Russia.
1740	Ivan VI crowned emperor of Russia.
1741	Elizabeth crowned empress of Russia.
1762	Peter III crowned emperor of Russia; abolishes compulsory state service for the gentry; Catherine II (the Great) crowned empress of Russia after Peter III's assassination.
1768–74	War with Ottoman Empire ends with Treaty of Kuchuk-Kainarji.
1772	Russia participates in first partition of Poland.
1773–74	Emel'yan Pugachev leads peasant revolt.
1785	Catherine II confirms nobility's privileges in Charter to the Nobility.
1787–92	War with Ottoman Empire ends with Treaty of Jassy; Ottomans recognize 1783 Russian annexation of Crimea.
1792	Government initiates Pale of Settlement, restricting Jews to western part of the empire.
1793 and 1795	Russia participates in second and third partitions of Poland.
1796	Paul crowned emperor of Russia; establishes new law of succession.
NINETEENTH CENTURY	
1801	Alexander I crowned emperor; conquest of Caucasus region begins.
1809	Finland annexed from Sweden and awarded autonomous status.
1812	Napoleon's army occupies Moscow but is then driven out of Russia.

Table A. (Continued) Chronology of Important Events

Period	Description
1817–19	Baltic peasants liberated from serfdom but given no land.
1825	Decembrist Revolt fails; Nicholas I crowned emperor.
1831	Polish uprising crushed by forces of Nicholas I.
1833	"Autocracy, Orthodoxy, and nationality" accepted as guiding principles by regime.
1837	First Russian railroad, from St. Petersburg to Tsarskoye Selo, opens; Aleksandr Pushkin, foremost Russian writer, dies in duel.
1840s and 1850s	Slavophiles debate Westernizers over Russia's future.
1849	Russia helps to put down anti-Habsburg Hungarian rebellion at Austria's request.
1853–56	Russia fights Britain, France, Sardinia, and Ottoman Empire in Crimean War; Russia forced to accept peace settlement dictated by its opponents.
1855	Alexander II crowned emperor.
1858	Treaty of Aigun signed with China; northern bank of Amur River ceded to Russia.
1860	Treaty of Beijing signed with China; Ussuri River region awarded to Russia.
1861	Alexander II emancipates serfs.
1863	Polish rebellion unsuccessful.
1864	Judicial system reformed; *zemstva* created.
1866	*Crime and Punishment* by Fedor Dostoyevskiy (1821–81) published.
1869	*War and Peace* by Lev Tolstoy (1828–1910) published.
1873–74	Army reformed; Russian radicals go "to the people."
1875	Kuril Islands yielded to Japan in exchange for southern Sakhalin Island.
1877–78	War with Ottoman Empire ends with Treaty of San Stefano; independent Bulgaria proclaimed; Russia forced to accept less advantageous terms of Congress of Berlin.
1879	Revolutionary society Land and Liberty splits; People's Will and Black Repartition formed.
1879–80	*The Brothers Karamazov* by Fedor Dostoyevskiy published.
1881	Alexander II assassinated; Alexander III crowned emperor.
1894	Nicholas II crowned emperor.
1898	Russian Social Democratic Labor Party established and holds first congress in March; Vladimir I. Lenin one of organizers of party.
TWENTIETH CENTURY	
1903	Russian Social Democratic Labor Party splits into Bolshevik and Menshevik factions.
1904–05	Russo-Japanese War ends with Russian defeat; southern Sakhalin Island ceded to Japan.
1905	Bloody Sunday massacre in January begins Revolution of 1905, a year of labor and ethnic unrest; government issues so-called October Manifesto, calling for parliamentary elections.

Table A. (Continued) Chronology of Important Events

Period		Description
1906		First Duma (parliament) elected.
1911		Petr Stolypin, prime minister since 1906, assassinated.
1914		World War I begins.
1916		Rasputin murdered.
1917	March	February Revolution, in which workers riot in Petrograd; Petrograd Soviet of Workers' and Soldiers' Deputies formed; Provisional Government formed; Emperor Nicholas II abdicates; Petrograd Soviet issues Order Number One.
	April	Demonstrations lead to Aleksandr Kerenskiy's assuming leadership in government; Lenin returns to Petrograd from Switzerland.
	July	Bolsheviks outlawed after attempt to topple government fails.
	November	Bolsheviks seize power from Provisional Government; Lenin, as leader of Bolsheviks, becomes head of state; Russian Soviet Federated Socialist Republic (Russian Republic) formed; Constituent Assembly elected.
	December	Cheka (secret police) created; Finns and Moldavians declare independence from Russia; Japanese occupy Vladivostok.
1918	January	Constituent Assembly dissolved; Ukraine declares its independence, followed, in subsequent months, by Armenia, Azerbaijan, Belorussia, Estonia, Georgia, Latvia, and Lithuania.
	February	Basmachi Rebellion begins in Central Asia; calendar changed from Julian to Gregorian.
	March	Treaty of Brest-Litovsk signed with Germany; Russia loses Poland, Finland, Baltic lands, Ukraine, and other areas; Russian Social Democratic Labor Party becomes Russian Communist Party (Bolshevik).
	April	Civil War begins.
	July	Constitution of Russian Republic promulgated; imperial family murdered.
	Summer	War communism established; intervention in Civil War by foreign expeditionary forces—including those of Britain, France, and United States—begins.
	August	Attempt to assassinate Lenin fails; Red Terror begins.
	November	Treaty of Brest-Litovsk repudiated by Soviet government after Germany defeated by Allied Powers.
1919	January	Belorussia established as theoretically independent Soviet republic.
	March	Communist International (Comintern) formally founded at congress in Moscow; Ukrainian Soviet established.
1920	January	Blockade of Russian Republic lifted by Britain and other Allies.
	February	Peace agreement signed with Estonia; agreements with Latvia and Lithuania follow.
	April	War with Poland begins; Azerbaijan Soviet republic established.
	July	Trade agreement signed with Britain.

Table A. (Continued) Chronology of Important Events

Period		Description
	October	Truce reached with Poland.
	November	Red Army defeats Wrangel's army in Crimea; Armenian Soviet republic established.
1921	March	War with Poland ends with Treaty of Riga; Red Army crushes Kronshtadt naval mutiny; New Economic Policy proclaimed; Georgian Soviet republic established.
	Summer	Famine breaks out in Volga region.
	August	Aleksandr Blok, foremost poet of Russian Silver Age, dies; large number of intellectuals exiled.
1922	March	Transcaucasian Soviet Federated Socialist Republic formed, uniting Armenian, Azerbaijan, and Georgian republics.
	April	Joseph V. Stalin made general secretary of party; Treaty of Rapallo signed with Germany.
	May	Lenin suffers his first stroke.
	June	Socialist Revolutionary Party members put on trial by State Political Directorate; Glavlit organized with censorship function.
	December	Union of Soviet Socialist Republics (Soviet Union) established, comprising Russian, Ukrainian, Belorussian, and Transcaucasian republics.
1924	January	Lenin dies; constitution of Soviet Union put into force.
	February	Britain recognizes Soviet Union; other European countries follow suit later in year.
	Fall	Regime begins to delimit territories of Central Asian nationalities; Turkmenistan and Uzbekistan elevated to Soviet republic status.
1925	April	Theoretician Nikolay Bukharin calls for peasants to enrich themselves.
	November	Poet Sergey Yesenin commits suicide.
	December	Russian Communist Party (Bolshevik) becomes All-Union Communist Party (Bolshevik).
1926	April	Grigoriy Zinov'yev ousted from Politburo.
	October	Leon Trotsky and Lev Kamenev ousted from Politburo.
1927	Fall	Peasants sell government less grain than demanded because of low prices; peasant discontent increases; grain crisis begins.
	December	Fifteenth Party Congress calls for large-scale collectivization of agriculture.
1928	January	Trotsky exiled to Alma-Ata.
	May	Shakhty trial begins; first executions for "economic crimes" follow.
	July	Sixth Congress of Comintern names socialist parties main enemy of communists.
	October	Implementation of First Five-Year Plan begins.
1929	January	Trotsky forced to leave Soviet Union.
	April	Law on religious associations requires registration of religious groups, authorizes church closings, and bans religious teaching.
	Fall	Red Army skirmishes with Chinese forces in Manchuria.

Table A. *(Continued) Chronology of Important Events*

Period		Description
	October	Tajikistan split from Uzbek Republic to form separate Soviet republic.
	November	Bukharin ousted from Politburo.
	December	Stalin formally declares end of New Economic Policy and calls for elimination of kulaks; forced industrialization intensifies, and collectivization begins.
1930	March	Collectivization slows temporarily.
	April	Poet Vladimir Mayakovskiy commits suicide.
	November	"Industrial Party" put on trial.
1931	March	Mensheviks put on trial.
	August	School system reformed.
1932	May	Five-year plan against religion declared.
	December	Internal passports introduced for domestic travel; peasants not issued passports.
1932–33		Terror and forced famine rage in countryside, primarily in southeastern Ukrainian Republic and northern Caucasus.
1933	November	Diplomatic relations with United States established.
1934	August	Union of Soviet Writers holds its First Congress.
	September	Soviet Union admitted to League of Nations.
	December	Sergey Kirov assassinated in Leningrad; Great Terror begins, causing intense fear among general populace, and peaks in 1937 and 1938 before subsiding in latter year.
1935	February	Party cards exchanged; many members purged from party ranks.
	May	Treaties signed with France and Czechoslovakia.
	Summer	Seventh Congress of Comintern calls for "united front" of political parties against fascism.
	August	Stakhanovite movement to increase worker productivity begins.
	September	New system of ranks issued for Red Army.
1936	June	Restrictive laws on family and marriage issued.
	August	Zinov'yev, Kamenev, and other high-level officials put on trial for alleged political crimes.
	September	Nikolay Yezhov replaces Genrikh Yagoda as head of NKVD (secret police); purge of party deepens.
	October	Soviet Union begins support for antifascists in Spanish Civil War.
	November	Germany and Japan sign Anti-Comintern Pact.
	December	New constitution proclaimed; Kazakstan and Kyrgyzia become Soviet republics; Transcaucasian Soviet Federated Socialist Republic splits into Armenian, Azerbaijan, and Georgian Soviet republics.
1937	January	Trial of "Anti-Soviet Trotskyite Center."
	June	Marshal Mikhail Tukhachevskiy and other military leaders executed.
1938	March	Russian language required in all schools in Soviet Union.

Table A. *(Continued)* Chronology of Important Events

Period		Description
	July	Soviet and Japanese forces fight at Lake Khasan.
	December	Lavrenti Beria replaces Yezhov as chief of secret police; Great Terror diminishes.
1939	May	Vyacheslav Molotov replaces Maksim Litvinov as commissar of foreign affairs; armed conflict with Japan at Halhin Gol in Mongolia continues until August.
	August	Nazi-Soviet Nonaggression Pact signed; pact includes secret protocol.
	September	Stalin joins Adolf Hitler in partitioning Poland.
	October	Soviet forces enter Estonia, Latvia, and Lithuania.
	November	Remaining (western) portions of Ukraine and Belorussia incorporated into Soviet Union; Soviet forces invade Finland.
	December	Soviet Union expelled from League of Nations.
1940	March	Finland sues for peace with Soviet Union.
	April	Polish officers massacred in Katyn Forest by Soviet troops.
	June	New strict labor laws enacted; northern Bukovina and Bessarabia seized from Romania and subsequently incorporated into Ukrainian Republic and newly created Moldavian Republic, respectively.
	August	Soviet Union annexes Estonia, Latvia, and Lithuania; Trotsky murdered in Mexico.
1941	April	Neutrality pact signed with Japan.
	May	Stalin becomes chairman of Council of People's Commissars.
	June	Nazi Germany attacks Soviet Union in Operation Barbarossa.
	August	Soviet and British troops enter Iran.
	November	Lend-Lease Law of United States applied to Soviet Union.
	December	Soviet counteroffensive against Germany begins.
1942	May	Red Army routed at Khar'kov; Germans halt Soviet offensive; treaty signed with Britain against Germany.
	July	Battle of Stalingrad begins.
	November	Red Army starts winter offensive.
1943	February	German army units surrender at Stalingrad; 91,000 prisoners taken.
	May	Comintern dissolved.
	July	Germans defeated in tank battle at Kursk.
	September	Stalin allows Russian Orthodox Church to appoint patriarch.
	November	Tehran Conference held.
1944	January	Siege of Leningrad ends after 870 days.
	May	Crimea liberated from German army.
	June	Red Army begins summer offensive.
	October	Tuva incorporated into Soviet Union; armed struggle against Soviet rule breaks out in western Ukrainian, western Belorussian, Lithuanian, and Latvian republics and continues for several years.

Table A. (Continued) Chronology of Important Events

Period		Description
1945	February	Stalin meets with Winston Churchill and Franklin D. Roosevelt at Yalta.
	May	Red Army captures Berlin.
	July–August	Potsdam Conference attended by Stalin, Harry S. Truman, and Churchill, who later is replaced by Clement R. Attlee.
	August	Soviet Union declares war on Japan; Soviet forces enter Manchuria and Korea.
1946	March	Regime abolishes Ukrainian Greek Catholic Church (Uniate); Council of People's Commissars becomes Council of Ministers.
	Summer	Beginning of "Zhdanovshchina," a campaign against Western culture.
1947		Famine in southern and central regions of European part of Soviet Union.
	September	Cominform established to replace Comintern.
1948	June	Blockade of Berlin by Soviet forces begins and lasts into May 1949.
	Summer	Trofim Lysenko begins his domination of fields of biology and genetics that continues until 1955.
1949	January	Council for Mutual Economic Assistance formed; campaign against "cosmopolitanism" launched.
	August	Soviet Union tests its first atomic bomb.
1952	October	All-Union Communist Party (Bolshevik) becomes Communist Party of the Soviet Union (CPSU); name of Politburo is changed to Presidium.
1953	January	Kremlin "doctors' plot" exposed, signaling political infighting, new wave of purges, and anti-Semitic campaign.
	March	Stalin dies; Georgiy Malenkov, Beria, and Molotov form troika (triumvirate); title of party chief changes from general secretary to first secretary.
	April	"Doctors' plot" declared a provocation.
	July	Beria arrested and shot; Malenkov, Molotov, and Nikita S. Khrushchev form new troika.
	August	Soviet Union tests hydrogen bomb.
	September	Khrushchev chosen CPSU first secretary; rehabilitation of Stalin's victims begins.
1955	February	Nikolay Bulganin replaces Malenkov as prime minister.
	May	Warsaw Pact organized.
1956	February	Khrushchev's "secret speech" at Twentieth Party Congress exposes Stalin's crimes.
	September	Minimum wage established.
	November	Soviet forces crush Hungarian Revolution.
1957	July	"Antiparty group" excluded from CPSU leadership.
	August	First Soviet intercontinental ballistic missile tested successfully.
	October	World's first artificial satellite, Sputnik I, launched.
1958	March	Khrushchev named chairman of Council of Ministers.

Table A. *(Continued) Chronology of Important Events*

Period		Description
	October	Nobel Prize for Literature awarded to Boris Pasternak; campaign mounted against Pasternak, who is forced to decline award.
1959	September	Khrushchev visits United States.
1960	May	Soviet air defense downs United States U–2 reconnaissance aircraft over Soviet Union.
1961	April	Cosmonaut Yuriy Gagarin launched in world's first manned orbital space flight.
	July	Khrushchev meets with President John F. Kennedy in Vienna.
	August	Construction of Berlin Wall begins.
	October	Stalin's remains removed from Lenin Mausoleum.
1962	June	Workers' riots break out in Novocherkassk.
	October	Cuban missile crisis begins, bringing United States and Soviet Union close to war.
	November	Aleksandr Solzhenitsyn's *One Day in the Life of Ivan Denisovich* published in Soviet journal.
1963	August	Limited Test Ban Treaty signed with United States and Britain.
1964	October	Khrushchev removed from power; Leonid I. Brezhnev becomes CPSU first secretary.
1965	August	Volga Germans rehabilitated.
1966	February	Dissident writers Andrey Sinyavskiy and Yuliy Daniel tried and sentenced.
	April	Brezhnev's title changes from first secretary to general secretary; name of Presidium is changed back to Politburo.
1967	April	Stalin's daughter, Svetlana Alliluyeva, defects to West.
	September	Crimean Tatars rehabilitated but not allowed to return home.
1968	June	Andrey Sakharov's dissident writings published in samizdat.
	July	Treaty on the Nonproliferation of Nuclear Weapons (Nuclear Nonproliferation Treaty) signed by Soviet Union.
	August	Soviet-led Warsaw Pact armies invade Czechoslovakia.
1969	March	Soviet and Chinese forces skirmish on Ussuri River.
	May	Major General Petr Grigorenko, a dissident, arrested and incarcerated in psychiatric hospital.
1970	October	Jewish emigration begins to increase substantially.
	December	Solzhenitsyn awarded Nobel Prize for literature.
1972	May	Strategic Arms Limitation Talks (SALT) result in signing of Anti-Ballistic Missile Treaty (ABM Treaty) and Interim Agreement on the Limitation of Strategic Offensive Arms; President Richard M. Nixon visits Moscow.
1973	June	Brezhnev visits Washington.
1974	February	Solzhenitsyn arrested and sent into foreign exile.
1975	July	Apollo/Soyuz space mission held jointly with United States.

Table A. (Continued) Chronology of Important Events

Period		Description
	August	Helsinki Accords signed, confirming East European borders and calling for enforcement of human rights.
	December	Sakharov awarded Nobel Prize for Peace.
1976		Helsinki watch groups formed to monitor human rights safeguards.
1977	June	Brezhnev named chairman of Presidium of Supreme Soviet.
	October	New constitution promulgated for Soviet Union.
1979	June	Second SALT agreement signed but not ratified by United States Senate.
	December	Soviet armed forces invade Afghanistan.
1980	January	Sakharov exiled to Gor'kiy.
	August	Summer Olympics held in Moscow and boycotted by United States and other Western nations.
1981	February	CPSU holds its Twenty-Sixth Party Congress.
1982	June	Strategic Arms Reduction Treaty (START) talks begin.
	November	Brezhnev dies; Yuriy V. Andropov named general secretary.
1983	September	Soviet fighter aircraft downs South Korean civilian airliner KAL 007 near Sakhalin Island.
1984	February	Andropov dies; Konstantin U. Chernenko becomes general secretary.
1985	March	Chernenko dies; Mikhail S. Gorbachev becomes general secretary.
	November	Gorbachev meets with President Ronald W. Reagan in Geneva.
1986	February–March	CPSU holds its Twenty-Seventh Party Congress.
	April	Nuclear power plant disaster at Chernobyl' releases large amounts of radiation over Russia, Ukraine, and Belorussia.
		Glasnost launched.
	October	Gorbachev and Reagan hold summit at Reykjavik.
	December	Ethnic riots break out in Alma-Ata.
1987	January	Gorbachev launches *perestroika.*
	December	Soviet Union and United States sign Intermediate-Range Nuclear Forces Treaty (INF Treaty).
1988	Winter	Ethnic disturbances begin in Caucasus.
	May	Soviet authorities stop jamming Voice of America broadcasts.
	May–June	Reagan visits Moscow.
	June	Millennium of establishment of Christianity in Kievan Rus' celebrated in Moscow.
	June–July	CPSU's Nineteenth Party Conference tests limits of *glasnost* and *perestroika* in unprecedented discussions.
	October	Gorbachev replaces Andrey Gromyko as chairman of Presidium of Supreme Soviet; Gromyko retires, and others are removed from Politburo.
	December	Supreme Soviet dissolves itself, preparing way for new elected parliament.

Table A. (Continued) Chronology of Important Events

Period		Description
1989	February	Soviet combat forces complete withdrawal from Afghanistan.
	March–April	Initial and runoff elections held for the 2,250 seats in Congress of People's Deputies (CPD); many reform candidates, including Boris N. Yeltsin, win seats.
	April	Soviet troops break up rally in Tbilisi, Georgia, killing at least twenty civilians.
	May	CPD openly criticizes past and present regimes; Gorbachev elected by CPD to new position of chairman of Supreme Soviet.
	June	Free elections in Poland begin rapid decline of Soviet Union's empire in Central Europe.
	July	Coal miners strike in Russia and Ukraine.
	August	Nationalist demonstrations in Chisinau, Moldavia, lead to reinstatement of Romanian as official language of republic. Russians and Ukrainians living along Dnestr River go on strike, demanding autonomy.
		Soviet Union admits existence of secret protocols to 1939 Nazi-Soviet Nonagression Pact, which allotted to Soviet Union the Baltic countries, parts of then eastern Poland, and Moldavia.
		Mass exodus from East Germany begins.
	September	Ukrainian Popular Movement for Perestroika (Rukh) holds founding congress in Kiev.
	October	Mass protests take place in Berlin and Leipzig.
	November	Berlin Wall falls. Bulgaria's Todor Zhivkov deposed. Communist party of Czechoslovakia falls from power.
	December	Violent revolution in Romania. Nicolae Ceaucescu arrested, tried, and shot.
		CPD condemns Nazi-Soviet Nonagression Pact and secret protocols.
		Lithuanian Communist Party leaves CPSU.
		Latvian parliament deletes from its constitution reference to communist party's "leading role."
		At hasty shipboard summit off Malta, Gorbachev and United States president George H.W. Bush declare Cold War ended.
1990	January	Azerbaijani demonstrators on Soviet side of border with Iran dismantle border posts.
		Gorbachev fails to heal rift with Lithuanian communists.
		Anti-Armenian pogroms in Azerbaijan. Gorbachev sends troops to Baku.
	February	Central Committee of CPSU votes to strike Article 6, which guarantees leading role of communist party, from Soviet constitution.
	March	In elections for Supreme Soviet of Russian Republic, Yeltsin wins seat.
		Newly elected Lithuanian parliament declares independence.
		Estonian parliament declares itself in a state of transition to independence.

Table A. (Continued) Chronology of Important Events

Period		Description
	May	Latvian parliament votes to declare independence after unspecified transition period.
		Anti-Soviet demonstrations break out in and around Yerevan.
		Yeltsin becomes chairman of Supreme Soviet of Russian Republic.
	June	Communists in Russian Republic vote to form Communist Party of the Russian Republic.
		Russia, Uzbekistan, and Moldavia issue declarations of sovereignty. By October most of the other Soviet republics have done likewise.
	July	Twenty-Eighth Party Congress: Yeltsin quits CPSU; Politburo stripped of almost all meaning.
		Meeting of Gorbachev and West German chancellor Helmut Kohl in Stavropol'. German unification within North Atlantic Treaty Organization (NATO) secured.
		Soviet government and republics open negotiations on a new treaty of union.
	August	Russia and Lithuania sign agreement on trade and economic cooperation.
		Armenia declares independence.
	October	Germany united; Conventional Forces in Europe Treaty (CFE Treaty) signed in Paris.
		Parliament of Russian Republic passes resolution proclaiming that no Soviet law can take effect in the republic without republican parliamentary approval.
		Parliament of Russian Republic approves radical economic reform plan, thereby undercutting all-union Supreme Soviet's economic reform package.
		Gorbachev awarded Nobel Prize for peace.
	November	Violence breaks out in Moldavia between Moldavians and Russian and Ukrainian separatists.
		Gorbachev proposes new union treaty.
	December	Eduard Shevardnadze resigns as minister of foreign affairs, warning of oncoming dictatorship.
		Parliament of Russian Republic votes to contribute to Soviet budget less than one-tenth of central government's request.
1991	January	Soviet crackdown on Lithuanian and Latvian independence movements.
		Soviet Ministry of Defense announces plan to send troops to seven union republics to enforce military conscription and to round up draft dodgers.
		Russian Republic and the Baltic republics sign mutual security pact.
	February	Baltic countries hold nonbinding plebiscites as demonstration of their people's will to secede from Soviet Union.
	March	Coal miners go on strike in Ukraine, Kazakstan, Arctic mines, and Siberia.
		Mass pro-Yeltsin rallies in Moscow.

Table A. (Continued) Chronology of Important Events

Period	Description
	Referendum held on preservation of Soviet Union: 70 percent vote to remain in union, but Armenia, Georgia, Moldavia, Lithuania, Latvia, and Estonia boycott.
	Warsaw Pact officially dissolves.
April	Georgia declares independence.
	Russian parliament grants Yeltsin emergency powers.
May	Yeltsin gains control over coal mines in Russian Republic.
	Russian government establishes foreign ministry and internal security organization. Russian television begins broadcasting on second all-union channel.
June	By universal suffrage, Yeltsin elected president of Russian Republic.
	Last Soviet troops leave Hungary and Czechoslovakia.
	Gorbachev and leaders of seven Soviet republics sign draft union treaty.
July	Yeltsin bans political activity at workplaces and government establishments in Russian Republic; Gorbachev signs START I agreement in Moscow with United States president Bush.
August	Hard-line officials attempt to unseat Gorbachev government; coup fails after three days, elevating Yeltsin's prestige.
	Ukraine, Belorussia, Moldavia, Azerbaijan, Uzbekistan, and Kyrgyz Republic declare independence. Armenia and Tajikistan follow in September, Turkmenistan in October, and Kazakstan in December.
October	Dzhokar Dudayev elected president of newly declared Chechen Republic.
November	Russian parliament grants Yeltsin sweeping powers to introduce radical economic reform. Yeltsin cuts off Russian funding of Soviet central ministries.
	Chechens demand independence. Ingush members of Chechen National Congress resign.
	Russia gains control of Soviet natural resources; Yeltsin places Russian economy above that of Soviet Union, ending possibility of Russia remaining in union.
	Gorbachev fails to win support of republics for new union treaty.
December	Presidents of Ukraine, Belarus, and Russia meet in Minsk and proclaim initial Commonwealth of Independent States (CIS).
	Yeltsin meets with Soviet defense officials and army commanders to gain support for CIS.
	Russian foreign minister Andrey Kozyrev asks United States secretary of state James Baker to recognize independence of Russia, Belarus, and Ukraine.
	Gorbachev announces that at year's end all central government structures will cease to exist.
	Eleven republics form CIS.
	Soviet Union ceases to exist. Russian flag rises over Kremlin. Control of nuclear arsenal handed over to Yeltsin.

Table A. *(Continued)* Chronology of Important Events

Period		Description
1992	January	Russian government lifts price controls on almost all goods.
		Beginning of rift between Yeltsin and speaker of Russian Supreme Soviet Ruslan Khasbulatov and Russian vice president Aleksandr Rutskoy.
	February	First United States-Russia summit.
		International airlift of food and medical supplies to Russian cities begins.
	March	Fighting breaks out between Moldovan forces and Russian and Ukrainian separatists along Dnestr River.
		Eighteen of twenty autonomous republics within Russian Federation sign Federation Treaty. Tatarstan and Chechnya refuse.
	April	At first post-Soviet session of Russian CPD, Yeltsin fends off vote of no-confidence in his economic program. CPD also changes name of Russian Socialist Federation of Soviet Republics to Russian Federation.
		Yeltsin calls for a referendum on new constitution that would abolish Russian CPD.
	May	Formation of Russian armed forces. Army general Pavel Grachev appointed minister of defense.
		Ten of the eleven CIS presidents sign mutual security treaty in Tashkent. Treaty acknowledges demise of unified CIS armed forces.
		United States and all four post-Soviet nuclear states vow to comply with START agreement.
	June	Russia joins International Monetary Fund (IMF).
		Russian Supreme Soviet establishes Republic of Ingushetia within Russian Federation.
		Russian troops complete withdrawal from Republic of Chechnya.
		General Aleksandr Lebed' takes command of 14th Army in Moldova.
	July	Yeltsin makes first appearance at Group of Seven (G–7) meeting.
		Russian Supreme Soviet ratifies CFE Treaty.
	August	Black Sea Fleet evacuates 1,700 Russians from Sukhumi in civil-war-torn Georgia.
	September	Russia completes troop withdrawal from Mongolia.
	October	Russia launches privatization.
		Last Russian combat troops leave Poland.
	November	Yeltsin declares state of emergency in North Ossetia and Ingushetia in order to halt outbreak of ethnic conflicts.
		Russian troops attack Georgian forces deployed in Abkhazia.
		Russian troops enter Ingushetia.
	December	Seventh Russian CPD opens. Yeltsin and parliament clash over economic reform and powers. Viktor Chernomyrdin becomes prime minister. Yeltsin and congress agree to hold referendum on presidential power. Part of same deal grants Yeltsin extraordinary powers.

Table A. (Continued) Chronology of Important Events

Period		Description
		Russia and China pull most of their troops back 100 kilometers along common border.
1993	March	CPD revokes December 1992 deal with Yeltsin, who then attempts to impose special rule, but fails.
		Russian troops deployed in Tajikistan as part of CIS peacekeeping operation.
	April	Referendum approves Yeltsin as president and Yeltsin's social and economic programs.
		Yeltsin and CPD issue differing draft versions of new Russian constitution.
	July	Constitutional assembly passes draft Russian constitution worked out by conciliatory committee.
		Parliament annuls presidential decrees on economic reforms.
		Marshal Yevgeniy Shaposhnikov, having resigned as commander in chief of CIS joint forces, hands over his launch authorization codes to Russian defense minister Grachev.
		Russian Central Bank (RCB) announces withdrawal from circulation of Soviet and Russian banknotes issued between 1961 and 1992. Yeltsin eases some of RCB's provisions.
		Yeltsin counters parliament's suspension of privatization. Two weeks later, parliament again suspends privatization. Yeltsin issues decree continuing program.
	August	Yeltsin formally requests that parliament hold early elections.
	September	Yeltsin suspends Vice President Rutskoy based on charges of corruption.
		Yeltsin dissolves the CPD and Supreme Soviet and sets date for elections in December.
		Supreme Soviet votes to impeach Yeltsin and swears in Rutskoy as president; CPD confirms decisions.
		Clashes in Moscow between Yeltsin and Supreme Soviet supporters.
	October	Church mediation of government split collapses; further clashes on Moscow streets.
		Top leaders of opposition surrender. Sniper fire continues for several days.
		Russia officially asks for revisions to CFE Treaty.
		Yeltsin suspends Constitutional Court and disbands city, district, and village soviets.
	November	Russian troops land in Abkhazia.
	December	Parliamentary elections and referendum on new constitution are held. Constitution approved. Chechnya does not participate in elections.
		Yeltsin and Turkmenistan's president Saparmyrat Niyazov sign accord on dual citizenship, first such agreement between Soviet successor states.
1994	January	Trilateral agreement among Russia, Ukraine, and United States prepares for denuclearizing Ukraine's armed forces.

Table A. *(Continued) Chronology of Important Events*

Period		Description
		Chernomyrdin states that radical economic reform has come to an end in Russia. Reformers quit posts. Western advisers withdraw their services as advisers to Russian government.
	February	United States Central Intelligence Agency arrests Aldrich Ames on charges of spying for Soviet Union and Russia.
		State Duma (lower house of parliament beginning with 1993 election) grants amnesty to leaders of 1991 coup against Gorbachev and leaders of parliamentary revolt of October 1993.
		Yeltsin gives speech calling for continued radical restructuring of economy.
	April	Russia and Belarus agree to monetary union.
		Central Asian republics, Georgia, and Armenia allow Russian participation in patrolling their borders.
		Political leaders meet to sign Civic Accord, which calls on signatories to refrain from violence in pursuing political goals. Three of 248 participants refuse to sign, among them Gennadiy Zyuganov, leader of Communist Party of the Russian Federation (KPRF).
	June	Yeltsin accelerates market reforms.
		Foreign Minister Kozyrev signs NATO Partnership for Peace (PfP) accord.
	July	Russian and United States troops conduct joint peacekeeping exercise in Orenburg, Russia. United States conducts maneuvers in Black Sea with Russia, Ukraine, and other Black Sea countries.
		Russian government issues statement that situation in Chechnya is getting out of control.
	August	Last Russian troops leave Germany, Estonia, and Latvia.
	September	Fighting breaks out in Chechnya between Dudayev's and opposition forces.
	October	Ruble loses one-fifth of its value in one day.
		Chernomyrdin and Prime Minister Sangheli of Moldova sign agreement on withdrawal of Russia's 14th Army from Moldova.
	November	Dudayev proclaims martial law throughout republic and mobilizes all men aged seventeen and older.
		Yeltsin issues ultimatum to warring parties in Chechnya to lay down their arms.
	December	Kozyrev suspends Russia's participation in PfP.
		Russian armored columns enter Chechnya.
1995	January	Russia and Kazakstan agree to unify their armies by end of 1995.
	April	Human rights activist Sergey Kovalev estimates 10,000 Russian soldiers and 25,000 Chechen civilians killed in Chechnya since 1994.
	June	State Duma votes no-confidence in Government (cabinet). Second no-confidence vote fails in State Duma.
	July	Yeltsin hospitalized, returns to work in August.
	October	Yeltsin again hospitalized, reappears in November.

Table A. *(Continued) Chronology of Important Events*

Period		Description
	December	In parliamentary elections, communists and nationalists gain strength, reformists split and in decline.
1996	January	Yeltsin replaces Foreign Minister Andrey Kozyrev with Yevgeniy Primakov. Leading liberal reformists dismissed or resign.
	March	After slowdown in privatization and increase in government spending, Russia granted loan agreement worth US$10 billion by IMF.
		Leaders of Kazakstan, Kyrgyzstan, and Belarus sign customs union treaty in Moscow.
	April	Russia and Belarus sign union treaty with substantial elements of reunification.
		Dzhokar Dudayev killed in rocket attack in Chechnya.
	May	Chechens sign cease-fire agreement, whose terms are immediately violated; fighting resumes.
	June	Yeltsin and Zyuganov, candidate of KPRF, finish first and second, respectively, in first round of presidential elections, qualifying them for second round.
		Yeltsin fires Grachev and other senior hard-line officials and appoints Lebed' chief of Security Council.
		Yeltsin disappears from public view because of undisclosed illness.
	July	Yeltsin defeats Zyuganov in second round of presidential election, 54 percent to 40 percent.
		Fighting in Chechnya intensifies.
		Lebed' associate Igor' Rodionov named minister of defense, promises military reform; Anatoliy Chubays named presidential chief of staff.
		Citing failure of Russian economic reform, IMF withholds tranche of 1996 assistance package.
		Yeltsin creates civilian Defense Council.
		Pravda, voice of communism since 1912, renamed *Pravda 5* and begins more objective reporting.
	August	Yeltsin staff announces Yeltsin will rest for prolonged period to recover from election campaign.
		Chernomyrdin confirmed for second term as prime minister; Yeltsin names new Government with reformists in key positions.
		Chechen guerrillas recapture Chechen capital Groznyy, exposing weakness of Russian military; Lebed' achieves cease-fire in direct talks with Chechen leaders.
		IMF resumes economic assistance payments.
		Bellona Foundation report exposes mishandling of nuclear materials in Arctic regions.
	September	As cease-fire terms hold, first Russian troops leave Chechnya.
		NATO offers Russia special terms of military cooperation.
		Yeltsin announces he will undergo heart surgery; under pressure, he temporarily cedes military command and control of internal security agencies to Chernomyrdin.

Table A. (Continued) Chronology of Important Events

Period		Description
		Controversy continues over locus of government authority.
		Election cycle begins in subnational jurisdictions, continues through March 1997.
	October	Lebed' dismissed as Security Council chief; negotiations with Chechnya continue under Ivan Rybkin.
		United States secretary of defense William Perry rebuffed in attempt to gain passage of START II by State Duma.
		Government establishes emergency tax commission to improve tax collection; collection rate remains poor in ensuing months.
		Chubays begins campaign for compliance of regional laws with federal constitution.
	October–December	Escalating conflict between military and civilian defense officials over military reform methods.
	November	Russia's first bond issue on international market nets US$1 billion.
		Yeltsin undergoes successful open-heart surgery.
		Primakov visits China, Japan, and Mongolia to expand markets.
		Third Kilo-class submarine sold to Iran.
		Yeltsin remains out of public view until February 1997, his administration inactive; opposition calls for impeachment on health grounds.
	December	Four-person Consultative Council formed to smooth differences between Government and parliament.
		Primakov agrees to negotiate charter giving Russia special status with NATO.
		Federation Council (upper house of parliament since 1993 elections) claims Ukrainian port of Sevastopol' as Russian territory, reopening dispute with Ukraine.
1997	January	Long-delayed new Criminal Code goes into effect.
		State Duma passes 1997 budget after long discussions and amendments; experts call revenue projections unrealistic.
		Opposing military reform programs issued by Ministry of Defense and civilian Defense Council.
		Presidential and legislative elections in Chechnya; moderate Aslan Maskhadov wins presidency on independence platform.
		Yeltsin approves Russia's participation in NATO's Bosnia peacekeeping force until 1998.
		IMF withholds loan payment because of continued tax system problems.
	February	Last Russian troops leave Chechnya.
		NATO talks with Russia bring modification of CFE Treaty demands on Russia, subject to ratification by members.
	February–March	NATO chief Javier Solana visits several CIS nations, which entertain closer NATO ties.
	March	Yeltsin reestablishes his leadership with vigorous state of the federation speech.

Table A. *(Continued)* Chronology of Important Events

Period	Description
	Government streamlining begins with appointments of Chubays and Boris Nemtsov to powerful positions; Chernomyrdin's power wanes.
	Second issue of Russian bonds sold on international market; third issue scheduled.
	Nationwide labor action gains lukewarm participation; uncoordinated local actions intensify.
	At CIS summit, Yeltsin fails to reassert Russian domination as several members take independent positions.
	Helsinki summit with President William J. Clinton yields some economic agreements, continued discord on NATO expansion.
	Bilateral treaty reaffirms integration of Russia and Belarus.
April	Moscow summit with Chinese president Jiang Zemin expresses disapproval of United States world domination, yields agreement to reduce troops along shared border.
	State Duma postpones ratification of Chemical Weapons Convention following United States Congress ratification.
	Government proposal to limit government housing subsidies brings strong political opposition.
	Prompted by revenue shortages, Finance Minister Chubays submits budget revision to State Duma, cutting US$19 billion in spending.
May	Peace treaty signed by Russia and Chechnya (Chechnya-Ichkeria); Chechen independence issue remains unresolved.
	Igor' Sergeyev replaces Igor' Rodionov as minister of defense following Rodianov's open conflict with other defense authorities.
	New privatization programs begin in housing, natural gas, railroads, and electric power.
	Security Council issues new national security doctrine.
	Terms set for new pipeline from Tengiz oil fields (Kazakstan) to Black Sea port of Novorossiysk.
	Russia signs "founding act" agreement with NATO, allowing participation in NATO decision making; Russia agrees to drop opposition to NATO expansion in Central Europe.
	Yeltsin and Ukraine's president Leonid Kuchma sign treaty of friendship and cooperation, nominally settling disputes over territory and ownership of Black Sea Fleet.
June	State Duma recesses for summer without acting on budget-cut proposal, leaving determination of cuts to Government.
	Yeltsin names his daughter Tat'yana Dyachenko an official adviser.
	Yeltsin participates in Denver G–8 (formerly G–7) meeting as full partner for first time.
	Government announces allocation of US$2.9 billion to pay long-overdue pensions.

Table A. (Continued) Chronology of Important Events

Period	Description
	Government announces sale of shares in six state-owned oil companies to increase revenues.
	Under pressure from Yeltsin, Duma approves new tax code aimed at broadening government's revenue base.
June–July	Mishaps aboard Mir space station reinforce international doubts about Russia's space program.
July	Yeltsin declares Russia's economy has "turned the corner" toward growth and stability; statistics show some improvement.
	New CFE treaty reduces arms in Europe, does not limit NATO movement into Czech Republic, Hungary, and Poland as Russia had demanded.
	Russia offers Japan new conditions for development of disputed Kuril Islands; bilateral talks address Japanese investment elsewhere in Russia's Far East.
	Constitutinal Court rejects Moscow's residency fees as unconstitutional.
	Yeltsin announces large-scale program for military reform and streamlining.
	First meeting of NATO-Russia joint council establishes operational procedures.
	Yeltsin vetoes law restricting activities of non-Orthodox religions, after both houses of parliament had overwhelmingly passed it, Russian Orthodox Church supported it, and human rights organizations condemned it.
	Yeltsin's drive against official corruption thwarted as high officials refuse to divulge personal finances.
August	Pro-Yeltsin party, Our Home Is Russia, shaken by resignation of parliamentary leader Sergey Belyayev.
	NATO's Sea Breeze 97 exercise in Ukraine modified from military to humanitarian maneuver after protest by Russia.
	Yeltsin announces ruble reform for January 1998, dropping three zeros from denomination of currency.
	Government submits privatization plan for 1998 and draft 1998 budget to Sate Duma; budget calls for 2 percent growth in GDP and annual inflation of 5 percent.
	Russia and Armenia sign friendship and cooperation treaty tightening military and economic ties.
September	Duma reconvenes; atop agenda are tax reform bill and consideration of 1998 budget proposal.
	Shakeups of military establishment continue as Yeltsin dismisses his Defense Council chief, Yuriy Baturin, and reorganizes Rosvooruzheniye, the foreign arms sales cartel.
	Overdue tax payments by Gazprom reach US$2.4 billion.
	Agreement with Chechnya sets terms for repair of Baku (Azerbaijan)-Novorossiysk pipeline through Chechnya, with October 1997 as completion deadline; negotiations continue on new pipelines from Central Asia westward.

Table A. (Continued) Chronology of Important Events

Period	Description
	Russia warns NATO against pressure on Bosnian Serb Karadzic faction.
	Foreign trade figures for first half of 1997 announced; overall surplus US$18.5 billion, down 3.9 percent from first half 1996, including decrease of 11.7 percent in CIS trade.
	Duma passes land code without provision for sale of land by owner, frustrating Yeltsin's long campaign for reform of land ownership.
	Worker protests spread across Russia as wage non-payment continues, especially among coal, defense industry, and scientific workers.
	Yeltsin signs revised bill on religious organizations after "Christianity" added to list of Russia's "traditional," unrestricted faiths; human rights and religious groups protest.

Country Profile

Country

Formal Name: Russian Federation.

Short Form: Russia.

Term for Citizen(s): Russian(s).

Capital: Moscow.

Flag: Three equal-sized horizontal bands of white (top), red, and blue.

Geography

Size: 17,075,200 square kilometers.

Topography: Broad plain with low hills west of Urals in European Russia and vast coniferous forests and tundra east of Urals in Siberia. Uplands and mountains along southern border regions in Caucasus Mountains. About 10 percent of land area swampland, about 45 percent covered by forest.

Climate: Ranges from temperate to Arctic continental. Winter weather varies from short-term and cold along Black Sea to long-term and frigid in Siberia. Summer conditions vary from warm on steppes to cool along Arctic coast. Much of Russia covered by snow six months of year. Weather usually harsh and unpredictable. Average annual temperature of European Russia 0°C, lower in Siberia. Precipitation low to moderate in most areas; highest amounts in northwest, North Caucasus, and Pacific coast.

Land Boundaries: Land borders extend 20,139 kilometers: Azerbaijan 284 kilometers, Belarus 959 kilometers, China 3,645 kilometers, Estonia 290 kilometers, Finland 1,313 kilometers, Georgia 723 kilometers, Kazakstan 6,846 kilometers, Democratic People's Republic of Korea 19 kilometers, Latvia 217 kilometers, Lithuania 227 kilometers, Mongolia 3,441 kilometers, Norway 167 kilometers, Poland 432 kilometers, and Ukraine 1,576 kilometers.

Water boundaries: Coastline makes up 37,653 kilometers of border. Arctic, Atlantic, and Pacific oceans touch shores.

Land Use: 10 percent arable, 45 percent forest, 5 percent meadows and pasture, and 40 percent other, including tundra.

Society

Population: According to United States government estimates, 149,909,089. According to official 1996 Russian statistics, 148,200,000.

Ethnic Groups: According to 1989 census, Russian 81.5 percent, Tatar 3.8 percent, Ukrainian 3.0 percent, Chuvash 1.2 percent, Bashkir 0.9 percent, Belorussian 0.8 percent, Mordovian 0.7 percent, and other 8.1 percent.

Languages: Official language Russian. Approximately 100 others spoken.

Religion: In 1996 about 75 percent of believers in Russia considered themselves Russian Orthodox, 19 percent Muslim, and 7 percent other. Religious activity increased sharply in post-Soviet period, given official government and constitutional sanction.

Education: About 98 percent of population over age fifteen literate. Constitution guarantees right to free preschool, basic general, and secondary vocational education. Basic general education compulsory until age fifteen. In 1995 about 500 postsecondary schools in operation, including forty-two universities. Postsecondary technical and vocational schools now offer comprehensive education. Private schools and universities emerging in mid-1990s.

Health: Health care free of charge in principle, but adequate treatment increasingly depends upon wealth. Doctors poorly paid and poorly trained, and hospitals decrepit. Shortages of nurses, specialized personnel, and medical supplies and equipment persist. National distribution of facilities and medical personnel highly skewed in favor of urban areas, especially politically sensitive cities. About 131 hospital beds per 10,000 population and one doctor for every 275 citizens. 1994 life expectancy 57.3 years for males, 71.1 years for females, having dropped sharply since 1990. Officially reported infant mortality rate 19.9 per 1,000 live births in 1994. Poor quality of water and air in many areas and excessive smoking and alcohol use exacerbate poor health of nation.

Labor Force: About 57 percent of population working age. Work force relatively well-educated but ill-suited for challenges of post-Soviet economy. In 1994 some 37 percent of labor force worked in services, 27.7 percent in industry, 14.9 percent in agriculture, 10.9 percent in construction, and 7.6 percent in transport and communications. More than 16 percent of labor force works for government.

Economy

Salient Features: After years of double-digit declines, gross domestic product (GDP) shrank by only 4 percent in 1995. GDP per capita in 1995 US$4,224. Unemployment rising steadily, to estimated 8.5 percent in 1996; official Russian numbers about half that amount. Inflation, very high in 1994, under much better control under new government policy in 1995–96; April 1997 rate 1.2 percent. Economy increasingly dependent on foreign investment, multilateral loan agencies, and rescheduling of foreign debt. Privatization nearly complete but meeting political opposition to transformation of large state firms. Most prices determined by market. Role of organized crime significant, and much economic activity officially unaccounted for.

Agriculture: 6.3 percent of GDP in 1994. Major products grain, sugar beets, sunflower seeds, vegetables, fruits, meat, and milk.

Manufacturing: 28.3 percent of GDP in 1994. Principal products machine tools, rolling mills, high-performance aircraft, space vehicles, ships, road and rail transportation equipment, communications equipment, agricultural machinery, tractors and construction equipment, electric-power generating and transmitting equipment, medical and scientific instruments, and consumer durables.

Services: 50 percent of GDP in 1994. Tourism important source of foreign currency. Expansion of financial, communications, and information enterprises contributes to growth. Shipping services also major foreign-exchange earner.

Mining: Considerable mineral wealth, especially iron ore, copper, phosphates, manganese, chromium, nickel, platinum, diamonds, and gold. Production declined steadily 1990–95.

Energy: Russia self-sufficient in fuels and energy production.

Natural gas and oil main fuels exploited, coal production declining but still significant; long-distance fuel transportation a significant problem. Main electricity sources: coal 18 percent, nuclear 13 percent, hydroelectric 19 percent, and natural gas 42 percent. Industry consumes 61 percent of energy production. Generation capacity 188 gigawatts. Energy exports most important source of foreign exchange.

Foreign Trade: Trade liberalization ongoing, abolishing export duties, restructuring import tariffs, and ending export registration in 1996. Main trading partners Germany, Italy, the Netherlands, Switzerland, Britain, the United States, Ukraine, Kazakstan, Belarus, China, and Japan. Exports for 1995 estimated at US$77.8 billion, imports US$57.9 billion. Balance of payments US$13.1 billion in 1995. Capital flight expected to drop to US$1 billion in 1996. Foreign investment strongly encouraged in some sectors, but unpredictable commercial conditions hinder growth. Outstanding Soviet-era debt by Third World countries, between US$100 and US$170 billion, could make Russia creditor country on balance.

Currency and Exchange Rate: Ruble. In July 1997, US$1 equaled 5,790 rubles.

Fiscal Year: Calendar year.

Transportation and Telecommunications

Roads: 934,000 kilometers in service in 1995, of which 725,000 kilometers paved or gravel and of which 445,000 kilometers serve only specific industries or farms. Automobile travel expanding, but roads inadequate in quality and quantity.

Railroads: 154,000 kilometers wide-gauge in 1995, of which 87,000 kilometers for common carrier service. 49,000 kilometers diesel, and 38,000 kilometers electrified. Proportion of cargo shipping by rail high by Western standards. System in need of large-scale repair.

Civil Aviation: 2,517 airports, of which fifty-four with paved runways over 3,047 meters. In 1990s hundreds of private airlines formed. Aeroflot, the state monopoly of Soviet Union, now joint-stock company with majority of stock held by government. Major international airports include Sheremet'evo in Moscow and Pulkovo in St. Petersburg. Flights to most major world capitals and major cities within

Commonwealth of Independent States (CIS).

Ports and Shipping: Main ports Arkhangel'sk, Astrakhan', Kaliningrad, Kazan', Khabarovsk, Kholmsk, Krasnoyarsk, Magadan, Moscow, Murmansk, Nakhodka, Nevel'sk, Novorossiysk, Petropavlovsk, Rostov-na-Donu, Sochi, St. Petersburg, Tuapse, Vladivostok, Volgograd, Vostochnyy, and Vyborg. Merchant fleet 800 vessels in 1995. Some 235 ships operating under Maltese, Cypriot, Liberian, Panamanian, St. Vincent and the Grenadines, Honduran, Marshall Islands, Bahamian, and Vanuatu registry.

Inland waterways: Total navigable routes in general use 101,000 kilometers.

Pipelines: Crude oil, 48,000 kilometers; petroleum products, 15,000 kilometers; natural gas, 140,000 kilometers.

Telecommunications: 24,400,000 telephones; 20,900,000 in urban areas and 3,500,000 in rural areas in 1995. Development of modern communications lines and acquisition of advanced equipment slow. Diversity in radio and television programming increasing since late 1980s. Access to Internet and cellular phones expanding, but poor state of telecommunications hinders country's modernization.

Government and Politics

Government: Democratic, federative form of government under 1993 constitution. Divided into executive, legislative, and judicial branches. President, elected to four-year term, sets basic tone of domestic and foreign policy, represents state at home and abroad. Prime minister appoints Government (cabinet) to administer executive-branch functions. Forty ministries, state committees, and services; reduction in Government size planned late 1996. Prime minister administers policy according to constitution, laws, and presidential decrees. New Government named August 1996 following presidential election, retaining some key members from previous administration. Boris N. Yeltsin president, first elected 1991. Viktor Chernomyrdin prime minister, reappointed August 1996. Parliament, bicameral Federal Assembly, has lower house, State Duma, with 450 members serving four-year terms; last election December 1995. Upper house, Federation Council, has 178 seats (two members representing the executive and legislative bodies of each of the eighty-nine subnational jurisdictions). Three highest judicial bodies Constitutional Court, Supreme Court, and Superior Court of Arbitration. Judges appointed by president with confirmation from the Federation Council required. Jurisprudence advancing slowly toward Western standards; jury trials held only in some regions.

Politics: Largest party representation in State Duma by Communist Party of the Russian Federation, Liberal-Democratic Party of Russia, Our Home Is Russia, and Yabloko coalition. More than a dozen other parties have representation in State Duma. Personal connections, personalities retain impact in politics as national parties develop slowly, government figures avoid party affiliation; shifting coalitions typical in State Duma. Seventy-eight nominal independents in State Duma.

Administrative Divisions: Twenty-one autonomous republics, forty-nine oblasts (provinces), six territories (*kraya*; sing., *kray*), ten autonomous regions (*okruga*; sing., *okrug*), one autonomous oblast. Cities of Moscow and St. Petersburg with separate status at oblast level.

Foreign Relations: In early 1990s, basically pro-Western, drastic change from Soviet era. Russia cofounded Commonwealth of Independent States (CIS) in 1991 and assumed Soviet Union seats in many international organizations. Dependence on foreign assistance greatly increased in 1990s. Beginning in 1993, substantial domestic political pressure mitigated stance toward participation in Western-dominated organizations and treaties, reemphasis of independent national power. So-called Eurasianism assumes unique role in world affairs and primary concerns in Asia rather than Europe. Chechnya crisis and nuclear transactions with Iran bring international criticism, although summits with United States president continue, 1997. Policy toward successor states marked by interest in reintegration of CIS countries and well-being of Russians living outside borders of Russian Federation. Expansion of North Atlantic Treaty Organization (NATO) into Central Europe major issue in 1996. Other key issues include improvement of relations with China and insistence on strict interpretation of the Anti-Ballistic Missile Treaty (ABM Treaty). Member of Council of Europe, European Bank for Reconstruction and Development (EBRD), International Labour Organisation (ILO), International Monetary Fund (IMF), International

Criminal Police Organization (Interpol), NATO Partnership for Peace (PfP), United Nations (UN) and its Security Council, and World Bank.

National Security

Armed Forces: Approximately 1.5 million personnel in 1996, but sharp cuts and reorganization forecast. Term of active duty two years. Units filled mainly by conscription, with some contract personnel. Women may serve if they possess specialized skills. Armed forces divided into ground forces, naval forces, air forces, air defense forces, strategic rocket forces. Ground forces personnel 670,000 (210,000 conscripts); naval forces 200,000 (40,000 conscripts); air forces 130,000 (40,000 conscripts); air defense forces 200,000 (60,000 conscripts); strategic rocket forces 100,000 (50,000 conscripts).

Military Presence Overseas: Transcaucasus Group of Forces—9,000 personnel in Armenia, with one air defense MiG–23 squadron. 22,000 personnel in Georgia, with one air force composite regiment of thirty-five aircraft. Azerbaijan refuses Russian troop presence. Forces in other former Soviet republics: Moldova 6,400 personnel, Tajikistan 12,000 personnel, Turkmenistan 11,000 personnel, and several thousand each in Kazakstan and Kyrgyzstan. Contributions to UN missions in Angola, Bosnia, Croatia, Georgia, Haiti, Iraq/Kuwait, Former Yugoslav Republic of Macedonia, Rwanda, and Western Sahara. Signal and intelligence personnel in Vietnam, Syria, Cuba, Mongolia, and parts of Africa.

Military Budget: 1997 defense budget submitted August 1996 allots 100.8 trillion rubles (about US$19 billion), of 260 trillion rubles requested by Ministry of Defense. Anticipated 1998 budget somewhat higher. Maintenance and salaries far below required levels. Anti-inflationary budget restraints cause dissension among ministries and continued military morale decline.

Internal Security Forces: Reorganized after fall of Soviet Union but with many extraconstitutional functions ongoing and only partial transparency. Power, but not effectiveness, grows as crime wave continues in mid-1990s. Ministry of Internal Affairs had 540,000 troops, including regular police and special units, in 1996. Federal Border Service, 135,000 troops in 1994, then augmented substantially. Main Guard Directorate (presidential guard), 20,000 troops, 1994. Troops of Federal Security Service and Ministry of Internal Affairs heavily involved in Chechnya conflict, 1994–96.

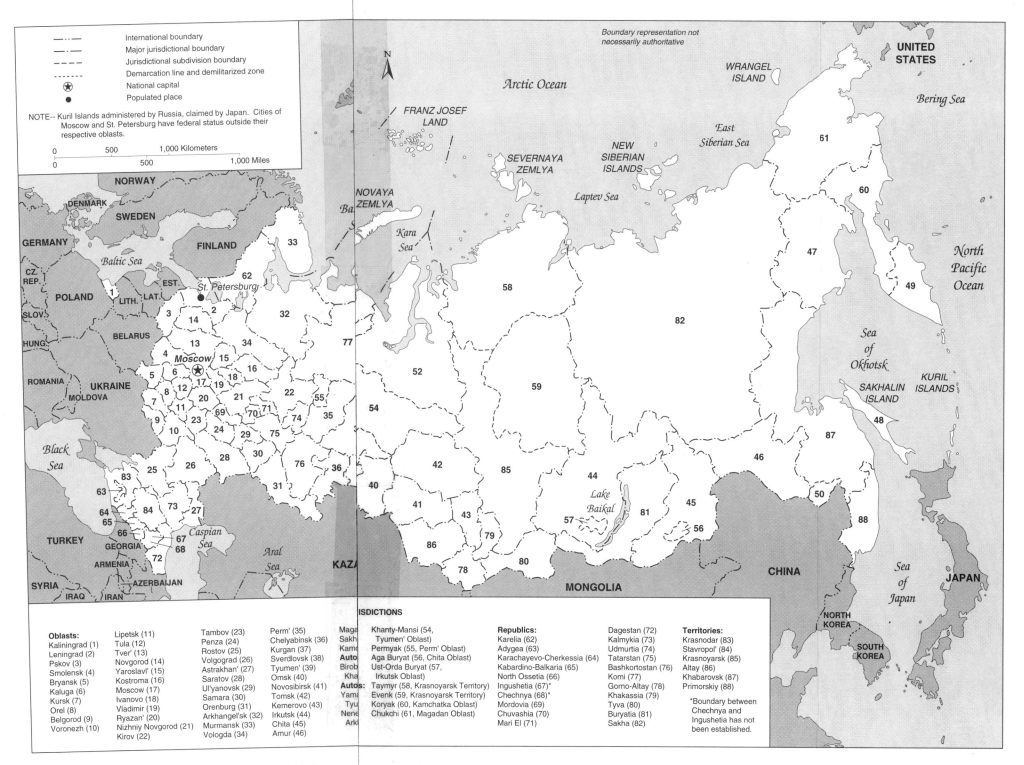

Legend:

- — · — International boundary
- — · · — Major jurisdictional boundary
- — — — Jurisdictional subdivision boundary
- · · · · · Demarcation line and demilitarized zone
- ⊛ National capital
- • Populated place

NOTE-- Kuril Islands administered by Russia, claimed by Japan. Cities of Moscow and St. Petersburg have federal status outside their respective oblasts.

1,000 Kilometers
1,000 Miles

Boundary representation not necessarily authoritative

JURISDICTIONS

Oblasts:
Kaliningrad (1)
Leningrad (2)
Pskov (3)
Smolensk (4)
Bryansk (5)
Kaluga (6)
Kursk (7)
Orel (8)
Belgorod (9)
Voronezh (10)

Lipetsk (11)
Tula (12)
Tver' (13)
Novgorod (14)
Yaroslavl' (15)
Kostroma (16)
Moscow (17)
Ivanovo (18)
Vladimir (19)
Ryazan' (20)
Nizhniy Novgorod (21)
Kirov (22)

Tambov (23)
Penza (24)
Rostov (25)
Volgograd (26)
Astrakhan' (27)
Saratov (28)
Ul'yanovsk (29)
Samara (30)
Orenburg (31)
Arkhangel'sk (32)
Murmansk (33)
Vologda (34)

Perm' (35)
Chelyabinsk (36)
Kurgan (37)
Sverdlovsk (38)
Tyumen' (39)
Omsk (40)
Novosibirsk (41)
Tomsk (42)
Kemerovo (43)
Irkutsk (44)
Chita (45)
Amur (46)

Maga[...]
Sakh[...]
Kam[...]

Auto[...]
Birob[...]
Kha[...]

Autos: Taymyr (58, Krasnoyarsk Territory)
Yama[...] Evenk (59, Krasnoyarsk Territory)
Tyu[...] Koryak (60, Kamchatka Oblast)
Nene[...] Chukchi (61, Magadan Oblast)
Ark[...]

Khanty-Mansi (54, Tyumen' Oblast)
Permyak (55, Perm' Oblast)
Aga Buryat (56, Chita Oblast)
Ust-Orda Buryat (57, Irkutsk Oblast)

Republics:
Karelia (62)
Adygea (63)
Karachayevo-Cherkessia (64)
Kabardino-Balkaria (65)
North Ossetia (66)
Ingushetia (67)*
Chechnya (68)*
Mordovia (69)
Chuvashia (70)
Mari El (71)

Dagestan (72)
Kalmykia (73)
Udmurtia (74)
Tatarstan (75)
Bashkortostan (76)
Komi (77)
Gorno-Altay (78)
Khakassia (79)
Tyva (80)
Buryatia (81)
Sakha (82)

Territories:
Krasnodar (83)
Stavropol' (84)
Krasnoyarsk (85)
Altay (86)
Khabarovsk (87)
Primorskiy (88)

*Boundary between Chechnya and Ingushetia has not been established.

Figure 1. Administrative Divisions of Russia, 1996

lii

Introduction

RUSSIA IS THE LARGEST of the fifteen geopolitical entities that emerged in 1991 from the Soviet Union. Covering more than 17 million square kilometers in Europe and Asia, Russia succeeded the Soviet Union as the largest country in the world. As was the case in the Soviet and tsarist eras, the center of Russia's population and economic activity is the European sector, which occupies about one-quarter of the country's territory. Vast tracts of land in Asian Russia are virtually unoccupied. Although numerous Soviet programs had attempted to populate and exploit resources in Siberia and the Arctic regions of the Russian Republic, the population of Russia's remote areas decreased in the 1990s. Thirty-nine percent of Russia's territory but only 6 percent of its population in 1996 was located east of Lake Baikal, the geographical landmark in south-central Siberia. The territorial extent of the country constitutes a major economic and political problem for Russian governments lacking the far-reaching authoritarian clout of their Soviet predecessors.

In the Soviet political system, which was self-described as a democratic federation of republics, the center of authority for almost all actions of consequence was Moscow, the capital of the Russian Republic. After the breakup of the Soviet Union in 1991, that long-standing concentration of power meant that many of the other fourteen republics faced independence without any experience at self-governance. For Russia, the end of the Soviet Union meant facing the world without the considerable buffer zone of Soviet republics that had protected and nurtured it in various ways since the 1920s; the change required complete reorganization of what had become a thoroughly corrupt and ineffectual socialist system.

Under those circumstances, Russia has undergone an agonizing process of self-analysis and refocusing of national goals. That process, which seemingly had only begun in the mid-1990s, has been observed and commented upon with more analytic energy than any similar transformation in the history of the world. As information pours out past the ruins of the Iron Curtain, a new, more reliable portrait of Russia emerges, but substantial mystery remains.

In a history-making year, the regime of President Mikhail S. Gorbachev of the Soviet Union was mortally injured by an unsuccessful coup in August 1991. After all the constituent republics, including Russia, had voted for independence in the months that followed the coup, Gorbachev announced in December 1991 that the nation would cease to exist. In place of the monolithic union, there remained the Commonwealth of Independent States (CIS—see Glossary), a loose confederation of eleven of the former Soviet republics, which now were independent states with an indefinite mandate of mutual cooperation. By late 1991, the Communist Party of the Soviet Union (CPSU—see Glossary) and the Communist Party of the Russian Republic had been banned in Russia, and Boris N. Yeltsin, who had been elected president of the Russian Republic in June 1991, had become the leader of the new Russian Federation.

In the late 1980s, Yeltsin's appeals for political reform gained him the enmity of the communist hierarchy, including Gorbachev, but he won the support of a Russian public whose self-expression had been liberated by Gorbachev's own policy of *glasnost* (literally, public voicing—see Glossary). In that period, the atmosphere of Russia, especially its main cities, Moscow and Leningrad, was one of expectation that significant political changes finally would occur after the sclerotic decades of the Brezhnev regime (1964–82). The first years of Yeltsin's presidency, which began with an overt challenge to the Soviet Union's authority over Russian affairs, brought a surge of activity that promised economic and political reform and an end to the economic stagnation and social malaise of the 1980s. Both Russians and Westerners hoped that Russia could make a short, painless transformation to democratic rule and free-market economics. Although events of the first five post-Soviet years provided some reasons for optimism, all observers soon realized that whatever transformation Russia was to experience would require much more time, and would yield much less predictable results, than initially expected.

At the time it became independent, the Russian Federation included nineteen autonomous republics, ten autonomous regions, and one autonomous oblast, each designated for a particular ethnic group. The ethnically Russian population was (and remains) the largest group in all but a handful of the republics and autonomous regions; most of the exceptions, where the local ethnic groups constitute a majority, are located in the North Caucasus.

In 1989 the Baltic republics' declarations of sovereignty within the Soviet Union began a cascade of similar declarations by jurisdictions within Russia. In the second half of 1990 alone, ten of Russia's autonomous republics declared sovereignty. When Russia became an independent state, perceptions of Moscow's weakness further encouraged separatist movements, which in turn prompted a long-term campaign by the Yeltsin government to maintain the federation intact. Although some experts predicted that the Russian Federation ultimately would suffer the same fragmentation as the Soviet Union, little evidence of such an outcome has been seen in the first five years of the post-Soviet era.

In 1992 Moscow began the struggle to preserve the federation by inducing all but two autonomous republics (Chechnya and Tatarstan) to sign the Federation Treaty defining the respective areas of jurisdiction of the national and regional governments. The treaty included definitions of sovereignty over natural resources and other economic assets. Since the treaty was signed, Moscow's hegemony has been threatened in several other instances, the most notable being the Republic of Chechnya's fulfillment of its 1991 declaration of independence by a coup against the republic's Russian-controlled government in 1993. Chechnya's defiance and the hapless military response that Russia initiated against the republic in 1994 encouraged other regions to seek more power. In most cases, including oil-rich Tatarstan and diamond-rich Sakha (Yakutia), the Yeltsin government has signed compromise bilateral treaties assuaging local demands, which are mostly economic. Some of Russia's fifty-five lesser jurisdictions—the six territories and the forty-nine oblasts—have made similar demands. Because the federal government has not been able to enforce its policies on a number of issues, the jurisdictions have taken varying approaches to economic and political reform, creating a patchwork effect that has inhibited interregional cooperation.

The military failure in Chechnya was the most obvious indication of a grave overall decline in post-Soviet Russia's military establishment. The Soviet military earned society's gratitude by its performance in the Great Patriotic War (as World War II is commonly called in Russia), a costly but unified and heroic defense of the homeland against invading Nazi armies. In the postwar era, the Soviet military maintained its positive image and budgetary support in good part because of incessant government propaganda about the need to defend the country against the capitalist West.

The demise of the Soviet Union also ended much of the threat of military confrontation between Russia and the West that had characterized the Cold War. Already in the mid-1980s, however, Soviet military doctrine had begun shifting to a more defensive posture in recognition of the country's economic limitations, even as Soviet occupation of the Warsaw Pact (see Glossary) nations and of Afghanistan continued. Beginning in 1988, the Soviet military establishment suffered a series of major blows. The military operation in Afghanistan, which had little success against fervid guerrilla forces, was declared a failure in 1988, and Soviet forces withdrew after nearly ten years of combat. In 1989 the Warsaw Pact alliance began to disintegrate as all the East European member nations rejected their communist governments; the alliance dissolved in 1991, and by 1994 all Russian forces had left Eastern Europe.

The third blow, the end of the Soviet Union itself, required withdrawal of troops stationed in the other fourteen republics; in this process, much equipment and weaponry was left behind and claimed by the newly independent states. The successive return of large numbers of troops into Russia after each of these three events caused an enormous logistical problem for the military; furthermore, the morale of the institution was seriously eroded by withdrawals of unprecedented magnitude from regions assumed to be permanent parts of the Soviet domain. At the same time, serious examples of corruption were exposed at the highest command levels of the armed forces.

In 1992 the Russian Federation inherited the bulk of the Soviet Union's armed forces as well as all of their problems. In the early 1990s, there were new ramifications of the morale and command problems that had surfaced earlier. In a new social environment of permissiveness and diversification, increasing numbers of Russia's youth rejected military service as a patriotic duty, many top individuals in the junior officer corps resigned because of poor pay and housing, and the incidence of crime increased significantly. At the same time, corruption and politicization destroyed the unity that had characterized the senior officer corps during the Soviet era. These changes all occurred as the need for a new set of national security guidelines became increasingly evident. Within a few years, both the geopolitical and the budgetary conditions of Russia's military had changed dramatically without appropriate adjustments in military doctrine. Although the size of the military was reduced between 1992 and 1996 from about 2.8 million personnel to about 1.5 million, reductions were disproportionately high in the enlisted ranks, leaving a bloated officer corps. In 1996 both the military doctrine (which was updated fragmentarily in 1993) and military equipment still reflected the Soviet-era priority of large-scale mechanized land war and/or nuclear war to be fought on the continent of Europe.

In 1996 elements of a new military doctrine appeared, but fundamental conflict remained between reformers and hard-liners in the policy-making establishment. The strong positions taken by the opposing sides suggested that enacting a comprehensive new doctrine would involve a long struggle. Despite the diminished capability of Russia's economy to support the military, hard-liners insisted that major reductions would damage national security. As budgetary support of routine military readiness has shrunk drastically in the mid-1990s, calls for large-scale reform have intensified. Among the main reform elements cited are downsizing the armed forces, shifting their emphasis to mobile warfare, eliminating much of the corrupt and flabby corps of senior officers, relying more heavily on contract volunteers rather than conscripts, and discarding the concept of military parity with the United States. In July 1996, the State Duma (the lower house of the Russian parliament) began hearings on reform measures. In December the Duma recommended the formation of a federal department to set military reform guidelines through 2005, together with a 25 percent increase in the military budget.

The condition of the military forces remains an important part of Russia's national self-image. The Chechnya conflict, the first post-Soviet test of those forces, revealed shocking insufficiencies even in elite units. In mid-1996 the dismissal of Minister of Defense Pavel Grachev, upon whom the most blame for Chechnya had been heaped, produced no visible improvement. In August 1996, the sudden loss of the Chechen capital of Groznyy, from which Russian forces had driven the Chechen guerrillas in 1995, forced the withdrawal of Russian forces under the terms of the cease-fire that followed.

In the second half of 1996, ultimate responsibility for military policy remained balanced uncertainly between civilian and military authorities, as it was when Grachev was minister of defense. In November 1996, a call for a new military doctrine by Yeltsin's civilian Defense Council met stiff resistance from the Ministry of Defense.

Grachev's successor, Igor' Rodionov, inherited a force with plummeting morale, gravely deteriorating matériel support, minimal training, and no clear doctrine. In the second draft call of 1996, an estimated 37,000 men out of a target number of 215,000 conscripts failed to report. This was the largest recorded episode of draft dodging since the establishment of the Soviet Union. The budget passed in January 1997 added only token amounts to the 1996 allotment of US$19 billion. The budget provided for only about 38 percent of the Ministry of Defense's budget request and made no allowance for inflation. The 1997 budget package caused Rodionov to curse the Ministry of Finance as Grachev had, intensifying tensions among the "power ministries" of the Government (cabinet). Meanwhile, in the last months of 1996 the pay arrears of the Ministry of Defense mounted steadily, and there were rumors that military strike committees had been formed. Already in August, an estimated US$2.8 billion was owed to Russia's military personnel. Rodionov also repeated Grachev's complaint that military units of the internal security agencies received funding that should go to the Ministry of Defense. The exact troop levels of those units are unknown, but in the second half of 1996 some estimates exceeded 1 million.

Rodionov predicted that the grandiose plans of Yeltsin and others for military restructuring and modernization would be frustrated without significant expenditures in the transition period. The plans included large-scale force reduction, a new military doctrine matching Russia's less stressful post-Cold-War geopolitical position, and possibly an all-volunteer force. In January 1997, the Ministry of Defense submitted a reform plan whose first step was increased funding. The Defense Council submitted a rival, long-term plan extending beyond 2005 and calling for 30 percent reductions in defense and non-defense troop levels as the first reform step, citing the country's low financial resources. The conflicting emphasis of the two plans exacerbated the existing disagreements in the defense establishment, specifically between Rodionov and Defense Council chief Yuriy Baturin, over the direction of reform.

Meanwhile, accusations of corruption and incompetence in the military establishment continued, with Duma Defense Committee chairman Lev Rokhlin, a retired general, levying the most serious charges. Those charges combined with the military's abject failure in Chechnya to further erode the authority of the Ministry of Defense under Rodionov. In December 1996, Yeltsin forced Rodionov to resign his commission in order to move the ministry toward civilian rather than military control.

As Russia's military deteriorated, the arms export activities of its defense industries continued to grow. In 1995 Russia exported more arms to developing countries than any other producer; China was its best customer. Total 1995 sales were estimated at US$6 billion, an increase of 62 percent over 1994. At the end of 1996, defense authorities announced that foreign arms sales would play a prominent role in financing military reform in coming years. In early 1997, Russia angered the West by selling S–300 missile systems to the Republic of Cyprus and by selling a third Kilo-class diesel submarine to Iran.

Some of the most visible domestic products of the arms industry suffered production delays in 1996. In November construction began on the *Yuriy Dolgorukiy*, the first in the new Severodvinsk class of strategic missile submarines described as superior to any existing model and expected to carry Russia's sea-based nuclear missiles after 2000. Plans had called for three such boats to go into production in 1996. The *Petr Velikiy*, a powerful, heavily armed cruiser whose keel was laid in 1986, finally took its maiden voyage in October 1996 after years of production delays. In March 1997, the Moscow Aviation Production Association (MAPO) postponed serial production of an advanced multifunctional fighter, targeting instead the MiG–35 fighter destined for overseas sales.

The agencies of internal security have fared better than the military in the post-Soviet era. Throughout the Soviet period, these agencies were among the most firmly entrenched and respected national institutions. A succession of internal security agencies, ending with the Committee for State Security (Komitet gosudarstvennoy bezopasnosti—KGB; see Glossary), struck fear in the Soviet population by thoroughly penetrating all of society and launching periodic purges (the most violent of which occurred in the 1930s) against elements of society deemed harmful to the socialist state.

In the post-Soviet era, internal security agencies generally have received more solid support from the Yeltsin government than the armed forces, although specific agencies have been favored. The Federal Security Service (FSB), the most direct successor to the KGB, has a broad mandate for intelligence gathering inside Russia and abroad when national security is threatened, and no concrete governmental oversight is prescribed in legislation. Human rights advocates in Russia and elsewhere, sensitive to the precedent of unbridled KGB power, have criticized the direct presidential control of internal security agencies such as the FSB, and human rights violations have been documented. Armed units of the FSB and the Ministry of Internal Affairs (MVD) were heavily involved in the Chechnya campaign.

Russia's still-powerful internal security agencies also were hit by scandal in 1996 when the former financial head of the Federal Agency for Government Communications and Information (FAPSI) was imprisoned by its sister agency, the FSB, for embezzling large sums from the FAPSI budget. Although the affair received no official acknowledgment, the independent press reported a major power struggle between powerful successor agencies of the KGB. Such a scenario would continue a series of rearrangements of the former KGB agencies that have occurred in the 1990s because of political power struggles rather than security considerations.

Rampant, well-publicized corruption in the security agencies has eroded public confidence in all of Russian law enforcement. In July 1996, the Ministry of Internal Affairs (MVD) reported that 1,400 employees of the regular police (militia) had been arrested in 1995 for various types of criminal activity, including participation in crimes by criminal organizations of the *mafiya*. That report was the result of the MVD's Clean Hands Campaign, a highly publicized public-confidence program begun in 1995 to purge law enforcement agencies of dishonest members. But, according to most accounts, the 1995 arrests removed only a very small part of Russia's internal security corruption.

Russia has experimented cautiously with Western-style jurisprudence and penal reform. In the mid-1990s, jury trials were introduced in some regions, and the rights of accused persons and prison inmates were stipulated more concretely. Nevertheless, major elements of the Soviet system remain in the jurisprudence of the Russian Federation. For example, procurators (public prosecutors) still have both investigative and prosecutorial functions, and expansion of the jury system has met substantial resistance among entrenched Soviet-era judges and procurators. In addition, prison conditions have deteriorated substantially because Russia's crime wave has increased the prison population but funding is not available for new facilities. In early 1997, more than one-quarter of the prison population was awaiting trial, and pretrial detention lasted as long as three years for some individuals. Russia's procurator general, Yuriy Skuratov, reported that his office had been overwhelmed in 1996 with 1.2 million court cases, for which it had only about 7,000 investigators. He noted that the same trend was continuing in 1997.

After many delays and amendments, a new Criminal Code went into effect on January 1, 1997. An estimated 150,000 criminal cases were expected to require review based on the new code, and many prisoners will be released because the laws under which they were convicted no longer exist. A separate criminal correction code defining conditions in the prison system was scheduled to go into effect in July 1997.

Compounding Russia's other problems are deteriorating environmental conditions, the extent of which became clear only gradually during the 1990s. Among the most serious hazards in Russia are pollution of ground water and bodies of water in most of European Russia; air pollution from the venting of unprocessed industrial by-products; large concentrations of waste chemicals from industry and agriculture; and actual and potential radiological pollution from civilian and military nuclear installations.

In August 1996, the Bellona Foundation of Oslo, long a vocal critic of Russia's nuclear waste procedures, issued a damning report on the threat posed to Arctic regions by Russia's nuclear waste disposal practices and at least thirty-six decommissioned nuclear submarines at anchor near Murmansk with their reactors on board. Bellona described the Murmansk region as having the world's largest concentration of active and defunct nuclear reactors, many of which are not maintained or disposed of properly. According to the report, the FSB obstructed the foundation's investigation and imprisoned Aleksandr Nikitin, the retired Russian naval officer who was a key author of the report. As Nikitin's trial was delayed repeatedly, his case attracted international protests.

Meanwhile, the interdepartmental Commission for Ecological Safety, headed by senior environmental authority Aleksey Yablokov, continued releasing shocking statistics about Russia's environmental quality. For example, in 1996 one in five tap-water samples failed to meet public health chemical standards, and about 40 percent of sewage was being dumped untreated into bodies of water, with Moscow and St. Petersburg among the regions most affected. In the second half of 1996, Yablokov lobbied Yeltsin unsuccessfully to expand the ecological safety commission and its funding.

Russian environmentalists won a battle in December 1996 when a regional referendum soundly rejected completion of the Kostroma Nuclear Power Station, on which construction had been suspended after the Chernobyl' disaster of 1986. This was Russia's first referendum on such an issue; the 59 percent turnout made the vote legally binding. In February 1997, the Republic of Sakha announced plans to conserve one-quarter of its vast Siberian territory, including the world's largest tract of virgin forest, protecting several endangered species and the shrinking indigenous population of Evenk nomads. That plan bypassed national authorities—an increasingly frequent trend in environmental and other matters. The Sakha government received a support grant directly from a Swiss environmental organization.

The "social umbrella" of the Soviet Union's socialist system, which nominally had guaranteed all citizens employment, health care, child care, pensions, and universal, high-quality education, also encountered problems. By the 1980s, many of the more than 200 million citizens covered by the umbrella began receiving fewer benefits or benefits of lesser quality. The Soviet education and health systems, which offered top-quality service only to the country's political, scientific, and cultural elite, were undermined by the infrastructural and organizational failures inherent in such centrally planned systems. The Soviet concept of guaranteed employment eroded the national economy by encouraging slipshod labor and malingering.

In the 1990s, the state's social welfare system retained the bureaucratic complexities of the Soviet era, but it did not keep pace with the needs of society. As runaway inflation devalued the fixed payments of the pension system, many citizens depending on fixed incomes fell below the official poverty line, which in late 1996 was about US$67 per month. In 1996 an estimated 30 percent of those with fixed incomes and about 24 percent of the total population were in that category. The government's failure to index welfare programs also reduced the value of a wide variety of other entitlements that had provided Soviet workers with substantial savings in the cost of living. Nevertheless, Soviet-era programs such as maternity leave, child care, free medical facilities, and housing subsidies remained substantially unchanged in the mid-1990s, continuing expectations that increasingly strained the federal budget.

Reforms such as pension indexation and differentiation of individual contributions to pension funds were only beginning to appear in the mid-1990s. By that time, the government's inability to collect taxes and other obligated funds had had a major impact on social programs. In the fall of 1996, an estimated US$3 billion in pension payments were overdue. At that point, the Pension Fund, which is administered by the Ministry of Social Protection, was owed US$8.5 billion by the enterprises that are the main contributors. The federal budget also owed money to the fund, which by mid-1996 had exhausted its commercial bank credits by taking loans to make pension payments.

Russia's health care system also deteriorated substantially in the 1990s. Equipment and medicines are in increasingly short supply, aging facilities have not been replaced, and existing facilities often are inaccessible. Medical personnel generally are not trained as rigorously as their contemporaries in the West, and chronic failures to pay doctors and nurses have exacerbated shortages in those professions. The 1997 national budget allocated US$1.6 billion for health, an increase of US$158 million over 1996, but most of the new money was targeted for medical centers in large cities. The 1997 figure was 2.6 percent of the gross domestic product (GDP—see Glossary), compared with the World Health Organization's recommended minimum share of 5 percent.

Failures in health care are one aspect of an increasingly grave health crisis afflicting the Russian population as a whole in the 1990s. Other elements of the crisis include widespread and acute environmental pollution of various types, which government programs and nongovernmental "green" organizations have not been able to ameliorate; the continued heavy use of tobacco and alcohol and a growing narcotics addiction problem; and poor hygiene and nutrition practices among large portions of the population.

In the first ten months of 1996, confirmed cases of human immunodeficiency virus (HIV) were four times more numerous than in all of 1995, with drug addicts accounting for about 70 percent of cases. Although the official estimate of HIV cases was fewer than 2,000 in 1996, other estimates placed the number at ten times that many. The Ministry of Health reported that only 50,000 of Russia's estimated 2 million drug addicts were under treatment for their addiction in 1996. In 1996 health experts identified alcoholism as the number-one cause of premature death in Russia, a situation exacerbated by the estimated 68 percent of alcohol products that contain foreign substances. By 1995 Russia's average life expectancy had fallen to only fifty-seven years for males and seventy-one for females, and natural population growth has been negative since 1992. In the first nine months of 1996, the population showed a net decrease of 350,000, dropping to 147.6 million according to the State Committee for Statistics.

Russia's education system has suffered from the same shortages and lack of support as its health system. And education, accorded high value in Soviet society, seems to have lost some of its esteem in a fragmented Russian society where many traditional institutions are viewed with unprecedented skepticism. In the 1990s, the centralized, rigid Soviet education system has given way to a system that gives localities substantial autonomy in shaping curricula and hiring teachers. This opportunity for creativity has been hampered, however, by two conditions: because many Soviet-trained Russian educators do not understand individual initiative and autonomy, many schools have perpetuated the rote memorization methods of the past; and, as in other aspects of Russian social policy, funding for personnel and infrastructure has been woefully inadequate. Teachers, always underpaid in the Soviet system, have been impoverished by the Russian system, and many have left the profession since 1992. In this atmosphere, private schools have begun to offer creative curricula to students who can afford to eschew public schooling. According to Deputy Prime Minister Viktor Ilyushin, by October 1996 education and culture had received only 65 percent and 30 percent, respectively, of the 1996 budget funds allotted to them. In late 1996 and early 1997, the highest proportion of striking workers were teachers.

Beginning in the late 1980s, religion assumed a more important role in the lives of many Russians, and in the life of the Russian state as well. Russian Orthodoxy, the dominant religion of Russia since the ruler Vladimir accepted Christianity in A.D. 988, was subservient to the state from the time of Peter the Great (r. 1682–1725) until 1917; nevertheless, it exerted a powerful influence on the spiritual lives of most Russians. In the Soviet period, the activities of the church were further restricted as most churches and monasteries were closed and religious observances strongly discouraged.

In the late 1980s, the Gorbachev regime began to restore the church's property and rights; official observance of the millennium of Russian Orthodoxy in 1988 was a watershed event in that process. Beginning in 1992, the Russian Orthodox patriarchate, which had been restored in 1917 only to be repressed for the next seventy years, assumed growing influence in state as well as spiritual affairs. Many churches were built and restored, and in the early 1990s millions of Russians returned to regular worship. However, by early 1997 Orthodox Russians attended church at about the same rate as religious believers in West European countries. In the 1990s, politicians have eagerly sought the opinion of the church on most important issues, and in 1996 even the communist presidential candidate, Gennadiy Zyuganov, made an appearance with Patriarch Aleksiy II an important element of his campaign.

Other religious groups also have enjoyed relative freedom in the post-Soviet period, with some limitations. Mainstream Protestant, Roman Catholic, and Muslim groups are fully accepted by the state and the Orthodox Church, but the Orthodox hierarchy often has used its dominant position to discourage or block the activities of their congregations. The new freedom of the Gorbachev era brought a wave of Western evangelical groups whose proselytizing the Orthodox hierarchy viewed with alarm and hostility. In mid-1996 the State Duma passed legislation establishing a state committee to monitor the activity of such groups. The law was introduced by nationalist allies of the Orthodox Church and opposed by democratic factions as unconstitutional. The Jewish community, whose religious and cultural activities have blossomed in Russia in the 1990s, still experiences subtle forms of discrimination.

The problems of post-Soviet Russia also are based directly in economic circumstances. Some of the reasons for Russia's uneven progress are found in the legacy of the Soviet era, others in post-Soviet economic policies. For the majority of Russian citizens, the ballyhooed economic reforms of the 1990s did not improve the quality of life; indeed, in 1996 the "shock" of Russia's transition to a free-enterprise system seemed to be intensifying rather than subsiding, as unemployment figures rose and more Russians slipped below the official poverty line. In the first half of 1996, the number of registered unemployed workers increased by 16 percent, totaling 2.7 million—but a much higher number of Russians remained unemployed and failed to register for meager state benefits. According to an official report, average real incomes decreased by about 40 percent between 1991 and October 1996.

Russia's society has become increasingly divided according to economic categories. As the majority of Russian citizens struggle to remain above the poverty line, a small minority have prospered through high-risk economic ventures that often involve connections with the *mafiya*, Russia's pervasive network of organized criminal organizations. Members of the successful minority increasingly are distinguished from the majority of society by conspicuous consumption, which has engendered strong feelings of resentment. Another type of post-Soviet success story is demonstrated by former members of the Soviet official elite, the *nomenklatura*, who have used Soviet-era connections to gain access to financial resources and influential enterprise positions in the new system. By 1997 experts had identified a new oligarchy—the post-Soviet entrepreneurs who have built personal empires and strong ties with the government at the expense of their fellow Russians. Russian society also is increasingly divided by generations. Older Russians have found adapting to the complexities and challenges of post-Soviet society much more difficult than have their younger compatriots, so the former often preserve as much as possible of their former lives, garnished with nostalgia for an idealized Soviet past.

Moscow has become the center of Russia's economic activity, both personal and corporate, far outstripping St. Petersburg, which in the Soviet era was the more cosmopolitan city. Many foreign investors have concentrated their activity in Moscow, where all of Russia's large banks are headquartered and where the energetic Mayor Yuriy Luzhkov has fostered rapid commercial expansion with active government participation. Meanwhile, the luxurious life of the new Moscow upper class has spread very little to the hinterlands.

The increasing availability of land and materials has enabled some individuals to escape dependency on the old housing subsidy system (which nevertheless remained active in 1997). In the transition to a fully privatized housing system that began in 1992, the scarcity of resources and high inflation drove private housing prices beyond the reach of most Russians; in the mid-1990s, the slow, uneven progress of housing reform meant the continued existence of long waiting lists and very crowded housing conditions, especially in the cities.

The Soviet and Russian economies have been supported by one of the richest supplies of natural resources in the world. Fuels, minerals, timber, and a well-educated labor force always have been strong principal assets of industry. But the location of Russia's raw materials often has presented a transportation problem. As the industrial centers of European Russia used up nearby fuels and other resources, the more distant supplies of Siberia have become critical but expensive alternatives. The sheer volume of available raw materials encouraged tremendous waste in the Soviet system; central planning took into account neither the possibility of running out of materials nor the grave environmental damage caused by uncontrolled exploitation.

Economic policy in the Soviet Union was the exclusive domain of planners in the central government, whose quotas and distribution decisions ruled virtually all economic activity in Russia and the other Soviet republics. Resource apportionment in that system favored heavy industry and the military-industrial complex at the expense of consumer production, token revival of which was attempted sporadically beginning with the regime of Nikita S. Khrushchev (in office 1953–64). The services sector remained underdeveloped, and agricultural production policy precluded private landownership and relied almost entirely on collective farms (see Glossary) and state farms (see Glossary). Central allocation of resources and price establishment created an inflexible economic system whose production and consumption sides had no relation to each other. The basic unit of planning, the five-year plan (see Glossary), set long-term goals whose basis in real economic conditions often was nonexistent by the end of the period. The Soviet planning system also produced a substantial class of state bureaucrats, many of whom preserved their influential and highly profitable positions in state enterprises (and hence their stubborn opposition to economic reform) well into the post-Soviet era.

The Soviet state also had full control of foreign trade. The vast majority of Russia's overseas commercial activity was conducted with the nations of the Community for Mutual Economic Assistance (Comecon—see Glossary), all of which followed the Soviet model of the centrally planned economy, and all of which were governed by Comecon's artificial system for allocation of production responsibilities. This closed commercial system included a high percentage of barter arrangements. The system was supplemented by equally regimented commercial links among the republics of the Soviet Union. An important result was that Russian products were exposed to very little genuine competition in world markets, despite periodic efforts to cultivate commercial relationships outside Comecon.

By 1980 the Soviet economy had entered a decline from which it never was to emerge. It became obvious that the strong central controls that traditionally guided economic development had failed to promote the creativity and productivity urgently needed in a highly developed, modern economy. As one of the two world superpowers, the Soviet Union was acutely conscious that the West, and especially the United States, was bypassing it in many areas outside the military field. So, beginning in the mid-1980s, Soviet leader Mikhail S. Gorbachev (in office 1985–91) experimented with unprecedented economic reforms, including limited application of free-market principles, in a policy called *perestroika* (rebuilding—see Glossary). However, the Gorbachev concessions were too small and too late, so the system's inherent flaws remained. The standard of living and productivity both continued to fall until the Soviet Union dissolved and central planning was discredited in 1991.

As president of the Russian Republic, Boris Yeltsin already had advocated substantial economic reform prior to Russia's independence, in order to begin resurrecting Russia's economy from the crisis of the last Soviet years. For the new Russian Federation, the Yeltsin administration set ambitious economic reform goals in 1992: strict limitation of government spending to cut inflation; redirection of state investment from the military-industrial complex and heavy industry toward consumer production; a new tax system to redistribute financial resources to more efficient sectors; cutting of government subsidies for enterprises and eliminating government price controls; and lifting of government control of foreign trade. Privatization of the major sectors of production, still virtually state monopolies in 1991, was another primary goal.

In 1992 worsening economic conditions brought a confrontation with the Supreme Soviet (legislature) over economic policy. The clash forced Yeltsin's dismissal of reform Prime Minister Yegor Gaydar and a general modification of reform goals under Gaydar's pragmatic successor, Viktor Chernomyrdin. At that point, failing enterprises still received easy credit from the banking system and from other enterprises—a continuation of Soviet-style fiscal management and a crucial flaw that began to be corrected only in 1995.

Many of the goals of the Yeltsin program were met at least partially in the first five post-Soviet years, depending on which statistics are used to define economic trends. Foreign trade has been liberalized significantly, and the list of Russia's trading partners now is dominated by West European rather than East European and former Soviet countries. The course of foreign investment has been uneven. Although Western and Japanese firms have shown great interest in joint ventures with Russian enterprises, Russia's unfinished and uncertain commercial and legal infrastructure has limited foreign participation, and protectionist laws restrict foreign activity in industries such as communications and automobiles. International lenders such as the International Monetary Fund (IMF—see Glossary), the Paris Club of Western government lenders, and the London Club of international commercial banks have provided substantial aid, with the caveat that Russia must improve economic indicators such as its inflation rate and budget deficits. In 1993 and 1994, soaring inflation and government deregulation of prices robbed consumers of much of their purchasing power before a government tight-money policy brought inflation under control in 1995 and 1996. In December 1996, prices rose by 1.4 percent, although wage arrears made that figure irrelevant for many Russians.

The Yeltsin privatization program began with small enterprises, a large proportion of which were in private hands by 1995. Sales of larger enterprises, accomplished in several phases, encountered substantial difficulties, however. In 1995 allegations of corruption slowed the process, as did persistent opposition from the antireform State Duma factions. Privatization was virtually halted during the 1996 presidential election campaign, but in July 1996 the administration announced new goals and a reformed system for ownership transition. Initially positive, Western evaluations of Russia's privatization program were tempered in 1996 by continued government favoritism toward former state enterprises, by the sale of investment shares to banks and other institutions with close state connections rather than to the public, and by the program's distinct slowdown in 1996. In October 1996, the government had collected only 14 percent of the year's targeted privatization revenue of US$2.2 billion. In November the planned public sale of stock in two major state-owned telecommunications firms, Rostelekom and Svyazinvest, was canceled in favor of stock sales to two large banks that had financed Yeltsin's 1996 campaign, heralding a new privatization scandal. The 1997 national budget set a privatization income goal for 1997 at US$1.1 billion, but already in February Vladimir Potanin, head of the privatization revenue collection commission, expressed doubt that the goal could be met.

Tax collection remained a major problem for Russia as of early 1997. Although some nominal tax reforms were put in place, tax collection remained inept, and the system still failed to promote private initiative or foreign investment. Despite constant government pleas, promises, and reform blueprints, and despite substantial pressure from the IMF, in 1997 taxation remained the main obstacle to budgetary solvency.

The government lost large amounts of tax revenue because unofficial and illegal commerce is widespread and because the State Taxation Service inspires so little respect from legitimate businesses. According to an official 1996 estimate, only 16 percent of Russia's 2.6 million firms were paying taxes regularly, and at least twice that number paid no taxes at all. On three different occasions, the IMF postponed installments of a US$10.1 billion loan to Russia because of the taxation problem—twice in the second half of 1996 and again in February 1997.

When the official tax shortfall reached US$24.4 billion in October 1996, the government began televising appeals for tax-law compliance. A new emergency tax commission, headed by Prime Minister Chernomyrdin and Chief of Staff Anatoliy Chubays, targeted seventeen of Russia's largest companies for bankruptcy proceedings if their huge tax arrears were not paid immediately. Among the most delinquent enterprises were three subsidiaries of Chernomyrdin's extremely wealthy former company, the State National Gas Company (Gazprom), which reportedly owed US$2.1 billion. Many large enterprises failed to comply, and much of Russia's extensive so-called shadow economy remained beyond the reach of the commission. Critics characterized the emergency commission as a stopgap tactic that delayed fundamental reform in the tax system. According to government statistics, in 1996 some 20,000 collection orders were issued for back taxes amounting to US$15.7 billion; the orders yielded only US$3.8 billion to the state budget. Early in 1997, Minister of Finance Aleksandr Livshits drafted a new tax code that would have saved the government an estimated US$30 billion annually. But the plan's anticipated closing of profitable loopholes attracted sharp resistance. In February 1997, Minister of Internal Affairs Anatoliy Kulikov, known as a hard-liner, was given the task of cracking down on tax violators. Yeltsin removed Livshits from his position during the Government reorganization of March 1997.

In March the Government threatened bankruptcy proceedings against a new group of ninety nonpaying enterprises, many of them quite large, hoping to encourage public sales of shares that would dislodge Soviet-era managers in favor of outside investors. At the same time, privatization chief Al'fred Kokh was given control of the inept State Taxation Service.

Besides the chronic tax collection failure, institutional remains of the Soviet era also continue to plague economic progress. In many large plants, the economic reforms of the early 1990s left control with the same managers who had run the plants for the state. In the post-Soviet years, managers have taken advantage of Russia's new free-market atmosphere, and the lack of effective commercial legislation, to line their own pockets—often in cooperation with criminal organizations—while paying little attention to plant productivity. In 1996 the Government increased subsidies to some major automobile and defense plants, reversing the direction of privatization and further diminishing incentives.

Another obstacle to economic stability is the pervasive influence on economic activity of the *mafiya*—as commonly used in Russia, a term including gangsters, dishonest businesspeople, and corrupt officials. In the 1990s, Russia is suffering the effects of an increasingly prosperous national network of criminals who extort protection money from an estimated 75 percent of businesses and banks. Individuals refusing such payments often are the victims of violent crimes. In 1995 gangs controlled an estimated 50,000 private and state enterprises and had full ownership of thousands more. Unlike organized criminal groups in the West, which specialize in illegal activity such as drug trafficking and prostitution, Russia's *mafiya* spans the entire range of the economy, discouraging private enterprise and siphoning off 10 to 20 percent of enterprise profits that are neither taxed nor reinvested in legitimate business. Organized crime also has been involved in the movement of a huge amount of capital—estimated at US$1 to US$2 billion per month—out of Russia in the mid-1990s. Such activity has prospered mainly because of strong links with corrupt officials; an estimated 30 to 50 percent of organized crime's proceeds is spent on bribes to procurators, police, and bureaucrats.

This connection is not new in the post-Soviet era; already in the Brezhnev era, officials took bribes from the underworld as the black market responded to gaps in Soviet production. In the early post-Soviet years, reformers implicitly condoned such activity in the hope that it would hasten the development of a legitimate private-enterprise sector. In 1993, however, government measures against criminals were stimulated by publicity about Russia's crime wave and by the success of ultranationalist political groups who stressed the crime issue. Many of the Yeltsin administration's law enforcement decrees of 1993 and 1994 were of questionable constitutionality, and they have had little overall effect in the mid-1990s because law enforcement agencies remain corrupt.

As Russia has attempted to meet the standards for inflation and budget deficits set by international lenders, a key element has been limiting the money supply, which was poorly controlled until 1995. The more stringent policies established that year brought loud complaints from regional governments, an increase in noncurrency payments that hampered the collection of state revenue, and continued wage arrears in state and private enterprises suffering cash shortages. Although the annual inflation rate for 1996 was 22 percent, compared with 131 percent in 1995, authorities in the Government and elsewhere blamed a new economic downturn on the tight-money policy because private enterprises lacked capital with which to expand their operations.

The 1997 monetary plan of the Russian Central Bank (RCB) called for increasing the money supply by 22 to 30 percent during that year, a level not projected to raise inflation above the 12 percent annual increase forecast by the 1997 national budget. At the end of 1996, the RCB planned for a ruble depreciation of 9 percent during 1997, which would maintain the exchange rate at between 5,750 and 6,350 rubles per United States dollar at the end of the year. During 1996 the exchange rate moved from 4,640 rubles to the dollar to 5,560, an increase of nearly 20 percent.

A Government goal for 1997 was reducing the interest rate for domestic bank loans to 20 or 25 percent to provide working capital for stagnant enterprises and limit the haphazard, uncontrolled interenterprise loans and in-kind payments that had proliferated as capital became scarce. However, shares in most enterprises remained unavailable to the general public, and the high-interest bonds sold by the Government in 1996 had attracted large amounts of bank capital away from more risky investment in private ventures.

The Government's draft 1997 budget, which had been revised by a conciliation commission of legislators and Government representatives, was approved by the State Duma in January after the four readings required by law. After the first two drafts were rejected, the Government added about US$6 billion in spending and new tax breaks to stimulate economic activity. The changes swung the votes of the Communist Party of the Russian Federation (Kommunisticheskaya partiya Rossiyskoy Federatsii—KPRF) and its allies, who had lobbied for additional government spending, but democratic parties such as Yabloko voted against the budget because of inadequate fiscal restraint. The Federation Council (the upper house of the parliament) approved the budget but expressed serious doubts about the realism of its revenue projections.

As approved, the budget was based on projections of 11.8 percent annual inflation and GDP growth of 2 percent for 1997. The planned budget deficit of about US$16.5 billion would be 3.5 percent of the projected GDP figure. However, Russian and Western experts, including Russia's minister of economics, Yevgeniy Yasin, called the GDP projection greatly exaggerated. Yasin's ministry forecast zero GDP growth for 1997, with recovery beginning in 1998 at the earliest. The budget did not include a 10 percent increase in Russia's minimum wage that went into effect in January 1997 and that would entail additional state spending. In 1996 the government's issue of bonds with interest rates exceeding 100 percent had complicated the budget-balancing process by tripling the government borrowing of 1995 and inflating the public debt from 16 to 26 percent of GDP.

Economic indicators for the first half of 1996 were mostly negative. According to an independent Russian survey, compared with December 1995 the real volume of production and services dropped by 11 percent, the number of employed persons dropped by 4 percent, the real volume of capital investment dropped by 54 percent, the average prices of manufactured products and purchased products rose by 14 percent and 25 percent, respectively, and the average wage rose by 10 percent. In the first nine months of 1996, total GDP dropped by 6 percent, and industrial output dropped by 5 percent compared with the same period in 1995. Light industry, construction materials, and machine building showed the sharpest drops in production, and domestic investment declined by 17 percent.

In the first nine months of 1996, agricultural production dropped by 8 percent. Russia's 1996 grain harvest was 69 million tons, one of the smallest in the last thirty years and only a 9 percent improvement over the disastrously low harvest of 1995. An estimated three-quarters of farms lost money, and only two-thirds of 1996 budget allotments for farm support were paid out. As of early 1997, the restructuring of the agricultural system was one of the major unfulfilled promises of Yeltsin's presidency.

Russia's foreign trade position did not improve significantly in 1996. Membership in the World Trade Organization (WTO—see Glossary), a top priority for acceptance in the international free market, continued to be delayed. Although some aspects of Russia's trade policy have been liberalized substantially, the WTO cited continuing price controls on oil, state subsidies to major industries, protective import duties, and abrupt changes in tariff and tax policies for foreign companies as defects that precluded Russia's membership. According to the WTO, stability and transparency were the major missing elements in Russia's trade policy. Although the United States pledged support for Russia's admittance in 1998, prospects were unclear in early 1997.

Foreign investment for 1996 was forecast to reach only slightly more than half the 1995 figure (US$1.5 billion), mainly because of continuing uncertainty in Russia's standards for taxation, accounting, and property rights. In October 1996, an international market consulting firm placed Russia below Brazil, Indonesia, Mexico, and Venezuela in desirability as an emerging market opportunity for investors. Corruption, fraud, and bureaucratic delays were cited as the main factors in that ranking. In November the failure of a Russian space mission to Mars lost foreign investors about US$180 million, as well as damaging the stature of a key remaining high-technology industry. In April the space program suffered further damage with the delay of the new Russia-United States International Space Station because the Government had not funded a critical aerospace contractor.

On the positive side, in October foreign investors paid nearly US$450 million for shares in Gazprom, the natural gas monopoly. About forty joint ventures were active in the oil industry in 1996, accounting for about 8 percent of Russia's total extraction. Foreign investment in Russia's extraction industries was expected to expand significantly beginning in 1997 as the State Duma expedited approval of the production-sharing agreements that are the basis of foreign participation.

In November 1996, Russia issued its first set of bonds on the European market after receiving an unexpectedly high bond rating from Western credit agencies. Following Russia's first bond rating since 1917, the bonds drew US$1 billion from United States, European, and South Korean investors attracted by the 9.25 percent interest rate. A place in the bond market was expected to help Russia raise money from other international sources. In March 1997, the issue of a second set of bonds, this time denominated in German marks, fetched US$1.2 billion. A third issue was planned for later in 1997; like the second, it was designated to pay overdue pensions and salaries.

In late 1996 and early 1997, labor groups showed some signs of ending their remarkably passive reaction to the chronic wage arrears in many of Russia's industries. (In March 1997, the total wage debt was estimated at US$8.5 billion.) Through most of 1996, with a few notable exceptions such as the coal workers, labor in Russia followed the Soviet pattern of expecting the government rather than enterprise managers to remedy their plight.

The older trade unions, many of whose leaders had been hand-picked by plant managers in the Soviet era, generally discouraged strong actions against employers in the early and mid-1990s. Unions formed after 1985 suffered from Russia's total lack of labor legislation, which allowed the government and enterprise officials to ignore union claims on behalf of the workers. Experts pointed to the lack of pressure from a united labor movement as a key reason the Yeltsin government failed to address the problem of overdue wages.

In the second half of 1996, strike activity intensified somewhat. According to government statistics, 356,000 workers at more than 3,700 enterprises participated in strikes in the first nine months of 1996, with the largest number of strikes in educational institutions and coal mines. (Doctors, miners, nurses, and teachers were the workers hardest hit by wage arrears.)

In November 1996 and March 1997, nationwide strikes and demonstrations called by the Federation of Independent Trade

Unions of Russia (Federatsiya nezavisimikh profsoyuzov Rossii—FNPR), the largest such organization in the country, failed to galvanize widespread support. In the March action, an estimated 2 million workers struck or demonstrated, but more than 80 percent of those were teachers, and the FNPR had predicted substantially heavier participation. Observers attributed the low turnout to apathy, lack of trust in the FNPR, and the expectation that Yeltsin's recent government reorganization would improve the situation.

The democratization of the political system has followed an equally bumpy path in Russia's first post-Soviet years. As with economic reform, some elements of political reform appeared under Gorbachev in the late 1980s. The policy of *glasnost* allowed public discussion of hitherto taboo subjects, including the wisdom of government economic policy in a time of serious economic decline. As the Soviet Union's regional jurisdictions clamored for various degrees of sovereignty, Boris Yeltsin led Russia's challenge to Soviet authority in a number of areas. In 1991 Russians elected Yeltsin president of their republic in a free election; the coup against Gorbachev in August 1991 made Yeltsin the most powerful man in Russia, which shortly became an independent state.

From the very beginning, Yeltsin's attempts to promulgate reform programs from the office of the presidency encountered stiff opposition from antireform factions in the legislative branch. Beginning in 1994, that opposition was centered in the State Duma. After Yeltsin used military force to overcome an open rebellion against his dismissal of the parliament in October 1993, he achieved passage of a new constitution that prescribed a strong executive and reduced the powers of the legislative branch. However, the first two legislative elections, in 1993 and 1995, seated large numbers of deputies from the KPRF, the Liberal-Democratic Party of Russia (Liberal'no-demokraticheskaya partiya Rossii—LDPR), and other nationalist and antireform groups. Under worsening economic conditions, a seemingly unstoppable crime wave, and a highly unpopular war in Chechnya, Yeltsin's popularity plummeted in 1995 and early 1996. His response was a contradictory series of personnel and agency shifts at top government levels, together with presidential decrees that often reversed the movement toward democratic governance. By early 1996, virtually all reformist officials had been removed from positions of influence, and a group of hard-liners, led by presidential security chief Aleksandr Korzhakov, Deputy Prime Minister Oleg Soskovets, and Minister of Internal Affairs Anatoliy Kulikov, seemingly had the president's ear.

By that time, Yeltsin's authoritarian use of executive power had combined with the Chechnya imbroglio to lose him the support of the democratic and reformist factions that had been active promoters of early reform policies. As he engaged in an uphill presidential campaign, Yeltsin made lavish promises of government aid to unemployed workers and state enterprises, and allegations of corruption in the latest phase of the privatization program forced him to remain silent about that aspect of his administration.

The 1996 presidential campaign yielded two distinctly opposed theories of governance: the KPRF's frank appeal for return to the central rule of Soviet days and Yeltsin's sometimes timid commitment to democratization and economic reform. In general, however, the national party system remained quite fluid. Although a large number of parties with national constituencies emerged, much shifting occurred among the smaller parties as coalitions formed and dissolved. Some forty-three parties and coalitions registered for the 1995 legislative elections. In 1995 Yeltsin attempted to dominate party politics by forming two nominally opposed parties with essentially pro-administration positions, but his strategy was unsuccessful. The one major party that emerged from his manipulations, Our Home Is Russia, captured relatively few seats in the State Duma in 1995 but retained national standing as a major party because of its identification with Chernomyrdin.

Of the proreform opposition groups, the Yabloko coalition remained the strongest in 1996, but its influence was limited because it refused to join forces with other reform parties. The candidates of Yabloko and other reformist groups fared poorly in the first round of the 1996 presidential election. Meanwhile, the KPRF had developed a unified and loyal following among Russians disillusioned with Yeltsin and nostalgic for the Soviet past.

As the presidential campaign developed, the KPRF candidate, former CPSU functionary Gennadiy Zyuganov, emerged as the prime competitor of Yeltsin. The president used his access to broadcast and print media (which feared the repression that would result from a KPRF victory) to climb steadily in the polls. In the first round, Yeltsin defeated Zyuganov narrowly. Before the second-round faceoff with Zyuganov, Yeltsin dismissed the most visible hard-liners in his administration, added popular third-place finisher Aleksandr Lebed' to his administration, and coaxed lukewarm endorsements from Yabloko and other reformist parties.

In the second round, Yeltsin easily defeated Zyuganov, a dull campaigner who could not convince undecided voters that a KPRF victory would not mean a return to the days of Soviet repression. In what amounted to a contest between anti-Yeltsin and anticommunist sides, Yeltsin attracted an estimated 17 million voters who had voted for Lebed' or Yabloko candidate Grigoriy Yavlinskiy in the first round, and for whom Yeltsin now was the lesser of two evils.

To gain acceptance as the main opposition faction at the national level, after the presidential election the KPRF attempted to broaden its constituency by forming a coalition called the National Patriotic Union of Russia. The coalition included the leftist and nationalist groups that had supported Zyuganov's 1996 presidential bid. To improve its national image from one of disruption to one of constructive cooperation, the coalition softened its antigovernment rhetoric. A prime example of the new approach was KPRF support of the Chernomyrdin government's draft budget in the State Duma deliberations of December 1996–January 1997.

The KPRF found this position tenable while Yeltsin was ill and the moderate Chernomyrdin had a strong position in the Government. However, the Government reorganization of March 1997 gave new power to reformists with whom the KPRF shared little common ground. The party also showed signs of a split between moderates and radicals who rejected compromise. Meanwhile, young Russians showed little interest in joining the KPRF, which offered few constructive ideas about Russia's future and whose membership increasingly was based on an old guard of Soviet-era activists.

Beginning his second term, Yeltsin filled his new cabinet with individuals with reformist credentials. Free-market advocate Aleksandr Livshits was appointed minister of finance, and reformist Yevgeniy Yasin retained his position as minister of the economy. In another indication that economic reform would continue, Yeltsin named reformist Al'fred Kokh as deputy prime minister for privatization. Retained from the previous Government were Minister of Foreign Affairs Yevgeniy Primakov (a 1996 appointee), recently appointed Minister of

Defense Igor' Rodionov, and hard-line Minister of Internal Affairs Anatoliy Kulikov.

The Ministry of Environmental Protection and Natural Resources was redesignated the Ministry of Natural Resources; environmental issues were shifted to a new, subcabinet agency, the State Environmental Protection Committee, headed by Viktor Danilov-Danil'yan, who had been minister of environmental protection and natural resources in the first Yeltsin administration. The only minister affiliated with the KPRF was Aman Tuleyev, a strong proponent of reintegration of the CIS states, who was appointed to head the Ministry of CIS Affairs.

In August 1996, Chernomyrdin listed among the new Government's goals a dramatic reduction of the state bureaucracy, including the elimination of twenty-four ministries and agencies. However, no streamlining occurred until March 1997, when Yeltsin dropped three of his deputy prime ministers and announced a large-scale Government reorganization as a remedy for what Yeltsin admitted was poor performance by his second-term appointees. The new, smaller Government was to include eight deputy prime ministers (compared with twelve previously), twenty-three ministries (three of which were headed by deputy prime ministers, and a reduction of one from the previous organization), sixteen state committees (compared with seventeen previously), and twenty other federal agencies.

A key appointment in this period was Boris Nemtsov as deputy prime minister in charge of social issues (including the crisis of wage and pension arrears) and the extremely problematic reform of state monopolies and housing subsidies. As governor of Nizhniy Novgorod Oblast, Nemtsov had gained international recognition for his brilliant regional economic reforms. Nemtsov's reputation for honesty also was expected to improve the tarnished image of Yeltsin's administration.

The Government reorganization process required much more time than expected because factions struggled to gain coveted posts and no qualified persons could be found for others. Reportedly at least twelve individuals refused appointments to head ministries and committees. The reorganization also sharpened the power struggle between the Government and the State Duma, the main political bastion of numerous special interests that the initiatives of Chubays and Nemtsov promised to attack, and whose patron, Chernomyrdin, now was fading.

In June 1996, the appointment of former general Aleksandr Lebed' as head of the Security Council improved the prospects of an already promising political figure. In this position, Lebed' remained in the public eye by making controversial speeches on matters of policy and by negotiating what turned out to be the conclusive cease-fire of the Chechen conflict. Lebed' had a base of avid supporters who craved charismatic, assertive leadership. Unlike most other Russian government figures, he created a positive image on television, which by 1996 was the most important source of news for most Russians. In October Yeltsin responded to continued criticism from Lebed' by dismissing him from the Security Council. In the months that followed his dismissal, Lebed' polished his public image in Russia and abroad. He began preparations for a future presidential campaign by seeking funds for future political activities, and by traveling to the United States and Western Europe. Although he virtually disappeared from the pro-Yeltsin television networks after his dismissal, in early 1997 polls indicated that Lebed' remained the most popular political figure in Russia. In March he established a new opposition party, the Russian People's Republican Party, which he described as an alternative to the KPRF and the ruling elite.

Early in Yeltsin's second term, the urgency of the Chechnya conflict receded as the two sides negotiated the long-term conditions of the so-called Khasavyurt accords that Lebed' had achieved in August 1996. The cease-fire was met with great relief by the Russian people as the end of a long ordeal, and this attitude contributed to the enduring popularity of Lebed'. In October the Khasavyurt accords survived the dismissal of their architect; the Chechens reluctantly continued negotiations after the moderate Ivan Rybkin was named to replace Lebed' as Security Council chief and head negotiator on the Russian side. In November Yeltsin announced the withdrawal of the two Russian brigades that had been designated for permanent occupation of Chechnya, a concession upon which Chechen negotiators had adamantly insisted. By February 1997, all Russian units had been withdrawn. After six Red Cross workers and six Russian civilians were murdered—apparently by renegade guerrillas—near Groznyy in December 1996, all international aid organizations except for the Organization for Security and Cooperation in Europe (OSCE—see Glossary) removed their personnel from Chechnya. Unreconciled Chechen guerrilla groups continued kidnappings in 1997, however, and the resettlement of Russian émigrés from Chechnya promised to strain the already meager resources of Russia's Federal Migration Service.

In late 1996, Russia took an increasingly conciliatory negotiating approach with the Chechens, offering agreements restoring trade, communications, customs relations, and road links and resuming oil and gas refining and transport. Russia's best hope of keeping Chechnya in the federation in 1997 was economic leverage, because the war had left the republic decimated and without international ties and because the infrastructure already existed for Russia to restore Chechnya's most vital industry, oil refining. The main Russian economic negotiator was Boris Berezovskiy, a controversial automotive and banking mogul who had contributed a large sum to Yeltsin's reelection campaign.

The ultimate status of Chechnya and the payment of war reparations remained unresolved in early 1997. The Khasavyurt accords called for a five-year waiting period before deciding the independence issue, but Russia insisted that the territorial integrity of the federation must not be threatened. In January 1997, Chechnya conducted its first presidential and legislative elections; international observers described the election procedure as fair and open, although refugees from Chechnya, including an estimated 350,000 Russians, were not permitted to vote. Russia's foreign policy establishment saw Aslan Maskhadov, the former military leader who easily won the presidency, as a potential partner in further negotiations, unlike the more radical presidential candidates. However, all sixteen presidential candidates based their platforms on Chechnya's full independence under the name "Republic of Chechnya-Ichkeria," and Maskhadov refused to take his rightful seat as a republic governor in Russia's Federation Council. Russia's official response to the January elections was muted; by March, the terms of a treaty of "peace and agreement" were under serious discussion.

As Yeltsin began his second term, the strength of the president's political position and the nature of his intentions remained unclear. Yeltsin ended his first term on an ominous note by retreating completely from public view immediately after his election victory. The heart attack that Yeltsin suffered between the two rounds of the election was identified only later as the cause of his disappearance.

Beginning with the first round of the presidential election, Yeltsin's physical condition exerted a growing influence over the political atmosphere in Russia. In the fall of 1996, news of the president's very serious heart condition intensified speculation about the identity of likely successors. As Yeltsin maintained a limited public schedule in that period, three figures, Chernomyrdin, Lebed', and Moscow's very popular mayor, Yuriy Luzhkov, jockeyed openly for advantage in the anticipated post-Yeltsin era—although Chernomyrdin clearly lacked the political appeal of his potential rivals. Those maneuvers continued after Yeltsin's heart surgery in November.

By early 1997, Russia's apparent lack of leadership caused intense concern and speculation in the international community, and Yeltsin's popularity again plummeted as workers and pensioners remained unpaid. In March 1997, Yeltsin used his annual state of the federation speech to the State Duma to reassure domestic and foreign opinion and to reassert his presidential power—a goal that he achieved by delivering a forceful and coherent speech. Accusing the Government of failing to execute his commands, Yeltsin repeated his unfulfilled 1996 promises of wage and pension payments, accelerated economic reform, and more efficient government.

During Yeltsin's absence, another figure bore the brunt of opposition attacks on the administration. In 1995 and early 1996, Yeltsin had dismissed reform economist Anatoliy Chubays from two high-level economic positions in response to strong criticism from antireform factions. However, after directing Yeltsin's successful 1996 presidential campaign, Chubays was rewarded with the chief of staff position in Yeltsin's second administration, at the same time increasing the prospects that the pace of reform would increase.

Although too unpopular to have a realistic chance at the presidency, Chubays maneuvered effectively within the Yeltsin administration. He formed an alliance with Yeltsin's ambitious daughter, Tat'yana Dyachenko, who was rumored to have substantial influence over her father's policy decisions. The work of Chubays was widely seen in the dismissal of the Aleksandr Korzhakov coterie in June and of Aleksandr Lebed' in October. Chubays was credited with maintaining some sort of order during Yeltsin's convalescence in the early stages of the second administration, even as Chubays's many enemies spread rumors of illegal campaign funding and links with organized crime.

Despite speculation that Yeltsin would limit Chubays's power by increasing the prestige of rivals—a technique Yeltsin had used throughout his presidency—in the Government reorganization of March 1997 Yeltsin advanced Chubays to the positions of deputy prime minister in charge of economic affairs and minister of the economy. Chubays now had direct control of the governmental restructuring that Yeltsin prescribed to end bureaucratic gridlock, and the new faces that Yeltsin appointed at that time improved the prospect that the new minister would be able to accelerate economic reform in 1997.

In July 1996, experts had seen Yeltsin's creation of a civilian advisory Defense Council as an effort to balance the power that Lebed' had gained as chief of the Security Council. In October the head of the Defense Council, Yuriy Baturin, supplanted Lebed' as the primary architect of military reform, dismissing six top generals and reassigning several who remained. By the end of 1996, Baturin was in a bitter battle with defense minister Rodionov for authority over reform policy. By March 1997, Rodionov's position in the administration was reported to be quite tenuous.

Late in 1996, another extraconstitutional organ was formed in the Yeltsin administration: a permanent, four-member Consultative Council that included the president, the prime minister, and the speakers of the two houses of the Federal Assembly. The council was to meet twice a month in an effort designed to smooth differences between the two branches of government. The inclusion of the State Duma speaker brought a prominent KPRF deputy, Gennadiy Seleznev, into a top advisory group—a move calculated by Yeltsin and Chubays to either divide or conciliate the strongest of the opposition parties. The fourth member of the council was Yegor Stroyev, speaker of the Federation Council and usually a Yeltsin supporter. During Yeltsin's illnesses, Chubays represented the president at council meetings.

Already in the mid-1990s, the executive branch contained numerous directorates and commissions answering only to the president. In 1996 the addition of extraconstitutional governing bodies such as the Defense Council and the Consultative Council continued Yeltsin's propensity to govern by decree and outside constitutionally prescribed lines of power. According to some experts, the existence of seemingly redundant presidential policy-making groups was a new manifestation of Russia's long tradition of arbitrary rule; according to others, such organs were necessary to circumvent the gridlock of opposition in the State Duma.

In the fall of 1996, Yeltsin's illness brought demands from all political factions for clarification of the 1993 constitution's vague language on replacing a disabled head of state: the conditions for such replacement are listed in the constitution, but the authority to make the decision is not specified. In this case, Yeltsin responded by temporarily delegating to Prime Minister Chernomyrdin his authority as commander in chief of the armed forces, head of internal security, and custodian of the codes needed to unleash a nuclear attack. Within hours of his successful heart bypass surgery in November, Yeltsin publicly reclaimed full control, apparently seeking to end the impression of a power vacuum in Moscow. In the months that followed, however, government assurances of Yeltsin's continued competence met increasing skepticism as the president appeared only in carefully edited news film. In the first months of 1997, KPRF deputies introduced motions in the State Duma to impeach Yeltsin on health grounds, and the Duma discussed constitutional amendments limiting the powers of the president.

Between September 1996 and March 1997, Yeltsin's administration faced a new political challenge when a series of regional elections provided the KPRF and its nationalist allies another opportunity to weaken Yeltsin's political base. Fifty-two of Russia's eighty-nine subnational jurisdictions were to elect chief executives during that period, and all of those executives are ex officio members of the Federation Council, the upper house of parliament and a bastion of Yeltsin support until 1997. (The chief executives of republics are called presidents; those of other jurisdictions carry the title governor or administrative head.)

Before the elections began, experts identified fifteen of those constituencies, primarily in the "Red Belt" along the southern border from the North Caucasus to the Far East, as sure to elect communist leaders. At the end of 1996, a Yeltsin-appointed incumbent chief executive had been defeated in twenty-four of the forty-four elections decided to that point. The KPRF had backed fifteen of the new officials, and six had had Yeltsin's support. Among the victors were former vice president and outspoken Yeltsin critic Aleksandr Rutskoy, who was elected governor of Kursk Oblast, and Vasiliy Starodubtsev, a central figure in the 1991 coup against the Gorbachev government, who was elected governor of Tula Oblast. In most cases, successful candidates took less partisan positions and were more ready to negotiate with their opposition than experts had predicted when the elections began. Incumbents generally fared better in northern and urban regions where economic conditions were the most favorable. Yeltsin's doubtful health and the rescinding of his 1996 campaign spending promises hampered some progovernment candidates. All the chief executives elected in 1996 were expected to wield greater political power because they now had direct mandates rather than presidential appointments, and that legitimacy also would bolster the power of the Federation Council vis-à-vis the State Duma in the Federal Assembly.

In 1996 the central government's economic and legislative control of subnational jurisdictions continued to slip away as the power of regional chief executives increased proportionally. Governors such as Yevgeniy Nazdratenko of strategically vital Maritime (Primorskiy) Territory on the Pacific coast and Eduard Rossel' of Sverdlovsk Oblast in the Urals already had established personal fiefdoms outside Moscow's control. Nazdratenko openly challenged the national administration on a number of issues, including the transfer of a small parcel of his territory's land to China as part of a Sino-Russian border treaty. In 1993 Sverdlovsk Oblast briefly declared itself a republic under Rossel'. As of January 1997, Moscow had signed bilateral agreements, establishing a wide variety of power-sharing relationships, with twenty-six subnational jurisdictions.

By 1996 regional governments raised 50 percent of taxes and accounted for 70 percent of government spending in Russia. Although only fifteen of eighty-nine subnational jurisdictions were net contributors to the federal budget and sixty-seven relied on federal subsidies for pensions, in 1996 Moscow still had no centralized system to account for movement of funds between the federal government and the regions. Many jurisdictions complained that the 1997 budget did not allocate sufficient funds to them to compensate for their tax payments to Moscow. As of March 1997, no subnational jurisdiction had received a full allotment of federal pension funds, and only ten jurisdictions had paid their federal taxes in full.

In October 1996, the emergency tax committee was forced to withdraw its threat of bankruptcy proceedings against the Kama Automobile Plant (KamAZ), one of the Republic of Tatarstan's largest industries, for nonpayment of federal taxes.

Citing the 1994 power-sharing treaty between the republic and the federal government, Tatarstan's president Mintimer Shaimiyev convinced Chernomyrdin that ending KamAZ's favorable tax status would intrude on the republic's economic sovereignty.

Experts predicted that tensions between Moscow and the subnational governments would intensify during the shaping of Russia's new federal system, especially as that system addresses the question of who controls the country's vast national resources. After the regional elections, a loose coalition of jurisdictions that were net contributors to the federal budget ("donor regions") was in a position to gain significant economic concessions from the federal government. At the same time, the eight regional economic associations, which include all of Russia's eighty-nine subnational jurisdictions except Chechnya, showed new cohesiveness and also were expected to gain greater autonomy and attention from Moscow in 1997. Those associations are: the Far East and Baikal Association; the Siberian Accord Association; the Greater Volga Association; the Central Russia Association; the Cooperation Association of North Caucasus Republics, Territories, and Oblasts; the Black Earth Association; the Urals Regional Association; and the North-West Association.

In October presidential chief of staff Chubays began a campaign to reverse the movement toward regional autonomy. Chubays called for a review of the many regional laws that contravene the national constitution, in an effort to curtail the autonomy that such legislation encourages. (Several of the regional constitutions adopted after 1991 contain language contradicting the national constitution, and the electoral laws of some twenty-seven regions reportedly violate federal law.) However, the project was postponed because regional procurators, who would be responsible for such an investigation, lack sufficient authority over regional officials. After the elections of 1996–97 gave most regional leaders a popular mandate, the lack of federal sanctions on subnational jurisdictions violating federal law became a more significant threat to the integrity of the federation as well as to human rights and the balance of political power within jurisdictions. Meanwhile, local and municipal administrations chafed under restrictions imposed by regional jurisdictions, just as the latter complained about Moscow's restrictions.

In the post-Soviet period, Russia's foreign policy has shifted significantly, most often in response to domestic rather than foreign conditions. The early Yeltsin administration, represented by Minister of Foreign Affairs Andrey Kozyrev, sought to bring Russia fully into the community of nations—especially Western nations—and to dispel the aura of the Evil Empire. The military and economic competition of the Cold War was replaced by a series of cooperative agreements with Western powers, including disarmament treaties, that brought economic and humanitarian aid to Russia. The vast set of Soviet commitments that spanned the world in the 1980s was reduced in an effort to concentrate limited resources in the most useful areas.

However, a strong nationalist faction in the parliament and elsewhere saw such complaisance as the surrender of the pre-eminent, rightful role in world politics that had been won in the Soviet era. This faction, which has been compared with the nineteenth-century Slavophile movement that sought to protect Russian culture from the harmful intrusion of Western civilization, has urged that Russia recapture as much influence as possible in the former Soviet Union and the former Soviet empire in Central Europe. This process would discourage the influence of the West in those regions, countering the ostensible drive of the North Atlantic Treaty Organization (NATO—see Glossary) to push Russia out of the continent of Europe. For many advocates of this position, the preferred area of closer foreign relations is Asia, and a new anti-Western alliance with China is the focal point.

In the early and mid-1990s, Yeltsin had improved Russia's international image by participating in several meetings of the Group of Seven (G–7—see Glossary) as well as his regular summit conferences with United States presidents. In maintaining such contacts, Yeltsin attempted to walk a line between making concessions to the West that would anger Russian nationalists and taking independent positions that would weaken the Western commitment to aid Russia during its transition period. As a result of these conflicting demands, in the mid-1990s Russia's foreign policy positions have been inconsistent, and Yeltsin, Minister of Foreign Affairs Yevgeniy Primakov, Chernomyrdin, and other official spokesmen often have issued contradictory statements on important issues.

On issues such as Chechnya and human rights in Russia, Western diplomats refrained in 1996 from criticizing Yeltsin for fear of damaging his prestige at home. Before the August 1996 cease-fire in Chechnya, the IMF offered Russia the second-largest loan in the bank's history, and the Council of Europe (see Glossary), considered a guardian of human rights in Europe, admitted Russia to its membership despite numerous reports of atrocities in Chechnya and noncompliance with the council's policy on capital punishment.

However, Yeltsin received substantial criticism from the West for some policies that failed to comply with international standards. Among them were the sale of nuclear reactors, submarines, and other critical items to Iran in violation of international sanctions; continued dumping and careless handling of nuclear materials by Russia's civilian and military agencies (criticism coming mainly from Japan and the Scandinavian countries, which were most directly affected); and Russia's failure to comply with the arms limitations of the Conventional Forces in Europe Treaty (CFE Treaty—see Glossary). Most of the summit meetings of the mid-1990s discussed some or all of those questions, but few solutions emerged. Early in 1997, Russia's relationship with Iran had become closer, its nuclear safety policies remained unchanged, and CFE Treaty modifications were under discussion.

In the mid-1990s, the major point of conflict in the struggle over Western influence in Russia was the projected expansion of NATO into former Warsaw Pact nations of what is now called Central Europe. In 1995 and 1996, numerous statements by the Russian government rejected the possibility that countries such as Poland and Hungary could enter NATO without dire consequences. Russia's statements predicted that, by isolating and impoverishing Russia, a NATO presence would in fact reactivate the Cold War. During 1996 government spokesmen threatened a variety of diplomatic and military reprisals if NATO membership were enlarged. Most experts labeled Russia's behavior as gamesmanship aimed at gaining the most advantageous possible position once an inevitable first round of NATO expansion occurred.

Despite Russia's threats, in 1996 eleven European countries, including the three Baltic states—Estonia, Latvia, and Lithuania—reiterated their enthusiasm for gaining NATO membership. In early 1997, Bulgaria declared its desire to join, and Georgia, Moldova, and Ukraine sought closer cooperation with the alliance.

A potentially important change appeared in the Russian position at the end of 1996. In September the United States had proposed a charter that would give Russia a special relationship with NATO, in an attempt to relieve tensions over the expansion issue. In January 1997, Primakov began to negotiate such an agreement with NATO secretary general Javier Solana. As negotiations proceeded, two of Russia's key goals emerged: obtaining more favorable terms in the CFE Treaty and limiting the NATO military presence in any new member nation in Central Europe. In keeping with Russia's position that NATO is an anachronistic leftover of the Cold War, Primakov and Chernomyrdin demanded a binding treaty obligating NATO to reform itself from a military to a "political" organization.

As conceived in the West, the agreement would offer Russia consultation but no veto on NATO expansion decisions; increased presence of Russian observers at various NATO command levels; and modification of existing arms reduction agreements to suit Russia's demands. At the March 1997 Helsinki summit, Yeltsin backed the agreement as a way around the issue of NATO expansion, which he still called "a mistake." By that time, Primakov and Solana had agreed on most of the charter's terms, including a permanent consultative council for discussion of issues such as nuclear security, crisis management, and peacekeeping operations. However, Primakov insisted on restricting the presence of NATO forces in any new member nation, a concession that NATO refused because it would interfere with the alliance's basic commitment to mutual defense. Because NATO had set a target date of July 1997 for the first official invitations to new member nations, little time was available for conflicting views to be mediated. (Russia demanded that the signing of the Russia-NATO charter precede and be separate from the NATO summit that would announce the invitations.)

During his first term in office, Boris Yeltsin continued the tradition, begun by Mikhail Gorbachev, of holding regular summit meetings with United States presidents. The second Strategic Arms Reduction Treaty (START II—see Glossary) was a product of a 1993 summit with President George H.W. Bush. Western experts saw the drastic nuclear arms reductions of START II as a way for Russia to cut military expenses without sacrificing national security, at a time when nuclear parity was an increasingly expensive proposition. But as Russia's conventional military forces deteriorated and funding declined in the mid-1990s, nuclear strike capability assumed a more prominent place in national security planning. Therefore, by late 1996 Russian authorities were demanding greater limitations on sea-based nuclear warheads, in which the United States has a distinct advantage; greater latitude for deployment of land-based missiles, in which Russia is strongest; and revision of the START II restrictions on the multiple-warhead weapons that Russia considers its most formidable threat.

In October 1996, United States secretary of defense William Perry met strong resistance when he tried to convince the State Duma and Ministry of Defense officials in Moscow that START II ratification would benefit both sides. At the same time, Russia also delayed finalizing an agreement on classification of anti-ballistic missiles (ABMs), indicating continuing sensitivity about the prospect of the United States building a missile interception system that would negate much of Russia's nuclear strike capacity. Early in 1997, Western defense experts began formulating a START III proposal that might leapfrog the START II deadlock by eliminating at least some of the most serious obstacles. But the largest obstacle was the NATO issue: already in 1995, nationalists and many moderates in the State Duma refused to even consider START II without assurances that NATO would not move eastward, and this linkage remained in early 1997.

In the early stages of Yeltsin's second term, high-level diplomatic contact with the West was fitful and unproductive. In September a Moscow visit by German chancellor Helmut Kohl, Yeltsin's most vocal supporter among Western leaders, failed to bridge the two countries' differences on sanctions on Iraq (which Russia opposed), NATO expansion, and conditions for expanded German investment in Russia. In late December, the first foreign leader to confer with Yeltsin after his convalescence was China's prime minister Li Peng rather than a Westerner. At that time, Russia and China signed new bilateral agreements on cooperation in banking, nuclear power plant construction, and the sale of two naval destroyers to China. In early 1997, visits by Kohl and French president Jacques Chirac to Moscow produced no breakthrough on the NATO expansion issue.

The Helsinki summit, the first such meeting since April 1996, yielded agreements on a range of economic matters; Russia was promised an increased role in the G–7, whose annual meetings were to be renamed the Summit of the Eight, and

Yeltsin received United States commitments for enhanced investment and integration of Russia in global markets and support for much-coveted entry into the World Trade Organization (WTO—see Glossary) in 1998. Yeltsin pledged renewed support for passage of START II in the State Duma, and he supported a START III agreement that would further reduce strategic arms. The two presidents pledged support for ratification of the 1993 Chemical Weapons Convention, which faced stiff opposition in the legislatures of both countries. Yeltsin also unexpectedly accepted an understanding of the Anti-Ballistic Missile Treaty (ABM Treaty—see Glossary) that would allow the United States to continue developing a limited ABM system.

Yeltsin's robust performance at the summit also allayed the health fears that had haunted his second administration. The president received strong criticism from communist and nationalist factions for the substantive output of the summit, but experts noted that Russia's position in the meeting provided little negotiating leverage.

Russia and NATO did cooperate successfully in Bosnia. In September 1996, Primakov expressed Russia's willingness to extend the assignment of Russian troops to the NATO international peacekeeping force, IFOR, with which they had functioned smoothly for more than a year. Russia's continued participation was conditioned on the lifting of international sanctions against Serbia. The sanctions ended in October; Russia took an active part in planning the next phase of the peacekeeping operation. In January 1997, Yeltsin approved extending Russia's participation through July 1998.

Recovery of the empire of the Soviet Union became a foreign policy goal of increasing importance in the mid-1990s. In the Duma elections of December 1995, every party and group mentioned reintegration of the CIS states in its foreign policy platform. In 1996 nationalists used a variety of strategies to encourage the government to extend Russia's influence in the CIS countries. In three former Soviet states plagued with internal conflict—Georgia, Moldova, and Tajikistan—Russian troops remained in ostensibly peacekeeping roles, and Russian negotiators continued to sponsor talks between hostile groups. Many experts called the diplomatic activity an insincere effort to achieve stability in areas where continued conflict was the only justification for a Russian military presence.

In late 1996, the State Duma overwhelmingly approved a permanent Russian force in the breakaway Dnestr Moldavian Republic (Transnistria) in Moldova, claiming erroneously that most of the republic's citizens are Russian and thus require protection. (A 1994 treaty with Moldova, which the State Duma never ratified, provided for withdrawal of all Russian forces.) Early in 1997, Russian officials promised that forces would be withdrawn when the Transnistria question was settled, while at the same time encouraging the separatists to push for full independence.

In December 1996, a Federation Council resolution officially claimed the city of Sevastopol', located on Ukraine's Black Sea coast, as Russian territory. This claim continued Russia's post-Soviet dispute with Ukraine over control of the Black Sea Fleet that the two countries had inherited from the Soviet Union. Moscow mayor Yuriy Luzhkov, hoping to gain national stature for future political advancement, became a main spokesman for the claim on Sevastopol'. In 1996 Yeltsin and Ukraine's president Leonid Kuchma had negotiated terms for dividing the fleet, but the new claims by Russian nationalists threatened to sour the recently improved relations between Russia and Ukraine. Spurred by Russia's territorial claims, in January 1997 Ukraine proposed a "special partnership" with NATO, ratification of which was expected at the midyear NATO summit.

The bitter border disputes that had erupted with Estonia and Latvia at the time of those republics' declarations of independence continued into 1997, although in both cases some concessions were made in late 1996 and early 1997. As progress was made on territorial issues, the main sticking point in 1997 was Russia's requirement that the two Baltic states change their policy against granting dual citizenship to their Russian populations.

Russia also struggled to maintain as much as possible of its Soviet-era access to the rich natural resources of the Caspian Sea, against the claims of former Soviet republics Azerbaijan, Kazakstan, and Turkmenistan. Allied with Iran, Russia called for joint jurisdiction of resources by all adjoining states rather than allocation according to national borders. The latter system, advocated by the other three former republics, would place most Caspian oil fields outside the jurisdiction of Iran and Russia. In October 1996, Russia amended its previous hard-line approach somewhat, but the issue promised to be under negotiation for an extended period.

Early in 1996, a customs union agreement was concluded among Belarus, Kazakstan, Kyrgyzstan, and Russia, significantly reducing trade barriers within that group (and simplifying the smuggling of narcotics from Central Asia into Russia). In November 1996, Russia reversed its recent policy of reducing credits to other CIS countries, increasing its credit allotment for CIS partners by about fifteen times in the 1997 draft budget. Those credits are limited, however, to the purchase of Russian goods. The total debt of CIS countries to Russia was estimated at US$6 billion, plus US$3 billion in unpaid energy bills, prior to the credit extension. Russia's CIS trade figures for early 1997 showed a decline in most categories, with natural gas accounting for the bulk of exports within the commonwealth.

Russia's stature in the CIS suffered setbacks in the 1990s as other CIS nations took independent positions on a variety of issues. From the beginning, charter members Turkmenistan and Azerbaijan took very independent positions: contrary to Russia's desire to maintain a military presence throughout the CIS, Azerbaijan allowed no Russian troops at all on its soil, and Turkmenistan maintained joint command of all military units. Kazakstan and Turkmenistan continued to seek Western support in bypassing the Russian pipelines upon which they previously had depended for their oil and natural gas shipments in the Soviet system. Early in 1997, Kazakstan's president Nursultan Nazarbayev, a consistent and influential advocate of economic integration of the newly independent states, criticized Russia's leadership of the CIS, calling for diversification of control in order to energize the moribund organization.

Belarus, whose president, Alyaksandr Lukashyenka, had pushed his country toward reunification with Russia, suffered a constitutional crisis late in 1996. Lukashyenka's bid for authoritarian power provoked strong nationalist opposition in the parliament of Belarus. It also brought unfavorable international attention to Russia's dominant position in the new bilateral relationship established by the 1996 Community of Sovereign Republics treaty. Unsuccessful in mediating the dispute between Lukashyenka and the Belarusian parliament, Russia continued staunch support for Lukashyenka in early 1997, although Russia's reform factions opposed closer relations that would require Russia to support Belarus's backward economy. A new agreement signed by Yeltsin and Lukashyenka in March 1997 reaffirmed the 1996 treaty but increased the controversy in Moscow between reformers—including Chubays and most of Yeltsin's new top-level Government appointees—and nationalists, who saw union with Belarus as the first step in restoring the Soviet Union.

In 1996 Uzbekistan, the strongest of the five Central Asian CIS states, began a concentrated effort to cultivate commercial and diplomatic relations with Western countries and Israel. In May 1996, Uzbekistan's president Islam Karimov criticized the Economic Cooperation Organization of Islamic nations, of which Uzbekistan is a member, for its anti-Israeli and anti-United States positions; then he made a state visit to the United States to improve bilateral relations. In January 1997, Karimov voiced support for expansion of NATO.

In November Kazakstan, Kyrgyzstan, and Uzbekistan announced plans for a Central Asian peacekeeping battalion to be used in United Nations-sponsored operations and to be trained within NATO's Partnership for Peace (PfP—see Glossary) program. The new unit's Western connections were a signal that the wealthiest Central Asian countries wished to reduce Russia's role in regional security. Russia responded by seeking joint action with the Central Asian republics in defending against infiltration by Afghanistan's aggressively fundamentalist Taliban movement. The Russian gambit gained support from Karimov and Tajikistan's president Imomali Rahmonov. At the CIS summit in March 1997, Yeltsin attempted to foster unity and to reassert Russia's dominance, but Georgia, Kazakstan, Turkmenistan, and Uzbekistan reiterated their individual national concerns, complained about the CIS's ineffectiveness, and defended their right to form relationships outside the context of the full organization. Yeltsin's chief vehicle for economic reintegration was to be his Concept for Integrated Economic Development of the CIS, which CIS foreign ministers refused to discuss pending modification.

In February 1997, NATO secretary general Javier Solana received a warm reception when he visited Georgia and Moldova. Moldova's president Petru Lucinschi requested a NATO security guarantee for the borders of his neutral country, showing concern for the continued presence of Russian forces in Transnistria. Georgia's president Eduard Shevardnadze was frustrated after more than two years of fruitless Russia-brokered negotiations with Georgia's separatist republic, Abkhazia. The failure to resolve territorial and refugee issues there postponed Georgia's unification and, ultimately, its independence from Russian military assistance. Georgia concluded several bilateral military agreements with NATO member countries in 1996. In his talks with Solana, Shevardnadze characterized Georgia as an integral part of the new European zone of security to be formed once NATO expanded. (Early in 1997, the Group of Russian Forces in the Transcaucasus began withdrawing units from Georgia into Russia as part of the overall military downsizing program.)

Of the countries Solana visited, only Armenia continues to seek extensive military assistance from Russia. In 1997 Armenia still was under blockade by Azerbaijan and Turkey, traditionally hostile Muslim states that nearly surround the country, and Russia supported Armenia in the Nagorno-Karabakh conflict with Azerbaijan—factors that made Russia Armenia's only alternative for regional economic and security assistance.

The appointment of the Arabist Primakov as minister of foreign affairs in January 1996 continued the turn of Russia's foreign policy from West to East, and diplomatic activity in the East increased in 1996—despite official protestations that Russia seeks a balance between East and West. By the end of 1996, Russia and China had resolved several of the issues that had split the major communist powers for several decades, and both sides seemed intent on forming additional ties in 1997. Meanwhile, accelerated commercial activity in Russia's Maritime (Primorskiy) Territory encouraged new agreements between Russia and the two Koreas, and progress was made in late 1996 in resolving the fifty-year stalemate with Japan over Russian occupation of four of the Kuril Islands. New initiatives also went to the prosperous member nations of the Association of Southeast Asian Nations (ASEAN), expanding the drive to make Russia a Pacific Rim commercial power. In November 1996, Primakov visited China, Japan, and Mongolia with the stated goal of improving Russia's position in vital Asian markets. Primakov visited Iran the following month. Russia also felt that establishing its identity as an Asian power was crucial because it had been excluded from several prosperous Pacific Rim trading groups and from talks on Korean unification. China's rapid emergence as a world economic power also was a primary concern.

In 1996 Russia saw the presence of Primakov in the Ministry of Foreign Affairs, Western sanctions against Iraq, and the election of a hard-line government in Israel as creating conditions in the Middle East that would favor a return to the Soviet

Union's role as champion of the Arab countries in the region. Russia had a special interest in freeing Iraq from economic sanctions because Iraq was to begin repaying its substantial debt to Russia once oil exports resumed, and lucrative new bilateral deals were negotiated in 1996. For this reason, in September 1996 the United States bombing of Iraqi targets and the threat of extended international sanctions brought harsh criticism from Moscow.

Meanwhile, Russia continued cultivating relations with Iran, another international pariah. A third Kilo-class submarine went from Russia to Iran in November 1996, and the transfer of nuclear-reactor technology continued despite Western objections. In the second half of 1996, as another token of Russia's importance in the region, Primakov also sought a more active role in Arab-Israeli peace talks.

Whatever its relations with foreign countries, however, no foreign power threatened Russia's security in the 1990s, and domestic conditions were the key determinant of Russia's future. In the 1990s, Russian society, until recently held together by the forced observance of Soviet power, seemed to lack any sort of glue that could be used to combat the forces of economic fragmentation. In the early post-Soviet years, religion re-emerged as an important factor in the lives of many Russians, but cultural and intellectual institutions showed signs of decline (production of art, literature, and scientific books dropped sharply in the mid-1990s, as did newspaper publication), and citizens showed little interest in forming independent civic groups. Despite guarantees of equal rights in the 1993 constitution, minority ethnic groups have experienced serious discrimination and even violence in Russia's cities, and hints of religious intolerance have emerged as well. Social resentments have festered as the economic status of most Russians deteriorated and a new elite flaunted its wealth.

The émigré sociologist Vladimir Shlapentokh observed in 1996 that personal gain had become the most important value in Russian society and that the newly democratized government institutions offered little authority against dishonest behavior because those institutions are themselves rife with corruption. The inability of government to maintain law and order through its democratic institutions has provoked authoritarian behavior by the Yeltsin administration, whose security agencies have maintained a large share of their Soviet-era autonomy.

Optimists point to the next generation of Russians, who will have formed their civic habits independent of Soviet influence, as the basis of democratic renewal and a new civil society. The three orderly and fair national elections of 1993–96 offer some hope for this prognosis. The relative calm with which Russians have accepted the agonies of transition has provided an opportunity for new institutions to develop, but such a passive public attitude may not bode well for participatory democracy. Western influences, which were vital to the postcommunist progress of Poland, Hungary, and the Czech Republic, have penetrated Russia only in random fashion, and they met increasing resistance in the mid-1990s. That resistance has dampened the government's commitment to economic and political reform and obscured the prognosis for the transition process.

By 1996 the reforms envisioned in 1992 had reached a plateau quite short of their final goals. Cynicism, corruption, and the president's long period of inactivity had sapped the momentum of reform programs, and an entrenched bureaucracy blocked further initiatives. In 1997 Russia remained an international power in some respects, but its search for ways to preserve that status was increasingly uncertain.

March 31, 1997

*　　　*　　　*

In the months following the preparation of this manuscript, several events of importance occurred. In April 1997, shortly after the United States Congress ratified the controversial Chemical Weapons Convention outlawing the manufacture and sale of chemical weapons, the State Duma refused passage on the grounds that the cost of destroying Russia's chemical weapons supply, the largest in the world, was prohibitively high. Although the Duma promised to reconsider the measure in the fall of 1997, its decision caused consternation in the United States, which had expected reciprocity on that issue.

In the spring of 1997, Russia continued to affirm its commitment to craft a foreign policy independent of international opinion. In April an official Moscow visit by Iranian head of parliament Ali Akbar Nateq-Noori—one day after a German court had found Iran guilty of assassinating exiled dissidents—was met by expressions of friendship from President Yeltsin. There were indications that Russia's military and economic deals with Iran, criticized sharply in the West because of Iran's support for terrorist groups, would continue or expand. Yeltsin and Minister of Foreign Affairs Yevgeniy Primakov also expressed support for Syria's position in peace talks with Israel, expanding Russia's effort to reestablish influence in the Middle East.

Shortly thereafter, a Moscow summit meeting with Jiang Zemin, president of China, produced a statement reinforcing the two nations' "multipolar" foreign policy as a balance against United States domination of the post-Soviet world. The leaders signed an agreement to reduce troops and equipment along the Sino-Russian border by 15 percent. The troop maximum was set at 130,000 for each side. Neighboring countries Kazakstan, Kyrgyzstan, and Tajikistan also signed the agreement. Yeltsin announced that military-industrial entrepreneur Arkadiy Vol'skiy would head the Russian delegation to a new Sino-Russian standing committee on friendship, peace, and development scheduled to go into operation sometime in 1997. In April Russia also announced that two new guided-missile destroyers, previously intended for the Russian naval forces, would be delivered to China in 1997. However, despite official rhetoric and new agreements, in mid-1997 a substantial part of Russia's foreign policy establishment saw China as a stopgap partner until permanent relationships could be forged with the United States, Western Europe, and/or Japan. In May 1997, Japan and Russia began high-level defense talks, Japan dropped its objection to Russia's membership in the G–7 organization, and Russia showed some signs of compromise in the continuing dispute over four Russian-held islands in the Kuril chain north of Japan. Based on Japan's change of policy, Yeltsin participated as a full member in the June meeting of the newly renamed G–8.

In May Primakov's long negotiations with NATO officials yielded an agreement defining special status for Russia in NATO in return for Russia's acceptance of a first round of NATO expansion into Central Europe. The most difficult obstacle, Russia's demand that no nuclear or conventional NATO forces be deployed in new NATO member nations, was overcome by a general statement that neither nuclear nor conventional forces would be deployed under normal circumstances. Both sides claimed that the agreement vindicated their position, although NATO made no firm commitment not to deploy forces. The centerpiece of the agreement, which Yeltsin signed in Paris on May 27, is a permanent council consisting of the secretary general of NATO, a Russian ambassador, and a representative of the full NATO membership. Although Yeltsin described this council as giving Russia a veto over NATO decisions, only specific security issues are to be discussed in the new body. The alliance's major political decision-making process remains separate. The first meeting of the council took place in July.

The agreement, officially termed a "founding act," is not legally binding and did not require ratification by the parliaments of the signatory countries. Having signed the act, Russia officially ended its objections to full NATO membership for the Czech Republic, Hungary, and Poland, which are expected to become full NATO members in 1999. The agreement also improved the prospect that the Russian economy would benefit from closer contacts with the West. Public reaction in Russia was muted, although nationalist politicians claimed that Russia had sustained a serious diplomatic defeat.

Meanwhile, the status of international arms treaties remained unclear. In July talks among the thirty signatory nations of the CFE Treaty—including Russia and all the NATO countries—yielded Russia some concessions on the ratio of NATO to Russian conventional arms in Europe. However, four CIS countries—Azerbaijan, Georgia, Moldova, and Ukraine—had objected that relaxation of CFE restrictions on Russia's flank quotas for troop deployment in or near CIS countries would threaten their national security. The final treaty modification made overall force reductions in Europe but did not include the limitations on NATO forces in Central Europe that Russia had demanded in return for approval of NATO expansion.

As of June 1997, Yeltsin had not made a renewed effort to gain State Duma ratification of the START II agreement, although he had promised President Clinton at the Helsinki summit that he would do so. At Helsinki the United States had eased some terms of START II to improve the treaty's prospects for passage in the Duma.

In May President Aslan Maskhadov of Chechnya (Chechnya-Ichkeria) signed a peace treaty with Russia. In the very brief treaty, both sides renounced the use of force against the other. The official categorization of the agreement as a peace treaty was a concession by Russia, which earlier had refused to sign such a treaty with what it considered an integral part of the federation. The document did not mention independence for the breakaway republic—a potentially divisive issue that both sides avoided in the interest of achieving peace—but the form of the treaty was that used between two equal states subject to international law, hence a tacit recognition of Chechnya-Ichkeria's independence.

Russia also signed agreements for economic aid to Chechnya, and Yeltsin's negotiator Boris Berezovskiy offered several major concessions, including an official apology for all of Russia's historical incursions into Chechnya, in an effort to stave off full independence. Meanwhile, radical Chechen groups continued kidnappings and terrorist acts, casting doubt on the authority of the Maskhadov government.

Chechnya continued to occupy a critical position in Russia's pipeline politics, which became increasingly complex in the mid-1990s as more countries sought participation in the oil wealth of Azerbaijan and Kazakstan. As its price for allowing oil to flow through Chechnya en route to export from Novorossiysk on the Black Sea, Chechnya demanded recognition as a full partner in the endeavor. Because an alternative line through Georgia and Turkey would eliminate both Novorossiysk and Chechnya—hence all Russian participation—from lucrative new shipments, in July Russia signed a trilateral agreement with Azerbaijan and Chechnya, granting Chechnya an equal role. Income from oil shipments was expected to be an important element in stabilizing Chechnya's still rocky internal security situation.

The international Caspian Pipeline Consortium, founded in 1992 to bring oil from Kazakstan to the West, has been plagued by internal friction among partner companies, which represent six countries (Britain, Italy, Kazakstan, Oman, Russia, and the United States). In early 1997, however, the consortium showed signs of agreement on the Russian section of a new line that would deliver oil from Kazakstan's Tengiz fields to Novorossiysk. In April Yeltsin signed the December 1996 agreement on division of shares among the consortium partners. Increased United States activity in the region's new oil fields was a major reason that Russia signed the trilateral pipeline agreement.

Russia's relations with other CIS countries continue to be unsettled. In April both houses of Russia's Federal Assembly ratified the treaty permitting long-term deployment of Russian forces in Armenia. This move caused alarm in neighboring Azerbaijan (still fighting and negotiating with Armenia over

Nagorno-Karabakh), Georgia (through which additional Russian troops would pass en route to Armenia), and Turkey (near whose border additional Russian troops might be stationed). Disclosures of secret deliveries of Russian arms to Armenia in 1994–96 already had alarmed Azerbaijan, and the military treaty seemingly committed Armenia to a long term as a Russian satellite. However, the terms of the July 1997 treaty with Azerbaijan implicitly reduced the prospect of future Russian support for Armenia in the Nagorno-Karabakh conflict. In May a friendship treaty with Ukraine resolved division of the Black Sea Fleet and jurisdiction in Sevastopol', the fleet's largest port, among other treaty provisions.

Meanwhile, other CIS countries continued to deemphasize CIS (largely Russian) investment and trade agreements in favor of Western and Japanese deals with more favorable conditions. According to an April 1997 report, 90 percent of Kazakstan's enterprises had at least some investments from non-CIS sources. Because Kazakstan's president Nazarbayev was a staunch supporter of CIS integration, this statistic was especially bad news for Russia's efforts to bind together and dominate the organization. In 1997 Russian authorities also were alarmed by an incipient trilateral agreement among Azerbaijan, Georgia, and Ukraine, which began cooperating in several critical areas of security and economics where Russia had enjoyed substantial influence.

In May 1997, Yeltsin's Security Council completed a long-awaited national security doctrine. The document, unpublished but leaked extensively, included economic, foreign-policy, and military elements in a general description of Russia's present security situation and its primary goals. Improvement of domestic economic and social conditions, rather than geopolitical advancement, was listed as the primary requirement for enhanced national security. The most aggressive element of the statement was a revocation of Mikhail Gorbachev's pledge that the Soviet Union never would initiate the use of nuclear weapons in a war. The new stance was described by Western experts as a volley in the diplomatic conflict over NATO expansion and a reflection of the acute deterioration of Russia's conventional forces. Because the legislative branch had not been consulted in the creative process, experts doubted that the anti-Yeltsin State Duma would grant the approval necessary for the doctrine to become official.

Russia's defense establishment remained unsettled in mid-1997 after Yeltsin, long dissatisfied with the pace of military reform, fired Chief of Staff Viktor Samsonov and Minister of Defense Igor' Rodionov. General Igor' Sergeyev was named to replace Rodionov. At the same time, Yeltsin created two new military reform commissions. The first, headed by Prime Minister Chernomyrdin, was to deal with military construction; the second, headed by First Deputy Prime Minister Chubays, was to deal with military finances. Experts saw these moves as a victory for civilian officials who advocated reassigning the military's "hidden reserves" rather than allocating additional funds for military reform. In July Yeltsin outlined a comprehensive plan for reducing the military and consolidating the five branches into two, again emphasizing reallocation of existing resources. The drafting procedure and content of the plan attracted strong criticism from government and military officials.

Russia's internal security situation also remained unstable in mid-1997 as the country's crime wave continued. The Ministry of Internal Affairs (MVD) reported a reduction of 12 percent in overall crime in the first quarter of the year, with substantial drops in murders, assaults, thefts, and robberies. However, there was no evidence of a reduction in *mafiya* protection activity and the corruption and crime associated with it. The 7,500 murders committed in 1996 were the most ever for a single year. Meanwhile, the MVD's "Clean Hands Campaign" reported that in 1996 some 21,000 police officials had been fired because of misconduct, including *mafiya* connections. Capital punishment continued to be a sensitive political issue: although Russia was obligated by its 1996 admission to the Council of Europe to end capital punishment, the crime wave continued to bolster strong public feeling against such a change. Human rights organizations estimated that 140 people were executed in 1996, the fourth-largest total in the world.

The prison system continued to suffer grave problems in 1997. In April an Amnesty International report listed torture, lack of bail, acute crowding, epidemics of tuberculosis, and long periods of pretrial detention as frequent conditions in Russia's prisons and jails. An estimated 300,000 prisoners (up from 233,000 in 1994) were in pretrial custody, which lasted for an average of ten months. In mid-1997 the Government announced an amnesty program that would affect as many as 440,000 Russian prisoners, targeting mainly those in pretrial detention. Because Russia's incarceration rate was about ten times that of West European nations, its 1997 prison budget was much higher than its health care budget. Prison reform received little support either from Minister of Internal Affairs Anatoliy Kulikov or from the majority of State Duma deputies.

Overdue wages were another continuing result of the national budget deficit. By midyear Russia's workers were owed an estimated US$9.5 billion, and the amount continued to grow. Although the nationwide labor shutdowns called by unions in November 1996 and March 1997 had failed to attract wide support, the number of local shutdowns increased noticeably in the first half of 1997. Miners, doctors, and teachers blockaded roads and railroads and occupied administrative buildings to protest continued wage arrears. Teacher strikes affected nineteen of Russia's eighty-nine subnational jurisdictions, and only fifteen jurisdictions did not owe money to their teachers.

Partly because of low budget allocations for health, in 1997 new reports indicated that Russia's health crisis was worsening. Although the life expectancy for males increased from 57.3 years to 59.6 years between 1994 and 1996, the drinking and smoking habits of Russians, together with continued air pollution in many areas, kept mortality rates from cardiac and circulatory diseases more than twice as high as those in the United States. The incidence of infectious and parasitic diseases continued to increase. Although a major diphtheria vaccination program in 1995–96 radically reduced the incidence of that disease, tuberculosis cases increased sharply, especially in Russia's prisons. In 1997 the minister of health predicted that sexual promiscuity and drug addiction would cause 800,000 new cases of HIV infection by the year 2000.

Meanwhile, the official government population prediction for 2010 called for a decrease of 7.3 million people, and one Russian expert predicted a decrease of 12 million by that year. In that period, fertility was expected to decline because of health problems among women of childbearing age and because of the overall aging of the population.

The overall economic situation continued to be overshadowed by the Government's inability to balance its budget. Continuing its effort to improve tax collection—the most often cited way of paying overdue state salaries and pensions—in May the Chernomyrdin government submitted a new tax code to the State Duma for approval. Under Yeltsin's implicit threat to dissolve the Duma, the body gave preliminary approval to the code in June. Meanwhile, major enterprises continued to avoid full tax payment. According to an April 1997 State Taxation Service report, Gazprom, the natural gas monopoly, used 140 separate bank accounts to shelter its assets. Of the Government's list of eighty leading tax-evading enterprises, fifty-three were in the fuel and energy industry.

Only 57 percent of projected revenues were collected in the first quarter of 1997, leaving arrears of US$12 billion, and only 63 percent of budgeted expenditures were made. By May the Government owed an estimated US$2.2 billion in pensions, US$2.3 billion in wages to state workers, and US$1.4 billion in child support allowances. The shortfall also reduced economic investment, which in the first half of 1997 was only about 95 percent of the amount invested in the same period of 1996.

In response to the shortfall, Minister of Finance Anatoliy Chubays submitted a proposal to the State Duma for sequestration of allotted funds, warning that the Government could not continue functioning if major cuts were not made. The revisions called for reducing spending by US$19 billion. Despite strong and widespread opposition to the level and allocation of the cuts, in June the Duma adjourned for its summer vacation without submitting an alternative plan.

Meanwhile, the "capital flight" of hard currency (see Glossary) from Russia continued at a rapid rate in 1997. International police authorities estimated that US$1 to US$2 billion dollars left the country every month, much of it connected with illegal activity and invested abroad by Russian émigrés. Experts identified this trend as a sign of continuing low confidence in the domestic economy.

For the first six months of 1997, Russia's GDP shrank by 0.2 percent, casting doubt on Yeltsin's July assertion that the economy had "turned the corner." Positive economic news of early 1997 included the continuing reduction of inflation, which reached an annual rate of 14.5 percent in June—the lowest rate since Russia's independence. Also, the reorganization of the Government in March caused the IMF to resume monthly payments on Russia's US$10 billion loan, which had been suspended since December. The World Bank also announced a two-year loan of US$6 billion to help pay overdue wages and pensions.

In April a series of presidential decrees moved Government policy closer to privatization in some sectors, although strong political support for the giant monopolies in the State Duma guaranteed that Deputy Prime Minister Boris Nemtsov would have a hard struggle in breaking them down. According to the new privatization goals, Government subsidies of housing and municipal services, which were budgeted at US$27 billion in 1997, were to be reduced. (The average Russian paid only 27 percent of such costs in 1997.) According to a sliding scale, subsidies would reach zero in 2003, although some state housing support would remain for the neediest individuals. In the spring of 1997, local increases in utility and housing costs brought demonstrations in St. Petersburg, and Moscow's powerful mayor, Yuriy Luzhkov, objected strongly to the national proposal.

Provisions were made for substantial modification of the pricing and/or structure of the state-controlled electric power industry and the railroad network, and Yeltsin ordered the sale of 49 percent of the telecommunications giant Svyazinvest, division of which was one of the most controversial privatization issues. In July 25 percent of total Svyazinvest shares were won at auction by a group including Russia's Uneximbank and German and United States investors. Because of the backward state of Russia's telephone system, telecommunications is considered potentially one of Russia's largest growth industries. The results of the Svyazinvest auction, which Boris Nemtsov touted as fully free and equitable, set off loud protests from the powerful business interests that failed to acquire shares. The issue threatened to split the large-business bloc that had supported Yeltsin before and after the 1996 election.

Russia's nineteen railroad companies, which accounted for 78 percent of freight traffic and 40 percent of passenger traffic in 1997, were to be removed from direct control of the Ministry of Transportation, under whose management fast-rising railroad fees had added enormous amounts to the overhead of railroad-dependent industries such as steel and coal. At the same time, rail customers owed the lines an estimated US$1.1 billion in 1997, and the companies' equipment was in desperate need of modernization.

In May Yeltsin announced that Gazprom henceforth would be run by a state commission, depriving the gas monopoly of the financial freedom that had gained it billions of dollars of untaxed profits. Yeltsin already had stripped Gazprom of its exclusive right to develop new natural gas deposits, and the Government now expected to recover much of Gazprom's unpaid taxes through the new commission. Prime Minister

Chernomyrdin remained a protector of the industry's special status, however.

In April Yeltsin renewed his appeal for Russia's consumers to "buy Russian" to support the domestic economy in the face of increased consumption of imported consumer goods. However, Russian manufacturers faced a circular dilemma: consistently low quality kept the demand for Russian goods from expanding, but firms were unable to improve quality without new profits or increasingly scarce government subsidies.

In politics, reformist members of the Kremlin's younger generation advanced in Yeltsin's Government reorganization. Boris Nemtsov, thirty-seven, gained immediate popularity with ordinary Russians in his new post as deputy prime minister by attacking monopolies and bureaucratic corruption; in April Nemtsov supplanted Aleksandr Lebed' as Russia's most trusted politician in two nationwide polls, although most experts called his reform program virtually impossible. Experts in Russia already were speaking of Nemtsov as the likely presidential candidate of the "young reformers" in 2000. In April forty-three-year-old Sergey Yastrzhembskiy, who had gained wide approval as Yeltsin's press secretary, was named deputy chief of staff and foreign policy coordinator while retaining his previous position.

The struggle for power continued at the echelon of government immediately below Yeltsin. The resignation of Chernomyrdin protégé Petr Rodionov from his post as Minister of Fuel and Energy deprived the prime minister of his most important Government ally. However, Chernomyrdin's position still gave him substantial power vis-à-vis Chubays, an important factor in Yeltsin's ongoing policy of checking the ambitions of his most powerful subordinates. (Experts also considered the presence of Nemtsov and Valentin Yumashev, whom Yeltsin made his chief of staff in March, as additional factors preventing Chubays and his powerful business allies from dominating the reform agenda.)

Human rights continued to have strong political ramifications in mid-1997 when both houses of the Federal Assembly passed a law restricting the activities of all but four "traditional" religions. The Russian Orthodox Church received special status; no other Christian religions were included in the "traditional" category. The law, successor to legislation introduced unsuccessfully by nationalist and communist factions earlier in the 1990s, attracted strong condemnation from the Vatican and human rights groups and strong support from the Russian Orthodox hierarchy and the Communist Party of Russia. In July Yeltsin vetoed the law—which experts saw as evidence of growing anti-Western sentiment in Russian society—as a violation of the constitution's human rights guarantees. The fate of that law, and the unresolved disputes between the executive and legislative branches over budget cuts, privatization, military reform, and tax collection were signs that Yeltsin's new government team still faced complex problems in their reform campaign.

August 20, 1997   Glenn E. Curtis

Chapter 1. Historical Setting: Early History to 1917

A beautiful princess, transformed from a white swan, presents herself to Gvidon, son of Tsar Saltan (design from lacquer box made in village of Mstera).

EACH OF THE MANY NATIONALITIES of Russia has a separate history and complex origins. The historical origins of the Russian state, however, are chiefly those of the East Slavs, the ethnic group that evolved into the Russian, Ukrainian, and Belorussian peoples. The major pre-Soviet states of the East Slavs were, in chronological order, medieval Kievan Rus', Muscovy, and the Russian Empire. Three other states—Poland, Lithuania, and the Mongol Empire—also played crucial roles in the historical development of Russia.

The first East Slavic state, Kievan Rus', emerged along the Dnepr River valley, where it controlled the trade route between Scandinavia and the Byzantine Empire. Kievan Rus' adopted Christianity from the Byzantine Empire in the tenth century, beginning the synthesis of Byzantine and Slavic cultures that defined Russian culture for the next thousand years. Kievan Rus' ultimately disintegrated as a state because of the armed struggles among members of the princely family that collectively possessed it. Conquest by the Mongols in the thirteenth century was the final blow in this disintegration; subsequently, a number of states claimed to be the heirs to the civilization and dominant position of Kievan Rus'. One of those states, Muscovy, was a predominantly Russian territory located at the far northern edge of the former cultural center. Muscovy gradually came to dominate neighboring territories, forming the basis for the future Russian Empire.

Muscovy had significant impact on the civilizations that followed, and they adopted many of its characteristics, including the subordination of the individual to the state. This idea of the dominant state derived from the Slavic, Mongol, and Byzantine heritage of Muscovy, and it later emerged in the unlimited power of the tsar. Both individuals and institutions, even the Russian Orthodox Church, were subordinate to the state as it was represented in the person of the autocrat.

A second characteristic of Russian history has been continual territorial expansion. Beginning with Muscovy's efforts to consolidate Russian territory as Tatar control waned in the fifteenth century, expansion soon went beyond ethnically Russian areas; by the eighteenth century, the principality of Muscovy had become the huge Russian Empire, stretching from Poland eastward to the Pacific Ocean. Size and military might made Russia a major power, but its acquisition of large territories inhabited by non-Russian peoples began an enduring pattern of nationality problems.

Expansion westward sharpened Russia's awareness of its backwardness and shattered the isolation in which the initial stages of expansion had taken place. Muscovy was able to develop at its own pace, but the Russian Empire was forced to adopt Western technology to compete militarily in Europe. Under this exigency, Peter the Great (r. 1682–1725) and subsequent rulers attempted to modernize the country. Most such efforts struggled with indifferent success to raise Russia to European levels of technology and productivity. The technology that Russia adopted brought with it Western cultural and intellectual currents that changed the direction in which Russian culture developed. As Western influence continued, native and foreign cultural values began a competition that survives in vigorous form in the 1990s. The nature of Russia's relationship with the West became an enduring obsession of Russian intellectuals.

Russia's defeat in the Crimean War (1853–56) triggered another attempt at modernization, including the emancipation of the peasants who had been bound to the land in the system of serfdom. Despite major reforms enacted in the 1860s, however, agriculture remained inefficient, industrialization proceeded slowly, and new social problems emerged. In addition to masses of peasants seeking land to till, a new class of industrial workers—the proletariat—and a small but influential group of middle-class professionals were dissatisfied with their positions. The non-Russian populations resented periodic official Russification campaigns and struggled for autonomy. Successive regimes of the nineteenth century responded to such pressures with a combination of halfhearted reform and repression, but no tsar was willing to cede autocratic rule or share power. Gradually, the monarch and the state system that surrounded him became isolated from the rest of society. In the last decades of the nineteenth century, some intellectuals became more radical, and groups of professional revolutionaries emerged.

In spite of its internal problems, Russia continued to play a major role in international politics. However, unexpected defeat in the Russo-Japanese War of 1904–05 sparked a revolution in 1905. At that stage, professionals, workers, peasants, minority ethnic groups, and soldiers demanded fundamental reforms. Reluctantly, Nicholas II responded to the first of Russia's revolutions by granting a limited constitution, but he increasingly circumvented its democratic clauses, and autocracy again took command in the last decade of the tsarist state. World War I found Russia unready for combat but full of patriotic zeal. However, as the government proved incompetent and conditions worsened, war weariness and revolutionary pressures increased, and the defenders of the autocracy grew fewer.

Early History

Many ethnically diverse peoples migrated onto the East European Plain, but the East Slavs remained and gradually became dominant. Kievan Rus', the first East Slavic state, emerged in the ninth century A.D. and developed a complex and frequently unstable political system that flourished until the thirteenth century, when it declined abruptly. Among the lasting achievements of Kievan Rus' are the introduction of a Slavic variant of the Eastern Orthodox religion and a synthesis of Byzantine and Slavic cultures. The disintegration of Kievan Rus' played a crucial role in the evolution of the East Slavs into the Russian, Ukrainian, and Belorussian peoples.

The Inhabitants of the East European Plain

Long before the organization of Kievan Rus', Iranian and other peoples lived in the area of present-day Ukraine. The best known of those groups was the nomadic Scythians, who occupied the region from about 600 B.C. to 200 B.C. and whose skill in warfare and horsemanship is legendary. Between A.D. 100 and A.D. 900, Goths and nomadic Huns, Avars, and Magyars passed through the region in their migrations. Although some of them subjugated the Slavs in the region, those tribes left little of lasting importance. More significant in this period was the expansion of the Slavs, who were agriculturists and beekeepers as well as hunters, fishers, herders, and trappers. By A.D. 600, the Slavs were the dominant ethnic group on the East European Plain.

Little is known of the origin of the Slavs. Philologists and archaeologists theorize that the Slavs settled very early in the Carpathian Mountains or in the area of present-day Belarus. By A.D. 600, they had split linguistically into southern, western, and eastern branches. The East Slavs settled along the Dnepr River in what is now Ukraine; then they spread northward to the northern Volga River valley, east of modern-day Moscow, and westward to the basins of the northern Dnestr and the western Bug rivers, in present-day Moldova and southern Ukraine. In the eighth and ninth centuries, many East Slavic tribes paid tribute to the Khazars, a Turkic-speaking people who adopted Judaism about A.D. 740 and lived in the southern Volga and Caucasus regions.

The East Slavs and the Varangians

By the ninth century, Scandinavian warriors and merchants, called Varangians, had penetrated the East Slavic regions. According to the *Primary Chronicle*, the earliest chronicle of Kievan Rus', a Varangian named Rurik first established himself in Novgorod, just south of modern-day St. Petersburg, in about 860 before moving south and extending his authority to Kiev. The chronicle cites Rurik as the progenitor of a dynasty that ruled in Eastern Europe until 1598. Another Varangian, Oleg, moved south from Novgorod to expel the Khazars from Kiev and founded Kievan Rus' about A.D. 880. During the next thirty-five years, Oleg subdued the various East Slavic tribes. In A.D. 907, he led a campaign against Constantinople, and in 911 he signed a commercial treaty with the Byzantine Empire as an equal partner. The new Kievan state prospered because it controlled the trade route from the Baltic Sea to the Black Sea and because it had an abundant supply of furs, wax, honey, and slaves for export. Historians have debated the role of the Varangians in the establishment of Kievan Rus'. Most Russian historians—especially in the Soviet era—have stressed the Slavic influence in the development of the state. Although Slavic tribes had formed their own regional jurisdictions by 860, the Varangians accelerated the crystallization of Kievan Rus'.

The Golden Age of Kiev

The region of Kiev dominated the state of Kievan Rus' for the next two centuries (see fig. 2). The grand prince of Kiev controlled the lands around the city, and his theoretically subordinate relatives ruled in other cities and paid him tribute. The zenith of the state's power came during the reigns of Prince Vladimir (r. 978–1015) and Prince Yaroslav (the Wise; r. 1019–54). Both rulers continued the steady expansion of Kievan Rus' that had begun under Oleg. To enhance their power, Vladimir married the sister of the Byzantine emperor, and Yaroslav arranged marriages for his sister and three daughters to the kings of Poland, France, Hungary, and Norway. Vladimir's greatest achievement was the Christianization of Kievan Rus', a process that began in 988. He built the first great edifice of Kievan Rus', the Desyatinnaya Church in Kiev. Yaroslav promulgated the first East Slavic law code, *Rus'ka pravda* (Justice of Rus'); built cathedrals named for St. Sophia in Kiev and Novgorod; patronized local clergy and monasticism; and is said to have founded a school system. Yaroslav's sons developed Kiev's great Peshcherskiy monastyr' (Monastery of the Caves), which functioned in Kievan Rus' as an ecclesiastical academy.

Vladimir's choice of Eastern Orthodoxy reflected his close personal ties with Constantinople, which dominated the Black Sea and hence trade on Kiev's most vital commercial route, the Dnepr River. Adherence to the Eastern Orthodox Church had long-range political, cultural, and religious consequences. The church had a liturgy written in Cyrillic (see Glossary) and a corpus of translations from the Greek that had been produced for the South Slavs. The existence of this literature facilitated the East Slavs' conversion to Christianity and introduced them to rudimentary Greek philosophy, science, and historiography without the necessity of learning Greek. In contrast, educated people in medieval Western and Central Europe learned Latin. Because the East Slavs learned neither Greek nor Latin, they were isolated from Byzantine culture as well as from the European cultures of their neighbors to the west.

In the centuries that followed the state's foundation, Rurik's purported descendants shared power over Kievan Rus'. Princely succession moved from elder to younger brother and from uncle to nephew, as well as from father to son. Junior members of the dynasty usually began their official careers as rulers of a minor district, progressed to more lucrative principalities, and then competed for the coveted throne of Kiev.

In the eleventh and twelfth centuries, the princes and their retinues, which were a mixture of Varangian and Slavic elites and small Finno-Ugric and Turkic elements, dominated the society of Kievan Rus'. Leading soldiers and officials received income and land from the princes in return for their political and military services. Kievan society lacked the class institutions and autonomous towns that were typical of West European feudalism. Nevertheless, urban merchants, artisans, and laborers sometimes exercised political influence through a city assembly, the *veche,* which included all the adult males in the population. In some cases, the *veche* either made agreements

7

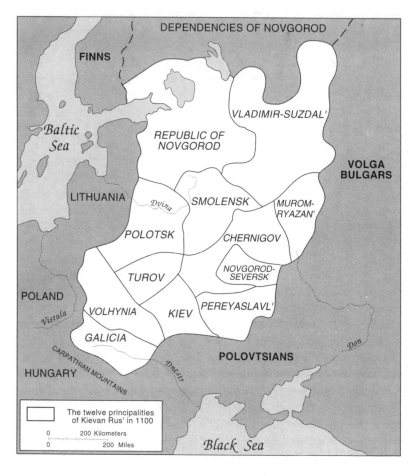

Source: Based on information from David MacKenzie and Michael W. Curran, *A History of Russia and the Soviet Union*, Chicago, 1987, 61.

Figure 2. The Principalities of Kievan Rus', 1136

with their rulers or expelled them and invited others to take their place. At the bottom of society was a small stratum of slaves. More important was a class of tribute-paying peasants, who owed labor duty to the princes; the widespread personal serfdom characteristic of Western Europe did not exist in Kievan Rus', however.

The Rise of Regional Centers

Kievan Rus' was not able to maintain its position as a powerful and prosperous state, in part because of the amalgamation of disparate lands under the control of a ruling clan. As the members of that clan became more numerous, they identified themselves with regional interests rather than with the larger patrimony. Thus, the princes fought among themselves, frequently forming alliances with outside groups such as the Polovtsians, Poles, and Hungarians. The Crusades brought a shift in European trade routes that accelerated the decline of Kievan Rus'. In 1204 the forces of the Fourth Crusade sacked Constantinople, making the Dnepr trade route marginal. As it declined, Kievan Rus' splintered into many principalities and several large regional centers. The inhabitants of those regional centers then evolved into three nationalities: Ukrainians in the southeast and southwest, Belorussians in the northwest, and Russians in the north and northeast.

In the north, the Republic of Novgorod prospered as part of Kievan Rus' because it controlled trade routes from the Volga River to the Baltic Sea. As Kievan Rus' declined, Novgorod became more independent. A local oligarchy ruled Novgorod; major government decisions were made by a town assembly, which also elected a prince as the city's military leader. In the twelfth century, Novgorod acquired its own archbishop, a sign of increased importance and political independence. In its political structure and mercantile activities, Novgorod resembled the north European towns of the Hanseatic League, the prosperous alliance that dominated the commercial activity of the Baltic region between the thirteenth and seventeenth centuries, more than the other principalities of Kievan Rus'.

In the northeast, East Slavs colonized the territory that eventually became Muscovy by intermingling with the Finno-Ugric tribes already occupying the area. The city of Rostov was the oldest center of the northeast, but it was supplanted first by Suzdal' and then by the city of Vladimir. By the twelfth century, the combined principality of Vladimir-Suzdal' had become a major power in Kievan Rus'.

In 1169 Prince Andrey Bogolyubskiy of Vladimir-Suzdal' dealt a severe blow to the waning power of Kievan Rus' when his armies sacked the city of Kiev. Prince Andrey then installed his younger brother to rule in Kiev and continued to rule his realm from Suzdal'. Thus, political power shifted to the northeast, away from Kiev, in the second half of the twelfth century. In 1299, in the wake of the Mongol invasion, the metropolitan of the Orthodox Church moved to the city of Vladimir, and Vladimir-Suzdal' replaced Kievan Rus' as the religious center.

To the southwest, the principality of Galicia-Volhynia had highly developed trade relations with its Polish, Hungarian, and Lithuanian neighbors and emerged as another successor to Kievan Rus'. In the early thirteenth century, Prince Roman Mstislavich united the two previously separate principalities, conquered Kiev, and assumed the title of grand duke of Kievan Rus'. His son, Prince Daniil (Danylo; r. 1238–64) was the first ruler of Kievan Rus' to accept a crown from the Roman papacy, apparently doing so without breaking with Orthodoxy. Early in the fourteenth century, the patriarch of the Orthodox Church in Constantinople granted the rulers of Galicia-Volhynia a metropolitan to compensate for the move of the Kievan metropolitan to Vladimir.

However, a long and unsuccessful struggle against the Mongols combined with internal opposition to the prince and foreign intervention to weaken Galicia-Volhynia. With the end of the Mstislavich Dynasty in the mid-fourteenth century, Galicia-Volhynia ceased to exist; Lithuania took Volhynia, and Poland annexed Galicia.

The Mongol Invasion

As it was undergoing fragmentation, Kievan Rus' faced its greatest threat from invading Mongols. In 1223 an army from Kievan Rus', together with a force of Turkic Polovtsians, faced a Mongol raiding party at the Kalka River. The Kievan alliance was defeated soundly. Then, in 1237–38, a much larger Mongol force overran much of Kievan Rus'. In 1240 the Mongols sacked the city of Kiev and then moved west into Poland and Hungary. Of the principalities of Kievan Rus', only the Republic of Novgorod escaped occupation, but it paid tribute to the Mongols. One branch of the Mongol force withdrew to Saray on the lower Volga River, establishing the Golden Horde (see Glossary). From Saray the Golden Horde Mongols ruled Kievan Rus' indirectly through their princes and tax collectors.

The impact of the Mongol invasion on the territories of Kievan Rus' was uneven. Centers such as Kiev never recovered from the devastation of the initial attack. The Republic of Novgorod continued to prosper, however, and a new entity, the city of Moscow, began to flourish under the Mongols. Although a Russian army defeated the Golden Horde at Kulikovo in 1380, Mongol domination of the Russian-inhabited territories, along with demands of tribute from Russian princes, continued until about 1480.

Historians have debated the long-term influence of Mongol rule on Russian society. The Mongols have been blamed for the destruction of Kievan Rus', the breakup of the "Russian" nationality into three components, and the introduction of the concept of "oriental despotism" into Russia. But most historians agree that Kievan Rus' was not a homogeneous political, cultural, or ethnic entity and that the Mongols merely accelerated a fragmentation that had begun before the invasion. Historians also credit the Mongol regime with an important role in the development of Muscovy as a state. Under Mongol occupation, for example, Muscovy developed its postal road network, census, fiscal system, and military organization.

Kievan Rus' also left a powerful legacy. The leader of the Rurik Dynasty united a large territory inhabited by East Slavs into an important, albeit unstable, state. After Vladimir accepted Eastern Orthodoxy, Kievan Rus' came together under a church structure and developed a Byzantine-Slavic synthesis in culture, statecraft, and the arts. On the northeastern periphery of Kievan Rus', those traditions were adapted to form the Russian autocratic state.

Muscovy

The development of the Russian state can be traced from Vladimir-Suzdal' through Muscovy to the Russian Empire. Muscovy drew people and wealth to the northeastern periphery of Kievan Rus'; established trade links to the Baltic Sea, the White Sea, and the Caspian Sea and to Siberia; and created a highly centralized and autocratic political system. Muscovite political traditions, therefore, exerted a powerful influence on Russian society.

The Rise of Muscovy

When the Mongols invaded the lands of Kievan Rus', Moscow was an insignificant trading outpost in the principality of Vladimir-Suzdal'. The outpost's remote, forested location offered some security from Mongol attack and occupation, and a number of rivers provided access to the Baltic and Black seas and to the Caucasus region. More important to Moscow's development in what became the state of Muscovy, however, was its rule by a series of princes who were ambitious, determined, and lucky. The first ruler of the principality of Muscovy, Daniil Aleksandrovich (d. 1303), secured the principality for his branch of the Rurik Dynasty. His son, Ivan I (r. 1325–40), known as Ivan Kalita ("Money Bags"), obtained the title "Grand Prince of Vladimir" from his Mongol overlords. He cooperated closely with the Mongols and collected tribute from other Russian principalities on their behalf. This relationship enabled Ivan to gain regional ascendancy, particularly over Muscovy's chief rival, the northern city of Tver'. In 1327 the Orthodox metropolitan transferred his residency from Vladimir to Moscow, further enhancing the prestige of the new principality.

In the fourteenth century, the grand princes of Muscovy began gathering Russian lands to increase the population and wealth under their rule (see table 2, Appendix). The most successful practitioner of this process was Ivan III (the Great; r. 1462–1505), who conquered Novgorod in 1478 and Tver' in 1485. Muscovy gained full sovereignty over the ethnically Russian lands in 1480 when Mongol overlordship ended officially, and by the beginning of the sixteenth century virtually all those lands were united. Through inheritance, Ivan obtained part of the province of Ryazan', and the princes of Rostov and Yaroslavl' voluntarily subordinated themselves to him. The northwestern city of Pskov remained independent in this period, but Ivan's son, Vasiliy III (r. 1505–33), later conquered it.

Ivan III was the first Muscovite ruler to use the titles of tsar and "Ruler of all Rus'." Ivan competed with his powerful northwestern rival Lithuania for control over some of the semi-independent former principalities of Kievan Rus' in the upper Dnepr and Donets river basins. Through the defections of some princes, border skirmishes, and a long, inconclusive war with Lithuania that ended only in 1503, Ivan III was able to push westward, and Muscovy tripled in size under his rule.

The Evolution of the Russian Aristocracy

Internal consolidation accompanied outward expansion of the state. By the fifteenth century, the rulers of Muscovy considered the entire Russian territory their collective property. Various semi-independent princes still claimed specific territories, but Ivan III forced the lesser princes to acknowledge the grand prince of Muscovy and his descendants as unquestioned rulers with control over military, judicial, and foreign affairs.

Gradually, the Muscovite ruler emerged as a powerful, autocratic ruler, a tsar. By assuming that title, the Muscovite prince underscored that he was a major ruler or emperor on a par with the emperor of the Byzantine Empire or the Mongol khan. Indeed, after Ivan III's marriage to Sophia Paleologue, the niece of the last Byzantine emperor, the Muscovite court adopted Byzantine terms, rituals, titles, and emblems such as the double-headed eagle. At first, the term *autocrat* connoted only the literal meaning of an independent ruler, but in the reign of Ivan IV (r. 1533–84) it came to mean unlimited rule. Ivan IV was crowned tsar and thus was recognized, at least by the Orthodox Church, as emperor. An Orthodox monk had claimed that, once Constantinople had fallen to the Ottoman Empire in 1453, the Muscovite tsar was the only legitimate Orthodox ruler and that Moscow was the Third Rome because it was the final successor to Rome and Constantinople, the centers of Christianity in earlier periods. That concept was to resonate in the self-image of Russians in future centuries.

Ivan IV

The development of the tsar's autocratic powers reached a peak during the reign of Ivan IV, and he became known as the Terrible (his Russian epithet, *groznyy*, means threatening or dreaded). Ivan strengthened the position of the tsar to an unprecedented degree, demonstrating the risks of unbridled power in the hands of a mentally unstable individual. Although apparently intelligent and energetic, Ivan suffered from bouts of paranoia and depression, and his rule was punctuated by acts of extreme violence.

Ivan IV became grand prince of Muscovy in 1533 at the age of three. Various factions of the boyars (see Glossary) competed for control of the regency until Ivan assumed the throne in 1547. Reflecting Muscovy's new imperial claims, Ivan's coronation as tsar was an elaborate ritual modeled after those of the Byzantine emperors. With the continuing assistance of a group of boyars, Ivan began his reign with a series of useful reforms. In the 1550s, he promulgated a new law code, revamped the military, and reorganized local government. These reforms undoubtedly were intended to strengthen the state in the face of continuous warfare.

During the late 1550s, Ivan developed a hostility toward his advisers, the government, and the boyars. Historians have not determined whether policy differences, personal animosities, or mental imbalance cause his wrath. In 1565 he divided Muscovy into two parts: his private domain and the public realm.

For his private domain, Ivan chose some of the most prosperous and important districts of Muscovy. In these areas, Ivan's agents attacked boyars, merchants, and even common people, summarily executing some and confiscating land and possessions. Thus began a decade of terror in Muscovy. As a result of this policy, called the *oprichnina,* Ivan broke the economic and political power of the leading boyar families, thereby destroying precisely those persons who had built up Muscovy and were the most capable of administering it. Trade diminished, and peasants, faced with mounting taxes and threats of violence, began to leave Muscovy. Efforts to curtail the mobility of the peasants by tying them to their land brought Muscovy closer to legal serfdom. In 1572 Ivan finally abandoned the practices of the *oprichnina.*

Despite the domestic turmoil of Ivan's late period, Muscovy continued to wage wars and to expand. Ivan defeated and annexed the Kazan' Khanate on the middle Volga in 1552 and later the Astrakhan' Khanate, where the Volga meets the Caspian Sea. These victories gave Muscovy access to the entire Volga River and to Central Asia. Muscovy's eastward expansion encountered relatively little resistance. In 1581 the Stroganov merchant family, interested in fur trade, hired a Cossack (see Glossary) leader, Yermak, to lead an expedition into western Siberia. Yermak defeated the Siberian Khanate and claimed the territories west of the Ob' and Irtysh rivers for Muscovy (see fig. 3).

Expanding to the northwest toward the Baltic Sea proved to be much more difficult. In 1558 Ivan invaded Livonia, eventually embroiling him in a twenty-five-year war against Poland, Lithuania, Sweden, and Denmark. Despite occasional successes, Ivan's army was pushed back, and Muscovy failed to secure a coveted position on the Baltic Sea. The war drained Muscovy. Some historians believe that Ivan initiated the *oprichnina* to mobilize resources for the war and to quell opposition to it. Regardless of the reason, Ivan's domestic and foreign policies had a devastating effect on Muscovy, and they led to a period of social struggle and civil war, the so-called Time of Troubles (Smutnoye vremya, 1598–1613).

The Time of Troubles

Ivan IV was succeeded by his son Fedor, who was mentally deficient. Actual power went to Fedor's brother-in-law, the boyar Boris Godunov. Perhaps the most important event of

Fedor's reign was the proclamation of the patriarchate of Moscow in 1589. The creation of the patriarchate climaxed the evolution of a separate and totally independent Russian Orthodox Church.

In 1598 Fedor died without an heir, ending the Rurik Dynasty. Boris Godunov then convened a *zemskiy sobor*, a national assembly of boyars, church officials, and commoners, which proclaimed him tsar, although various boyar factions refused to recognize the decision. Widespread crop failures caused a famine between 1601 and 1603, and during the ensuing discontent, a man emerged who claimed to be Dmitriy, Ivan IV's son who had died in 1591. This pretender to the throne, who came to be known as the first False Dmitriy, gained support in Poland and marched to Moscow, gathering followers among the boyars and other elements as he went. Historians speculate that Godunov would have weathered this crisis, but he died in 1605. As a result, the first False Dmitriy entered Moscow and was crowned tsar that year, following the murder of Tsar Fedor II, Godunov's son.

Subsequently, Muscovy entered a period of continuous chaos. The Time of Troubles included a civil war in which a struggle over the throne was complicated by the machinations of rival boyar factions, the intervention of regional powers Poland and Sweden, and intense popular discontent. The first False Dmitriy and his Polish garrison were overthrown, and a boyar, Vasiliy Shuyskiy, was proclaimed tsar in 1606. In his attempt to retain the throne, Shuyskiy allied himself with the Swedes. A second False Dmitriy, allied with the Poles, appeared. In 1610 that heir apparent was proclaimed tsar, and the Poles occupied Moscow. The Polish presence led to a patriotic revival among the Russians, and a new army, financed by northern merchants and blessed by the Orthodox Church, drove the Poles out. In 1613 a new *zemskiy sobor* proclaimed the boyar Mikhail Romanov as tsar, beginning the 300-year reign of the Romanov family.

Muscovy was in chaos for more than a decade, but the institution of the autocracy remained intact. Despite the tsar's persecution of the boyars, the townspeople's dissatisfaction, and the gradual enserfment of the peasantry, efforts at restricting the power of the tsar were only halfhearted. Finding no institutional alternative to the autocracy, discontented Russians rallied behind various pretenders to the throne. During that period, the goal of political activity was to gain influence over

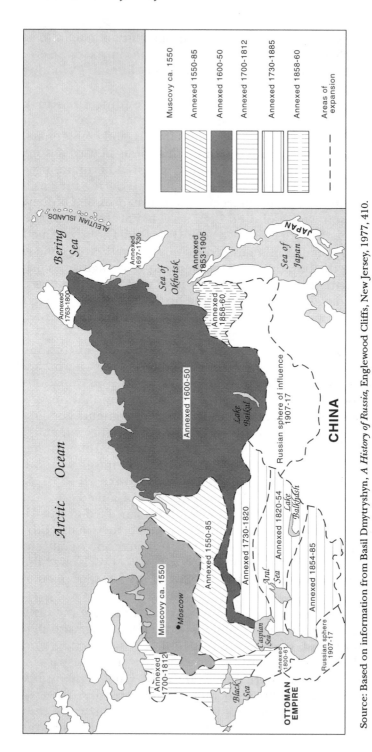

Source: Based on information from Basil Dmytryshyn, *A History of Russia*, Englewood Cliffs, New Jersey, 1977, 410.

Figure 3. Territorial Expansion of Muscovy and the Russian Empire, 1550–1917.

the sitting autocrat or to place one's own candidate on the throne. The boyars fought among themselves, the lower classes revolted blindly, and foreign armies occupied the Kremlin (see Glossary) in Moscow, prompting many to accept tsarist absolutism as a necessary means to restoring order and unity in Muscovy.

The Romanovs

The immediate task of the new dynasty was to restore order. Fortunately for Muscovy, its major enemies, Poland and Sweden, were engaged in a bitter conflict with each other, which provided Muscovy the opportunity to make peace with Sweden in 1617 and to sign a truce with Poland in 1619. After an unsuccessful attempt to regain the city of Smolensk from Poland in 1632, Muscovy made peace with Poland in 1634. Polish king Wladyslaw IV, whose father and predecessor Sigismund III had manipulated his nominal selection as tsar of Muscovy during the Time of Troubles, renounced all claims to the title as a condition of the peace treaty.

The early Romanovs were weak rulers. Under Mikhail, state affairs were in the hands of the tsar's father, Filaret, who in 1619 became patriarch of the Orthodox Church. Later, Mikhail's son Aleksey (r. 1645–76) relied on a boyar, Boris Morozov, to run his government. Morozov abused his position by exploiting the populace, and in 1648 Aleksey dismissed him in the wake of a popular uprising in Moscow.

The autocracy survived the Time of Troubles and the rule of weak or corrupt tsars because of the strength of the government's central bureaucracy. Government functionaries continued to serve, regardless of the ruler's legitimacy or the boyar faction controlling the throne. In the seventeenth century, the bureaucracy expanded dramatically. The number of government departments (*prikazy*; sing., *prikaz*) increased from twenty-two in 1613 to eighty by mid-century. Although the departments often had overlapping and conflicting jurisdictions, the central government, through provincial governors, was able to control and regulate all social groups, as well as trade, manufacturing, and even the Orthodox Church.

The comprehensive legal code introduced in 1649 illustrates the extent of state control over Russian society. By that time, the boyars had largely merged with the elite bureaucracy, who were obligatory servitors of the state, to form a new nobility, the *dvoryanstvo*. The state required service from both the old and the new nobility, primarily in the military. In return, they received land and peasants. In the preceding century, the state had gradually curtailed peasants' rights to move from one landlord to another; the 1649 code officially attached peasants to their domicile. The state fully sanctioned serfdom, and runaway peasants became state fugitives. Landlords had complete power over their peasants and bought, sold, traded, and mortgaged them. Peasants living on state-owned land, however, were not considered serfs. They were organized into communes, which were responsible for taxes and other obligations. Like serfs, however, state peasants were attached to the land they farmed. Middle-class urban tradesmen and craftsmen were assessed taxes, and, like the serfs, they were forbidden to change residence. All segments of the population were subject to military levy and to special taxes. By chaining much of Muscovite society to specific domiciles, the legal code of 1649 curtailed movement and subordinated the people to the interests of the state.

Under this code, increased state taxes and regulations exacerbated the social discontent that had been simmering since the Time of Troubles. In the 1650s and 1660s, the number of peasant escapes increased dramatically. A favorite refuge was the Don River region, domain of the Don Cossacks. A major uprising occurred in the Volga region in 1670 and 1671. Stenka Razin, a Cossack who was from the Don River region, led a revolt that drew together wealthy Cossacks who were well established in the region and escaped serfs seeking free land. The unexpected uprising swept up the Volga River valley and even threatened Moscow. Tsarist troops finally defeated the rebels after they had occupied major cities along the Volga in an operation whose panache captured the imaginations of later generations of Russians. Razin was publicly tortured and executed.

Expansion and Westernization

Muscovy continued its territorial growth through the seventeenth century. In the southwest, it acquired eastern Ukraine, which had been under Polish rule. The Ukrainian Cossacks, warriors organized in military formations, lived in the frontier areas bordering Poland, the Tatar lands, and Muscovy. Although they had served in the Polish army as mercenaries, the Ukrainian Cossacks remained fiercely independent and staged a number of uprisings against the Poles. In 1648 most of Ukrainian society joined the Cossacks in a revolt because of the political, social, religious, and ethnic oppression suffered under Polish rule. After the Ukrainians had thrown off Polish rule, they needed military help to maintain their position. In 1654 the Ukrainian leader, Bogdan Khmel'nitskiy (Bohdan Khmel'nyts'kyy), offered to place Ukraine under the protection of the Muscovite tsar, Aleksey I, rather than under the Polish king. Aleksey's acceptance of this offer, which was ratified in the Treaty of Pereyaslavl', led to a protracted war between Poland and Muscovy. The Treaty of Andrusovo, which ended the war in 1667, split Ukraine along the Dnepr River, reuniting the western sector with Poland and leaving the eastern sector self-governing under the suzerainty of the tsar.

In the east, Muscovy had obtained western Siberia in the sixteenth century. From this base, merchants, traders, and explorers pushed eastward from the Ob' River to the Yenisey River, then to the Lena River. By the middle of the seventeenth century, Muscovites had reached the Amur River and the outskirts of the Chinese Empire. After a period of conflict with the Manchu Dynasty, Muscovy made peace with China in 1689. By the Treaty of Nerchinsk, Muscovy ceded its claims to the Amur Valley, but it gained access to the region east of Lake Baikal and the trade route to Beijing. Peace with China consolidated the initial breakthrough to the Pacific that had been made in the middle of the century.

Muscovy's southwestern expansion, particularly its incorporation of eastern Ukraine, had unintended consequences. Most Ukrainians were Orthodox, but their close contact with the Roman Catholic Polish Counter-Reformation also brought them Western intellectual currents. Through Kiev, Muscovy gained links to Polish and Central European influences and to the wider Orthodox world. Although the Ukrainian link stimulated creativity in many areas, it also undermined traditional Russian religious practices and culture. The Russian Orthodox Church discovered that its isolation from Constantinople had caused variations to creep into its liturgical books and practices. The Russian Orthodox patriarch, Nikon, was determined to bring the Russian texts back into conformity with the Greek originals. But Nikon encountered fierce opposition among the many Russians who viewed the corrections as improper foreign intrusions, or perhaps the work of the devil. When the Orthodox Church forced Nikon's reforms, a schism resulted in 1667. Those who did not accept the reforms came to be called the Old Believers (*starovery*); they were officially pronounced heretics and were persecuted by the church and the state. The chief opposition figure, the archpriest Avvakum, was burned at the stake. The split subsequently became permanent, and many merchants and peasants joined the Old Believers.

The tsar's court also felt the impact of Ukraine and the West. Kiev was a major transmitter of new ideas and insight through the famed scholarly academy that Metropolitan Mogila (Mohyla) founded there in 1631. Among the results of this infusion of ideas into Muscovy were baroque architecture, literature, and icon painting. Other more direct channels to the West opened as international trade increased and more foreigners came to Muscovy. The tsar's court was interested in the West's more advanced technology, particularly when military applications were involved. By the end of the seventeenth century, Ukrainian, Polish, and West European penetration had undermined the Muscovite cultural synthesis—at least among the elite—and had prepared the way for an even more radical transformation.

Early Imperial Russia

In the eighteenth century, Muscovy was transformed from a static, somewhat isolated, traditional state into the more dynamic, partially Westernized, and secularized Russian Empire. This transformation was in no small measure a result of the vision, energy, and determination of Peter the Great. Historians disagree about the extent to which Peter himself transformed Russia, but they generally concur that he laid the foundations for empire building over the next two centuries. The era that Peter initiated signaled the advent of Russia as a major European power. But, although the Russian Empire would play a leading political role in the next century, its retention of serfdom precluded economic progress of any significant degree. As West European economic growth accelerated during the Industrial Revolution, which had begun in the second half of the eighteenth century, Russia began to lag ever farther behind, creating new problems for the empire as a great power.

Peter the Great and the Russian Empire

As a child of the second marriage of Tsar Aleksey, Peter at first was relegated to the background of Russian politics as various court factions struggled to control the throne. Aleksey was succeeded by his son from his first marriage, Fedor III, a sickly boy who died in 1682. Peter then was made co-tsar with his half brother, Ivan V, but Peter's half sister, Sofia, held the real power. She ruled as regent while the young Peter was allowed to play war games with his friends and to roam in Moscow's foreign quarters. These early experiences instilled in him an abiding interest in Western military practice and technology, particularly in military engineering, artillery, navigation, and shipbuilding. In 1689, using troops that he had drilled during childhood games, Peter foiled a plot to have Sofia crowned. When Ivan V died in 1696, Peter became the sole tsar of Muscovy.

War dominated much of Peter's reign. At first Peter attempted to secure the principality's southern borders against the Tatars and the Ottoman Turks. His campaign against a fort on the Sea of Azov failed initially, but after he created Russia's first navy, Peter was able to take the port of Azov in 1696. To continue the war with the Ottoman Empire, Peter traveled to Europe to seek allies. The first tsar to make such a trip, Peter visited Brandenburg, Holland, England, and the Holy Roman Empire during his so-called Grand Embassy. Peter learned a great deal and enlisted into his service hundreds of West European technical specialists. The embassy was cut short by the attempt to place Sofia on the throne instead of Peter, a revolt that was crushed by Peter's followers. As a result, Peter had hundreds of the participants tortured and killed, and he publicly displayed their bodies as a warning to others.

Peter was unsuccessful in forging a European coalition against the Ottoman Empire, but during his travels he found interest in waging war against Sweden, then an important power in northern Europe. Seeing an opportunity to break through to the Baltic Sea, Peter made peace with the Ottoman Empire in 1700 and then attacked the Swedes at their port of Narva on the Gulf of Finland. However, Sweden's young king, Charles XII, proved his military acumen by crushing Peter's army. Fortunately for Peter, Charles did not follow up his victory with a counteroffensive, becoming embroiled instead in a series of wars over the Polish throne. This respite allowed Peter to build a new, Western-style army. When the armies of the two leaders met again at the town of Poltava in 1709, Peter defeated Charles. Charles escaped to Ottoman territory, and Russia subsequently became engaged in another war with the Ottoman Empire. Russia agreed to return the port of Azov to the Ottomans in 1711. The Great Northern War, which in essence was settled at Poltava, continued until 1721, when Sweden agreed to the Treaty of Nystad. The treaty allowed Muscovy to retain the Baltic territories that it had conquered: Livonia, Estonia, and Ingria. Through his victories, Peter acquired a direct link with Western Europe. In celebration, Peter assumed the title of emperor as well as tsar, and Muscovy officially became the Russian Empire in 1721.

Peter achieved Muscovy's expansion into Europe and its transformation into the Russian Empire through several major initiatives. He established Russia's naval forces, reorganized the army according to European models, streamlined the government, and mobilized Russia's financial and human resources. Under Peter, the army drafted soldiers for lifetime terms from the taxpaying population, and it drew officers from the nobility and required them to give lifelong service in either the military or civilian administration. In 1722 Peter introduced the Table of Ranks, which determined a person's position and status according to service to the tsar rather than to birth or seniority. Even commoners who achieved a certain level on the table were ennobled automatically.

Peter's reorganization of the government structure was no less thorough. He replaced the *prikazy* with colleges or boards and created a senate to coordinate government policy. Peter's reform of local government was less successful, but his changes enabled local governments to collect taxes and maintain order. As part of the government reform, the Orthodox Church was partially incorporated into the country's administrative structure. Peter abolished the patriarchate and replaced it with a collective body, the Holy Synod, led by a lay government official.

Peter tripled the revenues of the state treasury through a variety of taxes. He levied a capitation, or poll tax, on all males except clergy and nobles and imposed a myriad of indirect taxes on alcohol, salt, and even beards. To provide uniforms and weapons for the military, Peter developed metallurgical and textile industries using serf labor.

Peter wanted to equip Russia with modern technology, institutions, and ideas. He required Western-style education for all male nobles, introduced so-called cipher schools to teach the alphabet and basic arithmetic, established a printing house, and funded the Academy of Sciences (see Glossary), which was established just before his death in 1725 and became one of

Russia's most important cultural institutions. He demanded that aristocrats acquire the dress, tastes, and social customs of the West. The result was a deepening of the cultural rift between the nobility and the mass of Russian people. The best illustration of Peter's drive for Westernization, his break with traditions, and his coercive methods was his construction in 1703 of a new, architecturally Western capital, St. Petersburg, situated on land newly conquered from Sweden on the Gulf of Finland. Although St. Petersburg faced westward, its Westernization was by coercion, and it could not arouse the individualistic spirit that was an important element in the Western ways Peter so admired.

Peter's reign raised questions about Russia's backwardness, its relationship to the West, the appropriateness of reform from above, and other fundamental problems that have confronted many of Russia's subsequent rulers. In the nineteenth century, Russians debated whether Peter was correct in pointing Russia toward the West or whether his reforms had been a violation of Russia's natural traditions.

The Era of Palace Revolutions

Peter changed the rules of succession to the throne after he killed his own son, Aleksey, who had opposed his father's reforms and served as a rallying figure for antireform groups. A new law provided that the tsar would choose his own successor, but Peter failed to do so before his death in 1725. In the decades that followed, the absence of clear rules of succession left the monarchy open to intrigues, plots, coups, and countercoups. Henceforth, the crucial factor for obtaining the throne was the support of the elite palace guard in St. Petersburg.

After Peter's death, his wife, Catherine I, seized the throne. But when she died in 1727, Peter's grandson, Peter II, was crowned tsar. In 1730 Peter II succumbed to smallpox, and Anna, a daughter of Ivan V, who had been co-ruler with Peter, ascended the throne. The clique of nobles that put Anna on the throne attempted to impose various conditions on her. In her struggle against those restrictions, Anna had the support of other nobles who feared oligarchic rule more than autocracy. Thus the principle of autocracy continued to receive strong support despite chaotic struggles for the throne.

Anna died in 1740, and her infant grandnephew was proclaimed tsar as Ivan VI. After a series of coups, however, he was replaced by Peter the Great's daughter Elizabeth (r. 1741–62).

During Elizabeth's reign, which was much more effective than those of her immediate predecessors, a Westernized Russian culture began to emerge. Among notable cultural events were the founding of Moscow University (1755) and the Academy of Fine Arts (1757) and the emergence of Russia's first eminent scientist and scholar, Mikhail Lomonosov.

During the rule of Peter's successors, Russia took a more active role in European statecraft. From 1726 to 1761, Russia was allied with Austria against the Ottoman Empire, which France usually supported. In the War of Polish Succession (1733–35), Russia and Austria blocked the French candidate to the Polish throne. In a costly war with the Ottoman Empire (1734–39), Russia reacquired the port of Azov. Russia's greatest reach into Europe was during the Seven Years' War (1756–63), which was fought on three continents between Britain and France with numerous allies on both sides. In that war, Russia continued its alliance with Austria, but Austria shifted to an alliance with France against Prussia. In 1760 Russian forces were at the gates of Berlin. Fortunately for Prussia, Elizabeth died in 1762, and her successor, Peter III, allied Russia with Prussia because of his devotion to the Prussian emperor, Frederick the Great.

Peter III had a short and unpopular reign. Although he was a grandson of Peter the Great, his father was the duke of Holstein, so Peter III was raised in a German Lutheran environment. Russians therefore considered him a foreigner. Making no secret of his contempt for all things Russian, Peter created deep resentment by forcing Prussian military drills on the Russian military, attacking the Orthodox Church, and depriving Russia of a military victory by establishing his sudden alliance with Prussia. Making use of the discontent and fearing for her own position, Peter III's wife, Catherine, deposed her husband in a coup, and her lover, Aleksey Orlov, subsequently murdered him. Thus, in June 1762 a German princess who had no legitimate claim to the Russian throne became Catherine II, empress of Russia.

Imperial Expansion and Maturation: Catherine II

Catherine II's reign was notable for imperial expansion, which brought the empire huge new territories in the south and west, and for internal consolidation. Following a war that broke out with the Ottoman Empire in 1768, the parties agreed to the Treaty of Kuchuk-Kainarji in 1774. By that treaty, Russia acquired an outlet to the Black Sea, and the Crimean Tatars were made independent of the Ottomans. In 1783 Catherine annexed Crimea, helping to spark the next war with the Ottoman Empire, which began in 1787. By the Treaty of Jassy in 1792, Russia expanded southward to the Dnestr River. The terms of the treaty fell far short of the goals of Catherine's reputed "Greek project"—the expulsion of the Ottomans from Europe and the renewal of a Byzantine Empire under Russian control. The Ottoman Empire no longer was a serious threat to Russia, however, and was forced to tolerate an increasing Russian influence over the Balkans.

Russia's westward expansion under Catherine was the result of the partitioning of Poland. As Poland became increasingly weak in the eighteenth century, each of its neighbors—Russia, Prussia, and Austria—tried to place its own candidate on the Polish throne. In 1772 the three agreed on an initial partition of Polish territory, by which Russia received parts of Belorussia and Livonia. After the partition, Poland initiated an extensive reform program, which included a democratic constitution that alarmed reactionary factions in Poland and in Russia. Using the danger of radicalism as an excuse, the same three powers abrogated the constitution and in 1793 again stripped Poland of territory. This time Russia obtained most of Belorussia and Ukraine west of the Dnepr River. The 1793 partition led to an anti-Russian and anti-Prussian uprising in Poland, which ended with the third partition in 1795. The result was that Poland was wiped off the map.

Although the partitioning of Poland greatly added to Russia's territory and prestige, it also created new difficulties. Having lost Poland as a buffer, Russia now had to share borders with both Prussia and Austria. In addition, the empire became more ethnically heterogeneous as it absorbed large numbers of Poles, Ukrainians, Belorussians, and Jews. The fate of the Ukrainians and Belorussians, who were primarily serfs, changed little at first under Russian rule. Roman Catholic Poles resented their loss of independence, however, and proved to be difficult to integrate. Russia had barred Jews from the empire in 1742 and viewed them as an alien population. A decree of January 3, 1792, formally initiated the Pale of Settlement, which permitted Jews to live only in the western part of the empire, thereby setting the stage for anti-Jewish discrimination in later periods (see Other Religions, ch. 4). At the same time, Russia abolished the autonomy of Ukraine east of the

Dnepr, the Baltic republics, and various Cossack areas. With her emphasis on a uniformly administered empire, Catherine presaged the policy of Russification that later tsars and their successors would practice.

Historians have debated Catherine's sincerity as an enlightened monarch, but few have doubted that she believed in government activism aimed at developing the empire's resources and making its administration more effective. Initially, Catherine attempted to rationalize government procedures through law. In 1767 she created the Legislative Commission, drawn from nobles, townsmen, and others, to codify Russia's laws. Although the commission did not formulate a new law code, Catherine's Instruction to the Commission introduced some Russians to Western political and legal thinking.

During the 1768–74 war with the Ottoman Empire, Russia experienced a major social upheaval, the Pugachev Uprising. In 1773 a Don Cossack, Emel'yan Pugachev, announced that he was Peter III. Other Cossacks, various Turkic tribes that felt the impingement of the Russian centralizing state, and industrial workers in the Ural Mountains, as well as peasants hoping to escape serfdom, all joined in the rebellion. Russia's preoccupation with the war enabled Pugachev to take control of a part of the Volga area, but the regular army crushed the rebellion in 1774.

The Pugachev Uprising bolstered Catherine's determination to reorganize Russia's provincial administration. In 1775 she divided Russia into provinces and districts according to population statistics. She then gave each province an expanded administrative, police, and judicial apparatus. Nobles no longer were required to serve the central government, as they had since Peter the Great's time, and many of them received significant roles in administering provincial governments.

Catherine also attempted to organize society into well-defined social groups, or estates. In 1785 she issued charters to nobles and townsmen. The Charter to the Nobility confirmed the liberation of the nobles from compulsory service and gave them rights that not even the autocracy could infringe upon. The Charter to the Towns proved to be complicated and ultimately less successful than the one issued to the nobles. Failure to issue a similar charter to state peasants, or to ameliorate the conditions of serfdom, made Catherine's social reforms incomplete.

The intellectual westernization of the elite continued during Catherine's reign. An increase in the number of books and periodicals also brought forth intellectual debates and social criticism (see Literature and the Arts, ch. 4). In 1790 Aleksandr Radishchev published his *Journey from St. Petersburg to Moscow,* a fierce attack on serfdom and the autocracy. Catherine, already frightened by the French Revolution, had Radishchev arrested and banished to Siberia. Radishchev was later recognized as the father of Russian radicalism.

Catherine brought many of the policies of Peter the Great to fruition and set the foundation for the nineteenth-century empire. Russia became a power capable of competing with its European neighbors on military, political, and diplomatic grounds. Russia's elite became culturally more like the elites of Central and West European countries. The organization of society and the government system, from Peter the Great's central institutions to Catherine's provincial administration, remained basically unchanged until the emancipation of the serfs in 1861 and, in some respects, until the fall of the monarchy in 1917. Catherine's push to the south, including the establishment of Odessa as a Russian port on the Black Sea, provided the basis for Russia's nineteenth-century grain trade.

Despite such accomplishments, the empire that Peter I and Catherine II had built was beset with fundamental problems. A small Europeanized elite, alienated from the mass of ordinary Russians, raised questions about the very essence of Russia's history, culture, and identity. Russia achieved its military preeminence by reliance on coercion and a primitive command economy based on serfdom. Although Russia's economic development was almost sufficient for its eighteenth-century needs, it was no match for the transformation the Industrial Revolution was causing in Western countries. Catherine's attempt at organizing society into corporate estates was already being challenged by the French Revolution, which emphasized individual citizenship. Russia's territorial expansion and the incorporation of an increasing number of non-Russians into the empire set the stage for the future nationalities problem. Finally, the first questioning of serfdom and autocracy on moral grounds foreshadowed the conflict between the state and the intelligentsia that was to become dominant in the nineteenth century.

Ruling the Empire

During the early nineteenth century, Russia's population, resources, international diplomacy, and military forces made it one of the most powerful states in the world. Its power enabled it to play an increasingly assertive role in Europe's affairs. This role drew the empire into a series of wars against Napoleon, which had far-reaching consequences for Russia and the rest of Europe. After a period of enlightenment, Russia became an active opponent of liberalizing trends in Central and Western Europe. Internally, Russia's population had grown more diverse with each territorial acquisition. The population included Lutheran Finns, Baltic Germans, Estonians, and some Latvians; Roman Catholic Lithuanians, Poles, and some Latvians; Orthodox and Uniate (see Glossary) Belorussians and Ukrainians; Muslim peoples along the empire's southern border; Orthodox Greeks and Georgians; and members of the Armenian Apostolic Church. As Western influence and opposition to Russian autocracy mounted, the regime reacted by creating a secret police and increasing censorship in order to curtail the activities of persons advocating change. The regime remained committed to its serf-based economy as the means of supporting the upper classes, the government, and the military forces. But Russia's backwardness and inherent weakness were revealed in the middle of the century, when several powers forced the surrender of a Russian fortress in Crimea.

War and Peace, 1796–1825

Catherine II died in 1796, and her son Paul (r. 1796–1801) succeeded her. Painfully aware that Catherine had planned to bypass him and name his son, Alexander, as tsar, Paul instituted primogeniture in the male line as the basis for succession. It was one of the few lasting reforms of Paul's brief reign. He also chartered a Russian-American company, which eventually led to Russia's acquisition of Alaska. Paul was haughty and unstable, and he frequently reversed his previous decisions, creating administrative chaos and accumulating enemies.

As a major European power, Russia could not escape the wars involving revolutionary and Napoleonic France. Paul became an adamant opponent of France, and Russia joined Britain and Austria in a war against France. In 1798–99 Russian troops under one of the country's most famous generals, Aleksandr Suvorov, performed brilliantly in Italy and Switzerland.

Paul reversed himself, however, and abandoned his allies. This reversal, coupled with increasingly arbitrary domestic policies, sparked a coup, and in March 1801 Paul was assassinated.

The new tsar, Alexander I (r. 1801–25), came to the throne as the result of his father's murder, in which he was implicated. Groomed for the throne by Catherine II and raised in the spirit of enlightenment, Alexander also had an inclination toward romanticism and religious mysticism, particularly in the latter period of his reign. Alexander tinkered with changes in the central government, and he replaced the colleges that Peter the Great had set up with ministries, but without a coordinating prime minister. The brilliant statesman Mikhail Speranskiy, who was the tsar's chief adviser early in his reign, proposed an extensive constitutional reform of the government, but Alexander dismissed him in 1812 and lost interest in reform.

Alexander's primary focus was not on domestic policy but on foreign affairs, and particularly on Napoleon. Fearing Napoleon's expansionist ambitions and the growth of French power, Alexander joined Britain and Austria against Napoleon. Napoleon defeated the Russians and Austrians at Austerlitz in 1805 and trounced the Russians at Friedland in 1807. Alexander was forced to sue for peace, and by the Treaty of Tilsit, signed in 1807, he became Napoleon's ally. Russia lost little territory under the treaty, and Alexander made use of his alliance with Napoleon for further expansion. He wrested the Grand Duchy of Finland from Sweden in 1809 and acquired Bessarabia from Turkey in 1812.

The Russo-French alliance gradually became strained. Napoleon was concerned about Russia's intentions in the strategically vital Bosporus and Dardenelles straits. At the same time, Alexander viewed the Grand Duchy of Warsaw, the French-controlled reconstituted Polish state, with suspicion. The requirement of joining France's Continental Blockade against Britain was a serious disruption of Russian commerce, and in 1810 Alexander repudiated the obligation. In June 1812, Napoleon invaded Russia with 600,000 troops—a force twice as large as the Russian regular army. Napoleon hoped to inflict a major defeat on the Russians and force Alexander to sue for peace. As Napoleon pushed the Russian forces back, however, he became seriously overextended. Obstinate Russian resistance combined with the Russian winter to deal Napoleon a disastrous defeat, from which fewer than 30,000 of his troops returned to their homeland.

As the French retreated, the Russians pursued them into Central and Western Europe and to the gates of Paris. After the allies defeated Napoleon, Alexander became known as the savior of Europe, and he played a prominent role in the redrawing of the map of Europe at the Congress of Vienna in 1815. In the same year, under the influence of religious mysticism, Alexander initiated the creation of the Holy Alliance, a loose agreement pledging the rulers of the nations involved—including most of Europe—to act according to Christian principles. More pragmatically, in 1814 Russia, Britain, Austria, and Prussia had formed the Quadruple Alliance. The allies created an international system to maintain the territorial status quo and prevent the resurgence of an expansionist France. The Quadruple Alliance, confirmed by a number of international conferences, ensured Russia's influence in Europe.

At the same time, Russia continued its expansion. The Congress of Vienna created the Kingdom of Poland (Russian Poland), to which Alexander granted a constitution. Thus, Alexander I became the constitutional monarch of Poland while remaining the autocratic tsar of Russia. He was also the limited monarch of Finland, which had been annexed in 1809 and awarded autonomous status. In 1813 Russia gained territory in the Baku area of the Caucasus at the expense of Persia. By the early nineteenth century, the empire also was firmly ensconced in Alaska.

Historians have generally agreed that a revolutionary movement was born during the reign of Alexander I. Young officers who had pursued Napoleon into Western Europe came back to Russia with revolutionary ideas, including human rights, representative government, and mass democracy. The intellectual Westernization that had been fostered in the eighteenth century by a paternalistic, autocratic Russian state now included opposition to autocracy, demands for representative government, calls for the abolition of serfdom, and, in some instances, advocacy of a revolutionary overthrow of the government. Officers were particularly incensed that Alexander had granted Poland a constitution while Russia remained without one. Several clandestine organizations were preparing for an uprising when Alexander died unexpectedly in 1825. Following his death, there was confusion about who would succeed him because the next in line, his brother Constantine, had relinquished his right to the throne. A group of officers commanding about 3,000 men refused to swear allegiance to the new tsar, Alexander's brother Nicholas, proclaiming instead their loyalty to the idea of a Russian constitution. Because these events occurred in December 1825, the rebels were called Decembrists. Nicholas easily overcame the revolt, and the Decembrists who remained alive were arrested. Many were exiled to Siberia.

To some extent, the Decembrists were in the tradition of a long line of palace revolutionaries who wanted to place their candidate on the throne. But because the Decembrists also wanted to implement a liberal political program, their revolt has been considered the beginning of a revolutionary movement. The Decembrist Revolt was the first open breach between the government and liberal elements, and it would subsequently widen.

Reaction under Nicholas I

Nicholas completely lacked his brother's spiritual and intellectual breadth; he saw his role simply as one paternal autocrat ruling his people by whatever means were necessary. Having experienced the trauma of the Decembrist Revolt, Nicholas I was determined to restrain Russian society. A secret police, the so-called Third Section, ran a huge network of spies and informers. The government exercised censorship and other controls over education, publishing, and all manifestations of public life. In 1833 the minister of education, Sergey Uvarov, devised a program of "autocracy, Orthodoxy, and nationality" as the guiding principle of the regime. The people were to show loyalty to the unlimited authority of the tsar, to the traditions of the Orthodox Church, and, in a vague way, to the Russian nation. These principles did not gain the support of the population but instead led to repression in general and to suppression of non-Russian nationalities and religions in particular. For example, the government suppressed the Uniate Church in Ukraine and Belorussia in 1839.

The official emphasis on Russian nationalism contributed to a debate on Russia's place in the world, the meaning of Russian history, and the future of Russia. One group, the Westernizers, believed that Russia remained backward and primitive and could progress only through more thorough Europeanization. Another group, the Slavophiles, idealized the Russia that had existed before Peter the Great. The Slavophiles viewed old Russia as a source of wholeness and looked askance at Western rationalism and materialism. Some of them believed that the

Russian peasant commune, or *mir,* offered an attractive alternative to Western capitalism and could make Russia a potential social and moral savior. The Slavophiles, therefore, represented a form of Russian messianism.

Despite the repressions of this period, Russia experienced a flowering of literature and the arts. Through the works of Aleksandr Pushkin, Nikolay Gogol', Ivan Turgenev, and numerous others, Russian literature gained international stature and recognition. Ballet took root in Russia after its importation from France, and classical music became firmly established with the compositions of Mikhail Glinka (1804–57) (see Literature and the Arts, ch. 4).

In foreign policy, Nicholas I acted as the protector of ruling legitimism and guardian against revolution. His offers to suppress revolution on the European continent, accepted in some instances, earned him the label of gendarme of Europe. In 1830, after a popular uprising had occurred in France, the Poles in Russian Poland revolted. Nicholas crushed the rebellion, abrogated the Polish constitution, and reduced Poland to the status of a Russian province. In 1848, when a series of revolutions convulsed Europe, Nicholas was in the forefront of reaction. In 1849 he intervened on behalf of the Habsburgs and helped suppress an uprising in Hungary, and he also urged Prussia not to accept a liberal constitution. Having helped conservative forces repel the specter of revolution, Nicholas I seemed to dominate Europe.

Russian dominance proved illusory, however. While Nicholas was attempting to maintain the status quo in Europe, he adopted an aggressive policy toward the Ottoman Empire. Nicholas I was following the traditional Russian policy of resolving the so-called Eastern Question by seeking to partition the Ottoman Empire and establish a protectorate over the Orthodox population of the Balkans, still largely under Ottoman control in the 1820s. Russia fought a successful war with the Ottomans in 1828 and 1829. In 1833 Russia negotiated the Treaty of Unkiar-Skelessi with the Ottoman Empire. The major European parties mistakenly believed that the treaty contained a secret clause granting Russia the right to send warships through the Bosporus and Dardanelles straits. By the London Straits Convention of 1841, they affirmed Ottoman control over the straits and forbade any power, including Russia, to send warships through the straits. Based on his role in suppressing the revolutions of 1848 and his mistaken belief that he had British diplomatic support, Nicholas moved against the Ottomans, who declared war on Russia in 1853. Fearing the results of an Ottoman defeat by Russia, in 1854 Britain and France joined what became known as the Crimean War on the Ottoman side. Austria offered the Ottomans diplomatic support, and Prussia remained neutral, leaving Russia without allies on the continent. The European allies landed in Crimea and laid siege to the well-fortified Russian base at Sevastopol'. After a year's siege the base fell, exposing Russia's inability to defend a major fortification on its own soil. Nicholas I died before the fall of Sevastopol', but he already had recognized the failure of his regime. Russia now faced the choice of initiating major reforms or losing its status as a major European power.

Transformation of Russia in the Nineteenth Century

The late nineteenth and early twentieth centuries were times of crisis for Russia. Not only did technology and industry continue to develop more rapidly in the West, but also new, dynamic, competitive great powers appeared on the world scene: Otto von Bismarck united Germany in the 1860s, the post-Civil War United States grew in size and strength, and a modernized Japan emerged from the Meiji Restoration of 1868. Although Russia was an expanding regional giant in Central Asia, bordering the Ottoman, Persian, British Indian, and Chinese empires, it could not generate enough capital to support rapid industrial development or to compete with advanced countries on a commercial basis. Russia's fundamental dilemma was that accelerated domestic development risked upheaval at home, but slower progress risked full economic dependency on the faster-advancing countries to the east and west. In fact, political ferment, particularly among the intelligentsia, accompanied the transformation of Russia's economic and social structure, but so did impressive developments in literature, music, the fine arts, and the natural sciences.

Economic Developments

Throughout the last half of the nineteenth century, Russia's economy developed more slowly than did that of the major European nations to its west. Russia's population was substantially larger than those of the more developed Western countries, but the vast majority of the people lived in rural communities and engaged in relatively primitive agriculture. Industry, in general, had greater state involvement than in Western Europe, but in selected sectors it was developing with private initiative, some of it foreign. Between 1850 and 1900, Russia's population doubled, but it remained chiefly rural well into the twentieth century. Russia's population growth rate from 1850 to 1910 was the fastest of all the major powers except for the United States. Agriculture, which was technologically underdeveloped, remained in the hands of former serfs and former state peasants, who together constituted about four-fifths of the rural population. Large estates of more than fifty square kilometers accounted for about 20 percent of all farmland, but few such estates were worked in efficient, large-scale units. Small-scale peasant farming and the growth of the rural population increased the amount of land used for agricultural development, but land was used more for gardens and fields of grain and less for grazing meadows than it had been in the past.

Industrial growth was significant, although unsteady, and in absolute terms it was not extensive. Russia's industrial regions included Moscow, the central regions of European Russia, St. Petersburg, the Baltic cities, Russian Poland, some areas along the lower Don and Dnepr rivers, and the southern Ural Mountains. By 1890 Russia had about 32,000 kilometers of railroads and 1.4 million factory workers, most of whom worked in the textile industry. Between 1860 and 1890, annual coal production had grown about 1,200 percent to over 6.6 million tons, and iron and steel production had more than doubled to 2 million tons per year. The state budget had more than doubled, however, and debt expenditures had quadrupled, constituting 28 percent of official expenditures in 1891. Foreign trade was inadequate to meet the empire's needs. Until the state introduced high industrial tariffs in the 1880s, it could not finance trade with the West because its surpluses were insufficient to cover the debts.

Reforms and Their Limits, 1855–92

Tsar Alexander II, who succeeded Nicholas I in 1855, was a conservative who saw no alternative but to implement change. Alexander initiated substantial reforms in education, the government, the judiciary, and the military. In 1861 he proclaimed the emancipation of about 20 million privately held serfs. Local commissions, which were dominated by landlords, effected emancipation by giving land and limited freedom to the serfs. The former serfs usually remained in the village commune, but they were required to make redemption payments to the government over a period of almost fifty years. The government compensated former owners of serfs by issuing them bonds.

The regime had envisioned that the 50,000 landlords who possessed estates of more than 110 hectares would thrive without serfs and would continue to provide loyal political and administrative leadership in the countryside. The government also had expected that peasants would produce sufficient crops for their own consumption and for export sales, thereby helping to finance most of the government's expenses, imports, and foreign debt. Neither of the government's expectations was realistic, however, and emancipation left both former serfs and their former owners dissatisfied. The new peasants soon fell behind in their payments to the government because the land they had received was poor and because Russian agricultural methods were inadequate. The former owners often had to sell their lands to remain solvent because most of them could neither farm nor manage estates without their former serfs. In addition, the value of their government bonds fell as the peasants failed to make their redemption payments.

Reforms of local government closely followed emancipation. In 1864 most local government in the European part of Russia was organized into provincial and district *zemstva* (sing., *zemstvo*), which were made up of representatives of all classes and were responsible for local schools, public health, roads, prisons, food supply, and other concerns. In 1870 elected city councils, or *dumy* (sing., *duma*), were formed. Dominated by property owners and constrained by provincial governors and the police, the *zemstva* and *dumy* raised taxes and levied labor to support their activities.

In 1864 the regime implemented judicial reforms. In major towns, it established Western-style courts with juries. In general, the judicial system functioned effectively, but the government lacked the finances and cultural influence to extend the court system to the villages, where traditional peasant justice continued to operate with minimal interference from provincial officials. In addition, the regime instructed judges to decide each case on its merits and not to use precedents, which would have enabled them to construct a body of law independent of state authority.

Other major reforms took place in the educational and cultural spheres. The accession of Alexander II brought a social restructuring that required a public discussion of issues and the lifting of some types of censorship. When an attempt was made to assassinate the tsar in 1866, the government reinstated censorship, but not with the severity of pre-1855 control. The government also put restrictions on universities in 1866, five years after they had gained autonomy. The central government attempted to act through the *zemstva* to establish uniform curricula for elementary schools and to impose conservative policies, but it lacked resources. Because many liberal teachers and school officials were only nominally subject to the reactionary Ministry of Education, however, the regime's educational achievements were mixed after 1866.

In the financial sphere, Russia established the State Bank in 1866, which put the national currency on a firmer footing. The Ministry of Finance supported railroad development, which facilitated vital export activity, but it was cautious and moderate in its foreign ventures. The ministry also founded the Peasant Land Bank in 1882 to enable enterprising farmers to acquire more land. The Ministry of Internal Affairs countered this policy, however, by establishing the Nobles' Land Bank in 1885 to forestall foreclosures of mortgages.

The regime also sought to reform the military. One of the chief reasons for the emancipation of the serfs was to facilitate the transition from a large standing army to a reserve army by instituting territorial levies and mobilization in times of need. Before emancipation, serfs could not receive military training and then return to their owners. Bureaucratic inertia, however, obstructed military reform until the Franco-Prussian War (1870–71) demonstrated the necessity of building a modern army. The levy system introduced in 1874 gave the army a role in teaching many peasants to read and in pioneering medical education for women. But the army remained backward despite these military reforms. Officers often preferred bayonets to bullets, expressing worry that long-range sights on rifles would induce cowardice. In spite of some notable achievements, Russia did not keep pace with Western technological developments in the construction of rifles, machine guns, artillery, ships, and naval ordnance. Russia also failed to use naval modernization as a means of developing its industrial base in the 1860s.

In 1881 revolutionaries assassinated Alexander II. His son Alexander III (r. 1881–94) initiated a period of political reaction, which intensified a counterreform movement that had begun in 1866. He strengthened the security police, reorganizing it into an agency known as the Okhrana, gave it extraordinary powers, and placed it under the Ministry of Internal Affairs. Dmitriy Tolstoy, Alexander's minister of internal affairs, instituted the use of land captains, who were noble overseers of districts, and he restricted the power of the *zemstva* and the *dumy.* Alexander III assigned his former tutor, the reactionary Konstantin Pobedonostsev, to be the procurator of the Holy Synod of the Orthodox Church and Ivan Delyanov to be the minister of education. In their attempts to "save" Russia from "modernism," they revived religious censorship, persecuted non-Orthodox and non-Russian populations, fostered anti-Semitism, and suppressed the autonomy of the universities. Their attacks on liberal and non-Russian elements alienated large segments of the population. The nationalities, particularly Poles, Finns, Latvians, Lithuanians, and Ukrainians, reacted to the regime's efforts to Russify them by intensifying their own nationalism. Many Jews emigrated or joined radical movements. Secret organizations and political movements continued to develop despite the regime's efforts to quell them.

Foreign Affairs after the Crimean War

After the Crimean War, Russia pursued cautious and well-calculated foreign policies until nationalist passions and another Balkan crisis almost caused a catastrophic war in the late 1870s. The 1856 Treaty of Paris, signed at the end of the Crimean War, had demilitarized the Black Sea and deprived Russia of southern Bessarabia and a narrow strip of land at the mouth of the Danube River. The treaty gave the West European powers the nominal duty of protecting Christians living in the Ottoman Empire, removing that role from Russia, which had been designated as such a protector in the 1774 Treaty of Kuchuk-Kainarji. Russia's primary goal during the first phase of Alexander II's foreign policy was to alter the Treaty of Paris to regain naval access to the Black Sea. Russian statesmen viewed Britain and Austria (redesignated as Austria-Hungary in 1867) as opposed to that goal, so foreign policy concentrated on good relations with France, Prussia, and the United States. Prussia (Germany as of 1871) replaced Britain as Russia's chief banker in this period.

Following the Crimean War, the regime revived its expansionist policies. Russian troops first moved to gain control of the Caucasus region, where the revolts of Muslim tribesmen—Chechens, Cherkess, and Dagestanis—had continued despite numerous Russian campaigns in the nineteenth century. Once the forces of Aleksandr Baryatinskiy had captured the legendary Chechen rebel leader Shamil in 1859, the army resumed the expansion into Central Asia that had begun under Nicholas I. The capture of Tashkent was a significant victory over the Ququon (Kokand) Khanate, part of which was annexed in 1866. By 1867 Russian forces had captured enough territory to form the Guberniya (Governorate General) of Turkestan, the capital of which was Tashkent. The Bukhoro (Bukhara) Khanate then lost the crucial Samarqand area to Russian forces in 1868. To avoid alarming Britain, which had strong interests in protecting nearby India, Russia left the Bukhoran territories directly bordering Afghanistan and Persia nominally independent. The Central Asian khanates retained a degree of autonomy until 1917.

Russia followed the United States, Britain, and France in establishing relations with Japan, and, together with Britain and France, Russia obtained concessions from China consequent to the Second Opium War (1856–60). Under the Treaty of Aigun in 1858 and the Treaty of Beijing in 1860, China ceded to Russia extensive trading rights and regions adjacent to the Amur and Ussuri rivers and allowed Russia to begin building a port and naval base at Vladivostok. Meanwhile, in 1867 the logic of the balance of power and the cost of developing and defending the Amur-Ussuri region dictated that Russia sell Alaska to the United States in order to acquire much-needed funds.

As part of the regime's foreign policy goals in Europe, Russia initially gave guarded support to France's anti-Austrian diplomacy. A weak Franco-Russian entente soured, however, when France backed a Polish uprising against Russian rule in 1863. Russia then aligned itself more closely with Prussia by approving the unification of Germany in exchange for a revision of the Treaty of Paris and the remilitarization of the Black Sea. These diplomatic achievements came at a London conference in 1871, following France's defeat in the Franco-Prussian War. After 1871 Germany, united under Prussian leadership, was the strongest continental power in Europe. In 1873 Germany formed the loosely knit League of the Three Emperors with

Russia and Austria-Hungary to prevent them from forming an alliance with France. Nevertheless, Austro-Hungarian and Russian ambitions clashed in the Balkans, where rivalries among Slavic nationalities and anti-Ottoman sentiments seethed. In the 1870s, Russian nationalist opinion became a serious domestic factor in its support for liberating Balkan Christians from Ottoman rule and making Bulgaria and Serbia quasi-protectorates of Russia. From 1875 to 1877, the Balkan crisis escalated with rebellions in Bosnia, Herzegovina, and Bulgaria, which the Ottoman Turks suppressed with such great cruelty that Serbia, but none of the West European powers, declared war.

In early 1877, Russia came to the rescue of beleaguered Serbian and Russian volunteer forces when it went to war with the Ottoman Empire. Within one year, Russian troops were nearing Constantinople, and the Ottomans surrendered. Russia's nationalist diplomats and generals persuaded Alexander II to force the Ottomans to sign the Treaty of San Stefano in March 1878, creating an enlarged, independent Bulgaria that stretched into the southwestern Balkans. When Britain threatened to declare war over the terms of the Treaty of San Stefano, an exhausted Russia backed down. At the Congress of Berlin in July 1878, Russia agreed to the creation of a smaller Bulgaria. Russian nationalists were furious with Austria-Hungary and Germany for failing to back Russia, but the tsar accepted a revived and strengthened League of the Three Emperors as well as Austro-Hungarian hegemony in the western Balkans.

Russian diplomatic and military interests subsequently returned to Central Asia, where Russia had quelled a series of uprisings in the 1870s, and Russia incorporated hitherto independent amirates into the empire. Britain renewed its concerns in 1881 when Russian troops occupied Turkmen lands on the Persian and Afghan borders, but Germany lent diplomatic support to Russian advances, and an Anglo-Russian war was averted. Meanwhile, Russia's sponsorship of Bulgarian independence brought negative results as the Bulgarians, angry at Russia's continuing interference in domestic affairs, sought the support of Austria-Hungary. In the dispute that arose between Austria-Hungary and Russia, Germany took a firm position toward Russia while mollifying the tsar with a bilateral defensive alliance, the Reinsurance Treaty of 1887 between Germany and Russia. Within a year, Russo-German acrimony led to Bismarck's forbidding further loans to Russia, and France replaced Germany as Russia's financier. When Kaiser Wilhelm II dismissed Bismarck in 1890, the loose Russo-Prussian entente collapsed after having lasted for more than twenty-five years. Three years later, Russia allied itself with France by entering into a joint military convention, which matched the dual alliance formed in 1879 by Germany and Austria-Hungary.

The Rise of Revolutionary Movements

Alexander II's reforms, particularly the lifting of state censorship, fostered the expression of political and social thought. The regime relied on journals and newspapers to gain support for its domestic and foreign policies. But liberal, nationalist, and radical writers also helped to mold public opinion that was opposed to tsarism, private property, and the imperial state. Because many intellectuals, professionals, peasants, and workers shared these opposition sentiments, the regime regarded the publications and the radical organizations as dangerous. From the 1860s through the 1880s, Russian radicals, collectively known as Populists (Narodniki), focused chiefly on the peasantry, whom they identified as "the people" (*narod*).

The leaders of the Populist movement included radical writers, idealists, and advocates of terrorism. In the 1860s, Nikolay Chernyshevskiy, the most important radical writer of the period, posited that Russia could bypass capitalism and move directly to socialism (see Glossary). His most influential work, *What Is to Be Done?* (1861), describes the role of an individual of a "superior nature" who guides a new, revolutionary generation. Other radicals such as the incendiary anarchist Mikhail Bakunin and his terrorist collaborator, Sergey Nechayev, urged direct action. The calmer Petr Tkachev argued against the advocates of Marxism (see Glossary), maintaining that a centralized revolutionary band had to seize power before capitalism could fully develop. Disputing his views, the moralist and individualist Petr Lavrov made a call "to the people," which hundreds of idealists heeded in 1873 and 1874 by leaving their schools for the countryside to try to generate a mass movement among the *narod*. The Populist campaign failed, however, when the peasants showed hostility to the urban idealists and the government began to consider nationalist opinion more seriously.

The radicals reconsidered their approach, and in 1876 they formed a propagandist organization called Land and Liberty (Zemlya i volya), which leaned toward terrorism. This orientation became stronger three years later, when the group renamed itself the People's Will (Narodnaya volya), the name under which the radicals were responsible for the assassination of Alexander II in 1881. In 1879 Georgiy Plekhanov formed a propagandist faction of Land and Liberty called Black Repartition (Chernyy peredel), which advocated redistributing all land to the peasantry. This group studied Marxism, which, paradoxically, was principally concerned with urban industrial workers. The People's Will remained underground, but in 1887 a young member of the group, Aleksandr Ul'yanov, attempted to assassinate Alexander III, and authorities arrested and executed him. The execution greatly affected Vladimir Ul'yanov, Aleksandr's brother. Influenced by Chernyshevskiy's writings, Vladimir joined the People's Will, and later, inspired by Plekhanov, he converted to Marxism. The younger Ul'yanov later changed his name to Lenin.

Witte and Accelerated Industrialization

In the late 1800s, Russia's domestic backwardness and vulnerability in foreign affairs reached crisis proportions. At home a famine claimed a half-million lives in 1891, and activities by Japan and China near Russia's borders were perceived as threats from abroad. In reaction, the regime was forced to adopt the ambitious but costly economic programs of Sergey Witte, the country's strong-willed minister of finance. Witte championed foreign loans, conversion to the gold standard, heavy taxation of the peasantry, accelerated development of heavy industry, and a trans-Siberian railroad. These policies were designed to modernize the country, secure the Russian Far East, and give Russia a commanding position with which to exploit the resources of China's northern territories, Korea, and Siberia. This expansionist foreign policy was Russia's version of the imperialist logic displayed in the nineteenth century by other large countries with vast undeveloped territories such as the United States. In 1894 the accession of the pliable Nicholas II upon the death of Alexander III gave Witte and other powerful ministers the opportunity to dominate the government.

Witte's policies had mixed results. In spite of a severe economic depression at the end of the century, Russia's coal, iron, steel, and oil production tripled between 1890 and 1900. Railroad mileage almost doubled, giving Russia the most track of any nation other than the United States. Yet Russian grain production and exports failed to rise significantly, and imports grew faster than exports. The state budget also more than doubled, absorbing some of the country's economic growth. Western historians differ as to the merits of Witte's reforms; some believe that domestic industry, which did not benefit from subsidies or contracts, suffered a setback. Most analysts agree that the Trans-Siberian Railroad (which was completed from Moscow to Vladivostok in 1904) and the ventures into Manchuria and Korea were economic losses for Russia and a drain on the treasury. Certainly the financial costs of his reforms contributed to Witte's dismissal as minister of finance in 1903.

Radical Political Parties Develop

During the 1890s, Russia's industrial development led to a significant increase in the size of the urban bourgeoisie and the working class, setting the stage for a more dynamic political atmosphere and the development of radical parties. Because the state and foreigners owned much of Russia's industry, the working class was comparatively stronger and the bourgeoisie comparatively weaker than in the West. The working class and peasants were the first to establish political parties because the nobility and the wealthy bourgeoisie were politically timid. During the 1890s and early 1900s, abysmal living and working conditions, high taxes, and land hunger gave rise to more frequent strikes and agrarian disorders. These activities prompted the bourgeoisie of various nationalities in the empire to develop a host of different parties, both liberal and conservative.

Socialists of different nationalities formed their own parties. Russian Poles, who had suffered significant administrative and educational Russification, founded the nationalistic Polish Socialist Party in Paris in 1892. That party's founders hoped that it would help reunite a divided Poland with the territories held by Austria-Hungary, Germany, and Russia. In 1897 Jewish workers in Russia created the Bund (league or union), an organization that subsequently became popular in western Ukraine, Belorussia, Lithuania, and Russian Poland. The Russian Social Democratic Labor Party was established in 1898. The Finnish Social Democrats remained separate, but the Latvians and Georgians associated themselves with the Russian Social Democrats. Armenians, inspired by both Russian and Balkan revolutionary traditions, were politically active in this period in Russia and in the Ottoman Empire. Politically minded Muslims living in Russia tended to be attracted to the pan-Islamic and pan-Turkic movements that were developing in Egypt and the Ottoman Empire. Russians who fused the ideas of the old Populists and urban socialists formed Russia's largest radical movement, the United Socialist Revolutionary Party, which combined the standard Populist mix of propaganda and terrorist activities.

Vladimir I. Ul'yanov was the most politically talented of the revolutionary socialists. In the 1890s, he labored to wean young radicals away from populism to Marxism. Exiled from 1895 to 1899 in Siberia, where he took the name Lenin from the mighty Siberian Lena River, he was the master tactician among the organizers of the Russian Social Democratic Labor Party. In December 1900, he founded the newspaper *Iskra* (Spark). In his book *What Is to Be Done?* (1902), Lenin developed the theory that a newspaper published abroad could aid in organizing a centralized revolutionary party to direct the overthrow of an autocratic government. He then worked to establish a tightly organized, highly disciplined party to do so in Russia. At the Second Party Congress of the Russian Social Democratic Labor Party in 1903, he forced the Bund to walk out and induced a split between his majority Bolshevik (see Glossary) faction and the minority Menshevik (see Glossary) faction, which believed more in worker spontaneity than in strict organizational tactics. Lenin's concept of a revolutionary party and a worker-peasant alliance owed more to Tkachev and to the People's Will than to Karl Marx and Friedrich Engels, the developers of Marxism. Young Bolsheviks, such as Joseph V. Stalin and Nikolay Bukharin, looked to Lenin as their leader.

Imperialism in Asia and the Russo-Japanese War

At the turn of the century, Russia gained room to maneuver in Asia because of its alliance with France and the growing rivalry between Britain and Germany. Tsar Nicholas failed to orchestrate a coherent Far Eastern policy because of ministerial conflicts, however. Russia's uncoordinated and aggressive moves in the region ultimately led to the Russo-Japanese War (1904–05).

By 1895 Germany was competing with France for Russia's favor, and British statesmen hoped to negotiate with the Russians to demarcate spheres of influence in Asia. This situation enabled Russia to intervene in northeastern Asia after Japan's victory over China in 1895. In the negotiations that followed,

Japan was forced to make concessions in the Liaotung Peninsula and Port Arthur in southern Manchuria. The next year, Witte used French capital to establish the Russo-Chinese Bank. The goal of the bank was to finance the construction of a railroad across northern Manchuria and thus shorten the Trans-Siberian Railroad. Within two years, Russia had acquired leases on the Liaotung Peninsula and Port Arthur and had begun building a trunk line from Harbin in central Manchuria to Port Arthur on the coast.

In 1900 China reacted to foreign encroachments on its territory with an armed popular uprising, the Boxer Rebellion. Russian military contingents joined forces from Europe, Japan, and the United States to restore order in northern China. A force of 180,000 Russian troops fought to pacify part of Manchuria and to secure its railroads. The Japanese were backed by Britain and the United States, however, and insisted that Russia evacuate Manchuria. Witte and some Russian diplomats wanted to compromise with Japan and trade Manchuria for Korea, but a group of Witte's reactionary enemies, courtiers, and military and naval leaders refused to compromise. The tsar favored their viewpoint, and, disdaining Japan's threats—despite the latter's formal alliance with Britain—the Russian government equivocated until Japan declared war in early 1904.

In the war that followed, Japan's location, technological superiority, and superior morale gave it command of the seas, and Russia's sluggishness and incompetent commanders caused continuous setbacks on land. In January 1905, after an eight-month siege, Russia surrendered Port Arthur, and in March the Japanese forced the Russians to withdraw north of Mukden. In May, at the Tsushima Straits, the Japanese destroyed Russia's last hope in the war, a fleet assembled from the navy's Baltic and Mediterranean squadrons. Theoretically, Russian army reinforcements could have driven the Japanese from the Asian mainland, but revolution at home and diplomatic pressure forced the tsar to seek peace. Russia accepted mediation by United States president Theodore Roosevelt, ceded southern Sakhalin Island to Japan, and acknowledged Japan's ascendancy in Korea and southern Manchuria.

The Last Years of the Autocracy

The Russo-Japanese War was a turning point in Russian history. It led to a popular uprising against the government that forced the regime to respond with domestic economic and political reforms. In the same period, however, counterreform and special-interest groups exerted increasing influence on the regime's policies. In foreign affairs, Russia again became an intrusive participant in Balkan affairs and in the international political intrigues of the major European powers. As a consequence of its foreign policies, Russia was drawn into a world war for which its domestic policies rendered it unprepared. Severely weakened by internal turmoil and lacking leadership, the regime ultimately was unable to overcome the traumatic events that would lead to the fall of tsarism and initiate a new era in Russian and world history.

Revolution and Counterrevolution, 1905–07

The Russo-Japanese War accelerated the rise of political movements among all classes and the major nationalities, including propertied Russians. By early 1904, Russian liberal activists from the *zemstva* and from the professions had formed an organization called the Union of Liberation. In the same year, they joined with Finns, Poles, Georgians, Armenians, and Russian members of the Socialist Revolutionary Party to form an antiautocratic alliance.

In January 1905, Father Georgiy Gapon, a Russian Orthodox priest who headed a police-sponsored workers' association, led a huge, peaceful march in St. Petersburg to present a petition to the tsar. Nervous troops responded to the throng with gunfire, killing several hundred people and initiating the Revolution of 1905. This event, which came to be called Bloody Sunday, combined with the embarrassing failures in the war with Japan to prompt more strikes, agrarian disorders, army mutinies, and terrorist acts organized by opposition groups. Workers formed a council, or soviet, in St. Petersburg. Armed uprisings occurred in Moscow, the Urals, Latvia, and parts of Poland. Activists from the *zemstva* and the broad professional Union of Unions formed the Constitutional Democratic Party, whose initials lent the party its informal name, the Kadets.

Some upper-class and propertied activists called for compromise with opposition groups to avoid further disorders. In late 1905, Witte pressured Nicholas to issue the so-called October Manifesto, which gave Russia a constitution and proclaimed basic civil liberties for all citizens. In an effort to stop the activity of liberal factions, the constitution included most of their demands, including a ministerial government responsible to the tsar, and a national Duma (see Glossary)—a parliament to be elected on a broad, but not wholly equitable, franchise. Those who accepted this arrangement formed a center-right political party, the Octobrists, and named Witte the first prime minister. Meanwhile, the Kadets held out for a ministerial government and equal, universal suffrage. Because of their political principles and continued armed uprisings, Russia's leftist parties were undecided whether to participate in the Duma elections, which had been called for early 1906. At the same time, rightist factions actively opposed the reforms. Several new monarchist and protofascist groups also arose to subvert the new order. Nevertheless, the regime continued to function through the chaotic year of 1905, eventually restoring order in the cities, the countryside, and the army. In the process, terrorists murdered several thousand officials, and the government executed an equal number of terrorists. Because the government had been able to restore order and to secure a loan from France before the first Duma met, Nicholas was in a strong position that enabled him to replace Witte with the much less independent functionary Petr Stolypin.

The First Duma was elected in March 1906. The Kadets and their allies dominated it, with the mainly nonparty radical leftists slightly weaker than the Octobrists and the nonparty center-rightists combined. The socialists had boycotted the election, but several socialist delegates were elected. Relations between the Duma and the Stolypin government were hostile from the beginning. A deadlock of the Kadets and the government over the adoption of a constitution and peasant reform led to the dissolution of the Duma and the scheduling of new elections. In spite of an upsurge of leftist terror, radical leftist parties participated in the election, and, together with the nonparty left, they gained a plurality of seats, followed by a loose coalition of Kadets with Poles and other nationalities in the political center. The impasse continued, however, when the Second Duma met in 1907.

The Stolypin and Kokovtsov Governments

In 1907 Stolypin instituted a series of major reforms. In June 1907, he dissolved the Second Duma and promulgated a new electoral law, which vastly reduced the electoral weight of lower-class and non-Russian voters and increased the weight of the nobility. This political coup had the desired short-term result of restoring order. New elections in the fall returned a more conservative Third Duma, which Octobrists dominated. Even this Duma quarreled with the government over a variety of issues, however, including the composition of the naval staff, the autonomous status of Finland, the introduction of *zemstva* in the western provinces, the reform of the peasant court system, and the establishment of workers' insurance organizations under police supervision. In these disputes, the Duma, with its appointed aristocratic-bureaucratic upper house, was sometimes more conservative than the government, and at other times it was more constitutionally minded. The Fourth Duma, elected in 1912, was similar in composition to the third, but a progressive faction of Octobrists split from the right and joined the political center.

Stolypin's boldest measure was his peasant reform program. It allowed, and sometimes forced, the breakup of communes as well as the establishment of full private property. Stolypin hoped that the reform program would create a class of conservative landowning farmers loyal to the tsar. Most peasants did not want to lose the safety of the commune or to permit outsiders to buy village land, however. By 1914 only about 10 percent of all peasant communes had been dissolved. Nevertheless, the economy recovered and grew impressively from 1907 to 1914, both quantitatively and through the formation of rural cooperatives and banks and the generation of domestic capital. By 1914 Russian steel production equaled that of France and Austria-Hungary, and Russia's economic growth rate was one of the highest in the world. Although external debt was very high, it was declining as a percentage of the gross national product (GNP—see Glossary), and the empire's overall trade balance was favorable.

In 1911 a double agent working for the Okhrana assassinated Stolypin, and Finance Minister Vladimir Kokovtsov replaced him. The cautious Kokovtsov was very able and a supporter of the tsar, but he could not compete with the powerful court factions that dominated the government.

Historians have debated whether Russia had the potential to develop a constitutional government between 1905 and 1914. The failure to do so was partly because the tsar was not willing to give up autocratic rule or share power. By manipulating the franchise, the government obtained progressively more conservative, but less representative, Dumas. Moreover, the regime sometimes bypassed the conservative Dumas and ruled by decree.

During this period, the government's policies waivered from reformist to repressive. Historians have speculated about whether Witte's and Stolypin's bold reform plans could have "saved" the Russian Empire. But court politics, together with the continuing isolation of the tsar and the bureaucracy from the rest of society, hampered all reforms. Suspensions of civil liberties and the rule of law continued in many places, and neither workers nor the Orthodox Church had the right to organize themselves as they chose. Discrimination against Poles, Jews, Ukrainians, and Old Believers was common. Domestic unrest was on the rise while the empire's foreign policy was becoming more adventurous.

Active Balkan Policy, 1906–13

Russia's earlier Far Eastern policy required holding Balkan issues in abeyance, a strategy Austria-Hungary also followed between 1897 and 1906. Japan's victory in 1905 had forced Russia to make deals with the British and the Japanese. In 1907 Russia's new foreign minister, Aleksandr Izvol'skiy, concluded agreements with both nations. To maintain its sphere of influence in northern Manchuria and northern Persia, Russia agreed to Japanese ascendancy in southern Manchuria and Korea, and to British ascendancy in southern Persia, Afghanistan, and Tibet. The logic of this policy demanded that Russia and Japan unite to prevent the United States from establishing a base in China by organizing a consortium to develop Chinese railroads. After China's republican revolution of 1911, Russia and Japan recognized each other's spheres of influence in Outer Mongolia. In an extension of this reasoning, Russia traded recognition of German economic interests in the Ottoman Empire and Persia for German recognition of various Russian security interests in the region. Russia also protected its strategic and financial position by entering the informal Triple Entente with Britain and France, without antagonizing Germany.

In spite of these careful measures, after the Russo-Japanese War Russia and Austria-Hungary resumed their Balkan rivalry, focusing on the Kingdom of Serbia and the provinces of Bosnia and Herzegovina, which Austria-Hungary had occupied since 1878. In 1881 Russia secretly had agreed in principle to Austria's future annexation of Bosnia and Herzegovina. But in 1908, Izvol'skiy foolishly consented to support formal annexation in return for Austria's support for revision of the agreement on the neutrality of the Bosporus and Dardanelles—a change that would give Russia special navigational rights of passage. Britain stymied the Russian gambit by blocking the revision, but Austria proceeded with the annexation. Then, backed by German threats of war, Austria-Hungary exposed Russia's weakness by forcing Russia to disavow support for Serbia.

After Austria-Hungary's annexation of Bosnia and Herzegovina, Russia became a major part of the increased tension and conflict in the Balkans. In 1912 Bulgaria, Serbia, Greece, and Montenegro defeated the Ottoman Empire in the First Balkan War, but the putative allies continued to quarrel among themselves. Then in 1913, the alliance split, and the Serbs, Greeks, and Romanians defeated Bulgaria in the Second Balkan War. Austria-Hungary became the patron of Bulgaria, which now was Serbia's territorial rival in the region, and Germany remained the Ottoman Empire's protector. Russia tied itself more closely to Serbia than it had previously. The complex system of alliances and Great Power support was extremely unstable; among the Balkan parties harboring resentments over past defeats, the Serbs maintained particular animosity toward the Austro-Hungarian annexation of Bosnia and Herzegovina.

In June 1914, a Serbian terrorist assassinated Archduke Franz Ferdinand, heir to the throne of Austria-Hungary, which then held the Serbian government responsible. Austria-Hungary delivered an ultimatum to Serbia, believing that the terms were too humiliating to accept. Although Serbia submitted to the ultimatum, Austria-Hungary declared the response unsatisfactory and recalled its ambassador. Russia, fearing another humiliation in the Balkans, supported Serbia. Once the Serbian response was rejected, the system of alliances began to operate automatically, with Germany supporting Austria-Hungary and France backing Russia. When Germany invaded France through Belgium, the conflict escalated into a world war.

Russia at War, 1914–16

Russia's large population enabled it to field a greater number of troops than Austria-Hungary and Germany combined, but its underdeveloped industrial base meant that its soldiers were as poorly armed as those of the Austro-Hungarian army. Russian forces were inferior to Germany's in every respect except numbers. In most engagements, the larger Russian armies defeated the Austro-Hungarians but suffered reverses against German forces.

In the initial phase of the war, Russia's offensives into East Prussia drew enough German troops from the western front to allow the French, Belgians, and British to stop the German advance. One of Russia's two invading armies was almost totally destroyed, however, at the disastrous Battle of Tannenberg—the same site at which Lithuanian, Polish, and Russian troops had defeated the German Teutonic Knights in 1410. Meanwhile, the Russians turned back an Austrian offensive and pushed into eastern Galicia, the northeastern region of the Austro-Hungarian Empire. The Russians halted a combined German-Austrian winter counteroffensive into Russian Poland, and in early 1915 they pushed more deeply into Galicia. Then in the spring and summer of that year, a German-Austrian offensive drove the Russians out of Galicia and Poland and destroyed several Russian army corps. In 1916 the Germans planned to drive France out of the war with a large-scale attack in the Verdun area, but a new Russian offensive against Austria-Hungary once again drew German troops from the west. These actions left both major fronts stable and both Russia and Germany despairing of victory—Russia because of exhaustion, Germany because of its opponents' superior resources. Toward the end of 1916, Russia came to the rescue of Romania, which had just entered the war, and extended the eastern front south to the Black Sea.

Wartime agreements among the Allies reflected the Triple Entente's imperialist aims and the Russian Empire's relative weakness outside Eastern Europe. Russia nonetheless expected impressive gains from a victory: territorial acquisitions in eastern Galicia from Austria, in East Prussia from Germany, and in Armenia from the Ottoman Empire, which joined the war on the German side; control of Constantinople and the Bosporus and Dardanelles straits; and territorial and political alteration of Austria-Hungary in the interests of Romania and the Slavic peoples of the region. Britain was to acquire the middle zone of Persia and share much of the Arab Middle East with France; Italy—not Russia's ally Serbia—was to acquire Dalmatia along the Adriatic coast; Japan, another ally of the entente, was to control more territory in China; and France was to regain Alsace-Lorraine, which it had lost to Germany in the Franco-Prussian War, and to have increased influence in western Germany.

The Fatal Weakening of Tsarism

The onset of World War I exposed the weakness of Nicholas II's government. A show of national unity had accompanied Russia's entrance into the war, with defense of the Slavic Serbs the main battle cry. In the summer of 1914, the Duma and the *zemstva* expressed full support for the government's war effort. The initial conscription was well organized and peaceful, and the early phase of Russia's military buildup showed that the empire had learned lessons from the Russo-Japanese War. But military reversals and the government's incompetence soon soured much of the population. German control of the Baltic Sea and German-Ottoman control of the Black Sea severed Russia from most of its foreign supplies and potential markets. In addition, inept Russian preparations for war and ineffective economic policies hurt the country financially, logistically, and militarily. Inflation became a serious problem. Because of inadequate matériel support for military operations, the War Industries Committee was formed to ensure that necessary supplies reached the front. But army officers quarreled with civilian leaders, seized administrative control of front areas, and refused to cooperate with the committee. The central government distrusted the independent war support activities that were organized by *zemstva* and cities. The Duma quarreled with the war bureaucracy of the government, and center and center-left deputies eventually formed the Progressive Bloc to create a genuinely constitutional government.

After Russian military reversals in 1915, Nicholas II went to the front to assume nominal leadership of the army, leaving behind his German-born wife, Alexandra, and Rasputin, a member of her entourage, who exercised influence on policy and ministerial appointments. Rasputin was a debauched faith healer who initially impressed Alexandra because he was able to stop the bleeding of the royal couple's hemophiliac son and heir presumptive. Although their true influence has been debated, Alexandra and Rasputin undoubtedly decreased the regime's prestige and credibility.

While the central government was hampered by court intrigue, the strain of the war began to cause popular unrest. In 1916 high food prices and fuel shortages caused strikes in some cities. Workers, who had won the right to representation in sections of the War Industries Committee, used those sections as organs of political opposition. The countryside also was becoming restive. Soldiers were increasingly insubordinate, particularly the newly recruited peasants who faced the prospect of being used as cannon fodder in the inept conduct of the war.

The situation continued to deteriorate. In an attempt to alleviate the morass at the tsar's court, a group of nobles murdered Rasputin in December 1916. But the death of the mysterious "healer" brought little change. Increasing conflict between the tsar and the Duma weakened both parts of the government and increased the impression of incompetence. In early 1917, deteriorating rail transport caused acute food and fuel shortages, which resulted in riots and strikes. Authorities summoned troops to quell the disorders in Petrograd (as St. Petersburg had been called since 1914, to Russianize the Germanic name). In 1905 troops had fired on demonstrators and saved the monarchy, but in 1917 the troops turned their guns over to the angry crowds. Public support for the tsarist regime simply evaporated in 1917, ending three centuries of Romanov rule.

*   *   *

Three excellent one-volume surveys of Russian history are Nicholas Riasanovsky's *A History of Russia*, David MacKenzie and Michael W. Curran's *A History of Russia and the Soviet Union*, and Robert Auty and Dmitry Obolensky's *An Introduction to Russian History*. The most useful thorough study of Russia before the nineteenth century is Vasily Kliuchevsky's five-volume collection, *The Course of Russian History*. Good translations exist, however, only for the third volume, *The Seventeenth Century*, and part of the fourth volume, *Peter the Great*. For the 1800–1917 period, two excellent comprehensive works are the second volume of Michael T. Florinsky's *Russia: A History and Interpretation* and Hugh Seton-Watson's *The Russian Empire, 1801–1917*. The roots and nature of Russian autocracy are probed in Richard Pipes's controversial *Russia under the Old Regime* and Geroid Tanquary Robinson's *Rural Russia under the Old Regime*, and Franco Venturi describes the development of populist and socialist movements in Russia in *Roots of Revolution*. Barbara Jelavich's *A Century of Russian Foreign Policy 1814–1914* studies the foreign relations of the last century of the autocracy. Jerome Blum treats social history in *Lord and Peasant in Russia from the Ninth to the Nineteenth Century*. Cultural history is discussed in James H. Billington's *The Icon and the Axe* and in Marc Raeff's *Russian Intellectual History*. (For further information and complete citations, see Bibliography.)

Chapter 2. Historical Setting: 1917 to 1991

Tsarevich Ivan pondering how he can obey his father and marry a frog. Fortunately for Ivan, the frog turns into Vasilisa the Wise and Clever, a maiden more beautiful than anyone had ever seen (design from lacquer box made in village of Fedoskino).

THE HISTORY OF RUSSIA between 1922 and 1991 is essentially the history of the Soviet Union (the Union of Soviet Socialist Republics—USSR). This ideologically based empire was roughly coterminous with the Russian Empire, whose last monarch, Tsar Nicholas II, ruled until 1917. The Soviet Union was established in December 1922 by the leaders of the Russian Communist Party (Bolshevik). At that time, the new nation included the Russian, Ukrainian, Belorussian, and Transcaucasian republics.

A spontaneous popular uprising in Petrograd, in response to the wartime decay of Russia's physical well-being and morale, culminated in the toppling of the imperial government in March 1917. Replacing the autocracy was the Provisional Government, whose leaders intended to establish democracy in Russia and to continue participating on the side of the Allies in World War I. At the same time, to ensure the rights of the working class, workers' councils, known as soviets, sprang up across the country. The radical Bolsheviks, led by Vladimir I. Lenin, agitated for socialist revolution in the soviets and on the streets. They seized power from the Provisional Government in November 1917. Only after the long and bloody Civil War of 1918–21, which included combat between government forces and foreign troops in several parts of Russia, was the new communist regime secure.

From its first years, government in the Soviet Union was based on the one-party rule of the communists, as the Bolsheviks called themselves beginning in March 1918. After unsuccessfully attempting to centralize the economy in accordance with Marxist dogma during the Civil War, the Soviet government permitted some private enterprise to coexist with nationalized industry in the 1920s. Debate over the future of the economy provided the background for Soviet leaders to contend for power in the years after Lenin's death in 1924. By gradually consolidating his influence and isolating his rivals within the party, Joseph V. Stalin became the sole leader of the Soviet Union by the end of the 1920s.

In 1928 Stalin introduced the First Five-Year Plan for building a socialist economy. In industry the state assumed control over all existing enterprises and undertook an intensive program of industrialization; in agriculture the state appropriated the peasants' property to establish collective farms. The plan's implementation produced widespread misery, including the deaths of millions of peasants by starvation or directly at the hands of the government during forced collectivization. Social upheaval continued in the mid-1930s, when Stalin began a purge of the party; out of this process grew a campaign of terror that led to the execution or imprisonment of untold millions from all walks of life. Yet despite this turmoil, the Soviet Union developed a powerful industrial economy in the years before World War II.

Although Stalin tried to avert war with Germany by concluding the Nazi-Soviet Nonaggression Pact in 1939, in 1941 Germany invaded the Soviet Union. The Red Army stopped the Nazi offensive at the Battle of Stalingrad in 1943 and drove through Eastern Europe to Berlin before Germany surrendered in 1945. Although ravaged by the war, the Soviet Union emerged from the conflict as an acknowledged great power.

During the immediate postwar period, the Soviet Union first rebuilt and then expanded its economy, with control always exerted exclusively from Moscow. The Soviet Union consolidated its hold on Eastern Europe, supplied aid to the eventually victorious communists in China, and sought to expand its influence elsewhere in the world. This active foreign policy helped bring about the Cold War, which turned the Soviet Union's wartime allies, Britain and the United States, into foes. Within the Soviet Union, repressive measures continued in force; Stalin apparently was about to launch a new purge when he died in 1953.

In the absence of an acceptable successor, Stalin's closest associates opted to rule the Soviet Union jointly, although a struggle for power took place behind the facade of collective leadership. Nikita S. Khrushchev, who won the power struggle by the mid-1950s, denounced Stalin's use of terror and eased repressive controls over party and society. Khrushchev's reforms in agriculture and administration, however, were generally unproductive, and foreign policy toward China and the United States suffered reverses. Khrushchev's colleagues in the leadership removed him from power in 1964.

Following the ouster of Khrushchev, another period of rule by collective leadership ensued, lasting until Leonid I. Brezhnev established himself in the early 1970s as the preeminent figure in Soviet political life. Brezhnev presided over a period of détente with the West while at the same time building up

Soviet military strength; the arms buildup contributed to the demise of détente in the late 1970s. Another contributing factor was the Soviet invasion of Afghanistan in December 1979.

After some experimentation with economic reforms in the mid-1960s, the Soviet leadership reverted to established means of economic management. Industry showed slow but steady gains during the 1970s, while agricultural development continued to lag. In contrast to the revolutionary spirit that accompanied the birth of the Soviet Union, the prevailing mood of the Soviet leadership at the time of Brezhnev's death in 1982 was one of aversion to change.

Two developments dominated the decade that followed: the increasingly apparent crumbling of the Soviet Union's economic and political structures, and the patchwork attempts at reforms to reverse that process. After the rapid succession of Yuriy V. Andropov and Konstantin U. Chernenko, transitional figures with deep roots in Brezhnevite tradition, the energetic Mikhail S. Gorbachev made significant changes in the economy and the party leadership. His policy of *glasnost* (see Glossary) freed public access to information after decades of government repression. But Gorbachev failed to address the fundamental flaws of the Soviet system; by 1991, when a plot by government insiders revealed the weakness of Gorbachev's political position, the end of the Soviet Union was in sight.

Revolutions and Civil War

The chaos and hardship that resulted from Russia's entry into World War I in 1914 were exacerbated in the years that followed. Russians saw the fall of the Romanov Dynasty, which had ruled for more than 300 years, followed by a long struggle for power between the Bolsheviks and a series of disparate armies, known collectively as the Whites, supported by Russia's erstwhile wartime allies. The combination of military occupation and economic disorder bled the country for three years until the Bolsheviks triumphed and began to establish a new order.

The February Revolution

By early 1917, the existing order in Russia was verging on collapse. The country's involvement in World War I had already cost millions of lives and severely disrupted Russia's already struggling economy. In an effort to reverse the worsening military situation, Nicholas II took personal command of

Russian forces at the front, leaving the conduct of government in Petrograd (St. Petersburg before 1914; Leningrad after 1924; St. Petersburg after 1991) to his unpopular wife and a series of incompetent ministers. As a consequence of these conditions, the morale of the people rapidly deteriorated.

The spark to the events that ended tsarist rule was ignited on the streets of Petrograd in February 1917 (according to the Julian calendar then still in use in Russia; according to the modern Gregorian calendar, which was adopted in February 1918, these events occurred in March). Driven by shortages of food and fuel, crowds of hungry citizens and striking workers began spontaneous rioting and demonstrations. Local reserve troops, called in to suppress the riots, refused to fire on the crowds, and some soldiers joined the workers and other rioters. A few days later, with tsarist authority in Petrograd disintegrating, two distinct groups emerged, each claiming to represent the Russian people. One was the Executive Committee, which the Duma (see Glossary), the lower house of the Russian parliament, had established in defiance of the tsar's orders. The other body was the Petrograd Soviet of Workers' and Soldiers' Deputies.

With the consent of the Petrograd Soviet, the Executive Committee of the Duma organized the Provisional Government on March 15. The government was a cabinet of ministers chaired by aristocrat and social reformer Georgiy L'vov. A legislature, the Constituent Assembly, also was to be created, but election of the first such body was postponed until the fall of 1917. Delegates of the new government met Nicholas that evening at Pskov, where rebellious railroad workers had stopped the imperial train as the tsar attempted to return to the capital. Advised by his generals that he lacked the support of the country, Nicholas informed the delegates that he was abdicating in favor of his brother, Grand Duke Michael. When Michael in turn refused the throne, imperial rule in Russia came to an end.

The Period of Dual Power

The collapse of the monarchy left two rival political institutions—the Provisional Government and the Petrograd Soviet—to share administrative authority over the country. The Petrograd Soviet, drawing its membership from socialist deputies elected in factories and regiments, coordinated the activities of other soviets that sprang up across Russia at this time. The

Petrograd Soviet was dominated by moderate socialists of the Socialist Revolutionary Party and by the Menshevik (see Glossary) faction of the Russian Social Democratic Labor Party. The Bolshevik (see Glossary) faction of the latter party provided the opposition. Although it represented the interests of Russia's working class, the Petrograd Soviet at first did not seek to undermine the Provisional Government's authority directly. Nevertheless, the Petrograd Soviet's first official order, which came to be known as Order Number One, instructed soldiers and sailors to obey their officers and the government only if their orders did not contradict the decrees of the Petrograd Soviet—a measure formulated to prevent continuation of Russia's war effort by crippling the Provisional Government's control of the military.

The Provisional Government, in contrast to the socialist Petrograd Soviet, chiefly represented the propertied classes. Headed by ministers of a moderate or liberal bent, the new government pledged to convene a constituent assembly that would usher in a new era of bourgeois democracy modeled on European constitutionalism. In the meantime, the government granted unprecedented rights—full freedom of speech, press, and religion, as well as legal equality—to all citizens. The government did not take up the matter of land redistribution, however, leaving that issue for the Constituent Assembly. Even more damaging, the ministers favored keeping Russia's military commitments to its allies, a position that became increasingly unpopular as the war dragged on. The government suffered its first crisis in the "April Days," when demonstrations against the government's war aims forced two ministers to resign, an event that led to the appointment of Aleksandr Kerenskiy—the only socialist among the government's ministers—as war minister. Quickly assuming de facto leadership of the government, Kerenskiy ordered the army to launch a major offensive in June. After early successes, that offensive turned into a full-scale retreat in July.

While the Provisional Government grappled with foreign foes, the Bolsheviks, who were opposed to bourgeois democracy, gained new strength. Lenin, the Bolshevik leader, returned to Petrograd in April 1917 from his wartime residence in Switzerland. Although he had been born into a noble family, from his youth Lenin espoused the cause of the common workers. A committed revolutionary and pragmatic Marxist thinker, he astounded the Bolsheviks in Petrograd with his

April Theses, in which he boldly called for the overthrow of the Provisional Government, the transfer of "all power to the soviets," and the expropriation of factories by workers and of land belonging to the church, the nobility, and the gentry by peasants. Lenin's dynamic presence quickly won the other Bolshevik leaders to his position, and the radicalized orientation of the Bolshevik faction attracted new members.

Inspired by Lenin's slogans, crowds of workers, soldiers, and sailors took to the streets of Petrograd in July to wrest power from the Provisional Government. But the spontaneity of the "July Days" caught the Bolshevik leaders by surprise, and the Petrograd Soviet, controlled by moderate Mensheviks, refused to take power or to enforce Bolshevik demands. After the uprising had died down, the Provisional Government outlawed the Bolsheviks and jailed Leon Trotsky, leader of a leftist Menshevik faction. Lenin fled to Finland.

In the aftermath of the "July Days," conservatives sought to reassert order in society. The army's commander in chief, General Lavr Kornilov, who protested the influence of the soviets on both the army and the government, appeared as a counterrevolutionary threat to Kerenskiy, now prime minister. Kerenskiy dismissed Kornilov from his command, but Kornilov, disobeying the order, launched an extemporaneous revolt on September 10 (August 28). To defend the capital, Kerenskiy sought help from all quarters and relaxed his ban on Bolshevik activities. Railroad workers sympathetic to the Bolsheviks halted Kornilov's troop trains, and Kornilov soon surrendered, ending the only serious challenge to the Provisional Government from the right.

The Bolshevik Revolution

Although the Provisional Government survived the Kornilov revolt, popular support for the government faded rapidly as the national mood swung to the left in the fall of 1917. Workers took control of their factories through elected committees; peasants expropriated lands belonging to the state, church, nobility, and gentry; and armies melted away as peasant soldiers deserted to take part in the land seizures. The Bolsheviks, skillfully exploiting these popular trends in their propaganda, achieved domination of the Petrograd and Moscow soviets by September. Trotsky, freed from prison after the Kornilov revolt, was recruited as a Bolshevik and named chairman of the Petrograd Soviet.

Realizing that the time was ripe to seize power by force, Lenin returned to Petrograd in October and convinced a majority of the Bolshevik Central Committee, which had hoped to take power legally, to accept armed uprising in principle. Trotsky won the Petrograd garrison over to the soviet, depriving the Provisional Government of its main military support in Petrograd.

The actual insurrection—the Bolshevik Revolution—began on November 6, when Kerenskiy ordered the Bolshevik press closed. Interpreting this action as a counterrevolutionary move, the Bolsheviks called on their supporters to defend the Petrograd Soviet. By evening, the Bolsheviks had taken control of utilities and most government buildings in Petrograd, thus enabling Lenin to proclaim the downfall of the Provisional Government on the morning of the next day, November 7. The Bolsheviks captured the Provisional Government's cabinet at its Winter Palace headquarters that night with hardly a shot fired in the government's defense. Kerenskiy left Petrograd to organize resistance, but his countercoup failed and he fled Russia. Bolshevik uprisings soon took place elsewhere; Moscow was under Bolshevik control within three weeks. The Second Congress of Soviets met in Petrograd to ratify the Bolshevik takeover after moderate deputies (mainly Mensheviks and right-wing members of the Socialist Revolutionary Party) quit the session. The remaining Bolsheviks and left-wing Socialist Revolutionaries declared the soviets the governing bodies of Russia and named the Council of People's Commissars (Sovet narodnykh kommissarov—Sovnarkom) to serve as the cabinet. Lenin became chairman of this council. Trotsky took the post of commissar of foreign affairs; Stalin, a Georgian, became commissar of nationalities. Thus, by acting decisively while their opponents vacillated, the Bolsheviks succeeded in effecting their coup d'état.

On coming to power, the Bolsheviks issued a series of revolutionary decrees ratifying peasants' seizures of land and workers' control of industries, abolished laws sanctioning class privileges, nationalized the banks, and set up revolutionary tribunals in place of the courts. At the same time, the revolutionaries now constituting the regime worked to secure power inside and outside the government. Deeming Western forms of parliamentary democracy irrelevant, Lenin argued for a "dictatorship of the proletariat" based on single-party Bolshevik rule, although for a time left-wing Socialist Revolutionaries also participated in the Sovnarkom. The new government created a secret police agency, the VChK (commonly known as the Cheka), to persecute enemies of the state (including bourgeois liberals and moderate socialists). Having convened the Constituent Assembly, which finally had been elected in November with the Bolsheviks winning only a quarter of the seats, the Soviet government dissolved the assembly in January after a one-day session, ending a short-lived experiment in parliamentary democracy.

In foreign affairs, the Soviet government, seeking to disengage Russia from World War I, called on the belligerent powers for an armistice and peace without annexations. The Allied Powers rejected this appeal, but Germany and its allies agreed to a cease-fire. Negotiations began in December 1917. After dictating harsh terms that the Soviet government would not accept, however, Germany resumed its offensive in February 1918, meeting scant resistance from disintegrating Russian armies. Lenin, after bitter debate with leading Bolsheviks who favored prolonging the war in hopes of precipitating class warfare in Germany, persuaded a slim majority of the Bolshevik Central Committee that peace must be made at any cost. On March 3, Soviet government officials signed the Treaty of Brest-Litovsk, relinquishing Poland, the Baltic lands, Finland, and Ukraine to German control and giving up a portion of the Caucasus region to Turkey. With the new border dangerously close to Petrograd, the government was soon transferred to Moscow. An enormous part of the population and resources of the Russian Empire was lost by this treaty, but Lenin understood that no other alternative could ensure the survival of the fledgling Soviet state.

Civil War and War Communism

Soon after buying peace with Germany, the Soviet state found itself under attack from other quarters. By the spring of 1918, elements dissatisfied with the radical policies of the communists (as the Bolsheviks started calling themselves) established centers of resistance in southern and Siberian Russia. Beginning in April 1918, anticommunist forces, called the Whites and often led by former officers of the tsarist army, began to clash with the Red Army, which Trotsky, named commissar of war in the Soviet government, organized to defend the new state. A civil war to determine the future of Russia had begun.

The White armies enjoyed varying degrees of support from the Allied Powers. Desiring to defeat Germany in any way possible, Britain, France, and the United States landed troops in Russia and provided logistical support to the Whites, whom the Allies trusted would resume Russia's struggle against Germany after overthrowing the communist regime. (In March 1918, the Russian Social Democratic Labor Party officially was renamed the Russian Communist Party [Bolshevik].) After the Allies defeated Germany in November 1918, they opted to continue their intervention in the Russian Civil War against the communists, in the interests of averting what they feared might become a world socialist revolution.

During the Civil War, the Soviet regime also had to deal with struggles for independence in regions that it had given up under the Treaty of Brest-Litovsk (which the regime immediately repudiated after Germany's defeat by the Allies in November 1918). By force of arms, the communists established Soviet republics in Belorussia (January 1919), Ukraine (March 1919), Azerbaijan (April 1920), Armenia (November 1920), and Georgia (March 1921), but they were unable to take back the Baltic region, where the independent states of Estonia, Latvia, and Lithuania had been founded shortly after the Bolshevik Revolution. In December 1917, the Soviet government recognized the independence of Finland as a gesture of support to the Finnish Reds. However, that strategy failed when Finland became a parliamentary republic in 1918. Poland, reborn after World War I, fought a successful war with Soviet Russia from April 1920 to March 1921 over the location of the frontier between the two states.

During its struggle for survival, the Soviet state relied heavily on the prospect that revolution would spread to other European industrialized countries. To coordinate the socialist movement under Soviet auspices, Lenin founded the Communist International (Comintern) in March 1919. Although no successful socialist revolutions occurred elsewhere immediately after the Bolshevik Revolution, the Comintern provided the communist leadership with the means for later control of foreign communist parties.

By the end of 1920, the communists had clearly triumphed in the Civil War. Although in 1919 Soviet Russia had shrunk to the size of sixteenth-century Muscovy, the Red Army had the advantage of defending the heartland with Moscow at its center (see fig. 4). The White armies, divided geographically and with-

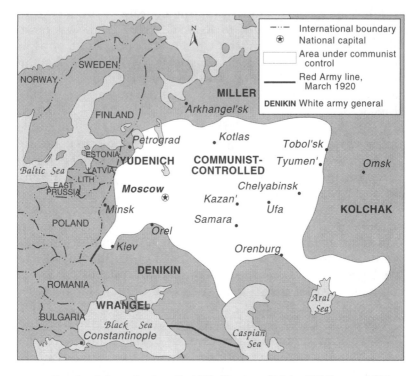

Source: Based on information from David MacKenzie and Michael W. Curran, *A History of Russia and the Soviet Union*, Chicago, 1987, 611.

Figure 4. Red Army Line, March 1920

out a clearly defined cause, went down to defeat one by one. Hopes of restoring the monarchy ended effectively when communists executed the imperial family in July 1918. The Allied governments, lacking support for intervention from their nations' war-weary citizenry, withdrew most of their forces by 1920. The last foreign troops departed Siberia in 1922, leaving the Soviet state unchallenged from abroad.

During the Civil War, the communist regime took increasingly repressive measures against its domestic opponents. The constitution of 1918 deprived members of the former "exploiting classes"—nobles, priests, and capitalists—of civil rights. Left-wing Socialist Revolutionaries, formerly partners of the Bolsheviks, became targets for persecution during what came to be known as the Red Terror, which followed an attempt on Lenin's life in August 1918 and lasted into 1920. In those desperate times, both Reds and Whites murdered and executed without trial large numbers of suspected enemies. The party also took measures to ensure greater discipline among its members by tightening its organization and creating specialized administrative organs.

In the economic life of the country, too, the communist regime sought to exert control through a series of drastic measures that came to be known as war communism. To coordinate what remained of Russia's economic resources after years of war, in 1918 the government nationalized industry and subordinated it to central administrations in Moscow. Rejecting workers' control of factories as inefficient, the regime brought in expert managers to run the factories and organized and directed the factory workers as in a military mobilization. To feed the urban population, the Soviet government requisitioned quantities of grain from the peasantry.

The results of war communism were unsatisfactory. Industrial production continued to fall. Workers received wages in kind because inflation had made the ruble practically worthless. In the countryside, peasants rebelled against payments in valueless currency by curtailing or consuming their agricultural production. In late 1920, strikes broke out in the industrial centers, and peasant uprisings sprang up across the land as famine ravaged the countryside. To the Soviet government, however, the most disquieting manifestation of dissatisfaction with war communism was the rebellion in March 1921 of sailors at the naval base at Kronshtadt (near Petrograd), which had earlier won renown as a bastion of the Bolshevik Revolution. Although Trotsky and the Red Army succeeded in putting down the mutiny, it signaled to the party leadership that war communism had to end. The harsh economic policies of the Civil War period, however, would have a profound influence on the future development of the country.

The Era of the New Economic Policy

The period of war communism was followed in the 1920s by a partial retreat from Bolshevik principles. The New Economic Policy (Novaya ekonomicheskaya politika—NEP; see Glossary) permitted certain types of private economic activity, so that the country might recover from the ravages of the Civil War. The interval was cut short, however, by the death of Lenin and the sharply different approach to governance of his successor, Joseph Stalin.

Lenin's Leadership

With the Kronshtadt base rebelling against war communism, the Tenth Party Congress of the Russian Communist Party (Bolshevik) met in March 1921 to hear Lenin argue for a new course in Soviet policy. Lenin realized that the radical approach to communism (see Glossary) was unsuited to existing conditions and jeopardized the survival of his regime. Now the Soviet leader proposed a tactical retreat, convincing the congress to adopt a temporary compromise with capitalism under the NEP program. Under the NEP, market forces and the monetary system regained their importance. The state scrapped its policy of grain requisitioning in favor of taxation, permitting peasants to dispose of their produce as they pleased. The NEP also denationalized service enterprises and much small-scale industry, leaving the "commanding heights" of the economy—large-scale industry, transportation, and foreign trade—under state control. Under the mixed economy called for under the NEP, agriculture and industry staged recoveries, with most branches of the economy attaining prewar levels of production by the late 1920s. In general, standards of living improved during this time, and the "NEP man"—the independent private trader—became a symbol of the era.

About the time that the party sanctioned partial decentralization of the economy, it also approved a quasi-federal structure for the state. During the Civil War, the non-Russian Soviet republics on the periphery of Russia were theoretically independent, but in fact they were controlled by the central government through the party and the Red Army. Some communists favored a centralized Soviet state, while nationalists wanted autonomy for the borderlands. A compromise between the two positions was reached in December 1922 with the formation of the USSR. The constituent republics of this "Soviet Union" (the Russian, Belorussian, Ukrainian, and Transcaucasian republics—the last combining Armenia, Azerbaijan, and Georgia) exercised a degree of cultural and linguistic autonomy, while the communist, predominantly Russian, leadership in Moscow retained political authority over the entire country. The giant Central Asian territory was given republic status piecemeal, beginning with the inclusion of the Turkmen and Uzbek republics in 1924 and concluding with the separation of Kazakstan and Kyrgyzstan in 1936. By that year, the Soviet Union included eleven republics, all with government structures and ruling communist parties identical to the one in the Russian Republic.

The party consolidated its authority throughout the country, becoming a monolithic presence in state and society. Potential rivals outside the party, including prominent members of the abolished Menshevik faction and the Socialist Revolutionary Party, were exiled. Within the party, Lenin denounced the formation of factions, particularly by radical-left party members. Central party organs subordinated local soviets to their authority. Party members perceived as less committed periodically were purged from the rosters. The Politburo (Political Bureau), which became the elite policy-making agency of the nation, created the new post of general secretary for the supervision of personnel matters and assigned Stalin to this office in April 1922. A minor member of the party's Central Committee at the time of the Bolshevik Revolution, Stalin was thought to be a rather lackluster personality and therefore well suited to the routine work required of the general secretary.

From the time of the Bolshevik Revolution and into the early NEP years, the actual leader of the Soviet state was Lenin. Although a collective of prominent communists nominally guided the party and the Soviet Union, Lenin commanded such prestige and authority that even such brilliant theoreticians as Trotsky and Nikolay Bukharin generally yielded to his will. But when Lenin became temporarily incapacitated after a stroke in May 1922, the unity of the Politburo fractured, and a troika (triumvirate) formed by Stalin, Lev Kamenev, and Grigoriy Zinov'yev assumed leadership in opposition to Trotsky. Lenin recovered late in 1922 and found fault with the troika, and particularly with Stalin. In Lenin's view, Stalin had used coercion to force non-Russian republics to join the Soviet Union, he was uncouth, and he was accumulating too much power through his office of general secretary. Although Lenin recommended that Stalin be removed from that position, the Politburo decided not to take action, and Stalin still was in office when Lenin died in January 1924.

As important as Lenin's activities were to the establishment of the Soviet Union, his legacy to the Soviet future was perhaps even more significant. By willingly changing his policies to suit new situations, Lenin had developed a pragmatic interpretation of Marxism (later called Marxism-Leninism—see Glossary) that implied that the party should follow any course that would ultimately lead to communism. His party, while still permitting intraorganizational debate, insisted that its members adhere to the organization's decisions once they were adopted, in accordance with the principle of democratic centralism. Finally, because the party embodied the dictatorship of the proletariat, organized opposition could not be tolerated, and adversaries would be prosecuted. Thus, although the Soviet regime was not totalitarian when he died, Lenin had nonetheless laid the foundation upon which such a tyranny would later arise.

Stalin's Rise to Power

After Lenin's death, two conflicting schools of thought about the future of the Soviet Union arose in party debates. Left-wing communists believed that world revolution was essential to the survival of socialism in the economically backward Soviet Union. Trotsky, one of the primary proponents of this position, called for Soviet support of a permanent world revolutionary movement. As for domestic policy, the left wing advocated the rapid development of the economy and the creation of a socialist society. In contrast to these militant communists, the right wing of the party, recognizing that world revolution was unlikely in the immediate future, favored the gradual development of the Soviet Union through continuation of pragmatic programs like the NEP. Yet even Bukharin, one of the major right-wing theoreticians, believed that socialism could not triumph in the Soviet Union without assistance from more economically advanced socialist countries.

Against this backdrop of contrasting perceptions of the Soviet future, the leading figures of the All-Union Communist Party (Bolshevik)—the new name of the Russian Communist Party (Bolshevik) as of December 1925—competed for influence. The Kamenev-Zinov'yev-Stalin troika, although it supported the militant international program, successfully maneuvered against Trotsky and engineered his removal as commissar of war in 1925. In the meantime, Stalin gradually consolidated his power base and, when he had sufficient strength, broke with Kamenev and Zinov'yev. Belatedly recognizing Stalin's political power, Kamenev and Zinov'yev made amends with Trotsky in order to join against their former partner. But Stalin countered their attacks on his position with his well-timed formulation of the theory of "socialism in one country." This doctrine, calling for construction of a socialist society in the Soviet Union regardless of the international situation, distanced Stalin from the left and won support from Bukharin and the party's right wing. With this support, Stalin ousted the leaders of the "Left Opposition" from their positions in 1926 and 1927 and forced Trotsky into exile in 1928. As the NEP era ended, open debate within the party became increasingly limited as Stalin gradually eliminated his opponents.

Foreign Policy, 1921–28

In the 1920s, as the new Soviet state temporarily retreated from the revolutionary path to socialism, the party also adopted a less ideological approach in its relations with the rest of the world. Lenin, ever the practical leader, having become convinced that socialist revolution would not break out in other countries in the near future, realized that his government required normal relations with the Western world for it to survive. Not only were good relations important to national security, but the economy also required trade with the industrial countries. Blocking Soviet attainment of these objectives were lingering suspicions about communism on the part of the Western powers and concern over foreign debts incurred by the tsarist government, which the Soviet government had unilaterally repudiated. In April 1922, the Soviet commissar of foreign affairs, Georgiy Chicherin, circumvented these difficulties by achieving an understanding with Germany, the other pariah state of Europe, in the Treaty of Rapallo. Under the treaty, Germany and Russia agreed on mutual recognition, cancellation of debt claims, normalization of trade relations, and secret cooperation in military development. Soon after concluding the treaty, the Soviet Union obtained diplomatic recognition from other major powers, beginning with Britain in February 1924. Although the United States withheld recognition until 1933, private American firms began to extend technological assistance and to develop commercial links in the 1920s.

Toward the non-Western world, the Soviet leadership limited its revolutionary activity to promoting opposition among the indigenous populations against "imperialist exploitation." The Soviet Union did pursue an active policy in China, aiding the Guomindang (Nationalist Party), a non-Marxist organization committed to reform and national sovereignty. After the triumph of the Guomindang in 1927, a debate developed among Soviet leaders concerning the future status of relations with China. Stalin wanted the Chinese Communist Party to join the Guomindang and infiltrate the government from within, while

Trotsky proposed an armed communist uprising and forcible imposition of socialism. Although Stalin's plan was finally accepted, it came to naught when in 1927 the Guomindang leader Chiang Kai-shek ordered the Chinese communists massacred and Soviet advisers expelled.

Society and Culture in the 1920s

In many respects, the NEP period was a time of relative freedom and experimentation in the social and cultural life of the Soviet Union. The government tolerated a variety of trends in these fields, provided they were not overtly hostile to the regime. In art and literature, numerous schools, some traditional and others radically experimental, proliferated. Communist writers Maksim Gor'kiy and Vladimir Mayakovskiy were active during this time, but other authors, many of whose works were later repressed, published work lacking socialist political content (see Literature and the Arts, ch. 4). Filmmaking, as a means of influencing a largely illiterate society, received encouragement from the state; much of legendary cinematographer Sergey Eisenstein's best work dates from this period.

Under Commissar Anatoliy Lunacharskiy, education entered a phase of experimentation based on progressive theories of learning. At the same time, the state expanded the primary and secondary school systems and introduced night schools for working adults. The quality of higher education suffered, however, because admissions policies gave preference to entrants from the proletarian class over those with bourgeois backgrounds, regardless of qualifications.

In family life, attitudes generally became more permissive. The state legalized abortion, and it made divorce progressively easier to obtain. In general, traditional attitudes toward such institutions as marriage were subtly undermined by the party's promotion of revolutionary ideals.

Transformation and Terror

The gradual accession of Stalin to power in the 1920s eventually brought an end to the liberalization of society and the economy, leading instead to a period of unprecedented government control, mobilization, and terrorization of society in Russia and the other Soviet republics. In the 1930s, agriculture and industry underwent brutal forced centralization, and Russian cultural activity was highly restricted. Purges eliminated thousands of individuals deemed dangerous to the Soviet state by Stalin's operatives.

Industrialization and Collectivization

At the end of the 1920s, a dramatic new phase in economic development began when Stalin decided to carry out a program of intensive socialist construction. To some extent, Stalin pressed economic development at this point as a political maneuver to eliminate rivals within the party. Because Bukharin and some other party members would not give up the gradualistic NEP in favor of radical development, Stalin branded them "right-wing deviationists" and during 1929 and 1930 used the party organization to remove them from influential positions. Yet Stalin's break with the NEP also revealed that his doctrine of building "socialism in one country" paralleled the line that Trotsky had originally supported early in the 1920s. Marxism supplied no basis for Stalin's model of a planned economy, although the centralized economic controls of the war communism years seemingly furnished a Leninist precedent. Between 1927 and 1929, the State Planning Committee (Gosudarstvennyy planovyy komitet—Gosplan) worked out the First Five-Year Plan (see Glossary) for intensive economic growth; Stalin began to implement this plan—his "revolution from above"—in 1928.

The First Five-Year Plan called for rapid industrialization of the economy, with particular emphasis on heavy industry. The economy was centralized: small-scale industry and services were nationalized, managers strove to fulfill Gosplan's output quotas, and the trade unions were converted into mechanisms for increasing worker productivity. But because Stalin insisted on unrealistic production targets, serious problems soon arose. With the greatest share of investment put into heavy industry, widespread shortages of consumer goods occurred, and inflation grew.

To satisfy the state's need for increased food supplies, the First Five-Year Plan called for the organization of the peasantry into collective units that the authorities could easily control. This collectivization program entailed compounding the peasants' lands and animals into collective farms (*kolkhozy;* sing., *kolkhoz*—see Glossary) and state farms (*sovkhozy;* sing., *sovkhoz*—see Glossary) and restricting the peasants' movement from these farms. The effect of this restructuring was to reintroduce a kind of serfdom into the countryside. Although the program was designed to affect all peasants, Stalin in particular sought to eliminate the wealthiest peasants, known as kulaks. Generally, kulaks were only marginally better off than other peasants, but the party claimed that the kulaks had ensnared the rest of the peasantry in capitalistic relationships. In any event, collectivization met widespread resistance not only from the kulaks but from poorer peasants as well, and a desperate struggle of the peasantry against the authorities ensued. Peasants slaughtered their cows and pigs rather than turn them over to the collective farms, with the result that livestock resources remained below the 1929 level for years afterward. The state in turn forcibly collectivized reluctant peasants and deported kulaks and active rebels to Siberia. Within the collective farms, the authorities in many instances exacted such high levels of procurement that starvation was widespread.

By 1932 Stalin realized that both the economy and society were under serious strain. Although industry failed to meet its production targets and agriculture actually lost ground in comparison with 1928 yields, Stalin declared that the First Five-Year Plan had successfully met its goals in four years. He then proceeded to set more realistic goals. Under the Second Five-Year Plan (1933–37), the state devoted attention to consumer goods, and the factories built under the first plan helped increase industrial output in general. The Third Five-Year Plan, begun in 1938, produced poorer results because of a sudden shift of emphasis to armaments production in response to the worsening international climate. In general, however, the Soviet economy had become industrialized by the end of the 1930s. Agriculture, which had been exploited to finance the industrialization drive, continued to show poor returns throughout the decade.

The Purges

The complete subjugation of the party to Stalin, its leader, paralleled the subordination of industry and agriculture to the state. Stalin had assured his preeminent position by squelching Bukharin and the "right-wing deviationists" in 1929 and 1930. To secure his absolute control over the party, however, Stalin began to purge leaders and rank-and-file members whose loyalty he doubted.

Stalin's purges began in December 1934, when Sergey Kirov, a popular Leningrad party chief who advocated a moderate policy toward the peasants, was assassinated. Although details remain murky, many Western historians believe that Stalin instigated the murder to rid himself of a potential opponent. In any event, in the resultant mass purge of the local Leningrad party, thousands were deported to camps in Siberia. Zinov'yev and Kamenev, Stalin's former political partners, received prison sentences for their alleged role in Kirov's murder. At the same time, the People's Commissariat for Internal Affairs (Narodnyy komissariat vnutrennikh del—NKVD), the secret police agency that was heir to the Cheka of the early 1920s, stepped up surveillance through its agents and informers and claimed to uncover anti-Soviet conspiracies among prominent long-term party members. At three publicized show trials held in Moscow between 1936 and 1938, dozens of these Old Bolsheviks, including Zinov'yev, Kamenev, and Bukharin, confessed to improbable crimes against the Soviet state. Their confessions were quickly followed by execution. (The last of Stalin's old enemies, Trotsky, who supposedly had masterminded the conspiracies against Stalin from abroad, was murdered in Mexico in 1940, presumably by the NKVD.) Coincident with the show trials of the original leadership of the party, unpublicized purges swept through the ranks of younger leaders in party, government, industrial management, and cultural affairs. Party purges in the non-Russian republics were particularly severe. The Yezhovshchina ("era of Yezhov," named for NKVD chief Nikolay Yezhov) ravaged the military as well, leading to the execution or incarceration of about half the officer corps. The secret police also terrorized the general populace, with untold numbers of common people punished after spurious accusations. By the time the purges subsided in 1938, millions of Soviet leaders, officials, and other citizens had been executed, imprisoned, or exiled.

The reasons for the period of widespread purges, which became known as the Great Terror, remain unclear. Western historians variously hypothesize that Stalin created the terror out of a desire to goad the population to carry out his intensive modernization program, or to atomize society to preclude dissent, or simply out of brutal paranoia. Whatever the causes, the purges must be viewed as having weakened the Soviet state.

In 1936, just as the Great Terror was intensifying, Stalin approved a new Soviet constitution to replace that of 1924. Hailed as "the most democratic constitution in the world," the 1936 document stipulated free and secret elections based on universal suffrage and guaranteed the citizenry a range of civil and economic rights. But in practice the freedoms implied by these rights were denied by provisions elsewhere in the constitution that indicated that the basic structure of Soviet society could not be changed and that the party retained all political power.

The power of the party, in turn, now was concentrated in the persons of Stalin and the members of his handpicked Politburo. As if to symbolize the lack of influence of the party rank and file, party congresses were convened less and less frequently. State power, far from "withering away" after the revolution as Karl Marx had prescribed, instead grew. With Stalin consciously building what critics would later describe as a cult of personality, the reverence accorded him in Soviet society gradually eclipsed that given to Lenin.

Mobilization of Society

Concomitant with industrialization and collectivization, society also experienced wide-ranging regimentation. Collective enterprises replaced individualistic efforts across the board. Not only did the regime abolish private farms and businesses, but it collectivized scientific and literary endeavors as well. As the 1930s progressed, the revolutionary experimentation that had characterized many facets of cultural and social life gave way to conservative norms.

Considerations of order and discipline dominated social policy, which became an instrument of the modernization effort. Workers came under strict labor codes demanding punctuality and discipline, and labor unions served as extensions of the industrial ministries. At the same time, higher pay and privileges accrued to productive workers and labor brigades. To provide greater social stability, the state aimed to strengthen the family by restricting divorce and abolishing abortion.

Literature and the arts came under direct party control during the 1930s, with mandatory membership in unions of writers, musicians, and other artists entailing adherence to established standards. After 1934 the party dictated that creative works had to express socialistic spirit through traditional forms. This officially sanctioned doctrine, called "socialist realism," applied to all fields of art. The state repressed works that were stylistically innovative or lacked appropriate content.

The party also subjected science and the liberal arts to its scrutiny. Development of scientific theory in a number of fields had to be based upon the party's understanding of the Marxist dialectic, which derailed serious research in certain disciplines. The party took a more active role in directing work in the social sciences. In the writing of history, the orthodox Marxist interpretation employed in the late 1920s was modified to include nationalistic themes and to stress the role of great leaders to create legitimacy for Stalin's dictatorship.

Education returned to traditional forms as the party discarded the experimental programs of Lunacharskiy after 1929. Admission procedures underwent modification: candidates for higher education now were selected on the basis of their academic records rather than their class origins. Religion suffered from a state policy of increased repression, starting with the closure of numerous churches in 1929. Persecution of clergy was particularly severe during the purges of the late 1930s, when many of the faithful went underground (see The Russian Orthodox Church, ch. 4).

Foreign Policy, 1928–39

Soviet foreign policy underwent a series of changes during the first decade of Stalin's rule. Soon after assuming control of the party, Stalin oversaw a radicalization of Soviet foreign policy that paralleled the severity of his remaking of domestic policy. To heighten the urgency of his demands for modernization, Stalin portrayed the Western powers, particularly France, as warmongers eager to attack the Soviet Union. The Great Depression, which seemingly threatened to destroy world capitalism in the early 1930s, provided ideological justification for the diplomatic self-isolation practiced by the Soviet Union in that period. To aid the triumph of communism, Stalin resolved to weaken the moderate social democratic parties of Europe, which seemed to be the communists' rivals for support among the working classes of the Western world.

Conversely, the Comintern ordered the Communist Party of Germany to aid the anti-Soviet National Socialist German Workers' Party (Nazi Party) in its bid for power, in the hopes that a Nazi regime would exacerbate social tensions and produce conditions that would lead to a communist revolution in Germany. In pursuing this policy, Stalin thus shared responsibility for Adolf Hitler's rise to power in 1933 and its tragic consequences for the Soviet Union and the rest of the world.

The dynamics of Soviet foreign relations changed drastically after Stalin recognized the danger posed by Nazi Germany. From 1934 through 1937, the Soviet Union tried to restrain

German militarism by building coalitions hostile to fascism. In the international communist movement, the Comintern adopted the "popular front" policy of cooperation with socialists and liberals against fascism, thus reversing its line of the early 1930s. In 1934 the Soviet Union joined the League of Nations, where Maksim Litvinov, the Soviet commissar of foreign affairs, advocated disarmament and collective security against fascist aggression. In 1935 the Soviet Union formed defensive military alliances with France and Czechoslovakia, and from 1936 to 1939 it gave assistance to antifascists in the Spanish Civil War. The menace of fascist militarism to the Soviet Union increased when Germany and Japan (which already posed a substantial threat to the Soviet Far East) signed the Anti-Comintern Pact in 1936. But the West proved unwilling to counter German provocative behavior, and after France and Britain acceded to Hitler's demands for Czechoslovak territory at Munich in 1938, Stalin abandoned his efforts to forge a collective security agreement with the West.

Convinced now that the West would not fight Hitler, Stalin decided to come to an understanding with Germany. Signaling a shift in foreign policy, Vyacheslav Molotov, Stalin's loyal assistant, replaced Litvinov, who was Jewish, as commissar of foreign affairs in May 1939. Hitler, who had decided to attack Poland despite the guarantees of Britain and France to defend that country, soon responded to the changed Soviet stance. While Britain and France dilatorily attempted to induce the Soviet Union to join them in pledging to protect Poland, the Soviet Union and Germany engaged in intense negotiations. The product of the talks between the former ideological foes—the Nazi-Soviet Nonaggression Pact (also known as the Molotov-Ribbentrop Pact) of August 23, 1939—shocked the world. The open provisions of the agreement pledged absolute neutrality in the event one of the parties should become involved in war, while a secret protocol partitioned Poland between the parties and assigned Romanian territory as well as Estonia and Latvia (and later Lithuania) to the Soviet sphere of influence. With his eastern flank thus secured, Hitler began the German invasion of Poland on September 1, 1939; Britain and France declared war on Germany two days later. World War II had begun.

The War Years

The security that Stalin bought with the German treaty was

short-lived. Hitler repudiated the agreement in 1941, and Russian, Belorussian, and Ukrainian territory subsequently became the scene of fierce fighting and the eventual repulsion of a huge Nazi invasion force. Stalin was able to rally patriotic support for the war effort, and Soviet forces entered Berlin triumphantly in April 1945. Together with the United States, the Soviet Union entered the postwar era as a superpower.

Prelude to War

When German troops invaded Poland, the Soviet Union was ill prepared to fight a major war. Although military expenditures had increased dramatically during the 1930s and the standing army was expanded in 1939, Soviet weaponry was inferior to that of the German army. More important, eight of the nation's top military leaders, including Marshal Mikhail Tukhachevskiy, had been executed in 1937 in the course of Stalin's purges; thus the armed forces' morale and effectiveness were diminished. The time gained through the pact with the Nazis was therefore critical to the recovery of Soviet defenses, particularly because Hitler's forces had overrun much of Western Europe by the summer of 1940. To strengthen its western frontier, the Soviet Union quickly secured the territory located in its sphere of interest. Soviet forces seized eastern Poland in September 1939; entered Estonia, Latvia, and Lithuania in October 1939; and seized the Romanian territories of Bessarabia (later incorporated into the Moldavian Republic) and northern Bukovina (later added to the Ukrainian Republic) in June 1940. Only Finland resisted Stalin's program of expansion, first by refusing to cede territory and then by putting up a determined defense along the Mannerheim Line when the Red Army invaded in November 1939. The Soviet-Finnish War (also known as the Winter War) of 1939–40 exposed grave deficiencies in Soviet military capabilities, which Hitler undoubtedly noted.

As the European war continued and the theaters of the conflict widened, Hitler began to chafe under his pact with the Soviet Union. The German dictator refused to grant Stalin a free hand in the Balkans, instead moving the German forces deeper into Eastern Europe and strengthening his ties with Finland. Hitler thus prepared for war against the Soviet Union under a plan that he officially approved in December 1940. At this point, however, Stalin still apparently believed that the Soviet Union could avert war by appeasing Germany. To achieve this goal, regular shipments of Soviet materials to Germany continued, and the Soviet armed forces were kept at a low stage of readiness. But despite Stalin's efforts to mollify Hitler, Germany declared war on the Soviet Union just as 180 German divisions swept across the border early on the morning of June 22, 1941.

The Great Patriotic War

The German blitzkrieg, known as Operation Barbarossa, nearly succeeded in breaking the Soviet Union in the months that followed. Caught unprepared, the Soviet forces lost whole armies and vast quantities of equipment to the German onslaught in the first weeks of the war. By November the German army had seized the Ukrainian Republic, besieged Leningrad, the Soviet Union's second largest city, and threatened Moscow itself (see fig. 5). The Great Patriotic War, as the Soviet Union and then Russia have called that phase of World War II, thus began inauspiciously for the Soviet Union.

By the end of 1941, however, the German forces had lost their momentum. German movements were increasingly restricted by harsh winter weather, attacks from bands of partisans, and difficulties in maintaining overextended supply lines. At the same time, the Red Army, after recovering from the initial blow, launched its first counterattacks against the invaders in December. To ensure the army's ability to fight the war, the Soviet authorities moved thousands of factories and their key personnel from the war zone to the interior of the country—often to Central Asia—where the plants began producing war matériel. Finally, the country was bolstered by the prospect of receiving assistance from Britain and the United States.

After a lull in active hostilities during the winter of 1941–42, the German army renewed its offensive, scoring a number of victories in the Ukrainian Republic, Crimea, and southern Russia in the first half of 1942. Then, in an effort to gain control of the lower Volga River region, the German forces attempted to capture the city of Stalingrad (present-day Volgograd) on the west bank of the river. Here, Soviet forces put up fierce resistance even after the Germans had reduced the city to rubble. Finally, Soviet forces led by General Georgiy Zhukov surrounded the German attackers and forced their surrender in February 1943. The Soviet victory at Stalingrad proved decisive; after losing this battle, the Germans lacked the strength to sustain their offensive operations against the Soviet Union.

After Stalingrad, the Soviet Union held the initiative for the rest of the war. By the end of 1943, the Red Army had broken through the German siege of Leningrad and recaptured much of the Ukrainian Republic. By the end of 1944, the front had moved beyond the 1939 Soviet frontiers into Eastern Europe. With a decisive superiority in troops and weaponry, Soviet forces drove into eastern Germany, capturing Berlin in May 1945. The war with Germany thus ended triumphantly for the Soviet Union.

In gaining the victory, the Soviet government had to rely on the support of the people. To increase popular enthusiasm for the war, Stalin reshaped his domestic policies to heighten patriotic spirit. Nationalistic slogans replaced much of the communist rhetoric in official pronouncements and the mass media. Active persecution of religion ceased, and in 1943 Stalin allowed the Russian Orthodox Church to name a patriarch (see Glossary) after the office had stood vacant for nearly two decades. In the countryside, authorities permitted greater freedom on the collective farms. Harsh German rule in the occupied territories also aided the Soviet cause. Nazi administrators of conquered Soviet territories made little attempt to exploit the population's dissatisfaction with Soviet political and economic policies. Instead, the Nazis preserved the collective farm system, systematically carried out genocidal policies against Jews, and deported others (mainly Ukrainians) to work in Germany. Given these circumstances, the great majority of the Soviet people chose to fight and work on their country's behalf, thus ensuring the regime's survival.

The war with Germany also brought about a temporary alliance with the two greatest powers in the "imperialist camp," namely Britain and the United States. Despite deep-seated mistrust between the Western democracies and the Soviet state, the demands of war made cooperation critical. The Soviet Union benefited from shipments of weaponry and equipment from the Western allies; during the course of the war, the United States alone furnished supplies worth more than US$11 billion. At the same time, by engaging considerable German resources, the Soviet Union gave the United States and Britain time to prepare to invade German-occupied Western Europe.

Relations began to sour, however, when the war turned in the Allies' favor. The postponement of the European invasion to June 1944 became a source of irritation to Stalin, whose country meanwhile bore the brunt of the struggle against Ger-

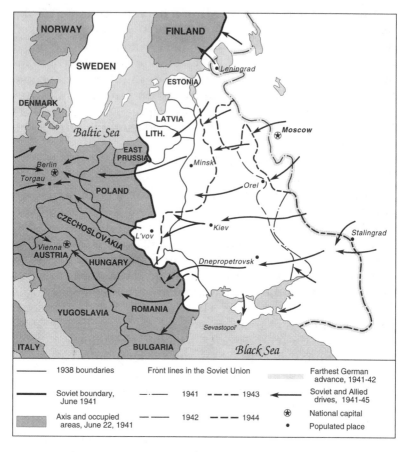

Source: Based on information from David MacKenzie and Michael W. Curran, *A History of Russia and the Soviet Union*, Chicago, 1987, 742.

Figure 5. Military Operations Against Germany, 1941–45

many. Then, as Soviet armies pushed into Eastern Europe, the question of the postwar order increased the friction within the coalition. At the Yalta Conference in February 1945, Stalin clashed with President Franklin D. Roosevelt and Prime Minister Winston Churchill over Stalin's plans to extend Soviet influence to Poland after the war. At the same time, however, Stalin promised to join the war against Japan ninety days after Germany had been defeated. Breaking the neutrality pact that the Soviet Union had concluded with Japan in April 1941, the Red Army entered the war in East Asia several days before Japan surrendered in August 1945. Now, with all common enemies defeated, little remained to preserve the alliance between the Western democracies and the Soviet Union.

The end of World War II saw the Soviet Union emerge as one of the world's two great military powers. Its battle-tested forces occupied most of Eastern Europe. The Soviet Union had won island holdings from Japan and further concessions from Finland (which had joined Germany in invading the Soviet Union in 1941) in addition to the territories seized as a consequence of the Nazi-Soviet Nonaggression Pact. But these achievements came at a high cost. An estimated 20 million Soviet soldiers and civilians perished in the war, the heaviest loss of life of any of the combatant countries. The war also inflicted severe material losses throughout the vast territory that had been included in the war zone. The suffering and losses resulting from the war made a lasting impression on the Soviet people and leaders that influenced their behavior in the postwar era.

Reconstruction and Cold War

The end of the common cause again exposed the underlying hostility between the capitalist countries and the Soviet Union. And the favorable position in which the Soviet Union finished World War II rapidly made it the prime postwar threat to world peace in the eyes of Western policy makers. The so-called Cold War that emerged from that situation featured Soviet domination of all of Eastern Europe, the development of nuclear weapons by the Soviet Union, and dangerous conflicts and near-conflicts in several areas of the world.

Reconstruction Years

Although the Soviet Union was victorious in World War II, its economy had been devastated in the struggle. Roughly a quarter of the country's capital resources had been destroyed, and industrial and agricultural output in 1945 fell far short of prewar levels. To help rebuild the country, the Soviet government obtained limited credits from Britain and Sweden but refused assistance proposed by the United States under the economic aid program known as the Marshall Plan (see Glossary). Instead, the Soviet Union compelled Soviet-occupied Eastern Europe to supply machinery and raw materials. Germany and former Nazi satellites (including Finland) made reparations to the Soviet Union. The Soviet people bore much of the cost of rebuilding because the reconstruction program emphasized heavy industry while neglecting agriculture and consumer goods. By the time of Stalin's death in 1953, steel production was twice its 1940 level, but the production of many consumer goods and foodstuffs was lower than it had been in the late 1920s.

During the postwar reconstruction period, Stalin tightened domestic controls, justifying the repression by playing up the threat of war with the West. Many repatriated Soviet citizens who had lived abroad during the war, whether as prisoners of war, forced laborers, or defectors, were executed or sent to prison camps. The limited freedoms granted in wartime to the church and to collective farmers were revoked. The party tightened its admission standards and purged many who had become party members during the war.

In 1946 Andrey Zhdanov, a close associate of Stalin, helped launch an ideological campaign designed to demonstrate the superiority of socialism over capitalism in all fields. This campaign, colloquially known as the Zhdanovshchina ("era of Zhdanov"), attacked writers, composers, economists, historians, and scientists whose work allegedly manifested Western influence. Although Zhdanov died in 1948, the cultural purge continued for several years afterward, stifling Soviet intellectual development. Another campaign, related to the Zhdanovshchina, lauded the real or purported achievements of past and present Russian inventors and scientists. In this intellectual climate, the genetic theories of biologist Trofim Lysenko, which were supposedly derived from Marxist principles but lacked a scientific foundation, were imposed upon Soviet science to the detriment of research and agricultural development. The anticosmopolitan trends of these years adversely affected Jewish cultural and scientific figures in particular. In general, a pronounced sense of Russian nationalism, as opposed to socialist consciousness, pervaded Soviet society.

Onset of the Cold War

Soon after World War II, the Soviet Union and its Western allies parted ways as mutual suspicions of the other's intentions and actions flourished. Eager to consolidate influence over a number of countries adjacent to the Soviet Union, Stalin pursued an aggressive policy of intervention in the domestic affairs of these states, provoking strong Western reaction. The United

States worked to contain Soviet expansion in this period of international relations that came to be known as the Cold War.

Mindful of the numerous invasions of Russia and the Soviet Union from the West throughout history, Stalin sought to create a buffer zone of subservient East European countries, most of which the Red Army (known as the Soviet army after 1946) had occupied in the course of the war. Taking advantage of its military occupation of these countries, the Soviet Union actively assisted local communist parties in coming to power. By 1948 seven East European countries—Albania, Bulgaria, Czechoslovakia, Hungary, Poland, Romania, and Yugoslavia—had communist governments. The Soviet Union initially maintained control behind the "Iron Curtain" (a phrase coined by Churchill in a 1946 speech) through the use of troops, security police, and the Soviet diplomatic service. Inequitable trade agreements with the East European countries permitted the Soviet Union access to valued resources.

Soviet actions in Eastern Europe generated hostility among the Western states toward their former ally, but they could do nothing to halt consolidation of Soviet authority in that region short of going to war. However, the United States and its allies had greater success in halting Soviet expansion in areas where Soviet influence was more tenuous. British and American diplomatic support for Iran forced the Soviet Union to withdraw its troops from the northeastern part of that country in 1946. Soviet efforts to acquire territory from Turkey and to establish a communist government in Greece were stymied when the United States extended military and economic support to those countries under the Truman Doctrine, a policy articulated by President Harry S. Truman in 1947. Later that year, the United States introduced the Marshall Plan for the economic recovery of other countries of Europe. The Soviet Union forbade the countries it dominated from taking part in the program, and the Marshall Plan contributed to a reduction of Soviet influence in the participating West European nations.

Tensions between the United States and the Soviet Union became especially strained over the issue of Germany. At the Potsdam Conference of July–August 1945, the Allied Powers confirmed their decision to divide Germany and the city of Berlin into zones of occupation (with the eastern sectors placed under Soviet administration) until such time as the Allies would permit Germany to establish a central government. Disagreements between the Soviet Union and the Western Allies soon arose over their respective occupation policies and the matter of reparations. In June 1948, the Soviet Union cut off the West's land access to the American, British, and French sectors of Berlin in retaliation for steps taken by the United States and Britain to unite Germany. Britain and the United States thereupon sponsored an airlift that kept the beleaguered sectors provisioned until the Soviet Union lifted the blockade in May 1949. Following the Berlin blockade, the Western Allies and the Soviet Union divided Germany into two countries, one oriented to the West, the other to the East. The crisis also provided the catalyst for the Western countries in 1949 to form the North Atlantic Treaty Organization (NATO— see Glossary), a collective security system under which conventional armies and nuclear weapons would offset Soviet forces.

While the Soviet Union gained a new satellite nation in the German Democratic Republic (East Germany), it lost its influence in Yugoslavia. The local communists in Yugoslavia had come to power without Soviet assistance, and their leader, Josip Broz Tito, refused to subordinate the country to Stalin's control. Tito's defiance led the Communist Information Bureau (Cominform—founded in 1947 to assume some of the functions of the Comintern, which had been abolished in 1943) to expel the Yugoslav party from the international communist movement in 1948. To avert the rise of other independent leaders, Stalin purged many of the chief communists in other East European states.

In Asia the Chinese communists, headed by Mao Zedong and assisted by the Soviet Union, achieved victory over the Guomindang in 1949. Several months afterward, in 1950, China and the Soviet Union concluded a mutual defense treaty against Japan and the United States. Hard negotiations over concessions and aid between the two communist countries served as an indication that China, with its independent party and enormous population, would not become a Soviet satellite, although for a time Sino-Soviet relations appeared particularly close. Elsewhere in Asia, the Soviet Union pursued a vigorous policy of support for national liberation movements, especially in Malaya and Indochina, which were still colonies of Britain and France, respectively. Thinking that the West would not defend the Republic of Korea (South Korea), Stalin allowed or encouraged the Soviet-equipped forces of the Democratic People's Republic of Korea (North Korea) to invade South Korea in 1950. But forces from the United States and other members of the United Nations came to the aid of South Korea, leading China to intervene militarily on behalf of North Korea, probably at Soviet instigation. Although the Soviet Union avoided direct participation in the conflict, the Korean War (1950–53) motivated the United States to strengthen its military capability and to conclude a peace treaty and security pact with Japan. Chinese participation in the war also strengthened China's independent position relative to the Soviet Union.

The Death of Stalin

In the early 1950s, Stalin, now an old man, apparently permitted his subordinates in the Politburo (enlarged and renamed the Presidium in October 1952) greater powers within their respective spheres. Also at the Nineteenth Party Congress, the name of the party was changed from the All-Union Communist Party (Bolshevik) to the Communist Party of the Soviet Union (CPSU—see Glossary). Indicative of the Soviet leader's waning strength was top aide Georgiy Malenkov's presentation of the political report to the congress in Stalin's stead. Although the general secretary took a smaller part in the day-to-day administration of party affairs, he maintained his animosity toward potential enemies. In January 1953, the party newspaper announced that a group of predominantly Jewish doctors had murdered high Soviet officials, including Zhdanov. Western historians speculate that the disclosure of this "doctors' plot" may have been a prelude to an intended purge directed against Malenkov, Molotov, and secret police chief Lavrenti Beria. When Stalin died in March 1953, under circumstances that remain unclear, his inner circle, which for years had lived in dread of their leader, secretly rejoiced.

During his quarter-century of dictatorial control, Stalin had overseen impressive development in the Soviet Union. From a comparatively backward agricultural society, the country had been transformed into a powerful industrial state. But in the course of that transformation, many millions of people had been killed, and Stalin's use of repressive controls had become an integral function of his regime. The extent to which Stalin's system would be maintained or altered would be a question of vital concern to Soviet leaders for years after his passing.

The Khrushchev Era

The end of the Stalin era brought immediate liberalization

in several aspects of Soviet life. Party leader Nikita S. Khrushchev denounced Stalin's tyrannical reign in 1956, signaling a sharp break with the past. Because Khrushchev lacked the all-encompassing power of Stalin, his time in office was marked by continuous maneuvering against political enemies much more real than Stalin's had been. Party control of cultural activity became much less restrictive with the onset of the first "thaw" in the mid-1950s. Khrushchev attempted reforms in both domestic and foreign policy, with mixed results. During his tenure (1953–64), world politics became much more complex as the insecurities of the Cold War persisted; Khrushchev ultimately was undone by a combination of failed policy innovations in agriculture, party politics, and industry.

Collective Leadership and the Rise of Khrushchev

Stalin died without naming an heir, and none of his associates had the power to make an immediate claim to supreme leadership. At first the deceased dictator's colleagues tried to rule jointly, with Malenkov holding the top position of prime minister. The first challenge to this arrangement occurred in 1953, when the powerful Beria plotted a coup. However, Beria, who had made many enemies during his bloody term as security chief, was arrested and executed by order of the Presidium. His death reduced the inordinate power of the secret police, although the party's strict control over the state security organs ended only with the demise of the Soviet Union itself (see Internal Security Before 1991, ch. 10).

After the elimination of Beria, the succession struggle became more subtle. Malenkov found a formidable rival in Khrushchev, whom the Presidium elected first secretary (Stalin's title of general secretary was abolished after his death) in September 1953. Of peasant background, Khrushchev had served as head of the Ukrainian party organization during and after World War II, and he was a member of the Soviet political elite during the late Stalin period. The rivalry between Malenkov and Khrushchev manifested itself publicly in the contrast between Malenkov's support for increased production of consumer goods and Khrushchev's stand-pat backing for continued development of heavy industry. After a poor showing by light industry and agriculture, Malenkov resigned as prime minister in February 1955. Because the new prime minister, Nikolay Bulganin, had little influence or real power, the departure of Malenkov made Khrushchev the most important figure within the collective leadership.

At the Twentieth Party Congress, held in February 1956, Khrushchev further advanced his position within the party by denouncing Stalin's crimes in a dramatic "secret speech." Khrushchev revealed that Stalin had arbitrarily liquidated thousands of party members and military leaders, thereby contributing to the initial Soviet defeats in World War II, and had established what Khrushchev characterized as a pernicious cult of personality. With this speech, Khrushchev not only distanced himself from Stalin and from Stalin's close associates, Molotov, Malenkov, and Lazar Kaganovich, but he also abjured the dictator's use of terror as an instrument of policy. As a direct result of the "de-Stalinization" campaign launched by Khrushchev's speech, the release of political prisoners, which had begun in 1953, was stepped up, and some of Stalin's victims were posthumously rehabilitated. Khrushchev intensified his campaign against Stalin at the Twenty-Second Party Congress in 1961, winning approval to remove Stalin's body from the Lenin Mausoleum, where it had originally been interred. De-Stalinization encouraged many in artistic and intellectual circles to speak out against the abuses of the former regime. Although Khrushchev's tolerance for critical creative works varied during his tenure, the new cultural period—known as the "thaw"—represented a clear break with the repression of the arts under Stalin.

After the Twentieth Party Congress, Khrushchev continued to expand his influence, although he still faced opposition. His rivals in the Presidium, spurred by reversals in Soviet foreign policy in Eastern Europe in 1956, potentially threatening economic reforms, and the de-Stalinization campaign, united to vote him out of office in June 1957. Khrushchev, however, demanded that the matter be put to the Central Committee of the CPSU, where he enjoyed strong support. The Central Committee overturned the Presidium's decision and expelled Khrushchev's opponents (Malenkov, Molotov, and Kaganovich), whom Khrushchev labeled the "antiparty group." In a departure from Stalinist procedure, Khrushchev did not order the imprisonment or execution of his defeated rivals but instead placed them in relatively minor offices.

Khrushchev moved to consolidate his power further in the ensuing months. In October he removed Marshal Zhukov (who had helped Khrushchev squelch the "antiparty group") from the office of defense minister, presumably because he feared Zhukov's influence in the armed forces. Khrushchev became prime minister in March 1958 when Bulganin resigned, thus formally confirming his predominant position in the state as well as in the party.

Despite his rank, Khrushchev never exercised the dictatorial authority of Stalin, nor did he ever completely control the party, even at the peak of his power. His attacks on members of the "antiparty group" at the Twenty-First Party Congress in 1959 and the Twenty-Second Party Congress in 1961 suggest that his opponents retained support within the party. Khrushchev's relative political insecurity probably accounted for some of his grandiose pronouncements, for example his 1961 promise that the Soviet Union would attain communism by 1980. His desire to undermine opposition and mollify critics explained the nature of many of his domestic reforms and the vacillations in his foreign policy toward the West.

Foreign Policy under Khrushchev

Almost immediately after Stalin died, the collective leadership began altering the conduct of Soviet foreign policy to permit better relations with the West and new approaches to the nonaligned countries. Malenkov introduced a change in tone by speaking out against nuclear war as a threat to civilization. Khrushchev initially contradicted this position, saying capitalism alone would be destroyed in a nuclear war, but he adopted Malenkov's view after securing his domestic political position. In 1955, to ease tensions between East and West, Khrushchev recognized permanent neutrality for Austria. Meeting President Dwight D. Eisenhower in Geneva later that year, Khrushchev confirmed a Soviet commitment to "peaceful coexistence" with capitalism. Regarding the developing nations, Khrushchev tried to win the goodwill of their national leaders, instead of following the established Soviet policy of shunning the governments while supporting local communist parties. Soviet influence over the international alignments of India and Egypt, as well as of other Third World countries, began in the middle of the 1950s. Cuba's entry into the socialist camp in 1961 was a coup for the Soviet Union.

With the gains of the new diplomacy came reversals as well. By conceding Yugoslavia's independent approach to communism in 1955 as well as by his de-Stalinization campaign, Khrushchev created an opening for unrest in Eastern Europe, where the policies of the Stalin era had been particularly onerous. In Poland, riots brought about a change in communist party leadership, which the Soviet Union reluctantly recognized in October 1956. A popular uprising against Soviet control then broke out in Hungary, where the local communist leaders, headed by Imre Nagy, called for a multiparty political system and withdrawal from the Warsaw Pact (see Glossary), the defensive alliance founded by the Soviet Union and its East European satellites in 1955. The Soviet army crushed the revolt early in November 1956, causing numerous casualties. Although the Hungarian Revolution hurt Soviet standing in world opinion, it demonstrated that the Soviet Union would use force if necessary to maintain control over its satellite states in Eastern Europe.

Outside the Soviet sphere of control, China grew increasingly restive under Chinese Communist Party chairman Mao Zedong. Chinese discontent with the new Soviet leadership stemmed from low levels of Soviet aid, feeble Soviet support for China in its disputes with Taiwan and India, and the new Soviet doctrine of peaceful coexistence with the West, which Mao viewed as a betrayal of Marxism-Leninism. Against Khrushchev's wishes, China embarked on a nuclear arms program, declaring in 1960 that communism could defeat "imperialism" in a nuclear war. The dispute between militant China and the more moderate Soviet Union escalated into a schism in the world communist movement after 1960. Albania left the Soviet camp and became an ally of China, Romania distanced itself from the Soviet Union in international affairs, and communist parties around the world split over whether they should be oriented toward Moscow or Beijing. The monolithic bloc of world communism had shattered.

Soviet relations with the West, especially the United States, seesawed between moments of relative relaxation and periods of tension and crisis. For his part, Khrushchev wanted peaceful coexistence with the West, not only to avoid nuclear war but also to permit the Soviet Union to develop its economy. Khrushchev's meetings with President Eisenhower in 1955 and President John F. Kennedy in 1961 and his tour of the United States in 1959 demonstrated the Soviet leader's desire for fundamentally smooth relations between the West and the Soviet Union and its allies. Yet Khrushchev also needed to demonstrate to Soviet conservatives and the militant Chinese that the Soviet Union was a firm defender of the socialist camp. Thus, in 1958

Khrushchev challenged the status of Berlin; when the West would not yield to his demands that the western sectors be incorporated into East Germany, he approved the erection of the Berlin Wall between the eastern and western sectors of the city in 1961. To maintain national prestige, Khrushchev canceled a summit meeting with Eisenhower in 1960 after Soviet air defense troops shot down a United States reconnaissance aircraft over Soviet territory. Finally, mistrust over military intentions clouded East-West relations during this time. The West feared the implications of Soviet innovations in space technology and saw in the buildup of the Soviet military an emerging "missile gap" in the Soviet Union's favor.

By contrast, the Soviet Union felt threatened by a rearmed Federal Republic of Germany (West Germany), by a United States alliance system that seemed to be encircling the Soviet Union, and by the West's superior strategic and economic strength. To offset the United States military advantage and thereby improve the Soviet negotiating position, Khrushchev in 1962 tried to install nuclear missiles in Cuba, but he agreed to withdraw them after Kennedy ordered a blockade around the island nation. After coming close to war during the Cuban missile crisis, the Soviet Union and the United States took steps to reduce the nuclear threat. In 1963 the two countries established a "hot line" between Washington and Moscow to provide instant communication that would reduce the likelihood of accidental nuclear war. In the same year, the United States, Britain, and the Soviet Union signed the Limited Test Ban Treaty, which forbade nuclear weapons testing in the atmosphere.

Khrushchev's Reforms and Fall

Throughout his years of leadership, Khrushchev attempted to carry out reform in a range of fields. The problems of Soviet agriculture, a major concern of Khrushchev's, had earlier attracted the attention of the collective leadership, which introduced important innovations in this area of the Soviet economy. The state encouraged peasants to grow more on their private plots, increased payments for crops grown on collective farms, and invested more heavily in agriculture. In his dramatic Virgin Lands campaign in the mid-1950s, Khrushchev opened vast tracts of land to farming in the northern part of the Kazak Republic and neighboring areas of the Russian Republic. These new farmlands turned out to be susceptible to droughts, but in some years they produced excellent harvests. Later innovations by Khrushchev, however, proved counterproductive. His plans for growing corn and increasing meat and dairy production failed miserably, and his reorganization of collective farms into larger units produced confusion in the countryside.

Khrushchev's attempts at reform in industry and administrative organization created even greater problems. In a politically motivated move to weaken the central state bureaucracy, in 1957 Khrushchev did away with the industrial ministries in Moscow and replaced them with regional economic councils. Although he intended these economic councils to be more responsive to local needs, the decentralization of industry led to disruption and inefficiency. Connected with this decentralization was Khrushchev's decision in 1962 to recast party organizations along economic, rather than administrative, lines. The resulting bifurcation of the party apparatus into industrial and agricultural sectors at the oblast (province) level and below contributed to the disarray and alienated many party officials at all levels. Symptomatic of the country's economic difficulties was the abandonment in 1963 of Khrushchev's special seven-year economic plan (1959–65) two years short of its completion.

By 1964 Khrushchev's prestige had been damaged in a number of areas. Industrial growth had slowed, while agriculture showed no new progress. Abroad, the split with China, the Berlin crisis, and the Cuban fiasco hurt the Soviet Union's international stature, and Khrushchev's efforts to improve relations with the West antagonized many in the military. Lastly, the 1962 party reorganization caused turmoil throughout the Soviet political chain of command. In October 1964, while Khrushchev was vacationing in Crimea, the Presidium voted him out of office and refused to permit him to take his case to the Central Committee. Khrushchev retired as a private citizen after his successors denounced him for his "hare-brained schemes, half-baked conclusions, and hasty decisions." Yet along with his failed policies, Khrushchev must also be remembered for his public disavowal of Stalinism and the greater flexibility he brought to Soviet leadership after a long period of monolithic terror.

The Brezhnev Era

The regime that followed Khrushchev took a much more conservative approach to most problems. Stalinism did not return, but there was less latitude for individual expression. Foreign relations continued to roller-coaster, with the invasion of Afghanistan in 1979 constituting a major setback for relations with the West. The Soviet economy continued to falter, reaping no apparent benefit from the end of Khrushchev's economic experimentation.

Collective Leadership and the Rise of Brezhnev

After removing Khrushchev from power, the leaders of the Politburo (as the Presidium was renamed in 1966 by the Twenty-Third Party Congress) and Secretariat again established a collective leadership. As was the case following Stalin's death, several individuals, including Aleksey Kosygin, Nikolay Podgornyy, and Leonid I. Brezhnev, contended for power behind a facade of unity. Kosygin accepted the position of prime minister, which he held until his retirement in 1980. Brezhnev, who took the post of first secretary, may have been viewed originally by his colleagues as an interim appointee.

Born to a Russian worker's family in 1906, Brezhnev became a Khrushchev protégé early in his career and through his patron's influence rose to membership in the Presidium. As his own power grew, Brezhnev built up a coterie of followers whom he, as first secretary, gradually maneuvered into powerful positions. At the same time, Brezhnev slowly demoted or isolated possible contenders for his office. For instance, in December 1965 he succeeded in elevating Podgornyy to the ceremonial position of chairman of the Presidium of the Supreme Soviet, the highest legislative organization in the government, thus eliminating him as a rival. But Brezhnev's rise was very gradual; only in 1971, when he succeeded in appointing four close associates to the Politburo, did it become clear that his was the most influential voice in the collective leadership. After several more personnel changes, Brezhnev assumed the chairmanship of the Presidium of the Supreme Soviet in 1977, confirming his primacy in both party and state.

The years after Khrushchev were notable for the stability of the cadres, groups of activists in responsible and influential positions in the party and state apparatus. By introducing the slogan "Trust in Cadres" in 1965, Brezhnev won the support of many bureaucrats wary of the constant reorganizations of the Khrushchev era and eager for security in established hierarchies. Indicative of the stability of the period is the fact that nearly half of the Central Committee members in 1981 were holdovers from fifteen years earlier. The corollary to this stability was the aging of Soviet leaders; the average age of Politburo members rose from fifty-five in 1966 to sixty-eight in 1982. The Soviet leadership (or the "gerontocracy," as it was referred to in the West) became increasingly conservative and ossified.

Conservative policies characterized the regime's agenda in the years after Khrushchev. Upon assuming power, the collective leadership not only reversed such Khrushchev policies as the bifurcation of the party, it also halted de-Stalinization. Indeed, favorable references to the dead dictator began to appear. The Soviet constitution of 1977, although differing in certain respects from the 1936 Stalin document, retained the general thrust of the latter. In contrast to the relative cultural freedom permitted during the early Khrushchev years, Brezhnev and his colleagues continued the more restrictive line of the later Khrushchev era. The leadership was unwilling or unable to employ Stalinist means to control Soviet society; instead, it opted to use repressive tactics against political dissidents even after the Soviet Union signed the Helsinki Accords of 1975, which bound signatory nations to higher standards of human rights observance. Dissidents persecuted during this time included writers and activists in outlawed religious, nationalist, and human rights movements. In the latter part of the Brezhnev era, the regime tolerated popular expressions of anti-Semitism. Under conditions of "developed socialism" (the historical stage that the Soviet Union attained in 1977, according to the CPSU), the precepts of Marxism-Leninism were taught and reinforced as a means to bolster the authority of the regime rather than as a tool for revolutionary action.

Foreign Policy of a Superpower

A major concern of Khrushchev's successors was to reestablish Soviet primacy in the community of communist states by undermining the influence of China. Although the new leaders originally approached China without hostility, Mao's condemnation of Soviet foreign policy as "revisionist" and his competition for influence in the Third World soon led to a worsening of relations between the two countries. The Sino-Soviet relationship reached a low point in 1969 when clashes broke out along the disputed Ussuri River boundary in the Far East. Later, the Chinese, intimidated by Soviet military strength, agreed not to patrol the border area claimed by the

Soviet Union; but strained relations between the two countries continued into the early 1980s.

Under the collective leadership, the Soviet Union again used force in Eastern Europe, this time in Czechoslovakia. In 1968 reform-minded elements of the Communist Party of Czechoslovakia rapidly began to liberalize their rule, loosen censorship, and strengthen Western ties. In response, Soviet and other Warsaw Pact troops entered Czechoslovakia and installed a new regime. Out of these events arose the so-called Brezhnev Doctrine (see Glossary), which warned that the Soviet Union would act to maintain its hegemony in Eastern Europe (see Central Europe, ch. 8). Soviet suppression of the reform movement reduced blatant gestures of defiance on the part of Romania and served as a threatening example to the Polish Solidarity trade union movement in 1980. But it also helped disillusion communist parties in Western Europe to the extent that by 1977 most of the leading parties embraced Eurocommunism, a pragmatic approach to ideology that freed them to pursue political programs independent of Soviet dictates.

Soviet influence in the developing world expanded somewhat during the 1970s. New communist or left-leaning governments having close relations with the Soviet Union took power in several countries, including Angola, Ethiopia, Mozambique, and Nicaragua. In the Middle East, the Soviet Union vied for influence by backing the Arabs in their dispute with Israel. After the June 1967 War in the Middle East, the Soviet Union rebuilt the defeated Syrian and Egyptian armies, but it suffered a setback when Egypt expelled Soviet advisers from the country in 1972 and subsequently entered into a closer relationship with the United States. The Soviet Union retained ties with Syria and supported Palestinians' claims to an independent state. But Soviet prestige among moderate Muslim states suffered in the 1980s as a result of Soviet military activities in Afghanistan (see The Middle East, ch. 8). Attempting to shore up a communist government in that country, Brezhnev sent in Soviet armed forces in December 1979, but a large part of the Afghan population resisted both the occupiers and the Marxist Afghan regime. The resulting war in Afghanistan continued to be an unresolved problem for the Soviet Union at the time of Brezhnev's death in 1982.

Soviet relations with the West first improved, then deteriorated in the years after Khrushchev. The gradual winding down of United States involvement in the war in Vietnam after 1968 opened the way for negotiations between the United States and the Soviet Union on the subject of nuclear arms. The Treaty on the Nonproliferation of Nuclear Weapons (commonly known as the Nuclear Nonproliferation Treaty—NPT; see Glossary) went into effect in 1970, and the two countries began the Strategic Arms Limitation Talks (SALT) the following year. At the Moscow summit meeting of May 1972, Brezhnev and President Richard M. Nixon signed the Anti-Ballistic Missile Treaty (ABM Treaty—see Glossary) and the Interim Agreement on the Limitation of Strategic Offensive Arms. Both agreements essentially froze the two countries' existing stockpiles of strategic defensive and offensive weapons. A period of détente, or relaxation of tensions, between the two superpowers emerged, with a further agreement concluded to establish ceilings on the number of offensive weapons on both sides in 1974. The crowning achievement of the era of détente was the signing in 1975 of the Helsinki Accords, which ratified the postwar status quo in Europe and bound the signatories to respect basic principles of human rights. In the years that followed, the Soviet Union was found to be in substantial violation of the accords' human rights provisions.

But even during the period of détente, the Soviet Union increased weapons deployments, with the result that by the end of the 1970s it achieved nuclear parity with—or even superiority to—the United States. The Soviet Union also intensified its condemnation of the NATO alliance in an attempt to weaken Western unity. Although a second SALT agreement was signed by Brezhnev and President Jimmy Carter in Vienna in 1979, after the Soviet invasion of Afghanistan the Carter administration withdrew the agreement from consideration by the United States Senate, and détente effectively came to an end. Also in reaction to the Soviet involvement in Afghanistan, the United States imposed a grain embargo on the Soviet Union and boycotted the Moscow Summer Olympics in 1980. Tensions between the United States and the Soviet Union continued up to Brezhnev's death.

The Economy under Brezhnev

Despite Khrushchev's tinkering with economic planning, the economic system remained dependent on central plans drawn up with no reference to market mechanisms. Reformers, of whom the economist Yevsey Liberman was most noteworthy, advocated greater freedom for individual enterprises from outside controls and sought to turn the enterprises' economic objectives toward making a profit. Prime Minister Kosygin championed Liberman's proposals and succeeded in incorporating them into a general economic reform program approved in September 1965. This reform included scrapping Khrushchev's regional economic councils in favor of resurrecting the central industrial ministries of the Stalin era. Opposition from party conservatives and cautious managers, however, soon stalled the Liberman reforms, forcing the state to abandon them.

After Kosygin's short-lived attempt to revamp the economic system, planners reverted to drafting comprehensive centralized plans of the type first developed under Stalin. In industry, plans stressed the heavy and defense-related branches, slighting the light consumer-goods branches (see The Postwar Growth Period, ch. 6). As a developed industrial country, the Soviet Union by the 1970s found it increasingly difficult to maintain the high rates of growth in the industrial sector that it had enjoyed in earlier years. Increasingly large investment and labor inputs were required for growth, but these inputs were becoming more difficult to obtain. Although the goals of the five-year plans of the 1970s had been scaled down from previous plans, the targets remained largely unmet. The industrial shortfalls were felt most sharply in the sphere of consumer goods, where the public steadily demanded improved quality and increased quantity. Agricultural development continued to lag in the Brezhnev years. Despite steadily higher investments in agriculture, growth under Brezhnev fell below that attained under Khrushchev. Droughts occurring intermittently throughout the 1970s forced the Soviet Union to import large quantities of grain from Western countries, including the United States. In the countryside, Brezhnev continued the trend toward converting collective farms into state farms and raised the incomes of all farmworkers. Despite the wage increases, peasants still devoted much time and effort to their private plots, which provided the Soviet Union with a disproportionate share of its agricultural goods (see Agriculture, ch. 6).

The standard of living in the Soviet Union presented a problem to the Brezhnev leadership after the growth of the late 1960s stalled at a level well below that of most Western industrial (and some East European) countries. Although certain appliances and other goods became more accessible during the 1960s and 1970s, improvements in housing and food supply were slight. Shortages of consumer goods encouraged pilferage of government property and the growth of the black market. Vodka, however, remained readily available, and alcoholism was an important factor in both the declining life expectancy and the rising infant mortality rate that the Soviet Union experienced in the later Brezhnev years (see Health Conditions, ch. 5).

Culture and the Arts in the 1960s and 1970s

Progress in developing the education system was mixed during the Brezhnev years. In the 1960s and 1970s, the percentage of working-age people with at least a secondary education steadily increased. Yet at the same time, access to higher education grew more limited. By 1980 the percentage of secondary-school graduates admitted to universities had dropped to only two-thirds of the 1960 figure. Students accepted into universities increasingly came from professional families rather than worker or peasant households. This trend toward the perpetuation of the educated elite was not only a function of the superior cultural background of elite families but also, in many cases, a result of their power to influence admissions procedures (see The Soviet Heritage, ch. 5).

Progress in science also was variable under Brezhnev. In the most visible test of its advancement—the race with the United States to put a man on the moon—the Soviet Union failed, but through persistence the Soviet space program continued to make headway in other areas. In general, despite leads in such fields as metallurgy and thermonuclear fusion, Soviet science lagged behind that of the West, hampered in part by the slow development of computer technology.

In literature and the arts, a greater variety of creative works became accessible to the public than had previously been available. As in earlier decades, the state continued to determine what could be legally published or performed, punishing persistent offenders with exile or prison. Nonetheless, greater experimentation in art forms became permissible in the 1970s, with the result that more sophisticated and subtly critical work began to be produced. The regime loosened the strictures of socialist realism; thus, for instance, many protagonists of the novels of author Yuriy Trifonov concerned themselves with problems of daily life rather than with building socialism. In music, although the state continued to frown on such Western phenomena as jazz and rock, it began to permit Western musical ensembles specializing in these genres to make limited appearances. But the native balladeer Vladimir Vysotskiy, widely popular in the Soviet Union, was denied official recognition because of his iconoclastic lyrics (see Literature and the Arts, ch. 4).

In the religious life of the Soviet Union, a resurgence in popular devotion to the major faiths became apparent in the late 1970s despite continued de facto disapproval on the part of the authorities. This revival may have been connected with the generally growing interest of Soviet citizens in their respective national traditions (see The Russian Orthodox Church, ch. 4).

The Death of Brezhnev

Shortly after his cult of personality began to take root in the mid-1970s, Brezhnev began to experience periods of ill health. After Brezhnev suffered a stroke in 1975, Politburo members Mikhail Suslov and Andrey Kirilenko assumed some of the leader's functions for a time. Then, after another bout of poor health in 1978, Brezhnev delegated more of his responsibilities to Konstantin U. Chernenko, a longtime associate who soon began to be regarded as the heir apparent. His prospects of succeeding Brezhnev, however, were hurt by political problems plaguing the general secretary in the early 1980s. Not only were economic failures damaging Brezhnev's prestige, but scandals involving his family and political allies also were undermining his stature. Meanwhile, Yuriy V. Andropov, chief of the Committee for State Security (Komitet gosudarstvennoy bezopasnosti—KGB; see Glossary), apparently also began a campaign to discredit Brezhnev. Andropov took over Suslov's functions after Suslov died in 1982, and he used his position to promote himself as the next CPSU general secretary. Although he suffered another stroke in March 1982, Brezhnev refused to relinquish his office. He died that November.

The Soviet Union paid a high price for the stability of the Brezhnev years. By avoiding necessary political and economic change, the Brezhnev leadership ensured the economic and political decline that the country experienced during the 1980s. This deterioration of power and prestige stood in sharp contrast to the dynamism that had marked the Soviet Union's revolutionary beginnings.

The Leadership Transition Period

By 1982 the decrepitude of the Soviet regime was obvious to the outside world, but the system was not yet ready for drastic change. The transition period that separated the Brezhnev and Gorbachev regimes resembled the former much more than the latter, although hints of reform emerged as early as 1983.

The Andropov Interregnum

Two days passed between Brezhnev's death and the announcement of the election of Andropov as the new general secretary, suggesting to many outsiders that a power struggle had occurred in the Kremlin. Once in power, however, Andropov wasted no time in promoting his supporters. In June 1983, he assumed the post of chairman of the Presidium of the Supreme Soviet, thus becoming the ceremonial head of state. Brezhnev had needed thirteen years to acquire this post. During his short rule, Andropov replaced more than one-fifth of the Soviet ministers and regional party first secretaries and more than one-third of the department heads within the Central Committee apparatus. But Andropov's ability to reshape the top leadership was constrained by his poor health and the influence of his rival Chernenko, who had previously supervised personnel matters in the Central Committee.

Andropov's domestic policy leaned heavily toward restoring discipline and order to Soviet society. He eschewed radical political and economic reforms, promoting instead a small degree of candor in politics and mild economic experiments similar to those that had been associated with Kosygin in the mid-1960s. In tandem with such economic experiments, Andropov launched an anticorruption drive that reached high into the government and party ranks. Andropov also tried to boost labor discipline. Throughout the country, police stopped and questioned people in parks, public baths, and shops during working hours in an effort to reduce the rate of job absenteeism.

In foreign affairs, Andropov continued Brezhnev's policy of projecting Soviet power around the world. United States-Soviet relations, already poor since the late 1970s, began deteriorating more rapidly in March 1983, when President Ronald W. Reagan described the Soviet Union as an "evil empire . . . the focus of evil in the modern world," and Soviet spokesmen responded by attacking Reagan's "bellicose, lunatic anticommunism." In September 1983, the downing of a South Korean passenger airplane by a Soviet jet fighter resulted in the deaths of many United States citizens and further chilled United States-Soviet relations. United States-Soviet arms control talks on intermediate-range nuclear weapons in Europe were suspended by the Soviet Union in November 1983 in response to the beginning of United States deployments of intermediate-range nuclear weapons in Europe. The next month, Soviet officials also walked out of negotiations on reducing the number of strategic nuclear weapons.

Whether Andropov could have found a way out of the depths to which United States-Soviet relations had fallen, or whether he could have managed to lead the country out of its stagnation, will never be known. The Andropov regime was to last only fifteen months. The general secretary's health declined rapidly during the tense summer and fall of 1983, and he died in February 1984 after disappearing from public view for several months.

Andropov's most significant legacy to the Soviet Union was his discovery and promotion of Mikhail S. Gorbachev. Beginning in 1978, Gorbachev advanced in two years through the Kremlin hierarchy to full membership in the Politburo. His responsibilities for the appointment of personnel allowed him to make the contacts and distribute the favors necessary for a future bid to become general secretary. At this point, Western experts believed that Andropov was grooming Gorbachev as his successor. However, although Gorbachev acted as a deputy to the general secretary throughout Andropov's illness, Gorbachev's time had not yet arrived when his patron died early in 1984.

The Chernenko Interregnum

At seventy-two, Konstantin Chernenko was in poor health and unable to play an active role in policy making when he was chosen, after lengthy discussion, to succeed Andropov. But Chernenko's short time in office did bring some significant policy changes. The personnel changes and investigations into corruption undertaken by the Andropov regime came to an end. Chernenko advocated more investment in consumer goods and services and in agriculture. He also called for a reduction in the CPSU's micromanagement of the economy and greater attention to public opinion. However, KGB repression of Soviet dissidents also increased. Stalin was rehabilitated as a diplomat and a military leader, and there was discussion of returning the name Stalingrad to the city whose name had been changed back to Volgograd during the anti-Stalinist wave of the 1950s. The one major personnel change that Chernenko made was the firing of the chief of the General Staff, Nikolay Ogarkov, who had advocated less spending on consumer goods in favor of greater expenditures on weapons research and development.

Although Chernenko had called for renewed détente with the West, little progress was made toward closing the rift in East-West relations during his rule. The Soviet Union boycotted the 1984 Summer Olympics in Los Angeles, retaliating for the United States boycott of the 1980 Summer Olympics in Moscow. In the late summer of 1984, the Soviet Union also prevented a visit to West Germany by East German leader Erich Honecker. Fighting in Afghanistan also intensified, but in the late autumn of 1984 the United States and the Soviet Union did agree to resume arms control talks in early 1985.

The poor state of Chernenko's health made the question of succession an acute one. Chernenko gave Gorbachev high party positions that provided significant influence in the Politburo, and Gorbachev was able to gain the vital support of Foreign Minister Andrey Gromyko in the struggle for succession. When Chernenko died in March 1985, Gorbachev was well positioned to assume power.

The Gorbachev Era

In contrast to the uncertain handling of leadership vacancies in 1982 and 1984, upon the death of Chernenko the Politburo acted within hours to choose unanimously the healthy and relatively youthful Gorbachev as general secretary. In his speech before the Central Committee, Gorbachev announced that he would emphasize policies of labor discipline and increased productivity, calling for a "scientific and technological revolution" to revive heavy industry.

Gorbachev's First Year

Gorbachev quickly changed the composition of the highest CPSU and government bodies, eliminating Brezhnev-era appointees and promoting allies. Among the major changes in the July 1985 Central Committee plenum, Gorbachev promoted Georgian party first secretary Eduard Shevardnadze to full membership in the Politburo and nominated him as minister of foreign affairs, while Boris N. Yeltsin made his national political debut as one of two members added to the CPSU Secretariat. In December Yeltsin advanced again, this time as first secretary of the Moscow city committee of the party.

At the Twenty-Seventh Party Congress in February 1986, Gorbachev reaffirmed much of the existing CPSU doctrine and policies, giving little indication of future reforms. While calling for "radical reforms" in the economy, he merely reemphasized the need to increase production and to use more advanced technology in heavy industry. The new party program contained no surprises, and the congress made few changes in high-level CPSU bodies. Among the significant changes that did occur were the appointment to the Central Committee Secretariat of Aleksandr Yakovlev, an advocate of radical reform and the exposure of Stalin's crimes, and the promotion of Yeltsin to candidate membership in the Politburo. It was at this party gathering that Yeltsin first offended conservatives by denouncing the hidden privileges of the party elite.

New Thinking: Foreign Policy under Gorbachev

"New Thinking" was Gorbachev's slogan for a foreign policy based on shared moral and ethical principles to solve global problems rather than on Marxist-Leninist concepts of irreconcilable conflict between capitalism and communism. Rather than flaunt Soviet military power, Gorbachev chose to exercise political influence, ranging from the enhancement of diplomatic relations and economic cooperation to personally greeting the public in spur-of-the-moment encounters at home and abroad. Gorbachev used the world media skillfully and made previously unimaginable concessions in the resolution of regional conflicts and arms negotiations. In addition to helping the Soviet Union gain wider acceptance among the family of nations, the New Thinking's conciliatory policies toward the West and the loosening of Soviet control over Eastern Europe ultimately led to the collapse of communism and the end of the Cold War.

United States-Soviet relations began to improve soon after Gorbachev became general secretary. The first summit meeting between Reagan and Gorbachev took place in Geneva in November 1985. The following October, the two presidents discussed strategic arms reduction in Reykjavik, without making significant progress. In the late summer of 1987, the Soviet

Union yielded on the long-standing issue of intermediate-range nuclear arms in Europe; at the Washington summit that December, Reagan and Gorbachev signed the Intermediate-Range Nuclear Forces Treaty (INF Treaty—see Glossary), eliminating all intermediate- and shorter-range missiles from Europe. In April 1988, Afghanistan and Pakistan signed an accord, with the United States and Soviet Union as guarantors, calling for withdrawal of Soviet troops from Afghanistan by February 1989. The Soviet Union subsequently met the accord's deadline for withdrawal.

Gorbachev also assiduously pursued closer relations with China. Improved Sino-Soviet relations had long depended on the resolution of several issues, including Soviet support for the Vietnamese military presence in Cambodia, the Soviet occupation of Afghanistan, and the large numbers of Soviet troops and weapons deployed along China's northern border. Soviet moves to resolve these issues led the Chinese government to agree to a summit meeting with Gorbachev in Beijing in May 1989, the first since the Sino-Soviet split in the 1950s.

Soviet relations with Europe improved markedly during the Gorbachev period, mainly because of the INF Treaty and Soviet acquiescence to the collapse of communist rule in Eastern Europe during 1989–90. Since the Soviet-led invasion of Czechoslovakia in 1968, the Soviet Union had adhered to the Brezhnev Doctrine upholding the existing order in socialist states. Throughout the first half of Gorbachev's rule, the Soviet Union continued this policy, but in July 1989, in a speech to the Council of Europe (see Glossary), Gorbachev insisted on "the sovereign right of each people to choose their own social system," a formulation that fell just short of repudiating the Brezhnev Doctrine. By then, however, the Soviet Union's control over its outer empire already was showing signs of disintegration.

That June the communist regime in Poland had held relatively free parliamentary elections, and the communists had lost every contested seat. In Hungary the communist regime had steadily accelerated its reforms, rehabilitating Imre Nagy, the reform communist leader of the 1956 uprising, and dismantling fortifications along Hungary's border with Austria. At the end of the summer, East German vacationers began escaping to the West through this hole in the Iron Curtain. They also poured into the West German embassy in Prague. The East German state began to hemorrhage as thousands of its citizens sought a better and freer life in the West.

With the East German government under increasing pressure to stem the outflow, East Germans who stayed behind demonstrated on the streets for reform. When the ouster of East German communist party leader Honecker failed to restore order, the authorities haphazardly opened the Berlin Wall in November 1989. The same night the Berlin Wall fell, the Bulgarian Communist Party deposed its longtime leader, Todor Zhivkov. Two weeks later, Czechoslovakia embarked on its "Velvet Revolution," quietly deposing the country's communist leaders. At an impromptu summit meeting in Malta in December 1989, Gorbachev and United States president George H.W. Bush declared an end to the Cold War.

Throughout 1990 and 1991, Soviet-controlled institutions in Eastern Europe were dismantled. At the January 1990 Council for Mutual Economic Assistance (Comecon—see Glossary) summit, several East European states called for disbanding that fundamental economic organization of the Soviet empire, and the summit participants agreed to recast their multilateral ties. At the next summit, in January 1991, Comecon dissolved itself. In March 1990, Gorbachev called for converting the Warsaw Pact to a political organization, but instead the body officially disbanded in July 1991. Soviet troops were withdrawn from Central Europe over the next four years—from Czechoslovakia and Hungary by mid-1991 and from Poland in 1993. By midsummer 1990, Gorbachev and West German chancellor Helmut Kohl had worked out an agreement by which the Soviet Union acceded to a unified Germany within NATO.

By the June 1990 Washington summit, the United States-Soviet relationship had improved to such an extent that Gorbachev characterized it as almost a "partnership" between the two countries, and President Bush noted that the relationship had "moved a long, long way from the depths of the Cold War." In August 1990, the Soviet Union joined the United States in condemning the Iraqi invasion of Kuwait and supported United Nations resolutions to restore Kuwait's sovereignty. In November 1990, the United States, the Soviet Union, and most of the European states signed the Conventional Forces in Europe Treaty (CFE Treaty—see Glossary), making reductions in battle tanks, armored combat vehicles, artillery, and fighter aircraft "from the Atlantic Ocean to the Ural Mountains."

During the Gorbachev years, improvements in United States-Soviet relations were not without complications. For example, in 1991 Soviet envoy Yevgeniy Primakov's attempted mediation of the Kuwait conflict threatened to undercut the allied coalition's demand that Iraq withdraw unconditionally from Kuwait. After the signing of the CFE Treaty, disputes arose over Soviet compliance with the treaty and the Soviet military's efforts to redesignate weapons or move them so that they would not be subject to the treaty's terms. United States pressure led to the resolution of these issues, and the CFE Treaty entered into force in 1992. The Soviet crackdown on Baltic independence movements in January 1991 also slowed the improvement of relations with the United States.

By the summer of 1991, the United States-Soviet relationship showed renewed signs of momentum, when Bush and Gorbachev met in Moscow to sign the Strategic Arms Reduction Treaty (START I—see Glossary). Under START, for the first time large numbers of intercontinental ballistic missiles were slated for elimination. The treaty foresaw a reduction of approximately 35 percent in United States ballistic missile warheads and about 50 percent in Soviet ballistic missile warheads within seven years of treaty ratification. Gorbachev recently had attended the Group of Seven (G–7; see Glossary) summit to discuss his proposals for Western aid. Gorbachev also established diplomatic relations with Saudi Arabia, South Korea, and, in the waning days of the Soviet Union's existence, Israel.

Gorbachev's foreign policy won him much praise and admiration. For his efforts to reduce superpower tensions around the world, he was awarded the Nobel Prize for Peace in 1990. Ironically, as a result of frequent rumors of a conservative coup, the leader of the Soviet empire, whose previous rulers had kept opposition figures Lech Walesa and Andrey Sakharov from collecting their Nobel prizes, was unable to collect his own until June 1991.

Perestroika

Domestic policy in the Gorbachev era was conducted primarily under three programs, whose names became household words: *perestroika* (rebuilding—see Glossary), *glasnost* (public voicing—see Glossary), and *demokratizatsiya* (democratization—see Glossary). The first of these was applied primarily to the economy, but it was meant to refer to society in general. Over the course of Soviet rule, society in the Soviet Union had grown more urbanized, better educated, and more complex. Old methods of exhortation and coercion were inappropriate, yet Brezhnev's government had denied change rather than mastered it. Despite Andropov's efforts to reintroduce some measure of discipline, the communist superpower remained stagnant. Once Gorbachev began to call for bolder reforms, the "acceleration" gave way to *perestroika.*

Throughout the early years of his rule, Gorbachev spoke of *perestroika,* but only in early 1987 did the slogan become a full-scale campaign and yield practical results. At that time, measures were adopted on the formation of cooperatives and joint ventures (see The *Perestroika* Program, ch. 6). At a plenum of the CPSU Central Committee in January 1987, Gorbachev explicitly applied the label to his program to devolve economic and political control. In economics, *perestroika* meant greater leeway in decision making for plant managers, allowance for a certain degree of individual initiative and the chance to make a profit.

In January 1988, the new Law on State Enterprises went into effect, allowing enterprises to set many of their own prices and wages. Results were disappointing, however, because workers demanded steep wage increases. As the government printed more money, products fetched higher prices outside the official economy. Thus, goods usually sold in state stores at fixed prices quickly disappeared as speculators snatched them up or producers ceased making deliveries. By September 1988, many staple products could not be found even in Moscow. During 1988–89 Gorbachev also issued orders to the oblast party committees to cease interfering in the economy, and he cut the staffs of state committees and ministries involved in the economy in order to prevent them from further tampering with it. Without the state and the party to hold it together and guide it, the economy went into free-fall (see Unforeseen Results of Reform, ch. 6).

In the summer of 1990, Yeltsin, who had been elected chairman of the Supreme Soviet of the Russian Republic in May, backed a radical economic reform plan that would have spelled the end of many special interests within the party. Gorbachev in turn presented a much less extreme "Presidential Plan," which the Supreme Soviet of the Soviet Union passed. Yeltsin threatened that the Russian Republic would proceed with the initial radical plan, but shortly thereafter he suspended it.

In January 1991, Gorbachev replaced Prime Minister Nikolay Ryzhkov, who had become identified with the regime's economic failures, with Valentin Pavlov, an opponent of radical reform. Pavlov immediately created a mass panic by withdrawing large-denomination banknotes from circulation and limiting the public's ability to convert them to lower-denomination notes. The move, designed to reduce the vast sums of money circulating and to punish "black marketeers" hoarding large banknotes, only intensified the people's mistrust of the Soviet government. The economy continued to spiral downward, and Gorbachev and Shevardnadze had to ask the West for financial aid in order to stave off collapse. Gorbachev's retreat marked the last time economic reform dominated the agenda of a Soviet government.

Glasnost

As *perestroika* was failing, the two policies designed to promote it, *glasnost* and *demokratizatsiya,* were moving out of control. To mobilize the populace in support of *perestroika,* Gorbachev and his aide Aleksandr Yakovlev introduced *glasnost,* a policy of liberalized information flow aimed at publicizing the corruption and inefficiency of Brezhnev's policies and colleagues—qualities that the Russian public long had recognized and accepted in its leadership but that had never been acknowledged by the Kremlin. Like *perestroika,* this policy had unintended results. Gorbachev had meant to shape the new information emanating from his government in a way that would encourage political participation in support of his economic and social programs. Instead, the process of calling into question the whole Stalinist system inevitably led to questions about the wisdom of Lenin, the man who had allowed Stalin to rise in the first place. Because Lenin was the undisputed founder of the Soviet Union, the process then moved even farther as open questioning signified that somehow the Soviet Union, supposedly immune to such doubts, had lost its raison d'être.

The official announcement of *glasnost,* scheduled for mid-1986, was overtaken by an event that lent new meaning to the term. In April 1986, a reactor explosion at the Chernobyl' Nuclear Power Station, located in northern Ukraine, covered Belorussia, the Baltics, parts of Russia, and Scandinavia with a cloud of radioactive dust (see table 3, Appendix). The efforts to contain the accident and its attendant publicity were handled with exceptional ineptitude, setting *glasnost* back by six months as official news sources scrambled to control the flow of information to the public.

Despite the clumsy reaction of the Soviet government to the Chernobyl' episode, Gorbachev turned the accident in his favor by citing it as an example of the need for economic *perestroika*. Taking their cue from Gorbachev, throughout the Soviet Union the news media reported numerous examples of mismanagement of resources, waste, ecological damage, and the effects of this damage on public health. In the Soviet republics, these revelations had the unintended effect of accelerating the formation of popular fronts pushing for autonomy or independence.

The officially controlled phase of *glasnost* began the examination of "blank pages" in Soviet history. Literary journals filled up with long-suppressed works by writers such as Anna Akhmatova, Joseph Brodsky, Mikhail Bulgakov, Boris Pasternak, and Andrey Platonov. Newspapers and magazines carried stories of Stalin-era acts of repression, concentration camps, and mass graves. The works of Marxist theoretician Nikolay Bukharin, shot in 1938 for alleged rightist deviation, appeared. By revealing communist party crimes against the Soviet peoples, and the peasants in particular, *glasnost* further undermined Soviet federalism and contributed to the breakup of the Soviet Union.

Demokratizatsiya

By 1987 Gorbachev had concluded that introducing his reforms required more than discrediting the old guard. He changed his strategy from trying to work through the CPSU as it existed and instead embraced a degree of political liberalization. In January 1987, he appealed over the heads of the party to the people and called for *demokratizatsiya*, the infusion of "democratic" elements into the Soviet Union's sterile, monolithic political process. For Gorbachev, *demokratizatsiya* meant the introduction of multicandidate—not multiparty—elections for local party and soviet offices. In this way, he hoped to rejuvenate the party with progressive personnel who would carry out his institutional and policy reforms. The CPSU would retain sole custody of the ballot box.

Despite Gorbachev's intentions, the elements of a multiparty system already were crystallizing. In contrast to previous Soviet rulers, Gorbachev had permitted the formation of unofficial organizations. In October 1987, the newspaper of the CPSU youth, *Komsomol'skaya pravda*, reported that informal groups, so-called *neformaly*, were "growing as fast as mushrooms in the rain." The concerns of these groups included the environment, sports, history, computers, philosophy, art, literature, and the preservation of historical landmarks. In August 1987, forty-seven *neformaly* held a conference in Moscow without interference from the authorities. In fact, one of the unofficial attendees was Yeltsin. In early 1988, some 30,000 *neformaly* existed in the Soviet Union. One year later, their number had more than doubled. These informal groups begot popular fronts, which in turn spawned political parties. The first of those parties was the Democratic Union, formed in May 1988.

Gorbachev's Reform Dilemma

Gorbachev increasingly found himself caught between criticism by conservatives who wanted to stop reform and liberals who wanted to accelerate it. When one of these groups pressed too hard, Gorbachev resorted to political methods from the Brezhnev era. For example, when Yeltsin spoke out in 1987 against the slow pace of reform, he was stripped of his Politburo and Moscow CPSU posts. At the party meeting where Yeltsin was removed from his post, Gorbachev personally subjected him to verbal abuse reminiscent of the Stalin era.

Despite some setbacks, reform efforts continued. In June 1988, at the CPSU's Nineteenth Party Conference, the first held since 1941, Gorbachev launched radical reforms meant to reduce party control of the government apparatus. He again called for multicandidate elections for regional and local legislatures and party first secretaries and insisted on the separation of the government apparatus from party bodies at the regional level as well. In the face of an overwhelming majority of conservatives, Gorbachev still was able to rely on party discipline to force through acceptance of his reform proposals. Experts called the conference a successful step in promoting party-directed change from above.

At an unprecedented emergency Central Committee plenum called by Gorbachev in September 1988, three stalwart old-guard members left the Politburo or lost positions of power. Andrey Gromyko retired from the Politburo, Yegor Ligachev was relieved of the ideology portfolio within the Secretariat, and Boris Pugo replaced Politburo member Mikhail Solomentsev as chairman of the powerful Party Control Committee. The Supreme Soviet then elected Gorbachev chairman of the Presidium of the Supreme Soviet. These changes meant that the Secretariat, until that time solely responsible for the development and implementation of party policies, had lost much of its power.

Meaningful changes also occurred in governmental structures. In December 1988, the Supreme Soviet approved formation of a Congress of People's Deputies, which constitutional amendments had established as the Soviet Union's new legislative body. The Supreme Soviet then dissolved itself. The amendments called for a smaller working body of 542 members, also called the Supreme Soviet, to be elected from the 2,250-member Congress of People's Deputies. To ensure a communist majority in the new parliament, Gorbachev reserved one-third of the seats for the CPSU and other public organizations.

The March 1989 election of the Congress of People's Deputies marked the first time that voters of the Soviet Union ever chose the membership of a national legislative body. The results of the election stunned the ruling elite. Throughout the country, voters crossed off the ballot unopposed communist candidates, many of them prominent party officials, taking advantage of the nominal privilege of withholding approval of the listed candidates. However, the Congress of People's Deputies that emerged still contained 87 percent CPSU members. Genuine reformists won only some 300 seats.

In May the initial session of the Congress of People's Deputies electrified the country. For two weeks on live television, deputies from around the country railed against every scandal and shortcoming of the Soviet system that could be identified. Speakers spared neither Gorbachev, the KGB, nor the military. Nevertheless, a conservative majority maintained control of the congress. Gorbachev was elected without opposition to the chairmanship of the new Supreme Soviet; then the Congress of People's Deputies elected a large majority of old-style party apparatchiks to fill the membership of its new legislative body. Outspoken party critic Yeltsin obtained a seat in the Supreme Soviet only when another deputy relinquished his position. The first Congress of People's Deputies was the last moment of real control for Gorbachev over the political life of the Soviet Union.

In the summer of 1989, the first opposition bloc in the Congress of People's Deputies formed under the name of the Interregional Group. The members of this body included almost all of the liberal members of the opposition. Its cochairmen were Yeltsin, Andrey Sakharov, historian Yuriy Afanas'yev, economist

Boris Yeltsin appears before crowds during 1991 coup, Moscow.
Courtesy Michael E. Samojeden

Gavriil Popov, and academician Viktor Pal'm. Afanas'yev summed up the importance of this event, saying, "It is difficult for Gorbachev to get used to the thought that he is no longer the sole leader of *perestroika.* Other forces are already fulfilling that role." Afanas'yev had in mind not only the Interregional Group. He also was referring to the miners striking in Ukraine, Kazakstan, and Siberia, and the popular fronts in the Baltics, which were agitating for independence. In January 1990, a group of reformist CPSU members announced the formation of Democratic Platform, the first such CPSU faction since Lenin banned opposition groups in the 1920s.

A primary issue for the opposition was the repeal of Article 6 of the constitution, which prescribed the supremacy of the CPSU over all the institutions in society. Faced with opposition pressure for the repeal of Article 6 and needing allies against hard-liners in the CPSU, Gorbachev obtained the repeal of Article 6 by the February 1990 Central Committee plenum. Later that month, before the Supreme Soviet, he proposed the creation of a new office of president of the Soviet Union, to be elected by the Congress of People's Deputies rather than the people. Accordingly, in March 1990 Gorbachev was elected for the third time in eighteen months to a position equivalent to Soviet head of state. Former first deputy chairman of the Supreme Soviet Anatoliy Luk'yanov became chairman of the Supreme Soviet.

By the time of the Twenty-Eighth Party Congress in July 1990, the CPSU was regarded by liberals, intellectuals, and the general public as anachronistic and unable to lead the country. The CPSU branches in many of the fifteen Soviet republics began to split into large pro-sovereignty and pro-union factions, further weakening central party control.

In a series of humiliations, the CPSU had been separated from the government and stripped of its leading role in society and its function in overseeing the national economy. For seventy years, it had been the cohesive force that kept the union together; without the authority of the party in the Soviet center, the nationalities of the constituent republics pulled harder than ever to break away from the union.

Nationality Ferment

The issue Gorbachev understood least of all was that of the nationalities. Stalin, a Georgian, had been a commissar for nationalities, Khrushchev had built his career suppressing

Ukrainian nationalism, and Brezhnev had risen through his work in Ukraine and Moldavia. Gorbachev was a Russian whose political background included little time outside Russia proper. His policies of *glasnost* and *demokratizatsiya,* which loosened authoritarian controls over society, facilitated and fueled the airing of national grievances in the republics. As the peoples of the Soviet Union began to assert their respective national characters, they clashed with ethnic minorities within their republics and with Soviet authorities (see table 4, Appendix).

As early as 1985, reports of clashes between Estonian and Russian students began seeping into the West. By 1987 the Baltic republics all had developed popular fronts and were calling for the restoration of their independence. In November 1988, Estonia issued a declaration of sovereignty, claiming that all Estonian laws superseded Soviet laws. Lithuania and Latvia followed with their own declarations of sovereignty in May and July 1989, respectively.

The first major flare-up of ethnic violence came in December 1986, when Gorbachev replaced the first secretary of the Communist Party of Kazakstan with an ethnic Russian. A large crowd gathered in the Kazakstani capital, Alma-Ata (renamed Almaty after independence), to protest the move. When a force of 10,000 Soviet troops was deployed in Alma-Ata to disperse the crowds, demonstrators rioted.

In 1987 citizens of the autonomous oblast of Nagorno-Karabakh, a landlocked enclave of Armenians inside Azerbaijani territory, petitioned the Central Committee, requesting that the region be made part of the Armenian Republic. The Central Committee's rejection of this petition was followed by demonstrations in the autonomous oblast and similar displays of sympathy in Yerevan, the capital of Armenia. A promise by Gorbachev to establish a commission to study the Karabakh issue provoked outrage in Azerbaijan. After an anti-Armenian pogrom took place outside Baku, the Azerbaijani capital, large-scale fighting erupted between Armenians and Azerbaijanis, with both groups claiming to have been victimized by the Soviet regime in Moscow. In both republics, people rallied around popular fronts, which later became movements for independence from the Soviet Union. By the end of 1988, Georgia had developed its own popular front as well. In April 1989, more than twenty Georgians were killed as Soviet troops brutally dispersed demonstrators in the Georgian capital, Tbilisi.

Ethnic violence became a frequent occurrence throughout the Soviet Union—in Uzbekistan's Fergana Valley between Uzbeks and Meskhetian Turks, and in Georgia, when that republic's Abkhazian Autonomous Republic and South Ossetian Autonomous Oblast sought status as separate Soviet republics. Wherever Soviet forces intervened, they either failed to master the situation or contributed to the violence. In January 1990, the Armenian Supreme Soviet enacted a measure giving its own legislation supremacy over Soviet law. In the Armenian government's view, this meant that the Soviet demarcation of autonomous jurisdictions such as Nagorno-Karabakh no longer was binding on Armenians in that enclave. That vote caused rioting to break out in Azerbaijan. When the Soviet government imposed a state of emergency in the Azerbaijani capital of Baku and deployed 11,000 troops to end the anti-Armenian and anticommunist riots, at least eighty-three Azerbaijanis were killed.

As it had in the republics along the Soviet southern perimeter, national consciousness reawakened in Ukraine and Belorussia. In Ukraine the first popular front, the Ukrainian Popular Movement for Perestroika, known as Rukh, held its founding congress in September 1989. On March 4, 1990, Ukraine and Belorussia elected new legislatures. In both cases, opposition movements and coalitions made good showings despite ballot tampering and legal obstacles erected by authorities.

In March 1990, Lithuania declared independence, and Gorbachev imposed a partial economic blockade in response. That same year, riots also took place in Tajikistan and in the Kyrgyz city of Osh, leading to hundreds of deaths and the imposition of a state of emergency in several areas of Kyrgyzstan. The Moldavian government also declared a state of emergency when Gagauz separatists tried to declare the independence of their region, prompting Gorbachev to deploy troops from the Ministry of Internal Affairs in Moldavia. Violence between ethic Romanian Moldavians and Russians broke out in the Transnistria region of the republic a few weeks later. In October 1990, multiparty legislative elections in Georgia resulted in victory for the pro-independence bloc, and the new Supreme Soviet in Tbilisi began to move toward declaring independence. The major challenge to Gorbachev, however, came not from the non-Russian constituent republics but from Russia itself.

Tanks on Red Square during 1991 coup, Moscow
Courtesy Michael E. Samojeden

Many institutions that existed in the other constituent republics did not exist in Russia. Russia had no television stations addressing specifically Russian interests. Unlike other republics, the Russian Republic had no academy of sciences (see Glossary). It also lacked a ministry of internal affairs, a republic-level KGB, and a Russian communist party. Between 1918 and 1925, the CPSU had been called the Russian Communist Party (Bolshevik), but it was known as the All-Union Communist Party (Bolshevik) from 1925 until 1952 when Stalin changed the name to the Communist Party of the Soviet Union.

Such a policy by the communists had aimed at tying the Russian people as closely as possible to the Soviet state. The strategy was based on the belief that, lacking internal security forces and the political base that would be furnished by a Russian communist party, the Russians would be unlikely to engage in opposition to the system. By 1990, however, Russians were beginning to think differently. Although the predominantly Russian CPSU promoted policies of Russification to facilitate its rule and to placate the large Russian population, in the late 1980s average Russians increasingly saw the CPSU's efforts to co-opt and coerce the other nationalities as debasing the Russian language and culture and depleting Russian natural and financial resources. Gorbachev viewed this growing body of opinion with fear, but Yeltsin, who had been learning from the Baltic republics' struggle, saw it as providing an opportunity. Yeltsin took up the cause of Russia's rights within the union, making alliances with both Russian nationalists and Russian liberals.

In July 1990, Gorbachev finally acceded to the founding of the Russian Communist Party, which became a bastion of Russian nationalist conservatism and opposition to Gorbachev. The party failed to gain control of the Russian Republic's legislative bodies, however. Instead, it faced formidable competition in the Russian Congress of People's Deputies, which by that time was dominated by Yeltsin. Yeltsin's May 1990 election as chairman of the Russian Supreme Soviet had made him the de facto president of the Russian Republic, just as Gorbachev's election as chairman of the Supreme Soviet of the Soviet Union had made him de facto president of the country in 1989.

Yeltsin's new position enabled him to pose a serious challenge to Gorbachev. On June 11, 1990, Russia issued its declaration of sovereignty, the first republic to do so after the Baltic states. This move challenged Soviet jurisdiction over the very heart of the union. By the end of November, another nine republics had followed Russia's lead. The last instance of cooperation between Yeltsin and Gorbachev in this period was their effort in the fall of 1990 to draft a common economic policy. However, Gorbachev's desire to protect the favored position of the military-industrial establishment caused the effort to founder and the two men's relationship to deteriorate rapidly.

As the leader of the most populous and richest union republic, Yeltsin became the champion of all the republics' rights against control from the center. However, he did not advocate the breakup of the Soviet Union. Yeltsin originally hoped for the creation of a new federation anchored by bilateral and multilateral treaties between and among the union republics, with Russia as the preeminent member. When Soviet forces cracked down on the Baltic states in January 1991, Yeltsin went to Estonia in a show of support for the Baltics, signing agreements with the Baltic states that recognized their borders and promising assistance in the event of an attack on them from the Soviet center.

In June 1990, Gorbachev already had initiated talks on a new union treaty. The Supreme Soviet debated provisions of a draft union treaty throughout 1990 and into 1991. With tensions increasing between the center and the constituent republics, Gorbachev scheduled a national referendum in March 1991. The Baltic states, Armenia, Georgia, and Moldavia refused to participate. In the Russian referendum, Yeltsin included a question on the creation of a Russian presidential post. The overall referendum vote gave approval to Gorbachev's position on preserving the union, but the voters in Russia also approved Yeltsin's call for a president elected directly by the people. On June 12, Yeltsin, whose popularity had risen steadily as Gorbachev's plummeted, was elected president of the Russian Republic with 57 percent of the vote.

The August Coup and Its Aftermath

Gorbachev hoped that he could at least hold the union together in a decentralized form. However, in the eyes of the remaining CPSU conservatives, he had gone too far because his new union treaty dispersed too much of the central government's power to the republics. On August 19, 1991, one day before Gorbachev and a group of republic leaders were due to sign the union treaty, a group calling itself the State Emergency Committee attempted to seize power in Moscow. The group announced that Gorbachev was ill and had been relieved of his state post as president. Soviet Union vice president Gennadiy Yanayev was named acting president. The committee's eight members included KGB chairman Vladimir Kryuchkov, Internal Affairs Minister Pugo, Defense Minister Dmitriy Yazov, and Prime Minister Pavlov, all of whom had risen to their posts under Gorbachev.

Large public demonstrations against the coup leaders took place in Moscow and Leningrad, and divided loyalties in the defense and security establishments prevented the armed forces from crushing the resistance that Yeltsin led from Russia's parliament building. On August 21, the coup collapsed, and Gorbachev returned to Moscow.

Once back in Moscow, Gorbachev acted as if he were oblivious to the changes that had occurred in the preceding three days. As he returned to power, Gorbachev promised to purge conservatives from the CPSU. He resigned as general secretary but remained president of the Soviet Union. The coup's failure brought a series of collapses of all-union institutions. Yeltsin took control of the central broadcasting company and key economic ministries and agencies, and in November he banned the CPSU and the Russian Communist Party.

By December 1991, all of the republics had declared independence, and negotiations over a new union treaty began anew. Both the Soviet Union and the United States had recognized the independence of the Baltic republics in September. For several months after his return to Moscow, Gorbachev and his aides made futile attempts to restore stability and legitimacy to the central institutions. In November seven republics agreed to a new union treaty that would form a confederation called the Union of Sovereign States. But Ukraine was unrepresented in that group, and Yeltsin soon withdrew to seek additional advantages for Russia. In the absence of the CPSU, there was no way to keep the Soviet Union together. From Yeltsin's perspective, Russia's participation in another union would be senseless because inevitably Russia would assume responsibility for the increasingly severe economic woes of the other republics.

On December 8, Yeltsin and the leaders of Belarus (which adopted that name in August 1991) and Ukraine met at Minsk, the capital of Belarus, where they created the Commonwealth of Independent States (CIS—see Glossary) and annulled the 1922 union treaty that had established the Soviet Union. Another signing ceremony was held in Alma-Ata on December 21 to expand the CIS to include the five republics of Central Asia, Armenia, and Azerbaijan. Georgia did not join until 1993; the three Baltic republics never joined. On December 25, 1991, the Soviet Union ceased to exist. Exactly six years after Gorbachev had appointed Boris Yeltsin to run the Moscow city committee of the party, Yeltsin now was president of the largest successor state to the Soviet Union.

*   *   *

A number of comprehensive texts cover the history of the Soviet Union through 1985. Most worthy of recommendation to the nonspecialist is *A History of Russia and the Soviet Union* by David MacKenzie and Michael W. Curran. A thoughtful survey can be found in Geoffrey A. Hosking's *The First Socialist Society.* Other general works covering the Soviet period include Robert V. Daniels's *Russia: The Roots of Confrontation,* Donald W. Treadgold's *Twentieth Century Russia,* and Adam B. Ulam's *A History of Soviet Russia.* Several excellent books cover the various phases of Soviet history. The recognized classic on the revolutionary and Civil War period is William H. Chamberlin's *The Russian Revolution, 1917–1921.* Recommended for the Stalin era is *Stalin: The Man and His Era* by Adam B. Ulam. For Khrushchev, the reader is referred to Carl A. Linden's *Khrushchev and the Soviet Leadership, 1957–1964.* Khrushchev's two-volume memoir, *Khrushchev Remembers,* makes fascinating reading. Harry Gelman's *The Brezhnev Politburo and the Decline of Detente* treats the Brezhnev period in detail.

Significant overviews of all or part of the post-Brezhnev era include Donald R. Kelley's *Soviet Politics from Brezhnev to Gorbachev,* Stephen White's *Gorbachev in Power,* and John B. Dunlop's *The Rise of Russia and the Fall of the Soviet Empire.* Important articles include Amy Knight's "Andropov: Myths and Realities"; Marc Zlotnik's "Chernenko Succeeds"; and Jerry Hough's "Andropov's First Year." Other useful sources are Martin Malia's *The Soviet Tragedy: A History of Socialism in Russia, 1917–1991,* David Remnick's *Lenin's Tomb,* and Hélène Carrère d'Encausse's *The End of the Soviet Empire.* (For further information and complete citations, see Bibliography.)

Chapter 3. Physical Environment and Population

A peasant named Ivan rides a humpbacked pony, which has very long ears, on a quest to the Palace of the Moon (design from lacquer box made in village of Palekh).

CURVING AROUND THE NORTH POLE in a huge arc, Russia (the Russian Federation) spans almost half the globe from east to west and about 4,000 kilometers from north to south. Divided into eleven time zones, Russia is by far the world's largest country. It occupies much of Eastern Europe and northern Asia. The country's terrain is diverse, with extensive stands of forest, numerous mountain ranges, and vast plains. On and below the surface of the land are extensive reserves of natural resources that provide the nation with enormous potential wealth. Russia ranks sixth in the world in population, trailing China, India, the United States, Indonesia, and Brazil. The population is as varied as the terrain. Slavs (Russians, Ukrainians, and Belarusians) are the most numerous of the more than 100 European and Asiatic nationalities.

The Ural Mountains, which extend more than 2,200 kilometers from north to south, form the boundary separating the unequal European and Asian sectors of Russia. The continental divide continues another 1,375 kilometers from the southern end of the Ural Mountains through the Caspian Sea and along the Caucasus Mountains. Asian Russia is about as large as China and India combined, occupying roughly three-quarters of the nation's territory. But it is the European western quarter that is home to more than 75 percent of Russia's inhabitants. This acutely uneven distribution of human and natural resources is a striking feature of Russian geography and population. Despite government attempts to settle people in sparsely populated Asian areas abundant in resources, this imbalance persists. Meanwhile, depletion of water and fuel resources in the European part outpaces exploitation of resource-rich Siberia, the famously forbidding land stretching from the Urals to the Pacific Ocean. From 1970 to 1989, the campaign to settle and exploit western Siberia's plentiful fuel and energy supplies was expensive and only partially successful. Since *glasnost* (see Glossary), revelations of extreme environmental degradation have tarnished the image of the Siberian development program.

The Soviet and Russian environmental record has been generally dismal. Seven decades of Soviet rule left irradiated landscapes and marine ecosystems, a desiccated inland sea, befouled rivers, and toxic urban air as reminders of the consequences of seeking industrialization at any price. Russia and the other Soviet republics responded to the pressures of the long and costly Cold War by developing a defense-oriented, production-obsessed economy amid ecological devastation. Without a genuine environmental movement until its final years, the Soviet Union left in its wake an environmental catastrophe that will take decades and perhaps trillions of dollars to repair even partially.

During the Soviet period, natural and geopolitical phenomena shaped the characteristics of Russia's population. In that period, wars, epidemics, famines, and state-sanctioned mass killings claimed millions of victims. Before the 1950s, each decade brought to the population of the former Russian Republic some form of cataclysmic demographic event. Demographers have calculated that a total of 33.6 million people died from a brutal collectivization process and the famine that ensued in the 1920s and 1930s, the Great Terror of Joseph V. Stalin (in office 1927–53) in the 1930s, and World War II (see Transformation and Terror, ch. 2). Although those events ended more than fifty years ago, such disasters have had significant long-term effects. In age-groups above forty-five, women greatly outnumber men.

In the 1990s, demographers and policy makers are concerned about alarming trends such as a plummeting birthrate, increasing mortality among able-bodied males, and declining life expectancy. Another demographic concern is the millions of Russians remaining in the other newly independent countries of the former Soviet Union, called by policy makers the "near abroad." These Russians or their forebears resettled under a variety of conditions. Russian authorities fear that social and ethnic upheaval in those states could trigger the mass migration of Russians into the federation, which is ill equipped to integrate such numbers into its economy and society. By the early 1990s, Russia had already become the destination of greatly increased numbers of immigrants.

In 1995 the population of the Russian Federation was estimated at slightly less than 150 million. Whereas Russians had accounted for only about 50 percent of the Soviet Union's population, in Russia they are a clear majority of 82 percent of the population in what remains a distinctively multicultural, multinational state (see Ethnic Composition, ch. 4).

Physical Environment

Russia's topography includes the world's deepest lake and Europe's highest mountain and longest river. The topography and climate, however, resemble those of the northernmost portion of the North American continent. The northern forests and the plains bordering them to the south find their closest counterparts in the Yukon Territory and in the wide swath of land extending across most of Canada. The terrain, climate, and settlement patterns of Siberia are similar to those of Alaska and Canada.

Global Position and Boundaries

Located in the northern and middle latitudes of the Northern Hemisphere, most of Russia is much closer to the North Pole than to the equator. Individual country comparisons are of little value in gauging Russia's enormous size (slightly less than twice that of the United States) and diversity. The country's 17.1 million square kilometers include one-eighth of the earth's inhabited land area. Its European portion, which occupies a substantial part of continental Europe, is home to most of Russia's industrial and agricultural activity. It was here, roughly between the Dnepr River and the Ural Mountains, that the Russian Empire took shape after the principality of Muscovy gradually expanded eastward to reach the Pacific Ocean in the seventeenth century (see Expansion and Westernization, ch. 1).

Russia extends about 9,000 kilometers from westernmost Kaliningrad Oblast, the now-isolated region cut off from the rest of Russia by the independence of Belarus, Latvia, and Lithuania, to Ratmanova Island (Big Diomede Island) in the Bering Strait. This distance is roughly equivalent to the distance from Edinburgh, Scotland, east to Nome, Alaska. Between the northern tip of the Arctic island of Novaya Zemlya to the southern tip of the Republic of Dagestan on the Caspian Sea is about 3,800 kilometers of extremely varied, often inhospitable terrain.

Extending for 57,792 kilometers, the Russian border is the world's longest—and, in the post-Soviet era, a source of substantial concern for national security. Along the 20,139-kilometer land frontier, Russia has boundaries with fourteen countries. New neighbors are eight countries of the near abroad—Kazakstan in Asia, and, in Europe, Estonia, Latvia,

Lithuania, Belarus, Ukraine, Georgia, and Azerbaijan. Other neighbors include the Democratic People's Republic of Korea (North Korea), China, Mongolia, Poland, Norway, and Finland. And, at the far northeastern extremity, eighty-six kilometers of the Bering Strait separate Russia from a fifteenth neighbor—the United States (see fig. 6).

Approximately two-thirds of the frontier is bounded by water. Virtually all of the lengthy northern coast is well above the Arctic Circle; except for the port of Murmansk, which receives the warm currents of the Gulf Stream, that coast is locked in ice much of the year. Thirteen seas and parts of three oceans—the Arctic, Atlantic, and Pacific—wash Russian shores.

Administrative and Territorial Divisions

With a few changes of status, most of the Soviet-era administrative and territorial divisions of the Russian Republic were retained in constituting the Russian Federation. In 1996 there were eighty-nine administrative territorial divisions: twenty-one republics, six territories (*kraya*; sing., *kray*), forty-nine oblasts (provinces), one autonomous oblast, and ten autonomous regions (*okruga*; sing., *okrug*). The cities of Moscow and St. Petersburg have separate status at the oblast level. Population size and location have been the determinants for a region's designation among those categories. The smallest political division is the *rayon* (pl., *rayony*), a unit roughly equivalent to the county in the United States.

The republics include a wide variety of peoples, including northern Europeans, Tatars, Caucasus peoples, and indigenous Siberians. The largest administrative territorial divisions are in Siberia. Located in east-central Siberia, the Republic of Sakha, formerly known as Yakutia, is the largest administrative division in the federation, twice the size of Alaska. Second in size is Krasnoyarsk Territory, which is southwest of Sakha in Siberia. Kaliningrad Oblast, which is somewhat larger than Connecticut, is the smallest oblast, and it is the only noncontiguous part of Russia. The two most populous administrative territorial divisions, Moscow Oblast and Krasnodar Territory, are in European Russia.

Topography and Drainage

Geographers traditionally divide the vast territory of Russia into five natural zones: the tundra zone; the taiga, or forest, zone; the steppe, or plains, zone; the arid zone; and the moun-

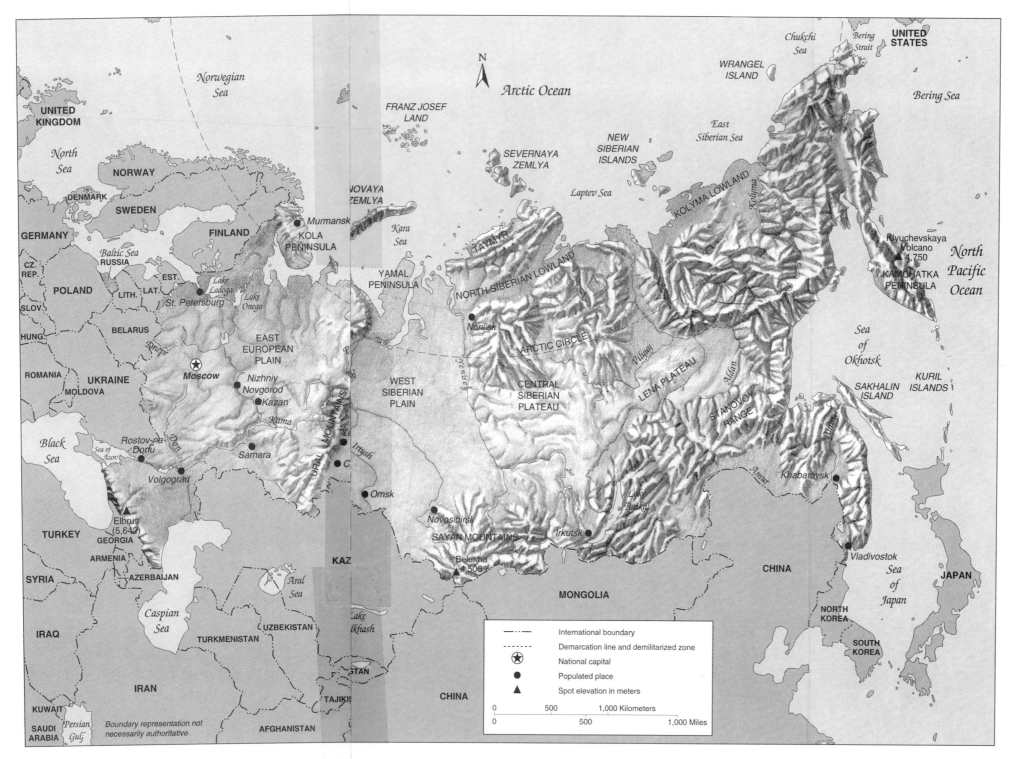

Figure 6. Topography and Drainage

128

tain zone. Most of Russia consists of two plains (the East European Plain and the West Siberian Plain), two lowlands (the North Siberian and the Kolyma, in far northeastern Siberia), two plateaus (the Central Siberian Plateau and the Lena Plateau to its east), and a series of mountainous areas mainly concentrated in the extreme northeast or extending intermittently along the southern border.

Topography

The East European Plain encompasses most of European Russia. The West Siberian Plain, which is the world's largest, extends east from the Urals to the Yenisey River. Because the terrain and vegetation are relatively uniform in each of the natural zones, Russia presents an illusion of uniformity. Nevertheless, Russian territory contains all the major vegetation zones of the world except a tropical rain forest.

About 10 percent of Russia is tundra, or treeless, marshy plain. The tundra is Russia's northernmost zone, stretching from the Finnish border in the west to the Bering Strait in the east, then running south along the Pacific coast to the northern Kamchatka Peninsula. The zone is known for its herds of wild reindeer, for so-called white nights (dusk at midnight, dawn shortly thereafter) in summer, and for days of total darkness in winter. The long, harsh winters and lack of sunshine allow only mosses, lichens, and dwarf willows and shrubs to sprout low above the barren permafrost (see Glossary). Although several powerful Siberian rivers traverse this zone as they flow northward to the Arctic Ocean, partial and intermittent thawing hamper drainage of the numerous lakes, ponds, and swamps of the tundra. Frost weathering is the most important physical process here, gradually shaping a landscape that was severely modified by glaciation in the last ice age. Less than 1 percent of Russia's population lives in this zone. The fishing and port industries of the northwestern Kola Peninsula and the huge oil and gas fields of northwestern Siberia are the largest employers in the tundra. With a population of 180,000, the industrial frontier city of Noril'sk is second in population to Murmansk among Russia's settlements above the Arctic Circle.

The taiga, which is the world's largest forest region, contains mostly coniferous spruce, fir, cedar, and larch. This is the largest natural zone of the Russian Federation, an area about the size of the United States. In the northeastern portion of this belt, long and severe winters frequently bring the world's coldest temperatures for inhabited areas. The taiga zone extends in a broad band across the middle latitudes, stretching from the Finnish border in the west to the Verkhoyansk Range in northeastern Siberia and as far south as the southern shores of Lake Baikal. Isolated sections of taiga also exist along mountain ranges such as the southern part of the Urals and in the Amur River valley bordering China in the Far East. About 33 percent of Russia's population lives in this zone, which, together with a band of mixed forest to its south, includes most of the European part of Russia and the ancestral lands of the earliest Slavic settlers.

The steppe has long been depicted as the typical Russian landscape. It is a broad band of treeless, grassy plains, interrupted by mountain ranges, extending from Hungary across Ukraine, southern Russia, and Kazakstan before ending in Manchuria. Most of the Soviet Union's steppe zone was located in the Ukrainian and Kazak republics; the much smaller Russian steppe is located mainly between those nations, extending southward between the Black and Caspian seas before blending into the increasingly desiccated territory of the Republic of Kalmykia. In a country of extremes, the steppe zone provides the most favorable conditions for human settlement and agriculture because of its moderate temperatures and normally adequate levels of sunshine and moisture. Even here, however, agricultural yields are sometimes adversely affected by unpredictable levels of precipitation and occasional catastrophic droughts.

Russia's mountain ranges are located principally along its continental divide (the Urals), along the southwestern border (the Caucasus), along the border with Mongolia (the eastern and western Sayan ranges and the western extremity of the Altay Range), and in eastern Siberia (a complex system of ranges in the northeastern corner of the country and forming the spine of the Kamchatka Peninsula, and lesser mountains extending along the Sea of Okhotsk and the Sea of Japan). Russia has nine major mountain ranges. In general, the eastern half of the country is much more mountainous than the western half, the interior of which is dominated by low plains. The traditional dividing line between the east and the west is the Yenisey Valley. In delineating the western edge of the Central Siberian Plateau from the West Siberian Plain, the Yenisey runs from near the Mongolian border northward into the Arctic Ocean west of the Taymyr Peninsula.

The Urals are the most famous of the country's mountain ranges because they form the natural boundary between Europe and Asia and contain valuable mineral deposits. The range extends about 2,100 kilometers from the Arctic Ocean to the northern border of Kazakstan. In terms of elevation and vegetation, however, the Urals are far from impressive, and they do not serve as a formidable natural barrier. Several low passes provide major transportation routes through the Urals eastward from Europe. The highest peak, Mount Narodnaya, is 1,894 meters, lower than the highest of the Appalachian Mountains.

To the east of the Urals is the West Siberian Plain, which covers more than 2.5 million square kilometers, stretching about 1,900 kilometers from west to east and about 2,400 kilometers from north to south. With more than half its territory below 500 meters in elevation, the plain contains some of the world's largest swamps and floodplains. Most of the plain's population lives in the drier section south of 55° north latitude.

The region directly east of the West Siberian Plain is the Central Siberian Plateau, which extends eastward from the Yenisey River valley to the Lena River valley. The region is divided into several plateaus, with elevations ranging between 320 and 740 meters; the highest elevation is about 1,800 meters, in the northern Putoran Mountains. The plain is bounded on the south by the Baikal mountain system and on the north by the North Siberian Lowland, an extension of the West Siberian Plain extending into the Taymyr Peninsula on the Arctic Ocean.

Truly alpine terrain appears in the southern mountain ranges. Between the Black and Caspian seas, the Caucasus Mountains rise to impressive heights, forming a boundary between Europe and Asia. One of the peaks, Mount Elbrus, is the highest point in Europe, at 5,642 meters. The geological structure of the Caucasus extends to the northwest as the Crimean and Carpathian mountains and southeastward into Central Asia as the Tian Shan and Pamirs. The Caucasus Mountains create an imposing natural barrier between Russia and its neighbors to the southwest, Georgia and Azerbaijan.

In the mountain system west of Lake Baikal in south-central Siberia, the highest elevations are 3,300 meters in the Western Sayan, 3,200 meters in the Eastern Sayan, and 4,500 meters at Mount Belukha in the Altay Range. The Eastern Sayan reach nearly to the southern shore of Lake Baikal; at the lake, there is an elevation difference of more than 4,500 meters between the nearest mountain, 2,840 meters high, and the deepest part of the lake, which is 1,700 meters below sea level. The mountain systems east of Lake Baikal are lower, forming a complex of minor ranges and valleys that reaches from the lake to the Pacific coast. The maximum height of the Stanovoy Range, which runs west to east from northern Lake Baikal to the Sea of Okhotsk, is 2,550 meters. To the south of that range is southeastern Siberia, whose mountains reach 2,800 feet. Across the Tatar Strait from that region is Sakhalin Island, where the highest elevation is about 1,700 meters.

Northeastern Siberia, north of the Stanovoy Range, is an extremely mountainous region. The long Kamchatka Peninsula, which juts southward into the Sea of Okhotsk, includes many volcanic peaks, some of which still are active. The highest is the 4,750-meter Klyuchevskaya Volcano, the highest point in the Russian Far East. The volcanic chain continues from the southern tip of Kamchatka southward through the Kuril Islands chain and into Japan. Kamchatka also is one of Russia's two centers of seismic activity (the other is the Caucasus). In 1994 a major earthquake largely destroyed the oil-processing city of Neftegorsk.

Drainage

Russia is a water-rich country. The earliest settlements in the country sprang up along the rivers, where most of the urban population continues to live. The Volga, Europe's longest river, is by far Russia's most important commercial waterway. Four of the country's thirteen largest cities are located on its banks: Nizhniy Novgorod, Samara, Kazan', and Volgograd. The Kama River, which flows west from the southern Urals to join the Volga in the Republic of Tatarstan, is a second key European water system whose banks are densely populated.

Russia has thousands of rivers and inland bodies of water, providing it with one of the world's largest surface-water resources. However, most of Russia's rivers and streams belong to the Arctic drainage basin, which lies mainly in Siberia but also includes part of European Russia. Altogether, 84 percent of Russia's surface water is located east of the Urals in rivers flowing through sparsely populated territory and into the Arctic and Pacific oceans. In contrast, areas with the highest concentrations of population, and therefore the highest demand for water supplies, tend to have the warmest climates and highest rates of evaporation. As a result, densely populated areas such as the Don and Kuban' river basins north of the Caucasus have barely adequate (or in some cases inadequate) water resources.

Forty of Russia's rivers longer than 1,000 kilometers are east of the Urals, including the three major rivers that drain Siberia as they flow northward to the Arctic Ocean: the Irtysh-Ob' system (totaling 5,380 kilometers), the Yenisey (4,000 kilometers), and the Lena (3,630 kilometers). The basins of those river systems cover about 8 million square kilometers, discharging nearly 50,000 cubic meters of water per second into the Arctic Ocean. The northward flow of these rivers means that source areas thaw before the areas downstream, creating vast swamps such as the 48,000-square-kilometer Vasyugane Swamp in the center of the West Siberian Plain. The same is true of other river systems, including the Pechora and the North Dvina in Europe and the Kolyma and the Indigirka in Siberia. Approximately 10 percent of Russian territory is classified as swampland.

A number of other rivers drain Siberia from eastern mountain ranges into the Pacific Ocean. The Amur River and its main tributary, the Ussuri, form a long stretch of the winding boundary between Russia and China. The Amur system drains most of southeastern Siberia. Three basins drain European Russia. The Dnepr, which flows mainly through Belarus and Ukraine, has its headwaters in the hills west of Moscow. The 1,860-kilometer Don originates in the Central Russian Upland south of Moscow and then flows into the Sea of Azov and the Black Sea at Rostov-na-Donu. The Volga is the third and by far the largest of the European systems, rising in the Valday Hills west of Moscow and meandering southeastward for 3,510 kilometers before emptying into the Caspian Sea. Altogether, the Volga system drains about 1.4 million square kilometers. Linked by several canals, European Russia's rivers long have been a vital transportation system; the Volga system still carries two-thirds of Russia's inland water traffic (see Transportation, ch. 6).

Russia's inland bodies of water are chiefly a legacy of extensive glaciation. In European Russia, the largest lakes are Ladoga and Onega northeast of St. Petersburg, Lake Peipus on the Estonian border, and the Rybinsk Reservoir north of Moscow. Smaller man-made reservoirs, 160 to 320 kilometers long, are on the Don, the Kama, and the Volga rivers. Many large reservoirs also have been constructed on the Siberian rivers; the Bratsk Reservoir northwest of Lake Baikal is one of the world's largest.

The most prominent of Russia's bodies of fresh water is Lake Baikal, the world's deepest and most capacious freshwater lake. Lake Baikal alone holds 85 percent of the freshwater resources of the lakes in Russia and 20 percent of the world's total. It extends 632 kilometers in length and fifty-nine kilometers across at its widest point. Its maximum depth is 1,713 meters. Numerous smaller lakes dot the northern regions of the European and Siberian plains. The largest of these are lakes Beloye, Topozero, Vyg, and Il'men' in the European northwest and Lake Chany in southwestern Siberia.

Climate

Russia has a largely continental climate because of its sheer size and compact configuration. Most of its land is more than 400 kilometers from the sea, and the center is 3,840 kilometers from the sea. In addition, Russia's mountain ranges, predominantly to the south and the east, block moderating temperatures from the Indian and Pacific oceans, but European Russia and northern Siberia lack such topographic protection from the Arctic and North Atlantic oceans.

Because only small parts of Russia are south of 50° north latitude and more than half of the country is north of 60° north latitude, extensive regions experience six months of snow cover over subsoil that is permanently frozen to depths as far as several hundred meters. The average yearly temperature of nearly all of European Russia is below freezing, and the average for most of Siberia is freezing or below. Most of Russia has only two seasons, summer and winter, with very short intervals of moderation between them. Transportation routes, including entire railroad lines, are redirected in winter to traverse rock-solid waterways and lakes. Some areas constitute important exceptions to this description, however: the moderate maritime climate of Kaliningrad Oblast on the Baltic Sea is similar to that of the American Northwest; the Russian Far East, under the influence of the Pacific Ocean, has a monsoonal climate that reverses the direction of wind in summer and winter, sharply differentiating temperatures; and a narrow, subtropical band of territory provides Russia's most popular summer resort area on the Black Sea.

Collective farm in Kultuk, at
southern tip of Lake Baikal
Courtesy Donna Kostka

In winter an intense high-pressure system causes winds to blow from the south and the southwest in all but the Pacific region of the Russian landmass; in summer a low-pressure system brings winds from the north and the northwest to most of the landmass. That meteorological combination reduces the wintertime temperature difference between north and south. Thus, average January temperatures are –8°C in St. Petersburg, –27°C in the West Siberian Plain, and –43°C at Yakutsk (in east-central Siberia, at approximately the same latitude as St. Petersburg), while the winter average on the Mongolian border, whose latitude is some 10° farther south, is barely warmer. Summer temperatures are more affected by latitude, however; the Arctic islands average 4°C, and the southernmost regions average 20°C. Russia's potential for temperature extremes is typified by the national record low of –94°C, recorded at Verkhoyansk in north-central Siberia and the record high of 38°C, recorded at several southern stations.

The long, cold winter has a profound impact on almost every aspect of life in the Russian Federation. It affects where and how long people live and work, what kinds of crops are grown, and where they are grown (no part of the country has a year-round growing season). The length and severity of the winter, together with the sharp fluctuations in the mean summer and winter temperatures, impose special requirements on many branches of the economy. In regions of permafrost, buildings must be constructed on pilings, machinery must be made of specially tempered steel, and transportation systems must be engineered to perform reliably in extremely low and extremely high temperatures. In addition, during extended periods of darkness and cold, there are increased demands for energy, health care, and textiles.

Because Russia has little exposure to ocean influences, most of the country receives low to moderate amounts of precipitation. Highest precipitation falls in the northwest, with amounts decreasing from northwest to southeast across European Russia. The wettest areas are the small, lush subtropical region adjacent to the Caucasus and along the Pacific coast. Along the Baltic coast, average annual precipitation is 600 millimeters, and in Moscow it is 525 millimeters. An average of only twenty millimeters falls along the Russian-Kazak border, and as little as fifteen millimeters may fall along Siberia's Arctic coastline. Average annual days of snow cover, a critical factor for agriculture, depends on both latitude and altitude. Cover varies from forty to 200 days in European Russia, and from 120 to 250 days in Siberia.

Environmental Problems

With the breakup of the Soviet Union in 1991, Moscow and the Russian Federation escaped direct responsibility for some of the world's worst environmental devastation because many of the Soviet disaster sites were now in other countries. Since then, however, the gravity and complexity of threats to Russia's own environment have become clear. During the first years of transition and reform, Russia's response to those conditions was sporadic and often ineffectual.

Only in the late 1980s and early 1990s was a linkage identified between the increasingly poor state of human health and the destruction of ecosystems in Russia. When that linkage was established, a new word was coined to sum up the environmental record of the Soviet era—"ecocide."

Environmental Conditions

In the Soviet system, environmentally threatening incidents such as the bursting of an oil pipeline received little or no public notice, and remedial actions were slow or nonexistent. Government officials felt that natural resources were abundant enough to afford waste, that the land could easily absorb any level of pollution, and that stringent control measures were an unjustifiable hindrance to economic advancement. In the 1990s, after decades of such practices, the government categorized about 40 percent of Russia's territory (an area about three-quarters as large as the United States) as under high or moderately high ecological stress. Excluding areas of radiation contamination, fifty-six areas have been identified as environmentally degraded regions, ranging from full-fledged ecological disaster areas to moderately polluted areas.

Major Crises

Dangerous environmental conditions came to the attention of the public in the Soviet Union under the *glasnost* policy of the regime of Mikhail S. Gorbachev (in office 1985–91), which liberated the exchange of information in the late 1980s. The three situations that gripped public attention were the April 1986 nuclear explosion at the Chernobyl' Nuclear Power Station in Ukraine, the long-term and ongoing desiccation of the Aral Sea between Uzbekistan and Kazakstan, and the irradiation of northern Kazakstan by the Semipalatinsk (present-day Semey) nuclear testing site. The overall cost of rectifying these three disasters is staggering, dwarfing the cost of cleanups elsewhere, such as the superfund campaign to eliminate toxic waste sites in the United States. By the time the Soviet Union dissolved in 1991, such conditions had become symbols of that system's disregard for the quality of the environment.

Since 1990 Russian experts have added to the list the following less spectacular but equally threatening environmental crises: the Dnepropetrovsk-Donets and Kuznets coal-mining and metallurgical centers, which have severely polluted air and water and vast areas of decimated landscape; the Urals industrial region, a strip of manufacturing cities that follows the southern Urals from Perm' in the north to Magnitogorsk near the Kazak border (an area with severe air and water pollution as well as radioactive contamination near the city of Kyshtym); the Kola Peninsula in the far northwest, where nonferrous mining and metallurgical operations, centered on the region's nickel reserves, have created air pollution that drifts westward across northern Scandinavia; the Republic of Kalmykia, where faulty agricultural practices have produced soil erosion, desertification, and chemical contamination; and the Moscow area, which suffers from high levels of industrial and vehicular air pollution and improper disposal of low-level radioactive waste. The experts also named five areas of severe water pollution: the Black Sea, the Caspian Sea, the Sea of Azov north of the Black Sea, the Volga River, and Lake Baikal.

Each of Russia's natural zones has suffered degradation of specific kinds. In the tundra, the greatest damage stems from extraction and transportation of mineral resources by crude techniques. In delicate tundra habitats, oil spills, leaks in natural gas pipelines, and the flaring of natural gas destroy northern marshland ecosystems, which take many years to purify naturally. Also endangered are reindeer grazing lands, upon which indigenous peoples traditionally have depended for their livelihood. In the permafrost zones that constitute about 40 percent of Russia's territory, lower air, water, and ground temperatures slow natural self-cleansing processes that mitigate contamination in warmer regions, magnifying the impact of every spill and leak.

In the taiga, or forest, zone, the overcutting of trees poses the greatest threat, particularly in northern European Russia, the Urals, and the Angara Basin in south-central Siberia. Uncontrolled mining operations constitute the second major source of damage in the taiga. In the broad-leafed forest zone, irrational land use has caused soil erosion on a huge scale. Urbanization and air and water pollution also are problems.

The forest-steppe and steppe regions are subjected to soil exhaustion, loss of humus, soil compacting, and erosion, creating an extremely serious ecological situation. The soil fertility of Russia's celebrated black-earth (chernozem—see Glossary) region has deteriorated significantly in the postwar period. Overgrazing is the main problem in the pasturage regions of the Russian steppe and has severely affected the Republic of Kalmykia in southwestern Russia and the region east of Lake Baikal. In Russia's limited semiarid and arid territories, poorly designed irrigation and drainage systems have caused salinization, pollution, and contamination of surface and underground water, but not to the degree that these problems exist in Uzbekistan, Turkmenistan, and Kazakstan.

Air Quality

Although reductions in industrial production caused air quality indexes to improve somewhat in the 1990s, Russia's air still rates among the most polluted in the world. According to one estimate, only 15 percent of the urban population breathes air that is not harmful. Experts fear that a return to full industrial production will mean even more dangerous levels of air pollution given Russia's current inefficient pollution control technology. Of the 43.8 million tons of pollutants discharged into the open air in 1993, about 18,000 industrial enterprises generated an estimated 24.8 million tons. Vehicle emissions added 19 million tons.

In the early 1990s, Russia's Hydrometeorological Service, which monitors air quality, reported that 231 out of 292 cities exceeded maximum permissible concentrations (MPCs) for particulate matter, sulfur dioxide, nitrogen oxides, or carbon monoxide. Pollution levels in eighty-six cities exceeded MPCs by a factor of ten. The most polluted cities are centers of heavy industry (ferrous and nonferrous metallurgy, petroleum refining, chemicals, and pulp production). Not surprisingly, the largest industrial cities head the list. In European Russia, these are Moscow and St. Petersburg; the Ural manufacturing centers of Yekaterinburg, Nizhniy Tagil, Magnitogorsk, and Ufa; and Astrakhan', Samara, and Volgograd on the lower Volga. In Asian Russia, the heaviest air pollution is in Omsk and Novokuznetsk in southwestern Siberia, Irkutsk on Lake Baikal, the Noril'sk industrial center in northwestern Siberia, and Khabarovsk in the Far East. Levels of airborne sulfur, nitrogen, and lead remain high.

Most vehicles in Russia continue to burn leaded fuel. In the early 1990s, motor vehicles contributed about one-third of total hazardous emissions in urban and industrial areas. Throughout the Soviet period and into the 1990s, trucks were the greatest vehicular polluters because privately owned vehicles were relatively scarce. As Russia adopts the culture of the privately owned vehicle, however, it is likely that transportation will increase its share of total emissions.

Water Quality

Soviet leaders took little action to protect the nation's inland bodies of water or surrounding oceans and seas from pollution, and Soviet planners gave low priority to risk-free treatment and transport of water. As a result, 75 percent of Russia's surface water is now polluted, 50 percent of all water is not potable according to quality standards established in 1992, and an estimated 30 percent of groundwater available for use is highly polluted. The most serious water pollution conditions relative to demand and availability of clean water are in the industrial regions of Krasnodar and Stavropol' territories north of the Caucasus, Rostov and Novosibirsk oblasts, the Republic of Chechnya, and the city of Moscow. In Krasnodar and Stavropol', inherent water shortages exacerbate the situation.

The quality of drinking water is a major concern. Poor water management standards have raised health concerns in many cities, and water safety also is doubtful in the countryside, where 59 percent of the population draws water from common wells affected by groundwater pollution. Unsanitary runoff from populated places and agricultural sites contributes heavily to pollution of sources that ultimately provide water for domestic use; the quality of drinking water declines noticeably during spring floods, when such runoff is heaviest. Rudimentary portable filters are not widely available. An estimated 8 percent of wastewater is fully treated prior to dumping in waterways; most water treatment facilities are obsolete, inefficient, and generally overwhelmed by the volume of material that now passes through them, but funding is not available to replace them.

In recent years, officials have identified many of Russia's rivers as carriers of waterborne diseases, epidemics of which were especially frequent in 1995. In July 1995, Moscow city health officials reported an outbreak of cholera-causing bacteria in the Moscow River. Officials have warned of increasing outbreaks of sewage-related diseases—including cholera, salmonella, typhoid fever, dysentery, and viral hepatitis—in many other Russian rivers. Citizens have been instructed to boil all water before use. In some areas, clean water is so scarce that water is imported from other regions. The highest consumption of imported water is in the republics of Sakha (Yakutia) and Kalmykia, Kamchatka and Magadan oblasts in the Far East, and Stavropol' Territory.

Among the chemicals and contaminants dumped frequently and indiscriminately have been compounds containing heavy metals, phenols, pesticides, and pathogenic bacteria. Chemical pollution was dramatized when fires ignited spontaneously on the Iset' River in Sverdlovsk (present-day Yekaterinburg) in 1965 and on the Volga River in 1970. Russian agriculture, like industry subject to centralized control and quota fulfillment in the Soviet era, continues to cause severe water pollution by overuse and improper handling and storage of toxic chemical fertilizers, herbicides, and pesticides. During the Soviet era, dioxin, a carcinogen, was used routinely as an agricultural

*Power plant discharging effluents into Amur River and into
atmosphere, Khabarovsk
Courtesy Donna Kostka*

insecticide, and it heavily tainted rural wells. In 1990 Soviet
authorities declared that dioxin, which enters the body
through drinking water, was the most serious health threat
from pollution.

In 1992 the Russian Federation's Committee on Fishing
reported 994 cases in which bodies of water were "completely
contaminated" by agricultural runoff. Runoff from fields
results in fish kills and groundwater contamination. Among the
largest river systems in European Russia, the Volga and Dnepr
rivers suffer from acute eutrophication—depletion of dissolved
oxygen by overnutrition of aquatic plant life—which distorts
natural life cycles. Large-scale fish kills have occurred in the
Kama, Kuban', North Dvina, Oka, and Ural rivers.

Pollution in the Gulf of Finland, the easternmost extension
of the Baltic Sea, includes untreated sewage from St. Peters-

burg, where heavy metals and other chemical substances are not properly removed prior to dumping. In late 1995, St. Petersburg city officials signed an agreement with a French water purification company to process the city's drinking water; the Finns hope that such a move also will improve the overall quality of the city's effluent water.

Water quality in Lake Ladoga, Europe's largest freshwater lake, came to the attention of government authorities in the mid-1990s. Factories on the lake, which is just east of St. Petersburg, have discharged tons of heavy metals and other toxic substances into local rivers. The shores of Lake Ladoga and Lake Onega to its east have been storage sites for fertilizers, livestock waste, and chemicals as well as for radioactive military waste. When local rivers emanating from the lakes reach the Gulf of Finland, their chemical burden changes the oxygen balance in the gulf. Similar situations affect the Arctic Ocean, into which Siberian rivers flow after passing through numerous industrial and power-generating centers, and the Baltic Sea, into which large amounts of military waste and chemical weapons were discarded from Poland and the Baltic republics during the Soviet era.

Marine biologists report that only five species of fish remain in the Black Sea, which once was a highly diverse marine ecosystem with twenty-six species. Between 1985 and 1994, the total fish catch in the Black Sea dropped from 675,000 to 45,000 kilograms. According to environmentalists, the entire sea is in danger of "dying" because only about 10 percent of its near-surface volume contains enough oxygen to support life. Deoxygenation is caused primarily by large-scale infusions of hydrogen sulfide, which comes mainly from the Danube, Don, South Bug, and Dnepr rivers that flow into the sea from the north and the west. Large amounts of mercury, cadmium, arsenic, and oil have been identified as well. In 1992 the littoral states of Bulgaria, Georgia, Romania, Russia, Turkey, and Ukraine signed an agreement to take specific measures against pollution of the Black Sea and the tributary rivers that flow through their territory. Conflicting goals and positions among the states involved, however, have hindered environmental cooperation.

The Caspian Sea is also beset with chemical pollution and the loss of indigenous species, and it now faces the danger that 1 million hectares of its coastline, including Russia's Volga River delta, will be flooded. According to a 1996 report,

Public beach on Amur River, downstream from polluting power plant,
Khabarovsk
Courtesy Donna Kostka

300,000 hectares in Dagestan already had been inundated. By 1993 the average water level of the sea had risen by more than two meters. Scientists blame the rise on the 1977 Soviet damming of the Garabogaz Gulf on the Caspian coast of Turkmenistan. Previously, the waters of the gulf intermixed with those of the Caspian, acting as the main thermal regulator and volume stabilizer of the larger body. In 1996 the Russian government allocated US$38 million for Caspian Sea conservation, to be matched by US$34 million from local budgets.

Water quality problems are most severe in European Russia, especially in the Volga Basin, where about 60 million people live. Of all water withdrawn from natural sources in Russia, 33 percent comes from the Volga. About half of that water returns to the Volga as polluted discharge, accounting for 37 percent of the total volume of such material generated in Russia. The Volga's water does not meet the norms for drinking water and is unsuitable for fish farming or irrigation. In the late 1980s and early 1990s, numerous government committees were formed to clean up the Volga. Few of the resulting restorative programs have been implemented, however, and the Volga remains under ecological stress.

Lake Baikal, a water resource of world importance located in south-central Siberia, long was the focal point of Soviet environmental efforts to end the pollution that the pulp and paper plants caused in the lake's watershed. A series of comprehensive Soviet and post-Soviet plans yielded limited success in protecting the lake's water and shoreline, which gradually have succumbed to chemical stresses. In 1995 the World Bank (see Glossary) and the European Union (EU—see Glossary) granted funds for cleaning up Lake Baikal, and in 1996 the Gore-Chernomyrdin Commission announced United States plans to aid Russia in overhauling paper plants in the Baikal region (see The United States, ch. 8).

Soil and Forests

Russia devotes about 10 percent of its land to agriculture, but land quality is declining. Erosion carries away as much as 1.5 billion tons of topsoil every year (see Agriculture, ch. 6). In the past twenty-five years, Russia's arable land area has decreased by an estimated 33 million hectares, with much of that loss attributable to poor land management. Experts fear that agricultural land management may deteriorate further under Russia's new land privatization as individual farmers try to squeeze short-term profit from their new property. In the early 1990s, an estimated 50 percent of arable land needed remediation and improved management for agricultural productivity to improve. Russia's southern regions, especially the Republic of Kalmykia, are losing about 6,400 hectares of agricultural land yearly to desertification. To the east, desiccation of the Aral Sea and expansion of the Qizilqum Desert in Kazakstan have a climatic drying effect that exacerbates desertification in Russia to the north and west.

In Russia an estimated 74 million hectares of agricultural land have been contaminated by industrial toxic agents, pesticides, and agricultural chemicals. Considerable land also is lost in the extraction of mineral resources. Unauthorized dumping of hazardous industrial, chemical, and household waste takes land out of production. Flooding is a problem near the Cas-

*High-rise apartment buildings on eroding sandstone banks of
Amur River, Khabarovsk
Courtesy Floyd Reichman*

pian Sea and in Stavropol' Territory, where the construction of
reservoirs has removed land from use.

In 1994 about 22 percent of the world's forests and 50 percent of its coniferous forests were in Russia, covering an area
larger than the continental United States. Of the 764 million
hectares of forested area, 78 percent was in Siberia and the Far
East. At that time, vast stands of Siberian forest remained
untouched. Such broad expanses have an important role in the
global carbon cycle and in biodiversity. In the 1990s, the atmosphere of economic stress and political decentralization has the
potential to accelerate drastically Russia's rate of deforestation
and land degradation, especially in remote areas. Environmentalists fear that timber sales will be used as a short-term stimu-
lus to regional economies; already, Chinese, Mongolian, and

North and South Korean companies have taken advantage of looser restrictions and the critical need for hard currency (see Glossary) to begin clear-cutting Siberian forests. Timber harvesting by Russian firms decreased dramatically in the 1990s, from 375 million cubic meters in 1989 to 110 million cubic meters in 1996.

Aleksey Yablokov, head of the nongovernmental Center for Russian Environmental Policy, has estimated that Siberia is losing 16 million hectares of forest annually to cutting, pollution, and fires—an amount six times the official government estimate and higher than the rate of loss in the Amazon rain forests. Fires, which normally improve biodiversity and long-term stability, cause excessive damage because of poor fire control measures. Large tracts of Russian forest, most notably 136,000 hectares in the vicinity of Chernobyl', have suffered radioactive contamination, which also increases the likelihood of forest fires. Because forests cannot be decontaminated, the distribution of radioactive particles in the trees remains constant over many years.

Inefficient lumbering procedures cause unnecessary loss of timber; as much as 40 percent of Russia's harvested trees never go to the mill, and unsystematic clear-cutting prevents productive regrowth. Forest management has improved gradually in the post-Soviet era. In 1993 the Supreme Soviet, then the lower house of Russia's parliament, passed the Principles of the Forest, national laws that include guidelines for management and protection. Because implementation of these laws has been quite slow, many regional jurisdictions have adopted their own management standards.

Acid rain from European and Siberian industrial centers and from power generation plants has reduced the Siberian forests by an estimated 730,000 hectares. Hydroelectric dams on Siberian rivers raise significantly the temperature of air and water, destabilizing the growing conditions of adjacent forests. Because of the enormous oxygen production and carbon dioxide absorption of the Russian forests (a capacity estimated to be second only to that of the Amazon rain forest), removal of large sections of those forests would have a drastic effect on the quality of land in Russia and the quality of air over the entire world.

Radioactive Contamination

Beginning with *glasnost* in the mid-1980s and continuing

with the establishment of an independent Russia in 1991, much disturbing information has become available about Soviet and Russian nuclear practices and mishaps. These disclosures have included deadly accidents on land and aboard naval vessels, a network of secret cities designed specifically for nuclear weapons production and material processing, detonation of nuclear blasts for "peaceful" purposes, and the dumping of nuclear waste at sea and its injection into subterranean cavities.

More than any other event, the Chernobyl' disaster prompted greater scrutiny and candor about Soviet nuclear programs. Although much of the contamination from Chernobyl' occurred in the now-independent countries of Ukraine and Belarus, the present-day Russian Federation also received significant fallout from the accident. Approximately 50,000 square kilometers of the then Russian Republic, particularly the oblasts of Bryansk, Orel, Kaluga, and Tula, were contaminated with cesium-137 (see table 3, Appendix). The total population of the nineteen oblasts and republics receiving fallout from Chernobyl' was 37 million in 1993.

The Soviet, now Russian, navy's disposal and accidental venting of radioactive materials pose particular problems. Beginning in 1965, twenty nuclear reactors, most with their fuel rods still inside, were dumped from nuclear submarines and an icebreaker into the Arctic Ocean north of Russia. In 1994 the Oslo-based Bellona Foundation estimated that radioactive dumping in the Kara Sea north of western Siberia and adjacent waters constituted two-thirds of all the radioactive materials that ever have entered the world's oceans. In 1996 Bellona identified fifty-two decommissioned Russian nuclear submarines that were scheduled for scrapping but were still afloat near Murmansk with nuclear fuel on board; a timetable for dismantling them has fallen far behind.

Japan has been engaged in a long struggle to stop Russia's Pacific Fleet from dumping radioactive waste into the Sea of Japan (see Japan, ch. 8). In 1994 Russia complied with Japan's demand to cease dumping entirely; after a long series of negotiations, in January 1996 Russia and Japan agreed on construction of a floating nuclear waste recycling plant and expansion of an existing facility to process nuclear waste generated by the Pacific Fleet. The United States and Japan are to fund the first project, and the United States and Norway the second. In the mid-1990s, Russia still was seeking methods of storing and disposing of first-generation radioactive waste in many regions, including the European Arctic. Under these conditions, experts predict that the country will be hard-pressed to comply with the requirements of the arms reduction agreements for disposal of waste from thousands of nuclear weapons scheduled for destruction later in the 1990s (see Nuclear Arms Issues, ch. 9). On the eve of the Group of Seven (G–7; see Glossary) nuclear safety summit meeting in Moscow in April 1996, Aleksey Yablokov and the Bellona Foundation complained that continued operation of Chernobyl'-type reactors presented an unacceptable risk to the Russian public. The Western leaders at the G–7 meeting generally muted their criticism on the issue to avoid embarrassing President Boris N. Yeltsin during his presidential campaign. Yablokov announced the formation of a new lobby of Russian nongovernmental organizations for greater government disclosure on the issue.

The Response to Environmental Problems

In the half-decade that began with the Chernobyl' disaster and culminated in the dissolution of the Soviet Union, substantial changes took place in the public's attitudes toward environmental crises. The public engaged in unprecedented discussion about the dangers the state's environmental policies posed to public health. According to surveys, the public's main concerns were local problems having immediate impact, such as polluted water supplies, violation of public health regulations, and air pollution. Russians were much less interested in more general and fundamental issues such as loss of biodiversity, deforestation, and acid rain. In 1989 a national poll placed environmental pollution fifth among citizens' major concerns, but only one-third of respondents expressed their willingness to sacrifice economically to improve the situation. Nevertheless, a substantial green movement arose in the late 1980s. Fragmented by disagreement over politicization and national versus local agendas, parts of the movement branched into other areas of activism such as human rights and regional autonomy, and no single green party emerged.

Public enthusiasm for environmental improvement followed the same curve as enthusiasm for democratic and economic reform; by 1992 economic hardship began to wilt the zeal for reform, and the vast majority of Russians remained skeptical of political change throughout the early 1990s. As worsening economic conditions heightened short-term insecurity, issues such as environmental protection paled, especially in cases where the shutting of a polluting plant threatened the livelihood of a town or city.

Politicians and government policy generally followed the same pattern as citizen concern in the early and mid-1990s. In 1988 the initial groundswell of environmental concern stimulated the Gorbachev government to form the State Committee for the Protection of Nature (Gosudarstvennyy komitet po okhrane prirody—Goskompriroda), an agency given broad responsibilities similar to those of the United States Environmental Protection Agency. In 1992 the Russian Federation used Goskompriroda as the model for a new Ministry of Environmental Protection and Natural Resources, which received a similar mandate.

In the 1990 elections for Russia's local legislative bodies (soviets) and the republic-level Congress of People's Deputies, virtually every candidate, whether democrat or communist, made the environment a major campaign issue, thus promoting the electorate's awareness that severe problems exist. In 1990 Yablokov was appointed to an influential position as environmental adviser to the president of Russia (a position he continued to hold in the Russian Federation after 1991), and powerful environmental commissions were formed in the local soviets of Moscow and other cities. In the early 1990s, such soviets blocked many large, environmentally dubious projects of the central government, such as the activation of the Northern Thermoelectric Center near Moscow, and of various local jurisdictions tied to national monopolies, such as the State Construction Committee (Goskomstroy) and the Ministry of Atomic Energy (Minatom).

By the time of the parliamentary elections of 1993, however, the political atmosphere had changed. Most environmental activists either abstained from political activity or merged their single-issue efforts with coalitions that might exceed the 5 percent threshold needed for a party to gain representation in the State Duma. Neither strategy had political impact because environmental views were lost in the coalitions' agendas. Among the major parties, only the Yabloko coalition had a separate department for environmental issues. Another major reform-minded party, Russia's Choice, which gained seventy-six seats in 1993, advocated environmental protection through market reform; Russia's minister of environmental protection and natural resources, former communist functionary Viktor Danilov-

Danil'yan, was a member of Russia's Choice. However, neither in the campaign nor after assuming office did Danilov-Danil'yan press the party's nominal program of tax stimulation for energy conservation and pollution control. In the 1995 legislative elections, Russia's Democratic Choice (the new name of Russia's Choice) declined dramatically, gaining only nine seats in the new State Duma, although Danilov-Danil'yan remained head of his ministry.

A crucial event was the 1992 appointment of Viktor Chernomyrdin as prime minister to replace Yegor Gaydar, head of Russia's Choice. Chernomyrdin, former head of the State Natural Gas Company (Gazprom), has made the reinvigoration of Russian industry, and especially the fuel industries, a top priority. A second important event was President Yeltsin's dismissal of the local soviets in his 1993 struggle to consolidate presidential power and curb the growth of regional autonomy. The local dumas that replaced the soviets have been much more solicitous of local economic ambitions.

In the parliamentary elections of 1995, the Kedr (Cedar) coalition (which also had presented a slate in the 1993 election) was the only group among forty-three parties calling itself environmental; however, the party was dominated by businesspeople rather than environmental activists. Kedr candidates received less than 1 percent of the vote and no seats in the new State Duma. Some nongovernmental groups have continued to have political impact, and in 1995 Yablokov hailed a new wave of the green movement. The annual Days of Defense Against Environmental Hazards, which began modestly in 1993, became a national phenomenon the next year and included a speech by President Yeltsin. Public organizations played a major role in establishing the All-Russian Congress for the Protection of Nature under the Ministry of Environmental Protection and Natural Resources. The national congress is preceded each year by eighty-nine regional congresses, one in each of Russia's political subdivisions. In late 1993, the new Commission on Ecological Security went into operation under the Security Council, with the assignment of assessing the most serious environmental problems as they endanger national security (see The Security Council, ch. 8). Although it was formed with great fanfare, the commission received little funding in its first three years.

In 1994 the Ministry of Environmental Protection and Natural Resources employed about 21,000 people. In addition, the

Research vessels on Lake Baikal
Courtesy Paul Hearn

official Russian environmental protection system included environmental agencies in each of the eighty-nine subnational jurisdictions and also several state committees responsible for the use of mineral, water, and forest resources. In 1993 some 65 percent of the ministry's expenditures went for protection of water quality and 26 percent for protection of air quality. However, the ministry's actions against major polluters remained infrequent despite the 1993 constitution's guarantee of the people's right to a clean environment, to receive information about environmental conditions, and to get compensation for damage to health and property that results from negative ecological conditions. In 1995 Danilov-Danil'yan reported that only twenty-two cases had been brought against alleged polluters in the previous year.

In 1993 Russia's total investment in environmental preservation was about US$2.3 billion, less than 4 percent of the national budget category entitled "industrial construction," in which environmental expenditures are included. That figure was 20 percent less than the 1990 investment. The structure of environmental spending remained substantially the same as it was in 1980: some 58 percent went for protection of water resources, 24 percent for prevention of air pollution, 7 percent for forest management, and only 0.04 percent for nature preserves and species protection (see table 5, Appendix). In most subnational jurisdictions, water pollution receives the most investment because of uniformly serious water conditions.

In 1993 state enterprises and organizations paid 39 percent of environmental costs. As state budget deficits occurred in subsequent years, the amounts from those sources decreased, but the percentage did not because the only other funding sources were local budgets and private environmental foundations. Budgets of subnational jurisdictions often suffered the same deficits as the federal government, and private organizations contributed only 1.4 percent of total investments in 1993. Meanwhile, local economic conditions have combined with weak enforcement funding to promote corruption among local authorities and to encourage poaching, especially in the fishing industry.

In 1991 Yeltsin signed Russia's first comprehensive environmental law, On Environmental Protection. Modeled after a similar Soviet law, it made many general statements about the environmental rights of citizens without setting any specific goals. The law also defined numerous environmental functions for every level of government as well as for citizens and nongovernmental organizations, and it specified environmental regulation of every aspect of society, from health resorts to electromagnetic radiation. The sheer inclusiveness of such provisions made practical enforcement impossible. The other major obstacle to enforcement has been the slow development of Russia's judiciary, which was only a rubber-stamp branch of government in the Soviet system and which totally lacked experience in the area of environmental law (as well as the general theory of Western-style jurisprudence) (see The Criminal Justice System, ch. 10). Before any enforcement could begin, the 1991 law stipulated that numerous other laws had to be passed. The same complex situation has existed at the regional and local government levels. In early 1995, the State Duma passed a law requiring environmental impact assessments for a variety of construction and development projects, including large-scale industrial development, large-scale use of natural resources, city planning, creation of new technology and materials, and modification of existing commercial facilities.

Russia is a signatory of most major international environmental treaties. Among them are the International Tropical Timber Agreement (1983), the Convention on International Trade in Endangered Species (CITES, 1973), the United Nations Convention on the Law of the Sea (1982), and the Montreal Protocol controlling substances harmful to the ozone layer.

Population

The population in what is now the Russian Federation has undergone several major shocks in the twentieth century, including large-scale rural famines in the 1920s and 1930s and the loss of millions of citizens in World War II. According to demographic experts, the early 1990s may be the start of a more gradual but potentially powerful new shift. Beginning in 1992, the population has suffered a net loss that is projected to continue at least through the first decade of the next century. This phenomenon is caused by a combination of economic, political, and ethnographic factors.

In the mid-1990s, Russians constituted about 82 percent of the population of the Russian Federation, and they dominate virtually all regions of the country except for the North Caucasus and parts of the middle Volga region (see Minority Peoples and Their Territories, ch. 4). The major ethnic minorities are Tatars (3.8 percent), Ukrainians (3.0 percent), Chuvash (1.2 percent), Bashkirs (0.9 percent), Belarusians (0.8 percent), and Mordovians (0.7 percent). The total population of the twenty-one ethnic republics, all designated for one or more of the minority groups in the federation, was about 24 million. However, only in eight of the republics was the population of the titular group (or groups, in the case of Kabardino-Balkaria and Karachayevo-Cherkessia) larger than the population of Russians, and Russians constitute more than half the population in nine republics. One other ethnic jurisdiction, the Khanty-Mansi Autonomous Region in the West Siberian Plain, has a population of more than 1 million; however, two-thirds of the autonomous region's population are Russian settlers, and the Khanty and Mansi, the tribes for which the region is named, together constitute less than 2 percent of the population.

Demographic Conditions

The range of estimates for Russia's 1995 population is between 147.5 and 149.9 million. Roughly 78 percent of Russia's population lives in the European part of Russia; most of the industrial cities with over 1 million inhabitants are located in the European part. In order of size, the largest Russian cities are Moscow (8.7 million people in 1992), St. Petersburg (4.4 million), Novosibirsk (1.4 million), Nizhniy Novgorod (1.4 million), Yekaterinburg (1.4 million), Samara (1.2 million), Omsk (1.2 million), Chelyabinsk (1.1 million), and Kazan' (1.1 million). Of those cities, only Novosibirsk and Omsk are located east of the Urals. In 1995 Russia's population density was 8.7 persons per square kilometer, but distribution varies from more than 200 persons per square kilometer in parts of European Russia, to 0.03 person per square kilometer in the Evenk Autonomous Region of Siberia.

According to most sources, the population of the present Russian Federation peaked in 1991 at 148,689,000. Even with significant increases in immigration in the early 1990s, the Russian population has been shrinking since 1992; according to projections by the Center for Economic Analysis of the Russian Federation, immigration will make a very small dent in a continued negative natural increase through the year 2005. Thus, for the period 1985–2005, projected total immigration is 3.3 million, whereas the natural population will decrease by 12.9 million. The annual rate of population change, which dropped from 0.7 percent in 1985 to its first negative figure of –0.3 percent in 1992, is projected to reach –0.6 percent in 1998 and to continue at that level through 2005.

Several reasons are given for the decline in Russia's population. First, the postwar baby boom, which began echoing in a secondary population rise in many Western countries in the early 1990s, had much less demographic impact in Russia. Second, a long history of Soviet ecological abuse has planted still unquantifiable seeds of demographic decline throughout the population, especially in areas of concentrated industry, military installations, and intensive agriculture. Third, post-Soviet Russia has experienced a general decline in health conditions and health care (see Health, ch. 5).

In addition, the prolonged economic downturn of the early and mid-1990s, in which an estimated 31 percent of the population (46.5 million people) had incomes below the poverty level, has increased the incidence of malnutrition, which in turn lowers resistance to common ailments. Only individuals who have their own gardens are assured a regular supply of fruits and vegetables (see table 6, Appendix). Even under the Soviet system, the average Russian's diet was classified as deficient, so the population now shows the cumulative effects of earlier living conditions as well as current limitations. Poor economic prospects, together with low confidence in the state's family benefits programs, discourage Russians from planning families; the least positive "reproductive attitudes" have been found in the Urals and in northeastern Siberia.

Experts have identified a number of general demographic trends that are likely to prevail between 1996 and 2005. Contrary to the trend in Western countries of a shrinking working population supporting an expanding community of retired individuals, in Russia a declining life expectancy and a declining birthrate will increase marginally the proportion of active workers in the population. The actual number of such people is not likely to rise appreciably, however, and some analyses project a decline in this figure as well. In 1992, for every 1,000 people of working age, 771 people were outside working age; the Center for Economic Analysis projects that in 2005 that proportion will drop to 560 per 1,000. The declining birthrate is projected to cause the ratio of younger-than-working-age individuals in the population to decrease dramatically from the 1992 figure of 421 per 1,000 in the working-age group to only 241 per 1,000 in 2005. According to that scenario, the overall percentage of the population in the working-age group would increase from 56.5 to 64.1.

Most of the demographic disasters that have beset Russia in the twentieth century have affected primarily males. In 1992 the sex ratio was 884 males per 1,000 females; in the years between 1994 and 2005, the imbalance is projected to increase slightly to a ratio of 875 males per 1,000 females (see table 7, Appendix). Gender disparity has increased because of a sharp drop in life expectancy for Russian males, from sixty-five years in 1987 to fifty-seven in 1994. (Life expectancy for females reached a peak of 74.5 years in 1989, then dropped to 71.1 by 1994.) Projected changes in life expectancy are negative for both sexes, however. Mortality figures that the Ministry of Labor released in mid-1995 showed that if the current conditions persist, nearly 50 percent of today's Russian youth will not reach the retirement ages of fifty-five for women and sixty for men.

The process of urbanization of the Russian population, ongoing since the 1930s, began a gradual reversal in 1991, when a peak of 74 percent of the population was classified as urban. This marked a significant increase from the 1970 figure of 62 percent. In 1995 the urban share fell below 73 percent. Meanwhile, rural areas continued to lose significant portions of their population. Between 1960 and 1995, about two-thirds of Russia's small villages (those with fewer than 1,000 residents) disappeared; of the 24,000 that remained in the mid-1990s, more than half the population was older than sixty-five and only 20 percent was younger than thirty-five (see Rural Life, ch. 5). Migration has exacerbated the negative population trend of lower marriage and birthrates in many rural settlements. As the young have left rural Russia, large rural sections of the country's central region have been deserted. As their aged inhabitants die, thousands more Russian villages are disappearing. Proposals have been put forth for resettling some of the Russian immigrants from the "near abroad" in rural areas in order to revive local economies, but in the mid-1990s migration authorities had little authority and few resources with which to organize such a program.

A particular demographic concern of the Russian government, as well as governments of the other states of the Commonwealth of Independent States (CIS—see Glossary), is the loss of highly skilled personnel. This problem had existed in the last decade of the Soviet Union; in 1989 some 2,653 employees of the Soviet Union's Academy of Sciences left the country, five times more than in 1988. A 1990 sociological forecast predicted that 1.5 million specialists would leave the country in the 1990s if conditions did not improve.

The easing of emigration restrictions in the early 1990s resulted in a significant increase in Russia's "brain drain." In the early 1990s, China, North Korea, the Republic of Korea (South Korea), Iran, Iraq, and several Latin American countries offered jobs to scientists in Russia, especially those with nuclear backgrounds. (Russia also loses scientific know-how when its scientists move into the growing financial and commercial fields; in 1994 the newspaper *Moskovskiye novosti* reported than one in three leaders of commercial structures was a former scientist or technical specialist.) An ongoing economic crisis and political uncertainty encourage individuals with marketable skills to leave Russia. A high percentage of immigrants from other CIS republics possess the same type of skills as those being lost, but in the mid-1990s Russia lacked a program for settling and apportioning the newcomers so that their presence would compensate for emigration losses.

Fertility

With the exception of a few ethnic groups in the North Caucasus, birthrates for all nationalities in Russia have generally declined in the postwar period (see Ethnic Composition, ch. 4). Throughout the Soviet period, urbanization was rapid, and urban families generally had fewer children than rural ones. The urbanization process ended in 1992, when for the first time in the postwar period a smaller percentage of the Russian population lived in cities than the year before. By that time, however, substantial reasons existed for Russians to limit the size of their families. The population decline of the Russians has been especially pronounced in comparison with other ethnic groups. In many of the twenty-one republics, the titular nationalities have registered higher birthrates and larger average family sizes than the Russian populations.

The birthrate of Russians already was falling dramatically in the 1960s, moving from 23.2 per 1,000 population at the beginning of the decade to 14.1 in 1968. By 1983 the rate had recovered to 17.3 per 1,000, stimulated by a state program that provided incentives for larger families, including increased maternity benefits. Another decline in the birthrate began in 1987, and by 1993 the rate was only 9.4 per 1,000. According to the projections of the Center for Economic Analysis, after reaching its lowest point (8.0 per 1,000) in 1995, the birthrate will rise gradually to 9.7 per 1,000 in 2005.

In the turnaround year of 1992, the number of births in Russia dropped by 207,000 (13 percent) compared with 1991, and the number of deaths increased by 116,000 (7 percent). The fertility rate has dropped in both urban and rural areas. In the early 1990s, the lowest rates were in the northwest, especially St. Petersburg and in central European Russia. The disparity between birth and death rates was especially pronounced in the cities of Moscow and St. Petersburg and in the European oblasts of Pskov, Tula, Tver', Belgorod, Leningrad, Novgorod, Yaroslavl', Moscow, Tambov, and Ivanovo. In 1992 natural population growth occurred only in the republics of Kalmykia, Dagestan, Kabardino-Balkaria, Karachayevo-Cherkessia, North Ossetia, Chechnya, Ingushetia, Gorno-Altay, Sakha, and Tyva, and in Tyumen' and Chita oblasts of western and eastern Siberia, respectively. However, although fertility rates in the predominantly Muslim republics of the North Caucasus and the Volga region continued to exceed those of the Slavic population, by 1995 the rate was declining even in Dagestan, the republic with the highest birthrate in Russia.

For Russians the total fertility rate, which is the average number of children a woman of childbearing age will have at current birthrates, fell from 2.0 in 1989 to 1.4 in 1993. The State Committee for Statistics (Goskomstat) estimates that the rate will decline further to 1.0 by the year 2000. Roughly half as many children were born in 1993 as in 1987. In 1994 the population of Russia fell by 920,000.

The sharp decline in the fertility rate in the 1990s was linked to the social and economic troubles triggered by the rapid transition to a market economy and resulting unemployment. Families have been destabilized, and living standards for many have fallen from even the modest levels of the Soviet era (see The Family, ch. 5). Under such circumstances, decisions on marriage and childbearing often are postponed. Particularly in the cities, housing has been extremely hard to acquire, and the percentage of working wives has increased significantly in the post-Soviet era (see The Role of Women, ch. 5). The number of common-law marriages, which produce fewer children than traditional marriages, has increased since the 1960s, as has the percentage of babies born to unattached women.

History also has affected the absolute number of births. The birthrate during World War II was very low, accounting for part of the low birthrate of females in the 1960s, which in turn lowered the rate in the 1990s. Between 1989 and 1993, the number of women in the prime childbearing age-group decreased by 1.3 million, or 12 percent, making a major contribution to the 27 percent decline in births during that period. Between 1990 and 1994, the government's official estimate of the infant mortality rate rose from 17.4 per 1,000 live births to 19.9, reflecting deterioration of Russia's child care and nutrition standards. But Russia has not used international viability standards for newborns, and one Western estimate placed the 1995 rate at 26.3. Between 1992 and 1995, the official maternal mortality rate also rose from forty-seven to fifty-two deaths per 100,000 births.

Abortion

Fertility in Russia has been adversely affected by the common practice of using abortion as a primary means of birth control. In 1920 the Soviet Union was the first country to legalize abortion. Sixteen years later it was prohibited, except in certain circumstances, to compensate for the millions of lives lost in the collectivization of agriculture and the widespread famine that followed in the 1930s. The practice was fully legalized once again in 1968, and an entire industry evolved offering abortion services and encouraging women to use them. Although abortions became easily available for most women, an estimated 15 percent of the Soviet total were performed illegally in private facilities. Because of the persistent lack of contraceptive devices in both Soviet and independent Russia (and the social taboo on discussion of contraception and sex in general, which continued in the 1990s), for most women abortion remains the only reliable method of avoiding unwanted pregnancy (see Health Conditions; Sexual Attitudes, ch. 5). Russia continues to have the highest abortion rate in the world, as did the Soviet Union. In the mid-1990s, the Russian average was 225 terminated pregnancies per 100 births and ninety-eight abortions for every 1,000 women of childbearing age per year—a yearly average of 3.5 million. An estimated one-quarter of maternal fatalities result from abortion procedures.

Mortality

The social and economic crises that gripped Russia in the early 1990s are reflected in increased mortality and declining life expectancy, especially among able-bodied males. Contributing to Russia's long-term population decline is a projected mortality rate increase from 11.3 per 1,000 population in 1985 to 15.9 per 1,000 in 2005. Russia's mortality rate reached its lowest level, 10.4 per 1,000 population, in 1986 (for which a state antialcohol campaign received substantial credit); then the figure rose steadily in the ensuing decade. The largest jump was from 12.2 to 14.6 per 1,000 between 1992 and 1993; after having reached 15.7 per 1,000 in 1995, the rate was projected to remain virtually flat over the next decade.

According to 1994 statistics, the life expectancy for Russian males had reached 57.3 years and for females 71.1 years. These are the lowest figures and the largest disparity by sex for any country reporting to the World Health Organization, and they are a sharp decline from the 1987 levels of 64.9 years for males and 74.6 years for females. In 1990 the Russian Republic ranked only seventh in this statistic among the fifteen republics of the Soviet Union. The lag in the average life expectancy of males was attributed to alcohol and tobacco abuse; to unsafe conditions at work, on the road, and in the home; and to declining heath care.

Mortality rates are especially high for able-bodied males in rural areas. Served poorly by the health care system and lacking basic sanitary facilities and conveniences, many farming communities have been transformed into enclaves for the elderly, the indigent, and the sick. Moreover, indigenous nationalities such as the Evenks and the Nenets have suffered catastrophic declines in life expectancy and high rates of sickness and death that have prompted speculation that some of those groups may become extinct. Geographically, the lowest average life expectancy in Russia is in the Siberian Republic of Tyva, and the highest figures are in the Caucasus Republic of Dagestan and in the Volga region. In the first half of the 1990s, the imbalance between the birth and death rates was especially acute in major cities. In Moscow and St. Petersburg, the number of deaths in 1992 was almost double the number of births.

Since 1987 mortality from accidents, injuries, and poisonings has risen significantly, from 101 to 228 per 100,000 population. Contributing to that figure are an estimated 8,000 fatal workplace accidents per year, largely the result of aging equipment, the proliferation of risky jobs in the unofficial "shadow economy," and the deterioration of work discipline. For the period between 1990 and 1994, the suicide rate rose by 57 percent to a total of nearly 62,000, putting Russia in third place among eighty-four developed countries. The stress of the transition period is one explanation for this rising statistic. The homicide rate rose by more than 50 percent in the same period (see Crime, ch. 10). In 1994 Russia's 35,000 motor vehicle deaths nearly equaled the 40,000 in the United States, although Russia has less than 1 percent as many automobiles. Deteriorating roads and declining police discipline are the main causes of that fatality statistic.

The chief natural cause of death is diseases of the circulatory system, which accounted for 769 deaths per 100,000 population in 1993. The next causes in order of frequency are cancer and respiratory diseases. Among people of working age, 41 percent of deaths are attributable to unnatural causes; the proportion of such deaths was highest in Leningrad Oblast, the Permyak Autonomous Region, the Republic of Tyva, and the Evenk Autonomous Region. The number of alcohol-related deaths also climbed in the mid-1990s; the 1994 figure was 25 percent higher than the 1993 total. In some regions, alcoholism has assumed epidemic proportions; in the Bikin Rayon of Khabarovsk Territory on the Pacific coast, nearly half the deaths between 1991 and 1995 were alcohol related (see Health Conditions, ch. 5).

The overall aging of the population also is an important factor in the higher mortality rate. Between 1959 and 1989, the percentage of retirees in the population and the percentage of Russians eighty or older nearly doubled, although declining life expectancy already was reducing the impact of that trend in the mid-1990s.

Migration

For most of the postwar period, the state tightly controlled migration into and emigration from the Soviet Union and movement within the nation. Nevertheless, in each year of the 1980s, about 15 million citizens changed their place of residence within the Soviet Union, and large numbers of some ethnic groups, most notably Jews, Germans, and Armenians, were successful in emigrating. An estimated 2 million Jews left the Soviet Union between 1945 and 1991 (see Other Religions, ch. 4). Overall, external migration played a relatively minor role in the structure of the Russian Republic's population.

With the introduction of the policies of *glasnost* and *perestroika* (see Glossary) in the late 1980s, migration policy began to change. In 1985 just 2,943 persons received official permission to emigrate. By 1990 the figure had risen to more than 100,000. After the breakup of the Soviet Union in 1991, legislative and administrative changes brought about new policies with respect to migration. First, the traditional internal passport (*propiska*) that conferred permission to work and live in a specific place was nominally abolished, enhancing freedom of movement within Russia. Second, the general right to emigrate was written into law in the 1993 constitution.

Prior to the breakup of the Soviet Union in 1991, major historical internal migration paths were from the western parts of Russia and the Soviet Union to the northern and eastern regions. In contrast to the American experience, Russia has had difficulty in stabilizing the population in newly settled eastern and northern areas of the federation, where the climate and living conditions are harsh. Despite pay and benefit incentives, turnover has continued to hamper the operations of the giant territorial production complexes, especially in the key energy sector.

In the Soviet period, immigration was not a problem because the Soviet Union was not a destination of preference for any class of refugee. For that reason, in the early 1990s Russia was not equipped with agencies or laws for dealing with a large-scale influx of asylum seekers and returning Russians. In light of new demographic movements in the 1990s, however, respected academician Dmitriy Likhachev has warned that in the next decade immigration may become a national concern of the same magnitude as national defense.

Issues and Procedures

In 1993 Russia signed the United Nations Convention on Refugees, which reclassified it as a "country of first resort" for foreigners fleeing countries outside the CIS. Under the 1951 United Nations convention, this status entails an international obligation to care for such individuals. At the same time, the decline in border security since the dissolution of the Soviet Union has made illegal immigration easier in many areas. In the early 1990s, the number of official refugees swelled when students from Third World nations, particularly Afghanistan, refused to leave Russia when their studies were completed. According to the United Nations High Commissioner for Refugees (UNHCR), about 28,000 foreign refugees were living illegally in Moscow in 1994; figures for other parts of Russia are not available. The UNHCR's Moscow total was divided among 20,000 Afghans, 6,000 Iraqis, 2,000 Somalis, and smaller numbers of Angolans, Ethiopians, and Zairians. A 1995 Moscow press report, however, estimated that 100,000 illegal immigrants were living in Moscow, including 50,000 Chinese and 15,000 Afghans.

The first major influx of refugees into the Russian Republic occurred in 1988 and 1989, when Azerbaijanis and Armenians (mainly the latter) fled the Nagorno-Karabakh conflict between their respective countries, and when Meskhetian Turks fled Uzbekistan following a massacre in that republic in 1989. However, only in 1992 did the Russian government establish its first agency for dealing with such conditions, the Federal Migration Service (FMS). That service monitors refugees and other migrants from both outside and within the CIS, but it is underfunded and understaffed. In 1994 UNHCR transit camps in Moscow had a capacity of 1,000, leaving a large number of Moscow's refugee population to live in primitive conditions. Given the FMS's limited resources, several international social and charitable organizations are active in aiding refugees and migrants, although their work has not been well coordinated with the FMS or among themselves. An additional complication in the early 1990s was the influx of tens of thousands of Russian military personnel withdrawn from former Warsaw Pact member nations and from other CIS nations.

In response to Russia's new status as a country of first resort, a series of laws on refugees and forced migrants were passed in 1993 and 1994. The laws define various categories of migrants, particularly refugees and forced migrants, according to the conditions and motivations that prompted their movement as well as the responsibilities of the state to care for them.

Local branches of the FMS conduct registration of refugees and forced migrants and are responsible for providing material support until they are classified. Individuals in both categories theoretically have some input in their new place of residence; the FMS provides a list of permissible urban destinations, or relatives may accept them elsewhere. Legally, the FMS is obliged to help find suitable employment, schools, and social security and to aid in compensation for lost property. FMS activities receive funding from the Russian state budget, other countries and international organizations according to bilateral agreements, and private donations. Russian citizenship is granted automatically to individuals who were permanent residents of the federation before the Law on Citizenship was passed in February 1992; migrants from elsewhere in the CIS (particularly the 25 million Russians in other former Soviet republics) also have a guarantee of Russian citizenship upon arrival, provided they are not already citizens of another state. A 1993 refinement of FMS regulations added compulsory annual reregistration and stricter requirements for proof of forced migrant status. It also modified the temporary housing guarantee.

As of mid-1996, however, little of the system for carrying out the laws' guarantees had been worked out. Transportation aid is available only in extreme cases, and financial support at the time of settlement is offered only to individuals and families below the poverty line. The FMS reported that, to comply with all aspects of the refugee law, each individual should receive about US$10,000, a sum far beyond the resources of the agency.

Most illegal immigrants enter the country on tourist visas; some take advantage of leaky borders and vague visa requirements. Most claim to be in transit to another country, usually in the West. Profitable businesses have sprung up smuggling refugees through Russia and then to the West. In 1994 Russian authorities announced plans for a central data bank to monitor all immigration and emigration and a new refugee agency, but no such system was in place in mid-1996. Meanwhile, the prospects of moving large numbers of immigrants to Western countries diminished with new immigration restrictions imposed there; at the same time, the United Nations convention substantially limits Russia's options by forbidding deportation of immigrants to "countries of persecution." The FMS has optimistically planned to deal with 400,000 refugees per year, but some estimates projected that as many as 2 million would immigrate in 1996 alone.

The proportion of non-Russian immigrants declined noticeably after 1992. In 1995 the estimated share of Russians was 63 percent of refugees and 75 percent of forced migrants, followed by overall immigration shares of 7 to 9 percent each for Armenians, Ossetians, and Tatars, 3 percent for Ukrainians, and 1 percent each for Georgians and Tajiks. Non-Slavic immigrants have encountered hostile attitudes from most Russian authorities. For example, beginning in 1993 Moscow authorities mounted "cleansing" campaigns to rid the city of individuals lacking residence permits; because immigrants from the Caucasus and Central Asia are easily distinguishable from Slavs, such campaigns have detained and deported disproportionately large numbers from those ethnic groups. International human rights organizations have criticized Moscow for such practices.

The Soviet-era internal passport system, which required documentary proof of an individual's place of residence for that person to receive housing, was simplified theoretically in October 1993 to allow an individual to take residence in any area without proof of registration in that location. However, local authorities have ignored this change, especially in cities such as Moscow that are chief targets of migration. In continuing the Soviet registration system, local authorities can restrict housing, education, and social security benefits to migrants, whatever their origin. In the mid-1990s, strict, "temporary" local restrictions on initial admittance of migrants spread rapidly to most of the oblast capitals, often with conditions in clear violation of the human rights provisions of the 1993 constitution, with the official backing of the FMS. Continued local limitations have had the effect of discouraging housing construction and employment, hence exacerbating the situation of nonresidents.

Such a discrimination policy has not stemmed the tide of migration into Russia's cities from other CIS states or from within the federation. Because the Soviet system usually allowed migrants to eventually register, find work, and settle at their destination, continuation of that system also has continued the expectations and the demographic movement that it promoted. As a result, the number of homeless people in Russia's cities has increased dramatically (see Social Welfare, ch. 5).

Migration Patterns

The increased numbers of Russians arriving from other CIS nations create both logistical and political problems. As in the case of non-Russian refugees, statistical estimates of intra-CIS migration vary widely, partly because Russia has not differentiated that category clearly from the refugee category and partly because actual numbers are assumed to be much higher than official registrations indicate. Many newly arrived Russians (like non-Russians) simply settle with friends or relatives without official registration.

During Russia's problematic economic transition period, the movement of comparatively large numbers of migrants has created substantial social friction, especially over the distribution of scarce urban housing. Nationalist extremist political groups have inflamed local resentment toward refugees of all types. Friction is exacerbated by the state's meager efforts to support migrant populations. Skilled immigrants show particular resentment against a state that fails to provide opportunities and even enough resources to survive, and these people often have drifted into progressively more serious types of criminal activity. Local populations uniformly resent resources provided to migrants in their midst, and they attribute their own economic difficulties to the "strangers" among them, especially if those people are not of the same nationality. Particular tension has been evident in North Ossetia, whose 17 percent immigration statistic is by far the highest in the Russian Federation, in Stavropol' and Krasnodar territories, and in Orenburg, Kaluga,

Voronezh, and Saratov oblasts, all of which have numbers of migrants exceeding 1 percent of their populations.

By 1992 the International Red Cross had estimated that about 150,000 ethnic Russians had migrated from CIS states, and at the end of 1993 the head of the FMS estimated that 2 million Russians and non-Russians had arrived from the near abroad in the first two post-Soviet years. As many as 300,000 of the 375,000 Russians in Tajikistan left that country in the first years of the civil war that began in 1992, and in 1994 more than half the Russian arrivals came from Chechnya, Azerbaijan, Georgia, and Tajikistan. However, the structure of this group changes according to security and political conditions in the CIS states; by the end of 1994, almost 60 percent of Russian arrivals came from Kazakstan, Kyrgyzstan, and Uzbekistan, driven not by armed conflict but by local discrimination, and the share of arrivals from the conflict states had declined to one-third. The official FMS estimate for 1995 was 963,000 people arriving in Russia from other CIS states, slightly lower than the 1994 total. The number of forced migrants rose by 300,000 in 1995, however. The states of origin showing the largest increases in 1995 were Kazakstan, Ukraine, and Uzbekistan, and the Central Asian republics continued to account for more than half the total CIS migrants.

Refugees and migrants from outside the federation have settled in most of the territory of Russia except for parts of the Far North and ethnic republics such as Sakha, Chechnya, and Adygea. The largest numbers of settlers are in the North Caucasus, the southern part of the chernozem agricultural zone of European Russia, the Volga region, and the industrial cities of the adjacent Ural Mountains. Forced migrants show a decided preference for cities. In the north and the east, almost 100 percent of all migrants settle in urban regions, but more than half of migrants to south-central European Russia, the North Caucasus, and the Urals settle in rural areas. Because there has been no state program for distributing forced migrants, they have chosen destinations according to accessibility from their starting point and the location of relatives. Russian refugees seldom settle in an ethnic republic or a region with a high proportion of non-Russians, such as Orenburg Oblast; for that reason, their share of total refugees in the republics is less than 10 percent. Armenian refugees, mainly from the Nagorno-Karabakh enclave of Azerbaijan, are concentrated in the North Caucasus and Saratov Oblast, as well as the large cities and

Kaliningrad Oblast on the Baltic Sea. Islamic refugees, mainly Tatar, Bashkir, Tajik, Uzbek, and Kyrgyz, prefer the republics of Tatarstan and Bashkortostan and adjacent regions with large numbers of Tatars. National groups also have varying long-term intentions. Russians and Tatars tend to remain permanently in their new locations; Chechens mostly plan to return to their homeland once conditions improve; and Armenians and Germans are predominantly transit migrants en route to another country.

Future Prospects

The Russian Federation possesses a unique variety and scale of geographic features, even after the collapse of the larger Soviet Union, but it faces grave problems in managing its abundant natural resources. Although the potential remains for constructive exploitation of Russia's environment, the economic and political condition of the country does not bode well for an organized effort in that direction. Meanwhile, a large percentage of Russia's population is threatened by numerous grave ecological hazards left behind by Soviet regimes as well as by the tolerance the post-Soviet government has for most of those conditions. In the mid-1990s, those threats combine with other health problems, a low birthrate, and a declining life expectancy to give Russia one of the least positive demographic profiles in the world.

*   *   *

Two classic authorities on the geography of Russia are Paul E. Lydolph's *Geography of the U.S.S.R.* and David Hooson's *The Soviet Union: People and Regions.* A post-Soviet treatment of the topic is found in *Russian Regions Today: Atlas of the New Federation,* published in 1994 by the International Center in Washington, D.C. Environmental problems are discussed at length in D.J. Peterson's *Troubled Lands: The Legacy of Soviet Environmental Destruction* and in *Ecocide in the USSR: Health and Nature under Siege,* edited by Murray Feshbach and Alfred Friendly. Information on the current demographic crisis is provided by Valentina Bodrova's "Reproductive Behaviour of Russia's Population in the Transition Period" and Penny Morvant's "Alarm over Falling Life Expectancy." (For further information and complete citations, see Bibliography.)

Chapter 4. Ethnic, Religious, and Cultural Setting

The Firebird tears herself from the grasp of Tsarevich Ivan, who manages to retain one of her beautiful tail feathers (design from lacquer box made in village of Palekh).

THE RUSSIAN STATE HAS EMERGED from the Soviet era dominated by an ethnic group, the Russians, whose language prevails in most educational and government institutions, and a religion, Russian Orthodoxy, that is professed by the vast majority of those citizens who admit to a religious preference. In some respects, Russia's relative homogeneity in language and religion is the result of the uniformity imposed by Soviet rule. As they had in the centuries of tsarist rule, Russians continued in the twentieth century to occupy a percentage of governing positions disproportionate even to their lopsided ethnic majority. Enforced use of the Russian language was a chief means of preserving Moscow's authority in the far-flung regions of the Russian Republic, as it was in the other fourteen Soviet republics. Although it was not spared the persecution meted out to all faiths practiced in the Soviet Union, Russian Orthodoxy retained its preeminence among religiously observant Russians throughout the seven decades of officially prescribed atheism.

In the 1990s, Russians continue to constitute the largest ethnic group in all but a handful of the Russian Federation's nominally ethnic republics, but leaders in many of the republics and smaller ethnic jurisdictions have pressed the central government to grant measures of autonomy and other concessions in the name of indigenous groups. The breakaway Republic of Chechnya has taken the process to its furthest extreme, but in the mid-1990s other republics—in the North Caucasus, Siberia, and the Volga and Ural regions—were pushing hard to achieve the local autonomy to which Soviet governments had only paid lip service.

Meanwhile, the Russian Orthodox Church, long forced to rubber-stamp the cultural decisions of Soviet governments, has moved rapidly in the 1990s toward a more balanced partnership in the governance of Russia's spiritual and secular life. Post-Soviet Western influences have brought new variety to the spectrum of religious practice, but the loyalty to Orthodoxy of average Russians and of the Russian government has become clear as the church has added millions of professed believers in the 1990s and the government has sought church advice on many critical decisions. This renewed alliance has posed a challenge to the freedom of religion nominally guaranteed in the 1993 constitution.

The issue of language diversity has risen in parallel with issues of local sovereignty. The Russian language retains its traditional dominance in official communications and in the education system; however, the increasing unofficial use of the federation's many minority languages shows that they survived Soviet repression with the capacity to flourish anew as the central government's power has diminished.

Ethnic Composition

Russia is a multinational state that has inherited many of the nationality problems that plagued the Soviet Union. The last official Soviet census, conducted in 1989, listed more than 100 nationalities. Several of those groups now predominantly inhabit the independent nations that formerly were Soviet republics. However, the Russian Federation—the most direct successor to the Soviet Union—still is home to more than 100 national minorities, whose members coexist uneasily with the numerically and politically predominant Russians (see table 8, Appendix).

Besides the Slavs (Russians, Ukrainians, and Belarusians), who account for about 85 percent of Russia's population, three main ethnic groups and a handful of isolated smaller groups reside within the federation. The Altaic group includes mainly speakers of Turkic languages widely distributed in the middle Volga, the southern Ural Mountains, the North Caucasus, and above the Arctic Circle. The main Altaic peoples in Russia are the Balkars, Bashkirs, Buryats, Chuvash, Dolgans, Evenks, Kalmyks, Karachay, Kumyks, Nogay, and Yakuts. The Uralic group, consisting of Finnic peoples living in the upper Volga, the far northwest, and the Urals, includes the Karelians, Komi, Mari, Mordovians, and Udmurts. The Caucasus group is concentrated along the northern slopes of the Caucasus Mountains; its main subgroups are the Adyghs, Chechens, Cherkess, Ingush, and Kabardins, as well as about thirty Caucasus peoples collectively classified as Dagestani (see Minority Peoples and Their Territories, this ch.).

In the Soviet Union, the Russian Soviet Federated Socialist Republic (RSFSR) contained thirty-one autonomous, ethnically based administrative units. When the Russian Federation proclaimed its sovereignty in the wake of the Soviet Union's collapse in late 1991, many of those entities also declared their sovereignty. Of the thirty-one, sixteen were autonomous republics, five were autonomous oblasts (provinces), and ten were autonomous regions (*okruga*; sing., *okrug*), which were part of larger subnational jurisdictions. During the Soviet era, the autonomy referred to in these jurisdictions' official titles was more fictitious than real—the executive committees that administered the jurisdictions had no decision-making authority. All major administrative tasks were performed by the central government or, in the case of some social services, by industrial enterprises in the area. In postcommunist Russia, however, many of the autonomous areas have staked claims to more meaningful sovereignty as the numerically superior Russians continue to dominate the center of power in Moscow (see The Federation Treaty and Regional Power, ch. 7). Even in the many regions where Russians are in the majority, such claims have been made in the name of the indigenous ethnic group or groups.

According to the 1989 Soviet census, Russians constituted 81.5 percent of the population of what is now the Russian Federation. The next-largest groups were Tatars (3.8 percent), Ukrainians (3.0 percent), Chuvash (1.2 percent), Bashkirs (0.9 percent), Belorussians (0.8 percent), and Mordovians (0.7 percent). Other groups totaling more than 0.5 percent of the population each were Armenians, Avars, Chechens, Germans, Jews, Kazaks, Mari, and Udmurts. In 1992 an estimated 7.8 million people native to the other fourteen former Soviet republics were living in Russia.

The Russians

The ethnic group that came to be known as the Russians sprang from the East Slavs, one of the three groups into which the original Slavic people divided sometime before the seventh century A.D. The West Slavs eventually became differentiated as the Poles, Czechs, and Slovaks; the South Slavs divided into the Bulgarians, Croats, Serbs, and Slovenes. The East Slavic tribes settled along the Dnepr River in present-day Ukraine in the first centuries A.D. From that region, they then spread northward and eastward. In the ninth century, these tribes constituted the largest part of the population of Kievan Rus', the medieval state ruled by a Varangian dynasty from Scandinavia (see The East Slavs and the Varangians, ch. 1).

The East Slavs became more politically united in the tenth century when they adopted Christianity as the state religion of

Kievan Rus'. Nevertheless, tribal and regional differences were exacerbated in subsequent centuries as the state expanded, bringing the East Slavs into contact with other ethnic groups on their borders. Thus, Baltic and Finno-Ugric tribes mixed with the East Slavs to the northwest and the northeast, respectively. By the time the state of Kievan Rus' began disintegrating into independent principalities in the twelfth century, the East Slavs had begun to evolve into three peoples with distinct linguistic and cultural characteristics: the Russians to the north and northeast of Kiev, the Belorussians to the northwest of Kiev, and the Ukrainians in the Kiev region and to its south and southwest. In the thirteenth century, the invasion of the Mongols brought the final collapse of Kievan Rus' as a political entity, accelerating differentiation and consolidation of the three ethnic groups (see The Golden Age of Kiev, ch. 1). Although the three groups remained related culturally, linguistically, and religiously, each of them also was influenced by different political, economic, religious, and social developments that further separated them.

Building a state of increasing vitality as the Mongol occupation weakened in the fourteenth century, the principality of Muscovy became the base from which the Russian cultural and political systems expanded under a series of strong rulers. By the end of the nineteenth century, Russians had settled the remote stretches of Siberia to the Pacific Ocean and colonized Central Asia and the Caucasus, becoming in the process the most numerous and ubiquitous of the Slavic peoples (see Ruling the Empire, ch. 1).

Minority Peoples and Their Territories

With a few changes in status in the post-World War II period, the autonomous republics, autonomous oblasts, and autonomous regions of the Russian Soviet Federated Socialist Republic retained the classifications assigned to them in the 1920s or 1930s. In all cases, the postcommunist Russian government officially changed the term "autonomous republic" to "republic" in 1992. According to the 1989 Soviet census, in only fifteen of the thirty-one ethnically designated republics and autonomous regions were the "indigenous" people the largest group. Of the twenty-one republics existing in Russia in the mid-1990s, nine fell into this category, with the smallest percentages of Russians in Chechnya, Dagestan, Ingushetia, and North Ossetia. Each region designated by ethnic group is home to the majority of Russia's population of that group (see table 9, Appendix).

The border-drawing process that occurred in tsarist times and in the first decades of Soviet rule sometimes divided rather than united ethnic populations. The Buryats of southern Siberia, for example, were divided among the Buryat Autonomous Republic and Chita and Irkutsk oblasts, which were created to the east and west of the republic, respectively; that population division remains in the post-Soviet era. By contrast, the Chechens and Ingush were united in a single republic until 1992, and smaller groups such as the Khanty and the Mansi were grouped together in single autonomous regions.

Of the sixteen autonomous republics that existed in Russia at the time of the Soviet Union's breakup, one (the Chechen-Ingush Autonomous Republic) split into two in 1992, with Chechnya subsequently declaring full independence as the Republic of Chechnya and with Ingushetia gaining recognition as a separate republic of the Russian Federation. Three Soviet-era autonomous oblasts (Gorno-Altay, Adygea, and Karacha-yevo-Cherkessia) were granted republic status under the Federation Treaty of 1992, which established the respective powers of the central and republic governments. Two republics, Chechnya and Tatarstan, did not sign the treaty at that time. Most provisions of the Federation Treaty were overtaken by provisions of the 1993 constitution or by subsequent bilateral agreements between the central government and the republics.

After the changes of the immediate post-Soviet years, twenty-one nationality-based republics existed in the Russian Federation and were recognized in the constitution of 1993 (see table 10, Appendix). They are Adygea, Bashkortostan, Buryatia, Chechnya, Chuvashia, Dagestan, Gorno-Altay, Ingushetia, Kabardino-Balkaria, Kalmykia, Karachayevo-Cherkessia, Karelia, Khakassia, Komi, Mari El, Mordovia, North Ossetia, Sakha (Yakutia), Tatarstan, Tyva (Tuva), and Udmurtia.

Besides the republics, the constitution recognizes ten autonomous regions, whose status, like that of the republics, is based on the presence of one or two ethnic groups. These jurisdictions typically are sparsely populated, rich in natural resources, and inclined to seek independence from the larger units to which they belong. The existence and configuration of Russia's other jurisdictions are determined by geographical or political factors rather than ethnicity. The ten autonomous regions are the Aga Buryat, Chukchi, Evenk, Khanty-Mansi, Koryak,

Nenets, Permyak, Taymyr, Ust'-Orda Buryat, and Yamalo-Nenets autonomous regions. A Jewish Autonomous Oblast (Yevreyskaya avtonomnaya oblast', now known as Birobidzhan) was established in 1934. Russians are the majority of the population in all but the Aga Buryat Autonomous Region (whose population is 55 percent Buryats) and the Permyak Autonomous Region (whose population is 60 percent Komi-Permyak, one of the three subgroups of the Komi people). More typical is the Evenk Autonomous Region in Siberia west of the Republic of Sakha, where the Evenks are outnumbered by Russians 17,000 to 3,000. In fact, the Evenks, originally a nomadic and clan-based group whose society was nearly destroyed by Soviet collectivization in the 1930s, are among the indigenous peoples of Russia whose survival experts fear is endangered.

The North Caucasus

The region of Russia adjoining the north slope of the Caucasus range includes eight republics—Adygea, Chechnya, Dagestan, Ingushetia, Kabardino-Balkaria, Kalmykia, Karachayevo-Cherkessia, and North Ossetia. The North Caucasus retains its historical reputation as a trouble spot, although the majority of the region's republics are relatively peaceful and undeveloped.

The Adygh (or Adygey) Autonomous Oblast was established in 1922 as part of Krasnoyarsk Territory; between 1922 and 1928, it was known as the Cherkess (Adygh) Autonomous Oblast. It was redesignated as the Republic of Adygea in 1992. A landlocked sliver of land, Adygea occupies 7,600 square kilometers just inland from the northeast coast of the Black Sea, reaching southward to the northern foothills of the Caucasus Mountains. The oblast was formed by the early Soviet government for the Adygh people, who are one of three branches of the Cherkess, or Circassian, tribes—the other two being the Cherkess and the Kabardins. The general group from which these three peoples descend has occupied the northern border of the Caucasus Mountains at least since the Greeks began exploring beyond the Black Sea in the eighth century B.C. The Adyghs, most of whom accepted Islam early in the nineteenth century, speak a Caucasian language.

In 1995 the Adyghs constituted 22 percent of the population of Adygea, which was estimated at 450,400. The rest consisted of 68 percent Russians, 3 percent Ukrainians, and 2 percent Armenians. Adygea is the only Muslim republic of the Russian

Federation where the Muslim share of the population has decreased in the last two decades. The official languages are Russian and Adygh. Rich soil is the basis for an agricultural economy specializing in grains, tobacco, sugar beets, vegetables, fruits, cattle, poultry, and beekeeping. Processing of meats, tobacco, dairy products, and canned goods is an important industry. The republic's only substantial mineral resource under exploitation is an extensive natural gas and oil deposit. The capital city, Maykop, is the main industrial center, with metallurgical, machine-building, and timber-processing plants.

Chechnya has been the scene of the most violent of the separatist movements against the Russian Federation (see Movements Toward Sovereignty, this ch.; Chechnya, ch. 9; Security Operations in Chechnya, ch. 10). The Chechens and Ingush belong to ancient Caucasian peoples, mainly Muslim, who have lived in the same region in the northern Caucasus Mountains since prehistoric times. The two groups speak similar languages but have different historical backgrounds. The Chechen-Ingush Autonomous Oblast was established in 1934 by combining two separate oblasts that had existed since the early 1920s. In 1936 the oblast was redesignated an autonomous republic, but both ethnic groups were exiled to Central Asia in 1944 for alleged collaboration with the invading Germans.

The republic was reinstated in 1957, and what was left of the original population was allowed to return. In the three decades following their return, the Chechen and Ingush populations recovered rapidly, accounting in 1989 for 66 percent of the population of their shared republic. At that time, the Chechen population was about 760,000, the Ingush about 170,000. This proportion reflects approximately the relative size of the two regions after they split into separate republics in 1992. (Ingushetia occupies a sliver of land between Chechnya and North Ossetia; in 1995 its population was estimated at 254,100.) In 1989 Russians constituted about 23 percent of the combined population of Chechnya and Ingushetia, their numbers having declined steadily for decades.

The most important product of what now is known as the Republic of Chechnya (and officially called the Republic of Chechnya-Ichkeria within the republic) is refined petroleum. The capital, Groznyy, was one of the most important refining centers in southern Russia prior to its virtual annihilation in the conflict of 1995–96. Several major pipelines connect Groznyy refineries with the Caspian Sea, the Black Sea, and

Russian industrial centers to the north. The republic's other important industries are petrochemical and machinery manufacturing and food processing. When the Chechen-Ingush Autonomous Republic split in June 1992, Chechnya retained most of the industrial base.

Both the Chechens and the Ingush remain strongly attached to clan and tribal relations as the structure of their societies. Primary use of their respective North Caucasian languages has remained above 95 percent, despite the long period that the two groups spent in exile. Chechnya was fully converted to Islam by the seventeenth century, Ingushetia only in the nineteenth century. But the region has a two-century history of holy war against Russian authority. When the indigenous populations were exiled in 1944, Soviet authorities attempted to expunge Islam entirely from the region by closing all mosques. Although the mosques remained closed when the Chechens and Ingush returned, clandestine religious organizations spread rapidly.

Despite the close ethnic relationship of the Ingush and Chechen peoples, the Ingush opted to remain within the Russian Federation after Chechnya initially declared its sovereignty in 1991. In June 1992, Ingushetia declared itself a sovereign republic within the Russian Federation. At that time, Ingushetia claimed part of neighboring North Ossetia as well. When hostilities arose between the Chechens and the Ingush following their split, Russian troops were deployed between the two ethnic territories. Ingushetia opposed Russia's occupation of Chechnya, but it supported the regime of President Boris N. Yeltsin on other issues in the mid-1990s. The capital of Ingushetia is Nazran.

The Republic of Dagestan, formerly the Dagestan (or Daghestan) Autonomous Soviet Socialist Republic (Dagestan ASSR), occupies 50,300 square kilometers along the western shore of the Caspian Sea, from the border with Azerbaijan in the south to a point about 150 kilometers south of the Volga River delta in the north. Arriving along the Volga, Russians first settled the area in the fifteenth century, but Dagestan was not annexed by the Russian Empire until 1813. During 1920–22 most of the Dagestani people joined the Chechens in a widespread revolt against Soviet power; some of the secret Islamic orders that led the revolt continued to practice terrorism through the Soviet period. Designated an autonomous republic in 1921, Dagestan lost some of its territory in 1941 and 1957;

most of the original republic was restored in 1957. In the Soviet period, the Muslim majority suffered severe religious repression.

Unlike the other autonomous republics, Dagestan does not derive its existence from the presence of one particular group. Besides its Russian population (9.2 percent of the total in 1989), Dagestan is home to an estimated thirty ethnic groups and eighty nationalities, who speak Caucasian, Iranian, and Turkic languages and account for more than 80 percent of the population. The ten non-Slavic groups identified by Soviet censuses within the population of about 2 million are, in order of size, Avars, Dargins, Kumyks, Lezgins, Laks, Tabasarans, Nogay, Rutuls, Tsakhurs, and Aguls. Colonies of Azerbaijanis (4.2 percent in 1989) and Chechens (3.2 percent) also exist. Knowledge of Arabic and the teachings of Islam are more widespread in Dagestan than in any other Russian republic. In the 1990s, tension has existed among the many ethnic groups, accompanied by a debate over whether the republic should be organized on a unitary or federative basis.

The Avars, known for their warrior heritage, live mostly in the isolated western part of the republic, retaining much of their traditional village lifestyle. Numbering nearly 600,000, the Avars are by far the largest ethnic group in Dagestan. The Lezgins (also seen as Lezghins and Lezgians) are the dominant group in southern Dagestan; because of the Lezgins' location, their society has been more affected by foreign cultural influence than the other groups. Like the Avars, the Dargins, divided into several distinct groups, maintain their village communities in relative isolation. The Kumyks, the largest Turkic group in the republic, are descendants of the Central Asian Kipchak tribes; they inhabit northern Dagestan.

The Laks, a small, homogeneous group, occupy central Dagestan; their region was the original center of Islam on the upper Caspian coast. The Tabasarans, who live in southern Dagestan, are strongly influenced by the more numerous Lezgins, although folk practices such as vendettas persist. The steppe-dwelling Nogay of Dagestan, the second Turkic group in the republic, are descendents of one of two Nogay hordes of the Middle Ages; the second and larger group settled to the west, in Stavropol' Territory, and speaks a different language. The Tsakhurs, Rutuls, and Aguls are small, isolated groups of mountain people who lack a written language and largely have preserved their traditional social structures. The capital city,

Makhachkala, is located in southern Dagestan, on the Caspian Sea, in a region dominated by the Lezgins.

Most of the rural population raises livestock in the republic's hilly terrain. Dagestan is rich in oil, natural gas, coal, and other minerals; swift rivers offer abundant hydroelectric-power potential. The polyglot nature of Dagestan has made linguistic unity impossible; among the major groups, only the Nogay language is said to be declining in usage. Besides Azerbaijani and Russian, six languages were recognized as official languages in the late Soviet period.

Kabardino-Balkaria, the territory of the Kabardin and Balkar peoples, is located along the north-central border of Georgia and the northern slope of the Caucasus Mountains. Occupying about 12,500 square kilometers, the autonomous republic was established in 1936 after fourteen years as an autonomous oblast. In 1944 the Balkars, like certain other North Caucasus groups, were deported to Central Asia because of their alleged collaboration with the Nazis, and the region was renamed the Kabardin Autonomous Oblast. Republic status was restored in 1957 when the Balkars were allowed to return. In 1992 both the Kabardins and the Balkars opted to establish separate republics within the Russian Federation, using an ethnic boundary established in 1863, but the incumbent parliament of the republic declared the separation unlawful. Since that time, the issue of the republic's configuration has awaited a referendum. In 1994 Kabardino-Balkaria signed a bilateral treaty with Russia defining respective areas of jurisdiction within the federation.

In the fifteenth century, Crimean Tatars and Ottoman Turks brought Sunni Islam of the Hanafi school to the territory that is now Kabardino-Balkaria, but Muslim precepts have been observed rather superficially since that time. A small group of Christian Kabardins remains. Despite Russian immigration into the republic, the Muslim Kabardins and Balkars now constitute nearly 60 percent of the republic's population, which was estimated at 800,000 in 1995. Of that number, 48 percent were Kabardin, 9 percent Balkar, and 32 percent Russian, according to the 1989 census.

Although the tribal system of the Kabardins disappeared with the first contact with Russians, some aspects of the traditional clan system persist in society, and family customs are carefully preserved. Unlike other ethnic groups in the region, the Kabardins were strongly pro-Russian in tsarist times; they did not participate in the numerous uprisings of Caucasus peoples between the eighteenth and twentieth centuries. This affinity survived into the Soviet period despite the dominant position of the aristocracy in Kabardin society.

The economy of Kabardino-Balkaria is based on substantial deposits of gold, chromium, nickel, platinum, iron ore, molybdenum, tungsten, and tin. The main industries are metallurgy, timber and food processing, the manufacture of oil-drilling equipment, and hydroelectric power generation. The republic's capital is Nalchik.

The former Kalmyk Autonomous Soviet Socialist Republic (Kalmyk ASSR) is located in the Caspian Lowland, on the northwestern shore of the Caspian Sea. It has an area of 75,900 square kilometers and a population of about 350,000 (in 1995).

The Kalmyks, also known as the Oirots, were seminomadic Mongol people who migrated from Central Asia in the sixteenth century. In the eighteenth and nineteenth centuries, much of the Kalmyk population was dispersed or extinguished by Russian authorities, and the nomadic lifestyle largely disappeared during this period.

The republic was established in 1920 as an autonomous oblast. The Kalmyk ASSR was established in 1935, dissolved in 1943, then reconstituted in 1958, when its indigenous people were allowed to return from the exile imposed in 1944 for alleged collaboration with the Nazis. The republic officially changed its name to Kalmykia in February 1992. In 1989 the republic's population was 45 percent Kalmyk, 38 percent Russian, 6 percent Dagestani peoples, 3 percent Chechen, 2 percent Kazak, and 2 percent German. The Kalmyk economy is based on the raising of livestock, particularly sheep, and the population is mainly rural; the capital and largest city, Elista, had about 85,000 people in 1989.

Until 1992 an autonomous oblast, the Republic of Karachayevo-Cherkessia occupies 14,100 square kilometers along the northern border of Georgia's Abkhazian Autonomous Republic. A single autonomous region was formed in 1922 for the Cherkess (Circassian) and Karachay peoples; then separate regions existed between 1928 and 1943. The regions were recombined in 1943 as an autonomous oblast. The Cherkess converted to Islam after contacts with Crimean Tatars and Turks; the Karachay are an Islamic Turkic group. The Cherkess are the remnants of a once-dominant Circassian group of tribes that were dispersed, mostly to the Ottoman Empire, by the Russian conquest of the Caucasus region in the early nineteenth century. The original Cherkess now inhabit three republics, divided among five tribal groups: the Adyghs, Kabardins, Balkars, Karachay, and Cherkess (who inherited the original generic name).

The Balkars and the Karachay belong to the same overall Turkic group, although the latter live in the Republic of Karachayevo-Cherkessia immediately west of Kabardino-Balkaria on the north slope of the Caucasus Mountains. Like the Chechens and the Ingush, the Karachay were exiled to Central Asia during World War II. The Cherkess and the Karachay were reunited when the latter were returned from exile in 1957. Established in 1992, the republic is mainly rural, with an economy based on livestock breeding and grain cultivation. Some mining, chemical, and wood-processing facilities also exist. The population, which was estimated at 422,000 in 1990, was 42 percent Russian, 31 percent Karachay, and 10 percent Cherkess. The capital city is Cherkessk.

North Ossetia, called Alania in the republic's 1994 constitution, is located along the northern border of Georgia, between the republics of Kabardino-Balkaria and Ingushetia. The Ossetians are of Iranian and Caucasian origin, and they speak an Iranian language. In the first centuries A.D., Ossetia was occupied by the Alani tribe, ancestors of the modern Ossetians. In the thirteenth century, the Tatars drove the Alani into the mountains; Russian settlers began arriving in the eighteenth century. Russia annexed Ossetia in 1861. In 1924 North Ossetia became an autonomous region of the Soviet Union; in 1936 it was declared an autonomous republic. In 1992 the campaign for separation waged by Georgia's South Ossetian Autonomous Oblast directly to the south drew significant support from compatriots to the north. North Ossetia is the only Caucasus republic of the Russian Federation to give official support to Russia's occupation of nearby Chechnya.

In 1995 the republic's population was estimated at 660,000, of which 53 percent were Ossetian, 29 percent Russian, 5 percent Ingush, 2 percent Armenian, and 2 percent Ukrainian. The area of North Ossetia totals about 8,000 square kilometers. The outputs of industry and agriculture were of approximately equal value in 1993. The main industries, concentrated in the capital city of Vladikavkaz, are metalworking, wood processing, textiles, food processing, and distilling of alcoholic beverages.

The main crops are corn, wheat, potatoes, hemp, and fruit. Lead, zinc, and boron are mined.

The Northern Republics

Karelia and Komi, the two northernmost republics of European Russia, occupy a sizable portion of the latitudes north of Moscow. Both are rich in natural resources, exploitation of which has caused considerable environmental damage.

At 172,400 square kilometers, Karelia is the fourth largest of the autonomous republics of the Russian Federation. The republic shares a border with Finland from the Kola Peninsula in the north to Lake Ladoga in the south. The Karelians are of the same ethnic stock as the Finns. The status of Karelia has changed several times in the twentieth century. When Karelia first became an autonomous republic of the Soviet Union in 1923, it included only the territory known as Eastern Karelia, which had been Russian territory since 1323. When Western Karelia was gained from the Finns in 1940, the enlarged Karelia became a full republic of the Soviet Union, called the Karelo-Finnish Republic. After World War II, the southwestern corner of the republic, including its only stretch of open-water sea-coast on the Gulf of Finland, became part of the Russian Republic. In 1956 the regime of Nikita S. Khrushchev (in office 1953–64) redesignated the artificial entity, which never came close to having a Karelian majority, as the Karelian ASSR. In 1994 the republic's population of about 800,200 was 74 percent Russian, only 10 percent Karelian, 7 percent Belarusian, and 4 percent Ukrainian. The dominant religion is Russian Orthodoxy.

In a region dominated by forests, lakes, and marshes, the Karelian economy is supported mainly by logging, mining, and fishing. The plentiful mineral resources include construction stone, zinc, lead, silver, copper, molybdenum, aluminum, nickel, platinum, tin, barite, and iron ore. Industries include timber and mineral processing, and the manufacturing of furniture, chemicals, and paper. The capital of Karelia is Petrozavodsk.

The Republic of Komi extends westward from the northern end of the Ural Mountains across the Pechora River basin; the republic's westernmost extension is about 250 kilometers east of Arkhangel'sk and the White Sea. The region, which as a republic occupies 415,900 square kilometers, was annexed by the principality of Muscovy in the fourteenth century, principally because of its rich fur-trading potential. In the eighteenth century, Russians began exploiting mineral and timber resources. The Komi people, a Finno-Ugric group, traditionally have herded reindeer, hunted, and fished. They nominally accepted Russian Orthodoxy in the fourteenth century. In 1921 the Soviet government designated an autonomous oblast for the Komi, and in 1936 the oblast became an autonomous republic. The Komi include three ethnic subgroups: the Perm-yaks, who inhabit the Permyak Autonomous Region south of the republic; the Yazua, who live in both the Republic of Komi and the Permyak region; and the Zyryan, who account for the majority of the republic's Komi population. Altogether, in 1994 the Komi constituted 23 percent of the 1.2 million people of their republic, which had a 58 percent Russian majority. Long isolated by the forbidding climate of their region, the Komi of the north have intermixed with other ethnic groups only in recent decades.

Located just southwest of the oil-rich Yamal Peninsula, Komi has become an important producer of oil and natural gas; in 1994 a pipeline leak caused extensive damage to the tundra and rivers in the Pechora Basin. Vorkuta, in the far northeast-ern corner of the republic near the Kara Sea, is an important Arctic coal-mining center. The capital of Komi is Syktyvkar.

The Volga and Ural Republics

Forming a crescent from the middle Volga to the southern extent of Russia's Ural Mountains, six republics represent a variety of ethnic and religious groups. Included in this group are the republics of Bashkortostan and Tatarstan, two of Rus-sia's richest and most independent republics.

Bashkortostan is the name assumed in 1992 by the former Bashkir ASSR, which also had been called Bashkiria. The republic occupies an area of 143,600 square kilometers in the far southeastern corner of European Russia, bounded on the east by the Ural Mountains and within seventy kilometers of the Kazakstan border at its southernmost point. The region was settled by nomads of the steppe, the Turkic Bashkirs, during the thirteenth-century domination by the Golden Horde (see Glossary; The Mongol Invasion, ch. 1). Russians arrived in the mid-sixteenth century, founding the city of Ufa, now the repub-lic's capital. Numerous local uprisings broke out in opposition to the settlement of larger Russian populations in the centuries that followed. The Bashkirs finally give up nomadic life in the nineteenth century, adopting the agricultural lifestyle that remains their primary means of support. The traditional clan-based social structure has largely disappeared. The predominant religions of the Bashkir population are Islam—observed by the majority—and Russian Orthodoxy. A major battleground of the Russian Civil War (1918–21), in 1919 Bashkiria was the first ethnic region to be designated an autonomous republic of Russia under the new communist regime. The republic declared its sovereignty within the Soviet Union in 1990, and in 1992 it declared full independence. Two years later, Bashkortostan agreed to remain within the legislative framework of the Russian Federation, provided that mutual areas of competence were agreed upon.

The republic has rich mineral resources, especially oil, natural gas, iron ore, manganese, copper, salt, and construction stone. The Soviet government built a variety of heavy industries on that resource base, and the republic's economy is relatively prosperous. The traditional Bashkir occupations of livestock raising and beekeeping remain important economic activities. Bashkortostan's population was about 4 million in 1995. In 1989 the major ethnic groups were Russians (39 percent), Tatars (28 percent), Bashkirs (22 percent), Chuvash (3 percent), and Mari (3 percent).

The Republic of Chuvashia, the former Chuvash ASSR, occupies about 18,000 square kilometers along the east bank of the Volga River, about sixty kilometers west of the river's confluence with the Kama River and some 700 kilometers east of Moscow. The Chuvash are a Turkic people whose territory first was settled and annexed by Ivan IV (the Terrible; r. 1533–84) in the sixteenth century (see Ivan IV, ch. 1). At that time, the Chuvash already were a settled agricultural people. In 1920 Chuvashia became an autonomous oblast, and in 1925 it was redesignated an autonomous republic. The republic declared its sovereignty within the Soviet Union in 1990. The primary economic activities are agricultural; grain and fruit production and logging are emphasized. Except for phosphates and gypsum, Chuvashia lacks significant amounts of minerals and fuels.

The Chuvash speak a unique Turkic language and are believed to have descended from the same stock as the modern Bulgarians, whose ancestors migrated from the area. The Chuvash also are the only Turkic ethnic group in Russia to have converted en masse to Russian Orthodoxy. In 1995 the Chuvash constituted 68 percent of the population of their republic, which totaled about 1.4 million. Other groups are Russians (27 percent), Tatars (3 percent), and Mordovians (1 percent). The capital city is Cheboksary.

The Republic of Mari El, formerly the Mari ASSR, is located in the middle Volga Basin on the north shore of the river, directly east of the city of Nizhniy Novgorod (formerly Gor'kiy). The Finno-Ugric Mari people, also known as Cheremiss, first came into contact with the Russians in the sixteenth century, when the major Tatar outpost of Kazan', just downstream from the current republic, fell to Ivan IV. The autonomous oblast of Mari was established in 1920; an autonomous republic was designated in 1936. The economy is based mainly on timber products, agriculture, and machine building; the region is not rich in mineral resources. In 1989 the largest ethnic group was the Russians, who make up 48 percent of the population, with Mari constituting 45 percent and Tatars 6 percent. The predominant religion is Russian Orthodoxy, although some traces of animism remain in the Mari population. The total population in 1995 was 754,000, about 60 percent of whom dwell in cities. The republic's area is 23,300 square kilometers. The capital city is Yoshkar Ola.

Formerly the Mordovian (or Mordvinian) ASSR, Mordovia (or Mordvinia) is located at the southwestern extreme of the middle Volga cluster of autonomous republics that also includes Tatarstan, Mari El, Udmurtia, and Chuvashia. Belonging to the Finno-Ugric ethnic group, the Mordovians were traditionally agriculturalists, known especially as beekeepers. The first Russians reached the area in the twelfth century, and Muscovy had taken full control of Mordovia by the seventeenth century. After receiving the status of autonomous oblast in 1930, Mordovia was declared an autonomous republic in 1934. Although the Mordovians nominally accepted Russian Orthodoxy in the seventeenth century, they retain significant remnants of their pre-Christian beliefs, as well as national costumes and social practices.

In 1995 Russians constituted about 61 percent of the republic's population of approximately 964,000. Another 33 percent were Mordovians, and 5 percent were Tatars. The total area of Mordovia is 26,200 square kilometers. The republic's economy is based mainly on agriculture, especially the cultivation of grains, tobacco, hemp, and vegetables. Industry includes some machine building and chemical manufacturing, as well as enterprises based on timber and metals. The capital of Mordovia is Saransk.

Located in the middle Volga east of Mari El and Chuvashia and west of Bashkortostan, Tatarstan was established as an autonomous republic in 1920 for one segment of the large and widespread Tatar population of the Russian Republic. In the 1980s, less than one-third of Russia's Tatars lived in the republic designated for them. Extensive populations of Tatars, who are predominantly Muslim, are scattered throughout Russia as well as most of the other former Soviet republics. In the late Soviet period, numerous Tatars migrated to the Central Asian republics, in particular Uzbekistan and Tajikistan. The population of Tatarstan, about 3.8 million in 1995, is second only to that of Bashkortostan among Russia's republics. According to the 1989 census, the population was 49 percent Tatar, 43 percent Russian, 4 percent Chuvash, 1 percent Ukrainian, and 1 percent Mordovian.

The Tatars are a Turkic people whose language belongs to the Kipchak group and has several regional dialects. The region of present-day Tatarstan was occupied by the Mongols when the Golden Horde swept across the middle Volga region in the early thirteenth century. When the Mongol Empire fragmented two centuries later, one of its constituent parts, the Tatar Kazan' Khanate, inherited the middle Volga and held the region until its defeat by Ivan IV. Shortly thereafter, Russian colonization began.

Tatarstan has a diversified, well-developed economy that has been the basis of bold claims of independence from the Russian Federation beginning in 1992 (see Movements Toward Sovereignty, this ch.). The first World Congress of Tatars was held in the republic's capital, Kazan', in June 1992. About 1,200 delegates attended from Tatarstan and the Tatar diaspora to discuss the republic's status. In 1994 a bilateral agreement with the Yeltsin administration satisfied some of the republic's claims to sovereignty.

In 1995 the discovery of a large oil field in northern Tatarstan promised to boost the sagging local economy; oil extraction already was Tatarstan's most important industry. Other major industries include chemical manufacturing, machine building, and the manufacture of vehicles and paper products. The agricultural sector produces grains, potatoes, sugar beets, hemp, tobacco, apples, dairy products, and livestock.

Udmurtia, formerly the Udmurt ASSR, occupies 42,100 square kilometers north of Tatarstan on the lower reaches of the Kama River, northeast of the confluence of the Kama and the Volga. The Udmurts are a Finno-Ugric people whose territory was occupied by the Kazan' Khanate in the fourteenth and fifteenth centuries, then passed to Russian control when Ivan IV captured Kazan' in 1552. Originally established as the Votyak Autonomous Oblast in 1920, the territory was renamed for the Udmurts in 1932, then redesignated an autonomous republic in 1934. In 1995 the republic's population was about 1.5 million, of which 59 percent was Russian, 31 percent Udmurt, 7 percent Tatar, 1 percent Ukrainian, and 1 percent Mari.

Located in the industrial zone of the south Ural Mountains, Udmurtia has a substantial and diversified industrial economy that emphasizes locomotives and rolling stock, metallurgy, machine tools, construction materials, clothing, leather, and food processing. The capital city, Izhevsk, is also the largest industrial center. The most important agricultural products are grains, vegetables, and livestock.

The Republics of Siberia

Of the five republics located east of the Urals in Asian Russia, four—Buryatia, Gorno-Altay, Khakassia, and Tyva—extend along Russia's southern border with Mongolia. The fifth, Sakha (formerly Yakutia), is Russia's largest subnational jurisdiction and the possessor of a large and varied supply of valuable natural resources.

The Republic of Buryatia, formerly the Buryat ASSR, occupies 351,300 square kilometers along the eastern shore of Lake Baikal and along the north-central border of Mongolia. The Buryats, a nomadic herding people of Mongolian stock, first faced colonization by Russian settlers in the seventeenth century. After initially resisting this intrusion, most of the Buryats eventually adapted to life in farming settlements, which continues to be the predominant mode of existence. In 1989 the Buryats constituted only about 24 percent of the republic's population; Russians made up about 70 percent. The total Buryat population of the Soviet Union in the 1980s was about 390,000, with about 150,000 living in the adjacent oblasts of Chita and Irkutsk. In 1994 the population of the republic was 1.1 million, of which more than one-third lived in the capital city, Ulan-Ude.

Buryatia possesses rich mineral resources, notably bauxite, coal, gold, iron, rare earth minerals, uranium, manganese, molybdenum, nickel, and tungsten. Livestock raising, fur farming, hunting, and fishing are important economic pursuits of the indigenous population. The main industries derive from coal extraction, timber harvesting, and engineering.

Gorno-Altay was established in 1922 as the Oirot Autonomous Oblast, for the Mongol people of that name. In 1948 the region was renamed the Gorno-Altay Autonomous Oblast. Redesignated a republic in 1992, the region took its present name—the Republic of Gorno-Altay, or simply Altay (the vernacular term omits *gorno*, which means mountainous in Russian)—in that year. Occupying 92,600 square kilometers on the north slope of the Altay Range on the northeast border of Kazakstan, Gorno-Altay had a population in 1995 of 200,000, of whom 60 percent were Russian and 31 percent Altay. About 83 percent of Russia's total Altay population lives in the Republic of Gorno-Altay. The Altay people comprise several Turkic-speaking tribes living in the Altay and Kuznetsk Alatau mountains. Several collective terms have been applied to the overall group, including "Oirot," which was used in tsarist times. The Altays first came into contact with Russians in the eighteenth century, when colonization of the region began. Some conversion to Christianity occurred in the nineteenth century, but substantial numbers of Altays returned to their previous Mongolian Lamaism in the early twentieth century, as part of a general movement against Russian domination. In the post-Soviet era, most of the republic's population is Orthodox Christian.

The economy of Gorno-Altay is primarily agricultural, supported mainly by livestock raising in the hillsides and valleys that dominate the republic's landscape. Gold and other precious and nonprecious minerals—especially the rare earth minerals tantalum and cesium—support a small mining industry, and Gorno-Altay possesses rich coniferous forests. The main industries, mostly based on local resources, are the manufacture of clothing, footwear, and foods, and the processing of chemicals and minerals. The capital of the republic is Gorno-Altaysk.

Khakassia, an autonomous oblast that was redesignated an autonomous republic in 1992, is located about 1,000 kilometers west of Lake Baikal on the upper Yenisey River. Before the arrival of the first Russians in the seventeenth century, Khakassia was a regional power in Siberia, based on commercial links with the khanates of Central Asia and with the Chinese Empire. The sparsely populated republic (total population in 1995 was about 600,000) occupies 61,900 square kilometers of hilly terrain at the far northwestern end of the Altay Range. The Khakass people are a formerly nomadic Turkic Siberian group whose modern-day sedentary existence depends on sheep and goat husbandry. Russians now constitute nearly 80 percent of the population of Khakassia, although in 1989 more than three-quarters of oblast residents spoke Khakass. The Khakass population is 11 percent of the total. The republic produces timber, copper, iron ore, gold, molybdenum, and tungsten. The capital of Khakassia is Abakan.

Sakha, whose name was changed from Yakutia in 1994, is by far the largest of the republics in size. It occupies about 3.1 million square kilometers that stretch from Russia's Arctic shores in the north to within 500 kilometers of the Chinese border in the south, and from the longitude of the Taymyr Peninsula in the west to within 400 kilometers of the Pacific Ocean in the east. Sakha was annexed by the Russian Empire in the first half of the seventeenth century. Russians slowly populated the valley of the Lena River, which flows northward through the heart of Sakha. In the nineteenth century, most of the nomadic Yakuts adopted an agricultural lifestyle.

Formed as the Yakut Autonomous Republic in 1922, Sakha had a population of 1.1 million in 1994, of which 50 percent were Russian, 33 percent Yakut, 7 percent Ukrainian, and 2 percent Tatar. The Yakuts are a Mongoloid people who originated through the combination of local tribes with Turkic tribes that migrated northward before the tenth century.

Climatic conditions preclude agriculture in most of Sakha. Where agriculture is possible, the main crops are potatoes, oats, rye, and vegetables. The republic's economy is supported mainly by its extensive mineral deposits, which include gold, diamonds, silver, tin, coal, and natural gas. Sakha produces most of Russia's diamonds, and natural gas deposits are thought to be large. The capital of Sakha is Yakutsk.

Tyva was called the Tuva ASSR until the new Russian constitution recognized Tyva, the regional form of the name, in 1993. The republic occupies 170,500 square kilometers on the border of Mongolia, directly east of Gorno-Altay. After being part of the Chinese Empire for 150 years and existing as the independent state of Tannu Tuva between 1921 and 1944, Tyva voluntarily joined the Soviet Union in 1944 and became an autonomous oblast. It became an autonomous republic in 1961. The Tuvinians are a Turkic people with a heritage of rule by tribal chiefs. The republic's predominant religion is Tibetan Buddhism. In 1995 the population of about 314,000 was 64 percent Tuvinian and 32 percent Russian.

Tyva is mainly an agricultural region with only five cities and a predominantly rural population. The main agricultural activity is cattle raising, and fur is an important product. Gold, cobalt, and asbestos are mined, and the republic has extensive hydroelectric resources. The capital is Kyzyl.

Other Ethnic Groups

Besides the ethnic groups granted official jurisdictions in the Russian Republic and later in the Russian Federation, several minority groups have played an important role at some stage of the country's development. Among those that exist in significant numbers in parts of post-Soviet Russia are Germans, Koreans, and Roma.

Germans

According to the Soviet census of 1989, a total of 842,000 Germans lived in Russia. The remains of a large enclave that was settled along the Volga River beginning in the time of Peter the Great (r. 1682–1725), the "Volga Germans" were the ethnic basis of an autonomous republic before World War II. When Germany attacked the Soviet Union in 1941, Joseph V. Stalin (in office 1927–53) dissolved the republic and dispersed the German population into Central Asia and Siberia. Although some German prisoners of war remained in the Soviet Union after the war, many others returned to Germany in the decades that followed. By 1991 less than half of the German Russians claimed German as their first language.

Because of the discrimination suffered by the Volga Germans, the postwar constitution of the Federal Republic of Germany (West Germany) granted ethnic Germans in Russia the right to citizenship if they moved to Germany. Russia's German population began lobbying for reestablishment of the prewar Volga German Autonomous Republic in 1990. In 1991 President Yeltsin began discussions with the German government on creation of a German autonomous republic on the lower Volga near Volgograd. A protocol of cooperation signed in 1992 arranged for such a republic in exchange for significant financial aid from Germany. However, the proposed German enclave encountered strong local resistance from populations that would have been displaced by the Germans on the lower Volga; official discussion of the issue ended in 1993. In 1995 about 75,000 Russian Germans settled in Germany.

Koreans

An increasing percentage of the approximately 321,000 Koreans living in the former Soviet republics of Central Asia, in particular Uzbekistan, began migrating to the Russian Federation in 1992 when various forms of discrimination against non-indigenous peoples increased in those republics. Most of these migrants to Russia have settled in Maritime (Primorskiy) Territory, where their commercial activities have competed with local merchants and stirred numerous anti-Korean incidents. In 1996 about 36,000 Koreans also were living on Sakhalin Island.

When economic conditions deteriorated in the Democratic People's Republic of Korea (North Korea) in the mid-1990s, the North Korean government allowed thousands of carefully chosen guest workers to find manual jobs in Vladivostok and other parts of the Russian Far East. As North Korean guest workers have sought asylum in Russia, the question of their repatriation has caused Russia a difficult diplomatic problem in its relations with North Korea and the Republic of Korea (South Korea), in view of Russia's intensified efforts to expand commercial ties with South Korea without alienating putative ally North Korea. Korean arrivals in Russia from Central Asia and from North Korea receive support from the Association of Ethnic Koreans and from South Korea. Another Korean émigré organization, the United Confederation of Koreans in Russia, lends vocal support to North Korea in its disputes with South Korea. Tensions between the two Korean populations were very strong by 1996. Russian migration officials feared a much larger influx of North Koreans if the North Korean government collapsed.

Roma

The 1989 Soviet census indicated that Russia was home to about 153,000 Roma, commonly known as Gypsies. However, the actual size of the population is unknown because many Roma do not register their nationality; experts assume that the true number is much higher than the official estimate. Most of the Roma currently in Russia are descended from people who

Members of Korean community gather at Korean Cultural Center,
Vladivostok.
Courtesy Youn-Cha Shin Chey

migrated from Europe in the eighteenth century; they now call themselves Russka Roma. Another group, called the Vlach Roma, arrived after 1850 from the Balkans. Other Roma travel seasonally to Moscow from Moldova and Romania and back. Members of this group are often seen begging on Moscow streets; this activity has figured largely in the negative stereotype of the Roma among ethnic Russians.

Most Roma have been unable or unwilling to gain employment in any but a few occupations. In the Soviet era, metalworking was a designated Roma trade, but street commerce—selling whatever goods become available—remains the most common occupation. Roma were much involved in the blackmarket trade of the last Soviet decades. Roma musical ensembles have prospered in Soviet and post-Soviet times, but few individuals have access to such a profession.

In general, post-Soviet Russian society has included the Roma with other easily identified non-Slavic groups, particularly those from the Caucasus, who are accused of exploiting or worsening the economic condition of the majority population. In the 1990s, violence has erupted between Russians and Roma on several occasions. The wide dispersion of the Russian Roma population—there are at least six distinct groups, with little contact among them—has limited their ability to organize. In the 1990s, some Russian Roma have participated in international movements to gain support abroad. The various groups have widely varying political views. The elite musical performers and intelligentsia, for example, supported the socialism of the Soviet Union, but the wealthy Lovari group, which the government persecuted in Soviet times, is strongly antisocialist.

Movements Toward Sovereignty

Beginning in 1990, many of the constituent autonomous republics and regions, delineated at various stages of tsarist or Soviet control, used the chaos and centrifugal force created by the breakup of the Soviet Union to move toward local sovereignty. The legislatures of most republics made official declarations of sovereignty over their land and natural resources between August and October 1990. Although the declaration of full independence by the Chechen Autonomous Republic was the most extreme result of such moves, some observers felt that the political and economic stability of the Russian Federation was threatened by the separatism of regions that were valuable because of their strategic location or natural resources (see The Separatism Question, ch. 7). Furthermore, Russia, acutely conscious of having lost its "near abroad"—the fourteen republics that constituted the Soviet Union together with the RSFSR—could ill afford the second blow to national self-image that the loss of ethnically based jurisdictions would inflict.

Occupying about three-quarters of the territory of the former Soviet Union, Russia is the largest country in the world. It never has existed as a country within its present borders, however. Intent upon preserving the territorial integrity of the Russian Federation, the government in Moscow maintains an uneasy relationship with the non-Russian (and particularly the non-Slavic) nationalities. This relationship stems from Russian racial, religious, and cultural stereotypes (for example, perceptions of the dark-skinned Muslims in the midst of white-skinned, Orthodox Slavs), a historical tendency toward xenophobia among Russian commoners and parts of the Russian intelligentsia, and a legacy of forcible incorporation of various ethnic and nationality groups into the Russian Empire and the Soviet Union. Further complicating the relationship is the fact that many of Russia's abundant natural resources lie in the territories of various regions now proclaiming exclusive sovereignty over those resources.

Although some tensions in ethnic and nationality relations stem from a desire for union between peoples on both sides of an internal or international border arbitrarily drawn by the tsars or by Soviet authorities, other motivations also underlie the assertiveness of national minorities in the federation. In the more liberal post-Soviet atmosphere, people no longer must suppress their anger over Soviet political and economic subjugation and Russification campaigns. Accordingly, non-Russian nationalities seek recompense for long periods of colonial-style exploitation of their indigenous resources for the benefit of the regime in Moscow. Another cause of dissatisfaction is the perceived failure of the Russian government to provide adequate support and protection for native schools and cultures. Finally, the end of the Russian government's monopolization and censorship of the news media acquainted minority groups with political trends, such as the spread of nationalism, with which the rest of the world has been familiar for some time.

Other tensions result from Russian policies that non-Russian groups perceive as discriminatory or confiscatory. Examples include unfair tax practices and the refusal of the Russian government to let various ethnic groups reap the income from sale of their indigenous products and natural resources.

Separatist agitation in many areas of Russia already had begun in the Soviet Union's twilight years. A full year before the Soviet Union's demise, more than half the autonomous republics in the RSFSR had adopted declarations of sovereignty. Every region of the vast RSFSR was affected by this trend, which was more an indication of the central government's waning authority—even in regions relatively close to Moscow—than it was an indication of intent by those declaring sovereignty.

In May 1990, the Tuva ASSR witnessed civil strife between the Russian and Tuvinian populations. Charging that Russia had failed to provide them with employment opportunities or suitable housing and had sought to eradicate their indigenous culture, the Tuvinians attacked Russian neighborhoods, setting fire to homes and forcing about 3,000 Russians to flee.

In October 1990, the Chuvash ASSR declared itself a full republic of the Soviet Union, a status that would have given it equal status with Russia, Ukraine, and the other thirteen Soviet republics. Although the announcement stated that Chuvashia would remain part of the Russian Federation, the republic would exercise complete control over all its natural resources and would make Chuvash equal with Russian as an official language. Also in 1990, the Mari ASSR, about 500 kilometers east of Moscow, proclaimed itself a full Soviet republic whose natural resources would become the exclusive property of its people and whose state languages would be Mari and Russian. The republic adopted the new vernacular name "Mari El," meaning "Mari Territory," and that name won official approval from the government in Moscow.

Also in 1990, the Gorno-Altay Autonomous Oblast and the Adygh Autonomous Oblast unilaterally upgraded themselves to autonomous-republic status. While declaring their intention to remain part of the RSFSR, these jurisdictions asserted the right to local control of their land and natural resources. Still another declaration of sovereignty came from the Buryat ASSR. The Buryats declared that their republic's laws henceforth would take precedence over those of the RSFSR.

In northwestern Russia, secessionist sentiment manifested itself among the ethnic minorities of the Karelian and Komi ASSRs. In the autumn of 1990, local Karelian authorities protested insufficient food shipments by refusing to deliver timber and paper products to Russia. Many Karelians, ethnically close to the Finns, want their republic to become part of Finland.

During the period leading to the collapse of the Soviet Union, local officials in the oil-rich Bashkir ASSR (renamed Bashkortostan in 1992) declared sovereignty, and the Chukchi Autonomous Region, which faces Alaska across the Bering Strait, declared itself autonomous and demanded control over its reindeer and fish resources. Commenting on the rash of separatist activity, an adviser to President Mikhail S. Gorbachev remarked, "It's getting to the point where sooner or later someone is going to declare his apartment an independent state."

In October 1991, the legislature of the Tatar ASSR, some 600 kilometers east of Moscow, adopted a declaration of independence from Moscow, and in 1992 Tatarstan approved a constitution that described the republic as being on an equal footing with the Russian Federation. And, in what was to become the most troublesome of the ethnic autonomy movements of the 1990s, Chechnya proclaimed its sovereignty in October 1991.

Among these nominally separatist political units, the transition from words to deeds has been uneven. In some cases, ethnic and nationality groups appear content with the mere form of sovereignty; in others, efforts are under way to give substance to the words of separatism. In republics such as Mordovia, Ingushetia, and Kabardino-Balkaria, relations with Russia are the defining issue among opposing political groups. Other republics, such as pro-Russian Kalmykia and independence-minded Bashkortostan, are firmly under the control of a single leader.

The enormous Republic of Sakha in north-central Siberia, rich in diamonds and other minerals, exemplifies the threat that secession poses to the Russian Federation. Sakha has declared that its local laws supersede those imposed from Moscow and that it will retain all revenues generated by the sale and use of its resources. The republic also has accepted substantial direct development investment from Japan and China. Many members of Sakha's Russian majority have sided with the indigenous population in supporting self-government or full independence. Experts believe that such regions as Sakha, Tatarstan, and Bashkortostan theoretically have sufficient natural wealth to become viable independent entities. According to estimates, these regions' secession from the Russian Federation would deprive Russia of half of its oil, most of its diamonds, and much of its coal, as well as a substantial portion of such industries as automobile manufacturing.

Against the backdrop of ethnic and nationality tensions, a tug-of-war developed in the early 1990s over the respective powers of the federal and local governments in Russia (see Local and Regional Government, ch. 7). In March 1992, representatives of all but two of the republics (Chechnya and Tatarstan) and most of the smaller ethnic jurisdictions signed the Federation Treaty, which was an attempt to forestall further separatism and define the respective jurisdictions of central and regional government. The treaty failed to resolve differences in the key areas of taxation and control of natural resources, however. In some cases, self-proclaimed independent entities in Siberia and elsewhere in the Russian Federation have forged links with foreign countries. Commercial and cultural accords between Turkey and Turkic republics such as Bashkortostan and Chuvashia especially worry the central government.

The Chechnya Dilemma

The only autonomous jurisdictions that refused to sign the 1992 Federation Treaty were Chechnya and Tatarstan, both of which are rich in oil. In the spring of 1994, President Yeltsin signed a special political accord with the president of Tatarstan granting many of the Tatar demands for greater autonomy. Yeltsin declined to carry out serious negotiations with Chechnya, however, allowing the situation to deteriorate into full-scale war at the end of 1994 (see Chechnya, ch. 9). In the first half of 1996, Chechnya continued to pose the biggest obstacle to the quelling of separatism among the components of the Russian Federation.

Chechnya long has had a reputation in Russia as a center of organized crime and corrupt business practices; the Chechen *mafiya* has a particularly fierce reputation. The proportion of Chechens and other Caucasians in Russia's emerging market economy is much higher than the representation of these nationalities in the population as a whole. In its propaganda campaign to justify military action against Chechnya, the Russian government played upon the stereotypes of the criminal and the dishonest businessman. It also illustrated the brutal practices of the Chechen rebels by broadcasting photos of the severed heads of victims along the roads in the breakaway republic. Meanwhile, Russians adopted the habit of including all individuals of non-Slavic appearance under the heading "Chechen," widening the existing strain of racism in Russia's society.

The first Russian invasion of Chechnya occurred during the time of Peter the Great, in the early eighteenth century. After a long series of fierce battles and bloody massacres, Chechnya was incorporated into Russia in the 1870s. In 1936 Stalin created the Chechen-Ingush Autonomous Republic. In 1943, when Nazi forces reached the gates of the Chechen capital, Groznyy, Chechen separatists staged a rebellion against Russian rule. In response, the next year Stalin deported more than 1 million Chechens, Ingush, and other North Caucasian peoples to Siberia and Central Asia on the pretext that they had collaborated with the Nazis. The remaining Muslim people of the Chechnya region were resettled among neighboring Christian communities. Stalin's genocidal policy virtually erased Chechnya from the map, but Soviet first secretary Nikita S. Khrushchev permitted the Chechen and Ingush peoples to return to their homeland and restored their republic in 1957.

The series of events since the Soviet Union's collapse flowed naturally from the Chechens' long-standing hatred of the Russians. In September 1991, the government of the Chechen-Ingush Autonomous Republic resigned under pressure from the proindependence Congress of the Chechen People, whose leader was former Soviet air force general Dzhokar Dudayev. The following month, Dudayev won overwhelming popular support to oust the interim, central government-supported administration and make himself president. Dudayev then issued a unilateral declaration of independence. In November 1991, President Yeltsin dispatched troops to Groznyy, but they were withdrawn when Dudayev's forces prevented them from leaving the airport.

The Chechen-Ingush Autonomous Republic split in two in June 1992. After Chechnya had announced its initial declaration of sovereignty in 1991, Ingushetia joined the Russian Federation; Chechnya declared full independence in 1993. In August 1994, when an opposition faction launched an armed campaign to topple Dudayev's government, Moscow supplied the rebel forces with military equipment, and Russian aircraft began to bomb Groznyy. In December, five days after Dudayev and Minister of Defense Pavel Grachev of Russia had agreed to avoid the further use of force, Russian troops invaded Chechnya.

The Russian government's expectations of a quick surgical strike followed by Chechen capitulation were misguided. The protracted war in Chechnya, which generated many reports of violence against civilians, ignited fear and contempt toward Russia among many other ethnic groups in the federation. Experts believe that the inability of Russian forces to subdue the Chechen "bandits" also might encourage other ethnic groups to defy the central government by proclaiming and defending their independence. As the war was reported to the Russian public on television and in newspaper accounts, the rising protests from Russia's independent news media and various political and other interest groups soon came to threaten Russia's democratic experiment. Chechnya was one of the heaviest burdens Yeltsin carried during the 1996 presidential election campaign.

In January 1996, the destruction of the Dagestani border village of Pervomayskoye by Russian forces in reaction to Chechen hostage taking brought strong criticism from the hitherto loyal Republic of Dagestan and escalated domestic dissatisfaction. Chechnya's declaration that it was waging a jihad (holy war) against Russia also raised the specter that Muslim "volunteers" from other regions and even outside Russia would enter the fray. However, Russia feared that a move to end the war short of victory would create a cascade of secession attempts by other ethnic minorities and present a new target to extreme nationalist Russian factions.

Some fighting occurred in Ingushetia in 1995, mostly when Russian commanders sent troops over the border in pursuit of Chechen rebels. Although all sides generally observed the distinction between the two peoples that formerly shared the autonomous republic, as many as 200,000 refugees from Chechnya and neighboring North Ossetia strained Ingushetia's already weak economy. On several occasions, Ingush president Ruslan Aushev protested incursions by Russian soldiers, even threatening to sue the Russian Ministry of Defense for damages inflicted.

Meanwhile, the war in Chechnya spawned a new form of separatist activity in the Russian Federation. Resistance to the conscription of men from minority ethnic groups to fight in Chechnya was widespread among other republics, many of which passed laws and decrees on the subject. For example, the government of Chuvashia passed a decree providing legal protection to soldiers from the republic who refused to participate in the Chechnya war and imposing limits on the use of the Russian army in ethnic or regional conflicts within Russia. Some regional and local legislative bodies called for a prohibition on the use of draftees in quelling internal uprisings; others demanded a total ban on the use of the armed forces in domestic conflicts.

The Caucasus Region in the Federation

The oil-rich region around Chechnya, between the Black Sea and the Caspian Sea, forms a southwestern corridor of Russian territory bounded on the west by Ukraine and the Black Sea, on the south by Georgia and Azerbaijan, and on the east by the Caspian Sea and Kazakstan. The region north of the Caucasus includes seven ethnic republics and four "Russian" jurisdictions: the territories of Krasnodar and Stavropol' and the oblasts of Rostov and Astrakhan'. With the thirty ethnically and linguistically distinct communities of Dagestan the most extreme example of the region's ethnic diversity, much of the region surrounding Chechnya is a cauldron of nationality and ethnic conflicts among warlike mountain clans. On the opposite slope of the Caucasus, the former Soviet republic of Georgia likewise includes a number of ethnic groups, two of which—the Abkhaz and the South Ossetians—declared outright independence in the early 1990s.

Tsarist Russia conducted a centuries-long process of expansion into the Caucasus region, subduing the nationalities of the area gradually and often at great expense. The region has assumed particular importance in the contemporary era because of its oil, its location astride Russia's transportation and communications arteries leading to the Middle East, and the central government's fear of resurgent Islam along the southern border of the former Soviet Union.

Not far from Chechnya, a self-styled Confederation of Mountain Peoples of the North Caucasus emerged in 1992 in southwestern Russia, where the borders of the Russian Federation abut the Transcaucasian republics of the former Soviet Union. That confederation, including representatives from Russia's seven republics bordering the Caucasus, aspires to establish a chain of independent, predominantly Muslim states along the federation's southern periphery. It also has provided a forum for Chechen leaders to enlist support against Russia and for separatist leaders from Abkhazia and South Ossetia to enlist support against Georgia. Terrorist acts in Chechnya and elsewhere have been attributed to confederation members.

Responses and Prospects

In the mid-1990s, the relationship of Russia's central government to its regional jurisdictions remains tentative; the Yeltsin administration's failure to contain separatist movements is a favorite target of the president's nationalist critics. The Yeltsin government's policy toward separatism grew from the theory that compromises made with individual ethnic groups would satisfy the need to express national identity. Such an approach rests on the proposition that the diverse inhabitants of the Russian Federation ultimately will identify closely enough with the federation to ensure its continuing territorial integrity, and that centrifugal impulses will not lead Russia to the fate suffered by the Soviet Union.

Theoretically, the secession of one component of the Russian Federation could encourage the movement of others in an irrational but uncontrollable domino effect. On the one hand, Russia's inability to reverse secession despite the deployment of a large-scale force in Chechnya is cited by experts as an inducement to other national units to break away. On the other hand, the fact that no minority ethnic group constitutes more than 4 percent of the federation's population militates against breakaway jurisdictions attaining the critical mass and political leverage needed to secede and function successfully as independent nations. In many respects, Russia's ethnic republics, many of which lie deep within the boundaries of the federation, remain heavily dependent on the center, especially in economic matters. For example, under the conditions of the mid-1990s, Tatarstan's oil cannot be processed or transported to the outside world without the utilization of facilities lying outside its borders, in Russia proper. Thus, the threat of secession has now been established as a bargaining chip in the struggle with the central government for political and economic advantage, but it is a threat of limited practical value.

Religion

The chief religion of Russia is Russian Orthodox Christianity, which is professed by about 75 percent of citizens who describe themselves as religious believers. Because the concept of separation of church and state never took root in Russia, the Russian Orthodox Church, a branch of Eastern Orthodoxy, was a pillar of tsarist autocracy. During the communist era, the church, like every other institution in the Soviet Union, was completely subordinate to the state, achieving a modus vivendi by ceding most of its autonomous identity. Under the officially atheist regimes of the Soviet Union, no official figures on the number of religious believers in the country were available to Western scholars. According to various Soviet and Western sources, however, more than one-third of the citizens of the Soviet Union regarded themselves as believers in the 1980s, when the number of adherents to Russian Orthodoxy was estimated at more than 50 million—although a high percentage of that number feared to express their religious beliefs openly.

Islam, professed by about 19 percent of believers in the mid-1990s, is numerically the second most important religion in Russia. Various non-Orthodox Christian denominations and a dwindling but still important Jewish population complete the list of major religious groups in the Russian Federation. In general, Russians of all religions have enjoyed freedom of worship since the collapse of the communist regime in 1991, and large numbers of abandoned or converted religious buildings have been returned to active religious use in the 1990s.

The Russian Orthodox Church

The Russian Orthodox Church has a thousand-year history of strong political as well as spiritual influence over the inhabitants of the Russian state. After enduring the Soviet era as a state-controlled religious facade, the church quickly regained both membership and political influence in the early 1990s.

Beliefs and Ritual

Orthodox belief holds that the Orthodox Church is Christianity's true, holy, and apostolic church, tracing its origin directly to the institution established by Jesus Christ. Orthodox beliefs are based on the Bible and on tradition as defined by seven ecumenical councils held by church authorities between A.D. 325 and 787. Orthodox teachings include the doctrine of the Holy Trinity and the inseparable but distinguishable union of the two natures of Jesus Christ—one divine, the other human. Among saints, Mary has a special place as the Mother of God. Russian Orthodox services, noted for their pageantry, involve the congregation directly by using only the vernacular form of the liturgy. The liturgy itself includes multiple elaborate systems of symbols meant to convey the content of the faith to believers. Many liturgical forms remain from the earliest days of Orthodoxy. Icons, sacred images often illuminated by candles, adorn the churches as well as the homes of most Orthodox faithful. The church also places a heavy emphasis on monasticism. Many of the numerous monasteries that dotted the forests and remote regions of tsarist Russia are in the process of restoration. The Russian Orthodox Church, like the other churches that make up Eastern Orthodoxy, is autonomous, or self-governing. The highest church official is the patriarch. Matters relating to faith are decided by ecumenical councils in which all member churches of Eastern Orthodoxy participate. Followers of the church regard the councils' decisions as infallible.

Church History

The Russian Orthodox Church traces its origins to the time of Kievan Rus', the first forerunner of the modern Russian state. In A.D. 988 Prince Vladimir made the Byzantine variant of Christianity the state religion of Russia (see The Golden Age of Kiev, ch. 1). The Russian church was subordinate to the patriarch (see Glossary) of Constantinople (present-day Istanbul), seat of the Byzantine Empire. The original seat of the metropolitan, as the head of the church was known, was Kiev. As power moved from Kiev to Moscow in the fourteenth century, the seat moved as well, establishing the tradition that the metropolitan of Moscow is the head of the church. In the Middle Ages, the church placed strong emphasis on asceticism, which evolved into a widespread monastic tradition. Large numbers of monasteries were founded in obscure locations across all of the medieval state of Muscovy. Such small settlements expanded into larger population centers, making the monastic movement one of the bases of social and economic as well as spiritual life.

After the fall of the Byzantine Empire in 1453, the Russian Orthodox Church evolved into a semi-independent (autocephalous) branch of Eastern Christianity. In 1589 the metropolitan of Moscow received the title of patriarch. Nevertheless, the Russian church retained the Byzantine tradition of authorizing the head of state and the government bureaucracy to participate actively in the church's administrative affairs. Separation of church and state thus would be almost unknown in Russia.

As Western Europe was emerging from the Middle Ages into the Renaissance and the Reformation, Russia remained isolated from the West, and Russian Orthodoxy was virtually untouched by the changes in intellectual and spiritual life being felt elsewhere. In the seventeenth century, the introduction by Ukrainian clergy of Western doctrinal and liturgical reforms prompted a strong reaction among traditionalist Orthodox believers, resulting in a schism in the church.

In the early eighteenth century, Peter the Great modernized, expanded, and consolidated Muscovy into what then became known as the Russian Empire. In the process of redefining his power as tsar, Peter curtailed the minimal secular influence of the Russian Orthodox Church, which was functioning principally as a pillar of the tsarist regime. In 1721 Peter the Great went so far as to abolish the patriarchate and establish a governmental organ called the Holy Synod, staffed by secular officials, to administer and control the church. As a result, the church's moral authority declined in the eighteenth and nineteenth centuries.

In the second half of the nineteenth century, the monastic tradition produced a number of church elders who gained the

*Cathedral of the Assumption at
Trinity-St. Sergey Monastery
(Troitse-Sergiyeva lavra),
Zagorsk
Courtesy Jim Howland*

*Religious procession with icon,
Kazan'
Courtesy Carolou Marquet*

respect of all classes in Russia as wise counselors on both secular and spiritual matters. Similarly, by 1900 a strong revival movement was calling for the restoration of church autonomy and organizational reform. However, few practical reforms had been implemented when the October Revolution of 1917 brought to power the Bolsheviks (see Glossary), who set about eliminating the worldly and spiritual powers of the church. Ironically, earlier in 1917 the moderate Provisional Government had provided the church a few months of restoration to its pre-Petrine stature by reestablishing the patriarchate and independent governance of the church. In the decades that followed, the communist leadership frequently used the restored patriarch as a propaganda agent, allowing him to meet with foreign religious representatives in an effort to create the impression of freedom of religion in the Soviet Union.

Karl Marx, the political philosopher whose ideas were nominally followed by the Bolsheviks, called religion "the opiate of the people." Although many of Russia's revolutionary factions did not take Marx literally, the Bolshevik faction, led by Vladimir I. Lenin, was deeply suspicious of the church as an institution and as a purveyor of spiritual values. Therefore, atheism became mandatory for members of the ruling Russian Communist Party (Bolshevik). To eliminate as soon as possible what was deemed the perverse influence of religion in society, the communists launched a propaganda campaign against all forms of religion.

By 1918 the government had nationalized all church property, including buildings. In the first five years of the Soviet Union (1922–26), twenty-eight Russian Orthodox bishops and more than 1,200 priests were executed, and many others were persecuted. Most seminaries were closed, and publication of most religious material was prohibited. The next quarter-century saw surges and declines in arrests, enforcement of laws against religious assembly and activities, and harassment of clergy. Antireligious campaigns were directed at all faiths; beginning in the 1920s, Buddhist and Shamanist places of worship in Buryatia, in the Baikal region, were destroyed, and their lamas and priests were arrested (a practice that continued until the 1970s). The League of the Militant Godless, established in 1925, directed a nationwide campaign against the Orthodox Church and all other organized religions. The extreme position of that organization eventually led even the Soviet government to disavow direct connection with its practices. In 1940 an estimated 30,000 religious communities of all denominations survived in all the Soviet Union, but only about 500 Russian Orthodox parishes were open at that time, compared with the estimated 54,000 that had existed before World War I.

In 1939 the government significantly relaxed some restrictions on religious practice, a change that the Orthodox Church met with an attitude of cooperation. When Germany invaded the Soviet Union in 1941, the government reluctantly solicited church support as it called upon every traditional patriotic value that might resonate with the Soviet people. According to witnesses, active church support of the national war effort drew many otherwise alienated individuals to the Soviet cause. Beginning in 1942, to promote this alliance, the government ended its prohibition of official contact between clergy and foreign representatives. It also permitted the traditional celebration of Easter and temporarily ended the stigmatization of religiosity as an impediment to social advancement.

The government concessions for the sake of national defense reinvigorated the Russian Orthodox Church. Thousands of churches reopened during the war. But the Khrushchev regime (1953–64) reversed the policy that had made such a revival possible, pursuing a violent six-year campaign against all forms of religious practice. Although the church retained its official sanction throughout that period, Khrushchev's campaign was continued less stringently by his successor, Leonid I. Brezhnev (in office 1964–82). By 1975 the number of operating Russian Orthodox churches had been reduced to about 7,000. Some of the most prominent members of the Russian Orthodox hierarchy and religious activists were jailed or forced to leave the church. Their place was taken by a docile clergy whose ranks were sometimes infiltrated by agents of the Committee for State Security (Komitet gosudarstvennoy bezopasnosti—KGB; see Glossary). Under these circumstances, the church espoused and propagated Soviet foreign policy and furthered the Russification of non-Russian believers, such as Orthodox Ukrainians and Belorussians.

Despite official repression in the Khrushchev and Brezhnev years, religious activity persisted. Although regular church attendance was common mainly among women and the elderly, special occasions such as baptisms and Easter brought many more Russians into the churches. An increase in church weddings in the 1950s and 1960s stimulated the establishment of secular "marriage palaces" offering the ceremonial trappings of marriage devoid of religious rites. When applications for seminary study increased significantly in the 1950s, the Communist Youth League (Komsomol) forced aspiring seminarians to endure interrogations that discouraged many and that succeeded, by 1960, in sharply reducing the number of candidates.

The general cultural liberalization that followed Stalin's death in 1953 brought a natural curiosity about the Russian past that especially caught the interest of younger generations; the ceremonies and art forms of the Russian Orthodox Church, an inseparable part of that past, attracted particular attention, to the dismay of the Khrushchev and Brezhnev regimes. Historian James Billington has pointed out that in that period religious belief was a form of generational rebellion by children against doctrinaire communist parents.

Although the Russian Orthodox Church did not play the activist role in undermining communism that the Roman Catholic Church played in Poland and elsewhere in Eastern Europe, it gained appreciably from the gradual discrediting of Marxist-Leninist ideology in the late Soviet period. In the mid-1980s, only about 3,000 Orthodox churches and two monasteries were active. As the grip of communism weakened in that decade, however, a religious awakening occurred throughout the Soviet Union. Symbolic gestures by President Gorbachev and his government, under the rubric of *glasnost* (see Glossary), indicated unmistakably that Soviet policy was changing. In 1988 Gorbachev met with Orthodox leaders and explicitly discussed the role of religion in the lives of their followers. Shortly thereafter, official commemoration of the millennium of Russian Orthodoxy sent a signal throughout Russia that religious expression again was accepted. Beginning in 1989, new laws specified the church's right to hold private property and to distribute publications. In 1990 the Soviet legislature passed a new law on religious freedom, proposed by Gorbachev; at the same time, some of the constituent republics began enacting their own laws on the same subject. In the fall of 1990, a new deputy to the parliament of the Russian Republic, the Orthodox priest Gleb Yakunin, guided the passage of an extraordinarily liberal law on religious freedom. That law remained in force when Russia became a separate nation the following year. (Yakunin was defrocked in 1994, however, for criticizing the church hierarchy.)

According to the head of the Russian Orthodox Church, Patriarch Aleksiy II, between 1990 and 1995 more than 8,000 Russian Orthodox churches were opened, doubling the number of active parishes and adding thirty-two eparchies (dioceses). In the first half of the 1990s, the Russian government returned numerous religious facilities that had been confiscated by its communist predecessors, providing some assistance in the repair and reconstruction of damaged structures. The most visible such project was the building of the completely new Christ the Savior Cathedral, erected in Moscow at an expense of about US$300 million to replace the showplace cathedral demolished in 1931 as part of the Stalinist campaign against religion. Financed mainly by private donations, the new church is considered a visible acknowledgment of the mistakes of the Soviet past.

In the first half of the 1990s, the church's social services also expanded considerably with the creation of departments of charity and social services and of catechism and religious education within the patriarchy. Because there is a shortage of priests, Sunday schools have been introduced in thousands of parishes. An agreement between the patriarchy and the national ministries of defense and internal affairs provides for pastoral care of military service personnel of the Orthodox faith. The patriarch also has stressed that personnel of other faiths must have access to appropriate spiritual guidance. In November 1995, Minister of Defense Grachev announced the creation of a post in the armed forces for cooperation with religious institutions.

Among the religious organizations that have appeared in the 1990s are more than 100 Russian Orthodox brotherhoods. Reviving a tradition dating back to the Middle Ages, these priest-led lay organizations do social and philanthropic work. In 1990 they formed the Alliance of Orthodox Brotherhoods, which organizes educational, social, and cultural programs and institutions such as child care facilities, hostels, hospitals, and agricultural communities. Although its nominal task is to foster religious and moral education, the alliance has taken actively nationalist positions on religious tolerance and political issues.

Public opinion surveys have revealed that the church emerged relatively unscathed from its association with the communist regime—although dissidents such as Yakunin accused Aleksiy II of having been a KGB operative. According to polls, in the first half of the 1990s the church inspired greater trust among the Russian population than most other social and political institutions. Similarly, Aleksiy II, elected to head the church upon the death of Patriarch Pimen in 1990, was found to elicit greater grassroots confidence than most other public figures in Russia. The political leadership regularly seeks the approval of the church as moral authority for virtually all types of government policy. Boris Yeltsin's appearance at a Moscow Easter service in 1991 was considered a major factor in his success in the presidential election held two months later. Patriarch Aleksiy officiated at Yeltsin's inauguration that year.

Although the status of Russian Orthodoxy has risen considerably, experts do not predict that it will become Russia's official state religion. About 25 percent of Russia's believers profess other faiths, and experts stated that in the mid-1990s the church lacked the clerics, the organizational dynamism, and the infrastructure to assume such a position.

Other Religions

Article 14 of the 1993 constitution stipulates that "the Russian Federation is a secular state. No religion may be established as the state religion or a compulsory religion. Religious associations are separated from the state and are equal before the law." However, such a constitutional guarantee existed even during the Stalinist era, when religious oppression was at its worst. In the 1990s, the Russian citizenry has shown that the traditional, deeply felt linkage between Russian Orthodoxy and the Russian state remains intact. That linkage has a palpable effect on Russian secular attitudes toward religious minorities, and hence on the degree to which the new constitutional guarantee of religious liberty is honored.

Even before the demise of the Soviet Union, the new openness of Russian society had attracted religious activists of many persuasions from all over the world. In Moscow evangelists and missionaries filled the airwaves and the streets. Notable among them were German Lutherans, a Roman Catholic missionary society, Swiss Protestant church groups, the Quakers, the Salvation Army, and the Sisters of Charity, a Roman Catholic order of nuns headed by Mother Teresa. Also present were members of such groups as the Hare Krishnas, the Unification Church, and the Church of Scientology.

The activity of such groups, which paralleled Russia's new enthusiasm for all things Western in the late 1980s and early 1990s, had begun to wane by 1994. However, it stimulated a strong reaction among conservative political and religious groups. In November 1992, the influential conservative wing of the Russian parliament reacted to the influx of non-Russian religious activists by proposing the creation of a so-called Experts' Consultative Council of church representatives and government officials. That body would have had the power to tighten the requirements for registration of a religious group or missionary activity.

After a flurry of criticism from international human rights and religious groups, President Yeltsin failed to sign the consultative council bill, which died in the fall of 1993. After a new parliament convened, additional versions of the bill appeared. In mid-1996 a somewhat milder bill requiring registration of foreign missionary groups was passed by parliament. Meanwhile, some eighteen jurisdictions in the federation passed a variety of bills restricting missionary activity or requiring registration. Non-Orthodox religious groups also found that the purchase of land and the rental of building space were blocked increasingly by local authorities.

In the 1990s, the Russian Orthodox hierarchy's position on the issue of religious freedom has been muted but negative in many respects, as church officials have seen themselves defending Russian cultural values from Western ideas. Patriarch Aleksiy lent his support to the restrictive legislation as it was being debated in 1993, and Western observers saw an emerging alliance between the Orthodox Church and the nationalist factions in Russian politics. In another indication of its attitude toward the proliferation of "foreign" religious activity in Russia, the hierarchy has made little active effort to establish contacts with new foreign religious groups or with existing groups, and experts see scant hope that an ecumenical council of churches will be established in the near future. In October 1995, the Orthodox Church's governing Holy Synod refused to participate in a congress of Orthodox hierarchs because the Orthodox patriarch of Constantinople had recognized the Orthodox community in Estonia and an autocephalous Orthodox Church in Ukraine.

In 1995 the Yeltsin administration formed a consultative body called the Council for Cooperation with Religious Associations, which included representatives from most of the major denominations. On the council, the Russian Orthodox and Roman Catholic churches and Islamic organizations have two members each, with one representative each for Buddhist, Jewish, Baptist, Pentecostal, and Seventh-Day Adventist representatives. Council decisions have only the status of recommendations to the government.

Non-Orthodox Christian Religions

The Soviet Union was home to large numbers of Christians who were not followers of the Russian Orthodox Church. Several other churches had numerous adherents, including the Georgian Orthodox Church, the Armenian Apostolic Church (also called the Armenian Orthodox Church), and the Ukrainian and Belorussian autocephalous Orthodox churches, which, like the Russian Orthodox Church, were rooted in Byzantine rather than Roman Christianity. All of these faiths likewise endured persecution by the Soviet state. A large number of Roman Catholics and Protestants of various denominations also resided in the Soviet Union. But, because the majority of non-Orthodox Christians were concentrated in the Soviet republics of Ukraine, Belorussia, Lithuania, Latvia, and Estonia, the representation of non-Russian Orthodox groups in post-Soviet Russia is much less than it was in the Soviet Union.

The first West European Protestants in Russia were German Mennonites who arrived in the second half of the seventeenth century. Throughout the twentieth century, the Baptists have been by far the most active and numerous Protestant group. During the repressive 1960s, enthusiastic Baptist groups attracted numerous young Russians away from the official Komsomol, and the fervor of the Baptists in a nominally atheist society earned them admiration even among communist officials. The number of Protestants in the Soviet Union was estimated at 5 million in 1980; in 1993 an estimated 3,000 Baptist communities were active under the administration of the Eurasian Federation of Unions of Evangelical Baptist Christians. Within that structure, the Union of Evangelical Baptist Churches includes about 1,000 communities and supports two missionary groups and one publication. Headquarters is in Moscow. The Council of Churches of Evangelical Baptist Christians was founded in 1961 as a splinter group from what was then the Union of Evangelical Baptist Christian Churches; it existed illegally in Russia until 1988 and is not registered officially as a religious group. In the mid-1990s, the council included 230 communities.

Other Protestant groups in Russia have far fewer members than the Baptists. The Union of Evangelical Christian

Churches was founded in 1992 to continue the tradition of the Union of Evangelical Christians, which had been founded in Russia in 1909 and then banned under communist rule. Pentecostals first became active in Russia in the early twentieth century. In 1945 one faction reunited with the main Baptist church; then in 1991 the remaining group formed the Union of Christians of the Evangelical Faith Pentecostal, which issues several publications and supports missions.

The Seventh-Day Adventists formed a Russian union in 1909, despite active government opposition. The church structure was largely destroyed during the Soviet period. Then, after World War II, the All-Union League of Seventh-Day Adventists was established. The union was inactive from 1960 until 1990, when it was included in the international General Assembly of Adventists. About 600 communities were active in the mid-1990s, with publications, one seminary, one religious school, and a radio broadcast center.

The Jehovah's Witnesses appeared in Russia in 1939; their center in St. Petersburg and their missionary work in Russia are supported by the Jehovah's Witnesses Center in Brooklyn, New York. Lutheranism appeared in Russia in the seventeenth century; in the mid-1990s, only a few churches were active. A few groups of Methodists, Presbyterians, Mormons, and Evangelical Reformed believers also are active in Russia.

The size of the Roman Catholic population of Russia has varied greatly according to the territorial extent of the country. For example, after the partitions of Poland at the end of the eighteenth century, large numbers of Polish Catholics became subjects of the Russian Empire. Accordingly, from the eighteenth century until 1917 a papal legate, or nuncio, represented the Vatican in St. Petersburg. A Roman Catholic academy operated in St. Petersburg, and a mission was established in Astrakhan'. After World War II, the absorption of the Baltic states added many Catholics to the Soviet Union's population, but relatively few of those individuals entered the Russian Republic. In 1993 twenty-nine Roman Catholic dioceses were active in the Russian Federation, with those in the European sector administered from Moscow and those in the Asian sector from Novosibirsk.

The 1990 establishment of new Roman Catholic dioceses in Russia has caused tension with the Russian Orthodox hierarchy. The two churches have an understanding that neither will proselytize in the "territory" of the other, so representatives of the patriarch have condemned expanding Catholic influence as an unwelcome Western intrusion.

Islam

In the 1980s, Islam was the second most widespread religion in the Soviet Union; in that period, the number of Soviet citizens identifying themselves as Muslims generally totaled between 45 and 50 million. The majority of the Muslims resided in the Central Asian republics of the Soviet Union, which now are independent countries. In 1996 the Muslim population of Russia was estimated at 19 percent of all citizens professing belief in a religion. Major Islamic communities are concentrated among the minority nationalities residing between the Black Sea and the Caspian Sea: the Adyghs, Balkars, Bashkirs, Chechens, Cherkess, Ingush, Kabardins, Karachay, and numerous Dagestani nationalities. In the middle Volga Basin are large populations of Tatars, Udmurts, and Chuvash, most of whom are Muslims. Many Muslims also reside in Ul'yanovsk, Samara, Nizhniy Novgorod, Moscow, Perm', and Leningrad oblasts (see Ethnic Composition, this ch.).

Virtually all the Muslims in Russia adhere to the Sunni branch of Islam. In a few areas, notably Chechnya, there is a tradition of Sufism, a mystical variety of Islam that stresses the individual's search for union with God. Sufi rituals, practiced to give the Chechens spiritual strength to resist foreign oppression, became legendary among Russian troops fighting the Chechens during tsarist times.

Relations between the Russian government and Muslim elements of the population have been marked by mistrust and suspicion. In 1992, for example, Sheikh Ravil Gainurtdin, the imam of the Moscow mosque, complained that "our country [Russia] still retains the ideology of the tsarist empire, which believed that the Orthodox faith alone should be a privileged religion, that is, the state religion." The Russian government, for its part, fears the rise of political Islam of the violent sort that Russians witnessed in the 1980s firsthand in Afghanistan and secondhand in Iran. Government fears were fueled by a 1992 conference held in Saratov by the Tajikistan-based Islamic Renaissance Party. Representatives attended from several newly independent Central Asian republics, from Azerbaijan, and from several autonomous jurisdictions of Russia, including the secessionist-minded autonomous republics of Tatarstan and Bashkortostan. The meeting's pan-Islamic complexion created

Traditional wooden homes, with new mosque in background, Tyumen'
Courtesy G. W. Meredith, Jr.

concern in Moscow about the possible spread of radical Islam
into Russia from the new Muslim states along the periphery of
the former Soviet Union. For that reason, the Russian government has provided extensive military and political support to
secular leaders of the five Central Asian republics, all of whom
are publicly opposed to political Islam. By the mid-1990s, the
putative Islamic threat was a standard justification for radical
nationalist insistence that Russia regain control of its "near
abroad" (see The Near Abroad, ch. 8).

The struggle to delineate the respective powers of the federal and local governments in Russia also has influenced Russian relations with the Islamic community. The Russian
Federation inherited two of the four spiritual boards, or mufti-
ates, created during the Stalinist era to supervise the religious
activities of Islamic groups in various parts of the Soviet Union;
the other two are located in Tashkent and Baku. One of the
two Russian boards has jurisdiction in European Russia and
Siberia, and the other is responsible for the Muslim enclaves of
the North Caucasus and Transcaspian regions. In 1992 several
Muslim associations withdrew from the latter muftiate and
attempted to establish their own spiritual boards. Later that

year, Tatarstan and Bashkortostan withdrew recognition from the muftiate for European Russia and Siberia and created their own muftiate.

There is much evidence of official conciliation toward Islam in Russia in the 1990s. The number of Muslims allowed to make pilgrimages to Mecca increased sharply after the virtual embargo of the Soviet era ended in 1990. Copies of the Quran (Koran) are readily available, and many mosques are being built in regions with large Muslim populations. In 1995 the newly established Union of Muslims of Russia, led by Imam Khatyb Mukaddas of Tatarstan, began organizing a movement aimed at improving interethnic understanding and ending Russians' lingering conception of Islam as an extremist religion. The Union of Muslims of Russia is the direct successor to the pre-World War I Union of Muslims, which had its own faction in the Russian Duma (see Glossary). The postcommunist union has formed a political party, the Nur All-Russia Muslim Public Movement, which acts in close coordination with Muslim clergy to defend the political, economic, and cultural rights of Muslims and other minorities. The Islamic Cultural Center of Russia, which includes a *medrese* (religious school), opened in Moscow in 1991. The Ash-Shafii Islamic Institute in Dagestan is the only such research institution in Russia. In the 1990s, the number of Islamic publications has increased. Among them are two magazines in Russian, *Ekho Kavkaza* and *Islamskiy vestnik*, and the Russian-language newspaper *Islamskiye novosti*, which is published in Makhachkala, Dagestan.

Judaism

Judaism began to have an influence on Russian culture and social attitudes in the sixteenth century, shortly after the expulsion of the Jews from Spain by Queen Isabella in 1492. In the centuries that followed, large numbers of Jews migrated to Poland, Lithuania, Ukraine, and Belorussia. Much of the anti-Semitism that developed subsequently among Russian peasants came from the identification of Jews with activities such as tax collection and the administration of the large estates on which the peasants worked, two of the few occupations Jews were allowed to pursue in tsarist Russia. Anti-Semitism followed the Jews from Western Europe, and already in the sixteenth century the culture of Muscovy contained a strong element of that attitude. When Poland was partitioned at the end of the eighteenth century, large numbers of Jews came into the Russian

Empire, giving Russia the largest Jewish population (about 1.5 million) in the world. For the next 120 years, tsarist governments restricted Jewish settlements to what was called the Pale of Settlement, established by Catherine II in 1792 to include portions of the Baltic states, Ukraine, Belorussia, and the northern shore of the Black Sea.

During the nineteenth century, restrictions on the Jewish population were alternately eased and tightened. Alexander II (r. 1855–81), for example, relaxed restrictions on settlement, education, and employment. Alexander's assassination in 1881 brought reimposition of all previous restrictions, which then remained in force until 1917. During that period, Jews were beaten and killed and their property destroyed in government-sanctioned pogroms led by a group called the Black Hundreds. Despite repressive conditions in Russia and high levels of emigration to the United States, the Jewish population grew rapidly in the nineteenth century; by the beginning of World War I, an estimated 5.2 million Jews lived in Russia.

Within their areas of settlement, the Russian Jews developed a flourishing culture, and many of them became active in the revolutionary movements that sprang up in the late nineteenth and early twentieth centuries. But much of the long period of violence that began with World War I in 1914 and continued until the Civil War ended in 1921 took place in the regions inhabited by the Jews, many of whom were killed indiscriminately by the various armies struggling for power. After World War I, parts of the western territory of the former Russian Empire became the independent nations of Lithuania, Latvia, and Poland, a development that left many Russian Jews outside the borders of what now was the Soviet Union. By 1922 Russia's Jewish population had been reduced by more than half.

In the early years of the Soviet Union, Jews gained much more freedom to enter the mainstream of Russian society. Although relatively few supported the explicit program of the Bolsheviks, the majority expected that the new state would offer much greater ethnic and religious tolerance than had the tsarist system. In the 1920s, hundreds of thousands of Jews were integrated into Soviet economic and cultural life, and many acquired prominent positions. Among them were communist leaders Leon Trotsky, Lazar Kaganovich, Maksim Litvinov, Lev Kamenev, and Grigoriy Zinov'yev; writers Isaak Babel', Veniamin Kaverin, Boris Pasternak, Osip Mandel'shtam, and Ilya Ehrenburg; and cinematographer Sergey Eisenstein. Special Jewish sections were established in the All-Union Communist Party (Bolshevik). Then, in the 1930s the purges initiated by Stalin targeted groups for their ethnic and social identities. As non-Russians stereotyped as intellectuals, the Jews were targets in two categories. As part of Soviet ethnic policy, the Jewish Autonomous Oblast (Yevreyskaya avtonomnaya oblast', later called Birobidzhan) was established in 1934. But the oblast never was the center of the Soviet Union's Jewish population. Only about 50,000 Jews settled in this jurisdiction, which is located along the Amur River in the farthest reaches of the Soviet Far East.

When Nazi Germany invaded the Soviet Union in 1941, about 2.5 million Jews were killed by the Germans or by their Slavic collaborators. Jews who escaped to areas untouched by the Nazis often suffered from the resentment of local populations who envied their education or supposed wealth.

Between World War II and the collapse of the Soviet Union, Russia's Jewish population declined steadily, thanks to emigration, a low birth rate, intermarriage, and concealment of identity. In 1989 the official total was 537,000. Of the number remaining at that point, only about 9,000 were living in the Jewish Autonomous Oblast, and, by 1995, only an estimated 1,500 Jews remained in the oblast. The Jews of Russia always have been concentrated overwhelmingly in the larger cities, especially Moscow, St. Petersburg, and Odessa—partly because of the traditional ban, continued from tsarist times, on Jews owning land. Although 83 percent of Jews claimed Russian as their native language in the 1979 census, the Soviet government recognized Yiddish as the national language of the Jewish population in Russia and the other republics.

In the early 1980s, the Kremlin's refusal to allow Jewish emigration was a major issue of contention in Soviet-American relations. In 1974 the United States Congress had passed the Jackson-Vanik Amendment, which offered the Soviet Union most-favored-nation trade status in return for permission for Soviet Jews to emigrate. The Soviet Union responded by relaxing its restrictions, and in the years that followed there was a steady flow of Jewish emigrants from the Soviet Union to Israel. But the intensification of the Cold War in the years after the 1979 invasion of Afghanistan brought new restrictions that were not lifted fully until 1989, when a new surge of emigration began. Between 1992 and 1995, the emigration of Jews from Russia averaged about 65,000 per year, after reaching a peak of

188,000 in 1990. In 1996 the Russian government began curtailing the activity of the Jewish Agency, an internationally funded organization that has sponsored Jewish emigration since the 1940s.

The Soviet and Russian governments have always regarded the Jews not only as a distinct religious group but also as a nationality. This attitude persists in the post-Soviet era despite a provision in Article 26 of the 1993 constitution prohibiting the state from arbitrarily determining a person's nationality or forcing a person to declare a nationality.

Although official anti-Semitism has ceased and open acts of anti-Semitism have been rare in Russian society since the collapse of the Soviet Union, Jews have remained mindful of their history in Russia and skeptical of the durability of liberalized conditions. Traditional anti-Semitism in the Russian Orthodox Church and the increasing power of ultranationalist and neofascist political forces are the principal causes of concern; Jews also fear that they might become scapegoats for economic difficulties. Nevertheless, in the early 1990s Judaism has shown a slow but sure revival, and Russia's Jews have experienced a growing interest in learning about their religious heritage. In January 1996, a major event was publication in Russia of a Russian translation of a volume of the Talmud. The first such publication since before the Bolshevik Revolution, the volume marks the start of a series of Talmudic translations intended to provide Russian Jews with information about their religion's teachings, which until 1996 had been virtually unavailable in Russia.

With Jews becoming more willing to identify themselves, official estimates of the Jewish population increased between 1992 and 1995, from 500,000 to around 700,000. The Jewish population of Moscow has been estimated in the mid-1990s at between 200,000 and 300,000. Of that number, about 15 percent are Sephardic (non-European).

The number of Jews participating in religious observances remains relatively small, even though organizations such as the Hasidic (Orthodox) Chabad Lubavitch actively encourage full observance of religious traditions. In Moscow the Lubavitchers, whose activism has met with hostility from many Russians, run two synagogues and several schools, including a yeshiva (academy of Talmudic learning), kindergartens, and a seminary for young women. The organization also is active in charity work.

In the 1990s, a number of organizations devoted to the fostering of Jewish culture and religion have been established in Moscow. These include a rabbinical school, a Jewish youth center, a union of Hebrew teachers, and a Jewish cultural and educational society. The orthodox Jewish community also campaigned successfully for the return of the Shneerson books, a collection of manuscripts that had been stored in the Lenin State Library in Moscow since Soviet authorities confiscated them in the 1920s.

Religion and Foreign Policy

In the 1990s, there have been indications that religious considerations can influence certain areas of Russian foreign policy, as they have in the past. Relations with the newly independent Muslim states of Central Asia are a case in point. In all five republics of that region, the Russian government has strongly supported secular, autocratic Islamic leaders whose hold on power is justified in part by an ostensible threat of Muslim political activism. However, only in Tajikistan has a faction with any sort of connection to Islamic groups attempted to take power. There, a nominally secular Islamic party has played a central role in a prolonged guerrilla war against the Russian-supported regime, with assistance from Afghan forces.

Beginning in 1992, the conflict between Muslims and Orthodox Serbs in Bosnia and Herzegovina has tested the deeply ingrained tradition within the Orthodox Church of protecting coreligionists in the Middle East, the Balkans, and elsewhere beyond Russia's borders (see Central Europe, ch. 8). Russia's former minister of foreign affairs, Andrey Kozyrev, cautioned against making the Orthodox religion a determinant of Russian foreign policy, lest such a policy promote a split in Russia itself between Orthodox and Muslim believers. Nevertheless, nationalist sentiment in Russia caused the Yeltsin government to limit its participation in international sanctions and military actions against Serbia.

The Russian Language

The Russian language has dominated cultural and official life throughout the history of the nation, regardless of the presence of other ethnic groups. Linguistic groups in Russia run the gamut from Slavic (spoken by more than three-quarters of the population) to Turkic, Caucasian, Finno-Ugric, Eskimo,

Yiddish, and Iranian. Russification campaigns during both the tsarist and communist eras suppressed the languages and cultures of all minority nationalities. Although the Soviet-era constitutions affirmed the equality of all languages with Russian for all purposes, in fact language was a powerful tool of Soviet nationality policy. The governments of both the Soviet Union and the Russian Federation have used the Russian language as a means of promoting unity among the country's nationalities, as well as to provide access to literary and scientific materials not available in minority languages. According to the Brezhnev regime, all Soviet peoples "voluntarily" adopted Russian for use in international communication and to promote the unity of the Soviet Union.

Beginning in 1938, the Russian language was a compulsory subject in the primary and secondary schools of all regions. In schools where an indigenous language was used alongside Russian, courses in science and mathematics were taught in Russian. Many university courses were available only in Russian, and Russian was the language of public administration in all jurisdictions in all fifteen Soviet republics. Nevertheless, the minority peoples of the Russian Republic, as well as the peoples of the other fourteen Soviet republics, continued to consider their own language as primary, and the general level of Russian fluency was low (see The Post-Soviet Education Structure, ch. 5). In the mid-1990s, in every area of the federation, Russian remains the sole language of public administration, of the armed forces, and of the scientific and technical communities. Russian schools grant diplomas in only two minority languages, Bashkir and Tatar, and higher education is conducted almost entirely in Russian.

Although Russian is the lingua franca of the Russian Federation, Article 26 of the 1993 constitution stipulates that "each person has the right to use his native language and to the free choice of language of communication, education, instruction, and creativity." Article 68 affirms the right of all peoples in the Russian Federation "to retain their mother tongue and to create conditions for its study and development." Although such constitutional provisions often prove meaningless, the non-Slavic tongues of Russia have retained their vitality, and they even have grown more prevalent in some regions. This trend is especially visible as autonomy of language becomes an important symbol of the struggle to preserve distinct ethnic identities. In the 1990s, many non-Russian ethnic groups have issued laws or decrees giving their native languages equal status with Russian in their respective regions of the Russian Federation. In the mid-1990s, some 80 percent of the non-Slavic nationalities—or 12 percent of the population of the Russian Federation—did not speak Russian as their first language.

Literature and the Arts

Russian civilization has produced classic works of art in all genres, including innovations of lasting significance in literature, music, and ballet. The artistic process often has collided with political dogma, and outside influences have combined with "pure Russian" art forms in a sometimes uneasy harmony.

Literature

In the course of Russia's thousand-year history, Russian literature has come to occupy a unique place in the culture, politics, and linguistic evolution of the Russian people. In the modern era, literature has been the arena for heated discussion of virtually all aspects of Russian life, including the place that literature itself should occupy in that life. In the process, it has produced a rich and varied fund of artistic achievement.

The Beginnings

Literature first appeared among the East Slavs after the Christianization of Kievan Rus' in the tenth century (see The Golden Age of Kiev, ch. 1). Seminal events in that process were the development of the Cyrillic (see Glossary) alphabet around A.D. 863 and the development of Old Church Slavonic as a liturgical language for use by the Slavs. The availability of liturgical works in the vernacular language—an advantage not enjoyed in Western Europe—caused Russian literature to develop rapidly. Through the sixteenth century, most literary works had religious themes or were created by religious figures. Among the noteworthy works of the eleventh through fourteenth centuries are the *Primary Chronicle*, a compilation of historical and legendary events, the *Lay of Igor's Campaign*, a secular epic poem about battles against the Turkic Pechenegs, and *Zadonshchina*, an epic poem about the defeat of the Mongols in 1380. Works in secular genres such as the satirical tale began to appear in the sixteenth century, and Byzantine literary traditions began to fade as the Russian vernacular came into greater use and Western influences were felt.

Folk dance performance,
Volgograd
Courtesy Robert Schlickewitz

Written in 1670, the *Life of the Archpriest Avvakum* is a pioneering realistic autobiography that avoids the flowery church style in favor of vernacular Russian. Several novellas and satires of the seventeenth century also used vernacular Russian freely. The first Russian poetic verse was written early in the seventeenth century.

Peter and Catherine

The eighteenth century, particularly the reigns of Peter the Great and Catherine the Great (r. 1762–96), was a period of strong Western cultural influence. Russian literature was dominated briefly by European classicism before shifting to an equally imitative sentimentalism by 1780. Secular prose tales—many picaresque or satirical—grew in popularity with the middle and lower classes, as the nobility read mainly literature from Western Europe. Peter's secularization of the Russian Orthodox Church decisively broke the influence of religious themes on literature. The middle period of the eighteenth century (1725–62) was dominated by the stylistic and genre innovations of four writers: Antiokh Kantemir, Vasiliy Trediakovskiy, Mikhail Lomonosov, and Aleksandr Sumarokov. Their work was a further step in bringing Western literary concepts to Russia.

Under Catherine, the satirical journal was adopted from Britain, and Gavriil Derzhavin advanced the evolution of Russian poetry. Denis Fonvizin, Yakov Knyazhnin, Aleksandr Radishchev, and Nikolay Karamzin wrote controversial and innovative drama and prose works that brought Russian literature closer to its nineteenth-century role as an art form liberally furnished with social and political commentary (see Imperial Expansion and Maturation: Catherine II, ch. 1). The lush, sentimental language of Karamzin's tale *Poor Lisa* set off a forty-year polemic pitting advocates of innovation against those of "purity" in literary language.

The Nineteenth Century

By 1800 Russian literature had an established tradition of representing real-life problems, and its eighteenth-century practitioners had enriched its language with new elements. On this basis, a brilliant century of literary endeavor followed.

Russian literature of the nineteenth century provided a congenial medium for the discussion of political and social issues whose direct presentation was censored. The prose writers of this period shared important qualities: attention to realistic, detailed descriptions of everyday Russian life; the lifting of the taboo on describing the vulgar, unsightly side of life; and a satirical attitude toward mediocrity and routine. All of those elements were articulated primarily in the novel and short story forms borrowed from Western Europe, but the poets of the nineteenth century also produced works of lasting value.

The Age of Realism, generally considered the culmination of the literary synthesis of earlier generations, began around 1850. The writers of that period owed a great debt to four men of the previous generation: the writers Aleksandr Pushkin, Mikhail Lermontov, and Nikolay Gogol', and the critic Vissarion Belinskiy, each of whom contributed to new standards for language, subject matter, form, and narrative techniques. Pushkin is recognized as the greatest Russian poet, and the critic Belinskiy was the "patron saint" of the influential "social message" writers and critics who followed. Lermontov contributed innovations in both poetic and prose genres. Gogol' is accepted as the originator of modern realistic Russian prose, although much of his work contains strong elements of fantasy. The rich language of Gogol' was much different from the direct, sparse lexicon of Pushkin; each of the two approaches to the language of literary prose was adopted by significant writers of later generations.

By mid-century a heated debate was under way on the appropriateness of social questions in literature. The debate filled the pages of the "thick journals" of the time, which remained the most fertile site for literary discussion and innovation into the 1990s; traces of the debate appeared in the pages of much of Russia's best literature as well. The foremost advocates of social commentary were Nikolay Chernyshevskiy and Nikolay Dobrolyubov, critics who wrote for the thick journal *Sovremennik* (The Contemporary) in the late 1850s and early 1860s.

The best prose writers of the Age of Realism were Ivan Turgenev, Fedor Dostoyevskiy, and Lev Tolstoy. Because of the enduring quality of their combination of pure literature with eternal philosophical questions, the last two are accepted as Russia's premier prose artists; Dostoyevskiy's novels *Crime and Punishment* and *The Brothers Karamazov*, like Tolstoy's novels *War and Peace* and *Anna Karenina*, are classics of world literature.

Other outstanding writers of the Age of Realism were the playwright Aleksandr Ostrovskiy, the novelist Ivan Goncharov, and the prose innovator Nikolay Leskov, all of whom were closely involved in some way with the debate over social commentary. The most notable poets of mid-century were Afanasiy Fet and Fedor Tyutchev.

An important tool for writers of social commentary under strict tsarist censorship was a device called Aesopic language—a variety of linguistic tricks, allusions, and distortions comprehensible to an attuned reader but baffling to censors. The best practitioner of this style was Mikhail Saltykov-Shchedrin, a prose satirist who, along with the poet Nikolay Nekrasov, was considered a leader of the literary left wing in the second half of the century.

The major literary figure in the last decade of the nineteenth century was Anton Chekhov, who wrote in two genres: the short story and drama. Chekhov was a realist who examined the foibles of individuals rather than society as a whole. His plays *The Cherry Orchard*, *The Seagull*, and *The Three Sisters* continue to be performed worldwide.

In the 1890s, Russian poetry was revived and thoroughly reshaped by a new group, the symbolists, whose most prominent representative was Aleksandr Blok. Two more groups, the futurists and the acmeists, added new poetic principles at the start of the twentieth century. The leading figure of the former was Vladimir Mayakovskiy, and of the latter, Anna Akhmatova. The premier prose writers of the period were the realist writers Leonid Andreyev, Ivan Bunin, Maksim Gor'kiy, Vladimir Korolenko, and Aleksandr Kuprin. Gor'kiy became the literary figurehead of the Bolsheviks and of the Soviet regimes of the 1920s and 1930s; shortly after the Bolshevik Revolution, Bunin and Kuprin emigrated to Paris. In 1933 Bunin became the first Russian to receive the Nobel Prize for Literature.

The Soviet Period and After

The period immediately following the Bolshevik Revolution was one of literary experimentation and the emergence of numerous literary groups. Much of the fiction of the 1920s described the Civil War or the struggle between the old and new Russia. The best prose writers of the 1920s were Isaak Babel', Mikhail Bulgakov, Veniamin Kaverin, Leonid Leonov, Yuriy Olesha, Boris Pil'nyak, Yevgeniy Zamyatin, and Mikhail Zoshchenko. The dominant poets were Akhmatova, Osip Mandel'shtam, Mayakovskiy, Pasternak, Marina Tsvetayeva, and Sergey Yesenin. But under Stalin, literature felt the same restrictions as the rest of Russia's society. After a group of "proletarian writers" had gained ascendancy in the early 1930s, the communist party Central Committee forced all fiction writers into the Union of Soviet Writers in 1934. The union then established the standard of "socialist realism" for Soviet literature, and many of the writers in Russia fell silent or emigrated (see Mobilization of Society, ch. 2). A few prose writers adapted by describing moral problems in the new Soviet state, but the stage was dominated by formulaic works of minimal literary value such as Nikolay Ostrovskiy's *How the Steel Was Tempered* and Yuriy Krymov's *Tanker Derbent.* A unique work of the 1930s was the Civil War novel *The Quiet Don,* which won its author, Mikhail Sholokhov, the Nobel Prize for Literature in 1965, although Sholokhov's authorship is disputed by some experts. The strict controls of the 1930s continued until the "thaw" following Stalin's death in 1953, although some innovation was allowed in prose works of the World War II period.

Between 1953 and 1991, Russian literature produced a number of first-rate artists, all still working under the pressure of state censorship and often distributing their work through a sophisticated underground system called samizdat (literally, self-publishing). The poet Pasternak's Civil War novel, *Doctor*

Zhivago, created a sensation when published in the West in 1957. The book won the Nobel Prize for Literature in 1958, but the Soviet government forced Pasternak to decline the award. Aleksandr Solzhenitsyn, whose *One Day in the Life of Ivan Deniso-vich* (1962) also was a watershed work, was the greatest Russian philosophical novelist of the era; he was exiled from the Soviet Union in 1974 and eventually settled in the United States. In the 1960s and 1970s, a new generation of satirical and prose writers, such as Fazil' Iskander, Vladimir Voinovich, Yuriy Kaza-kov, and Vladimir Aksyonov, battled against state restrictions on artistic expression, as did the noted poets Yevgeniy Yevtush-enko, Andrey Voznesenskiy, and Joseph Brodsky. Aksyonov and Brodsky emigrated to the United States, where they remained productive. Brodsky won the Nobel Prize for Literature in 1987. The most celebrated case of literary repression in the 1960s was that of Andrey Sinyavskiy and Yuliy Daniel, iconoclas-tic writers of the Soviet "underground" whose 1966 sentence to hard labor for having written anti-Soviet propaganda brought international protest.

Another generation of writers responded to the liberalized atmosphere of Gorbachev's *glasnost* in the second half of the 1980s, openly discussing previously taboo themes: the excesses of the Stalin era, a wide range of previously unrecognized social ills such as corruption, random violence, anti-Semitism, and prostitution, and even the unassailably positive image of Vladimir I. Lenin himself. Among the best of this generation were Andrey Bykov, Mikhail Kurayev, Valeriy Popov, Tat'yana Tolstaya, and Viktor Yerofeyev—writers not necessarily as tal-ented as their predecessors but expressing a new kind of "alter-native fiction." The *glasnost* period also saw the publication of formerly prohibited works by writers such as Bulgakov, Solzhenitsyn, and Zamyatin.

Beginning in 1992, Russian writers experienced complete creative freedom for the first time in many decades. The change was not entirely for the better, however. The urgent mission of the Russian writers, to provide the public with a kind of truth they could not find elsewhere in a censored society, had already begun to disappear in the 1980s, when *glasnost* opened Russia to a deluge of information and entertainment flowing from the West and elsewhere. Samizdat was tacitly accepted by the Gorbachev regime, then it disappeared entirely as private publishers appeared in the early 1990s. Writ-ers' traditional special place in society no longer is recognized by most Russians, who now read literature much less avidly than they did in Soviet times. For the first time since their appearance in the early 1800s, the "thick journals" are disregarded by large portions of the intelligentsia, and in the mid-1990s several major journals went bankrupt. Under these circumstances, many Russian writers have expressed a sense of deep loss and frustration.

Music

Until the eighteenth century, Russian music consisted mainly of church music and folk songs and dances. In the 1700s, Italian, French, and German operas were introduced to Russia, making opera a popular art form among the aristocracy.

In the nineteenth century, Russia began making an original contribution to world music nearly as significant as its contribution in literature. In the first half of the nineteenth century, Mikhail Glinka (1804–57) initiated the application of purely Russian folk and religious music to classical compositions. His best operas, *Ruslan and Lyudmila* and *A Life for the Tsar*, are considered pioneering works in the establishment of Russian national music, although they are based on Italian models.

In 1859 the Russian Music Society was founded to foster the performance and appreciation of classical music, especially German, from Western Europe; the most influential figures in the society were the composer Anton Rubinstein and his brother Nikolay, who founded influential conservatories in Moscow and St. Petersburg. Anton Rubinstein also was one of the best pianists of the nineteenth century.

In the second half of the nineteenth century, a group of composers that came to be known as the "Mighty Five"—Miliy Balakirev, Aleksandr Borodin, César Cui, Modest Musorgskiy, and Nikolay Rimskiy-Korsakov—continued Glinka's movement away from imitation of European classical music. The Mighty Five challenged the Russian Music Society's conservatism with a large body of work thematically based on Russia's history and legends and musically based on its folk and religious music. Among the group's most notable works are Rimskiy-Korsakov's symphonic suite *Scheherezade* and the operas *The Snow Maiden* and *Sadko*, Musorgskiy's operas *Boris Godunov* and *Khovanshchina*, and Borodin's opera *Prince Igor'*. Balakirev, a protégé of Glinka, was the founder and guiding spirit of the group.

Outside that group stood Peter Ilich Tchaikovsky (Chaykovskiy), who produced a number of enduring symphonies, operas, and ballets more imitative of Western music. During his lifetime, Tchaikovsky already was acknowledged as one of the world's premier composers. Among his most-performed works are the ballets *Swan Lake, Sleeping Beauty,* and *The Nutcracker,* and his Sixth Symphony, known as the Pathétique. At the end of the 1800s, the generation that followed the Mighty Five and Tchaikovsky included talented and innovative figures such as Sergey Rachmaninov, a master pianist and composer who emigrated to Germany in 1906; Rimskiy-Korsakov's student Aleksandr Glazunov, who emigrated in 1928; and the innovator Aleksandr Skryabin, who injected elements of mysticism and literary symbolism in his works for piano and orchestra.

In the twentieth century, Russia continued to produce some of the world's foremost composers and musicians, despite the suppression by Soviet authorities of both music and performances. Restrictions on what musicians played and where they performed caused many artists to leave the Soviet Union either voluntarily or through forced exile, but the works of the émigrés continued to draw large audiences whenever they were performed. The Gorbachev era loosened the restrictions on émigrés returning. The pianist Vladimir Horowitz, who left the Soviet Union in 1925, made a triumphal return performance in Moscow in 1986, and émigré cellist Mstislav Rostropovich made his first tour of the Soviet Union in 1990 as conductor of the National Symphony Orchestra in Washington, D.C.

Igor' Stravinskiy, who has been called the greatest of the twentieth-century Russian composers, emigrated permanently in 1920 after having composed his three best-known works, the scores for the ballets *The Firebird, Petrushka,* and *The Rite of Spring.* Stravinskiy enjoyed a productive career of several decades in exile, making return visits to Russia in his last years. The composers Aram Khachaturyan, Sergey Prokof'yev, and Dmitriy Shostakovich spent their entire careers in the Soviet Union; all three were condemned in 1948 in the postwar Stalinist crackdown known as the Zhdanovshchina (see Reconstruction and Cold War, ch. 2). Prokof'yev, best known for his ballet music, had achieved enough international stature by 1948 to avoid official disgrace. Shostakovich, who enjoyed triumph and suffered censure during the Stalin era, wrote eleven symphonies and two well-known operas based on nineteenth-century Russian stories, *The Nose* by Gogol' and *Lady Macbeth of Mtsensk*

District by Leskov. He enjoyed substantial recognition after the "thaw" that liberated artistic activities after 1953. Khachaturyan based much of his work on Armenian and Georgian folk music.

Composers of modern music received much criticism in the Soviet period for digressing from realistic or traditional styles. Both official Soviet artistic standards and the traditional expectations of the Russian public restricted the creation and performance of innovative pieces. The most notable avant-garde symphonic composer was Alfred Schnittke, who remained in the Soviet Union, where his work won approval. Aleksey Volkonskiy was a notable member of Schnittke's generation who left the Soviet Union to compose in the West. The restraints of the 1970s and 1980s stimulated a musical underground, called *magnitizdat*, which recorded and distributed forbidden folk, rock, and jazz works in small batches. Two notable figures in that movement were Bulat Okudzhava and Vladimir Vysotskiy, who set their poetry to music and became popular entertainers with a satirical message. Vysotskiy, who died in 1980, was rehabilitated in 1990; Okudzhava continued his career into the mid-1990s.

Jazz performances were permitted by all Soviet regimes, and jazz became one of Russia's most popular music forms. In the 1980s, the Ganelin Trio was the best-known Russian jazz combo, performing in Europe and the United States. Jazz musicians from the West began playing regularly in the Soviet Union in the 1980s.

Rock music was controlled strictly by Soviet authorities, with only limited recording outside *magnitizdat*, although Russia's youth were fascinated with the rock groups of the West. In the more liberal atmosphere of the late 1980s, several notable Soviet rock groups emerged with official approval as more innovative, unsanctioned groups proliferated. The Leningrad Rock Club, which became a national network of performance clubs in 1986, was the most important outlet for sanctioned rock music. In the 1990s, much of Russia's rock music lost the innovative and satirical edge of the *magnitizdat* period, and experts noted a tendency to simply imitate Western groups.

Ballet

Russia has made a unique contribution to the development of ballet. Ballet was introduced in Russia together with other aristocratic dance forms as part of Peter the Great's Westernization program in the early 1700s. The first ballet school was established in 1734, and the first full ballet company was founded at the Imperial School of Ballet in St. Petersburg in the 1740s. Italian and French dancers and choreographers predominated in that period, but by 1800 Russian ballet was assimilating native elements from folk dancing as nobles sponsored dance companies of serfs. European ballet critics agreed that the Russian dance had a positive influence on West European ballet. Marius Petipa, a French choreographer who spent fifty years staging ballets in Russia, was the dominant figure during that period; his greatest triumphs were the staging of Tchaikovsky's ballets. Other noted European dancers, such as Marie Taglioni, Christian Johansson, and Enrico Cecchetti, performed in Russia throughout the nineteenth and early twentieth centuries, bringing new influences from the West.

The most influential figure of the early twentieth century was the impresario Sergey Diaghilev, who founded an innovative touring ballet company in 1909 with choreographer Michel Fokine, dancer Vaslav Nijinksy, and designer Alexandre Benois. After the staging of Stravinskiy's controversial *The Rite of Spring*, World War I and the Bolshevik Revolution kept Diaghilev from returning to Russia. Until Diaghilev died in 1929, his Russian dance company, the Ballet Russe, was headquartered in Paris. In the same period, the émigré dancer Anna Pavlova toured the world with her troupe and exerted a huge influence on the art form.

After Diaghilev, several new companies calling themselves the Ballet Russe toured the world, and new generations of Russian dancers filled their ranks. George Balanchine, a Georgian émigré and protégé of Diaghilev, formed the New York City Ballet in 1948. Meanwhile, the Soviet government sponsored new ballet companies throughout the union. After a period of innovation and experimentation in the 1920s, Russia's ballet reverted under Stalin to the traditional forms of Petipa, even changing the plots of some ballets to emphasize the positive themes of socialist realism. The most influential Russian dancer of the mid-twentieth century was Rudolf Nureyev, who defected to the West in 1961 and is credited with establishing the dominant role of the male dancer in classical ballet. A second notable émigré, Mikhail Baryshnikov, burnished an already brilliant career in the United States after defecting from Leningrad's Kirov Ballet in 1974. The large cities of Russia traditionally have their own symphony orchestras and ballet and opera houses. Although funding for such facilities has diminished in the 1990s, attendance at performances remains high. The ballet companies of the Bol'shoy Theater in Moscow and the Kirov Theater in St. Petersburg are world renowned and have toured regularly since the early 1960s.

Architecture and Painting

Early Slavic tribes created handsome jewelry, wall hangings, and decorated leather items that have been recovered from burial mounds. The folk-art motifs made liberal use of animal forms and representations of natural forces. Subsequently, the strongest single influence on Russian art was the acceptance of Christianity in A.D. 988. Transmitting the idea that the beauty of the church's physical attributes reflects the glory of God, Byzantine religious art and architecture penetrated Kiev, which was the capital of the early Russian state until about 1100 (see The Golden Age of Kiev, ch. 1). The northern cities of Novgorod and Vladimir developed distinctive architectural styles, and the tradition of painting icons, religious images usually painted on wooden panels, spread as more churches were built. The Mongol occupation (1240–1480) cut Muscovy's ties with the Byzantine Empire, fostering the development of original artistic styles. Among the innovations of this period was the iconostasis, a carved choir screen on which icons are hung. In the early fifteenth century, the master icon painter Andrey Rublev created some of Russia's most treasured religious art.

As the Mongols were driven out and Moscow became the center of Russian civilization in the late fifteenth century, a new wave of building began in Russia's cities. Italian architects brought a West European influence, especially in the reconstruction of Moscow's Kremlin, the city's twelfth-century wooden fortress. St. Basil's Cathedral in Red Square, however, combined earlier church architecture with styles from the Tatar east. In the 1500s and 1600s, the tsars supported icon painting, metalwork, and manuscript illumination; as contact with Western Europe increased, those forms began to reflect techniques of the West. Meanwhile, folk art preserved the forms of the earlier Slavic tribes in house decorations, clothing, and tools.

Under Peter the Great, Russia experienced a much stronger dose of Western influence. Many of the buildings in Peter's new capital, St. Petersburg, were designed by the Italian architects Domenico Trezzini and Bartolomeo Rastrelli under the direction of Peter and his daughter, Elizabeth. The most productive Russian architects of the eighteenth century, Vasiliy Bazhenov, Matvey Kazakov, and Ivan Starov, created lasting monuments in Moscow and St. Petersburg and established a base for the more Russian forms that followed.

The Academy of Fine Arts, founded by Elizabeth in 1757 to train Russia's artists, brought Western techniques of secular painting to Russia, which until that time had been dominated by icon painting. Catherine the Great (r. 1762–96), another energetic patron of the arts, began collecting European art objects that formed the basis of the collections for which Russia now is famous. Aleksey Venetsianov, the first graduate of the academy to fully embrace realistic subject matter such as peasant life, is acknowledged as the founder of Russia's realistic school of painting, which blossomed in the second half of the 1800s.

In the 1860s, a group of critical realists, led by Ivan Kramskoy, Il'ya Repin, and Vasiliy Perov, portrayed aspects of Russian life with the aim of making social commentary. Repin's *Barge Haulers on the Volga* is one of the most famous products of this school. In the late 1800s, a new generation of painters emphasized technique over subject, producing a more impressionistic body of work. The leaders of that school were Valentin Serov, Isaak Levitan, and Mikhail Vrubel'. In 1898 the theatrical designer Alexandre Benois and the dance impresario Sergey Diaghilev founded the World of Art group, which extended the innovation of the previous generation, played a central role in introducing the contemporary modern art of Western Europe to Russia, and acquainted West Europeans with Russia's art through exhibitions and publications.

In the nineteenth century, Russia's architecture and decorative arts combined European techniques and influences with the forms of early Russia, producing the so-called Russian Revival seen in churches, public buildings, and homes of that period. The European-trained goldsmith, jeweler, and designer Karl Fabergé, the most notable member of a brilliant artistic family, established workshops in Moscow, St. Petersburg, and London. His work, including jeweled enamel Easter eggs produced for the Russian royal family, is an important example of the decorative art of the period.

The Russian artists of the early twentieth century were exposed to a wide variety of Russian and European movements. Among the most innovative and influential of that generation were the painters Marc Chagall, Natal'ya Goncharova, Vasiliy

Kandinskiy, Mikhail Larionov, and Kazimir Malevich. The constructivists of the 1920s found parallels between their architectural and sculptural work and the precepts of the Bolshevik Revolution. By the 1930s, the government was limiting all forms of artistic expression to the themes of socialist realism, forbidding abstract forms and the exhibition of foreign art for more than thirty years. An "unofficial" art movement appeared in the 1960s under the leadership of sculptor Ernest Neizvestnyy and painters Mikhail Chemyakhin, Oskar Rabin, and Yevgeniy Rukhin. In the 1970s and the early 1980s, informal art exhibits were held in parks and social clubs. Like the other arts, painting and sculpture benefited from the policy of *glasnost* of the late 1980s, which encouraged artistic innovation and the exhibition of works abroad.

Outlook

In the mid-1990s, the Russian Federation remains an amalgam of widely varying ethnic groups and cultures. In fact, the differentiation among groups has increased since the demise of the Soviet Union. The much less repressive grasp of Russia's central government has encouraged both cultural and political autonomy, although ethnic Russians constitute about 80 percent of the population and about 75 percent of religious believers are Russian Orthodox. Many minority groups maintain their ethnic traditions, continue wide use of their languages, and demand economic and political autonomy partially based on ethnic differences.

In the 1990s, Islam, which has the second largest body of religious believers in Russia, has prospered among many of the ethnic groups. The Russian Orthodox Church also has experienced a renaissance after emerging from Soviet repression; the church's membership, secular influence, and infrastructure expanded rapidly in the 1990s.

Russia's long and rich literary history came to a new crossroads beginning in the late 1980s, as freedom of expression seemingly ended the traditional role of literature as the antidote to authoritarian dogma. Like literature, other elements of the federation's cultural and artistic life, all of them with notable past accomplishments, remained in a transitional stage in the 1990s.

*　　*　　*

The *Handbook of Major Soviet Nationalities,* edited by Zev Katz, is a somewhat dated but detailed listing of ethnic groups. *National Identity and Ethnicity in Russia and the New States of Eurasia,* edited by Roman Szporluk, provides a discussion of the unique viewpoints of all the major ethnic groups of the former Soviet Union, including those remaining in the Russian Federation. In *Islamic Peoples of the Soviet Union,* Shirin Akiner lists and describes all the Islamic ethnic groups in that category; that book is supplemented by *Muslims of the Soviet Empire: A Guide* by Alexandre Bennigsen, Marie Broxup, and S. Enders Wimbush. Religion as an ongoing element of Russian culture is described in *Russian Culture in Modern Times,* edited by Robert P. Hughes and Irina Paperno; Michael Bourdeaux discusses religion in post-Soviet Russia in *The Politics of Religion in Russia and the New States of Eurasia.* The evolution of Russian literature is discussed in the introductions and explanatory texts of anthologies such as *Medieval Russia's Epics, Chronicles, and Tales,* edited by Serge A. Zenkovsky, and *The Literature of Eighteenth-Century Russia,* edited by Harold B. Segel, and in Marc Slonim's *The Epic of Russian Literature from Its Roots Through Tolstoy* and Edward J. Brown's *Russian Literature since the Revolution.* (For further information and complete citations, see Bibliography.)

Chapter 5. The Society and Its Environment

The girl with the golden hair sits on a stone at the water's edge (design from lacquer box made in village of Kholuy).

THE DEMISE OF THE SOVIET UNION in 1991 brought a measure of freedom to Russia's people, but at the same time this change removed or severely weakened certain elements of the social safety net, which for many years had included a guarantee of employment, basic medical care, and government subsidies for food, clothing, shelter, and transportation. For the average citizen, social and economic conditions worsened considerably in the early postcommunist era. Although some components of state support remained close to their Soviet-era levels, the government lacked the resources to compensate Russia's citizens for the stresses of the transition period.

The end of the Soviet Union meant the disappearance of a reliable, if mediocre, set of social expectations for every Russian. Lacking such guidance, various elements of Russian society moved in very different directions. A small segment took immediate action—both legal and illegal—to make the most of its newfound range of opportunities for self-expression and economic advancement. Although few such adventurers found success, those who did coalesced into a new class of wealthy Russians independent of the government. The vast majority, however, met the prospect of reduced predictability in their lives with suspicion, confusion, or resentment. Remembering the security of Soviet life, many clung to symbolic or real remnants of that life, particularly in the workplace.

As the economic controls of centralized government were eased, prices for basic necessities rose—sometimes precipitously—and society was buffeted by marked increases in crime, infectious diseases, drug addiction, homelessness, and suicide. Growing pollution and other environmental hazards added to the malaise.

Social Structure

In the mid-1990s, Russian society was in the midst of a wrenching transition from a totalitarian structure to a protodemocracy of unknown character. During most of the Soviet era, society was atomized, so that the communist regime and its "transmission belts" (officially sanctioned organizations and institutions of every kind, from trade unions to youth groups) could fully monitor and control each individual. Civil society was nonexistent. The lines of control ran from the top down, through a rigid hierarchy constructed and staffed by the ruling Communist Party of the Soviet Union (CPSU—see Glossary).

Post-Soviet Russia is slowly striving to create a civil society and restore the family and other basic institutions as functional units within the society. In the mid-1990s, habits of trust, personal responsibility, community service, and citizen cooperation remained unformed in much of Russia's society, as the social attitudes of previous decades remained intact. Those holding such attitudes envisioned little between the extremes of totalitarianism and social anarchy; having moved away from the simplistic guidance of the former, much of society was strongly tempted to embrace the latter.

Social Stratification

Perhaps the most significant fact about Russia's social structure is that ideology no longer determines social status. During the Soviet era, membership in the CPSU was the surest path to career advancement and wealth. Political decisions rather than market forces determined social status. Despite Marxist-Leninist (see Glossary) notions of a classless society, the Soviet Union had a powerful ruling class, the *nomenklatura,* which consisted of party officials and key personnel in the government and other important sectors such as heavy industry. This class enjoyed privileges such as roomy apartments, country dachas, and access to special stores, schools, medical facilities, and recreational sites. The social status and income of members of the *nomenklatura* increased as they were promoted to higher positions in the party.

The social structure of the Soviet Union was characterized by self-perpetuation and limited mobility. Access to higher education, a prerequisite to political and social advancement, was steadily constrained in the postwar decades. The so-called period of stagnation that coincided with the long tenure of CPSU chief Leonid I. Brezhnev (in office 1964–82) had social as well as political connotations. Moreover, the sluggish economy of that period reduced opportunities for social mobility, thus accentuating differences among social groups and further widening the gap between the *nomenklatura* and the rest of society.

Members of the urban working class (proletariat), in whose name the party purported to rule, generally lived in cramped apartment complexes, spent hours each day standing in line to buy food and other necessities, and attended frequent obligatory sessions of political indoctrination. Similarly, the peasantry eked out a meager existence, with little opportunity for relief. Agricultural workers constituted the bottom layer of Soviet society, receiving the least pay, the least opportunity for social advancement, and the least representation in the nominally all-inclusive CPSU leadership.

Postcommunist society also is characterized by a wide disparity in wealth and privilege. Although there is no rigid class structure, social stratification based on wealth is evident and growing. The *nomenklatura* as it existed in Soviet times disappeared with the demise of the CPSU, but many of its members used their continuing connections with industry and finance to enrich themselves in the emerging capitalist system. According to a 1995 study conducted by the Russian Academy of Sciences, more than 60 percent of Russia's wealthiest millionaires, and 75 percent of the new political elite, are former members of the communist *nomenklatura*, and 38 percent of Russia's businesspeople held economic positions in the CPSU. The wealth of the new capitalists, who constitute 1 to 2 percent of the population, derives from the ownership of private property, which was prohibited under the communist regime; from former black-market transactions that now are pursued legally; and from repatriation of funds that were secretly transferred abroad during the Soviet era. Entrepreneurs have purchased former state-owned enterprises privatized by the government (often using connections with government authorities to gain favorable treatment) and have opened banks, stock exchanges, and other ventures typical of a market economy (see Banking and Finance; Privatization, ch. 6). By the mid-1990s, Russia had by no means established a full-fledged market economy, but the era of capitalism, which the Bolshevik Revolution had cut short, was ascendant.

The most successful of the new capitalists practice conspicuous consumption on an extravagant scale, driving flashy Western cars, sporting expensive clothing and jewelry, and frequenting stylish restaurants and clubs that are far beyond the reach of ordinary Russians. Russian *biznesmeny* with cash-filled briefcases purchase expensive real estate in exclusive areas of Western Europe and the United States. Other areas of the world, such as the city of Limassol, Cyprus, have been transformed into virtual Russian enclaves where illicit commercial transactions help fuel the economy. Russian capitalists attempting to achieve at a high level using legitimate means must nonetheless pay protection money to criminal groups, especially in the larger cities.

In the first half of the 1990s, the gap between the richest and poorest citizens of Russia grew steadily, and it became a source of social alienation because newly successful Russians are resented and often are assumed to have criminal connections. In 1995 the World Bank (see Glossary) ranked Russia's dichotomy between the highest and lowest economic echelons on a par with the wide gaps between rich and poor in Argentina and Turkey. However, by 1996 the gap had decreased slightly. According to the State Committee for Statistics (Goskomstat), in 1995 the wealthiest 10 percent of Russians earned 13.5 times as much as the poorest 10 percent. In 1996 the ratio had shrunk to 12.8 percent, suggesting that more people were sharing in the wealth. According to reports in 1996, the flaunting of luxurious automobiles, clothing, and other forms of material wealth became less prevalent in Russia's largest cities, especially Moscow, which is the center of the nouveau riche population.

Nonreporting of incomes by the highest socioeconomic level likely makes the real gap wider than the official statistics indicate. The overall decline in living standards in 1995 is revealed by an 8 percent decrease in retail trade and by opinion surveys. For instance, in early 1995 some 56 percent of respondents said that their material situation had declined, and 17 percent said that it had improved. Another survey identified 68 percent of respondents claiming to live below the poverty line in 1995, compared with 56 percent the previous year. Such self-perceptions of victimization promote the platforms of antireform political parties that promise a return to the guaranteed well-being of the Soviet era (see The Elections of 1995, ch. 7).

A subclass of young businesspeople, mainly bankers and stockbrokers, runs the new trading and investment markets in Moscow and St. Petersburg, remaining aloof from the tangled, state-dominated manufacturing sector. This group, a very visible part of life in the larger cities in the mid-1990s, has profited from the youthful flexibility that enabled it to embrace an entirely new set of rules for economic success, while Russia's older generations—with the exception of the astute *nomenklatura* members who became part of the nouveau riche—were much less able to adapt to the post-Soviet world.

Street musicians, St. Petersburg
Courtesy Carolou Marquet

Puppeteer in Sokol'niki Park, Moscow
Courtesy A. James Firth, United States
Department of Agriculture

Conditions for the working class and the peasants are sharply at variance with those of the new capitalist class. Political repression has eased, but economic privations have increased. Although more goods are available, they are often beyond the means of the average worker. Full employment, the virtually guaranteed basis of survival under communism, no longer is the norm (see Unemployment, ch. 6). At the lower end of the social scale, the "working poor" toil predominantly in agriculture, education, culture, science, and health, most of which are considered middle-class fields of employment in the West. State employees, who suffer especially from inflation because of infrequent wage adjustments, often fall below the official poverty line.

Young parents with little work experience and more than one child are especially likely to be members of the working poor. In 1993 some 57 percent of families classified as poor by the World Bank had one or more children, and 86 percent of families with three or more children were classified in the lowest income group. Most single-parent families also belonged to this group. In the lower- income groups, people with relatives generally fare better than those with none (especially single pensioners), as the informal subsistence networks formed during the Soviet era continue to provide support to a substantial segment of society.

The *glasnost* (see Glossary) policy of the late 1980s brought a new youth culture that took up the nonconformist dress, drug use, music, and antiestablishment stance of young people in the West, while earnestly seeking answers to questions about Russia's past and its potential future. The social and economic stresses and disappointments of the 1990s have pushed the majority of young Russians completely out of the youth culture, while the few who have won some sort of success have moved to further extremes, such as hedonism and wild economic speculation. In the cities, clubs and bars, all making heavy protection payments to the *mafiya*—as Russia's growing organized crime groups are termed—are gathering places that feature a variety of narcotics (including mushrooms gathered in the woods near St. Petersburg), alcohol, and a form of Russian rock music that was full of protest in the late 1980s but has since been diluted to widen its market appeal. This small but highly visible class of youth is divided into hundreds of *tusovki* (sing., *tusovka*), mutually exclusive social circles that provide a sense of identity but isolate their members from the rest of society. What the *tusovki* have in common are decadence, an appetite for risk, and a readiness to indulge in faddish forms of mass behavior.

Wages and Work

In the post-Soviet era, social mobility is unlimited in theory, but in the mid-1990s economic factors play an important role in restricting upward movement for most Russians. Those without an established source of wealth generally are unable to purchase land, real estate, or enterprises, or to take advantage of other financial opportunities to increase their income and status. Because individuals under such limitations also lack opportunities to pursue higher education, they tend to remain at or below the socioeconomic level of their parents. In many cases, the younger generation has less earning power than the one that preceded it.

In 1995 official government estimates placed 39 million people, or 26 percent of the population, below the poverty line. Living standards, which dropped drastically in 1992, recovered somewhat in 1993 and 1994 before falling again in 1995 as the government tightened its social support spending policy (see Social Welfare, this ch.; table 11, Appendix). Other factors, such as inflation, changes in the minimum wage and minimum pension, and income from nonwage sources such as business activity and property, also influence annual income in a given period. Raised in mid-1994, then not again until April 1995, the minimum wage has provided little protection against intermittent periods of high inflation. Official income statistics are skewed because many Russians underreport their incomes to avoid taxes and because such statistics ignore important nonincome sources of well-being such as property.

The real incomes of state-sector employees fell as much as 30 percent in the first three quarters of 1995. Wages in the private sector have kept pace with inflation more consistently, unless an enterprise has financial difficulties such as debts owed to other enterprises. In both sectors, long-term failure to pay wages has become a chronic problem; it affected an estimated 13 million people in mid-1995. Enterprises also have responded to financial difficulties by laying off employees and by shortening work weeks, pushing more workers below the poverty line. Although many of the working poor retain the housing, health, and free holidays associated with employment, enterprises are rapidly withdrawing those Soviet-era privileges.

The economic condition of many Russians is ameliorated by earnings from additional jobs or by access to private plots of land. In a 1994 survey, 47 percent of respondents reported some form of additional material support, and 23 percent reported having supplementary employment. In some cases, unofficial employment is quite profitable. Of the "working unemployed," Russians who consider themselves out of work but nevertheless hold some sort of job, 11 percent had incomes at least three times higher than the average wage in 1994. The large number of pensioners with unofficial jobs (approximately one in four) generally fare much better than those on fixed incomes, generating a disparity of status within the oldest segment of society. The easing of travel restrictions in post-Soviet Russia and the overall diversification of the private sector increased opportunities to earn supplementary income, through such activities as buying goods abroad and selling them inside Russia and offering a variety of private services such as repair work, sewing, and translation. In general, these opportunities are most accessible to young, well-educated Russians in large cities. But in many cases, well-educated individuals must sacrifice their social status by accepting unskilled jobs to make ends meet.

Some professional positions that are accorded high prestige carry a salary below that for certain categories of skilled labor. The upper echelons of the political, artistic, and scientific elites form the top of the occupation pyramid in terms of status and income. That category is followed by the professional, intellectual, and artistic intelligentsia; the most highly skilled industrial workers; white-collar workers; relatively prosperous farmers; and average workers. The bottom of the status and pay scales includes people employed as semiskilled or unskilled workers in light industry, agriculture, food processing, education, health care, retail trade, and the services sector.

Among the low-paying jobs are some that require higher or specialized education and that carry some level of prestige. Women predominate in these job categories, which include engineers, veterinarians, agronomists, accountants, legal advisers, translators, schoolteachers, librarians, organizers of clubs and cultural events, musicians, and even doctors. A 1994 World Bank report identified an increasing likelihood that positions offering lower wages would be filled by women, in most sectors and occupations of the Russian economy. Many women, however, reportedly accept jobs at lower levels of skill and remuneration in exchange for nonmonetary benefits, such as short commuting distances, minimum overtime hours, and access to child care or shopping facilities in the workplace (see The Role of Women, this ch.).

Rural Life

For rural society in both Soviet and post-Soviet times, agriculture has been the primary source of employment. Before 1992, however, the CPSU and its predecessors constituted the sole form of political organization, and all village communities were organized around the economic institution of the collective farm (*kolkhoz*—see Glossary) or state farm (*sovkhoz*—see Glossary) and the village soviet (council) administration—organizations that employed the elite of rural society, nearly all of whose members were men.

As in the past, the post-Soviet nonpolitical elite includes schoolteachers, agronomists, veterinary surgeons, and engineers. Teachers are held in high esteem, partly because of their role in determining who in the next generation will have upward social mobility. Despite this status, teachers receive low pay and often must maintain private garden plots to support themselves. Agricultural machinery specialists, including operators and mechanics, emerged as increasingly important and well-paid members of rural society in the 1970s and 1980s. In general, however, workers who remain in the countryside have less possibility of upward mobility than do urban dwellers. Managers and white-collar workers in rural agricultural and other organizations generally are brought in from outside.

Rural dwellers tend to spend more time in their homes than residents of urban areas. Rural homes generally are larger than those in the city and have private garden plots. The tastes of country people are simpler and less Western-oriented than those of their urban counterparts, and they have less money to spend on leisure pursuits. The routine of life in many rural villages has scarcely changed over many generations; the central concerns continue to be the weather and the condition of crops and livestock.

The end of Soviet rule cast a shadow over the villages' guarantee of medical care, job training, and entertainment, and rural areas benefited much less from the increased pace of information exchange characteristic of urban centers. Rural young people continue to leave their families to seek a better life elsewhere because village life has improved little since their grandparents were young. In this process, the family, the foundation of peasant society, has become fragmented. Villages with fewer than 1,000 inhabitants are disappearing at a rapid rate: between 1960 and 1995, the entire population of an estimated two-thirds of such villages either died or moved away. In the remaining rural villages, health care and education are increasingly inadequate, and essential commodities such as propane gas have become extremely expensive.

Many young people return to their rural homes after acquiring the type of education or technical training that is available only in cities and that is increasingly necessary to run mechanized farming operations and agroindustrial enterprises. They are joined by Russian émigrés from former Soviet republics, especially Central Asia, for whom it is easier to start life in Russia in a rural rather than an urban setting. However, most of those additions to the rural population are only stopping temporarily until they find more satisfying situations elsewhere. According to most experts, the long-term prospects of the traditional Russian village became grim in the immediate post-Soviet period.

Social Organizations

In the mid-1990s, the structure of Russia's civil society was still in flux, but by that time the country had developed a large and growing network of social organizations, including trade unions, professional societies, veterans' groups, youth organizations, sports clubs, women's associations, and a variety of support groups. Whereas all types of organization during the Soviet era functioned as "transmission belts" for the communist party, in the years that followed the emergence of a large number of diverse, autonomous nongovernmental groups was an important aspect of the growth of civil society.

The Federation of Independent Trade Unions of Russia (Federatsiya nezavisimykh profsoyuzov Rossii—FNPR) is one of the largest trade union organizations. Created as the official trade union movement was reconstituted following the disintegration of the Soviet Union, the federation includes thirty-six unions—many of them quite small in the mid-1990s—grouped by type of occupation. Among the FNPR's activities is the collection of contributions to the Social Insurance Fund by Russia's enterprises, each of which is required to earmark 4.5 percent of its total payroll for the fund.

Breaking the legal stranglehold of the Soviet-era trade union structure on the provision of social security benefits was a complicated but essential stage in enabling new unions to gain legitimacy in the eyes of workers. In the early 1990s, most workers saw the FNPR as representing the interests of management and the government, so they relied more heavily on unofficial, independent unions and a variety of worker-oriented organizations. However, in 1995 and early 1996 the FNPR, now a partner with top businesspeople in an umbrella party called Trade Unions and Industrialists of Russia, played a central role in organizing large-scale rallies and picketing actions to protest chronic late wage payments by enterprises all over the Russian Federation.

In the 1990s, substantial independent union activity has also occurred in the coal industry. There, the Independent Miners' Union (Nezavisimyy profsoyuz gornyakov—NPG) and the Independent Trade Union of Workers in the Coal-Mining Industry (Nezavisimyy profsoyuz rabochikh ugol'noy promyshlennosti—NPRUP), a reformed version of the official Soviet-era trade union, share power and have organized large-scale strikes.

In the 1990s, independent individuals and groups have begun establishing professional, research, educational, and cultural organizations. This activity has included a substantial upswing in the number of voluntary charitable and philanthropic organizations. In 1995 about 5,000 nonprofit organizations and 550 formal charities were operating in Russia. In Moscow more than 10,000 volunteers worked for these organizations in 1996. These numbers are low by Western standards, and a legal framework for the existence of charities and nonprofit organizations still did not exist as of mid-1996. However, the starting point in 1992 was nearly zero in both categories.

A significant token of citizen awareness is the proliferation of local and regional ecological and environmental cleanup groups throughout the Russian Federation (see The Response to Environmental Problems, ch. 3). For example, Epitsentr, an umbrella organization in St. Petersburg, has spawned numerous smaller groups that focus on controlling pollution in the city's water supply, stopping the construction of a controversial dam in the Gulf of Finland, and preserving St. Petersburg's historic buildings and cultural monuments. Students at Moscow State University and other educational institutions have played an important role in directing public attention to the massive

environmental degradation that plagues Russia. The Socio-Eco-
logical Union, which was founded at Moscow State University
in 1988, has become one of the Russian Federation's most
influential umbrella organizations committed to environmental protection.

The Family

As the Soviet Union became urbanized, families grew more
numerous and smaller in average size. Between the censuses of
1959 and 1989, the number of family units increased 41 percent, from 28.5 million to more than 40 million. Average family
size in the Russian Republic declined from 3.4 persons in 1970
to 3.1 in 1989. Already in the late 1970s, more than 80 percent
of urban families had two children or fewer. In 1989 some 87
percent of the population lived in families, of which about 80
percent were based on a married couple.

In the 1980s, the divorce rate in the Soviet Union was second
in the world only to that of the United States, although "unofficial divorces" and separations also were common. Crowded
housing and lack of privacy contributed heavily to the divorce
rate, especially for couples forced to live with the parents of
one spouse. Drunkenness and infidelity were other major
causes. Divorce procedures were relatively simple, although
courts generally attempted to reconcile couples. Custody of
children normally was awarded to the mother. In the first half
of the 1990s, the conditions contributing to the majority of
Russia's divorces did not change, and the divorce rate
increased.

In post-Soviet attitudes, the family continues to be viewed as
the most important institution in society. In a 1994 poll funded
by the Commission on Women's, Family, and Demographic
Problems, less than 3 percent of respondents named "living
alone without a family" as the best choice for a young person.
Although the size of the average Russian family has decreased
steadily over the past quarter-century, nearly 80 percent of
respondents named children as the essential element of a good
marriage. At the same time, about three-quarters of respondents said that a bad marriage should be terminated rather
than prolonged; the poll also showed that, generally, the Russian attitude toward divorce is more positive than it was in the
Soviet era.

According to the 1994 survey, the dynamics of the average
Russian family have changed somewhat. Compared with 1989,

about 3 percent fewer individuals characterized their marriages as in conflict, and 9 percent fewer called their marriages "egalitarian" in the distribution of authority between the partners. The average distribution of common household tasks was shown to be far from equal, with women performing an average of about 75 percent of cooking, cleaning, and shopping chores. Between 1989 and 1994, women's expression of dissatisfaction with their family situation increased 13 percent, while that of men rose only 2 percent. Women reporting family satisfaction were predominantly young or elderly, with adequate-to-high incomes and at least a secondary education. According to experts, social and economic crises have caused Russians to rely more heavily than ever on the family as a source of personal satisfaction. But these same crises have caused the standard of living to fall, and they have required that more time be spent at work to keep it from falling further, thus making it harder for families to sustain their most cherished attributes.

The Role of Women

In the post-Soviet era, the position of women in Russian society remains at least as problematic as it was in previous decades. In both cases, a number of nominal legal protections for women either have failed to address the existing conditions or have failed to supply adequate support. In the 1990s, increasing economic pressures and shrinking government programs left women with little choice but to seek employment, although most available positions were as substandard as in the Soviet period, and generally jobs of any sort were more difficult to obtain. Such conditions contribute heavily to Russia's declining birthrate and the general deterioration of the family. At the same time, feminist groups and social organizations have begun advancing the cause of women's rights in what remains a strongly traditional society.

The Soviet constitution of 1977 stipulated that men and women have equal rights, and that women have equal access to education and training, employment, promotions, remuneration, and participation in social, cultural, and political activity. The Soviet government also provided women special medical and workplace protection, including incentives for mothers to work outside the home and legal and material support of their maternal role. In the 1980s, that support included 112 days of maternity leave at full pay. When that allowance ended, a woman could take as much as one year of additional leave without pay without losing her position. Employer discrimination against pregnant and nursing women was prohibited, and mothers with small children had the right to work part-time. Because of such provisions, as many as 92 percent of women were employed at least part-time, Soviet statistics showed.

Despite official ideology, Soviet women did not enjoy the same position as men in society or within the family. Average pay for women in all fields was below the overall national average, and the vaunted high percentage of women in various fields, especially health care, medicine, education, and economics, did not hold true in the most prestigious and high-paying areas such as the upper management of organizations in any of those fields. Women were conspicuously underrepresented in the leadership of the CPSU; in the 1980s, they constituted less than 30 percent of party membership and less than 5 percent of the party Central Committee, and no woman ever achieved full membership in the Politburo.

Most of the nominal state benefit programs for women continued into the post-Soviet era (see Social Welfare, this ch.). However, as in the Soviet era, Russian women in the 1990s predominate in economic sectors where pay is low, and they continue to receive less pay than men for comparable positions. In 1995 men in health care earned an average of 50 percent more than women in that field, and male engineers received an average of 40 percent more than their female colleagues. Despite the fact that, on average, women are better educated than men, women remain in the minority in senior management positions. In the Soviet era, women's wages averaged 70 percent of men's; by 1995 the figure was 40 percent, according to the Moscow-based Center for Gender Studies. According to a 1996 report, 87 percent of employed urban Russians earning less than 100,000 rubles a month (for value of the ruble—see Glossary) were women, and the percentage of women decreased consistently in the higher wage categories.

According to reports, women generally are the first to be fired, and they face other forms of on-the-job discrimination as well. Struggling companies often fire women to avoid paying child care benefits or granting maternity leave, as the law still requires. In 1995 women constituted an estimated 70 percent of Russia's unemployed, and as much as 90 percent in some areas.

Sociological surveys show that sexual harassment and violence against women have increased at all levels of society in the 1990s. More than 13,000 rapes were reported in 1994, meaning that several times that number of that often-unreported crime probably were committed. In 1993 an estimated 14,000 women were murdered by their husbands or lovers, about twenty times the figure in the United States and several times the figure in Russia five years earlier. More than 300,000 other types of crimes, including spousal abuse, were committed against women in 1994; in 1996 the State Duma (the lower house of the Federal Assembly, Russia's parliament) drafted a law against domestic violence.

Working women continue to bear the "double burden" of a job and family-raising responsibilities, in which Russian husbands generally participate little. In a 1994 survey, about two-thirds of women said that the state should help families by paying one spouse enough to permit the other to stay at home. Most women also consider their role in the family more difficult than that of their husband. Such dissatisfaction is a factor in Russia's accelerating divorce rate and declining marriage rate. In 1993 the divorce rate was 4.5 per 1,000 population, compared with 4.1 ten years earlier, and the marriage rate declined from 10.5 per 1,000 population in 1983 to 7.5 in 1993. In 1992 some 17.2 percent of births were to unmarried women. According to 1994 government statistics, about 20 percent of families were run by a single parent—the mother in 94 percent of cases.

Often women with families are forced to work because of insufficient state child allowances and unemployment benefits. Economic hardship has driven some women into prostitution. In the Soviet period, prostitution was viewed officially as a form of social deviancy that was dying out as the Soviet Union advanced toward communism. In the 1990s, organized crime has become heavily involved in prostitution, both in Russia and in the cities of Central and Western Europe, to which Russian women often are lured by bogus advertisements for match-making services or modeling agencies. According to one estimate, 10,000 women from Central Europe, including a high proportion of Russians, have been lured or forced into prostitution in Germany alone.

Independent women's organizations—a form of activity that was suppressed in the Soviet era—have been formed in large numbers in the 1990s at the local, regional, and national levels. One such group is the Center for Gender Studies, a private research institute. The center analyzes demographic and social problems of women and acts as a link between Russian and Western feminist groups. A traveling group called Feminist Alternative offers women assertiveness training. Many local groups have emerged to engage in court actions on behalf of women, to set up rape and domestic violence awareness programs (about a dozen of which were active in 1995), and to aid women in establishing businesses. Another prominent organization is the Women's Union of Russia, which focuses on job-training programs, career counseling, and the development of entrepreneurial skills that will enable women to compete more successfully in Russia's emerging market economy. Despite the proliferation of such groups and programs, in the mid-1990s most Russians (including many women) remain contemptuous of their efforts, which many regard as a kind of Western subversion of traditional social values.

The rapidly expanding private sector offers women new employment opportunities, but many of the Soviet stereotypes remain; the most frequently offered job in new businesses is that of secretary, and advertisements often specify physical attractiveness as a primary requirement. Russian law provides for as much as three years' imprisonment for sexual harassment, but the law rarely is enforced. Although the Fund for Protection from Sexual Harassment has blacklisted 300 Moscow firms where sexual harassment is known to have taken place, demands for sex and even rape still are common on-the-job occurrences.

Women's higher profile in post-Soviet Russia also has extended to politics. At the national level, the most notable manifestation of women's newfound political success has been the Women of Russia party, which won 11 percent of the vote and twenty-five seats in the 1993 national parliamentary elections. Subsequently, the party became active in a number of issues, including the opposition to the military campaign in Chechnya that began in 1994. In the 1995 national parliamentary elections, the Women of Russia chose to maintain its platform unchanged, emphasizing social issues such as the protection of children and women rather than entering into a coalition with other liberal parties. As a result, the party failed to reach the 5 percent threshold of votes required for proportional representation in the new State Duma, gaining only three seats in the single-seat portion of the elections (see The Elections of 1995, ch. 7). The party considered running a candidate in the 1996 presidential election but remained outside the crowded field.

A smaller organization, the Russian Women's Party, ran as part of an unsuccessful coalition with several other splinter parties in the 1995 elections. A few women, such as Ella Pamfilova of the Republican Party, Socialist Workers' Party chief Lyudmila Vartazarova, and Valeriya Novodvorskaya, leader of the Democratic Union, have established themselves as influential political figures. Pamfilova has gained particular stature as an advocate on behalf of women and elderly people.

The Soldiers' Mothers Movement was formed in 1989 to expose human rights violations in the armed forces and to help youths resist the draft. The movement has gained national prominence through its opposition to the war in Chechnya. Numerous protests have been organized, and representatives have gone to the Chechen capital, Groznyy, to demand the release of Russian prisoners and locate missing soldiers. The group, which claimed 10,000 members in 1995, also has lobbied against extending the term of mandatory military service.

Women have occupied few positions of influence in the executive branch of Russia's national government. One post in the Government (cabinet), that of minister of social protection, has become a "traditional" women's position; in 1994 Ella Pamfilova was followed in that position by Lyudmila Bezlepkina, who headed the ministry until the end of President Boris N. Yeltsin's first term in mid-1996. Tat'yana Paramanova was acting chairman of the Russian Central Bank for one year before Yeltsin replaced her in November 1995, and Tat'yana Regent has been head of the Federal Migration Service since its inception in 1992. Prior to the 1995 elections, women held about 10 percent of the seats in parliament: fifty-seven of 450 seats in the State Duma and nine of 178 seats in the upper house of parliament, the Federation Council. The Soviet system of mandating legislative seats generally allocated about one-third of the seats in republic-level legislatures and one-half of the seats in local soviets to women, but those proportions shrank drastically with the first multiparty elections of 1990.

Sexual Attitudes

In the 1990s, Russian sexual values and attitudes generally moved toward liberalization and autonomy, with distinct differences according to age, sex, region, and level of education. In the Soviet era, the Russian attitude toward sexuality itself paralleled that toward artistic expression of the erotic: it simply was concealed. Most Soviet philosophical, psychological, and biological reference works made little or no mention of sexuality as a major characteristic of human beings. Soviet psychology, notoriously backward and misused, ignored almost completely the influence of sexual behavior and motivation on overall psychological makeup.

After decades of Stalinist repression, Russian erotic art, literature, and theater began a gradual revival in the 1970s as censorship and ideological control weakened somewhat. Access to Western novels with erotic motifs, such as Henry Miller's *Tropic of Cancer* and Vladimir Nabokov's *Lolita*, also improved in this period. In 1992 restrictions on the publication of erotic literature were loosened in Russia, heralding a rapid output of erotic and pornographic material of all sorts. A collection of children's erotic folklore was prepared in 1995, and erotic film festivals and photography exhibits began to appear in the 1990s. The public seemingly has accepted the frequent use of nudity in Russian television, dance, and drama.

Especially in film and literature, the shift has produced many instances of gratuitous or cruel sex and arbitrarily introduced nudity. Violence against women frequently is a central motif of movies, and violence and sex often are linked. Russian observers have expressed alarm that the release of long-repressed sexual expression in art will be accompanied by a similar deluge of sex and violence in Russian society. Indeed, the incidence of violence and sexual attacks against women in the first half of the 1990s seems to confirm these fears (see The Role of Women, this ch.).

Objections to the trend toward sexual liberation are concentrated in the older generations. In surveys younger and better-educated Russians generally voice approval, and new enterprises selling cosmetics, high-fashion clothing, and health products play to a new public interest in attractive display of the human body. The individuality implicit in such marketing—and especially obvious in the new Russian youth culture—is a drastic change from the strict standards of dress and grooming imposed in the Soviet era. The wearing of shorts, for example, only was accepted in Russia in the 1980s; in the Soviet era, women could not wear trousers in public without harassment or arrest; and vigilantes often forcibly cut the hair of youths who exceeded the standard for hair length.

According to surveys taken in the early 1990s, most Russians feel that romantic love is a precondition to marriage and to sexual intimacy. But there are great differences in attitude toward this ideal between the older and younger generations, between the sexes, and between rural and urban Russians. Russians in larger cities tend to take a more liberal outlook on premarital sex. The younger generations in Russia show a much more casual attitude toward commitment to a long-term relationship than do the older generations. However, in surveys younger males showed a much stronger identification of sex with pleasure, and younger females a stronger identification of sex with love. Russians' attitudes toward premarital sex became somewhat more liberal in the 1990s; in a 1993 survey, the percentage of those disapproving was substantially lower than it had been in previous years.

The official policy of the Soviet Union toward homosexuality was one of persecution and intimidation. Until the late 1980s, Russian social scientists and society in general were completely silent on the subject. Under those conditions, homosexuals, known as "blues," lived in an underground culture circumscribed by the brutality of gangs and the police and by employment discrimination.

With the advent of *glasnost* and the appearance of acquired immune deficiency syndrome (AIDS) in the Soviet Union, open scientific and journalistic discussion of homosexuality began in 1987. The issue became politicized in 1990 as gays and lesbians began attacking discrimination as a human rights issue. At this point, strong arguments appeared for abolishing Article 121 of the Criminal Code, which stipulated that sex between men (but not between women) was a crime. Despite increasingly strong opinion against Article 121, in the early 1990s nationalists and communists joined some religious organizations in opposing decriminalization. Meanwhile, the number of convictions under Article 121 decreased steadily. Although Russia's new Criminal Code had not been ratified as of mid-1996, substantial modifications had been made to Article 121 by that time.

Hundreds of gay rights organizations appeared in Russia in the 1990s, mostly in urban centers. Moscow became the center of Russia's gay and lesbian communities, both of which remained substantially less overt than their Western equivalents. Despite a gradual increase in public tolerance in the 1990s, substantial residues of homophobia remain in Russian society. The neofascist group Pamyat', for example, remained violently antigay in the mid-1990s, and the communist and extreme nationalist media have launched strident homophobic attacks. In the late 1980s and early 1990s, numerous surveys identified homosexuals as the most hated group in Russian society, although the number of Russians calling for their extermination or isolation decreased noticeably between 1989 and the mid-1990s.

Education

In the Soviet period, education was highly centralized, and indoctrination in Marxist-Leninist theory was a major element of every school's curriculum. The schools' additional ideological function left a legacy in the post-Soviet system that has proved difficult for educators to overcome. In the 1990s, reform programs are aimed at overhauling the Soviet-era pedagogical philosophy and substantially revising curricula. Inadequate funding has frustrated attainment of these goals, however, and the teaching profession has lost talented individuals because of low pay.

The Soviet Heritage

The Soviet government operated virtually all the schools in Russia. The underlying philosophy of Soviet schools was that the teacher's job was to transmit standardized materials to the students, and the student's job was to memorize those materials, all of which were put in the context of socialist ethics. That set of ethics stressed the primacy of the collective over the interests of the individual. Therefore, for both teachers and students, creativity and individualism were discouraged. The Soviet system also maintained some traditions from tsarist times, such as the five-point grading scale, formal and regimented classroom environments, and standard school uniforms—dark dresses with white collars for girls, white shirts and black pants for boys.

As in other areas of Soviet life, the need for reform in education was felt in the 1980s. Reform programs in that period called for new curricula, textbooks, and teaching methods. The chief aim of those programs was to create a "new school" that would better equip Soviet citizens to deal with the modern, technologically advanced nation that Soviet leaders foresaw in the future. Nevertheless, in the 1980s facilities generally were inadequate, overcrowding was common, and equipment and materials were in short supply. The schools and universities failed to supply adequately skilled labor to almost every sector of the economy, and overgrown bureaucracy further compromised education's contribution to society. At the same time, young Russians became increasingly cynical about the Marxist-Leninist philosophy they were forced to absorb, as well as the stifling of self-expression and individual responsibility. In the last years of the Soviet Union, funding was inadequate for the large-scale establishment of "new schools," and requirements of ideological purity continued to smother the new pedagogical creativity that was heralded in official pronouncements.

The dissolution of the Soviet Union and the transition toward democracy had a profound effect on national education policy. In 1992 a reform philosophy was set forth in the Law on Education. The fundamental principle of that law was the removal of state control from education policy. In regions with non-Russian populations, that meant that educational institutions could base their curricula and teaching methods on national and historical traditions. In all regions, enactment of the law meant significant autonomy for local authorities to choose education strategies most appropriate to the time and place. Post-Soviet education reform also stressed teaching objectively, thus discarding all forms of the narrow, institutional views that had dominated the previous era and preparing young people to deal with all aspects of the society they would encounter by presenting a broader interpretation of the world.

Post-Soviet educational philosophy also has sought to integrate education with the production and economic processes into which graduates will pass in adult life. Envisioning a program of continuous education lasting throughout the lifetime of an individual, this concept has as its goal converting the education process from an economic burden on the state to an engine of economic progress. Especially important in this program is the reorientation of vocational training to complement the economic reforms of the 1990s. New systems of education for farmers and various types of on-the-job training for adults have been introduced, and new curricula in economics stress understanding of market economies.

The Post-Soviet Education Structure

Article 43 of the 1993 constitution affirms each citizen's

right to education. It stipulates that "basic general education is compulsory" and that parents or guardians are responsible for ensuring that children obtain schooling. "General access to free preschool, basic general, and secondary vocational education in state or municipal educational establishments and in enterprises is guaranteed," according to the constitution. Although such access continued to exist in principle in the mid-1990s, various components of the system were increasingly inadequate. In 1993 some 35.2 million students were enrolled in Russian schools at all levels, including 20.5 million in general primary and secondary schools, 1.8 million in professional and technical schools, 2.1 million in special secondary schools, and 2.6 million in institutions of higher learning (see table 12, Appendix). A total of 70,200 general primary and secondary schools and 82,100 preschools were in operation at that time. Of the former category, 48,800 were in rural areas and 21,000 in urban areas.

In 1995 the projected budgetary expenditure for education was about 3.6 percent of the total state budget, a level Russian experts agreed could not maintain the system as it was, to say nothing of implementing the changes called for by post-Soviet legislation. The financing system made educational institutions fully dependent on state funds; outside sources of funding did not exist because no tax advantages accrued from investing in education.

Infrastructure

Because the Soviet Union had not built enough schools to accommodate increasing enrollment, Russia inherited a system of very large, overcrowded schools with a decaying infrastructure. By the late 1980s, 21 percent of students were attending schools with no central heating, and 30 percent were learning in buildings with no running water. In 1992 Russia had nearly 67,000 primary and secondary schools, which provided an average per-pupil space of 2.6 square meters, one-third the official standard. About one-quarter of schools housed 900 or more students. In 1993 Russia was forced to close about 20,000 of its schools because of physical inadequacy, and an estimated one-third of the national school capacity was in need of large-scale repair. In 1994 one of every two students attended a school operating on two or three shifts. Rural schools, which make up about 75 percent of the national total, were in especially bad condition.

Children in middle school, Tyumen'
Courtesy G.W. Meredith, Jr.

Teachers

The Soviet Union suffered a shortage of teachers for decades before the 1990s. Although society held the profession in high regard, teacher salaries were among the lowest of all professions, at least partly because women dominated the field at the primary and secondary levels. The emerging market economy of the 1990s improved the pay and career opportunities outside teaching for many who would have remained in education under the more rigid Soviet system; thus, the shortage was exacerbated. In the 1992–93 school year, Russian schools had about 29,000 teacher vacancies, and in the following year 25 percent of all foreign-language teaching positions were unfilled. Although low pay has damaged morale among Russian teachers, they are more disillusioned by the end of the idealistic first post-Soviet years of innovation and freedom of speech and the continued decline of their material environment. In the mid-1990s, rural schools experienced particular difficulty retaining teachers, as qualified young adults sought opportunities in larger communities.

Curriculum

The end of the communist system has led to extensive curriculum revision. A new paradigm has been developed to guide education, and more attention has gone to the arts, humanities, and social sciences. The 1992 Law on Education stressed the humanistic nature of education, common values, freedom of human development, and citizenship. Curriculum changes were laid out in another document, the Basic Curriculum of the General Secondary School; the overall curriculum reform program is to be put in place over a five-year period ending in 1998. In the mid-1990s, many public schools have designed special curricula, some returning to the classical studies prevalent in the early 1900s. Local development of curricula and materials became legal in 1992, although financial constraints have limited experimentation and the Soviet era left educators with a strong bias toward standardized instruction and rote memorization. In contrast to the Soviet era, the quality and content of curricula vary greatly among public schools. A major factor encouraging local initiative is the disarray of federal education agencies, which often leave oblast, regional, and municipal authorities to their own devices. Nevertheless, only about one-third of primary and secondary schools have taken advantage of the opportunity to develop their own curricula; many administrations have been unwilling to make such large-scale decisions independently.

Grade Structure

Russian parents have the option of sending their children to preschool until age seven, when enrollment in elementary school becomes mandatory. Because the overwhelming majority of mothers still have full-time employment, many preschool facilities are colocated with enterprises. As businesses become increasingly profit oriented, however, many have ceased or reduced their support of such facilities. The number of child-care facilities for working parents declined significantly after 1991, mainly because many such facilities lacked the funding to continue operation without state support. Of about 82,100 preschools in operation in 1993, more than one-third were housed in inadequate facilities.

Although the 1992 Law on Education lowered the upper age of the compulsory education range from seventeen to fifteen, in the mid-1990s more than 60 percent of students remained in school for the previously required ten years. Among Russia's educational reforms is a regulation authorizing school officials to expel students fourteen years of age or older who are failing their courses. By the end of 1992, about 200,000 students had been expelled, and two to three times that number had dropped out. In the mid-1990s, Russia had five types of secondary school: regular schools featuring a core curriculum; schools offering elective subjects; schools offering intensive study in elective subjects; schools designed to prepare students for entrance examinations to an institution of higher education (*vyssheye uchebnoye zavedeniye*—VUZ; pl., VUZy); and alternative schools with experimental programs.

Private Schools

State education is free, but by 1992 several state higher-education institutions had begun charging tuition. At that point, almost half of the students above the secondary level were paying fees of some sort. The 1992 Law on Education provides explicitly for private educational institutions; in the ensuing years, several organizations for private education have appeared, and a variety of private schools and colleges have opened. By 1992 about 300 nonstate schools were being attended by more than 20,000 students.

As public schools debated what to do with their new academic freedom, private schools and preschools became centers of innovation, with programs rediscovering prerevolutionary pedagogy and freely borrowing teaching methods from Western Europe and the United States. Serving largely Western-oriented families intent on making progress up the newly reconstructed social ladder, private schools emphasize learning English and other critical skills. Student-to-teacher ratios are very low, and teacher salaries average about US$170 per month (about three times the average for a public school teacher). Tuition may be as much as US$3,000 per year, but some private schools charge parents according to their means, surviving instead on donations of money and time from wealthy parents. Unlike public schools, all private schools must pay for rent, utilities, and textbooks, and many have struggled to retain adequate building space.

Educational Achievement

The literacy rate in Russia is nearly 100 percent except in some areas dominated by ethnic minorities, where the rate may be considerably lower. According to the 1989 census, three-fifths of Russia's people aged fifteen and older had completed secondary school, and 8 percent had completed higher education. Wide variations in educational attainment exist between urban and rural areas. The 1989 census indicated that two-thirds of the country's urban population aged fifteen and older had finished secondary school, as compared with just under one-half of the rural population. Schools can award diplomas only in three languages—Russian, Tatar, and Bashkir—a requirement that puts many of the country's more than 100 ethnic groups at a disadvantage.

Higher Education

The VUZ category includes all of Russia's postsecondary educational institutions; in 1995 these totaled about 500, including forty-two universities. The other two types of VUZ are the institute and the polytechnic institute. Institutes, the largest of the three groups, train students in a specific field such as law, economics, art, agriculture, medicine, or technology. The polytechnic institutes teach the same range of subjects but without specialization in a single area. Most universities teach the arts and pure sciences.

The institute program consists of two phases. After completing two years of general studies, a student receives a certificate; he or she then may take an entrance examination to continue for two more years or terminate the program and seek a job. Completion of the next two years results in conferral of a baccalaureate degree. The next level of higher education is specialized study based on a research program in the area of future professional activity. This phase lasts at least two years, at the end of which the individual is designated a specialist in the chosen field. The top level of higher education is graduate work, which entails a three-year program of study and research leading to a degree of candidate (*kandidat*), then finally to a degree of doctor of sciences (*doktor nauk*).

In the post-Soviet era, the system of higher education has undergone a more drastic transformation than the primary and secondary systems. Authority has moved from the center to agencies in local and subnational jurisdictions. About 14 percent of institutions of higher learning are located in the twenty-one republics of the federation (see table 13, Appendix). Under the new system, each VUZ can determine its own admissions policy and the content of its academic programs. These institutions also have their own financial resources and statutes of operation.

Most of Russia's universities are located in large cities. Moscow State University, which was founded in 1755 and has about 28,000 students and 8,000 teachers, enjoys the highest reputation. The Russian People's Friendship University in Moscow has about 6,500 students and 1,500 teachers, and St. Petersburg State University has about 21,000 students and 2,100 teachers.

The Soviet Union concentrated its vocational training resources in areas such as space and military technology. It lagged behind the West in technical and vocational training in other sectors because of the practice of ending students' preparation in these areas at the secondary level. In Russia vocational schools traditionally have had a poor image; only in the early 1990s was comprehensive vocational education introduced for postsecondary students. In 1993 some 400 VUZ offered specialized training in specific vocational areas ranging from engineering and electricity to agricultural specialties. Some vocational schools have combined general and vocational curricula, with the goal of giving specialists a broader educational background. Another trend is the integration of higher technical education with on-the-job training by linking educational institutions with enterprises and factories.

In the post-Soviet era, business education has expanded dramatically because the demand for competent managers far outstrips the supply. Experts believe that Russia's business education programs will play an important role in transforming social attitudes toward the market economy and capitalism and establishing a new economic infrastructure. The primary goal of the new programs is to create familiarity with the principles of the market economy while casting aside Marxist economic ideology. In the first two years after the Soviet Union dissolved, more than 1,000 business schools and training centers were established.

Three types of institution offer business management education: state and private business schools and private consulting firms. Many in the last category simply offer high-priced lectures, but some business schools have developed sophisticated programs. Examples are the International Business School of Moscow State University, the Graduate School of International Business of the Academy of the National Economy in Moscow, and the International Management Institute in St. Petersburg. Several schools offer full master of business administration (MBA) degree programs based on Western models. Business schools are funded by the state and by private enterprise. Competent faculty are at a premium in this field; many have been trained by Western firms such as IBM.

Education and Society

Education plays a crucial role in determining social status in Russia. People who leave school after eight years generally can find only unskilled jobs. Even those who complete secondary education may rise no higher than skilled labor or low-level white-collar work. A college or university education is necessary for most professional and bureaucratic positions and appears to be highly desirable for a position of political power. For example, a very high percentage of the members of Russia's parliament are university graduates.

Access to higher education is roughly proportionate to the social and financial situation of an individual's family. Children whose parents have money and status usually have an advantage in gaining admission to an institution of higher education. The reasons lie not only with the parents' possible influence and connections but increasingly with the better quality of primary and secondary education that has become available to such children, enhancing their ability to pass difficult university entrance examinations. Moreover, such families can afford to hire tutors for their children in preparation for the examinations and can more readily afford to pay university tuition in case the children do not receive stipends.

By the mid-1990s, the new phenomenon of individual commercial success began influencing the attitude of Russian society toward education and its goals. At the same time, the last generation of Soviet-educated Russians was finding itself ill prepared to deal with a new set of conditions for social and economic survival. In the new order, acquisition of money is much more important for both self-respect and practical survival, and career prestige by itself is of relatively less worth than it was in the Soviet system, where every career label ensured a known level of comfort. Significantly, in post-Soviet years, the phrase *delat' den'gi* (to make money) has passed into common usage in colloquial Russian. Together with the employment insecurity felt in the 1990s by well-educated Russians, the new values have dampened the educational ambitions of many, particularly with regard to higher education. Although most older Russians resent those who achieve commercial success in the new "system," the generation now in school shows increasing interest in advancement in the private sector of the economy. At the same time, polls show that education ranks ninth among the most pressing concerns of Russians.

Health

Russia has an entrenched, albeit underfunded, system of socialized medicine. Basic medical care is available to most of the population free of cost, but its quality is extremely low by Western standards, and in the mid-1990s the efficiency of the system continued the decline that had begun before the collapse of the Soviet system. In the first four post-Soviet years, that decline was typified by significant increases in infant and maternal mortality and contagious diseases and by decreases in fertility and life expectancy.

Health Conditions

The decline in health is attributable in part to such environmental and social factors as air and water pollution, contamination (largely from nuclear accidents or improper disposal of radioactive materials), overcrowded living conditions, inadequate nutrition, alcoholism, and smoking, and in part to a lack of modern medical equipment and technology. In 1991 life expectancy in Russia was 74.3 years for females and 63.5 years for males. By 1994 the figure for males was 57.3 years. The male-to-female ratio in the population reflects the higher male mortality rate and the enduring impact of losing millions more males than females in World War II. (In all age-groups below thirty-five, there are more males than females.) In 1993 the overall ratio was 884 males per 1,000 females, and experts predicted that the figure for males would decline to around 875 by the year 2005 (see Demographic Conditions, ch. 3).

By the mid-1990s, Russia's death rate had reached its highest peacetime level in the twentieth century. Curable infectious diseases such as diphtheria and measles have reached epidemic levels unseen since the Bolshevik Revolution, and the rates of tuberculosis, cancer, and heart disease are the highest of any industrialized country.

In 1993 the incidence of a number of infectious diseases increased significantly over the previous year: tuberculosis by 1.25 times, brucellosis by 1.9 times, diphtheria by 3.9 times, and syphilis by 2.6 times (see table 14, Appendix). In 1995 the Russian health system was overwhelmed by the return of epidemic diseases such as cholera and typhoid fever, even as it faced chronic staff and equipment shortages. In the winter of 1995–96, Russia suffered its most severe epidemic of influenza in decades. An estimated 1 million people were infected in Moscow alone, and numerous schools and public institutions were closed to prevent the spread of the disease. Experts attributed the virulence of the epidemic to the generally low level of resistance of much of the Russian population, the result of poor overall health care and stressful economic conditions. Other causes were the uneven availability of influenza shots and the population's general belief that injections enhance rather than decrease an individual's chances of becoming ill.

Between 1980 and 1989, cancer and its complications increased from 15 percent to 18 percent among causes of death. In 1990 the most common types of cancer were breast cancer, cancer of the stomach and liver, and skin cancer. In the last years of the Soviet Union, about 680,000 new cases were diagnosed annually. The causes of cancer are varied and complex, but contributing factors in Russia are heavy smoking, radiation exposure, and contact with pervasive toxic emissions and chemicals in soil, food, and water. According to the deputy minister of environmental protection and natural resources, about 50 percent of all cancer-related illnesses can be attributed to environmental factors. Heavy-manufacturing regions show especially high rates; in Noril'sk, the metallurgical center located above the Arctic Circle, the incidence of lung cancer among males is the highest in the world (see Environmental Conditions, ch. 3).

Russia's birthrate has shown an increasingly steep decline in the 1990s, amounting to what one commentator calls "the quiet suicide of a nation." For example, the annual birthrate for the first six months of 1992 was 11.2 per 1,000 population— a 12 percent decline from the same period in the previous year. In some areas, the rate was even lower, for instance, 9.2 in St. Petersburg and 8.2 in the Moscow region.

Funeral procession with coffin on flatbed truck, village of Pertominsk
Courtesy Al Levine

Russia's Ministry of Health reported in June 1991 that the country had a negative rate of population change for the first time since records have been kept. The declining number of births is attributed in part to a drop in fertility, which presumably stems from a combination of physiological and environmental factors, and in part to women's reluctance to bear children in a time of economic uncertainty.

Maternity, Infant Care, and Birth Control

Some of the same factors shortening the lives of adults cause needless premature deaths of newborns in Russia. Poor overall health care and lack of medicines, especially in rural areas, reduce infants' survival chances. In Russia an estimated 40 to 50 percent of infant deaths are caused by respiratory failure, infectious and parasitic diseases, accidents, injuries, and trauma. For developed countries, this share ranges between 4 and 17 percent.

Infant mortality rates vary considerably by region. Central and northern European Russia's rates have been more in line with West European rates. In the intermediate category are the Urals, western Siberia, and the Volga Basin. The highest rates are found in the North Caucasus, eastern Siberia, and the Far East. Several autonomous republics, including Kalmykia, Chechnya, Ingushetia, Dagestan, and Tyva, consistently record the highest rates in the Russian Federation. In these areas, social and economic underdevelopment, poor health care, and environmental degradation have had an impact on the health of mothers and newborns.

Unwanted pregnancies are common because of the limited availability and substandard quality of contraceptives and a reluctance to discuss sexual issues openly at home or to provide sex education at school. No social stigma is attached to children born out of wedlock, and unmarried mothers receive maternity benefits. Medical care for expectant mothers is among the least adequate aspects of the country's generally substandard system of health care. A high percentage of pregnant women suffer from anemia and poor diets—factors that have a negative effect on their babies' birth weight and general health.

In the mid-1990s, modern forms of contraception are unavailable or unknown to most Russian women. The Soviet Union legalized abortion for medical reasons in 1955 and overall in 1968. But information about Western advances in birth control—and all modern means of birth control—was systematically kept from the public throughout the remaining Soviet decades. As a result of that policy, today's Russian gynecologists lack the training to advise women on contraception, and public knowledge of the subject remains incomplete or simply mistaken. Even in Moscow in the mid-1990s, most contraceptives were paid for by voluntary funds and international charities. In the early 1990s, an estimated 22 percent of women of childbearing age were using contraceptives; the percentage was much lower in rural areas.

Abortion remains the most widely practiced form of birth control in Russia. In 1995 some 225 abortions were performed for every 100 live births, up from a rate of 196 per 100 in 1991. According to one study, 14 percent of the women in Russia with sixteen or more years of school had undergone eight to ten abortions. The conditions under which abortions are performed often are primitive. Moreover, it is estimated that nearly three-quarters of abortions take place after the first trimester of pregnancy, involving substantially greater maternal risk than those performed earlier. The number of abortions is much higher among Russian women than among Muslims and other minority groups, however. Statistically, the higher her social status and the extent of her Russification, the more likely a Muslim woman is to seek an abortion.

Infant and child health in Russia is significantly worse than in other industrialized countries. According to official statistics, only one child in five is born healthy. The inability of more than half of all new mothers to breast-feed, mainly because of poor diet, further undermines infants' health in a country where diets generally are unbalanced. Another problem is that most women of childbearing age are employed and thus must place their young children in day care centers, where they often contract contagious diseases. Illnesses such as cholera, typhoid fever, diphtheria, pertussis, and poliomyelitis, which have been virtually eradicated in other advanced industrial societies, are widespread among Russia's children. Vaccines are scarce. Even when immunizations are available, parents often refuse them for their children because they fear infection from dirty needles.

Alcohol, Narcotics, and Tobacco

Russia's rate of alcohol consumption, traditionally among the highest in the world and rising significantly in the 1990s, is a major contributor to the country's health crisis, as well as to low job productivity. Rated as Russia's third most critical health problem after cardiovascular diseases and cancer, alcoholism has reached epidemic proportions, particularly among males. In the twentieth century, periodic government campaigns against alcohol consumption have resulted in thousands of deaths from the consumption of alcohol surrogates. The latest such campaign was undertaken from 1985 to 1988, during the regime of Mikhail S. Gorbachev (in office 1985–91). Although some authorities credited reduced alcohol consumption with a concurrent drop in Russia's mortality rate, by 1987 the production of *samogon* (home-brewed liquor) had become a large-scale industry that provided alcohol to Russians while depriving the state of tax revenue. When restrictions were eased in 1988, alcohol consumption exceeded the pre-1985 level.

According to one study, between 1987 and 1992 annual per capita consumption rose from about eleven liters of pure alcohol to fourteen liters in 1992; current consumption is estimated at about fifteen liters. (According to World Health Organization standards, consumption of eight liters per year is likely to cause major medical problems.)

A 1995 Russian study found that regular drunkenness affected between 25 and 60 percent of blue-collar workers and 21 percent of white-collar workers, with the highest incidence found in rural areas. Because alcohol remains cheap relative to food and other items, and because it is available in most places day and night, unemployed people are especially prone to drunkenness and alcohol poisoning. In 1994 some 53,000 people died of alcohol poisoning, an increase of about 36,000 since 1991. If vodka is unavailable or unaffordable, Russians sometimes imbibe various combinations of dangerous substances. The Russian media often report poisonings that result from consumption of homemade alcohol substitutes. Production of often-substandard alcohol has become a widespread criminal activity in the 1990s, further endangering consumers. Alcohol consumption among pregnant women is partly responsible for Russia's rise in infant mortality, birth defects, and childhood disease and abnormalities.

Smoking, a widespread habit, especially among women and teenagers, compounds Russia's health crisis. Chain-smoking is endemic in Russia; in 1996 an estimated 55 percent of Russians were regular smokers, and health authorities believed that the figure was rising. However, rather than urge patients to quit, doctors often recommend the purchase of American cigarettes, which are more expensive but have less tar and nicotine than Russian brands. When import restrictions ended in the early 1990s, the American cigarette industry found a large new market in Russia. A modest government antismoking campaign paralleling Gorbachev's anti-alcohol campaign in the late 1980s had little effect. In January 1996, cigarette advertising in the print media was prohibited, and smoking in theaters and workplaces generally was restricted to designated locations.

The increasing incidence of drug abuse was belatedly acknowledged by the Russian government as a public health problem. In 1995 an estimated 2 million Russians used narcotics, more than twenty times the total recorded ten years earlier in the entire Soviet Union, with the number of users increasing 50 percent every year in the mid-1990s. In the Soviet era, drugs were viewed officially as a capitalist vice, but that attitude disappeared soon after the Soviet Union dissolved. Russia legalized drug use (but not possession or sale) in 1991. According to experts, laws against possession are not dissuasive. Narcotics use has spread to new elements of society in recent years, including alcoholics seeking a new means of escape. Russian experts rate the new class of Russian businesspeople as the group with the highest percentage of drug users; for them, success often includes the ability to purchase the most expensive narcotic. The drug scene, once dominated by students and intellectuals, now includes large numbers of housewives and workers. Synthetic drugs now are manufactured in small laboratories by professional chemists; some are easily fabricated by amateurs as well. Legally produced drugs often are stolen and move into the black market (see The Crime Wave of the 1990s, ch. 10).

Medical treatment and educational programs now include hot lines in major cities and walk-in clinics that provide advice and treatment on an anonymous basis. Some schoolteachers have begun class discussions of drug-related issues and have distributed antidrug literature to students. Nevertheless, Russia's drug problem remains largely intractable. Many addicts overdose, and some who cannot afford heroin inject themselves with other substances that cause illness or death.

Acquired Immune Deficiency Syndrome

Acquired immune deficiency syndrome (AIDS) likely was brought to the Soviet Union by students from countries with high levels of incidence of the disease. In 1987, after the first case of AIDS was confirmed in Russia, the Supreme Soviet of the Soviet Union passed the strictest anti-AIDS law in the world, making the knowing transmittal of the infection a criminal offense punishable by up to eight years in jail. A 1995 law, which has been criticized vehemently for its human rights implications and the cost of its administration, stipulates that all visitors remaining more than three months must prove that they are not infected with the AIDS-causing human immunodeficiency virus (HIV).

The government has established a diagnostic and screening infrastructure for AIDS prevention and control at the central and subnational levels. This system has been criticized heavily, however, because it tests only populations with little chance of infection, and because it fails to allocate scarce funds to root causes of AIDS transmittal such as infection from hospital procedures and reuse of hypodermic needles. The release of statistics on the incidence of AIDS and other sexually transmitted diseases has been extremely slow. In late 1995, the Ministry of Health reported that 1,023 Russians, including 278 children, had been registered as having HIV, and that to that point 160 Russians, of whom seventy-three were children, had died of AIDS. Before 1992 several mass infections of children occurred in medical facilities.

Official diagnoses of HIV increased 50 percent from 1993 to 1994. However, according to an official of the Imena AIDS support group, which is devoted to rehabilitation of HIV victims, the official statistics are understated at least tenfold because Russians in the groups most at risk—prostitutes, homosexuals, and drug users—have reason to fear that results will not remain confidential and so refuse AIDS testing. Although the 1990 Law on Prevention of AIDS mandates confidentiality of medical records, in practice jobs often are lost and social services denied after a positive diagnosis. The highest incidence of HIV is in Moscow, St. Petersburg, Rostov-na-Donu, Volgograd, and the Republic of Kalmykia, the last three of which have medical facilities where unsanitary procedures have resulted in mass transmission of the virus. The majority of reported HIV-positive individuals are drug users.

As in the Soviet period, the public receives little information about precautions against AIDS or the identity of the high-risk categories in society, and AIDS sufferers meet much intolerance in Russian society. Because the disease has been associated with foreigners, government officials and the public have ignored the need for preventive measures among Russians. AIDS transmittal is increased by a chronic shortage of condoms (which Soviet medical officials euphemistically called "Article Number 2") and by the lack of disposable hypodermic syringes in hospitals and clinics, which results in the repeated use of unsterilized needles.

The Health System

The *glasnost* period of the late 1980s first revealed the decay of the Soviet system of socialized medicine, which nominally guaranteed full health protection to all citizens without charge. That system had been installed under Joseph V. Stalin (in office 1927–53) with an emphasis on preserving a healthy work force as a matter of national economic policy. In the 1980s,

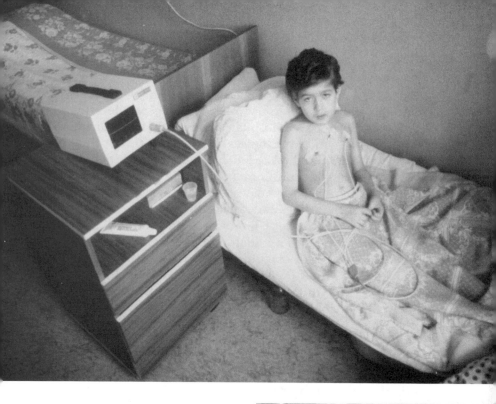

Child undergoing an EKG at children's hospital, Khabarovsk
Courtesy Barry Peril

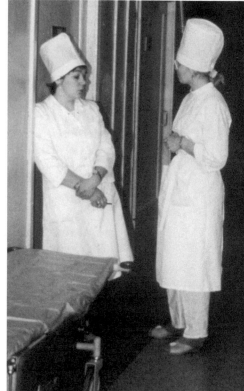

Hospital staff members talking in hospital hallway, Novgorod
Courtesy Judy Kramer

Russia had a huge network of neighborhood and work-site clinics and first-aid facilities to provide readily accessible primary care, together with large hospitals and polyclinics to diagnose and treat more complex illnesses and to perform surgery. In 1986 the Soviet Union had 23,500 hospitals with more than 3.6 million beds. Such facilities included about 28,000 women's consultation centers and pediatric clinics, together with emergency ambulance services and sanatoriums.

In the 1980s, the Soviet Union was first in the world in the ratio of hospital beds to population. Behind this system was a huge, multilevel bureaucracy directed from Moscow in consultation with organs of the CPSU. All aspects of health service had nationwide annual programs with complex statistical accounting and goals. Physicians devoted an estimated 50 percent of their time to filling out forms, and every year a large part of the national health care budget went to construction of new facilities.

The structure of the Soviet system, which specified the length of treatment for every disease, often caused people suffering from relatively minor ailments such as influenza to be hospitalized. The result was a serious overcrowding problem in hospitals despite the large number of beds available. Patients preferred hospital treatment because hospitals were better equipped than clinics and because crowded living conditions made recuperation at home difficult. Many large enterprises operated clinics that provided workers health care without requiring them to leave the work site. Such clinics aimed at reducing the incidence of sick leave, which averaged 3 percent of the workforce per day in the 1980s.

The most outdated and abuse-ridden aspect of Soviet health care was psychiatric treatment. That system never advanced from the methodology of the 1950s, which included Pavlovian conditioned-response treatment, heavy reliance on drug therapy, and little practice of individual or group counseling. Therefore, most citizens preferred to suffer rather than submit themselves to treatment. In addition, Soviet psychiatry was at the service of the government to declare dissenters "insane," commit them to psychiatric hospital-prisons, and administer powerful psychotropic drugs. In the mid-1980s, estimates of the number of political prisoners in such institutions ranged from 1,000 to several thousand, and in 1983 the Soviet Union withdrew from the World Psychiatric Association to avoid censure for its abuses of the profession. In 1988 the special psychiatric hospitals to which political dissidents had been committed were transferred from the jurisdiction of the Ministry of Internal Affairs to that of the Ministry of Health.

In 1986 the Soviet Union had about 1.2 million doctors and about 3.2 million paramedical and nursing personnel. Medical training emphasized practical work over basic research and pure science; only nine medical institutes were attached to universities. In the late 1980s, the average doctor's salary was roughly comparable to that of the average industrial worker. In 1996 the average Moscow specialist made about US$75 per month, and senior doctors made about US$150 per month. Paramedics and nurses needed only two years of training and no scientific background; however, in rural areas, which suffered a shortage of doctors, such individuals often were the only medical personnel available.

Despite the nominally equitable nature of Soviet socialized medicine, the actual system was highly stratified according to location, with far inferior care and facilities available in rural areas, and especially according to political status. The Ministry of Health maintained a completely separate, vastly superior system of clinics, hospitals, and sanatoriums for top party and government officials and other elite groups such as writers, actors, musicians, and artists.

The outline of the Soviet system did not change appreciably in the first half of the 1990s, but quality declined in nearly every aspect except the facilities designated for the elite. In 1992 Russia had 662,700 doctors, a drop of about 32,000 since 1990, and 131 hospital beds per 10,000 population, a drop of 97,000 beds (about 5 percent) since 1990. Among the doctors, 78,600 were surgeons, 77,600 pediatricians, 39,600 gynecologists, 20,300 psychiatrists, and 18,500 neurologists.

In the early 1990s, the public health delivery system in Russia was in crisis. Although the number of doctors and paramedics has remained sufficiently high to ensure the provision of adequate treatment, most such personnel are poorly trained, lack modern equipment, and are badly paid. In 1995 Russia had one doctor for every 275 citizens (compared with one for every 450 in the United States), but about half of medical school graduates cannot diagnose simple ailments or read an electrocardiogram when they enter practice. In 1993 about forty institutions offered medical training, but the quality of training varied considerably. Many medical schools suffer from shortages of instructors, textbooks, current medical journals, contacts with Western experts, and equipment.

Low salaries have made corruption common among medical personnel, who often extract bribes for both materials and services. Thus, although health care is free in principle, the chances of receiving adequate treatment may depend on the patient's wealth. The combination of bribes and authorized charges puts many types of medical treatment beyond the reach of all but the wealthy. Elderly people are hit especially hard by this situation. Meanwhile, a sharp decline in state funding has affected all aspects of medical care, from prevention to emergency treatment. Between 1990 and 1994, state funding declined from 3.4 percent of the national budget to 1.8 percent.

Although Russia pioneered in some specialized fields of medicine such as laser eye surgery and heart surgery, the country's medical establishment is generally deficient in hospital equipment, technology, and pharmaceuticals. For example, preventable infant deaths result from an absence of fetal heart monitors, ultrasound units, and various other equipment for monitoring labor and delivery; needless deaths from heart disease occur because hospitals lack the equipment needed to perform bypass surgery and angioplasty.

Facilities for the disabled, of whom about 6 million reside in Russia, also fall far below Western standards. Wheelchairs and artificial limbs are in very short supply, rehabilitation centers are few, and wheelchair ramps are virtually nonexistent. A 1995 law, On the Social Protection of Disabled Persons in the Russian Federation, provides for a wide range of benefits and services, including equal access to education, employment, transportation, and services. The law requires businesses to set aside at least 3 percent of their jobs for the disabled. However, no funding was available for any of the law's programs in 1996.

The shortage of medicines in Russia is chronic and catastrophic. Soviet-era supplies of materials and drugs have been depleted and are not being adequately replenished. Domestic production has plummeted because of the obsolescence of pharmaceutical factories and shortages of requisite raw materials and supplies. Many of the items produced are ineffective. Russia relies increasingly on imports from former Soviet-bloc nations in Central Europe, which formerly accepted barter transactions and payment in rubles but now demand hard currency (see Glossary), a scarce item in Russia, for their products.

The nonconvertibility of the ruble also has hindered Russia's ability to purchase medicines abroad. Even when pharmaceuticals are available in Russia, they often are priced beyond the reach of doctors and patients.

Russia's hospitals and polyclinics are generally old (about 15 percent were built before 1940), and they lack basic amenities. Roughly 42 percent of the country's hospitals and 30 percent of its clinics lack hot water, and 12 percent and 7 percent, respectively, have no running water at all. About 18 percent of hospitals and 15 percent of clinics are not connected to a sewerage system, and only 12 percent in both categories have central heating. Even in the best hospitals, medical personnel do not regularly wash their hands, surgical instruments are not always properly sterilized, and rates of infection are abnormally high.

Aside from shortfalls in Russia's health facilities and the quality of medical personnel, much of the country's public health crisis stems from poor personal hygiene and diet and lack of exercise. Preventive medicine and wellness programs are virtually nonexistent, as are programs to educate the public about personal sanitation, proper diet, and vitamins. The average Russian does not consume a balanced diet. Vegetables often are scarce in Russia, except in rural areas where they are homegrown, and fruits never have constituted an important element of the Russian diet. Per capita meat consumption also has fallen in the 1990s (see table 6, Appendix).

Russia's government is attempting to equalize the distribution of health care by fragmenting the Soviet-era network of top-level medical facilities for exclusive use of the elite. In the spring of 1993, President Yeltsin signed a decree entitled On Immediate Measures to Provide Health Care for the People of the Russian Federation. The proclaimed goal, which already had been established in the 1980s, was the creation by 2000 of a "unified system of health care" for the entire population. However, economic constraints are likely to stymie achievement of that goal in the near future. In 1995 less than 1 percent of Russia's budget was earmarked for public health, compared with 6 percent in Britain and more than 12 percent in the United States. Experts forecast that such a meager outlay will not address the major shortfalls in Russia's health care system, not to mention the air, water, and soil pollution that continue to contribute insidiously to worsening public health.

The impersonality and inaccessibility of national health system facilities, with patients often standing in line at clinics for an entire day before receiving brief diagnoses and prescriptions for drugs they cannot afford, has encouraged many Russians to turn to unorthodox alternatives such as faith healing, herbal medicine, and mysticism. By the mid-1990s, private medical clinics were serving a growing number of Russians able to afford their care.

In the Soviet era, the state discouraged alternative medicine by arresting practitioners. By 1995, however, the number of such individuals was estimated at 300,000, and as many as 80 percent of Russians needing medical assistance have turned to them, according to a Yeltsin adviser on social policy. Traditional folk healers constitute the largest group of nontraditional practitioners. They offer personalized attention and affordable cures such as birch bark and cranberries to cure a variety of complaints. Russians with access to a plot of land often grow their own herbs, and books describing home cures have become popular. Long-practiced cures such as wrapping oneself in a vinegar-soaked blanket and drinking one's own urine have become more widespread in the 1990s.

Housing

Always in short supply in the Soviet era, housing continues to be at a premium in the 1990s. However, the old, state-controlled system has begun giving way to private enterprise and a rudimentary housing market. Despite severe inequalities in housing opportunity and daunting financial disadvantages, many Russians have been able to establish private homes that would have been beyond their reach under the Soviet system. Nevertheless, in 1996 housing subsidies remained a significant drain on the national budget as the state continued the attempt to protect citizens from the inequities of a nascent housing market.

The Soviet Era

In the Soviet era, all land and most buildings belonged to the state; in rural areas, private home ownership was permitted, but the law limited such houses to a floor space of forty square meters. The occupants of state-owned housing enjoyed the rights to lifetime occupancy and to bequeath their housing units to the next generation, as well as virtually complete protection against eviction. Rental rates remained at the same extremely low, universal level—0.132 ruble per square meter—from 1927 until 1992. Maintenance of existing buildings and construction of new housing were both financed from other parts of the state budget; only 3 percent of funds used for these purposes came from residents. State enterprises covered a significant share of housing expenses as part of their employees' benefits. The design and construction of new housing had no relation to aesthetics or even to cost; in cities the State Construction Committee (Gosstroy) simply erected monolithic high-rise buildings containing a given number of housing units, following the dictates of the five-year plan for that locality. In 1990 nearly 100 percent of the housing stock in Moscow and St. Petersburg was publicly owned, and more than one-quarter of Russia's total housing stock had been built before 1917.

As in other aspects of daily Soviet life, the elite were allotted the best and most spacious housing, and influential friends helped them avoid long waiting lists that sometimes lasted more than ten years for ordinary Russians. The average urban Russian family either occupied a very small single apartment or shared an apartment with one or more other families, with joint access to the bathroom and the kitchen. According to a 1980 Soviet estimate, 20 percent of urban families (and 53 percent in Leningrad) shared apartments; that percentage had dropped slightly by the end of the Soviet era. Young, unmarried Russians often found housing only in crowded hostels operated by their employer; young married couples frequently lived with one set of parents until they could locate an apartment. Housing in rural areas was more spacious, but it usually had few amenities—the traditional wooden farmhouse contained two rooms divided by a raised corridor, with living space for people on one side and for animals on the other. In 1990 the average floor area per person in Moscow was 17.8 square meters, and in Russia as a whole it was 16.4 square meters, compared with averages in Western countries of between thirty and forty-five square meters per person.

Post-Soviet Conditions

The economic reforms of the post-Soviet era brought drastic and problematic changes in the Russian housing system. In the first years of that period, state support for new construction dwindled dramatically, making enterprises a more important source of financing in the absence of large-scale private invest-ment. Privatization of existing housing increased substantially in the mid-1990s, and more types of dwelling became eligible for privatization. The rate of new construction did not keep pace with demand, so waiting lists continued to exist, and the beginning of landownership law reform encouraged construc-tion of fully private housing by Russians who could afford it. However, in mid-1996 the average Russian still spent less than 3 percent of his or her budget on rent because a large share of Soviet-era state housing subsidies remained in place.

The establishment of a full market system in housing was complicated by several factors. First, the notion of private own-ership of land and housing was diametrically opposed to the concepts at the base of Soviet society, so the advantages of privatization were not immediately understood—especially as low-rent state housing continued to exist alongside expensive private property. Second, high inflation priced most Russians out of the housing market, especially as the inflation-adjusted incomes of most social groups declined. Third, continuing monopolies in construction materials, finance, and urbanized land kept construction costs very high; the first steps toward privatization were taken in the building industry only in 1993. Finally, a relatively high percentage of existing housing stock remained in the public sector, which promised to remain a sig-nificant housing owner through the near future.

After a relatively slow beginning in 1992, privatization of housing stock increased dramatically. The Soviet privatization law of 1989 began the process, which was continued in Russia by the 1991 Law on Privatization of Housing. But the newness of the laws, the lack of administrative procedures, and the con-tinuing attractiveness of low rents in state-owned housing lim-ited the total number of units privatized in 1991 to about 122,000 units, or 0.3 percent of urban housing stock in the Rus-sian Republic. By the end of 1993, more than 40 percent of urban housing stock (about 8.6 million units) in Russia had been privatized, and the total was between 55 and 60 percent one year later. Often the privatization process involved renters buying the apartments in which they were living. An important step in this process was a 1992 constitutional amendment that allowed free distribution of housing, broadened the categories of housing that could be privatized, and simplified privatiza-tion procedures. In the mid-1990s, the growing problem of how to house military families formerly domiciled outside Russia caused the Ministry of Defense and agencies dependent upon it to withhold their housing stock from privatization; in 1993 defense budgets financed 15 percent of Russia's total housing investment.

Availability of new private housing improved somewhat by the mid-1990s, after a sharp decline in the first post-Soviet years. In 1993 the output of new housing was 57 percent of the peak Soviet-era output reached in 1987, and in the early 1990s the ratio of unfinished projects to usable housing output was more than three to one (compared with 84 percent in 1988) because incentives promoted new starts rather than completions. Between 1986 and 1992, the number of names on housing waiting lists increased from about 8 million to some 10 million, mainly because in that period Russians began to change jobs and places of residence more frequently and because family units became smaller. In 1993 more than 21 percent of urban households were on waiting lists for housing. The waiting lists began to shrink in 1993, and by the end of 1994 about 9.1 million Russian households (including single-person households) were registered for housing. Inflation also played a major role in housing availability; in 1994 the price of a typical Moscow apartment of fifty-five square meters increased by five times over the 1993 average. A housing allowance program has been established to bridge the gap between rental costs and family incomes.

Because they felt the direct pressure of longer waiting lists and the support costs associated with the movement of people into their jurisdictions, local housing authorities lobbied against abolition of the internal passport (*propiska;* see Glossary) system that had restrained internal migration in the Soviet period. In 1993 the system was officially abolished in all jurisdictions except Moscow and St. Petersburg (see Social Welfare, this ch.).

Housing maintenance has been problematic in the post-Soviet era because local housing authorities, to whom full maintenance responsibility was shifted in 1991, have reallocated funds from maintenance to more pressing needs. Meanwhile, individual attitudes toward routine maintenance have been slow to compensate for this shift. In Soviet-era collective living quarters such as urban high-rise apartment buildings, which housed as many as 1,000 people, housing managers were expected to uphold minimum standards of cleanliness and service. In the 1990s, those complexes still house people from all economic levels (a survival of Stalin-era policy), but, given the newly fragmented condition of Russian society and economic distractions facing tenants, initiatives by residents often give way to disregard for voluntary maintenance of common property. Housing officials demand bribes for routine services, and housing complexes have become increasingly shabby. In some cases, the suspicion and anonymity of the Soviet era have been reinforced among people of disparate backgrounds forced to live in a more cramped environment than in Soviet times. However, in some apartment buildings condominium associations have been formed to advance the common welfare of families in a building or neighborhood.

Land Reform and Private Enterprise

Experts consider reform of landownership and condominium laws an important step toward full privatization of housing. Privatization of land, both urban and agricultural, has been a controversial issue for Russian legislators; there is a strong body of opinion that land is fundamentally public property that cannot belong to any single person. In the late Soviet period, new landownership laws confused rather than simplified the legal status of various types of land. Consequently, housing privatization has been hindered because ownership of a residence may not include ownership of the land on which it stands—a disparity rare in Western property law. Legislation passed in August 1993 legalized the sale of land, allowed villages to give away plots of land to individuals, and removed the space limitation on private homes on collective farms. Although dwellings built on suburban garden plots technically still could be no bigger than a summer cottage, such land increasingly was used to build year-round housing, thus expanding the number of available residences in Moscow and other cities.

In general, Moscow was the center of land-use innovation because it was the center of new commercial activity and foreign influence. The constitution of 1993 recognized for the first time the right to private ownership of land, a departure that experts believed would have a major impact on overall real estate ownership. In late 1993, a presidential decree established Russia's first set of provisional condominium regulations, which were considered an important clarification of housing ownership policy. But additional legislation, drafted by the Yeltsin administration to expedite landownership, was blocked in the State Duma in 1996.

Especially in Moscow, the emergence of Western-style enterprises associated with housing construction, such as finance companies, real estate offices, plumbing suppliers, and lumberyards, heralds more growth. The rapidly rising cost of existing apartments has fueled a brisk property business, as speculators buy privatized property in the hope that prices will continue to rise. In the mid-1990s, private houses began to appear rapidly just outside the ring of Soviet-era high-rises that surrounds Moscow. According to a 1995 report, prices for private land and housing in Moscow ranged from US$900 for an unimproved small plot to US$300,000 for a four-bedroom villa in a compound with security guards. As of mid-1996, mortgage loans were not yet offered by the Russian banking system, so buyers had to pay cash. Many Russians build their own dwellings, bribing city officials and contractors when necessary and collecting materials wherever possible. The demand for materials has prompted the emergence of numerous building supply stores and a parallel rise in the price of materials. Thus, although many Russians remain on waiting lists for existing housing, others have begun what they hope will be a Western-style progression from a first modest dwelling to something larger. The same divergence has appeared in housing as in other aspects of socioeconomic activity: individuals with financial resources or unusual initiative have taken advantage of the new opportunities of the 1990s. Those not so fortunate remain dependent on state housing subsidies.

Social Welfare

As Russia makes the transition from a command economy to a partial free-market system, the provision of an effective social safety net for its citizens assumes increasing urgency. A 1994 World Bank report described the current social-protection system as inappropriate for the market-oriented economy toward which Russia supposedly was striving. Among the major shortcomings noted in the report were the continued major role played by enterprises as suppliers of welfare services, as they had been in the Soviet period; the absence of any coverage for large groups of people and the inadequate level of benefits in some regions; a growing disparity between a shrinking wage base and the demands placed on the system; and the failure to target the neediest recipients. As the economic transition of the 1990s forces more of Russia's citizens into poverty, the state has tried to maintain the comprehensive Soviet system with severely constrained resources.

The system's inefficiency is exacerbated by its fragmentation. As in the Soviet period, allowances and benefits are administered and financed by diverse agencies, including four extrabudgetary funds, several ministries, and the lower levels of government. The Ministry of Social Protection is the primary federal agency handling welfare programs. However, that ministry focuses almost exclusively on the needs of people who are retired or disabled; other vulnerable groups receive much less attention. The four extrabudgetary funds that provide cash and in-kind social welfare benefits at the federal level are the Social Insurance Fund, the Pension Fund, the Employment Fund, and the Fund for Social Support.

Social security and welfare programs provide modest support for the most vulnerable segments of Russia's population: elderly pensioners, veterans, infants and children, expectant mothers, families with more than one child, invalids, and people with disabilities. These programs are inadequate, however, and a growing proportion of Russia's population lives on the threshold of poverty. Inflation has a particularly deleterious effect on households that rely on social subsidies. Women traditionally have outnumbered men in such households.

The Fund for Social Support supplements a variety of in-kind social assistance programs in Russia. It is financed through the Ministry of Social Protection and supplements social welfare programs at the subnational level. The federal government has transferred most responsibility for social welfare, health, and education programs to subnational organs but has failed to ensure their access to adequate revenue. The total allocation of transfers from the federal budget to localities amounted to less than 2 percent of Russia's gross domestic product (GDP—see Glossary) in 1992. Thus, the quantity and quality of social services at the local level—including the provision of food vouchers and cash payments to cover specific items such as heating bills—are far from certain as time passes. Under these conditions, local jurisdictions have come to rely increasingly on extrabudgetary sources, the instability of which makes long-term planning difficult.

Pensions

Pensions are the largest expenditure of the social safety program. The Pension Fund accounts for 83 percent of Russia's extrabudgetary allocations. At the end of 1994, about 36 million citizens, or 24 percent of the country's population, were receiving pensions, an increase of about 5 percent in the first three post-Soviet years. Two broad categories of pensions are paid in Russia: labor pensions, which are disbursed on the basis of a worker's payroll contributions, and social pensions, which are paid to individuals who have worked for less than the five years needed to qualify for a labor pension. All Russian citizens who have worked for twenty years are entitled to at least a minimum pension. In 1994 about 75 percent of all pensioners received labor pensions. The Pension Fund also finances some child allowances and other entitlements.

The Pension Fund is administered by the Ministry of Social Protection and financed by a 29 percent payroll tax and by transfers from the state budget. Between 1991 and 1993, the real income of pensioners was cut in half as prices rose rapidly and pension indexation failed to keep pace. Inflation also severely eroded the value of the life savings of retirees, and a disproportionate number of pensioners were victimized by financial scams. A 1994 law requires quarterly indexation of pensions, but the law was not observed consistently in its first year, and in mid-1995 the average pension fell below the subsistence minimum for pensioners. Beginning in 1994, the government's failure to pay pensions on time led to large rallies in several cities. In August 1994, an estimated 10 million pensioners did not receive their checks on time, and pension arrears mounted in the two years that followed. By mid-1996 the payment backlog was estimated at US$3 billion. The present system includes an important provision that has kept many pensioners above the poverty line: it allows workers to draw pensions while continuing to work. In 1995 as many as 27 percent of Russian pensioners continued to work after retiring from their primary job.

Russian and Western experts agree that the pension system requires comprehensive reform—although its rate of payment compliance by enterprises is substantially better than that of the State Taxation Service. The most pressing needs are an effective system of indexation of pensions to purchasing power, an insurance mechanism, individualized contributions, higher retirement ages, and the closing of loopholes that allow early retirement. In 1995 the Ministry of Social Protection began work on a reform that would establish a three-tier pension system including a basic pension, a work-related pension in proportion to years of service, and an optional private pension program. In 1995 Prime Minister Viktor Chernomyrdin admitted that the state budget lacked the money to continue indexing pensions according to living costs. In November 1995, a decree by President Yeltsin, On Additional Measures to Strengthen Payments Discipline for Settling Accounts with the Pension Fund, set stricter reporting standards for payments to the fund by organizations and citizens, in an effort to preclude nonpayment. In the midst of his campaign to be reelected president, Yeltsin then approved two laws increasing minimum pension levels in three stages, by 5, 10, and 15 percent, between November 1995 and January 1996.

Women are entitled to retire when they reach age fifty-five, and men when they reach age sixty. Nevertheless, financial hardship leads many women to remain in the labor force past retirement age, even while continuing to receive pensions, in order to prevent a drop in their families' standard of living. In 1991 women constituted an estimated 72 percent of pensioners. The disproportion between the genders stems from women's earlier permissible retirement age and their greater longevity. Aside from pensions, women receive other retirement privileges. Mothers of five or more children are entitled to a pension at age fifty. "Mother Heroines"—women with ten or more children—receive an allowance equal in sum to the pension, and the time they spent on child care leave counts toward the minimum twenty years of work required for labor pensions. For these reasons, many women retire before age fifty-five, while most men wait until they reach sixty-two. (Many job categories routinely allow retirement for both sexes before the standard ages.)

Worker Protection and Benefits

Legislation has established numerous protective devices at the enterprise level to provide a social safety net that is particularly attuned to the needs of women of childbearing age. Thus, family policy and employment policy are inextricably linked. In addition to basic allowances for all workers, special allowances exist for children of military personnel, children with unmarried, divorced, or widowed mothers, and children who are disabled. Women who have an employment contract are entitled to paid maternity leave from seventy days prior to giving birth until seventy days afterward. Maternity leave benefits are based on the minimum wage rather than on a woman's current wage, however.

Russia also provides a maternity grant, which is a onetime payment totaling three times the minimum wage or 45 percent of the minimum wage in the case of mothers who have worked less than one year. In order to receive a maternity allowance (or sickness benefits), a woman must have an employment contract. The maternity allowance amounts to 100 percent of the mother's salary, regardless of her length of employment.

Maternity allowances in Russia are followed by a monthly child allowance of 80 percent of the minimum wage in the case of children up to eighteen months old. This allowance may be supplemented by a child-care allowance, set at 35 percent of the minimum wage, to compensate for earnings lost in the course of caring for children in this age bracket. The latter allowance is paid to mothers over the age of eighteen who have been in the labor force at least one year. An additional compensatory child-care allowance, equivalent to 35 percent of the minimum wage, is available to mothers or other caretakers of children under the age of three.

Russia also has an extended child allowance of 45 percent of the minimum wage (60 percent for children of military personnel, children living with a guardian or in an orphanage, and children with AIDS) to assist families with the care of children between the ages of eighteen months and six years. Single mothers and those who receive no child support from the father of their child may obtain an additional 45 percent of the minimum wage up to their child's sixth birthday; this figure is then increased to 50 percent and remains effective until the child is sixteen. In May 1992, special cost-of-living compensations were introduced to cover the increased expense of meeting children's basic needs. These compensations ranged from 30 percent of the minimum wage in the case of children less than six years old to 40 percent in the case of those ages thirteen to sixteen.

Among other benefits provided by enterprises to their workers are access to special shops that sell subsidized milk for families with low incomes and small children and an allowance to children for the purchase of a school uniform when they start school and again at the age of thirteen. Other regulations focus more specifically on families with small children. These include protective legislation prohibiting the dismissal of pregnant women or women with children under the age of three, banning night work and overtime for mothers of small children, stipulating workload concessions to pregnant women and mothers of young children, and providing flextime, part-time work, home-based employment, nursing intervals, and additional paid and unpaid leave to mothers to care for sick children. Many workplaces also permit informal leave arrangements for the purpose of food shopping.

A significant portion of Russian workers have entitlements to housing, child care, and paid vacations, regardless of their rank within an enterprise. Housing entitlements involve either outright provision of a low-rent apartment (most apartment rents are very low) or various forms of cash or in-kind assistance. Moreover, occupants obtain an implicit ownership right extending beyond their term of employment. They may also have the legal title of the apartment transferred to their own names without paying any purchase price (see Housing, this ch.).

Besides housing allowances, most large and medium-sized enterprises provide on-site medical facilities or they contract for outside health care facilities for their employees. The medical care provided through the auspices of enterprises is free and often is of much higher quality than the care available in government-run facilities (see The Health System, this ch.). Finally, enterprises provide their employees with goods ranging from foodstuffs to consumer durables. The enterprises procure these items through direct purchase, barter, or from their own farms, and make them available at below-market prices.

The Social Insurance Fund is the administrative mechanism for payments to workers of birth, maternity, and sickness allowances, and child allowances for children between the ages of six and sixteen. The fund is managed by the largest union organization in Russia, the Federation of Independent Trade Unions of Russia (Federatsiya nezavisimykh profsoyuzov Rossii—FNPR) and serves as the repository of enterprise contributions consisting of 5.4 percent of the total payroll (see Social Organizations, this ch.). Nominally an independent institution since its establishment in 1991, the Social Insurance Fund is in fact responsible to the FNPR.

In 1993 an overhaul of the fund's administrative structure began as a result of enterprises' low levels of compliance with contribution requirements, charges of serious abuse by trade union officials, and the government's desire to promote democratic accountability. Since 1993 the management system has

Salvation Army young people's group, Red Square, Moscow
Courtesy Debbie Horrell

been in flux, and the quality of administration varies considerably throughout the country. Most worker contributions to the fund are retained by the enterprise for distribution. About one-half of the money goes to sick pay and one-fifth to subsidize treatment at sanatoriums. Family support includes birth and maternal allowances intended to replace lost wages, but child allowances do not address poverty directly because payments are not in proportion to household income.

Russia also has an overall system of family benefits. These can be grouped into three broad categories: those payable to all families with children, regardless of income or other qualifying conditions; those payable to working mothers; and those payable to disadvantaged families.

The communist system, for all its economic and moral deformities, provided virtually universal employment, so that every able-bodied citizen had an opportunity to earn income and thus social security. In postcommunist Russia, the phenomenon of unemployment is openly acknowledged and growing (see Unemployment, ch. 6). At the end of 1995, some 8.2 million people were registered as unemployed, indicating a far higher actual number. Three years earlier, about 5 million were registered. The "new poor," in the parlance of the World Bank, put a considerable strain on the resources available in Russia for social welfare.

Administered by the Ministry of Labor, the Employment Fund, which is financed by a 2 percent payroll tax from all enterprises, disburses compensation to jobless people. The level of compensation, already low in 1995, was expected to drop further if unemployment rose. As part of its assistance package to Russia, the World Bank is providing a computerized system that will help the country register claimants for unemployment and pay adequate benefits.

The Ministry of Labor's subsistence minimum is based on the cost of nineteen staple items considered sufficient to ensure survival, plus an estimated minimum cost for utilities, transportation, and other necessities. The calculation varies according to age-group and region; trade unions use other formulas that usually expand the number of people identified as living below the poverty line. In early 1996, the State Duma considered a law that would make the Ministry of Labor's figure the legal basis for establishing minimum wages, pensions, and other levels of social support. Barring such legislation, the subsistence minimum has no legal status.

The Homeless

The urban homeless are a category of the socially disadvantaged that received no official recognition in the Soviet era. Because Soviet law banned beggars and vagrants, the homeless (meaning anyone who lost his or her place of residence for any reason) were imprisoned or expelled from the cities. When the ban ended in the early 1990s, thousands of homeless people, mostly men, appeared in Russia's cities; the majority had migrated to urban areas seeking work or were refugees from the armed conflicts that erupted in the Caucasus and Central Asia when the Soviet Union dissolved.

In 1995 Moscow authorities estimated that city's homeless population at 30,000, but Western experts put the figure as high as 300,000. An estimated 300 homeless people died in Moscow in the first half of the winter of 1995–96, and on-site medical personnel reported widespread disease. At that point, Moscow had one shelter, with a capacity of twenty-four, and other Russian cities offered no sanitation or temporary residence centers of any sort. In the mid-1990s, the government of mayor Yuriy Luzhkov followed the Soviet pattern of forcibly removing vagrants from the city, especially at times when large numbers of Western visitors were expected. Police routinely harass and beat vagrants found on the streets. The Soviet *propiska* system of residency permits, which granted housing and employment to individuals only in the place where they were officially registered, has been found unconstitutional several times by Russia's Constitutional Court. However, many local authorities, including those in Russia's largest European cities, continue to require Soviet-era documentation; in 1995 Moscow assessed a fee of 35 million rubles (about US$7,000) for registration as a permanent resident of the city, and several other cities adopted similar measures. In the face of such restrictions, many homeless individuals are unable to change their status.

Through the first half of the 1990s, no specific agency of the Russian government has borne responsibility for aiding the homeless; the Federal Migration Service, a badly underfunded and understaffed agency created in 1992, has not been able to carry out its legal responsibility to locate housing and employment for internal and external migrants (see Migration, ch. 3). A number of Western humanitarian organizations, such as the Salvation Army and Doctors Without Borders, are the main source of assistance. In late 1995, the many deaths of homeless people prompted the Moscow government to announce plans to build ten new shelters and to ease the procedure for obtaining residency permits.

Private charities in Russia have suffered from an absence of government support and a general lack of social acceptance. In 1995, for example, the soup kitchen of the Christian Mercy Society in Moscow, which fed 400 poor people daily, had to pay city officials to stay open, and the organization was unable to obtain a designated space in which to operate. In fact, Russian law gives no status whatever to private charities, so such organizations must fend for themselves in helping the increasingly large number of urban poor. Russian society generally distrusts charities, partly because no such institutions existed either in tsarist times (royalty and the nobility provided whatever assistance went to the needy) or in the Soviet era, and partly because society has become fragmented by the difficult economic conditions of the 1990s.

According to Western experts, a comprehensive system of social protection is an urgent need of the Russian government, both for humanitarian reasons and as a prerequisite to financial stabilization and economic restructuring. The quality of future Russian society also will depend on reversing a steep downward trend in the quality of education and health care that has eroded the ability of Russians to improve their economic standing and to feel the sense of basic security that the Soviet system provided to some degree. Under Russia's conditions of drastic social and economic change, such forms of support are especially missed in the mid-1990s.

*   *   *

A number of useful monographs published in the 1990s include discussion of various aspects of Russia's social conditions. In *Redefining Russian Society and Polity*, Mary Buckley discusses major changes in housing, health care, and social expectations, with substantial background on the Soviet period. The *Environmental and Health Atlas of Russia*, edited by Murray Feshbach, provides useful details on the health crisis and its causes. *Education and Society in the New Russia*, edited by Anthony Jones, includes discussion of education trends as they apply to changes in post-Soviet society. *Local Power and Post-Soviet Politics*, edited by Theodore Friedgut and Jeffrey Hahn, illuminates the role of local governments in areas such as welfare and housing. The World Bank's 1995 report *Russia, Housing Reform and Privatization* gives a full picture of the economic forces and existing traditions at work in forming a new housing market. Igor Kon's *The Sexual Revolution in Russia* is a detailed and well-documented analysis of sexual attitudes in the Soviet and post-Soviet periods. *Russia's Youth and Its Culture* by Hilary Pilkington is a sociological study of groupings and behavior. A series of articles by Penny Morvant, published in the Open Media Research Institute's biweekly *Transition* in 1995, are concise studies of poverty, the role of women, and the health crisis in Russia. (For further information and complete citations, see Bibliography.)

Chapter 6. The Economy

The beautiful Vasilisa walks into the forest holding her magical doll while a horseman rides by (design from lacquer box made in village of Palekh).

LIKE MANY OTHER ASPECTS OF RUSSIAN LIFE, the Russian economy underwent a journey through uncharted waters in the early 1990s. First came the disintegration of the centrally planned economy that was a hallmark of the state-controlled economy and then its replacement by an economy operating on the basis of market forces. Some of the former communist states of Central Europe began their process of economic transition two years before Russia and have provided positive models. But Russia lacks experience with market economies and the institutions needed to operate them. Moreover, deeply entrenched remnants of central planning present challenges in Russia that other countries were able to avoid.

Russia undertakes the transition with advantages and obstacles. Although only half the size of the former Soviet economy, the Russian economy includes formidable assets. Russia possesses ample supplies of many of the world's most valued natural resources, especially those required to support a modern industrialized economy. It also has a well-educated labor force with substantial technical expertise. At the same time, Soviet-era management practices, a decaying infrastructure, and inefficient supply systems hinder efficient utilization of those resources.

For nearly 60 years, the Russian economy and that of the rest of the Soviet Union operated on the basis of central planning—state control over virtually all means of production and over investment, production, and consumption decisions throughout the economy. Economic policy was made according to directives from the communist party, which controlled all aspects of economic activity. The central planning system left a number of legacies with which the Russian economy must deal in its transition to a market economy.

Much of the structure of the Soviet economy that operated until 1987 originated under the leadership of Joseph V. Stalin (in office 1927–53), with only incidental modifications made between 1953 and 1987. Five-year plans (see Glossary) and annual plans were the chief mechanisms the Soviet government used to translate economic policies into programs. According to those policies, the State Planning Committee (Gosudarstvennyy planovyy komitet—Gosplan) formulated countrywide output targets for stipulated planning periods.

Regional planning bodies then refined these targets for economic units such as state industrial enterprises and state farms (*sovkhozy*; sing., *sovkhoz*—see Glossary) and collective farms (*kolkhozy*; sing., *kolkhoz*—see Glossary), each of which had its own specific output plan. Central planning operated on the assumption that if each unit met or exceeded its plan, then demand and supply would balance.

The government's role was to ensure that the plans were fulfilled. Responsibility for production flowed from the top down. At the national level, some seventy government ministries and state committees, each responsible for a production sector or subsector, supervised the economic production activities of units within their areas of responsibility. Regional ministerial bodies reported to the national-level ministries and controlled economic units in their respective geographical areas.

The plans incorporated output targets for raw materials and intermediate goods as well as final goods and services. In theory, but not in practice, the central planning system ensured a balance among the sectors throughout the economy. Under central planning, the state performed the allocation functions that prices perform in a market system. In the Soviet economy, prices were an accounting mechanism only. The government established prices for all goods and services based on the role of the product in the plan and on other noneconomic criteria. This pricing system produced anomalies. For example, the price of bread, a traditional staple of the Russian diet, was below the cost of the wheat used to produce it. In some cases, farmers fed their livestock bread rather than grain because bread cost less. In another example, rental fees for apartments were set very low to achieve social equity, yet housing was in extremely short supply (see Housing, ch. 5). Soviet industries obtained raw materials such as oil, natural gas, and coal at prices below world market levels, encouraging waste.

The central planning system allowed Soviet leaders to marshal resources quickly in times of crisis, such as the Nazi invasion, and to reindustrialize the country during the postwar period. The rapid development of its defense and industrial base after the war permitted the Soviet Union to become a superpower.

The record of Russian economic reform through the mid-1990s is mixed. The attempts and failures of reformers during the era of *perestroika* (restructuring—see Glossary) in the regime of Mikhail S. Gorbachev (in office 1985–91) attested to

the complexity of the challenge. Since 1991, under the leadership of Boris N. Yeltsin, the country has made great strides
toward developing a market economy by implanting basic
tenets such as market-determined prices. Critical elements
such as privatization of state enterprises and extensive foreign
investment went into place in the first few years of the post-
Soviet period. But other fundamental parts of the economic
infrastructure, such as commercial banking and authoritative,
comprehensive commercial laws, were absent or only partly in
place by 1996. Although by the mid-1990s a return to Soviet-era
central planning seemed unlikely, the configuration of the
post-transition economy remained unpredictable.

Economists have struggled to achieve accurate measurement
of the Russian economy, and they have questioned the accuracy
of official Russian economic data. Although the market now
determines most prices, the Government (Russia's cabinet)
still fixes prices on some goods and services, such as utilities
and energy. Furthermore, the exchange rate of the ruble (for
value of the ruble—see Glossary) to the United States dollar
has changed rapidly, and the Russian inflation rate has been
high. These conditions make it difficult to convert economic
measurements from rubles to dollars to make statistical comparisons with the United States and other Western countries.

According to official Russian data, in 1994 the national gross
domestic product (GDP—see Glossary) was 604 trillion rubles
(about US$207 billion according to the 1994 exchange rate),
or about 4 percent of the United States GDP for that year. But
this figure underestimates the size of the Russian economy.
Adjusted by a purchasing-power parity formula to account for
the lower cost of living in Russia, the 1994 Russian GDP was
about US$678 billion, making the Russian economy approxi-
mately 10 percent of the United States economy. In 1994 the
adjusted Russian GDP was US$4,573 per capita, approximately
19 percent of that of the United States. A second important
measurement factor is the extremely active so-called shadow
economy, which yields no taxes or government statistics but
which a 1996 government report quantified as accounting for
about 50 percent of the economy and 40 percent of its cash
turnover.

Historical Background

The Soviet economic system was in place for some six
decades, and elements of that system remained in place after

the dissolution of the Soviet Union in 1991. The leaders exerting the most substantial influence on that system were its founder, Vladimir I. Lenin, and his successor Stalin, who established the prevailing patterns of collectivization and industrialization that became typical of the Soviet Union's centrally planned system. By 1980, however, intrinsic defects became obvious as the national economy languished; shortly thereafter, reform programs began to alter the traditional structure. One of the chief reformers of the late 1980s, Boris Yeltsin, oversaw the substantial dissolution of the central planning system in the early 1990s.

The Eras of Lenin and Stalin

The basic foundation of the Soviet economic system was established after the Bolsheviks (see Glossary) assumed power in November 1917 (see Revolutions and Civil War, ch. 2). The Bolsheviks sought to mold a socialist society from the ruins of post-World War I tsarist Russia by liberally reworking the ideas of political philosophers Karl Marx and Friedrich Engels.

Soon after the revolution, the Bolsheviks published decrees nationalizing land, most industry (all enterprises employing more than five workers), foreign trade, and banking. The peasants took control of the land from the aristocracy and farmed it in small parcels.

Beginning in 1918, the new regime already was fighting for its survival in the Russian Civil War against noncommunist forces known as the Whites. The war forced the regime to organize the economy and place it on a war footing under a stringent policy known as war communism. Under such conditions, the economy performed poorly. In 1920 agricultural output had attained only half of its pre-World War I level, foreign trade had virtually ceased, and industrial production had fallen to only a small fraction of its prewar levels. Beginning in 1921, Lenin led a tactical retreat from state control of the economy in an effort to reignite production. His new program, called the New Economic Policy (Novaya ekonomicheskaya politika—NEP; see Glossary), permitted some private activity, especially in agriculture, light industry, and services (see Lenin's Leadership, ch. 2). However, heavy industry, transportation, foreign trade, and banking remained under state control.

Lenin died in 1924, and by 1927 the government had nearly abandoned the NEP. Stalin sought a rapid transformation from an agricultural, peasant-based country into a modern industrial power and initiated the country's First Five-Year Plan (1928–32). Under the plan, the Soviet government began the nationwide collectivization of agriculture to ensure production and distribution of food supplies to the growing industrial sector and to free labor for industry (see Industrialization and Collectivization, ch. 2). By the end of the five-year period, however, agricultural output had declined by 23 percent, according to official statistics. The chemical, textile, housing, and consumer goods and services industries were also performing poorly. Heavy industry exceeded the plan targets, but only at a great cost to the rest of the economy.

By the Third Five-Year Plan (1938–41), the Soviet economy was once again on a war footing, devoting increasing amounts of resources to the military sector in response to the rise of Nazi Germany. The Nazi invasion in 1941 forced the government to abandon the five-year plan and concentrate all resources on support for the military sector. This period also included the large-scale evacuation of much of the country's industrial production capacity from European Russia to the Urals and Central Asia to prevent further war damage to its economic base. The Fourth Five-Year Plan (1946–50) was one of repairing and rebuilding after the war.

Throughout the Stalin era, the government forced the pace of industrial growth by shifting resources from other sectors to heavy industry. The Soviet consumer received little priority in the planning process. By 1950 real household consumption had climbed to a level only marginally higher than that of 1928. Although Stalin died in 1953, his emphasis on heavy industry and central control over all aspects of economic decision making remained virtually intact well into the 1980s.

The Postwar Growth Period

Soviet economic growth rates during the postwar period appeared impressive. Between the early 1950s and 1975, the Soviet gross national product (GNP—see Glossary) increased an average of about 5 percent per year, outpacing the average growth of the United States and keeping pace with many West European economies—albeit after having started from a much lower point.

However, these aggregate growth figures hid gross inefficiencies that are typical of centrally planned systems. The Soviet Union was able to attain impressive growth through "extensive investments," that is, by infusing the economy with large inputs of labor, capital, and natural resources. But the state-set prices did not reflect the actual costs of inputs, leading to enormous misallocation and waste of resources. In addition, the heavily bureaucratic economic decision-making system and the strong emphasis on meeting targets discouraged the introduction of new technologies that could improve productivity. Central planning also skewed the distribution of investments throughout the economy.

The aggregate Soviet growth figures also did not reveal either the generally poor quality of Soviet goods and services that resulted from the state monopoly over production or the lack of priority given the consumer sector in the planning process. Eventually, diminishing returns from labor, capital, and other inputs led to a severe slowdown in Soviet economic growth. Furthermore, the availability of inputs, especially capital, labor, and technology, was decreasing. Declining birth rates, particularly in the European republics of the Soviet Union, placed constraints on the labor supply. By the mid-1970s and into the 1980s, average Soviet GNP growth rates had plummeted to about 2 percent, less than half the rates of the immediate postwar period.

Although such rates might have been acceptable in a mature, modern industrialized economy, the Soviet Union still trailed far behind the United States, other Western economies, and Japan, and in the 1980s another challenge arose from the newly industrializing countries of East Asia. Furthermore, the standard of living of the average Russian citizen, which had always been below that of the United States, was declining. In the 1980s, with the advent of modern communications that even Soviet censors found impossible to restrict, Soviet citizens began to recognize their relative position and to question the rationale of their country's economic policies. This was the atmosphere in which the Gorbachev regime undertook serious economic reform in the late 1980s.

Reform and Resistance

During several distinct periods, Soviet leaders attempted to reform the economy to make the Soviet system more efficient. In 1957, for example, Nikita S. Khrushchev (in office 1953–64) tried to decentralize state control by eliminating many national ministries and placing responsibility for implementing plans under the control of newly created regional economic councils. These reforms produced their own inefficiencies. In 1965

Soviet prime minister Aleksey Kosygin (in office 1964–80) introduced a package of reforms that reestablished central government control but reformed prices and established new bonuses and production norms to stimulate economic productivity. Under reforms in the 1970s, Soviet leaders attempted to streamline the decision-making process by combining enterprises into associations, which received some localized decision-making authority.

Because none of these reforms challenged the fundamental notion of state control, the root cause of the inefficiencies remained. Resistance to reform was strong because central planning was heavily embedded in the Soviet economic structure. Its various elements—planned output, state ownership of property, administrative pricing, artificially established wage levels, and currency inconvertibility—were interrelated. Fundamental reforms required changing the whole system rather than one or two elements. Central planning also was heavily entrenched in the Soviet political structure. A huge bureaucracy was in place from the national to the local level in both the party and the government, and officials within that system enjoyed the many privileges of the Soviet elite class. Such vested interests yielded formidable resistance to major changes in the Soviet economic system; the Russian system, in which many of the same figures have prospered, suffers from the same handicap.

Upon assuming power in March 1985, Gorbachev took measures intended to immediately resume the growth rates of earlier decades. The Twelfth Five-Year Plan (1986–90) called for the Soviet national income to increase an average of 4.1 percent annually and labor productivity to increase 4.6 percent annually—rates that the Soviet Union had not achieved since the early 1970s. Gorbachev sought to improve labor productivity by implementing an anti-alcohol campaign that severely restricted the sale of vodka and other spirits and by establishing work attendance requirements to reduce chronic absenteeism. Gorbachev also shifted investment priorities toward the machine-building and metalworking sectors that could make the most significant contribution to retool and modernize existing factories, rather than building new factories. Gorbachev changed Soviet investment strategy from extensive investing to intensive investing that focused on elements most critical to achieving the stated goal.

During his first few years, Gorbachev also restructured the government bureaucracy (see *Perestroika,* ch. 2). He combined ministries responsible for high-priority economic sectors into bureaus or state committees in order to reduce staff and red tape and to streamline the administration. In addition, Gorbachev established a state organization for quality control to improve the quality of Soviet production.

The *Perestroika* Program

The Soviet economic reforms during Gorbachev's initial period (1985–86) were similar to the reforms of previous regimes: they modified the Stalinist system without making truly fundamental changes. The basic principles of central planning remained. The measures proved to be insufficient, as economic growth rates continued to decline and the economy faced severe shortages. Gorbachev and his team of economic advisers then introduced more fundamental reforms, which became known as *perestroika* (restructuring). At the June 1987 plenary session of the Central Committee of the Communist Party of the Soviet Union (CPSU—see Glossary), Gorbachev presented his "basic theses," which laid the political foundation of economic reform for the remainder of the decade.

In July 1987, the Supreme Soviet passed the Law on State Enterprises. The law stipulated that state enterprises were free to determine output levels based on demand from consumers and other enterprises. Enterprises had to fulfill state orders, but they could dispose of the remaining output as they saw fit. Enterprises bought inputs from suppliers at negotiated contract prices. Under the law, enterprises became self-financing; that is, they had to cover expenses (wages, taxes, supplies, and debt service) through revenues. No longer was the government to rescue unprofitable enterprises that could face bankruptcy. Finally, the law shifted control over the enterprise operations from ministries to elected workers' collectives. Gosplan's responsibilities were to supply general guidelines and national investment priorities, not to formulate detailed production plans.

The Law on Cooperatives, enacted in May 1987, was perhaps the most radical of the economic reforms during the early part of the Gorbachev regime. For the first time since Lenin's NEP, the law permitted private ownership of businesses in the services, manufacturing, and foreign-trade sectors. The law initially imposed high taxes and employment restrictions, but it later revised these to avoid discouraging private-sector activity. Under this provision, cooperative restaurants, shops, and manufacturers became part of the Soviet scene.

Gorbachev brought *perestroika* to the Soviet Union's foreign economic sector with measures that Soviet economists considered bold at that time. His program virtually eliminated the monopoly that the Ministry of Foreign Trade had had on most trade operations. It permitted the ministries of the various industrial and agricultural branches to conduct foreign trade in sectors under their responsibility rather than having to operate indirectly through the bureaucracy of trade ministry organizations. In addition, regional and local organizations and individual state enterprises were permitted to conduct foreign trade. This change was an attempt to redress a major imperfection in the Soviet foreign trade regime: the lack of contact between Soviet end users and suppliers and their foreign partners.

The most significant of Gorbachev's reforms in the foreign economic sector allowed foreigners to invest in the Soviet Union in the form of joint ventures with Soviet ministries, state enterprises, and cooperatives. The original version of the Soviet Joint Venture Law, which went into effect in June 1987, limited foreign shares of a Soviet venture to 49 percent and required that Soviet citizens occupy the positions of chairman and general manager. After potential Western partners complained, the government revised the regulations to allow majority foreign ownership and control. Under the terms of the Joint Venture Law, the Soviet partner supplied labor, infrastructure, and a potentially large domestic market. The foreign partner supplied capital, technology, entrepreneurial expertise, and, in many cases, products and services of world competitive quality.

Although they were bold in the context of Soviet history, Gorbachev's attempts at economic reform were not radical enough to restart the country's chronically sluggish economy in the late 1980s. The reforms made some inroads in decentralization, but Gorbachev and his team left intact most of the fundamental elements of the Stalinist system—price controls, inconvertibility of the ruble, exclusion of private property ownership, and the government monopoly over most means of production.

By 1990 the government had virtually lost control over economic conditions. Government spending increased sharply as an increasing number of unprofitable enterprises required state support and consumer price subsidies continued. Tax revenues declined because revenues from the sales of vodka plummeted during the anti-alcohol campaign and because republic and local governments withheld tax revenues from the central government under the growing spirit of regional autonomy. The elimination of central control over production decisions, especially in the consumer goods sector, led to the breakdown in traditional supplier-producer relationships without contributing to the formation of new ones. Thus, instead of streamlining the system, Gorbachev's decentralization caused new production bottlenecks.

Unforeseen Results of Reform

Gorbachev's new system bore the characteristics of neither central planning nor a market economy. Instead, the Soviet economy went from stagnation to deterioration. At the end of 1991, when the union officially dissolved, the national economy was in a virtual tailspin. In 1991 the Soviet GDP had declined 17 percent and was declining at an accelerating rate. Overt inflation was becoming a major problem. Between 1990 and 1991, retail prices in the Soviet Union increased 140 percent.

Under these conditions, the general quality of life for Soviet consumers deteriorated. Consumers traditionally faced shortages of durable goods, but under Gorbachev, food, wearing apparel, and other basic necessities were in short supply. Fueled by the liberalized atmosphere of Gorbachev's *glasnost* (literally, public voicing—see Glossary) and by the general improvement in information access in the late 1980s, public dissatisfaction with economic conditions was much more overt than ever before in the Soviet period. The foreign-trade sector of the Soviet economy also showed signs of deterioration. The total Soviet hard-currency (see Glossary) debt increased appreciably, and the Soviet Union, which had established an impeccable record for debt repayment in earlier decades, had accumulated sizable arrearages by 1990.

In sum, the Soviet Union left a legacy of economic inefficiency and deterioration to the fifteen constituent republics after its breakup in December 1991. Arguably, the shortcomings of the Gorbachev reforms had contributed to the economic decline and eventual destruction of the Soviet Union, leaving Russia and the other successor states to pick up the

Economist Yegor Gaydar, acting prime minister under Boris Yeltsin in 1992 and major advocate of economic reform Courtesy Michael E. Samojeden

pieces and to try to mold modern, market-driven economies. At the same time, the Gorbachev programs did start Russia on the precarious road to full-scale economic reform. *Perestroika* broke Soviet taboos against private ownership of some types of business, foreign investment in the Soviet Union, foreign trade, and decentralized economic decision making, all of which made it virtually impossible for later policy makers to turn back the clock.

Economic Reform in the 1990s

Two fundamental and interdependent goals—macroeconomic stabilization and economic restructuring—mark the transition from central planning to a market-based economy. The former entails implementing fiscal and monetary policies that promote economic growth in an environment of stable prices and exchange rates. The latter requires establishing the commercial, legal, and institutional entities—banks, private property, and commercial legal codes—that permit the economy to operate efficiently. Opening domestic markets to foreign trade and investment, thus linking the economy with the rest of the world, is an important aid in reaching these goals. Under Gorbachev, the regime failed to address these fundamental goals. At the time of the Soviet Union's demise, the Yeltsin government of the Russian Republic had begun to attack the problems of macroeconomic stabilization and economic restructuring. As of mid-1996, the results were mixed.

The Yeltsin Economic Program

In October 1991, two months before the official collapse of the Soviet regime and two months after the August 1991 coup against the Gorbachev regime, Yeltsin and his advisers, including reform economist Yegor Gaydar, established a program of radical economic reforms. The Russian parliament, the Supreme Soviet, also extended decree powers to the president for one year to implement the program. The program was ambitious, and the record to date indicates that the goals for macroeconomic stabilization and economic restructuring programs may have been unrealistically high. Another complication in the Yeltsin reform program is that since 1991 both political and economic authority have devolved significantly from the national to the regional level; in a series of agreements with the majority of Russia's twenty-one republics and several other subnational jurisdictions, Moscow has granted a variety of special rights and powers having important economic overtones.

Macroeconomic Stabilization Measures

The program laid out a number of macroeconomic policy measures to achieve stabilization. It called for sharp reductions in government spending, targeting outlays for public investment projects, defense, and producer and consumer subsidies. The program aimed at reducing the government budget deficit from its 1991 level of 20 percent of GDP to 9 percent of GDP by the second half of 1992 and to 3 percent by 1993. The government imposed new taxes, and tax collection was to be upgraded to increase state revenues. In the monetary sphere, the economic program required the Russian Central Bank (RCB) to cut subsidized credits to enterprises and to restrict money supply growth. The program called for the shrinkage of inflation from 12 percent per month in 1991 to 3 percent per month in mid-1993.

Economic Restructuring Measures

Immediately after the dissolution of the Soviet Union was announced, the Government lifted price controls on 90 percent of consumer goods and 80 percent of intermediate goods. It raised, but still controlled, prices on energy and food staples such as bread, sugar, vodka, and dairy products. These measures were to establish a realistic relationship between production and consumption that had been lacking in the central planning system.

To encourage the development of the private sector, fundamental changes were made in the tax system, including introduction of a value-added tax (VAT—see Glossary) of 28 percent on most transactions, a progressive income tax, and a tax on business income; revisions in the system of import tariffs and export taxes; new taxes on domestic energy use to encourage conservation (a necessary step because energy prices were still controlled); and new taxes on oil and natural gas exports to narrow the gap between subsidized domestic prices and world prices and to prevent domestic energy shortages (see Taxation, this ch.). A fixed exchange rate was to be established for the ruble, which then would become convertible. Many restrictions on foreign trade and investment also were to be lifted to expose Russia to the discipline of world prices.

Monetary and Fiscal Policies

In 1992 and 1993, the Government expanded the money supply and credits at explosive rates that led directly to high inflation and to a deterioration in the exchange rate of the ruble. In January 1992, the Government clamped down on money and credit creation at the same time that it lifted price controls. However, beginning in February the RCB loosened the reins on the money supply. In the second and third quarters of 1992, the money supply had increased at especially sharp rates of 34 and 30 percent, respectively, and by the end of 1992, the Russian money supply had increased by eighteen times.

The sharp increase in the money supply was influenced by large foreign currency deposits that state-run enterprises and individuals had built up and by the depreciation of the ruble. Enterprises drew on these deposits to pay wages and other expenses after the Government had tightened restrictions on monetary emissions. Commercial banks monetized enterprise debts by drawing down accounts in foreign banks and drawing on privileged access to accounts in the RCB (see Banking and Finance, this ch.).

Government efforts to control credit expansion also proved ephemeral in the early years of the transition. Domestic credit increased about nine times between the end of 1991 and 1992. The credit expansion was caused in part by the buildup of interenterprise arrears and the RCB's subsequent financing of those arrears. The Government restricted financing to state enterprises after it lifted controls on prices in January 1992, but enterprises faced cash shortages because the decontrol of prices cut demand for their products. Instead of curtailing production, most firms chose to build up inventories. To support continued production under these circumstances, enterprises relied on loans from other enterprises. By mid-1992, when the amount of unpaid interenterprise loans had reached 3.2 trillion rubles (about US$20 billion), the government froze interenterprise debts. Shortly thereafter, the government provided 181 billion rubles (about US$1.1 billion) in credits to enterprises that were still holding debt.

The Government also failed to constrain its own expenditures in this period, partially under the influence of the conservative Supreme Soviet, which encouraged the Soviet-style financing of favored industries. By the end of 1992, the Russian budget deficit was 20 percent of GDP, much higher than the 5 percent projected under the economic program and stipulated under the International Monetary Fund (IMF—see Glossary) conditions for international funding. This budget deficit was financed largely by expanding the money supply. These ill-advised monetary and fiscal policies resulted in an inflation rate of over 2,000 percent in 1992.

In late 1992, deteriorating economic conditions and a sharp conflict with the parliament led Yeltsin to dismiss economic reform advocate Yegor Gaydar as prime minister. Gaydar's successor was Viktor Chernomyrdin, a former head of the State Natural Gas Company (Gazprom), who was considered less favorable to economic reform.

Chernomyrdin formed a new government with Boris Fedorov, an economic reformer, as deputy prime minister and finance minister. Fedorov considered macroeconomic stabilization a primary goal of Russian economic policy. In January 1993, Fedorov announced a so-called anticrisis program to control inflation through tight monetary and fiscal policies. Under the program, the Government would control money and credit emissions by requiring the RCB to increase interest rates on credits by issuing government bonds, by partially financing budget deficits, and by starting to close inefficient state enterprises. Budget deficits were to be brought under control by limiting wage increases for state enterprises, by establishing quarterly budget deficit targets, and by providing a more efficient social safety net for the unemployed and pensioners.

The printing of money and domestic credit expansion moderated somewhat in 1993. In a public confrontation with the parliament, Yeltsin won a referendum on his economic reform policies that may have given the reformers some political clout to curb state expenditures. In May 1993, the Ministry of Finance and the RCB agreed to macroeconomic measures, such as reducing subsidies and increasing revenues, to stabilize the economy. The RCB was to raise the discount lending rate to reflect inflation. Based on positive early results from this policy, the IMF extended the first payment of US$1.5 billion to Russia from a special Systemic Transformation Facility (STF) the following July.

Fedorov's anticrisis program and the Government's accord with the RCB had some effect. In the first three quarters of 1993, the RCB held money expansion to a monthly rate of 19 percent. It also substantially moderated the expansion of credits during that period. The 1993 annual inflation rate was around 1,000 percent, a sharp improvement over 1992, but still very high. The improvement figures were exaggerated, however, because state expenditures had been delayed from the last quarter of 1993 to the first quarter of 1994. State enterprise arrears, for example, had built up in 1993 to about 15 trillion rubles (about US$13 billion, according to the mid-1993 exchange rate).

In June 1994, Chernomyrdin presented a set of moderate reforms calculated to accommodate the more conservative elements of the Government and parliament while placating reformers and Western creditors. The prime minister pledged to move ahead with restructuring the economy and pursuing fiscal and monetary policies conducive to macroeconomic stabilization. But stabilization was undermined by the RCB, which issued credits to enterprises at subsidized rates, and by strong pressure from industrial and agricultural lobbies seeking additional credits.

By October 1994, inflation, which had been reduced by tighter fiscal and monetary policies early in 1994, began to soar once again to dangerous levels. On October 11, a day that became known as Black Tuesday, the value of the ruble on interbank exchange markets plunged by 27 percent. Although experts presented a number of theories to explain the drop, including the existence of a conspiracy, the loosening of credit and monetary controls clearly was a significant cause of declining confidence in the Russian economy and its currency.

In late 1994, Yeltsin reasserted his commitment to macroeconomic stabilization by firing Viktor Gerashchenko, head of the RCB, and nominating Tat'yana Paramonova as his replacement. Although reformers in the Russian government and the IMF and other Western supporters greeted the appointment with skepticism, Paramonova was able to implement a tight monetary policy that ended cheap credits and restrained interest rates (although the money supply fluctuated in 1995). Furthermore, the parliament passed restrictions on the use of monetary policy to finance the state debt, and the Ministry of Finance began to issue government bonds at market rates to finance the deficits.

The Government also began to address the interenterprise debt that had been feeding inflation. The 1995 budget draft, which was proposed in September 1994, included a commitment to reducing inflation and the budget deficit to levels acceptable to the IMF, with the aim of qualifying for additional international funding. In this budget proposal, the Chernomyrdin government sent a signal that it no longer would tolerate soft credits and loose budget constraints, and that stabilization must be a top government priority.

During most of 1995, the government maintained its commitment to tight fiscal constraints, and budget deficits remained within prescribed parameters. However, in 1995 pressures mounted to increase government spending to alleviate wage arrearages, which were becoming a chronic problem within state enterprises, and to improve the increasingly tattered social safety net. In fact, in 1995 and 1996 the state's failure to pay many such obligations (as well as the wages of most state workers) was a major factor in keeping Russia's budget deficit at a moderate level (see Social Welfare, ch. 5). Conditions changed by the second half of 1995. The members of the State Duma (beginning in 1994, the lower house of the Federal Assembly, Russia's parliament) faced elections in December, and Yeltsin faced dim prospects in his 1996 presidential reelection bid. Therefore, political conditions caused both Duma deputies and the president to make promises to increase spending.

In addition, late in 1995 Yeltsin dismissed Anatoliy Chubays, one of the last economic reform advocates remaining in a top Government position, as deputy prime minister in charge of economic policy. In place of Chubays, Yeltsin named Vladimir Kadannikov, a former automobile plant manager whose views were antireform. This move raised concerns in Russia and the West about Yeltsin's commitment to economic reform. Another casualty of the political atmosphere was RCB chairman Paramonova, whose nomination had remained a source of controversy between the State Duma and the Government. In November 1995, Yeltsin was forced to replace her with Sergey Dubinin, a Chernomyrdin protégé who continued the tight-money policy that Paramonova had established.

By mid-1996 many Duma deputies raised concerns about the Government's failure to meet its tax revenue targets. Revenue shortages were blamed on a number of factors, including a heavy tax burden that encourages noncompliance and an inefficient and corrupt tax collection system. A variety of tax collection reforms were proposed in the parliament and the Government, but by 1996 Russian enterprises and regional authorities had established a strong pattern of noncompliance with national tax regulations, and the Federal Tax Police Service was ineffectual in apprehending violators (see Ministry of Internal Affairs (MVD), ch. 10).

Inflation

In 1992, the first year of economic reform, retail prices in Russia increased by 2,520 percent. A major cause of the increase was the decontrol of most prices in January 1992, a step that prompted an average price increase of 245 percent in that month alone. By 1993 the annual rate had declined to 840 percent, still a very high figure. In 1994 the inflation rate had improved to 224 percent.

Trends in annual inflation rates mask variations in monthly rates, however. In 1994, for example, the Government managed to reduce monthly rates from 21 percent in January to 4 percent in August, but rates climbed once again, to 16.4 percent by December and 18 percent by January 1995. Instability in Russian monetary policy caused the variations. After tightening the flow of money early in 1994, the Government loosened its restrictions in response to demands for credits by agriculture, industries in the Far North, and some favored large enterprises. In 1995 the pattern was avoided more successfully by maintaining the tight monetary policy adopted early in the year and by passing a relatively stringent budget. Thus, the monthly inflation rate held virtually steady below 5 percent in the last quarter of the year. For the first half of 1996, the inflation rate was 16.5 percent. However, experts noted that control of inflation was aided substantially by the failure to pay wages to workers in state enterprises, a policy that kept prices low by depressing demand.

Exchange Rates

An important symptom of Russian macroeconomic instability has been severe fluctuations in the exchange rate of the ruble. From July 1992, when the ruble first could be legally exchanged for United States dollars, to October 1995, the rate of exchange between the ruble and the dollar declined from 144 rubles per US$1 to around 5,000 per US$1. Prior to July 1992, the ruble's rate was set artificially at a highly overvalued level. But rapid changes in the nominal rate (the rate that does not account for inflation) reflected the overall macroeconomic instability. The most drastic example of such fluctuation was the Black Tuesday (1994) 27 percent reduction in the ruble's value.

In July 1995, the RCB announced its intention to maintain the ruble within a band of 4,300 to 4,900 per US$1 through October 1995, but it later extended the period to June 1996. The announcement reflected strengthened fiscal and monetary policies and the buildup of reserves with which the Government could defend the ruble. By the end of October 1995, the ruble had stabilized and actually appreciated in inflation-adjusted terms. It remained stable during the first half of 1996. In May 1996, a "crawling band" exchange rate was introduced to allow the ruble to depreciate gradually through the end of 1996, beginning between 5,000 and 5,600 per US$1 and ending between 5,500 and 6,100.

Another sign of currency stabilization was the announcement that effective June 1996, the ruble would become fully convertible on a current-account basis. This meant that Russian citizens and foreigners would be able to convert rubles to other currencies for trade transactions.

Privatization

The essence of economic restructuring, and a critical consideration for foreign loans and investment in Russia's economy, is

Central meat market, Moscow
Courtesy Michael E. Samojeden

the privatization program. In most respects, between 1992 and 1995 Russia kept pace with or exceeded the rate established in the original privatization program of October 1991. As deputy prime minister for economic policy, the reformist Chubays was an effective advocate of privatization during its important early stages. In 1992 privatization of small enterprises began through employee buyouts and public auctions. By the end of 1993, more than 85 percent of Russian small enterprises and more than 82,000 Russian state enterprises, or about one-third of the total in existence, had been privatized.

On October 1, 1992, vouchers, each with a nominal value of 10,000 rubles (about US$63), were distributed to 144 million Russian citizens for purchase of shares in medium-sized and large enterprises that officials had designated and reorganized for this type of privatization. However, voucher holders also could sell the vouchers, whose cash value varied according to the economic and political conditions in the country, or they could invest them in voucher funds.

By the end of June 1994, the voucher privatization program had completed its first phase. It succeeded in transferring ownership of 70 percent of Russia's large and medium-sized enterprises to private hands and in privatizing about 90 percent of small enterprises. By that time, 96 percent of the vouchers issued in 1992 had been used by their owners to buy shares in firms directly, invest in investment funds, or sell on the secondary markets. According to the organizers of the voucher system, some 14,000 firms employing about two-thirds of the industrial labor force had moved into private hands.

The next phase of the privatization program called for direct cash sales of shares in remaining state enterprises. That phase would complete the transfer of state enterprises and would add to government revenues. After that procedure met stiff opposition in the State Duma, Yeltsin implemented it by decree in July 1994. But the president's commitment to privatization soon came into question. In response to the monetary crisis of October 1994, Yeltsin removed Chubays from his position as head of the State Committee for the Management of State Property, replacing him with little-known official Vladimir Polevanov. Polevanov stunned Russian and Western privatization advocates by suggesting renationalization of some critical enterprises. Yeltsin reacted by replacing Polevanov with Petr Mostovoy, a Chubays ally. In the ensuing eighteen months, Yeltsin made two more changes in the chairmanship position.

In 1995 and 1996, political conditions continued to hamper the privatization program, and corruption scandals tarnished the program's public image. By 1995 privatization had gained a negative reputation with ordinary Russians, who coined the slang word *prikhvatizatsiya,* a combination of the Russian word for "grab" and the Russianized English word "privatize," producing the equivalent of "grabification." The term reflects the belief that the privatization process most often shifted control of enterprises from state agencies to groups of individuals with inside connections in the Government, the *mafiya,* or both. Distrust of the privatization process was part of an increasing public cynicism about the country's political and economic leaders, fueled by the seeming failure of Yeltsin's highly touted reform to improve the lot of the average Russian (see Social Stratification, ch. 5).

The second phase of the privatization program went ahead with the sale of state-held shares for cash. Although the process was virtually complete by the end of the first quarter of 1996, the Government failed to garner expected revenues. Meanwhile, Yeltsin's June 1996 bid for reelection brought a virtual halt in privatization of state enterprises during the campaign period. In February 1996, the Procuracy announced a full-scale investigation into privatization practices, in particular a 1995 transaction in which state banks awarded loans to state firms in return for "privatization" shares in those enterprises (see The Procuracy, ch. 10). This loans-for-shares type of transaction characterized the second phase of privatization; banks provided the government badly needed cash based on the collateral of enterprise shares that banks presumably would be able to sell later. But most of the twenty-nine state enterprises originally slated to participate withdrew, and the banks that received shares appeared to have a conflict of interest based on their role in setting the rules of the bidding procedure. In the most widely publicized deal, the Uneximbank of Moscow received a 38 percent interest in the giant Noril'sk Nickel Joint-Stock Company at about half of a competing bid. Other banks and commercial organizations joined the traditional opponents of privatization in attacking the loans-for-shares program, and in 1996 the Government admitted that the program had been handled badly. As a result of corruption allegations, the State Duma formed a committee to review the privatization program. And Prime Minister Chernomyrdin requested off-budget funds to buy back shares from the banks.

Because the faults of the Yeltsin privatization program were an important plank in the 1996 presidential election platform of the Communist Party of the Russian Federation (Kommunisticheskaya partiya Rossiyskoy Federatsii—KPRF), the strongest opposition party, Yeltsin's campaign strategy was to reduce privatization as far as possible as a campaign issue (see The Executive Branch, ch. 7). Part of that strategy was to shift the privatization process from Moscow to the regions. In February 1996, a presidential decree simply granted shares in about 6,000 state-controlled firms to regional governments, which could auction the shares and keep the profits.

After Yeltsin's reelection in July 1996, his financial representatives announced continuation of the privatization program, with a new focus on selling ten to fifteen large state enterprises, including the joint-stock company of the Unified Electric Power System of Russia (YeES Rossii), the Russian State Insurance Company (Rosgosstrakh), and the St. Petersburg Maritime Port. The Communications Investment Joint-Stock Company (Svyazinvest), sale of which had failed in 1995, was to be offered to Western telecommunications companies in 1996.

The new, postelection privatization stage also was to reduce the role of enterprise workers in shareholding. Within the first years of such ownership, most worker shares had been sold at depressed prices, devaluing all shares and cutting state profits from enterprise sales. Therefore, to reach the budget target of 12.4 trillion rubles (about US$2.4 billion) of profit from privatization sales in 1996, distribution was to target recipients who would hold shares rather than sell them immediately.

Despite periodic delays, the inept administration of the program's more recent phases, and allegations of favoritism and corrupt transactions in the enterprise and financial structures, in 1996 international experts judged Russia's privatization effort a qualified success. The movement of capital assets from state to private hands has progressed without serious reversal of direction—despite periodic calls for reestablishing state control of certain assets. And the process has contributed to the creation of a new class of private entrepreneur.

Economic Conditions in Mid-1996

As of mid-1996, four and one-half years after the launching of Russia's post-Soviet economic reform, experts found the results promising but mixed. The Russian economy has passed through a long and wrenching depression. Official Russian economic statistics indicate that from 1990 to the end of 1995, Russian GDP declined by roughly 50 percent, far greater than the decline that the United States experienced during the Great Depression. (However, alternative estimates by Western analysts described a much less severe decline, taking into account the upward bias of Soviet-era economic data and the downward bias of post-Soviet data.) Such a decline, however, was to be expected in an economy going through the transition from central planning to a market structure. Much of the decline in production has occurred in the military-industrial complex and other heavy industries that benefited most from the skewed economic priorities of Soviet planners but have much less robust demand in a freer market.

But other major sectors such as agriculture, energy, and light industry also suffered from the transition. To enable these sectors to function in a market system, inefficient enterprises had to be closed and workers laid off, with resulting short-term declines in output and consumption. Analysts had expected that Russia's GDP would begin to rise in 1996, but data for the first six months of the year showed a continuing decline, and

Cossack running money-changing operation, Krasnodar
Courtesy A. James Firth, United States Department of Agriculture

some Russian experts predicted a new phase of economic crisis in the second half of the year.

The pain of the restructuring has been assuaged somewhat by the emergence of a new private sector. Western experts believe that Russian data overstate the dimensions of Russia's economic collapse by failing to reflect a large portion of the country's private-sector activity. The Russian services sector, especially retail sales, is playing an increasingly vital role in the economy, accounting for nearly half of GDP in 1995. The services sector's activities have not been adequately measured. Data on sector performance are skewed by the underreporting or nonreporting of output that Russia's tax laws encourage. According to Western analysts, by the end of 1995 more than half of GDP and more than 60 percent of the labor force were based in the private sector.

An important but unconventional service in Russia's economy is "shuttle trading"—the transport and sale of consumer goods by individual entrepreneurs, of whom 5 to 10 million were estimated to be active in 1996. Traders buy goods in foreign countries such as China, Turkey, and the United Arab Emirates and in Russian cities, then sell them on the domestic market where demand is highest. Yevgeniy Yasin, minister of economics, estimated that in 1995 some US$11 billion worth of

319

goods entered Russia in this way. Shuttle traders have been vital in maintaining the standard of living of Russians who cannot afford consumer goods on the conventional market. However, domestic industries such as textiles suffer from this infusion of competing merchandise, whose movement is unmonitored, untaxed, and often *mafiya*-controlled.

The geographical distribution of Russia's wealth has been skewed at least as severely as it was in Soviet times. By the mid-1990s, economic power was being concentrated in Moscow at an even faster rate than the federal government was losing political power in the rest of the country. In Moscow an economic oligarchy, composed of politicians, banks, businesspeople, security forces, and city agencies, controlled a huge percentage of Russia's financial assets under the rule of Moscow's energetic and popular mayor, Yuriy Luzhkov. Unfortunately, organized crime also has played a strong role in the growth of the city (see The Crime Wave of the 1990s, ch. 10). Opposed by a weak police force, Moscow's rate of protection rackets, contract murders, kickbacks, and bribes—all intimately connected with the economic infrastructure—has remained among the highest in Russia. Most businesses have not been able to function without paying for some form of *mafiya* protection, informally called a *krysha* (the Russian word for roof).

Luzhkov, who has close ties to all legitimate power centers in the city, has overseen the construction of sports stadiums, shopping malls, monuments to Moscow's history, and the ornate Christ the Savior Cathedral. In 1994 Yeltsin gave Luzhkov full control over all state property in Moscow. In the first half of 1996, the city privatized state enterprises at the rate of US$1 billion per year, a faster rate than the entire national privatization process in the same period. Under Luzhkov's leadership, the city government also acquired full or major interests in a wide variety of enterprises—from banking, hotels, and construction to bakeries and beauty salons. Such ownership has allowed Luzhkov's planners to manipulate resources efficiently and with little or no competition. Meanwhile, Moscow also became the center of foreign investment in Russia, often to the exclusion of other regions. For example, the McDonald's fast-food chain, which began operations in Moscow in 1990, enjoyed immediate success but expanded only in Moscow. The concentration of Russia's banking industry in Moscow gave the city a huge advantage in competing for foreign commercial activity.

In mid-1996 the national government appeared to have achieved some degree of macroeconomic stability. However, longer-term stability depends on the ability of policy makers to withstand the inflationary pressures of demands for state subsidies and easier credits for failing enterprises and other special interests. (Chubays estimated that spending promises made during Yeltsin's campaign amounted to US$250 per voter, which if actually spent would approximately double the national budget deficit; most of Yeltsin's pledges seemingly were forgotten shortly after his reelection.)

By 1996 the structure of Russian economic output had shifted far enough that it more closely resembled that of a developed market economy than the distorted Soviet central-planning model. With the decline in demand for defense industry goods, overall production has shifted from heavy industry to consumer production (see The Defense Industry, ch. 9). However, in the mid-1990s the low quality of most domestically produced consumer goods continued to limit enterprises' profits and therefore their ability to modernize production operations. On the other side of the "vicious circle," reliance on an outmoded production system guaranteed that product quality would remain low and uncompetitive.

Most prices are left to the market, although local and regional governments control the prices of some staples. Energy prices remain controlled, but the Government has been shifting these prices upward to close the gap with world market prices.

Natural Resources

Russia is the largest country in the world; it covers a vast amount of topographically varied territory, including much that is inaccessible by conventional modes of transportation. The traditional centers of economic activity are almost exclusively located in the more hospitable European part of Russia, which once offered considerable coal and natural gas to drive heavy industry (see fig. 7). But the European fuel base was largely depleted by the 1980s, forcing Russia to rely on Siberian deposits much farther from the industrial heartland.

Russia is one of the world's richest countries in raw materials, many of which are significant inputs for an industrial economy. Russia accounts for around 20 percent of the world's production of oil and natural gas and possesses large reserves of both fuels. This abundance has made Russia virtually self-suf-

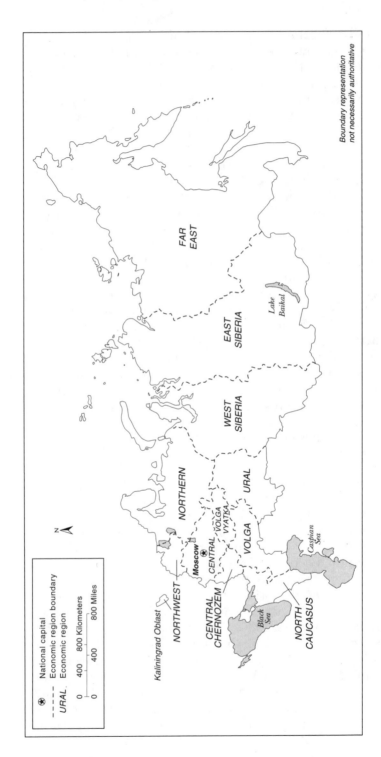

Figure 7. Economic Regions, 1996

ficient in energy and a large-scale exporter of fuels. Oil and gas were primary hard-currency earners for the Soviet Union, and they remain so for the Russian Federation. Russia also is self-sufficient in nearly all major industrial raw materials and has at least some reserves of every industrially valuable nonfuel mineral—even after the productive mines of Ukraine, Kazakstan, and Uzbekistan no longer were directly accessible. Tin, tungsten, bauxite, and mercury were among the few natural materials imported in the Soviet period. Russia possesses rich reserves of iron ore, manganese, chromium, nickel, platinum, titanium, copper, tin, lead, tungsten, diamonds, phosphates, and gold, and the forests of Siberia contain an estimated one-fifth of the world's timber, mainly conifers (see fig. 8; Environmental Conditions, ch. 3).

The iron ore deposits of the Kursk Magnetic Anomaly, close to the Ukrainian border in the southwest, are believed to contain one-sixth of the world's total reserves. Intensive exploitation began there in the 1950s. Other large iron ore deposits are located in the Kola Peninsula, Karelia, south-central Siberia, and the Far East. The largest copper deposits are located in the Kola Peninsula and the Urals, and lead and zinc are found in North Ossetia.

Agriculture

Climatic and geographic factors limit Russia's agricultural activity to about 10 percent of the country's total land area. Of that amount, about 60 percent is used for crops, the remainder for pasture and meadow (see table 15, Appendix). In the European part of Russia, the most productive land is in the Central Chernozem Economic Region and the Volga Economic Region, which occupy the grasslands between Ukraine and Kazakstan. More than 65 percent of the land in those regions is devoted to agriculture. In Siberia and the Far East, the most productive areas are the southernmost regions. Fodder crops dominate in the colder regions, and intensity of cultivation generally is higher in European Russia. The last expansion of cultivated land occurred in the late 1950s and early 1960s, when the Virgin Lands program of Nikita Khrushchev opened land in southwestern Siberia (and neighboring Kazakstan) for cultivation. In the mid-1990s, about 15 percent of the working population was occupied in agriculture, with the proportion dropping slowly as the younger population left rural areas to seek economic opportunities elsewhere (see Rural Life, ch. 5).

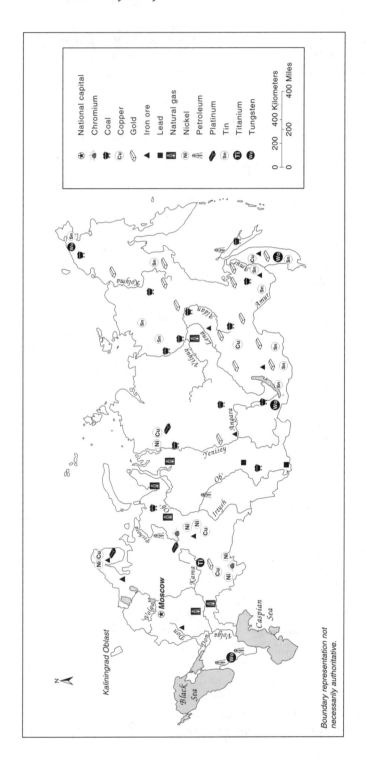

Figure 8. Major Mineral Deposits, 1996

Crops

Grains are among Russia's most important crops, occupying more than 50 percent of cropland. Wheat is dominant in most grain-producing areas. Winter wheat is cultivated in the North Caucasus and spring wheat in the Don Basin, in the middle Volga region, and in southwestern Siberia. Although Khrushchev expanded the cultivation of corn for livestock feed, that crop is only suitable for growth in the North Caucasus, and production levels have remained low compared with other grains. Barley, second to wheat in gross yield, is grown mainly for animal feed and beer production in colder regions as far north as 65° north latitude (the latitude of Arkhangel'sk) and well into the highlands of southern Siberia. Production of oats, which once ranked third among Russia's grains, has declined as machines have replaced horses in farming operations.

Legumes became a common crop in state farms in the 1980s. Potatoes, a vital crop for food and for the production of vodka, are grown in colder regions between 50° and 60° north latitude. Sugar beet production has expanded in recent years; the beets are grown mainly in the rich black-earth districts of European Russia. Flax, also a plant tolerant of cold and poor soils, is Russia's most important raw material for textiles, and the country produced about half the world's flax crop in the 1980s. Flax also yields linseed oil, which together with sunflowers (in the North Caucasus) and soybeans (in the Far East) is an important source of vegetable oil. Production of fruits and vegetables increased as private farms began to expand around 1990. In the mid-1990s, the largest yields in that category were in cabbages, apples, tomatoes, and carrots.

Increased production of fodder crops and expansion of pastureland have supported Russia's livestock industry, although economic conditions have caused cutbacks in animal holdings. Cattle are the most common form of livestock except in the drier areas, where sheep and goats dominate. The third-largest category is pigs, which are raised in areas of European Russia and the Pacific coast that offer grain, potatoes, or sugar beets as fodder. Only very small numbers of chickens are kept, and frozen chicken has become one of Russia's largest import items.

Agricultural Policy

Agricultural reform has proved to be a tough challenge for

Russia during its transition to a market economy. The challenge comes from the legacy of the Soviet period and from deeply imbedded cultural biases against individualism. Because of agriculture's vital economic role, large-scale agricultural reform is necessary for success in other sectors. In the mid-1990s, however, private initiative was not rewarded, and inefficient input distribution and marketing structures failed to take advantage of agricultural assets.

Soviet Policy

Under Stalin the government socialized agriculture and created a massive bureaucracy to administer policy. Stalin's campaign of forced collectivization, which began in 1929, confiscated the land, machinery, livestock, and grain stores of the peasantry. By 1937 the government had organized approximately 99 percent of the Soviet countryside into state-run collective farms. Under this grossly inefficient system, agricultural yields declined rather than increased. The situation persisted into the 1980s, when Soviet farmers averaged about 10 percent of the output of their counterparts in the United States.

During Stalin's regime, the government assigned virtually all farmland to one of two basic agricultural production organizations—state farms and collective farms. The state farm was conceived in 1918 as the ideal model for socialist agriculture. It was to be a large, modern enterprise directed and financed by the government. The work force of the state farm received wages and social benefits comparable to those enjoyed by industrial workers. By contrast, the collective farm was a self-financed producer cooperative that farmed parcels of land that the state granted to it rent-free and that paid its members according to their contribution of work.

In their early stages, the two types of organization also functioned differently in the distribution of agricultural goods. State farms delivered their entire output to state procurement agencies in response to state production quotas. Collective farms also received quotas, but they were free to sell excess output in collective-farm markets where prices were determined by supply and demand. The distinction between the two types of farms gradually narrowed, and the government converted many collective farms to state farms, where the state had more control.

Private plots also played a role in the Soviet agricultural system. The government allotted small plots to individual farming households to produce food for their own use and for sale as an income supplement. Throughout the Soviet period, the productivity rates of private plots far exceeded their size. With only 3 percent of total sown area in the 1980s, they produced over a quarter of agricultural output.

A number of factors made the Soviet collectivized system inefficient throughout its history. Because farmers were paid the same wages regardless of productivity, there was no incentive to work harder and more efficiently. Administrators who were unaware of the needs and capabilities of the individual farms decided input allocation and output levels, and the high degree of subsidization eliminated incentives to adopt more efficient production methods.

The Gorbachev Reforms

The Gorbachev agricultural reform program aimed to improve production incentives. Gorbachev sought to increase agricultural labor productivity by forming contract brigades consisting of ten to thirty farmworkers who managed a piece of land leased from a state or collective farm. The brigades were responsible for the yield of the land, which in turn determined their remuneration. After 1987 the government legalized family contract brigades and long-term leasing of land, removing the restrictions on the size of private agricultural plots and cutting into the state's holdings of arable land.

Although Gorbachev's reforms increased output in the agricultural sector in 1986, they failed to address fundamental problems of the system, such as the government's continued control over the prices of agricultural commodities, the distribution of agricultural inputs, and production and investment decisions. In the contract brigade system, farmers still had no real vested interest in the farms on which they worked, and production suffered accordingly. In the 1980s, the Soviet Union went from being self-sufficient in food production to becoming a net food importer.

Yeltsin's Agricultural Policies

The Yeltsin regime has attempted to address some of the fundamental reform issues of Russian agriculture. But agricultural reform has moved very slowly, causing output to decline steadily through the mid-1990s. Reform began in Russia shortly before the final collapse of the Soviet Union. In December 1990, the Congress of People's Deputies of the Russian Republic enacted a number of laws that were designed to restructure the agricultural sector and make it more commercially viable. The Law on Peasant Farms legalized private farms and allowed them to operate alongside state and collective farms, to hire labor, and to sell produce without state supervision. The same session of the congress passed the Law on Land Reform, which permitted land to be bequeathed as an inheritance from one generation to the next, but not to be bought or sold. The government also established the State Committee for Agrarian Reform, whose responsibility was to oversee the transfer of available land to private farming.

The main thrust of Yeltsin's agricultural reform has been toward reorganizing state and collective farms into more efficient, market-oriented units. A decree of December 1991 and its subsequent amendments provided several options to state and collective farmers for the future structure of their farms. The decree required that farmers choose either to reorganize into joint-stock companies, cooperatives, or individual private farms, or to maintain their existing structure. Under the first two arrangements, workers would hold shares in the farms and be responsible for managing the enterprises. An individual farmer could later decide to break from the larger unit and establish private ownership of his or her share of the land, as determined by an established procedure.

This restructuring program has progressed slowly. Although 95 percent of the state and collective farms underwent some form of reorganization, about one-third of them retained essentially their earlier structure. Most of the others, fearing the unstable conditions of market supply and demand that faced individual entrepreneurs, chose a form of collective ownership, either as joint-stock companies or as cooperatives. The conservatism of Russia's farmers prompted them to preserve as much as possible of the inefficient but secure Soviet-era controlled relationships of supply and output.

As of 1996, individual private farming had not assumed the significance in Russian agriculture that reformers and Western supporters had envisioned. Although the number of private farms increased considerably following the reforms of 1990, by the early 1990s the growth of farms had stalled, and by the mid-1990s the number of private farms actually may have dropped as some individuals opted to return to a form of cooperative enterprise or left farming entirely. By the end of 1995, Russia's

Waiting for grocery store to open in small town, Republic of Tyva
Courtesy Eugene Zakusilo

280,000 private farms accounted for only 5 percent of the arable land in Russia.

A number of factors have contributed to the slow progress of agricultural reform. Until the mid-1990s, the state government continued to act as the chief marketing agent for the food sector by establishing fixed orders for goods, thus guaranteeing farmers a market. The government also subsidized farms through guaranteed prices, which reduced the incentive of farmers to become efficient producers.

Perhaps most important, effective land reform has not been accomplished in Russia. The original land reform law and subsequent decrees did not provide a clear definition of private property, and they did not prescribe landholders' rights and protections. The nebulous status of private landholders under the new legislation made farmers reluctant to take the risk of proprietorship. In March 1996, President Yeltsin issued a decree that allows farmers to buy and sell land. However, in April 1996 the State Duma, heavily influenced by the antire-form KPRF and its ally, the Agrarian Party of Russia (representing the still formidable vested interests of collective and state farms), passed a draft law that prohibits land sales by anyone but the state. Recent opposition to the new notion of private landownership is based in a strong traditional Russian view that land must be held as collective rather than individual property.

However, in 1996 several factors were exerting pressure on the agricultural sector to become commercially viable. The federal government has retreated from its role as a guaranteed purchaser and marketer, although some regional governments are stepping in to fill the role. And private markets are emerging slowly. Increasingly, Russian agricultural production must compete with imported goods as the gap between domestic prices and world prices narrows. In addition, the fiscal position of the federal government has forced it to reduce subsidies to many sectors of the economy, including agriculture. Subsidies are among the targets of major budget cuts to comply with the standards of the IMF and other Western lenders and achieve macroeconomic stabilization.

Agricultural Production

Like the rest of the economy, the Russian agricultural sector has experienced a long, severe recession in the 1990s. Even before the dissolution of the Soviet Union, the output of grains and other crops began to decline, and it decreased steadily through 1996 because of the unavailability of fertilizers and other inputs, bad weather, and major readjustments during the period of transition. In 1995 overall agricultural production declined 8 percent, including a drop of 5 percent in crop production and 11 percent in livestock production. That year Russia suffered its worst grain harvest since 1963, with a yield of 63.5 million tons.

The most dramatic declines occurred in livestock production. Farmers reduced their holdings of animals as the price of grains and other inputs increased. As meat prices rose, the composition of the average consumer's diet included less meat and more starches and vegetables. Reduced demand in turn exacerbated the decline in livestock production.

Energy

Energy plays a central role in the Russian economy because it drives all the other elements of the system—the industrial, agricultural, commercial, and government sectors. In addition, energy, particularly petroleum and natural gas, is the most important export and source of foreign exchange for the Russian economy. Experts forecast that the energy sector will continue to occupy this central position until Russian manufacturing reaches a level competitive with the West.

Exploitation and Consumption

Russia's self-sufficiency in fuels and power generation puts the country in a good position for future economic growth and development. But Russia is also one of the most energy-dependent countries. The International Energy Agency of the Organisation for Economic Co-operation and Development (OECD—see Glossary) estimated that in 1993 it took 4.46 tons of oil equivalent (TOE) to produce US$1,000 of Russia's GDP, compared with an average of 0.23 TOE to produce US$1,000 of GDP for the OECD member countries.

Russia's excessive consumption of energy results from the Soviet system, which artificially priced energy far below the level of world market prices and thus subsidized it. Soviet energy-pricing policies disregarded resource utilization in the quest for higher output volumes and discouraged the adoption of conservation measures. Soviet planners also skewed resources toward the defense-related and heavy industries, which consume energy more intensively than other sectors of the economy. Until the 1980s, the national economy managed to survive under such policies because of the Soviet Union's rich endowment of natural resources.

The problems that plagued the Russian energy sector in the last decades of the Soviet Union were exacerbated during the transition period. Since 1991 the output of all types of fuel and energy has declined, partly because of plummeting demand for energy during a time of general economic contraction. But the energy sectors also have suffered from the intrinsic structural defects of the central planning system: poor management of resources, underinvestment, and outdated technology and equipment.

The structure of energy and fuel production began to change dramatically in the 1980s with the exploitation of large natural gas deposits. In the mid-1990s, natural gas accounted for more than half of Russia's energy consumption, a share that is expected to increase in the next decades. Oil accounts for another 20 percent, a proportion that is expected to remain approximately constant. Coal and other solid fuels, water power, and nuclear energy account for smaller shares that experts predict likely will decline after 2000. Despite the waste of fuel in the Russian economy, Russia manages to produce a surplus of energy for export. Exports, particularly of natural gas and oil, have accounted for 30 percent of Russian energy production, and this share is expected to hold steady.

Russia's drive to become a market economy should help to alleviate some of the problems of the energy sector. Russian energy pricing policies have changed. Since January 1992, energy has been gradually deregulated, closing the gap between world market prices and domestic prices and forcing consumers to conserve. Russia is also adopting Western technology and more efficient management techniques that will improve productivity in the sector.

Oil

Russia ranks third in the world in oil production, after Saudi Arabia and the United States. Estimates place proven and potential oil reserves at 8 to 11 billion tons. Russia's oil production peaked in 1987, then began a decline that continued through 1995. In the latter year, the yield was 741 million barrels, 13 million barrels less than the previous year. Output for the first quarter of 1996 was 182 million barrels.

Wasteful Soviet oil exploration and extraction techniques depleted wells, which often fell far below their potential capacity. Soviet technology was not capable of exploring and extracting as deeply and efficiently as Western technology. These handicaps have been instrumental in Russia's plummeting oil production during the last two decades. In 1994 the number of oil wells drilled was only one-quarter the number drilled in 1983. About two-thirds of Russia's oil comes from Siberia, mostly from huge fields in the northwest part of the region. The main European oil and gas fields are located in the Volga-Ural region, the North Caucasus, and the far north of the Republic of Komi (see fig. 9).

Russian oil companies are vertically integrated units that control the entire production process from exploration to transmission. The largest company is Lukoil, which, according

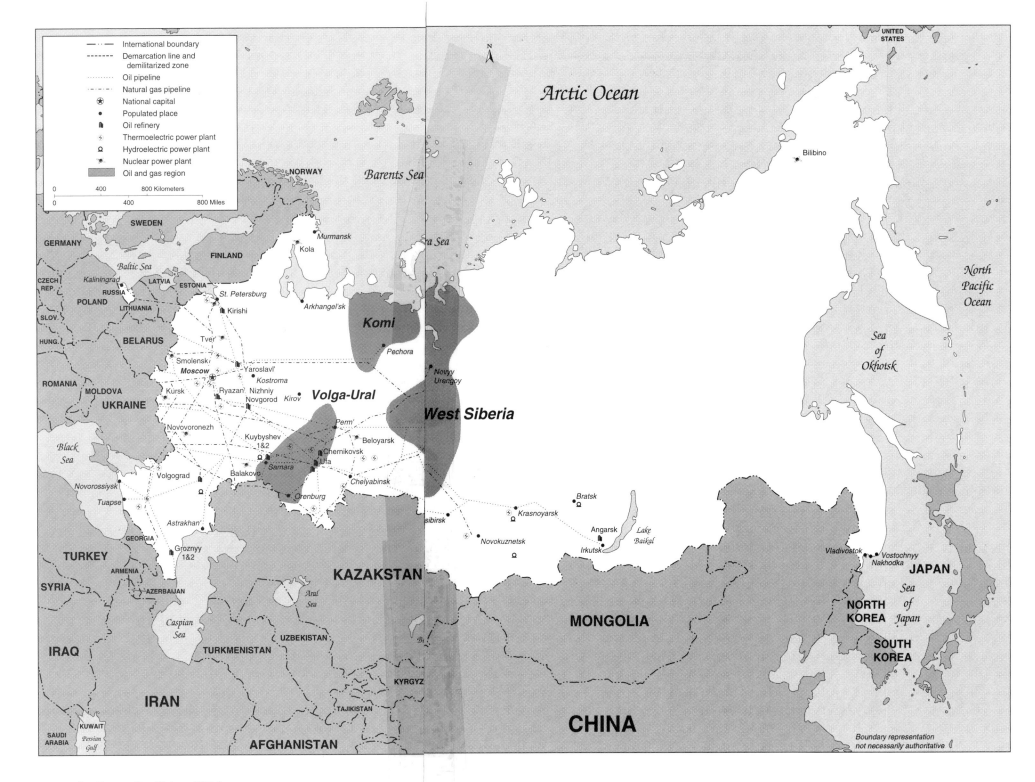

Figure 9. Energy Facilities, 1996

19

some measurements, is the largest oil company in the world. he dominance of a few large companies has made all stages of etroleum exploitation and sale extremely inefficient. National id local government policies have discouraged individual tailers from establishing independent gasoline storage facili- es and stations; therefore, retail gasoline likely will continue be in very short supply (only 8,900 stations were operating in ussia in 1995). Until January 1995, government policy pplied quotas to oil exports, and until July 1996 tariffs were pplied to oil exports. Both policies, resulting from the gap tween controlled domestic prices and world market prices, med at ensuring a sufficient supply of oil to meet domestic :mand; both were lifted as the gap narrowed.

The search for new oil deposits has been a primary force in ussia's foreign policy toward states to the south. Russia has aked its claim to the Caspian oil reserves that Western compa- es are exploring in conjunction with Azerbaijani, Turkmeni- ani, and Kazakstani state companies. The presence of estern interests and the strong role being played by Iran and irkey, Russia's traditional regional rivals, have complicated is policy, which aims to achieve maximum benefit from Rus- i's position on the shore of the north Caspian. Also a source international controversy is Russia's insistence that Caspian l flow northward through Russian pipelines rather than west- ird via new lines built through Georgia and Turkey (see For- gn Investment in Oil and Gas, this ch.).

atural Gas

Russia is also one of the world's largest natural gas produc- s. Its proven reserves have been estimated at 49 billion cubic eters, or roughly 35 percent of the world's total. Natural gas is also been one of the most successful parts of the Russian onomy. In the early 1980s, it replaced oil as the Soviet rowth fuel," offering cheaper extraction and transportation. though output has dropped in the 1990s, the decline has not en as severe as that for other energy sources or the rest of the onomy. Natural gas production peaked in 1991 at 727 mil- in cubic meters, then dropped throughout the early 1990s. it 1995 production, 596 million cubic meters, was an increase m the previous year. After European gas fields in the Volga- ral region dominated the industry through the 1970s, pro- iction shifted to giant fields in Siberia. The Urengoy and mburg fields in the West Siberia region are among the most productive; the former is the largest field in the world. Soviet plans called for rapid development of new reserves in the Yamal Peninsula in the Arctic Ocean north of Urengoy, but environmental problems and infrastructure costs slowed development. Hasty construction and poor maintenance have caused chronic breakdowns and accidents in the long pipeline of Russia's natural gas delivery system (see Transportation, this ch.).

The State Natural Gas Company (Gazprom) has a virtual monopoly over Russia's gas production and transmission. A vertically organized enterprise, the company has been reorganized into a joint-stock company, in which 40 percent of the shares remain under state control. Company employees hold another 15 percent, managers of the company hold 10 percent, and the remaining 35 percent were sold at public auction. Gazprom controls a network of regional production associations. Its management, which once was headed by Prime Minister Viktor Chernomyrdin, has been accused of corruption and tax evasion.

Coal

For more than 150 years, coal was the dominant fuel supporting Russia's industries, and many industrial centers were located near coal deposits. In the 1960s, oil and natural gas overtook coal when plentiful reserves of those fuels became available and the coal shafts of the European Soviet Union (located primarily in what is today Ukraine) were being exhausted. Russian coal reserves are estimated at 200 billion tons, an amount that experts say is more than ample for current usage trends. Siberia and the Far East produce about three-quarters of Russia's coal, with the European contributions coming largely from the Vorkuta field (Pechora Basin) in Komi, the Urals, the eastern Donets Basin in the southwest, and the Moscow Basin. Largely untapped coal fields lie in the Siberian Tunguska and Lena basins. Productive fields in Siberia are located along the Trans-Siberian Railroad, making their exploitation more economical. The largest operational sources in that region are the Kuznetsk, Kansk-Achinsk, and Cheremkhovo fields. Coal is one of the less important sources of energy because its labor-intensive extraction makes production much more costly than other fuels. Rossugol', the Russian coal company, controls coal production through regional associations that are organized as joint-stock companies. Russian coal production has declined markedly over the last decade, and the coal industry has suffered a long series of strikes. Coal miners, among the best paid industrial workers of the Soviet period, have organized strikes that have gained national attention to protest the industry's long delays in paying wages. Experts predict that coal output will continue to dwindle as its relative usefulness in industry and domestic applications is reduced. In 1994 Russia produced 249 million tons of coal, and in 1995 the total rose to 255 million tons. Production for the first quarter of 1996 was 71 million tons.

Nuclear Energy

In 1996 some twenty-nine nuclear reactors were operating at nine sites: Balakovo on the northwest border of Kazakstan, Beloyarsk in the southern Urals, Bilibino in northeastern Siberia (the only station east of the Urals), Kola in the far northwest, Kursk near the Ukrainian border, Novovoronezh on the Don River, St. Petersburg, Smolensk west of Moscow, and Tver' northwest of Moscow. Altogether these facilities accounted for 10 percent of Russia's energy generating capacity in 1994. The plants are operated by regional joint-stock companies in which the Ministry of Atomic Energy (Minatom) controls 51 percent of the shares. The nuclear energy sector has undergone financial problems because of government funding reductions. The industry has turned to selling goods related to nuclear energy—equipment and instruments, nuclear fuel, medical isotopes, and fertilizers.

The industry's financial problems, along with the disaster that occurred at the Chernobyl' plant in Ukraine in 1986, have raised questions about nuclear safety. Western countries have provided financial assistance in some cases because of their concern about Russia's lax standards of handling nuclear materials and the continued use of outmoded equipment. Russia's piecemeal environmental laws have led to indiscriminate dumping and burial of radioactive wastes, which are creating severe environmental problems. The theft of nuclear materials has become another source of danger emanating from Russia's nuclear energy program (see Environmental Conditions, ch. 3; The Crime Wave of the 1990s, ch. 10).

Nevertheless, experts predict that nuclear energy probably will play an important role in the Russian economy if enough investment is available to expand existing capacity. In 1992 Minatom announced plans to double nuclear energy capacity by 2010, but ensuing financial problems have caused a reduction of that goal, and no new capacity has been added since the breakup of the Soviet Union. The International Atomic Energy Agency (IAEA) projects that construction of new capacity will not begin until after 2005, even if the investment climate is favorable.

Conventional Power Generation

Much of the conventional fuel produced in Russia is burned to produce electric power. The Unified Electric Power System operates Russia's electric power plants through seventy-two regional power distribution companies. The power system consists of 600 thermal generating systems, more than 100 hydroelectric plants, and Russia's nine nuclear plants. Of the total rated generating capacity of 205 gigawatts, only about 188 gigawatts were available as of 1996. In 1995 Russia's power plants generated a total of 846 million kilowatt-hours, compared with 859 million kilowatt-hours in 1994. Generation for the first quarter of 1996 (normally the peak demand period of the year) was 268 million kilowatt-hours.

In 1993 natural gas provided 42 percent of electricity production; hydroelectric plants, 19 percent; coal, 18 percent; nuclear power, 13 percent; and other sources such as solar and geothermal plants, 8 percent. Natural gas and coal are burned at thermoelectric plants, which produce only electricity, and at cogeneration plants, which produce electricity and heat for urban centers. The largest hydroelectric plants are located on the Volga, Kama, Ob', Yenisey, and Angara rivers, where large reservoirs were built in massive Soviet energy projects. Thermoelectric and hydroelectric plants—located in Siberia because of available fuels and water power—send power to European Russia through a system of high-voltage transmission lines.

Consumption of electric power divides into the following categories: industrial, 61 percent; residential, 11 percent; the services sector, 11 percent; transportation, 9 percent; and agriculture, 8 percent. Regional energy commissions control the price of electricity.

Foreign Investment in Oil and Gas

In the mid-1990s, many analysts consider the oil and gas industries to be the best targets for foreign investment in Russia. The record of foreign investment in that period illustrates both the potentials and the pitfalls of such ventures. Experts have concluded that the Russian oil and gas sector will require large amounts of foreign capital to improve output. According to some estimates, the oil sector will require US$30 to US$50 billion in new investment just to maintain the mid-1990s level of production. To return production to its peak levels will require an estimated US$70 to US$130 billion in new investments, which clearly would have to come from foreign sources. The Russian oil and gas sector also would benefit from infusions of Western technology and expertise. However, according to a 1995 report by Cambridge Energy Research Associates, key figures in the oil industry, most of whom were schooled in the isolated Soviet-era approach to commerce, have been indifferent or hostile to Western management methods.

By the end of 1994, the oil and gas sector accounted for about 38 percent of total foreign direct investment in Russia, but the total input was only about US$1.4 billion. Although Western companies are poised to commit large amounts of capital for exploration, as of 1996 most foreign investment had gone to repairing and maintaining current facilities. Some analysts have estimated that foreign investment in the oil and gas sector could reach US$70 billion by the year 2000.

Among several United States oil companies active in Russia, Texaco heads a consortium in the largest project, the development of oil fields in the Timan-Pechora section of the Komi region north of the Arctic Circle. The project, under negotiation since 1989, has an estimated potential of US$45 billion in investment over the next fifty years. Conoco, a subsidiary of the DuPont de Nemours chemical firm, leads a consortium of United States and European firms and a Russian firm in the Polar Lights project to explore Siberian oil fields. Two United States companies, Marathon Oil and McDermott, along with the Japanese companies Mitsui and Mitsubishi and Britain's Royal Dutch Shell, are engaged in one of several projects to explore for oil off Sakhalin Island on the Pacific coast. The last two projects each could bring in as much as US$10 billion.

Nevertheless, Russia's generally poor investment climate and other obstacles such as special taxes have discouraged additional investment in gas and oil. As of mid-1996, a tax of about US$5 per barrel was imposed on oil exports, and a tax of about US$2.60 was levied per 1,000 cubic meters of natural gas exported. Foreign and domestic firms were also subject to royalty payments to the Government for the privilege of drilling for oil. Foreign investors have argued that reduced profit margins are a substantial obstacle to the support of some projects. Some major oil investors have received tax exemptions, but delays in rebate payments have created additional deterrents.

Banking and Finance

Experts have agreed that establishing a viable financial sector is a vital requirement for Russia to have a successful market economy. In the first five years of the post-Soviet era, the development of Russia's financial sector as an efficient distributor of money and credit to other parts of the economic structure has mirrored the ups and downs of the rest of the economy. In 1996 some elements of the central planning system remained obstacles to further progress.

The Soviet Financial System

The financial system of the Soviet period was a rudimentary mechanism for state control of the economy. The government owned and managed the banking system. The State Bank (Gosudarstvennyy bank—Gosbank) was the central bank and the only commercial bank. In its capacity as a central bank, Gosbank handled all significant banking transactions, including the issuance and control of currency and credit, the management of gold reserves, and the oversight of transactions among enterprises. Enterprises were issued money and credits in accordance with the government's planned allocation of wages and its management strategy for other expenses.

Wages were paid only in cash, and households used cash exclusively for making payments. Checkbooks, credit cards, and other alternative forms of payment were not available in the Soviet Union. Wage earners could keep savings deposits in the Savings Bank (Sberbank), where they earned low interest, and these funds were available to the government as a source of revenue. Two other banks also existed prior to 1987. The Construction Bank (Stroybank) provided investment credits to enterprises, and the Foreign Trade Bank (Vneshtorgbank) handled financial transactions pertaining to trade.

In 1987 and 1988, the Gorbachev regime separated commercial banking operations from Gosbank and replaced the two specialized banks with three banks to provide credit to designated sectors of the economy: the Agro-Industrial Bank (Agroprombank), the Industry and Construction Bank (Promstroybank), and the Social Investment Bank (Zhilsotsbank), which managed credits for the social welfare sector. The Soviet economy also had state-controlled insurance firms, but other forms of finance such as stocks and bonds did not exist.

The Financial Sector in the 1990s

In the 1990s, Russia's financial sector, particularly its banking system, has been one of the fastest changing elements of the economy. Although changes have moved clearly in the direction of market principles, in the mid-1990s much additional reform was necessary to achieve stability.

Reform of the Banking System

The Russian banking system has developed from the centralized system of the Soviet period into a two-tier system, including a central bank and commercial banks, that is the standard structure in market-based economies. The Russian Central Bank (RCB) assumed the functions of Gosbank in November 1991, and Gosbank was eliminated when the Soviet Union dissolved one month later. In its first years of existence, the RCB functioned under the guidelines of the 1977 Soviet constitution and Russian laws passed in 1990, which made the bank essentially an arm of the Russian parliament, whose members manipulated bank policy to help favored enterprises.

Russia's 1993 constitution gave the RCB more autonomy. However, the president has substantial influence on bank policies through his power to appoint the bank chairman, who in turn wields extensive authority over bank operations and policy. (The nomination is subject to the approval of the State Duma.)

Viktor Gerashchenko, a former Gosbank chairman, was the first chairman of the RCB. In late 1994, he resigned under pressure from President Yeltsin after the so-called Black Tuesday plunge of the ruble's value on exchange markets (see Monetary and Fiscal Policies, this ch.). Yeltsin named Tat'yana Paramonova to replace Gerashchenko, but she remained acting chairman throughout her tenure because the State Duma refused to approve her appointment. Powerful Duma members opposed Paramonova's policy of restricting credits to favored industrial sectors. In November 1995, the Duma approved Yeltsin's nomination of Sergey Dubinin to replace State Paramonova; Dubinin remained in that position through the end of Yeltsin's first term as president in mid-1996.

The Law on the Central Bank, enacted in April 1995, provides the statutory authority for the RCB. Under the law, the RCB is responsible for controlling the country's money supply, monitoring transactions among banks, implementing the federal budget and servicing Russia's foreign debt, monitoring the foreign-exchange rate of the ruble, implementing Russian exchange-rate policies, maintaining foreign currency reserves and gold reserves, licensing commercial banks, and regulating and supervising commercial banks.

The RCB has had the greatest impact on Russia's economy through its role in monetary policy. The RCB controls the money supply by lending funds to commercial banks and by establishing their reserve requirements. For several years after its establishment, the RCB issued direct credits to enterprises and to the agricultural sector at subsidized rates. Such credits were directed via commercial banks to politically influential sectors: agriculture, the industrial and energy enterprises of the northern regions, the energy sector in general, and other large, state-run enterprises.

In the early years, the RCB also financed state budget deficits by issuing credits to cover Government expenditures. The availability of such credits played a central role in the high inflation that the Russian economy endured between 1991 and 1994. In 1995 new legislation and regulations reduced this type of credit by prohibiting the use of credit to finance state budget deficits, and recent RCB chairmen have raised discount rates for RCB borrowing by commercial banks. Such restrictions have been heavily influenced by requirements of the IMF to maintain strict fiscal and monetary standards to be eligible for international financial assistance (see Foreign Debt, this ch.).

Initially, the RCB's regulation of commercial banks also was lax because the banking sector grew rapidly as the centralized economy collapsed and because Russia had no experience in establishing a market-based system. In the early and mid-1990s, the failure of regulation led to a plethora of new commercial banks, most of which were of dubious quality.

In the mid-1990s, the World Bank (see Glossary) assisted the Russian government in establishing a core of large banks, called international standard banks, that met the standards of the Bank for International Settlements (BIS—see Glossary). The new banks must conform to strict standards for the size and interest rates of loans; the size of a bank's capital base; the volume of loan reserves that banks must maintain; and the scrutiny under which banking activities will be monitored. The International Standard Bank program anticipates that the core of banks that meet its requirements will grow until the entire banking system conforms to the BIS criteria.

Meanwhile, plans called for the RCB to remain the foundation of the Russian banking system. Its success will depend greatly on its retaining as much independence as possible from both the executive and the legislative branches of government and on bank officials' ability to maintain credible monetary policies.

Commercial Banks

By the end of 1995, Russia had nearly 3,000 commercial banks. However, most of these banks were small and had little capitalization. A large portion of them are financially linked to companies and act exclusively as conduits of subsidized credits to these enterprises. The financial health of such institutions is highly questionable, and experts forecast that many of them will merge into larger, more viable institutions or go bankrupt as the RCB continues to tighten its requirements and as the role of cheap credits diminishes.

The commercial banking system has a core of large, viable banks that have attained financial credibility and that experts expect to remain in operation under any foreseeable economic conditions. The former state-controlled specialized banks of the Soviet system form the foundation of the current commercial banking system, including the six largest commercial banks in Russia. In 1991 three of the banks—the Agroprombank (subsequently renamed Rossel'bank), the Promstroybank, and the Zhilsotsbank (reorganized into Mosbusinessbank)—were reorganized into joint-stock companies and became independent commercial operations, forming the foundation of the commercial banking system.

The Soviet-era Savings Bank (Sberbank) was reorganized as the Sberbank of Russia, with the RCB holding controlling shares. In 1996 the Sberbank held between 60 and 70 percent of Russians' total household savings; that figure decreased from 90 percent in 1991 as other commercial banks began to provide competition. The Foreign Trade Bank (Rosvneshtorgbank) also remains state-controlled, and it continues to handle most foreign transactions, although by the mid-1990s it received competition from newer, privately owned banks. The

Moscow International Bank handles business between the large Russian banks and Western banks. Sberbank and Rossel'bank have systems of nationwide branches.

The types and quality of services that the Russian banking system offers to the public are still rudimentary according to the standards of Western industrialized countries. They are unable to offer diverse and efficient customer services because the Soviet Union had no retail banking tradition and because Russia lacks the sophisticated infrastructure, especially high-speed telecommunications and trained staffs, on which modern Western financial institutions depend.

Most of the commercial banks offer their customers savings deposit accounts, and the more established banks provide foreign-exchange services, investment services, and corporate services. Bank checks are still rarely used in Russia because check clearance is a long process. Some banks offer debit cards that allow customers to have payments for goods and services deducted directly from their bank balances. Some banks also offer credit cards to customers with impeccable credit ratings. The continued predominance of cash transactions has slowed the rate of Russia's commerce.

Although foreign banks have played a larger role in the Russian economy in the mid-1990s, that role has met substantial resistance from nationalist factions. In early 1996, the State Duma passed a statute prohibiting the RCB from licensing foreign banks that did not have operations in Russia before November 1993. However, opponents of such a policy have pointed out that efforts to protect the fledgling domestic banking sector from foreign competition also deny access to Western financial techniques that eventually would improve the competitiveness of Russian banks.

Other Financial Institutions

A Russian securities market has evolved with the rest of the economy. When the first Russian stock market was established in 1991, few private companies existed to offer shares, so trading activity was quite low. The securities market got a large boost from the Russian government's privatization campaign. Shares in privatized firms were issued, and then a secondary market emerged for the privatization vouchers that the government issued to each citizen (see Privatization, this ch.). As the first phase of the privatization program ended and companies' capital requirements rose, an efficient securities market became increasingly important.

Russian laws and regulations of the stock market and other elements of the securities market have not kept pace with the growth in the industry, fostering irregularities in the market. Among the most infamous was the operation of the MMM investment company, which developed into a pyramid scheme guaranteeing investors very high returns on their investments. A number of Russian small investors, whose savings had been eroded severely by inflation, were attracted to the scheme and eventually lost large sums of money. The head of MMM, Sergey Mavrodi, was arrested and jailed on tax fraud, but the MMM case underlined the lack of Western-style commercial laws in the Russian legal system. The Russian securities market also lacks a modern communications infrastructure, so registration and reporting of financial transactions are very slow.

In 1993 the Government added a new element to the securities market by issuing treasury bonds to help finance its budget deficits. In addition, Russian citizens are able to buy and sell rubles for foreign currency at selected banks. The exchange rate is established through weekly auctions on the Moscow International Currency Exchange (MICEX).

Insurance remains a small part of the Russian financial market. In 1996 approximately 200 insurance companies were operating in Russia, including the privatized versions of former Soviet state insurance companies. According to experts, Russia's relatively new financial institutions are likely to face a long period of adjustment as weaker banks close or merge with stronger banks, and a regulatory framework must be developed to ensure public confidence in the banking system and enable banks to offer reliable support in the development of private enterprise—a role that has expanded rapidly in the first five post-Soviet years. Other aspects of the financial system, such as securities markets, also lack the degree of standardized regulation required for large-scale domestic participation. However, as the private sector's role in the national economy grows and as Russia develops needed regulations and infrastructure, the securities markets and other nonbank financial institutions are expected to follow the banks as important elements of the economy.

Taxation

Throughout the first half of the 1990s, international financial institutions warned Russia that major adjustments were needed in the structure and the administration of the country's tax-collection system. However, in 1996 few meaningful changes had emerged. Tax reforms until that time had emphasized revenue from income, consumption, and trade, with the value-added tax (VAT—see Glossary), corporate profits taxes, and personal income taxes accounting for 60 to 70 percent of total revenue (see table 16, Appendix). Beginning in 1993, experts have pointed to changes in the bases and rates of the profit tax and the VAT as a major cause of declining revenues. Between 1993 and 1994, the ratio of taxes collected to GDP declined from 41 percent to 36 percent, although the percentage of GDP paid in taxes already was lower in Russia than in any of the Western market economies. In the first quarter of 1996, only 56 percent of planned tax revenue was realized.

The system in place in 1996 taxed the profits of enterprises heavily, especially in comparison with the tax burden of personal income. In 1993 business profit taxes were three to seven times higher than in Western economies, and personal income taxes were two to four times lower. That emphasis was not conducive to expanding investment, and many non-wage sources of income were not captured by personal income tax standards. According to a 1996 estimate, Russians kept US$30 billion to US$60 billion in foreign banks to avoid taxation.

The VAT, which is levied on imported and domestic goods, is set at 21.5 percent for most purchases and 10 percent for a specified list of foods. Administration of that tax is complicated by uneven compliance and accounting rules that do not define clearly the amounts to be classified as value added. Taxation on the extraction and sale of natural resources is a major revenue source, but the current system yields disproportionately little revenue from the energy sector, especially the natural gas industry. Excise taxes are levied on merchandise of both domestic and foreign origin. The tax on imported luxury items ranges from 10 to 400 percent, and the rate on imports has been kept higher than for domestic products in order to protect domestic industries.

Taxes on trade are a major revenue source. In the mid-1990s, export taxes became a more important source of revenue as other types of trade control were eliminated. Frequent changes in the tariff schedule for imported goods have led to confusion among importers. The average tariff rate in mid-

1995 was 17 percent, but a reduction of maximum rates was announced for the medium term.

Russia's taxation agency is the State Taxation Service (STS), which was established to administer the new market-based tax system installed in 1991 and 1992. Although in the mid-1990s its staff of 162,000 employees was much larger than tax agencies in Western countries, the STS has been hampered by poor organization, inadequate automation, and an untrained staff. Training and reorganization programs were announced in 1995, and some streamlining has resulted in separating the roles of various levels of government, identification of tax-eligible individuals and corporations, and application of penalties for tax evasion and tax arrears.

Experts have identified the most serious defect of the tax administration system as the ad hoc granting of tax exemptions, which distorts the overall revenue system and undermines the authority of administrators. The most problematic examples of this practice are exemptions granted to agricultural producers and the oil and natural gas industries.

The Labor Force

Literacy and education levels among the Russian population (148 million in 1996) are relatively high, largely because the Soviet system placed great emphasis on education (see The Soviet Heritage, ch. 5). Some 92 percent of the Russian people have completed at least secondary school, and 11 percent have completed some form of higher education (university and above). In 1995 about 57 percent of the Russian population was of working age, which the government defined as between the ages of sixteen and fifty-five for women and between the ages of sixteen and sixty for men, and 20 percent had passed working age. Women make up more than half the work force.

Although size, age, and education would seem to place the Russian labor force in a good position to participate in developing a modern, industrialized economy, it is not clear that the skills that Russian workers attained during the Soviet period are those required for a market economy. In 1994 the construction, industry, and agriculture sectors employed 53.5 percent of the work force, and the services sector employed 37 percent, a distribution typical of developing economies. By contrast, 67 percent of the United States labor force is in the services sector, and 22 percent is in agriculture, industry, and construction, a configuration typical of modern industrialized market economies. The Russian pattern reflects the emphasis that Soviet economic planners placed on the nonservice sectors. Even among the highly skilled labor force, the Soviet economy (and the national education system as a whole) skewed training toward the sciences, mathematics, and engineering and gave little attention to education in management and entrepreneurship. This pattern of work training and general education has continued in the 1990s; according to experts, its continued presence indicates that the economy may not be able to depend on younger workers to expand the fund of service-sector skills needed for a modern market economy. In any case, as the Russian economy progresses toward a market structure, middle-aged and older workers will increasingly find themselves playing a marginal role.

The living standards of Russia's workers have been eroded by two factors. First, the severe depression of the country's extended economic transition has left a large share of the work force either unemployed, underemployed, or receiving reduced wages. Second, labor lacks an effective organization to protect its interests. Neither trade unions from the Soviet era nor new, independent organizations have provided effective, united representation. As of mid-1996, negative conditions had not yielded the large-scale unrest that many experts had predicted in the working class.

Unemployment

The growth of unemployment has been the bane of many of the Central and East European countries in the transition from centrally planned to market economies. Russia's unemployment rate has been hard to measure accurately because many firms unofficially furlough workers but leave them on company rolls. This practice is a vestige of the paternalistic Soviet era, when the presence of workers in an enterprise often had no relation to that enterprise's actual production. Many of these furloughed workers find gainful employment in the private sector, where wages often go unreported. Such a system results in a haphazard, inefficient allocation of the labor force.

Western and Russian analysts have relied on International Labour Organisation measurements, which indicate that at the end of 1995, Russian unemployment had reached 8.2 percent (see table 17, Appendix). The Russian journal *Ekonomika i zhizn'* estimated the figure at 8.6 percent, or 6.3 million people, for the first quarter of 1996. Although the last figure still is below the unemployment rates of Poland and some other countries in transition, the full extent of unemployment has been masked by extended subsidies that delayed the shutdown of large Russian enterprises. In 1995 nearly half of plant directors surveyed said that they had more workers than they needed.

Unemployment varies considerably according to region. Moscow's unemployment rate, the lowest in Russia, was 0.6 percent in March 1996. The Republic of Ingushetia, which also has had the highest immigration rate because of its proximity to Chechnya, reported a rate of 23.5 percent in December 1995. In March 1996, Ivanovo, a textile center east of Moscow, had a rate of 13 percent, and the Republic of Udmurtia, a center of the struggling military-industrial complex, reported 9.4 percent (see The Defense Industry, ch. 9). At that time, women constituted 62 percent of Russia's officially unemployed, and 37 percent of the total were people below the age of thirty.

The Federal Employment Service (Federal'naya sluzhba zanyatosti—FSZ), the agency in charge of issuing unemployment benefits and placing unemployed workers, had only 3.7 percent of the working population registered for benefits in March 1996; many jobless workers do not register because benefits are so small (averaging US$22 per month in 1995) and because, after the guaranteed employment of the Soviet era, joblessness entails a significant stigma for many Russians. However, as the average term of unemployment grew from six to eight months between 1994 and 1995, more workers participated in FSZ programs. In 1995 the service placed an estimated 1.7 million workers in new jobs. That year, 9.8 million workers left positions and 8.7 million were hired, and the majority of those who left did so voluntarily—many because wages were not paid—rather than because of dismissal. Shortages exist in some types of skilled labor, and some companies actively recruit workers.

Wages

By 1995 delays in wage payment had become a chronic problem even in profitable Russian enterprises. In many cases, enterprises simply passed along the burden of late payments of state subsidies and customer debts. At the end of 1995, the Government owed a total of US$112 billion of subsidies, of which about 27 percent were more than three months overdue. Most of its debt was to the military and energy sectors. Through 1995 an average of 19 percent of wages were paid late, and in January 1996 a total of US$2.1 billion was overdue in agriculture, construction, industry, and transportation. The State Committee for Statistics (Goskomstat) began keeping separate statistics for wages formally paid and those actually delivered. The payment record of privatized enterprises was worse than that of state enterprises, and in many cases workers were paid in merchandise rather than in cash. In early 1996, the average rates of overdue payment were 62 percent in ferrous metallurgy, 86 percent in oil extraction, and 22 percent in food processing.

In his presidential campaign, Yeltsin promised to abolish state-sector wage arrears and to encourage improvement in the private sector. By squeezing the national budget, Yeltsin achieved temporary results in the state sector, but his promise had no effect on other enterprises. Officials proposed several programs to raise average wages and streamline the inefficient system by which wages are delivered, but no meaningful reform had been achieved by mid-1996. In July 1996, coal strikes in the Far East, southwestern Russia, southern Siberia, and the Urals threatened a nationwide shutdown in response to continued payment failures in that industry.

Manufacturing

Beginning in 1921, Lenin's Soviet government made industrial modernization a priority. But it was under Stalin that the system of central planning was fully developed and the industrialization of the Russian Republic reached its peak. Throughout the Stalin period, investment resources were directed into heavy manufacturing at the expense of consumer or light industry.

During the later Soviet period, economic reformers such as Nikita Khrushchev attempted to shift some resources to the consumer industries, but the emphasis eventually shifted back to heavy and military industries. This emphasis was especially strong while the Soviet Union was building its military base during the Cold War. In the 1970s, manufacturing productivity declined. As part of his *perestroika* program in the late 1980s, Gorbachev redirected resources to consumer goods, but the effort proved insufficient to forestall the decay of the manufacturing sector.

In the 1990s, Russia urgently needed a revival of the manufacturing sector to provide employment and steer the restructuring of industrial priorities away from the impractical Soviet emphasis on subsidized heavy industry and the military-industrial complex (MIC). Although a substantial share of Russia's MIC enterprises underwent full or partial conversion to civilian production and most manufacturers were partially or fully privatized, manufacturing output continued a general decline in the mid-1990s (see table 18, Appendix). This trend had slowed by 1995, when the decrease in total industrial production was 4 percent compared with 1994; the 1994 total had been 23 percent below that of 1993.

Ferrous Metallurgy

The Soviet Union's ferrous metallurgy industry was a showpiece of centralized planning of heavy industry. The fast-growing industry, vital in supplying other heavy industries with semifinished inputs, led the world in output in the 1970s and the 1980s. Beginning in the mid-1980s, however, ferrous metallurgy did not keep pace with the demands of domestic industry and foreign markets for more sophisticated and stronger metal materials. Many older plants with outmoded technology remained in full production; Soviet plans called for refitting the industry in the 1990s, but Russia's resources have not been sufficient for such a massive project.

In 1994 the ferrous and nonferrous metallurgical industries accounted for about 16 percent of industrial output. In 1996 more than 80 percent of Russia's steel output came from eight plants, although about 100 plants were in operation. Among the industry's most important products are pipe, pig iron, smelted steel, finished rolled metal, and shaped section steel. The four largest steel enterprises are the Novolipetsk and Cherepovets metallurgical plants, located southeast and north of Moscow, respectively, and the Magnitogorsk and Nizhniy Tagil metallurgical combines, located in the Ural industrial region. In 1995 the Cherepovets plant was re-formed as the Severstal' (Northern Steel) Joint-Stock Company. In the mid-1990s, more than half of Russia's steel production came from the outmoded open-hearth furnace process; the more modern continuous casting method accounted for only 24 percent of output.

In the first half of the 1990s, the steel industry was hit especially hard by Russia's overall economic decline, which caused domestic consumption to drop sharply; by 1996 only 50 to 60 percent of capacity was in use. Between 1991 and 1994, output of rolled steel dropped from 55.1 million tons to 35.8 millions tons. Foreign sales were especially important as the only source of hard currency for some enterprises, accounting for as much as 60 percent of output in some cases. In 1995 Russian exports increased by 30 percent, making Russia the second largest exporter of ferrous metals in the world. The profitability of such sales dropped substantially between 1994 and 1996, however. Much of the steel industry's domestic business was payment in kind to input suppliers and railroads. Production costs are raised by the prices of such domestic inputs as coal and iron ore and transportation, which averaged at or above world levels in 1996. Another major cost to the ferrous metallurgy sector is social support programs for workers. Those costs in turn raise domestic metal prices above international levels.

Nonferrous Metallurgy

The Noril'sk Nickel Joint-Stock Company dominates Russia's nonferrous metallurgy industries. It controls nearly all of the country's aluminum and nickel production and 60 percent of copper production. The largest operations in the industry are Noril'sk Nickel in northwestern Siberia and Bratsk Aluminum, Krasnoyarsk Aluminum, and Sayan Aluminum in south-central Siberia. More than 90 percent of Russia's aluminum comes from six smelters. Some smelters have been privatized and export their semifinished products. Inputs, especially alumina (of which Russia has little), became much more expensive in the mid-1990s, as did transportation and electricity costs. At the same time, export revenues fell.

The Automotive Industry

In 1993 Russia's automotive industry produced 956,000 passenger automobiles, a decrease from the 1991 figure of 1,030,000 automobiles. During the Soviet period, the industry had gained a reputation for extremely slow production of very unreliable vehicles. In the mid-1990s, the plant rated most efficient, the Volga Automotive Plant (Avtovaz) at Tol'yatti, required about thirty times as long to assemble an automobile as the leading plants in Japan. All Russian vehicle plants operated at far below capacity, with outmoded machinery and bloated work forces. Avtovaz, the most productive plant, operated at about 70 percent of capacity, and the Gor'kiy Automotive Plant (GAZ) in Nizhniy Novgorod was the only other major plant operating above 30 percent in 1995. The two main truck manufacturers, the Likhachev Automotive Plant (ZIL) in Mos-

New "American car"
dealership, Moscow
Courtesy Michael E. Samojeden

cow and the Kama Automotive Plant (KamAZ) in Naberezh-
nyye Chelny, have suffered especially from reductions in orders
by their main customers—the armed forces and collective
farms. GAZ has successfully marketed a light truck, of which it
sold 75,000 in 1995, mainly to small businesses. The traditional
Soviet truck was a heavy diesel model with limited service life.

Although demand for passenger automobiles has increased
substantially in Russia over the last twenty-five years, output has
not responded even in the post-Soviet period. In 1994 only
eighty-four autos were registered per 1,000 people. In the mid-
1990s, all automobile plants retained the Soviet style of organization, which is incapable of self-financing or effective marketing. The lack of post-Soviet government subsidies has placed
most enterprises in danger of extinction. Some Russian enterprises have proposed joint ventures with Western firms, but in
many cases the Russian partners lack funding for such ventures. Meanwhile, foreign imports further endanger the industry: in 1994 only 65,000 automobiles were imported legally, but
another 250,000 to 500,000 entered Russia illegally. Therefore,
most new cars in Russian cities are foreign. (In 1996 government vehicles were exclusively Audi, Mercedes-Benz, Saab, or
Volvo). Exports of Russian passenger cars declined in the early
1990s.

Machine Building

In the Soviet period, the machine-building industry was at the center of the industrial modernization programs that required a steady supply of capital equipment to respond to new demands. However, the inefficient organization of industrial planning caused bottlenecks in crucial programs and generally unreliable performance. The industry is concentrated in the European part of Russia, with major facilities in Moscow, St. Petersburg, Nizhniy Novgorod, and the Ural industrial region. (Russian machine building includes the automotive, construction equipment, and aviation industries as well as the tractor, electrical equipment, instrument making, consumer appliance, and machine industries.)

Between 1985 and 1995, production of most categories of machines decreased significantly, mainly because of declining domestic orders. For example, by 1992 production of metalcutting machines had dropped by 20 percent, washing machines by 47 percent, turbines by 36 percent, and tractors by 45 percent. In 1993 production of about one-third of sixty-two major categories of products declined by at least 50 percent. In 1995 production for the entire machine-building complex was about 4 percent below the 1994 level.

Light Industry

The most important branch of light industry is cotton textiles, which has production centers in Ivanovo, Kostroma, Yaroslavl', and about two dozen smaller cities between the Volga and Oka rivers east of Moscow. The economic slump of the 1990s had a dramatic effect on textile production and other light industries. In 1995 Russia's light industry suffered the sharpest drop in production of all economic sectors, slumping by an estimated 25 to 30 percent compared with the previous year. Prices for light-industry goods increased by an average of 2.9 times in 1995 after having increased by 5.6 times in 1994.

Unemployment in Russia's textile production centers has been among the highest in the country. In early 1996, an estimated 70 percent of workers in the industry were on furlough or working part-time. The chief cause is the Russian consumers' decline in personal income, hence in demand. In the mid-1990s, consumers purchased most of their textile products at flea markets, which offered both a wider variety of merchandise and cheaper prices than most stores. By the end of 1995, orders for all types of light-industrial production were 48 percent of the average for the previous years. Production declined by 20 percent in fabrics, 21 percent in leather shoes, and 44 percent in knitted goods, but stocks of finished products grew because demand decreased at a faster rate.

The high price of cotton also has hampered the textile industry, which had been accustomed to paying low prices for its raw material when the major suppliers in Central Asia were part of the Soviet economic system. Although their cotton is not of high quality, Central Asian sellers now charge world market prices. (Cotton from the "far abroad," outside the former Soviet Union, is even more expensive, however.) In 1996 industry experts expect some improvement because of expanding export markets in Europe and new investment in light industry by Russia's banks. They also expect an increase in domestic shoe manufacturing in the 1990s because the high import duties on foreign shoes make them twice as expensive as Russian shoes—although in 1996 some 65 percent of shoes sold in Russia were imported. The former member countries of the Council for Mutual Economic Assistance (Comecon—see Glossary) were the chief source of such goods.

Chemicals

The centers of the chemical industry traditionally have been areas where critical raw materials and allied industries were available. Before 1960 plants were near mineral deposits, potato farms, coking coal, and nonferrous metallurgy plants. When oil and natural gas became prime raw materials for chemical production, plants were built near the Volga-Ural and North Caucasus gas and oil fields or along pipelines. In the 1980s, major plants were built at Omsk, Tobol'sk, Urengoy, and Surgut in the western Siberia oil region and at Ufa and Nizhnekamsk in the Volga-Ural region. In the same period, the government gave strong investment and research support to chemical production because of its importance to the rest of heavy industry.

The major divisions of the chemical industry are paints and varnishes, rubber and asbestos products, synthetic tar and plastic products, mined chemical products, household chemicals and washing compounds, mineral fertilizers, chemical fibers and filaments, and paper and pulp. In the 1990s, output has decreased in all of those areas. Among representative products, between 1985 and the early 1990s production of mineral fertilizers dropped by 29 percent, agricultural pesticides by 74 percent, industrial carbon by 28 percent, sulfuric acid by 19 percent, synthetic tars and plastics by 16 percent, paints and varnishes by 43 percent, household soaps by 25 percent, and caustic soda by 15 percent.

Based on Russia's huge supply of timber, a substantial lumber-processing and pulp industry developed in the Soviet period as a subsidiary of the chemical industry. In 1996 Russia's largest pulp and paper enterprises were at Kondopoga near the Finnish border, Bratsk west of Lake Baikal, Syktyvkar in the Republic of Komi, and Kotlas southeast of Arkhangel'sk. Most pulp and paper companies do not own timber resources, but timber suppliers, who lease timberland from the state, generally sell raw materials at below world prices, giving Russian manufacturers a competitive advantage. Some mergers have occurred between suppliers and manufacturing operations.

In the early 1990s, production of raw timber dropped by about 25 percent, mainly because of equipment depletion, lack of credit, higher railroad transport fees, and a drop in construction of lumber roads. In 1993 production of raw timber was 450,000 cubic meters, 75 percent of the 1992 total; production of commercial cellulose was 79 percent of the previous year's total; and of cardboard, 73 percent (see Environmental Conditions, ch. 3).

Transportation and Telecommunications

As with the rest of the economy, the transportation and telecommunications infrastructures of the Russian economy continue to bear the imprint of Soviet central planning. CPSU priorities shaped those systems, and they are generally inappropriate to serve the needs of a market economy. Many analysts contend that inferior transportation and communications constitute a major impediment to Russian economic growth.

Transportation

The transportation system during the Soviet period was organized in the form of vertically integrated monopolies controlled by the central government. Thus, for example, the same administrative agency owned and operated the airports, airlines, and enterprises that manufactured aircraft. The infrastructure eroded seriously in the late Soviet period and

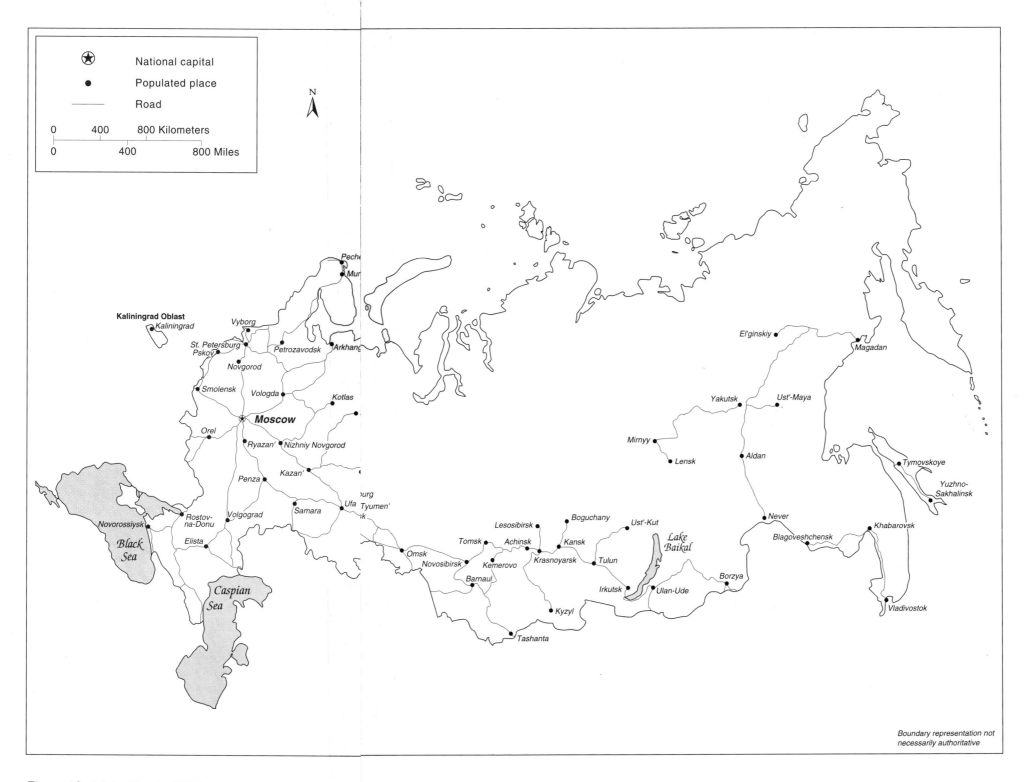

Figure 10. Major Roads, 1996

requires much modernization and reform, for which Russia relies heavily on foreign investment and aid.

Roads

Roads were one of the least-used forms of transportation in the Soviet Union, a characteristic that has continued in the Russian Federation. Soviet industry placed little emphasis on the production of automobiles and other modes of personal transport, and the privately owned vehicle was a relatively rare phenomenon; therefore, the demand for road construction was small. The dominance of the railroads for cargo transport also constrained the demand for the construction of roads. In 1995 Russia had 934,000 kilometers of roads, compared with 6.3 million kilometers in the United States (see fig. 10). Of Russia's total, 209,000 kilometers were unpaved, and 445,000 kilometers were not available for public use because they served specific industries or farms.

The World Bank has estimated that in twenty years the demands of Russia's new economy will increase the road system's share of transportation to 41 percent from its 1992 level of 13 percent. However, in 1992 some 38 percent of Russia's highway system required rehabilitation or reconstruction, and another 25 percent required repaving. Many major bridges also required large-scale repair in the mid-1990s.

Railroads

Railroads are the dominant mode of transportation. In 1995 Russia had some 154,000 kilometers of railroads, 26 percent of which were electrified, but 67,000 kilometers of that total served specific industries and were not available for general use (see fig. 11). The entire system is 1.52-meter gauge. In 1993 railroads accounted for 1,608 billion ton-kilometers of cargo traffic, compared with the 26 billion ton-kilometers provided by trucks. The prominence of railroads is the result of several factors: the vast distances that need to be covered; the penchant of Soviet economic planners for locating manufacturing facilities in politically expedient areas rather than where raw materials and other inputs were available; and the conditions for granting state fuel subsidies, which provided no incentives to break up cargo transportation into shorter-haul operations that could be covered by road. Cargo traffic is the predominant use of railroads, in contrast to the emphasis on passenger traffic in West European railroad systems (see table 19; table 20,

Appendix). This pattern is a product of the Soviet emphasis on heavy industry and production rather than on consumers. In 1992 Russia's railroads accounted for 253,000 passenger-kilometers, and by 1994 the total had dropped to 227,000 passenger-kilometers.

Railroad traffic has plummeted since the beginning of Russian economic reform, reflecting a general decline in economic activity. Between 1992 and 1994, freight haulage dropped from 1.9 million ton-kilometers to 1.2 million ton-kilometers, and Russia's rolling stock and roadbeds deteriorated, mainly because of insufficient maintenance funding. In 1993 an estimated 8.5 percent of Russian rail lines were defective. As a market economy takes shape, experts forecast a smaller relative role for the railroads. The combination of fuel and material costs, substantially higher in the absence of government subsidies, and new alternative routing will likely prompt Russian manufacturers to find more efficient means of transporting goods. For shorter hauls, trucks will replace rail service, and intermodal transportation will receive greater emphasis as an outgrowth of marketization.

Air Transportation

Of the modest amount of passenger traffic in Russia, air service accounts for a relatively large portion, although the volume of traffic declined in the first half of the 1990s. In 1990 the monopoly service of Aeroflot, the Soviet Union's state-owned airline, accounted for 22 percent of the total distance passengers traveled, a proportion comparable with the proportion of travel on the airlines of the United States and Canada. However, the contribution of air service to total travel had dropped to 12.5 percent by 1993, and the number of passengers flying was less than half the 1990 total. Subsidized air fares and long-distance flights between cities accounted for much of the air activity in the early 1990s. In 1994 Russia had a total of 2,517 airports, of which fifty-four had runways longer than 3,000 meters, 202 had runways between 2,400 and 3,000 meters, and another 108 had runways between 1,500 and 2,400 meters.

As with the rest of the economy, air travel has declined substantially as prices have increased and travelers' incomes have declined. The airline industry also has undergone major adjustments in the 1990s. Aeroflot, since 1995 a joint-stock company with majority state ownership, remains the main Russian airline. However, more than 200 regional carriers have

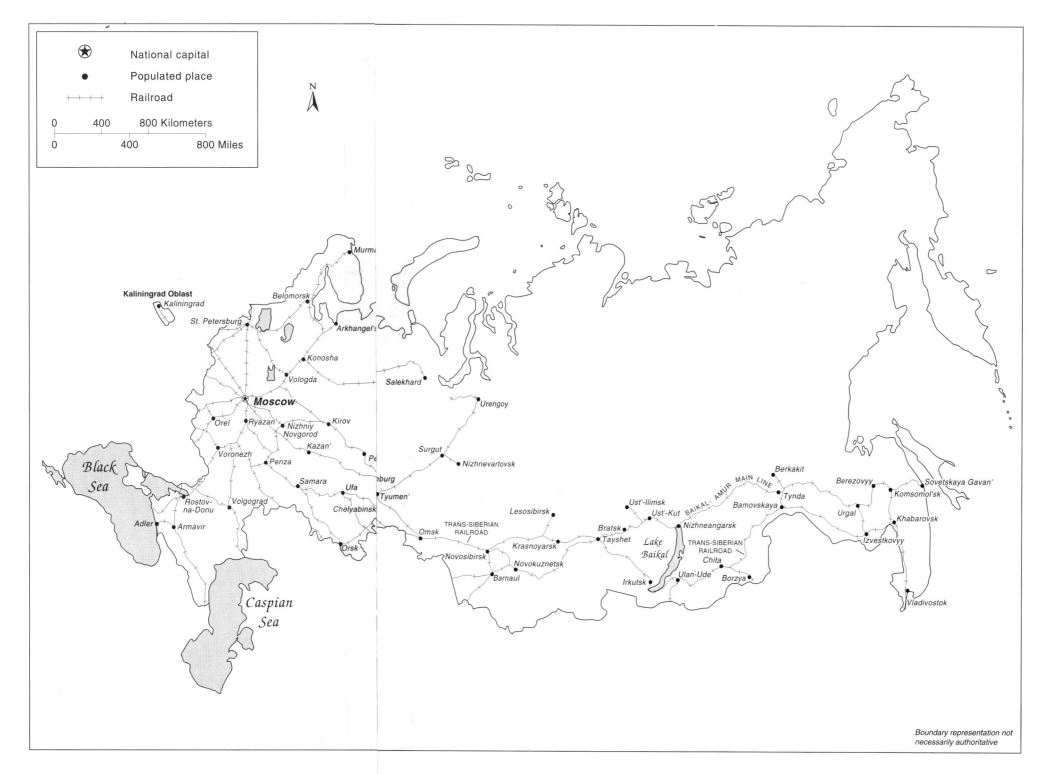

Figure 11. Major Railroads, 1996

362

emerged in the former Soviet Union, and most of them are in Russia. With flights from so many carriers, direct service is now available between regions, including direct flights from the Russian Far East to Japan and Alaska, without the previously obligatory stop in Moscow or St. Petersburg.

At the same time that airlines decentralized, so did reservation systems and navigation control networks, making those aspects of airline travel less efficient. Experts predict that as market forces continue to work in the sector, higher fuel costs and declining passenger demand will force mergers and bankruptcies that eventually will lead to a more efficient system.

The airline industry also must deal with an aging capital stock. As of 1993, some 48 percent of the national system's aircraft were more than fifteen years old. To upgrade, Russian airline services have purchased aircraft from Western firms and demanded more modern aircraft from domestic manufacturers.

Water Transportation

Maritime transportation plays an important role in Russian transit, but the country's geography and climate limit the capacity of shipping. Many Russian rivers run from south to north rather than from east to west, constraining their use during the Russian winters.

Russia's major ports providing access to the Baltic Sea are St. Petersburg and Kaliningrad, and Novorossiysk and Sochi are the main Black Sea ports (see fig. 12). Vladivostok, Nakhodka, Magadan, and Petropavlovsk-Kamchatskiy account for the bulk of maritime transportation on the Pacific coast. The largest Arctic port, Murmansk, maintains an ice-free harbor despite its location on the northern shore of the Kola Peninsula. In 1995 Russia's merchant marine had about 800 ships with a gross tonnage of more than 1,000, of which half are standard cargo vessels, about 100 oil tankers, and eighty container ships. Russia also owns 235 ships that are over 1,000 tons and sail under foreign registry. In 1991 the merchant marine carried 464 million tons of cargo.

Navigable inland waterways extend 101,000 kilometers, of which 16,900 kilometers are man-made and 60,400 are navigable at night. Boats of the Russian River Fleet do most of the inland shipping, which accounted for 514 million tons of cargo in 1991. The Russian government has made efforts to decentralize control over water transportation and to separate control of liners from ports.

Pipelines

Natural gas and petroleum pipelines play a crucial role in Russia's economy, both in distributing fuel to domestic industrial consumers and in supporting exports to Europe and countries of the Commonwealth of Independent States (CIS—see Glossary). Their complex network connects production regions with virtually all of Russia's centers of population and industry. Pipelines are especially important because of the long distances between Siberian oil and gas fields and Russia's European industrial centers as well as countries to the west.

In 1993 Russia had 48,000 kilometers of pipeline carrying crude oil, 15,000 kilometers for petroleum products, and 140,000 kilometers for natural gas. In recent decades, the natural gas lines have expanded at a much faster rate than the crude oil lines. The main natural gas pipeline, one of the Soviet Union's largest international trade projects, connects the natural gas fields of northern Siberia with most of the countries of Western Europe. Completed in 1984, the line passes nearly 4,000 kilometers across the Ural Mountains, the Volga River, and many other natural obstacles to connect Russian lines with the European system.

Also completed in the early 1980s, the Northern Lights natural gas line runs from the Vuktyl field in the Republic of Komi to Eastern Europe. The Orenburg pipeline was built in the late 1970s to bring gas from the Orenburg field in Russia and the Karachaganak field in northern Kazakstan to Eastern Europe.

Many of Russia's major oil pipelines parallel gas lines. A trunk oil line runs eastward from the Volga-Ural fields to Irkutsk on Lake Baikal, westward from those fields into Ukraine and Latvia, and southwest to connect with the North Caucasus oil fields and refineries; the line is joined by a line from the oil center at Surgut in the West Siberian Plain.

Public Transportation

Although the high price and scarcity of passenger automobiles required Soviet citizens to rely on public transportation, Soviet policy makers gave low priority to civilian transportation. Only six Russian cities have underground systems—Moscow, St. Petersburg, Yekaterinburg, Nizhniy Novgorod, Novosibirsk, and Samara. The extensive and decorative Moscow subway sys-

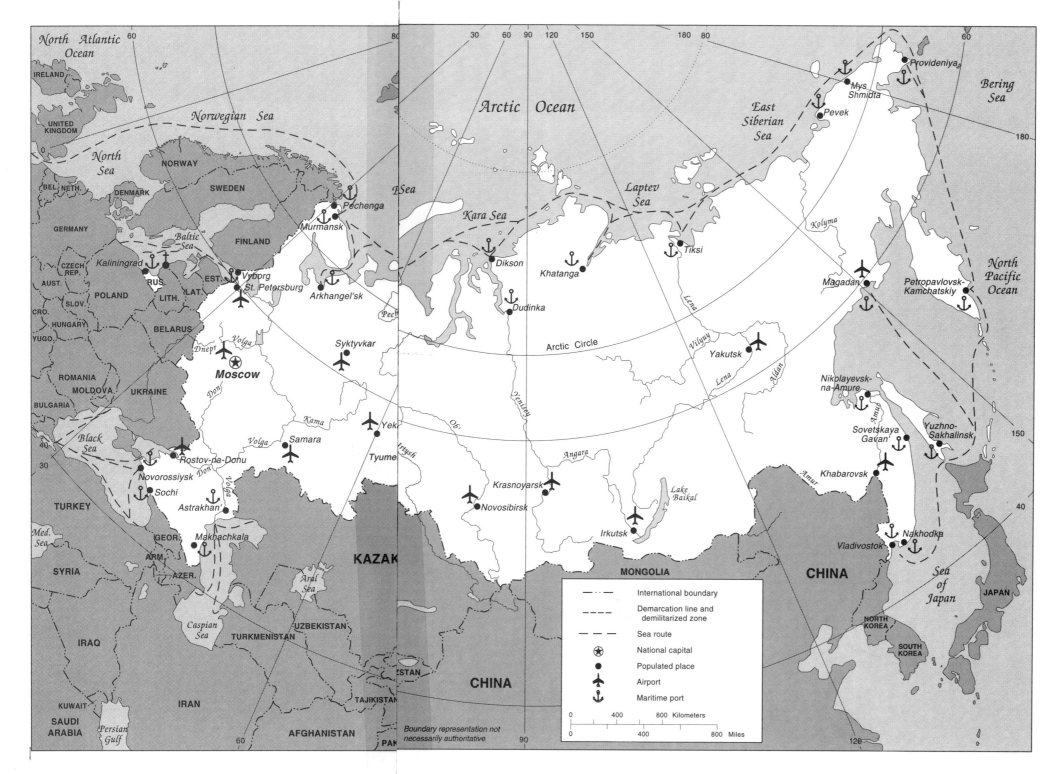

Figure 12. Major Maritime Ports, Airports, and Sea Routes, 1996

366

tem, built in the 1930s as a showpiece of Stalinist engineering, remains the most reliable and inexpensive means of transportation in the nation's capital.

Elsewhere, buses are the main form of public transportation. In cities, tramways supplement bus service, accounting for one-third of the passenger-kilometers that buses travel. The Russian Federation continues the Soviet-era 70 percent state subsidy, which keeps fares artificially low. This subsidy has been a drain on the budget and has blunted the public's demand for alternative modes of transportation. The system's infrastructure and vehicle fleets require extensive repair and modernization.

Transportation Reform

In the first half of the 1990s, market forces shifted some of the demand among the various transportation services. Russian policy makers had not prescribed the proper role of the transportation sector in the new economy. However, officials indicated that Russia will follow the Western model of assuming government regulation of transportation systems while reducing state ownership of those systems.

Many state-owned transportation monopolies have been dissolved, but some monopolies such as public transportation are expected to remain in place. The role of government will be to ensure that the systems are commercially viable and allow private systems to emerge. The government also will continue to be responsible for maintaining the quality and availability of the road, air, and water infrastructure and for maintaining standards of transportation safety.

Telecommunications

By various measures, Russia's telecommunications infrastructure is inferior to that of most developed industrialized countries. In 1991 only 33 percent of Russian households had telephones, compared with 94 percent in the United States. In 1995 Russia had seventeen telephone lines per 100 inhabitants, compared with thirty-six in Spain, forty-four in Belgium, and sixty-nine in Switzerland.

The Soviet Period

During the Soviet period, the state controlled all means of communications and used them primarily to convey decisions and to facilitate the execution of government directives affecting the economy, national security, and administrative governmental functions. The Ministry of Communications had responsibility for most nonmilitary communications, and the Ministry of Defense controlled military communications. Other ministries, including the Ministry of Culture, controlled specialized elements of the communications infrastructure.

Moscow maintained control over communications, and regional and local jurisdictions enjoyed little autonomy. This centralization forced the Soviet Union to acquire the means to deliver signals over a vast area and provided the impetus for the development of satellite communications, which began with the launching of the Molniya satellite communications system in 1965. Despite the success of the satellite system, Soviet technology was unable to meet the rapidly growing informational demands of the 1980s. In that period, the Soviet government began to import digital switching equipment from the West in an effort to modernize the national telephone system. The priority given to military and government applications skewed the distribution of new equipment, and officials dedicated relatively few telephone lines and communications facilities to commercial and residential use. In addition, most communications facilities remained concentrated in a few urban areas at the expense of smaller cities and rural regions.

Telecommunications in the 1990s

Since the breakup of the Soviet Union, Russia has been engaged in the reorganization and modernization of its communications systems. In this process, control over communications has been decentralized and in large part privatized. In domestic telephone and related communications, control devolved to regional and local enterprises, which were then reorganized into joint-stock companies. Long-distance and international service operations were grouped together into a new organization, Russian Telecommunications (Rostelekom), which itself became a joint-stock company. The federal government has retained control over the national satellite system, telecommunications research and development, and education systems through the Ministry of Communications. Despite ownership changes, in 1995 only about 14 percent of Russia's 24.4 million telephones were located outside urban areas, the waiting list for telephone installation included more than 10 million names, and only 34,100 pay telephones were available for long-distance calls.

Hydrofoil on Don River, Rostov-na-Donu
Courtesy Jim Howland

By mid-1994 the Russian telephone communications system had been privatized through the voucher program. Employees of the reorganized companies received about 25 percent of company stock, the government retained some shares, and the remainder were sold at public auction. Telecommunications stocks reportedly have been among the most coveted items on the fledgling Russian stock market. Domestic and foreign investors have been especially attracted to stocks in major regional telephone enterprises such as the Moscow and St. Petersburg telephone systems and Rostelekom. But the state has not relinquished its remaining telecommunications shares, showing reluctance to cede full control to the private sector.

Development of the telecommunications infrastructure depends heavily on foreign funding and joint ventures. The Ministry of Communications expected foreign investment in telecommunications to increase by 24 percent in 1996 over 1995, matching domestic investment of US$520 million. In the mid-1990s, state subsidies continue to fall. According to Western experts, that investment level is far below the amount needed over a prolonged period to modernize Russian lines or even to upgrade existing equipment. However, Russia faces stiff competition for foreign capital because Western and Japanese companies already have made substantial commitments to telecommunications modernization and privatization projects in a number of other countries.

Russia's goals for 1996 were the laying of 1,815 kilometers of cable and the installation of 9,500 kilometers of wireless lines, 5,000 long-distance exchanges, and 1.5 million new private telephone lines in urban and rural areas. The latter addition would bring the national total to 26 million lines.

The regulatory framework for telecommunications in Russia remains weak, but it is maturing. The Law on Communications, enacted in 1995, is the chief statute, but the lines of regulatory authority have not been clearly defined. The Ministry of Communications is the chief regulatory agency for "civilian" communications, but military and national security authorities control their own communications networks outside the purview of the Law on Communications.

As Russia's telecommunications systems develop, the regulatory issues facing the Ministry of Communications include frequency assignments, standardization of equipment, levels of competition, and establishment of optimal user rates. The military and internal security agencies traditionally have had priority use of most wireless frequencies, but the newer and expanding commercial and individual users require more access to frequencies. Standardization is needed so that older equipment can operate with the new models on expanded systems. A uniform policy is needed for regulation of telecommunications competition, which varied in the early post-Soviet years. And the Ministry of Communications has not yet established telephone rates that are affordable to the users but provide enough profit for the company to operate and expand.

The government has promoted competition in some sectors. An example is the licensing of a number of companies to provide specialized, dedicated service networks. For cellular telephone lines, the government has encouraged competition in densely populated areas, such as Moscow and St. Petersburg, while developing single provider systems for small areas where demand is limited. For long-distance service, in the mid-1990s Rostelekom competed with local telephone companies for revenues in the potentially lucrative area of interzonal communications. In addition, Rostelekom is facing competition from newer companies that are able to provide long-distance service through their own cables and via satellite. Under these conditions, the shape and size of the Russian telephone system is changing rapidly and responding to the demands of the market.

Experts estimate that Russia must expand its telephone networks from around 24 million telephones to between 75 million and 80 million and provide the modern switching equipment with which they can operate. They further expect that Russia will require an investment of US$150 billion to bring its telephone system up to modern standards. Russia has imported Western equipment in the modernization effort, but this strategy has proved very costly. The Russian equipment industry is trying to revive itself and develop indigenous technology to fulfill its needs.

Foreign investors could be an important source of capital and technology in the Russian telecommunications sector, but in the mid-1990s Russian laws and regulations limited foreign participation to the supply of equipment and services that would not hurt domestic producers. The Law on Communications gives preference to domestically produced equipment, with the major exception of cellular phone production, where officials have welcomed foreign participation. Domestic telephone services are the domain of Russian companies, but foreign companies have established a presence in domestic and international long-distance service.

Russian radio and television are undergoing similar changes (see The Broadcast Media, ch. 7). The programming facilities and transmission operations are separate, as they were in the Soviet system when the central government controlled all of these facilities. After the breakup of the Soviet Union, Russian radio and television programming operations were decentralized at the regional and local levels.

In the mid-1990s, three major countrywide state-owned programming companies provide most programming for the country. They are Russian Public Television (Obshchestvennoye rossiyskoye televideniye—ORT), Russian State Television, and St. Petersburg Television, which primarily serves the St. Petersburg metropolitan area. In 1995 Russian State Television was partially privatized when 49 percent of its shares were sold to private companies, but the company remains under state control.

The privatization process moved large blocks of shares into the hands of banks and powerful entrepreneurs, who formed communications and newspaper empires and used close connections in the Government to lobby for the release of additional state shares in the broadcasting enterprises. In 1996 the two most powerful broadcast entrepreneurs were former banker Vladimir Gusinskiy, head of the Media-Most holding company including the Independent Television (Nezavisimoye televideniye—NTV) network and several prominent periodicals, and Boris Berezovskiy, an automobile entrepreneur whose organization, Logovaz, now controls ORT as well as banking, oil, aviation, and print media enterprises.

Privately owned and operated, independent programming companies are playing a growing role in Russian radio and television programming. As of 1995, some 800 companies were in existence. In 1996 the largest private television channels are TV–6, which reaches sixty cities in Russia and elsewhere with a potential audience of 600 million viewers, and NTV, which serves European Russia and has a potential audience of 100 million viewers. Both companies were founded in 1993.

Transmission facilities are state-owned, and programmers must pay fees to the transmission companies to have their material broadcast. The fee establishment mechanism remains an issue in Russian telecommunications policy. Control over transmission gives the government powerful leverage over the content of broadcasts. In 1996 independent companies were considering cable and direct satellite television services to get into the state-dominated market as transmission providers. In 1992 some 48.5 million radios and 54.9 million televisions were in use.

Because the Law on Communications does not address the question of airtime allocation, policy makers also must grapple with that issue. Subsidies for radio and television broadcasters, including state-owned operations, have been reduced drastically in the first half of the 1990s, meaning that programmers must rely on advertising revenues.

Foreign Economic Relations

Integrating the Russian economy with the rest of the world through commerce and expanded foreign investment has been a high priority of Russian economic reform. Russia has joined the IMF and the World Bank and has applied to join the World Trade Organization (WTO—see Glossary) and the OECD. It also has been included in some functions of the Group of Seven (G–7; see Glossary).

Sellers from Mongolia at outdoor market, Khabarovsk
Courtesy Floyd Reichman

Foreign Trade

By the end of 1993, the Russian government had liberalized much of its import regime. It eliminated nontariff customs barriers on most imports, although it still requires some licenses for health and safety reasons. In mid-1992 the government took control of imports of some critical goods, including industrial equipment and food items, which it sold to end users at subsidized prices. In the early 1990s, government-controlled imports constituted about 40 percent of total Russian imports, but by 1996 most such controls had been phased out.

Russia also established a two-column tariff regime in harmony with the United States and other members of the General Agreement on Tariffs and Trade (GATT), which in January 1995 became the WTO. Russia differentiates between those trade partners that receive most-favored-nation trade treatment and, therefore, relatively low tariffs, and those that do not.

Although Russia has eliminated many nontariff import barriers, it still maintains high tariffs and other duties on imports of goods to raise revenue and protect domestic producers. All imports are subject to a 3 percent special tax in addition to import tariffs that vary with the category of goods. Some of the high tariffs include those of 40 to 50 percent on automobiles and aircraft and 100 percent on alcoholic beverages. Excise taxes ranging between 35 and 250 percent are applied to certain luxury goods that include automobiles, jewelry, alcohol, and cigarettes.

The Government has used licensing and quotas to restrict the export of certain key commodities, such as oil and oil products, to ease the effect of price differentials between controlled domestic prices and world market prices. Without such restrictions, Russian policy makers have argued, the domestic market would experience shortages of critical materials. The government finally eliminated quotas on oil exports in 1995 and export taxes on oil in 1996. In addition to customs restrictions, the government imposes other costs on exporters. It charges a 20 percent VAT on most cash-transaction exports and a 30 percent VAT on barter transactions. It applies additional tariffs on the exports of industrial raw materials. By the mid-1990s, much of Russia's foreign trade, even that with the former communist countries of Central Europe, was conducted on the basis of market-determined prices. Immediately after the dissolution of the Soviet-dominated Comecon in 1991, the Soviet Union sought to maintain commercial relations in Central Europe through bilateral agreements. But as market economies developed in those countries, their governments lost control over trade flows. Since 1993 Russian trade with former Comecon member countries has been at world prices and in hard currencies.

In the mid-1990s, Russia still maintained hybrid trade regimes with the other former Soviet states, reflecting the web of economic interdependence that had dominated commercial relations within the Soviet Union. The sharp decrease in central economic control that occurred just before and after the breakup of the Soviet Union virtually destroyed distribution channels between suppliers and producers and between producers and consumers throughout the region. Many of the non-Russian republics were dependent on Russian oil and natural gas, timber, and other raw materials. Russia bought food and other consumer goods from some of the other Soviet republics. To ease the effects of the transition, Russia concluded bilateral agreements with the other former Soviet states to maintain the flow of goods. But, as in the case of the Central European agreements, such arrangements proved impractical; by the mid-1990s, they covered only a small range of goods.

Russia now conducts trade with former Soviet states under various regimes, including free-trade arrangements and most-favored-nation trading status.

The volume of Russia's foreign trade has generally declined since the beginning of the economic transition. Trade volume peaked in 1990 and then declined sharply in 1991 and 1992. Between 1992 and 1995, however, exports rose from US$39.7 billion to US$77.8 billion, and imports rose from US$34.7 billion to US$57.9 billion. Many factors contributed to the decline of the early 1990s: the collapse of Comecon and trade relations with Eastern/Central Europe; the rapid decline of the domestic demand for imports; contraction in foreign currency reserves; a decline in the real exchange value of the ruble; the Government's imposition of high tariffs, VATs, and excess taxes on imports; and the reduction of state subsidies on some key imports. Russia's declining production of crude oil, a key export, also has contributed significantly. Until 1994 Russia's arms exports declined sharply because the military-industrial complex's production fell and international sanctions were placed on large-scale customers such as Iraq and Libya (see Foreign Arms Sales, ch. 9).

The geographical distribution of Russian foreign trade changed radically in the first half of the 1990s (see table 21; table 22, Appendix). In 1985 some 55 percent of Soviet exports and 54 percent of Soviet imports were with the Comecon countries. By contrast, 26 percent of Soviet exports and 28 percent of Soviet imports were with the fully developed market economies of Western Europe, Japan, the United States, and Canada. By the end of 1991, Russia and its former allies of Central Europe were actively seeking new markets. In 1991 only 23 percent of Russian exports and 24 percent of Russian imports were with the former Comecon member states. In 1994 some 27 percent of Russian imports and 22 percent of exports involved partners from Central Europe, with Poland, Hungary, and the Czech Republic generating the largest volume in both directions. Western Europe's share of Russian trade continued to grow, and in 1994 some 35 percent of Russia's imports and 36 percent of its exports were with countries in that region. Germany was by far the West European leader in exports and imports, and Switzerland and Britain were other large export customers. In 1994 the United States accounted for US$2.1 billion (5.3 percent) of imports and US$3.7 billion (5.9 percent) of exports; however, United States purchases of Russian goods had increased by more than 500 percent between 1992 and 1994. The total value of trade with the United States in 1995 was US$7 billion; trade for the first half of 1996 proceeded at virtually the same rate (see table 23, Appendix).

Russian trade with the so-called near abroad—the other former Soviet states—has greatly deteriorated. This trend began before the final collapse of the Soviet Union as Russian producers sought hard-currency markets for raw materials and other exportables. As Russia raised fuel prices closer to world market levels, the other republics found it increasingly difficult to pay for Russian oil and natural gas. The RCB extended credits to these countries to permit some shipments, but eventually the accumulation of large arrearages forced the Russian government to curtail shipments. At the end of 1995, Russian trade with the near abroad accounted for 17 percent of total Russian trade, down from 59 percent in 1991. Belarus, Kazakstan, and Ukraine remained Russia's largest partners, as they had been in the Soviet era. The failure to restore inter-republic trade was an important factor in the economic collapse that gripped the region around 1990.

Raw materials, especially oil, natural gas, metals, and minerals, have dominated Russia's exports, accounting for 65 percent of total exports in 1993. Exports as a whole are heavily concentrated in a few product categories. In 1995 ten commodities, all of which are raw materials, accounted for 70 percent of Russian exports. By contrast, for the United States the top ten export commodities account for only 37 percent of its exports.

The lack of diversity in Russian exports is a legacy of the Soviet period, when the central planning regime called for production of manufactured goods for domestic consumption with little consideration for the export market. Given this priority, most of the Soviet Union's consumer goods were of low quality by world standards. Post-Soviet concentration of Russian exportables in a few categories restricts Russia's potential sources of foreign currency to a few markets. And the frequent price fluctuations typical of world raw materials markets also make Russia's export revenues vulnerable to unforeseen change.

Manufactured goods dominate Russian imports, accounting for 68 percent of total imports in 1992. The largest categories of imported manufactured goods are machinery and equipment (29 percent of the total); foods, 16 percent; and textiles and shoes, 13 percent.

Foreign Investment

Foreign investment is the second major element of Russia's reform strategy to strengthen international economic links. From the late 1920s to the late 1980s, the Soviet government prohibited foreign investment because it would have undermined the state's decision-making prerogatives on investment, production, and consumption.

The *perestroika* economic reforms of the late 1980s permitted limited foreign investment in the Soviet Union in the form of joint ventures. The first joint-venture law, which went into effect in June 1987, restricted foreign ownership to 49 percent of the venture and required that Soviet administrators fill the positions of chairman and general manager. By 1991, however, the Soviet government allowed foreign entities 100 percent ownership of subsidiaries in Russia.

Although limited in scope, the joint-venture law did open the door to direct foreign investment in the Soviet Union, which provided Russia's economy wider access to Western capital, technology, and management know-how. But the overall limitations of *perestroika* hampered the joint-venture program. The nonconvertibility of the Russian ruble was an impediment to repatriation of profits by foreign investors, private property was not recognized, government price controls remained in effect, and most of the Soviet economy remained under state control.

The Yeltsin government's commitment to foreign investment has been hampered in some cases by Russia's ongoing debates about the appropriate relationship with the West and about the amount of assistance that Russia should accept from the capitalist countries. Substantial political factions view the infusion of foreign capital as a device for Western governments to intrude on Russia's sovereignty and manipulate its economic condition, and they advocate a more independent course.

The Foreign Investment Law of 1991 provides the statutory foundation for the treatment of foreign investment. The law provides for "national treatment" of foreign investments; that is, foreign investors and investments are to be treated no less favorably than domestically based investments. The law also permits foreign investment in most sectors of the Russian economy and in all the forms available in the Russian economy: portfolios of government securities, stocks, and bonds, and direct investment in new businesses, in the acquisition of existing Russian-owned enterprises, in joint ventures, in property acquisition, and in leasing the rights to natural resources. Foreign investors are protected against nationalization or expropriation unless the government declares that such a procedure is necessary in the public interest. In such cases, foreign investors are to receive just compensation.

In response to demands by foreign oil investors for stronger legal guarantees before making large capital commitments, in July 1995 the State Duma passed the Law on Oil and Gas. It provides a basic framework for other laws and regulations pertaining to exploration, production, transportation, and security of oil and gas. In late 1995, the Duma passed the Production-Sharing Agreement bill, which provides for foreign investors to share output with domestic partners. Among other things, the bill lifts many of the financial impediments by removing excise and customs duties on the exportation of oil by joint ventures, and it requires contract sanctity for the life of the project. But in a clause that drew criticism from the United States business community, the bill requires State Duma approval of new joint-venture agreements on a case-by-case basis. As of mid-1996, the United States Department of Commerce considered the Duma's veto power over such agreements a key obstacle to expanded United States investment in Russia.

By the end of 1995, foreign investment in Russia since 1991 had totaled an estimated US$6 billion, a small amount considering the size of the Russian economy. Of that amount, US$3.2 billion had been invested between 1991 and 1993 and US$1 billion in 1994. Of the approximately US$2 billion invested in 1995, about 28 percent came from the United States, 13 percent from Germany, 9 percent from Switzerland, and 6 percent from Belgium. By sector, 15 percent of 1995 investments went to trade and catering; 13 percent to finance, insurance, and pensions; 10 percent to the fuel industries; and 8 percent to chemical industries. Telecommunications, food processing and agriculture, pharmaceuticals and medical equipment, and housing are in particular need of additional foreign investment.

Russia's overall investment climate has not been robust because of high inflation, a plunging GDP, an unstable exchange rate, an uncertain legal and political environment, and the capricious enactment and implementation of tax and regulatory regimes. Nevertheless, experts predict that improvement in those conditions will bring a strong increase in foreign activity.

Foreign Debt

Russia inherited a large foreign debt burden from the Soviet Union that clouds its economic situation. Throughout its history, the Soviet Union was a conservative borrower of foreign credits. Its ability to manage international accounts allowed the Soviet Union to obtain both government-guaranteed and commercial credits on favorable terms. But, by the end of the 1980s, the Soviet hard-currency debt had increased appreciably. At the end of 1991, the debt was estimated at US$65 billion, an increase of over 100 percent since the end of 1986.

By arrangement with the other former Soviet states and its creditors, Russia accepted responsibility for repayment of the Soviet Union's entire debt, in exchange for control of some of the overseas assets of the other republics. In January 1996, Russia's total foreign debt was US$120.4 billion, including US$103 billion of the Soviet Union's debt that Russia assumed. Russia has been hard pressed to service that amount.

In March 1996, the IMF approved a three-year loan of US$10.1 billion to Russia. At that point, Russia already had US$10.8 billion in outstanding IMF debts. The first loan payment of US$340 million was paid almost immediately, and it helped Russia to overcome a large budget deficit that it had been trying to cover by issuing securities. The IMF made the early monthly payments of the loan during Russia's 1996 presidential election campaign, despite Russia's failure to comply with several loan requirements. However, once Yeltsin had been reelected, the IMF withheld the July payment because Russia's hard-currency reserves had been severely depleted during the campaign and the tax collection system remained unsatisfactory.

In April 1996, the Paris Club of seventeen lending nations agreed to the largest debt rescheduling procedure in the history of the organization by postponing US$40 billion of Russian debt in order to assist Russia in meeting its international debt payments. The agreement followed the November 1995 provisional accord with the London Club of international commercial bank lenders (which spread repayment of US$32.5 billion over a twenty-five-year period) and the IMF loan of US$10.1 billion in March 1996. The new schedule gave Russia a six-year grace period for repayment on the principal it owes.

The Economic Outlook

In the first half-decade after the end of the Soviet Union, Russia made significant strides in restructuring its economy and providing an environment for the operation of market forces rather than state control as the fundamental principle of the economic system. By 1995 more than half of the recorded GDP came from the private sector, with considerable unreported private activity also contributing to the vitality of the economy. Almost all prices are now market determined. Most of Russia's state enterprises have been placed under some degree of private control, although many continue to operate in much the same way as before privatization. By making the ruble convertible in foreign trade and other current-account transactions, Russia has accelerated the integration of its economy with those of the rest of the world.

These strides have come at a cost, however. The Russian economy has endured a severe contraction that experts predict will not end before late 1996 or 1997. Many Russians are experiencing the new and disillusioning phenomenon of unemployment as the growing private sector slowly absorbs an increasingly large labor pool jettisoned in the restructuring of the state sector. Many, particularly those of middle age, are finding it difficult to adjust to the loss of the cradle-to-grave social safety net of the Soviet system. The gap between Russia's "haves" and "have-nots," which is determined by the possession of skills, audacity, and connections needed to be successful under the new economic system, widened alarmingly in the mid-1990s.

Despite major problems, Russia is not likely to turn back the clock on economic reform, although periodic slowdowns are likely to recur. Western experts consider the results of the June–July 1996 presidential elections an encouraging sign that the government will not leave the path of conversion upon which Yeltsin embarked in 1990. But Russia's market economy remains partially formed, with some parts far advanced and others lagging behind. Critical, unfilled needs include the following: substantial improvement in the taxation system, which is poorly enforced and fails to encourage private initiative or foreign investment; a comprehensive rather than a piecemeal set of commercial laws to establish consistent business conditions; continued reform of the banking system, including removal of corrupt elements and ineffectual commercial banks; continuation of meaningful privatization, including reform of voucher distribution, expansion of the entrepreneurial class, and restoration of public confidence in privatization as more than redistribution of wealth among the entrepreneurial elite; continued government spending discipline (something forsaken completely during Yeltsin's 1996 campaign) to keep exchange rates, budget deficits, and inflation under control; establishment of agencies to promote trade and distribute information; and wage reform to ensure timely payment and gradually relieve the intense social pressure caused by the increase of the have-not part of Russia's population.

Yeltsin's appointment of reform economist Anatoliy Chubays as his chief of staff in July 1996 was a signal that the advocates of strong reform might overcome the factions that had blocked or weakened reform legislation in the State Duma. But political battles will continue over the speed and wisdom of market-oriented reform because strong vested interests continue to advocate state control of remaining economic assets, or even reassumption of state control of privatized assets. As the first five years have demonstrated, the road to economic reform in Russia is not straight or short, but, given continued outside assistance and political stability, the chances of further progress seem reasonably good.

$$* \quad * \quad *$$

A number of recent studies provide in-depth coverage of various aspects of the Russian economy. The PlanEcon series *Review and Outlook for the Former Soviet Republics* offers short summaries of most aspects of the economy, with forecasts of trends for the near future. The Economist Intelligence Unit's quarterly *Country Report: Russia* analyzes key economic indicators against the background of political and international conditions, with statistical information. The Congressional Research Service of the Library of Congress and the World Bank have issued series of useful studies on individual aspects of the economy and the reform program, with the latter concentrating on conditions for investment and business activity. The Organisation for Economic Co-operation and Development (OECD) offers its 1995 economic survey on the Russian Federation, a detailed analysis of the entire domestic economic structure and its supporting elements. *Energy Policies of the Russian Federation: 1995 Survey*, from the OECD's International Energy Agency, analyzes the status and potential of Russia's energy sector.

Anders Aslund's *How Russia Became a Market Economy* describes the reform process from the 1980s through 1995. The World Bank's *Statistical Handbook 1995: States of the Former USSR* provides indicative statistics on various economic categories. The Foreign Broadcast Information Service's *Daily Report: Central Eurasia* includes periodic economic reviews devoted to statistical and textual analysis of economic trends in Russia and elsewhere in the CIS. *Russian Federation: Report on the National Accounts* is an in-depth 1995 report on Russia's financial status by a team from the World Bank and Russia's State Committee for Statistics (Gosudarstvennyy komitet po statistike). (For further information and complete citations, see Bibliography.)

Chapter 7. Government and Politics

Lyudmila, a captive of the evil dwarf Chernomor, walks in the dwarf's beauti-ful garden while awaiting rescue (design from lacquer box made in village of Kholuy).

SINCE GAINING ITS INDEPENDENCE with the collapse of the Soviet Union at the end of 1991, Russia (formally, the Russian Federation) has faced serious challenges in its efforts to forge a political system to follow nearly seventy-five years of centralized, totalitarian rule. For instance, leading figures in the legislative and executive branches have put forth opposing views of Russia's political direction and the governmental instruments that should be used to follow it. That conflict reached a climax in September and October 1993, when President Boris N. Yeltsin used military force to dissolve the parliament and called for new legislative elections. This event marked the end of Russia's first constitutional period, which was defined by the much-amended constitution adopted by the Russian Republic in 1978. A new constitution, creating a strong presidency, was approved by referendum in December 1993.

With a new constitution and a new parliament representing diverse parties and factions, Russia's political structure subsequently showed signs of stabilization. However, since that time Russians have continued to debate the future of their political system, with Western-style democracy and authoritarianism being two widely considered alternatives. As the transition period extended into the mid-1990s, the power of the national government continued to wane as Russia's regions gained political and economic concessions from Moscow. Although the struggle between the executive and the legislative branches was partially resolved by the new constitution, the two branches continued to represent fundamentally opposing visions of Russia's future. The executive was the center of reform, and the lower house of the parliament, the State Duma, was a bastion of antireform communists and nationalists.

Historical Background

The Soviet Union formally came into being under the treaty of union in December 1922, which was signed by Russia and three other union republics—Belorussia (now Belarus), Ukraine, and what was then the Transcaucasian Soviet Federated Socialist Republic (an entity including Armenia, Azerbaijan, and Georgia). Under the treaty, Russia became known officially as the Russian Soviet Federated Socialist Republic

(RSFSR). The treaty of union was incorporated into the first Soviet constitution, which was promulgated in 1924. Nominally, the borders of each subunit were drawn to incorporate the territory of a specific nationality. The constitution endowed the new republics with sovereignty, although they were said to have voluntarily delegated most of their sovereign powers to the Soviet center. Formal sovereignty was evidenced by the existence of flags, constitutions, and other state symbols, and by the republics' constitutionally guaranteed "right" to secede from the union. Russia was the largest of the union republics in terms of territory and population. Ethnic Russians dominated Soviet politics and government; they also controlled local administration.

Because of the Russians' dominance in the affairs of the union, the RSFSR failed to develop some of the institutions of governance and administration that were typical of public life in the other republics: a republic-level communist party, a Russian academy of sciences, and Russian branches of trade unions, for example. As the titular nationalities of the other fourteen union republics began to call for greater republic rights in the late 1980s, however, ethnic Russians also began to demand the creation or strengthening of various specifically Russian institutions in the RSFSR. Certain policies of Soviet leader Mikhail S. Gorbachev (in office 1985–91) also encouraged nationalities in the union republics, including the Russian Republic, to assert their rights. These policies included *glasnost* (literally, public voicing—see Glossary), which made possible open discussion of democratic reforms and long-ignored public problems such as pollution. *Glasnost* also brought constitutional reforms that led to the election of new republic legislatures with substantial blocs of pro-reform representatives.

In Russia a new legislature, called the Congress of People's Deputies, was elected in March 1990 in a largely free and competitive vote. Upon convening in May, the congress elected Boris N. Yeltsin, a onetime Gorbachev protégé who had been exiled from the top party echelon because of his radical reform proposals, as president of the congress's permanent working body, the Supreme Soviet. The next month, the congress declared Russia's sovereignty over its natural resources and the primacy of Russia's laws over those of the central Soviet government. During 1990–91, the RSFSR enhanced its sovereignty by establishing republic branches of organizations such as the communist party, the Academy of Sciences (see Glossary) of the Soviet Union, radio and television broadcasting facilities, and the Committee for State Security (Komitet gosudarstven-noy bezopasnosti—KGB; see Glossary). In 1991 Russia created a new executive office, the presidency, following the example of Gorbachev, who had created such an office for himself in 1990. Russia held a popular election that conferred legitimacy on the office, whereas Gorbachev had eschewed such an election and had himself appointed by the Soviet parliament. Despite Gorbachev's attempts to discourage Russia's electorate from voting for him, Yeltsin was popularly elected as president in June 1991, handily defeating five other candidates with more than 57 percent of the vote.

Yeltsin used his role as president to trumpet Russian sovereignty and patriotism, and his legitimacy as president was a major cause of the collapse of the coup by hard-line government and party officials against Gorbachev in August 1991. The coup leaders had attempted to overthrow Gorbachev in order to halt his plan to sign a confederation treaty that they believed would wreck the Soviet Union. Yeltsin defiantly opposed the coup plotters and called for Gorbachev's restoration, rallying the Russian public. Most important, Yeltsin's opposition led elements in the "power ministries" that controlled the military, the police, and the KGB to refuse to obey the orders of the coup plotters. The opposition led by Yeltsin, combined with the irresolution of the plotters, caused the coup to collapse after three days.

Following the failed coup, Gorbachev found a fundamentally changed constellation of power, with Yeltsin in de facto control of much of a sometimes recalcitrant Soviet administrative apparatus. Although Gorbachev returned to his position as Soviet president, events began to bypass him. Communist party activities were suspended. Most of the union republics quickly declared their independence, although many appeared willing to sign Gorbachev's vaguely delineated confederation treaty. The Baltic states achieved full independence, and they quickly received diplomatic recognition from many nations. Gorbachev's rump government recognized the independence of Estonia, Latvia, and Lithuania in August and September 1991.

In late 1991, the Yeltsin government assumed budgetary control over Gorbachev's rump government. Russia did not declare its independence, and Yeltsin continued to hope that some form of confederation could be established. In December, one week after the Ukrainian Republic approved independence by referendum, Yeltsin and the leaders of Ukraine and Belarus met to form the Commonwealth of Independent States (CIS—see Glossary). In response to calls by the Central Asian and other union republics for admission, another meeting was held in Alma-Ata, on December 21, to form an expanded CIS. At that meeting, all parties declared that the 1922 treaty of union creating the Soviet Union was annulled and that the Soviet Union had ceased to exist. Gorbachev announced the decision officially December 25. Russia gained international recognition as the principal successor to the Soviet Union, receiving the Soviet Union's permanent seat on the United Nations Security Council and positions in other international and regional organizations. The CIS states also agreed that Russia initially would take over Soviet embassies and other properties abroad.

In October 1991, during the "honeymoon" period after his resistance to the Soviet coup, Yeltsin convinced the legislature to grant him important special executive powers for one year so that he might implement his economic reforms. In November 1991, he appointed a new government, with himself as acting prime minister, a post he held until the appointment of Yegor Gaydar as acting prime minister in June 1992.

During 1992 Yeltsin and his reforms came under increasing attack by former communist party members and officials, extreme nationalists, and others calling for reform to be slowed or halted in Russia. A locus of this opposition was increasingly the bicameral parliament, whose upper house was the Congress of People's Deputies (CPD) and lower house the Supreme Soviet. The lower house was headed by Ruslan Khasbulatov, who became Yeltsin's most vocal opponent. Under the 1978 constitution, the parliament was the supreme organ of power in Russia. After Russia added the office of president in 1991, the division of powers between the two branches was ambiguous.

Although Yeltsin managed to beat back most challenges to his reform program when the CPD met in April 1992, in December he suffered a significant loss of his special executive powers. The CPD ordered him to halt appointments of administrators in the localities and also the practice of naming additional local oversight emissaries (termed "presidential representatives"). Yeltsin also lost the power to issue special decrees concerning the economy, while retaining his constitu-

Placard of Mikhail Gorbachev
as Nazi at procommunist rally,
Moscow, 1991
Courtesy Michael E. Samojeden

tional power to issue decrees in accordance with existing laws. When his attempt to secure confirmation of Gaydar as prime minister was rejected, Yeltsin appointed Viktor Chernomyrdin, whom the parliament approved because he was viewed as more economically conservative than Gaydar. After contentious negotiations between the parliament and Yeltsin, the two sides agreed to hold a national referendum to allow the population to determine the basic division of powers between the two branches of government. In the meantime, proposals for extreme limitation of Yeltsin's power were tabled.

However, early 1993 saw increasing tension between Yeltsin and the parliament over the language of the referendum and power sharing. In mid-March 1993, an emergency session of the CPD rejected Yeltsin's proposals on power sharing and canceled the referendum, again opening the door to legislation that would shift the balance of power away from the president. Faced with these setbacks, Yeltsin addressed the nation directly to announce a "special regime," under which he would assume extraordinary executive power pending the results of a referendum on the timing of new legislative elections, on a new constitution, and on public confidence in the president and vice president. After the Constitutional Court declared his announcement unconstitutional, Yeltsin backed down (see The Judiciary, this ch.).

Despite Yeltsin's change of heart, a second extraordinary session of the CPD took up discussion of emergency measures to defend the constitution, including impeachment of the president. Although the impeachment vote failed, the CPD set new terms for a popular referendum. The legislature's version of the referendum asked whether citizens had confidence in Yeltsin, approved of his reforms, and supported early presidential and legislative elections. Under the CPD's terms, Yeltsin would need the support of 50 percent of eligible voters, rather than 50 percent of those actually voting, to avoid an early presidential election. In the vote on April 25, Russians failed to provide this level of approval, but a majority of voters approved Yeltsin's policies and called for new legislative elections. Yeltsin termed the results, which were a serious blow to the prestige of the parliament, a mandate for him to continue in power.

In June 1993, Yeltsin decreed the creation of a special constitutional convention to examine the draft constitution that he had presented in April. This convention was designed to circumvent the parliament, which was working on its own draft constitution. As expected, the two main drafts contained contrary views of legislative-executive relations. The convention, which included delegates from major political and social organizations and the eighty-nine subnational jurisdictions, approved a compromise draft constitution in July 1993, incorporating some aspects of the parliament's draft. The parliament failed to approve the draft, however.

In late September 1993, Yeltsin responded to the impasse in legislative-executive relations by repeating his announcement of a constitutional referendum, but this time he followed the announcement by dissolving the parliament and announcing new legislative elections for December. The CPD again met in emergency session, confirmed Vice President Aleksandr Rutskoy as president, and voted to impeach Yeltsin. On September 27, military units surrounded the legislative building (popularly known as the White House), but 180 delegates refused to leave the building. After a two-week standoff, Rutskoy urged supporters outside the legislative building to overcome Yeltsin's military forces. Firefights and destruction of property resulted at several locations in Moscow. The next day, under the direction of Minister of Defense Pavel Grachev, tanks fired on the White House, and military forces occupied the building and the rest of the city. This open, violent confrontation remained a backdrop to Yeltsin's relations with the legislative branch for the next three years.

The Constitution and Government Structure

During 1992–93 Yeltsin had argued that the existing, heavily amended 1978 constitution of Russia was obsolete and self-contradictory and that Russia required a new constitution granting the president greater power. This assertion led to the submission and advocacy of rival constitutional drafts drawn up by the legislative and executive branches. The parliament's failure to endorse a compromise was an important factor in Yeltsin's dissolution of the body in September 1993. Yeltsin then used his presidential powers to form a sympathetic constitutional assembly, which quickly produced a draft constitution providing for a strong executive, and to shape the outcome of the December 1993 referendum on Russia's new basic law. The referendum vote resulted in approval by 58.4 percent of Russia's registered voters. The announced 54.8 percent turnout met the requirement that at least 50 percent of registered voters participate in the referendum.

The 1993 constitution declares Russia a democratic, federative, law-based state with a republican form of government. State power is divided among the legislative, executive, and judicial branches. Diversity of ideologies and religions is sanctioned, and a state or compulsory ideology may not be adopted. The right to a multiparty political system is upheld. The content of laws must be made public before they take effect, and they must be formulated in accordance with international law and principles. Russian is proclaimed the state language, although the republics of the federation are allowed to establish their own state languages for use alongside Russian (see The Russian Language, ch. 4).

The Executive Branch

The 1993 constitution created a dual executive consisting of a president and prime minister, but the president is the dominant figure. Russia's strong presidency sometimes is compared with that of Charles de Gaulle (in office 1958–69) in the French Fifth Republic. The constitution spells out many prerogatives specifically, but some powers enjoyed by Yeltsin were developed in an ad hoc manner.

Presidential Powers

Russia's president determines the basic direction of Russia's domestic and foreign policy and represents the Russian state within the country and in foreign affairs. The president appoints and recalls Russia's ambassadors upon consultation with the legislature, accepts the credentials and letters of recall of foreign representatives, conducts international talks, and signs international treaties. A special provision allowed Yeltsin to complete the term prescribed to end in June 1996 and to exercise the powers of the new constitution, although he had been elected under a different constitutional order.

In the 1996 presidential election campaign, some candidates called for reducing or eliminating the presidency, criticizing its powers as dictatorial. Yeltsin defended his presidential powers, claiming that Russians desire "a vertical power structure and a strong hand" and that a parliamentary government would result in indecisive talk rather than action.

Several prescribed powers put the president in a superior position vis-à-vis the legislature. The president has broad authority to issue decrees and directives that have the force of law without legislative review, although the constitution notes that they must not contravene that document or other laws. Under certain conditions, the president may dissolve the State Duma, the lower house of parliament (as a whole, now called the Federal Assembly). The president has the prerogatives of scheduling referendums (a power previously reserved to the parliament), submitting draft laws to the State Duma, and promulgating federal laws.

The executive-legislative crisis of the fall of 1993 prompted Yeltsin to emplace constitutional obstacles to legislative removal of the president. Under the 1993 constitution, if the president commits "grave crimes" or treason, the State Duma may file impeachment charges with the parliament's upper house, the Federation Council. These charges must be confirmed by a ruling of the Supreme Court that the president's actions constitute a crime and by a ruling of the Constitutional Court that proper procedures in filing charges have been followed (see The Judiciary, this ch.). The charges then must be adopted by a special commission of the State Duma and confirmed by at least two-thirds of State Duma deputies. A two-thirds vote of the Federation Council is required for removal of the president. If the Federation Council does not act within three months, the charges are dropped. If the president is

*Mikhail Gorbachev and Boris Yeltsin confer at session of Supreme
Soviet after 1991 coup, Moscow.
Courtesy Michael E. Samojeden*

removed from office or becomes unable to exercise power
because of serious illness, the prime minister is to temporarily
assume the president's duties; a presidential election then must
be held within three months. The constitution does not provide for a vice president, and there is no specific procedure for
determining whether the president is able to carry out his
duties.

The president is empowered to appoint the prime minister
to chair the Government (called the cabinet or the council of
ministers in other countries), with the consent of the State
Duma. The president chairs meetings of the Government,
which he also may dismiss in its entirety. Upon the advice of the
prime minister, the president can appoint or remove Government members, including the deputy prime ministers. The
president submits candidates to the State Duma for the post of
chairman of the Russian Central Bank (RCB) and may propose
that the State Duma dismiss the chairman (see Banking and
Finance, ch. 6). In addition, the president submits candidates
to the Federation Council for appointment as justices of the
Constitutional Court, the Supreme Court, and the Superior

Court of Arbitration, as well as candidates for the office of procurator general, Russia's chief law enforcement officer (see The Procuracy, ch. 10). The president also appoints justices of federal district courts.

Informal Powers and Power Centers

Many of the president's powers are related to the incumbent's undisputed leeway in forming an administration and hiring staff. The presidential administration is composed of several competing, overlapping, and vaguely delineated hierarchies that historically have resisted efforts at consolidation. In early 1996, Russian sources reported the size of the presidential apparatus in Moscow and the localities at more than 75,000 people, most of them employees of state-owned enterprises directly under presidential control. This structure is similar to, but several times larger than, the top-level apparatus of the Soviet-era Communist Party of the Soviet Union (CPSU—see Glossary).

Former first deputy prime minister Anatoliy Chubays was appointed chief of the presidential administration (chief of staff) in July 1996. Chubays replaced Nikolay Yegorov, a hardline associate of deposed Presidential Security Service chief Aleksandr Korzhakov. Yegorov had been appointed in early 1996, when Yeltsin reacted to the strong showing of antireform factions in the legislative election by purging reformers from his administration. Yeltsin now ordered Chubays, who had been included in that purge, to reduce the size of the administration and the number of departments overseeing the functions of the ministerial apparatus. The six administrative departments in existence at that time dealt with citizens' rights, domestic and foreign policy, state and legal matters, personnel, analysis, and oversight, and Chubays inherited a staff estimated at 2,000 employees. Chubays also received control over a presidential advisory group with input on the economy, national security, and other matters. Reportedly that group had competed with Korzhakov's security service for influence in the Yeltsin administration.

Another center of power in the presidential administration is the Security Council, which was created by statute in mid-1992 (see The Security Council, ch. 8). The 1993 constitution describes the council as formed and headed by the president and governed by statute. Since its formation, it apparently has gradually lost influence in competition with other power cen-

Aleksandr Rutskoy, vice president of Russian Republic, speaks to crowd at parliament building during 1991 coup, Moscow.
Courtesy Michael E. Samojeden

ters in the presidential administration. However, the June 1996 appointment of former army general and presidential candidate Aleksandr Lebed' to head the Security Council improved prospects for the organization's standing. In July 1996, a presidential decree assigned the Security Council a wide variety of new missions. The decree's description of the Security Council's consultative functions was especially vague and wide-ranging, although it positioned the head of the Security Council directly subordinate to the president. As had been the case previously, the Security Council was required to hold meetings at least once a month (see The President, ch. 8).

Other presidential support services include the Control Directorate (in charge of investigating official corruption), the Administrative Affairs Directorate, the Presidential Press Service, and the Protocol Directorate. The Administrative Affairs Directorate controls state dachas, sanatoriums, automobiles, office buildings, and other perquisites of high office for the executive, legislative, and judicial branches of government, a function that includes management of more than 200 state industries with about 50,000 employees. The Committee on Operational Questions, until June 1996 chaired by antireformist Oleg Soskovets, has been described as a "government within a government." Also attached to the presidency are more than two dozen consultative commissions and extrabudgetary "funds."

The president also has extensive powers over military policy. As the commander in chief of the armed forces, the president approves defense doctrine, appoints and removes the high command of the armed forces, and confers higher military ranks and awards (see Command Structure, ch. 9). The president is empowered to declare national or regional states of martial law, as well as states of emergency. In both cases, both chambers of the parliament must be notified immediately. The Federation Council, the upper chamber, has the power to confirm or reject such a decree. The regime of martial law is defined by federal law. The circumstances and procedures for the president to declare a state of emergency are more specifically outlined in federal law than in the constitution. In practice, the Constitutional Court ruled in 1995 that the president has wide leeway in responding to crises within Russia, such as lawlessness in the separatist Republic of Chechnya, and that Yeltsin's action in Chechnya did not require a formal declaration of a state of emergency (see Movements Toward Sovereignty, ch. 4; Chechnya, ch. 9; Security Operations in Chechnya, ch. 10). In 1994 Yeltsin declared a state of emergency in Ingushetia and North Ossetia, two republics beset by intermittent ethnic conflict.

Presidential Elections

The constitution sets few requirements for presidential elections, deferring in many matters to other provisions established by law. The presidential term is set at four years, and the president may serve only two terms. A candidate for president must be a citizen of Russia, at least thirty-five years of age, and a resident of the country for at least ten years. If a president becomes unable to continue in office because of health problems, resignation, impeachment, or death, a presidential election is to be held not more than three months later. In such a situation, the Federation Council is empowered to set the election date.

The Law on Presidential Elections, ratified in May 1995, establishes the legal basis for presidential elections. Based on a draft submitted by Yeltsin's office, the new law included many provisions already contained in the Russian Republic's 1990 election law; alterations included the reduction in the number of signatures required to register a candidate from 2 million to 1 million. The law, which set rigorous standards for fair campaign and election procedures, was hailed by international analysts as a major step toward democratization. Under the law, parties, blocs, and voters' groups register with the Central Electoral Commission (CEC) and designate their candidates. These organizations then are permitted to begin seeking the 1 million signatures needed to register their candidates; no more than 7 percent of the signatures may come from a single federal jurisdiction. The purpose of the 7 percent requirement is to promote candidacies with broad territorial bases and eliminate those supported by only one city or ethnic enclave.

The law requires that at least 50 percent of eligible voters participate in order for a presidential election to be valid. In State Duma debate over the legislation, some deputies had advocated a minimum of 25 percent (which was later incorporated into the electoral law covering the State Duma), warning that many Russians were disillusioned with voting and would not turn out. To make voter participation easier, the law required one voting precinct for approximately every 3,000 voters, with voting allowed until late at night. The conditions for absentee voting were eased, and portable ballot boxes were to be made available on demand. Strict requirements were established for the presence of election observers, including emissaries from all participating parties, blocs, and groups, at polling places and local electoral commissions to guard against tampering and to ensure proper tabulation.

The Law on Presidential Elections requires that the winner receive more than 50 percent of the votes cast. If no candidate receives more than 50 percent of the vote (a highly probable result because of multiple candidacies), the top two vote-getters must face each other in a runoff election. Once the results of the first round are known, the runoff election must be held within fifteen days. A traditional provision allows voters to check off "none of the above," meaning that a candidate in a two-person runoff might win without attaining a majority. Another provision of the election law empowers the CEC to request that the Supreme Court ban a candidate from the election if that candidate advocates a violent transformation of the constitutional order or the integrity of the Russian Federation.

The presidential election of 1996 was a major episode in the struggle between Yeltsin and the Communist Party of the Russian Federation (Kommunisticheskaya partiya Rossiyskoy Federatsii—KPRF), which sought to oust Yeltsin from office and return to power. Yeltsin had banned the Communist Party of the Russian Republic for its central role in the August 1991 coup against the Gorbachev government. As a member of the Politburo and the Secretariat of the banned party, Gennadiy Zyuganov had worked hard to gain its relegalization. Despite Yeltsin's objections, the Constitutional Court cleared the way for the Russian communists to reemerge as the KPRF, headed by Zyuganov, in February 1993. Yeltsin temporarily banned the party again in October 1993 for its role in the Supreme Soviet's just-concluded attempt to overthrow his administration. Beginning in 1993, Zyuganov also led efforts by KPRF deputies to impeach Yeltsin. After the KPRF's triumph in the December 1995 legislative elections, Yeltsin announced that he would run for reelection with the main purpose of safeguarding Russia from a communist restoration.

Although there was speculation that losing parties in the December 1995 election might choose not to nominate presidential candidates, in fact dozens of citizens both prominent and obscure announced their candidacies. After the gathering and review of signature lists, the CEC validated eleven candidates, one of whom later dropped out.

In the opinion polls of early 1996, Yeltsin trailed far behind most of the other candidates; his popularity rating was below 10 percent for a prolonged period. However, a last-minute, intense campaign featuring heavy television exposure, speeches throughout Russia promising increased state expenditures for a wide variety of interest groups, and campaign-sponsored concerts boosted Yeltsin to a 3 percent plurality over Zyuganov in the first round. At that point, Yeltsin took the tactically significant step of appointing first-round presidential candidate Aleksandr Lebed', who had placed third behind Yeltsin and Zyuganov, as head of the Security Council. Yeltsin followed the appointment of Lebed' as the president's top adviser on national security by dismissing several top hard-line members of his entourage who were widely blamed for human rights violations in Chechnya and other mistakes. Despite his virtual disappearance from public view for health reasons shortly thereafter, Yeltsin was able to sustain his central message that Russia should move forward rather than return to its communist past. Zyuganov failed to mount an energetic or convincing second campaign, and three weeks after the first phase of the election, Yeltsin easily defeated his opponent, 54 percent to 40 percent (see table 24, Appendix).

Turnout in the first round was high, with about 70 percent of 108.5 million voters participating. Total turnout in the second round was nearly the same as in the first round. A contingent of almost 1,000 international observers judged the election to be largely fair and democratic, as did the CEC.

Most observers in Russia and elsewhere concurred that the election boosted democratization in Russia, and many asserted that reforms in Russia had become irreversible. Yeltsin had strengthened the institution of regularly contested elections when he rejected calls by business organizations and other groups and some of his own officials to cancel or postpone the balloting because of the threat of violence. The high turnout indicated that voters had confidence that their ballots would count, and the election went forward without incident. The democratization process also was bolstered by Yeltsin's willingness to change key personnel and policies in response to public protests and by his unprecedented series of personal campaign appearances throughout Russia.

The Government (Cabinet)

The constitution prescribes that the Government of Russia, which corresponds to the Western cabinet structure, consist of a prime minister (chairman of the Government), deputy prime ministers, and federal ministers and their ministries and departments. Within one week of appointment by the president and approval by the State Duma, the prime minister must submit to the president nominations for all subordinate Government positions, including deputy prime ministers and federal ministers. The prime minister carries out administration in line with the constitution and laws and presidential decrees. The ministries of the Government, which numbered twenty-four in mid-1996, execute credit and monetary policies and defense, foreign policy, and state security functions; ensure the rule of law and respect for human and civil rights; protect property; and take measures against crime. If the Government issues implementing decrees and directives that are at odds with legislation or presidential decrees, the president may rescind them.

The Government formulates the state budget, submits it to the State Duma, and issues a report on its implementation. In late 1994, the parliament successfully demanded that the Government begin submitting quarterly reports on budget expenditures and adhere to other guidelines on budgetary matters, although the parliament's budgetary powers are limited. If the State Duma rejects a draft budget from the Government, the budget is submitted to a conciliation commission including members from both branches.

Besides the ministries, in 1996 the executive branch included eleven state committees and forty-six state services and agencies, ranging from the State Space Agency (Glavkosmos) to the State Committee for Statistics (Goskomstat). There were also myriad agencies, boards, centers, councils, commissions, and committees. Prime Minister Viktor Chernomyrdin's personal staff was reported to number about 2,000 in 1995.

Chernomyrdin, who had been appointed prime minister in late 1992 to appease antireform factions, established a generally smooth working relationship with Yeltsin. Chernomyrdin proved adept at conciliating hostile domestic factions and at presenting a positive image of Russia in negotiations with other nations. However, as Yeltsin's standing with public opinion plummeted in 1995, Chernomyrdin became one of many Government officials who received public blame from the president for failures in the Yeltsin administration. As part of his presidential campaign, Yeltsin threatened to replace the Chernomyrdin Government if it failed to address pressing social welfare problems in Russia. After the mid-1996 presidential election, however, Yeltsin announced that he would nominate Chernomyrdin to head the new Government.

The Parliament

The 628-member parliament, termed the Federal Assembly, consists of two chambers, the 450-member State Duma (the lower house) and the 178-member Federation Council (the upper house). Russia's legislative body was established by the constitution approved in the December 1993 referendum. The first elections to the Federal Assembly were held at the same time—a procedure criticized by some Russians as indicative of

Yeltsin's lack of respect for constitutional niceties. Under the constitution, the deputies elected in December 1993 were termed "transitional" because they were to serve only a two-year term. In April 1994, legislators, Government officials, and many prominent businesspeople and religious leaders signed a "Civic Accord" proposed by Yeltsin, pledging during the two-year "transition period" to refrain from violence, calls for early presidential or legislative elections, and attempts to amend the constitution. This accord, and memories of the violent confrontation of the previous parliament with Government forces, had some effect in softening political rhetoric during the next two years.

The first legislative elections under the new constitution included a few irregularities. The republics of Tatarstan and Chechnya and Chelyabinsk Oblast boycotted the voting; this action, along with other discrepancies, resulted in the election of only 170 members to the Federation Council. However, by mid-1994 all seats were filled except those of Chechnya, which continued to proclaim its independence. All federal jurisdictions participated in the December 1995 legislative races, although the fairness of voting in Chechnya was compromised by the ongoing conflict there.

The Federal Assembly is prescribed as a permanently functioning body, meaning that it is in continuous session except for a regular break between the spring and fall sessions. This working schedule distinguishes the new parliament from Soviet-era "rubber-stamp" legislative bodies, which met only a few days each year. The new constitution also directs that the two chambers meet separately in sessions open to the public, although joint meetings are held for important speeches by the president or foreign leaders.

Deputies of the State Duma work full-time on their legislative duties; they are not allowed to serve simultaneously in local legislatures or hold Government positions. A transitional clause in the constitution, however, allowed deputies elected in December 1993 to retain their Government employment, a provision that allowed many officials of the Yeltsin administration to serve in the parliament. After the December 1995 legislative elections, nineteen Government officials were forced to resign their offices in order to take up their legislative duties.

Despite its "transitional" nature, the Federal Assembly of 1994–95 approved about 500 pieces of legislation in two years. When the new parliament convened in January 1996, deputies were provided with a catalog of these laws and were directed to work in their assigned committees to fill gaps in existing legislation as well as to draft new laws. A major accomplishment of the 1994–95 legislative sessions was passage of the first two parts of a new civil code, desperately needed to update antiquated Soviet-era provisions. The new code included provisions on contract obligations, rents, insurance, loans and credit, partnership, and trusteeship, as well as other legal standards essential to support the creation of a market economy. Work on several bills that had been in committee or in floor debate in the previous legislature resumed in the new body. Similarly, several bills that Yeltsin had vetoed were taken up again by the new legislature.

Structure of the Federal Assembly

The composition of the Federation Council was a matter of debate until shortly before the 1995 elections. The legislation that emerged in December 1995 over Federation Council objections clarified the constitution's language on the subject by providing ex officio council seats to the heads of local legislatures and administrations in each of the eighty-nine subnational jurisdictions, hence a total of 178 seats. As composed in 1996, the Federation Council included about fifty chief executives of subnational jurisdictions who had been appointed to their posts by Yeltsin during 1991–92, then won popular election directly to the body in December 1993. But the law of 1995 provided for popular elections of chief executives in all subnational jurisdictions, including those still governed by presidential appointees. The individuals chosen in those elections then would assume ex officio seats in the Federation Council.

Each legislative chamber elects a chairman to control the internal procedures of the chamber. The chambers also form committees and commissions to deal with particular types of issues. Unlike committees and commissions in previous Russian and Soviet parliaments, those operating under the 1993 constitution have significant responsibilities in devising legislation and conducting oversight. They prepare and evaluate draft laws, report on draft laws to their chambers, conduct hearings, and oversee implementation of the laws. As of early 1996, there were twenty-eight committees and several ad hoc commissions in the State Duma, and twelve committees and two commissions in the Federation Council. The Federation Council has established fewer committees because of the part-time status of its members, who also hold political office in the subnational jurisdictions. In 1996 most of the committees in both houses were retained in basic form from the previous parliament. According to internal procedure, no deputy may sit on more than one committee. By 1996 many State Duma committees had established subcommittees.

Committee positions are allocated when new parliaments are seated. The general policy calls for allocation of committee chairmanships and memberships among parties and factions roughly in proportion to the size of their representation. In 1994, however, Vladimir Zhirinovskiy's Liberal-Democratic Party of Russia (Liberal'no-demokraticheskaya partiya Rossii—LDPR), which had won the second largest number of seats in the recent election, was denied all but one key chairmanship, that of the State Duma's Committee on Geopolitics.

Legislative Powers

The two chambers of the Federal Assembly possess different powers and responsibilities, with the State Duma the more powerful. The Federation Council, as its name and composition implies, deals primarily with issues of concern to the subnational jurisdictions, such as adjustments to internal borders and decrees of the president establishing martial law or states of emergency. As the upper chamber, it also has responsibilities in confirming and removing the procurator general and confirming justices of the Constitutional Court, the Supreme Court, and the Superior Court of Arbitration, upon the recommendation of the president. The Federation Council also is entrusted with the final decision if the State Duma recommends removing the president from office. The constitution also directs that the Federation Council examine bills passed by the lower chamber dealing with budgetary, tax, and other fiscal measures, as well as issues dealing with war and peace and with treaty ratification.

In the consideration and disposition of most legislative matters, however, the Federation Council has less power than the State Duma. All bills, even those proposed by the Federation Council, must first be considered by the State Duma. If the Federation Council rejects a bill passed by the State Duma, the two chambers may form a conciliation commission to work out a compromise version of the legislation. The State Duma then votes on the compromise bill. If the State Duma objects to the proposals of the upper chamber in the conciliation process, it may vote by a two-thirds majority to send its version to the president for signature. The part-time character of the Federation Council's work, its less developed committee structure, and its lesser powers vis-à-vis the State Duma make it more a consultative and reviewing body than a law-making chamber.

Because the Federation Council initially included many regional administrators appointed by Yeltsin, that body often supported the president and objected to bills approved by the State Duma, which had more anti-Yeltsin deputies. The power of the upper chamber to consider bills passed by the lower chamber resulted in its disapproval of about one-half of such bills, necessitating concessions by the State Duma or votes to override upper-chamber objections. In February 1996, the heads of the two chambers pledged to try to break this habit, but wrangling appeared to intensify in the months that followed.

The State Duma confirms the appointment of the prime minister, although it does not have the power to confirm Government ministers. The power to confirm or reject the prime minister is severely limited. According to the 1993 constitution, the State Duma must decide within one week to confirm or reject a candidate once the president has placed that person's name in nomination. If it rejects three candidates, the president is empowered to appoint a prime minister, dissolve the parliament, and schedule new legislative elections.

The State Duma's power to force the resignation of the Government also is severely limited. It may express a vote of no-confidence in the Government by a majority vote of all members of the State Duma, but the president is allowed to disregard this vote. If, however, the State Duma repeats the no-confidence vote within three months, the president may dismiss the Government. But the likelihood of a second no-confidence vote is virtually precluded by the constitutional provision allowing the president to dissolve the State Duma rather than the Government in such a situation. The Government's position is further buttressed by another constitutional provision that allows the Government at any time to demand a vote of confidence from the State Duma; refusal is grounds for the president to dissolve the Duma.

The Legislative Process

Draft laws may originate in either legislative chamber, or they may be submitted by the president, the Government, local legislatures, the Supreme Court, the Constitutional Court, or the Superior Court of Arbitration. Draft laws are first considered in the State Duma. Upon adoption by a majority of the full State Duma membership, a draft law is considered by the Federation Council, which has fourteen days to place the bill on its calendar. Conciliation commissions are the prescribed procedure to work out differences in bills considered by both chambers.

A constitutional provision dictating that draft laws dealing with revenues and expenditures may be considered "only when the Government's findings are known" substantially limits the Federal Assembly's control of state finances. However, the legislature may alter finance legislation submitted by the Government at a later time, a power that provides a degree of traditional legislative control over the purse. The two chambers of the legislature also have the power to override a presidential veto of legislation. The constitution provides a high hurdle for an override, however, requiring at least a two-thirds vote of the total number of members of both chambers.

Clashes of Power, 1993–96

Although the 1993 constitution weakened their standing vis-à-vis the presidency, the parliaments elected in 1993 and 1995 nonetheless used their powers to shape legislation according to their own precepts and to defy Yeltsin on some issues. An early example was the February 1994 State Duma vote to grant amnesty to the leaders of the 1991 Moscow coup. Yeltsin vehemently denounced this action, although it was within the constitutional purview of the State Duma. In October 1994, both legislative chambers passed a law over Yeltsin's veto requiring the Government to submit quarterly reports on budget expenditures to the State Duma and adhere to other budgetary guidelines.

In the most significant executive-legislative clash since 1993, the State Duma overwhelmingly voted no confidence in the Government in June 1995. The vote was triggered by a Chechen rebel raid into the neighboring Russian town of Budennovsk, where the rebels were able to take more than 1,000 hostages. Dissatisfaction with Yeltsin's economic reforms also was a factor in the vote. A second motion of no confidence failed to carry in early July. In March 1996, the State Duma again incensed Yeltsin by voting to revoke the December 1991 resolution of the Russian Supreme Soviet abrogating the 1922 treaty under which the Soviet Union had been founded. That resolution had prepared the way for formation of the Commonwealth of Independent States.

In his February 1996 state of the federation speech, Yeltsin commended the previous parliament for passing a number of significant laws, and he noted with relief the "civil" resolution of the June 1995 no-confidence conflict. He complained, however, that the Federal Assembly had not acted on issues such as the private ownership of land, a tax code, and judicial reform. Yeltsin also was critical of legislation that he had been forced to return to the parliament because it contravened the constitution and existing law, and of legislative attempts to pass fiscal legislation in violation of the constitutional stricture that such bills must be preapproved by the Government. He noted that he would continue to use his veto power against ill-drafted bills and his power to issue decrees on issues he deemed important, and that such decrees would remain in force until suitable laws were passed. The State Duma passed a resolution in March 1996 demanding that Yeltsin refrain from returning bills to the parliament for redrafting, arguing that the president was obligated either to sign bills or to veto them.

The Judiciary

The Ministry of Justice administers Russia's judicial system. The ministry's responsibilities include the establishment of courts and the appointment of judges at levels below the federal district courts. The ministry also gathers forensic statistics and conducts sociological research and educational programs applicable to crime prevention.

Many Western observers consider the judicial and legal systems weak links in Russia's reform efforts, stymieing privatization, the fight against crime and corruption, the protection of civil and human rights, and the general ascendancy of the rule of law. Many judges appointed by the regimes of Leonid I. Brezhnev (in office 1964–82) and Yuriy V. Andropov (in office 1982–84) remained in place in the mid-1990s. Such arbiters were trained in "socialist law" and had become accustomed to basing their verdicts on telephone calls from local CPSU bosses rather than on the legal merits of cases.

For court infrastructure and financial support, judges must depend on the Ministry of Justice, and for housing they must depend on local authorities in the jurisdiction where they sit. In 1995 the average salary for a judge was US$160 per month, substantially less than the earnings associated with more menial positions in Russian society. These circumstances, combined with irregularities in the appointment process and the continued strong position of the procurators, deprived judges in the lower jurisdictions of independent authority (see The Procuracy, ch. 10).

Judicial Reform

In 1992 a new Law on the Status of Judges was passed. The law was intended to confer greater status on the judicial profession by raising salaries and benefits. The 1993 constitution provides for some degree of judicial reform by establishing an independent judiciary and specifying that justices may only be removed or their powers curtailed or terminated in accordance with the law. Sitting justices also enjoy immunity from prosecution. However, judicial reform has moved slowly despite those two legislative developments, and in 1996 the judiciary remained subject to the influence of security agencies and politicians. A large case backlog, trial delays, and lengthy pretrial detention also remain problems (see How the System Works, ch. 10).

According to a provision approved in 1994, trial by jury may take place in specific types of cases, including those involving the death penalty. This reform supersedes in part the older system of trial by judges and lay "people's assessors" who usually acceded to the judges' verdicts. In practice, trial by jury has made little headway in the hidebound court system. In 1995 jury trials were only available in nine of the eighty-nine subnational jurisdictions, although other jurisdictions sought permission to introduce them.

In the mid-1990s, a total of about 14,000 judges were active in approximately 2,500 courts at all judicial levels. To be eligible for appointment as a judge, an individual must be at least twenty-five years of age, have a higher education in law, and have at least five years of experience in the legal profession.

Structure of the Judiciary

The twenty-three-member Supreme Court is Russia's highest court of origination and of appeals for consideration of criminal, civil, and administrative cases. Its chairman in 1996, Vyacheslav Lebedev, had been a judge in Leningrad and Moscow for nineteen years before his appointment in 1989. The Superior Court of Arbitration, which is headed by a board of one chairman and four deputy chairmen, is the highest court for the resolution of economic disputes. Courts of arbitration also exist at lower jurisdictional levels. The nineteen-member Constitutional Court decides whether federal laws, presidential and federal decrees and directives, and local constitutions, charters, and laws comply with the federal constitution. Treaties between the national government and a regional jurisdiction and between regional jurisdictions are subject to the same oversight. The Constitutional Court also resolves jurisdictional disputes between federal or local organs of power, and it also may be asked to interpret the federal constitution. The Constitutional Court temporarily ceased to exist after Yeltsin dissolved the parliament in October 1993. Although prescribed in the new constitution, the court remained moribund in 1994 because no new law was passed governing its procedures and composition. In 1995 the Federation Council finally approved appointments to the Constitutional Court, and it resumed operation that year.

Under the constitution, judges of the three highest courts serve for life and are appointed by the Federation Council after nomination by the president. The president appoints judges at the next level, the federal district courts. The minister of justice is responsible for appointing judges to regional and city courts. However, in practice many appointments below the national level still are made by the chief executives of subnational jurisdictions, a practice that has perpetuated local political influence on judges' decisions (see Local and Regional Government, this ch.).

Local and Regional Government

In the Soviet period, some of Russia's approximately 100 nationalities were granted their own ethnic enclaves, to which varying formal federal rights were attached (see Minority Peoples and Their Territories, ch. 4). Other smaller or more dispersed nationalities did not receive such recognition. In most of these enclaves, ethnic Russians constituted a majority of the population, although the titular nationalities usually enjoyed disproportionate representation in local government bodies. Relations between the central government and the subordinate jurisdictions, and among those jurisdictions, became a political issue in the 1990s.

The Russian Federation has made few changes in the Soviet pattern of regional jurisdictions. The 1993 constitution establishes a federal government and enumerates eighty-nine subnational jurisdictions, including twenty-one ethnic enclaves with the status of republics. There are ten autonomous regions, or *okruga* (sing., *okrug*), and the Jewish Autonomous Oblast (Yevreyskaya avtonomnaya oblast', also known as Birobidzhan). Besides the ethnically identified jurisdictions, there are six territories (*kraya*; sing., *kray*) and forty-nine oblasts (provinces). The cities of Moscow and St. Petersburg are independent of surrounding jurisdictions; termed "cities of federal significance," they have the same status as the oblasts. The ten autonomous regions and Birobidzhan are part of larger jurisdictions, either an oblast or a territory (see fig. 1). As the power and influence of the central government have become diluted, governors and mayors have become the only relevant government authorities in many jurisdictions.

The Federation Treaty and Regional Power

The Federation Treaty was signed in March 1992 by President Yeltsin and most leaders of the autonomous republics and other ethnic and geographical subunits. The treaty consisted of three separate documents, each pertaining to one type of regional jurisdiction. It outlined powers reserved for the central government, shared powers, and residual powers to be exercised primarily by the subunits. Because Russia's new constitution remained in dispute in the Federal Assembly at the time of ratification, the Federation Treaty and provisions based on the treaty were incorporated as amendments to the 1978 constitution. A series of new conditions were established by the 1993 constitution and by bilateral agreements.

Local Jurisdictions under the Constitution

The constitution of 1993 resolved many of the ambiguities and contradictions concerning the degree of decentralization under the much-amended 1978 constitution of the Russian Republic; most such solutions favored the concentration of power in the central government. When the constitution was ratified, the Federation Treaty was demoted to the status of a subconstitutional document. A transitional provision of the constitution provided that in case of discrepancies between the federal constitution and the Federation Treaty, or between the constitution and other treaties involving a subnational jurisdiction, all other documents would defer to the constitution.

The 1993 constitution presents a daunting list of powers reserved to the center. Powers shared jointly between the federal and local authorities are less numerous. Regional jurisdictions are only allocated powers not specifically reserved to the federal government or exercised jointly. Those powers include managing municipal property, establishing and executing regional budgets, establishing and collecting regional taxes, and maintaining law and order (see table 25, Appendix). Some of the boundaries between joint and exclusively federal powers are vaguely prescribed; presumably they would become clearer through the give and take of federal practice or through adjudication, as has occurred in other federal systems. Meanwhile, bilateral power-sharing treaties between the central government and the subunits have become an important means of clarifying the boundaries of shared powers. Many subnational jurisdictions have their own constitutions, however, and often those documents allocate powers to the jurisdiction inconsistent with provisions of the federal constitution. As of 1996, no process had been devised for adjudication of such conflicts.

Under the 1993 constitution, the republics, territories, oblasts, autonomous oblast, autonomous regions, and cities of federal designation are held to be "equal in their relations with the federal agencies of state power"; this language represents an attempt to end the complaints of the nonrepublic jurisdictions about their inferior status. In keeping with this new equality, republics no longer receive the epithet "sovereign," as they did in the 1978 constitution. Equal representation in the Federation Council for all eighty-nine jurisdictions furthers the equalization process by providing them meaningful input into legislative activities, particularly those of special local concern (see The Parliament, this ch.). However, Federation Council officials have criticized the State Duma for failing to represent regional interests adequately. In mid-1995 Vladimir Shumeyko, then speaker of the Federation Council, criticized the current electoral system's party-list provision for allowing some parts of Russia to receive disproportionate representation in the lower house. (In the 1995 elections, Moscow Oblast received nearly 38 percent of the State Duma's seats based on the concentration of party-list candidates in the national capital.) Shumeyko contended that such misallocation fed potentially dangerous popular discontent with the parliament and politicians (see The Elections of 1995, this ch.).

Despite constitutional language equalizing the regional jurisdictions in their relations with the center, vestiges of Soviet-era multitiered federalism remain in a number of provisions, including those allowing for the use of non-Russian languages in the republics but not in other jurisdictions, and in the definitions of the five categories of subunit. On most details of the federal system, the constitution is vague, and clarifying legislation had not been passed by mid-1996. However, some analysts have pointed out that this vagueness facilitates resolution of individual conflicts between the center and the regions.

Power Sharing

Flexibility is a goal of the constitutional provision allowing bilateral treaties or charters between the central government and the regions on power sharing. For instance, in the bilateral treaty signed with the Russian government in February 1994, the Republic of Tatarstan gave up its claim to sovereignty and accepted Russia's taxing authority, in return for Russia's acceptance of Tatar control over oil and other resources and the republic's right to sign economic agreements with other countries. This treaty has particular significance because Tatarstan was one of the two republics that did not sign the Federation Treaty in 1992. By mid-1996 almost one-third of the federal subunits had concluded power-sharing treaties or charters.

The first power-sharing charter negotiated by the central government and an oblast was signed in December 1995 with Orenburg Oblast. The charter divided power in the areas of economic and agricultural policy, natural resources, international economic relations and trade, and military industries. According to Prime Minister Chernomyrdin, the charter gave Orenburg full power over its budget and allowed the oblast to participate in privatization decisions. By early 1996, similar charters had been signed with Krasnodar Territory and Kaliningrad and Sverdlovsk oblasts. In the summer of 1996, Yeltsin wooed potential regional supporters of his reelection by signing charters with Perm', Rostov, Tver', and Leningrad oblasts and with the city of St. Petersburg, among others, granting these regions liberal tax treatment and other economic advantages.

By the mid-1990s, regional jurisdictions also had become bolder in passing local legislation to fill gaps in federation statutes rather than waiting for the Federal Assembly to act. For example, Volgograd Oblast passed laws regulating local pensions, the issuance of promissory notes, and credit unions. The constitution upholds regional legislative authority to pass laws that accord with the constitution and existing federal laws.

Presidential Power in the Regions

The president retains the power to appoint and remove presidential representatives, who act as direct emissaries to the jurisdictions in overseeing local administrations' implementation of presidential policies. The power to appoint these overseers was granted by the Russian Supreme Soviet to Yeltsin in late 1991. The parliament attempted several times during 1992–93 to repeal or curtail the activities of these appointees, whose powers are only alluded to in the constitution. The presence of Yeltsin's representatives helped bring out the local vote on his behalf in the 1996 presidential election.

The governments of the republics include a president or prime minister (or both) and a regional council or legislature. The chief executives of lower jurisdictions are called governors or administrative heads. Generally, in jurisdictions other than republics the executive branches have been more sympathetic to the central government, and the legislatures (called soviets until late 1993, then called dumas or assemblies) have been the center of whatever separatist sentiment exists. Under the power given him in 1991 to appoint the chief executives of territories, oblasts, autonomous regions, and the autonomous oblast, Yeltsin had appointed virtually all of the sixty-six leaders of those jurisdictions. By contrast, republic presidents have been popularly elected since 1992. Some of Yeltsin's appointees have encountered strong opposition from their legislatures; in 1992 and 1993, in some cases votes of no-confidence brought about popular elections for the position of chief executive.

After the Moscow confrontation of October 1993, Yeltsin sought to bolster his regional support by dissolving the legislatures of all federal subunits except the republics (which were advised to "reform" their political systems). Accordingly, in 1994 elections were held in all the jurisdictions whose legislatures had been dismissed. In some cases, that process placed local executives at the head of legislative bodies, eliminating checks and balances between the branches at the regional level.

Election results in the subnational jurisdictions held great significance for the Yeltsin administration because the winners would fill the ex officio seats in the Federation Council, which until 1996 was a reliable bastion of support. The election of large numbers of opposition candidates would end the Federation Council's usefulness as a balance against the anti-Yeltsin State Duma and further impede Yeltsin's agenda. In 1995 some regions held gubernatorial elections to fill the administrative posts originally granted to Yeltsin appointees in 1991. Faced with an escalating number of requests for such elections, Yeltsin decreed December 1996 as the date for most gubernatorial and republic presidential elections. This date was confirmed by a December 1995 Federation Council law. The decree also set subnational legislative elections for June or December 1997. (In July 1996, the State Duma advanced these elections to late 1996.) Observers noted that by calling for most of these elections to take place after the presidential election, Yeltsin prevented unfavorable outcomes from possibly reducing his reelection chances—even though voter apathy after the presidential election had the potential to help opposition candidates.

The Separatism Question

In the first half of the 1990s, observers speculated about the possibility that some of the jurisdictions in the federation might emulate the former Soviet republics and demand full independence (see Minority Peoples and Their Territories, ch. 4). Several factors militate against such an outcome, however. Russia is more than 80 percent ethnic Russian, and most of the thirty-two ethnically based jurisdictions are demographically dominated by ethnic Russians, as are all of the territories and oblasts. Many of the subnational jurisdictions are in the interior of Russia, meaning that they could not break away without joining a bloc of seceding border areas, and the economies of all such jurisdictions were thoroughly integrated with the national economy in the Soviet system. The 1993 constitution strengthens the official status of the central government in relation to the various regions, although Moscow has made significant concessions in bilateral treaties. Finally, most of the differences at the base of separatist movements are economic and geographic rather than ethnic.

Advocates of secession, who are numerous in several regions, generally appear to be in the minority and are unevenly dispersed. Some regions have even advocated greater centralization on some matters. By 1996 most experts believed that the federation would hold together, although probably at the

413

expense of additional concessions of power by the central government. The trend is not toward separatism so much as the devolution of central powers to the localities on trade, taxes, and other matters.

Some experts observe that the Russian republics pressing claims for greater subunit rights fall into three groups. The first is composed of those jurisdictions most vociferous in pressing ethnic separatism, including Chechnya and perhaps other republics of the North Caucasus, and the Republic of Tyva. The second group consists of large, resource-rich republics, including Karelia, Komi, and Sakha (Yakutia). Their differences with Moscow center on resource control and taxes rather than demands for outright independence. A third, mixed group consists of republics along the Volga River, which straddle strategic water, rail, and pipeline routes, possess resources such as oil, and include large numbers of Russia's Muslim and Buddhist populations. These republics include Bashkortostan, Kalmykia, Mari El, Mordovia, Tatarstan, and Udmurtia.

In addition to the republics, several other jurisdictions have lobbied for greater rights, mainly on questions of resource control and taxation. These include Sverdlovsk Oblast, which in 1993 proclaimed itself an autonomous republic as a protest against receiving fewer privileges in taxation and resource control than the republics, and strategically vital Maritime (Primorskiy) Territory on the Pacific coast, whose governor in the mid-1990s, Yevgeniy Nazdratenko, defied central economic and political policies on a number of well-publicized issues.

Some limited cooperation has occurred among Russia's regional jurisdictions, and experts believe there is potential for even greater coordination. Eight regional cooperation organizations have been established, covering all subnational jurisdictions except Chechnya: the Siberian Accord Association; the Central Russia Association; the Northwest Association; the Black Earth Association; the Cooperation Association of North Caucasus Republics, Territories, and Oblasts; the Greater Volga Association; the Ural Regional Association; and the Far East and Baikal Association. The Federation Council formally recognized these interjurisdictional organizations in 1994. Expansion of the organizations' activities is hampered by economic inequalities among their members and by inadequate interregional transportation infrastructure, but in 1996 they began increasing their influence in Moscow.

Regional and ethnic conflicts have encouraged proposals to abolish the existing subunits and resurrect the tsarist-era *guberniya,* or large province, which would incorporate several smaller subunits on the basis of geography and population rather than ethnic considerations. Russian ultranationalists such as Vladimir Zhirinovskiy have been joined in supporting this proposal by some officials of the national Government and oblast and territory leaders who resent the privileges of the republics. Some have called for these new subunits to be based on the eight interregional economic associations.

Political Parties and Legislative Elections

After early 1990, when the Soviet constitution was amended to delete the provision that the CPSU was the "leading and guiding" force in the political system, many political groups began to operate more openly in Russia. The constitution of 1993 guarantees Russians' right to a multiparty system. Political party development has lagged, however, because many Russians associate parties with the repressiveness of the CPSU in the Soviet era. In the mid-1990s, most of Russia's parties were based on personal followings, had few formal members, and lacked broad geographical bases and coherent platforms. Prior to the legislative elections of 1993 and 1995, much shifting occurred as parties formed and abandoned coalitions, sometimes involving partners with which they had little in common politically. Even the KPRF, direct heir to the CPSU, waffled on many central economic and foreign policy issues in the 1996 presidential campaign. One observer noted that for most Russian voters, the two major sides in the 1996 election had no identification with broad national issues; they were simply the anti-Yeltsins and the anti-communists. Experts identified the lack of focused national party organizations as a key factor in the diffusion of political power to subnational jurisdictions in the mid-1990s (see The Federation Treaty and Regional Power, this ch.).

The Elections of 1993

In November 1993, Yeltsin issued decrees prescribing procedures for multiparty parliamentary elections, which would be the first since tsarist times. Besides setting the configuration of the new bicameral parliament, the Yeltsin plan called for half of the 450 State Duma deputies to be elected from national party lists with representation proportional to the overall votes received by each party. The other half would be elected locally, in single-member districts (see The Parliament, this ch.). The party-list procedure, a new feature in Russian elections, was designed to strengthen the identification of candidates with parties and to foster the concept of the multiparty system among the electorate. To achieve proportional representation in the State Duma, a party would need to gain at least 5 percent of the nationwide vote.

The CEC declared thirteen parties eligible for the party list, and 2,047 individual candidates were selected to compete for Federation Council seats (490) and State Duma single-mandate seats (1,567), allotted to individuals regardless of their parties' overall performance vis-à-vis the 5 percent threshold. Although the CEC reported some voting irregularities, the vast majority of the more than 1,000 international observers termed the elections largely free and fair, with some reservations expressed about manipulation of results. In several republics, the referendum results were invalidated by low turnouts caused by boycotts, or because voters failed to approve the constitution.

Many experts divided the myriad parties of the 1993 elections roughly into three main blocs: pro-Yeltsin reformists, centrists advocating a slower pace of reform, and hard-liners opposing reforms. The main reformist party was Russia's Choice, led by former prime minister Yegor Gaydar. The main centrist parties were the Yavlinskiy-Boldyrev-Lukin bloc, commonly referred to as Yabloko (the Russian word for apple), headed by economist Grigoriy Yavlinskiy and former ambassador to the United States Vladimir Lukin, and the Democratic Party of Russia, headed by Nikolay Travkin. The main hard-line parties were the LDPR, the KPRF, headed by Gennadiy Zyuganov, and the Agrarian Party, which represented state- and collective-farm interests and was headed by Mikhail Lapshin.

In 1993 the strongly nationalist, antireform LDPR emerged with the largest vote on the State Duma party lists, followed by Russia's Choice. By faring much better in the single-member districts, however, Russia's Choice emerged with sixty-six seats, the most in the State Duma. The LDPR followed with sixty-four seats. Altogether, reformist and centrist parties emerged with the greatest number of seats in the State Duma, followed by nationalist and antireform parties. Some 127 State Duma seats were won by individuals not formally affiliated with a party, many of whom were former CPSU members.

Of the thirteen parties participating in the December 1993 legislative elections on the party lists, eight exceeded the 5 percent threshold to win seats in the State Duma. In addition, all thirteen parties, as well as some local parties, won seats in single-member districts. Once the new parliament was seated, the parties aggregated into several factions. A number of deputies coalesced into the Union of December 12 faction. Sixty-five centrist deputies formed the New Regional Policy faction, and some LDPR members shifted their affiliation to the KPRF or the Agrarian Party, or supported former vice president Aleksandr Rutskoy's Concord in the Name of Russia policy agenda.

The Elections of 1995

In June 1995, the Federal Assembly passed—and Yeltsin signed—a new law to govern the next legislative elections, which were planned for December. This legislation echoed many provisions of Yeltsin's 1993 electoral decree, such as the division of the State Duma seats into party-list and single-member districts. Yeltsin had urged a change in this provision because he feared that Zhirinovskiy's LDPR might again gain many seats in the party-list voting, but the Duma had insisted on retaining the even-split voting procedure that gave such meaning to the party lists. The 1993 election had demonstrated that voting by party lists generally encouraged party formation and program pledges, whereas voting by district encouraged loyalty by deputies to local interests. The 5 percent threshold for party-list voting also was retained. In September 1995, Yeltsin decreed that the Federation Council seats would not be filled by regional elections; instead, the upper house would be composed of regional and republic executive and legislative leaders—a group with which Yeltsin had close contacts and from which he could expect strong loyalty. All of the suggested provisions were incorporated into the new election law (see The Parliament, this ch.).

In anticipation of the legislative races, early in 1995 Yeltsin encouraged the creation of two political parties that would lend support to his policies and form the basis of a stable, moderate, two-party system in Russia. One party would be led by State Duma speaker Ivan Rybkin, the other by Chernomyrdin (who by that time had proven himself a loyal and competent manager of the Yeltsin agenda). The unnamed "Rybkin bloc" was designed to attract centrist and leftist voters, and Chernomydin's party, Our Home Is Russia, was envisioned as a right-center coalition. Both parties would occupy the moderate band of the political spectrum. Having attracted the support of many Russian Government ministers and regional leaders, Our Home Is Russia became known as the "party of power." The Rybkin bloc, which was supposed to serve as the loyal opposition in the parliament, attracted several tiny parties, but major parties and groups refused to join the bloc because of opposition to some or all of Yeltsin's reforms. As a result, Rybkin's unification effort received little practical support.

To qualify for the party-list voting, parties were required to obtain 200,000 signatures, with no more than 7 percent of signatures coming from any single federal jurisdiction. The latter requirement was designed to encourage the emergence of broad-based rather than regionally based parties. Candidates wishing to run in single-member districts had to obtain signatures from at least 1 percent, or about 5,000, of their district's voters. Forty-three parties succeeded in getting on the party-list ballot, and more than 2,600 candidates were registered in 225 single-member district races. Many individuals listed on the party ballot also ran in single-member districts. This was especially true of locally popular candidates whose minor parties could not surpass the 5 percent national threshold needed to get on the national party-list ballot.

In the legislative elections of December 1995, voter turnout was high (about 65 percent), and international observers again evaluated the balloting as largely free and fair. The second such evaluation in two years boosted the image of electoral democratization in Russia. Dissatisfaction with the Yeltsin administration was conspicuous in the election results, but the showing of the reformist and centrist parties that supported some or all of Yeltsin's program was undermined by the disunity of that part of the political spectrum. Among the forty-three parties participating in the party-list vote, only four met the 5 percent requirement to win seats for their national party lists, although several other parties won seats in individual races. In the aggregate of party-list voting, reformists and centrists performed much better than they did in the single-member phase, receiving almost as many votes as the hard-liners. But pro-reform and centrist votes were dispersed among a multitude of parties, negating almost two-thirds of the party-list votes they received and costing these parties dozens of seats by keeping them below the 5 percent threshold. In contrast, the KPRF and its allies suffered much less from such dispersion and gained many seats from the party-list vote.

Although centrists and reformers split single-mandate seats about evenly with the antireform parties, nonaffiliated candidates gained more than one-third of these seats. About 40 percent of the sitting State Duma deputies were reelected, and fifteen Federation Council deputies entered the State Duma, providing some continuity of legislative expertise. Under a provision of the new constitution, Government officials were obligated to resign their positions if elected to the parliament.

Overall, reformist parties did not do as well in the 1995 elections as they had in 1993. Gaydar's party, now renamed Russia's Democratic Choice, failed to meet the 5 percent requirement. Altogether, reformists and centrists won 129 seats in the State Duma (less than one-third of the total), and independent, nominally nonaffiliated candidates won seventy-seven seats (about one-sixth). The KPRF and its ally, the Agrarian Party, gained 179 seats as the KPRF achieved a plurality of seats, and the anti-Yeltsin nationalist parties won another sixty-five. Zhirinovskiy's LDPR received much less electoral support than in 1993, gaining 11 percent of the vote—a distant second to the KPRF—and fifty-one seats (see table 26, Appendix).

More than in the 1993 alignment, parties now tended to be either for or against reform, with former centrists moving either left or right. In the 1996 State Duma, the main reformist parties were Chernomyrdin's "official" Our Home Is Russia, the main advocate of Yeltsin's programs, and Yavlinskiy's Yabloko coalition, which was highly critical of Yeltsin's approach to reform but supportive of reform principles. The main hardline, antireform parties in the Duma were the KPRF, headed by Zyuganov, and the LDPR, headed by Zhirinovskiy.

Altogether, in 1996 communist, nationalist, and agrarian parties controlled slightly more than half the State Duma seats. Their strength enabled them to pass some bills and resolutions if they voted together, but they still lacked enough votes to override Federation Council votes or presidential vetoes (see The Executive Branch, this ch.). The numerical proportions also did not permit antireformists to approve changes in the constitution, which require a two-thirds majority, that is, at least 300 votes of the full chamber.

Civil Rights

The constitution of 1993 includes a wide range of provisions guaranteeing the civil and human rights of Russia's citizens. However, inadequacies in the criminal justice system and other institutional flaws have hindered consistent observance of those provisions.

General Civil Rights Guarantees

The constitution establishes wide-ranging civil and human rights and social guarantees, several of which remained unattainable or unrealized in the mid-1990s. Social guarantees have been difficult to meet because of Russia's persistent economic crisis. Such guarantees include the right to a minimum wage and welfare for the "family, mothers, fathers, children, invalids, and elderly citizens." Protection of unemployed people and the right to a safe and hygienic work environment also are proclaimed. The right to housing is guaranteed, including free or low-cost housing for needy people and others. The right to free health care and secondary-level education is also upheld, in an echo of the promises of Soviet constitutions. Perhaps in recognition of the economic burden of such widely inclusive state social guarantees, the constitution calls for adult children to care for disabled parents, and it safeguards the existence of private charitable and insurance operations, which were forbidden or discouraged under the Soviet system.

Equality before the law is proclaimed regardless of sex, race, nationality, language, national origin, property and position, ideological conviction, membership in public associations, and other attributes and circumstances. Freedom of religion and conscience is upheld, and alternatives to military service are to be accepted, although neither the law in force nor military practice has upheld the latter provision. Individual privacy is protected, including that of correspondence and other communications and of housing. Nationality rights are upheld, including the right to use a language other than Russian in communications and education. The constitution asserts freedom of internal and foreign travel and the right to choose one's place of domicile. No one may be expelled or exiled from Russia. Freedom of the press is upheld, and censorship is prohibited. People have the right to assemble peaceably and to hold peaceful meetings and demonstrations of all types. The right to own, dispose of, and inherit private property, including land, is upheld, and private property may not be expropriated except with full compensation.

Constitutionally guaranteed civil rights may only be restricted upon the legal proclamation of a national or local state of emergency. Even in a state of emergency, however, the constitution prescribes that no one may be tortured or denied judicial rights, although an individual may be held for an unspecified period without being charged. The right of dual citizenship for ethnic Russians residing in the near abroad (the other fourteen former republics of the Soviet Union) is proclaimed. Presumably, such a right also exists for non-Russians residing in Russia. The constitution also includes a pledge that Russia will protect its citizens abroad. However, most member nations of the Commonwealth of Independent States (CIS) have resisted Russia's demand that they grant ethnic Russians such dual citizenship, viewing it as an infringement on their sovereignty (see Migration, ch. 3).

Massive civil and human rights violations have been committed in the Republic of Chechnya by Russian military units as well as by Chechen guerrillas, resulting in tens of thousands of deaths and injuries and the displacement of more than 300,000 people. Official human rights monitoring of the conflict was undermined in 1995 when the State Duma dismissed human rights activist Sergey Kovalev as its ombudsman for human rights. Kovalev was removed because of his strident condemnation of Russian military and police atrocities in Chechnya. Kovalev resigned as chairman of the presidential Human Rights Commission in January 1996, accusing Yeltsin of backtracking on human rights in Chechnya and throughout Russia. No figure of similar stature had filled Kovalev's position as of mid-1996.

Criminal Justice Protections

According to Russia's 1993 constitution, the death penalty is applicable to some crimes "until its abolition" by federal law. Although the annual number of executions reportedly had decreased by mid-1996, the public outcry at Russia's growing crime wave made the death penalty a politically sensitive issue. In cases where the death penalty may be applied, the accused is guaranteed the right to trial by jury, although this provision was only partly in force in the mid-1990s (see How the System Works, ch. 10). A condition of Russia's admittance to the Council of Europe (see Glossary), which it achieved in January 1996, was abolition of the death penalty within three years. Much international pressure was applied toward that end both before and after Russia was approved for council membership.

For all types of crime, punishment without trial and prosecution ex post facto are forbidden. The constitution also bars torture and other "brutal or humiliating" treatment and punishment. Citizens have nominal protection against arbitrary arrest without a judicial decision, and they may not be held for more than forty-eight hours without being charged, except in a state of emergency. However, this constitutional provision has been directly contravened by Yeltsin's 1994 decree on combating organized crime, which allows police to detain persons suspected of involvement with organized crime for as much as thirty days without a criminal charge and without access to a lawyer. This decree was used widely in 1995 to detain persons without judicial permission beyond the mandated maximum period. Russian human rights monitors reported in 1995 that the few detainees who were aware of their rights and complained of violations were subject to beatings. Nonetheless, about one in six cases of arrest was appealed to the courts in 1995, and judges released one in six of those on grounds of insufficient evidence or breach of procedure (see Criminal Law Reform in the 1990s, ch. 10).

According to the constitution, judicial sentences may be appealed to higher courts, as may decisions of government organs at all levels. Those organs may be sued for damages caused by action or inaction. Nominally, all citizens are guaranteed their "day in court," have the right to choose their own defense counsel, or may be provided with free legal counsel if required. Legal aid may be requested from the earliest moment a person is detained, placed in custody, or indicted, a change from previous practice whereby the individual could receive counsel only upon being formally charged and after being interrogated. Few citizens are aware of these rights, however. A person is considered innocent until proven guilty, but where jury trials do not occur, the accused generally are expected to prove their innocence rather than defend themselves against prosecutors' efforts to prove their guilt. In cases where a judge imposes sentence, the average rate of conviction is more than 99 percent, as opposed to an 84 percent conviction rate in jury trials.

The Media

For most of the Soviet era, the news media were under full

state control. The major newspapers, such as *Pravda, Izvestiya, Krasnaya zvezda,* and *Komsomol'skaya pravda,* were the official organs of party or government agencies, and radio and television were state monopolies. In the late 1980s, these monopolies began to weaken as stories such as the Chernobyl' disaster reached the public in detail, an occurrence that would not have been possible before *glasnost.* Then, after seventy-five years of state control, the media began an era of significantly less restricted activity in 1992.

In the post-Soviet era, the news media have played a central role in forming public opinion toward critical national concerns, including the Chechnya conflict, the economic crisis, and government policies and personalities. In the environment of freewheeling expression of opinion, public figures such as Boris Yeltsin and government actions such as the Chechnya campaign have received ruthless criticism, and the deterioration of Russia's environment, public health, national defense, and national economy has been exposed thoroughly, if not always accurately. However, the national and local governments have exerted heavy pressure on the print and broadcast media to alter coverage of certain issues. Because most media enterprises continue to depend on government support, such pressure often has been effective.

The Print Media

In the first post-Soviet years, major newspapers presented varied approaches to critical issues. Among the most influential titles were *Izvestiya* (in Soviet times, the organ of the Politburo, but after 1991 an independent periodical owned by its employees, with a daily circulation in 1995 of about 604,765); *Nezavisimaya gazeta,* 1995 daily circulation about 50,400; and the weekly *Argumenty i fakty* (1995 circulation about 3.2 million) (see table 27, Appendix). But by the mid-1990s, a new atmosphere of intense competition was bringing rapid change to the print media. In 1995 an estimated 10,000 newspapers and periodicals were registered, including more than twenty daily newspapers published in Moscow. The thousands of small regional newspapers that appeared after 1991 were plagued by low advertising revenue, high production costs, an increasingly apathetic public, and intense pressure from local authorities to slant content. But in the mid-1990s, local newspapers gained readers because of increased regional independence; they also benefited from the competition that television gave to national newspapers in providing the regions with news from Moscow and the rest of the world.

In 1995 the Moscow daily *Nezavisimaya gazeta,* which for five years remained true to its name (the independent newspaper) by refusing advertising and state subsidies, was forced to close because circulation had dropped to about 35,000 and many top journalists had left for more lucrative positions. The paper subsequently resumed publication under the ownership of a large bank consortium (the Unified Bank) with close ties to the Government. *Pravda,* formerly the main organ of the CPSU and still representing antireform positions, underwent numerous crises in the early and mid-1990s. Purchased by a Greek publishing firm in 1992, its circulation dropped from about 10 million in the 1980s to around 165,000 in 1995. After changing its name to *Pravda 5* in mid-1996, the newspaper broadened its procommunist position somewhat. The decline of *Pravda* left *Sovetskaya Rossiya* and *Zavtra* as the chief organs of the antireform faction of the legislature.

Official organs still have a place in the media, however; *Rossiyskaya gazeta,* the heavily subsidized organ of the Government, publishes most of that body's official documents, including laws and decrees. *Rossiyskiye vesti,* organ of the office of the president, reaches about 150,000 Russians daily. Both newspapers feature strongly pro-Government positions. The third official national newspaper, *Krasnaya zvezda,* representing the Ministry of Defense, acquired a reputation in the 1990s as strongly pro-Yeltsin.

Although Russia's newspapers offer readers diverse opinions on most issues, the quality of Russian journalism remains relatively low, and objectivity is random. Journalists generally do not verify their sources fully or are denied access to relevant individuals. A 1995 official report on press freedom indicated that reporters without special connections have no better access to state officials than their counterparts did in the Soviet era. Most newspapers make no clear distinction between objective reports and editorials, and, according to a 1995 report by the trade magazine *Zhurnalist,* most have some connection to a political party or faction.

The Broadcast Media

In 1992 some 48.5 million radios were in use in Russia. Domestic radio programming is provided by two state communications companies, the Federal Television and Radio Service of Russia and the All-Russian Television and Radio Company. The Voice of Russia (Golos Rossii) is the main foreign-language broadcast service, providing programs in thirty languages, including Arabic, Chinese, English, Japanese, Farsi, and Spanish.

In the 1990s, television reached an increasing number of Russians with increasingly diversified programming. In 1992 about 55 million televisions were in use. For most Russians, television is the chief source of news. Television channels and transmission facilities gradually have been privatized, although in 1996 the most prominent "private" stockholders were entrepreneurs with strong ties to the Yeltsin administration. The largest of the four major networks, Russian Public Television (Obshchestvennoye rossiyskoye televideniye—ORT, formerly Ostankino), which reaches an estimated 200 million people, remained 51 percent state-owned after partial privatization in 1994. However, ORT has offered regular programs, such as one hosted by Aleksandr Solzhenitsyn, that are critical of the Government. ORT's news broadcasts tend to favor Government policies.

The second-largest network, the All-Russian Television and Radio Company (Vserossiyskaya gosudarstvennaya teleradio-kompaniya, commonly called Russia Television—RTV), was fully state-owned in 1996 and reaches about 140 million viewers with relatively balanced news coverage. The largest private network is Independent Television (Nezavisimoye televideniye—NTV), which reaches about 100 million people. NTV has received praise in the West for unbiased news reporting. Its Chechnya coverage forced other networks to abandon pro-Government reporting of the conflict. The TV–6 commercial network brings its estimated 70 million viewers in European Russia mainly entertainment programs. Its founder, Eduard Sagalayev, was strongly influenced by an earlier partnership with United States communications magnate Ted Turner.

Besides the four networks, state-run channels are offered in every region, and an estimated 400 private television stations were in operation in 1995. More than half of such stations produce their own news broadcasts, providing mainly local rather than national or international coverage. The Independent Broadcasting System was established in 1994 to link some fifty stations with shared programming.

By 1995 the administration of state television had become heavily politicized. After the 1995 legislative elections, Yeltsin dismissed Oleg Poptsov, the head of RTV, for having aired what the president considered unfairly negative coverage of his administration. In exerting such overt political pressure, Yeltsin likely had in mind the prominent role television would play in the 1996 presidential election. In fact, all candidates in that election were represented in an unprecedented wave of televised campaign advertising, some of which was quite similar to that in the United States and little of which provided useful information to voters. Convinced that their independence would be jeopardized if KPRF candidate Gennadiy Zyuganov won, television broadcasters provided virtually no coverage of his main campaign events, and even the independent NTV aided Yeltsin by muting its criticism during the election. Critical coverage of the Chechen conflict and other issues resumed once Yeltsin's reelection seemed assured, however.

The Political Outlook

Russia's political culture made long strides toward democracy in the first five years of the post-Soviet era. By mid-1996 numerous political parties with widely varying agendas and viewpoints had participated in three free national elections—two legislative, one presidential. Although the sitting president enjoyed a distinct advantage in media coverage, all sides agreed after the 1996 election that the people had spoken. Observers noted the similarity of the 1996 campaign to those in the West, including barnstorming speeches, generous promises to special interests, and ample use of "photo opportunities." Never in the history of Russia had a head of state been subjected to open public evaluation and then been peacefully assured of a new term in power. Certainly this was a complete reversal of the Soviet Union's programmed, one-party political rituals.

Although the process of choosing a leader has been democratized, the process of governance remains a hybrid of Soviet and Western practices. The first administration of Boris Yeltsin was a combination of bold democratic initiatives and secretive decision making by committees and individuals beyond public view and responsibility. As criticism of Yeltsin grew in 1993 and 1994, his hold on power depended increasingly on presidential decrees rather than on open consultation with other branches of government or with the Russian people. Yeltsin's relatively easy reelection in mid-1996 fueled hopes that a second administration would revive some of the democratic processes that had enthused Russians as Yeltsin struggled with Gorbachev for

Russia's sovereignty before the demise of the Soviet Union. As a leader, however, Yeltsin showed little interest in the routine of day-to-day governance, and he often exercised poor judgment in delegating authority. Meanwhile, a formidable array of anti-reform factions retained their power base in the State Duma, and Yeltsin's precarious health further endangered the continuation of his reform program.

According to many analysts, the long-term well-being of Russia's political system will be determined by the next generation of political figures, who will not have been schooled in Soviet-style power politics. The question is how well democratic institutions will fare in the meantime.

*   *   *

Richard Sakwa covers Russian politics since the collapse of the Soviet Union in his textbook *Russian Politics and Society.* Boris Yeltsin offers an account of his forcible dissolution of the legislature in October 1993 and other Russian political events in *The Struggle for Russia.* Among books with useful sections on Russian politics are *After the Soviet Union: From Empire to Nation,* edited by Timothy J. Colton and Robert Legvold, and *Russia and the New States of Eurasia* by Karen Dawisha and Bruce Parrott. Prognoses of the future of reform in Russia are given in Anders Aslund's "Russia's Success Story," the "Russia Symposium" in the *Journal of Democracy* on the theme "Is Russian Democracy Doomed?," and *Russia 2010* by Daniel Yergin and Thane Gustafson. Informative articles on federalism and local politics include Susan L. Clark and David R. Graham's "The Russian Federation's Fight for Survival," Paul B. Henze's "Ethnic Dynamics and Dilemmas of the Russian Republic," and Robert Sharlet's "The Prospects for Federalism in Russian Constitutional Politics." In her article "Wrestling Political and Financial Repression," Laura Belin describes the situation of Russia's print and broadcast media in the mid-1990s. Information on current events in government and politics is provided by the Foreign Broadcast Information Service's *Daily Report: Central Eurasia,* the Open Media Research Institute's journal *Transition,* and the Jamestown Foundation's *Prism,* a monthly bulletin on Russia and the CIS. (For further information and complete citations, see Bibliography.)

Chapter 8. Foreign Relations

Alyonushka, an orphan, with her little brother, Ivanushka, who has turned into a goat (design from lacquer box made in village of Fedoskino)

ONCE A PARIAH DENIED DIPLOMATIC RECOGNITION by most countries, the Soviet Union progressed from being an outsider in international organizations and negotiations during the interwar period to being one of the arbiters of Europe's fate after World War II. The Soviet Union had official relations with the majority of nations by the late 1980s. In the 1970s, after achieving rough nuclear parity with the United States, the Soviet Union proclaimed that its own involvement was essential to the solution of any major international problem. At that time, regimes in countries containing about one-quarter of the world's population emulated the socialist form of political and economic organization proselytized by the Soviet Union. That web of influence was built upon the political doctrine of class struggle and the geopolitical philosophy of a proletarian internationalism that would link together the workers of the world. Although the spirit of those concepts remained at the base of the Soviet Union's international attitudes even in 1991, pragmatic considerations often were the primary determinants of policy in specific cases.

Among the many bureaucracies involved in the formation and execution of Soviet foreign policy, the Politburo of the Communist Party of the Soviet Union (CPSU—see Glossary) determined the major policy guidelines. The foremost objectives of that foreign policy were the maintenance and enhancement of national security and the maintenance of the hegemony gained over Eastern Europe following World War II. Relations with the United States and with Western Europe also were of major concern; the strategic significance of individual nations in the so-called Third World of developing nations determined, at least partly, the relations with those nations.

The Twenty-Seventh Party Congress of the CPSU in 1986 produced the last formal enumeration of Soviet foreign policy goals. That listing included ensuring favorable external conditions for building communism in the Soviet Union; eliminating the threat of world war; disarmament; strengthening the "world socialist system"; developing equal and friendly relations with so-called liberated (Third World) countries; peaceful coexistence with capitalist countries; and solidarity with communist and revolutionary-democratic parties, the international workers' movement, and national liberation struggles.

In the years that followed, the emphasis and ranking of these priorities changed in response to domestic and international stimuli. After Mikhail S. Gorbachev assumed power as CPSU general secretary in 1985, for instance, some Western analysts discerned in the ranking of priorities a deemphasis of Soviet support for national liberation movements. As such shifts occurred, two basic goals of Soviet foreign policy remained constant: national security (safeguarding CPSU rule at home and maintenance of adequate military forces) and influence over Eastern Europe.

After the demise of the Soviet Union, Russia claimed to be the legal successor to Soviet foreign policies. That position would allow Russia to assume a ready-made role as a leading world power. At the outset, Russia accepted or built upon many tenets of the conciliatory foreign policy toward the West of Gorbachev, the last Soviet leader, who had termed his revised policy "New Thinking." New Thinking defined international politics in common ethical and moral terms rather than military force, largely abandoning the Marxist-Leninist (see Glossary) idea that peaceful coexistence was merely a breathing spell in the worldwide class war. The most important practical result of Gorbachev's approach came in 1989 with the release of the Soviet Union's forty-four-year hold on the states of Eastern Europe. Superpower competition between the Soviet Union and the United States, known as the Cold War, gave way to increased cooperation with the United States on issues such as arms reduction, peace in the Middle East, and the Persian Gulf War.

In the early period after Russia became independent, Russian foreign policy built upon Gorbachev's legacy by decisively repudiating Marxism-Leninism as a putative guide to action, emphasizing cooperation with the West in solving regional and global problems, and soliciting economic and humanitarian aid from the West in support of internal reforms. In that early period, Russian foreign policy defended itself against arguments from former communists and ultranationalists that Russia had capitulated to the West and should renounce entanglements such as Western foreign aid. Russia also faced the challenge of reconciling the international commitments and obligations it inherited from the former Soviet Union with new and sometimes conflicting Russian interests, such as the desire to sell arms and missile technology abroad. Although Russia's leaders described Europe as its natural ally, they grappled with defining new relations with the East European (now termed Central European) states, the new states formed upon the disintegration of Yugoslavia, and Western Europe. In Asia, Russia faced territorial claims from China and Japan at the same time that closer Russian relations with these states and the Republic of Korea (South Korea) and Taiwan became possible. Several challenges emerged in Russia's relations with the fourteen other former Soviet republics, now called the "near abroad." Among the most serious confrontations were Russia's dispute with Ukraine over the status of Crimea, long and complicated conflicts between Armenia and Azerbaijan and within Georgia, and numerous new economic frictions. The problem of discrimination and ethnic violence against the 25 million ethnic Russians living in the new states was a growing concern in relations with several of the former Soviet republics, especially those in Central Asia. Russia also faced adapting to and competing with changing regional politics along its borders, such as the growing ties between the Central Asian states and Iran and Turkey (see Federal Border Service and Border Security, ch. 10).

The Emergence of Russian Foreign Policy

The Russian Soviet Federated Socialist Republic (RSFSR) of the Soviet Union began developing a separate foreign policy and diplomacy some time before the collapse of the Soviet Union at the end of 1991. The Russian Republic had possessed a foreign ministry and the "right" to conduct foreign policy since the 1936 Soviet constitution was amended in 1944. This power remained undeveloped, however, until the election of Boris N. Yeltsin as president of Russia and Russia's declaration of sovereignty in June 1990. Among the foreign policy institutions and procedures that emerged in Russia in this early period, some paralleled and others competed with those of the Soviet Union.

Recognized by world states and international organizations as the Soviet Union's successor state after its collapse, Russia aggressively assumed Soviet assets and most of the Soviet Union's treaty obligations. The assets included diplomatic properties worldwide and a large portion of the existing diplomatic personnel staffing those posts. Most foreign states simply reassigned their ambassadors from the Soviet Union to Russia, and international organizations allowed Russia to assume the Soviet seat. Most notably, Russia took over the permanent seat of the Soviet Union in the United Nations (UN) Security Council, which allowed it to join the elite power group with Britain, China, France, and the United States.

The Search for Objectives

In early 1992, Russian foreign minister Andrey Kozyrev announced that Russian foreign policy would differ from foreign policy under Gorbachev's New Thinking because democratic principles would drive it. These principles would provide a solid basis for peaceful policies. Kozyrev also stressed that the basis for the new foreign policy would be Russia's national interests rather than the so-called international class interests that theoretically underlay Soviet foreign policy. For two years (1992–93), Russian foreign policy was generally low key and conciliatory toward the West with endorsement of many Western foreign policy positions on world conflicts. Pressing domestic problems were a major determinant of this direction. Kozyrev argued that good relations with the West were possible because "no developed, democratic, civil society . . . can threaten us."

Domestic politics placed increasing pressure on this pro-Western and generally benign attitude. Bureaucratic infighting broke out in the government over foreign policy goals and the means of implementing them, and the same questions stimulated a major conflict between the legislative and executive branches of power. In this period, conflict and confusion exacerbated or triggered foreign policy problems with Ukraine, Japan, and the former Yugoslavia.

The lack of clarity in many aspects of foreign policy also reflected opposing Russian viewpoints over Russia's place in the world. Public debates raged over whether Russia should orient itself toward the West or the East, whether Russia was still a superpower, and what the intentions of the West were toward Russia—all indicating Russia's general search for a new identity to replace the accepted truths of Marxism-Leninism and the Cold War. In the debate, ultranationalists and communists strongly criticized what they viewed as pro-Western policies and argued that close relations with the West constituted a danger to Russia's national security because the West remained Russia's chief enemy. As early as December 1990, Soviet foreign minister Eduard Shevardnadze had cited harsh criticism of his conciliatory position toward the West as a major reason for his resignation.

To allay Russians' broad uncertainty about their country's place in the world, in early 1992 Kozyrev presented the Supreme Soviet (parliament) with his concept of three main foreign policy objectives, but the conservative legislators did not accept them. In January 1993, the Ministry of Foreign Affairs prepared another draft, which also met substantial criticism. Finally, in April 1993, the newly created Interdepartmental Foreign Policy Commission of the Security Council finalized a foreign policy concept that the parliament approved (see The Security Council, this ch.).

According to the 1993 foreign policy concept, Russia is a great power with several foreign policy priorities: ensuring national security through diplomacy; protecting the sovereignty and unity of the state, with special emphasis on border stability; protecting the rights of Russians abroad; providing favorable external conditions for internal democratic reforms; mobilizing international assistance for the establishment of a Russian market economy and assisting Russian exporters; furthering integration of the Commonwealth of Independent States (CIS—see Glossary) and pursuing beneficial relations with other nearby foreign states, including those in Central Europe; continuing to build relations with countries that have resolved problems similar to those that Russia faces; and ensuring Russia an active role as a great power. The concept also called for enhanced ties with Asian Pacific countries to balance relations with the West. Beginning in 1993, public statements about foreign policy placed greater emphasis on the protection of Russia's vital interests and less emphasis on openly pro-Western policies.

The 1993 concept disclosed a dispute between liberals and conservatives over the nature of Russian foreign policy toward the CIS. Liberals warned of the great human and material costs Russia would be forced to shoulder if it reabsorbed the former Soviet republics, a step the conservatives increasingly advocated in the 1990s. Liberals argued that Russia could be a great power without pursuing that policy. Both liberals and conservatives agreed, however, that Russia should play an active role in safeguarding the human rights of the 25 million ethnic Russians who found themselves in a foreign country for the first time after the breakup of the Soviet Union.

The 1993 foreign-policy concept called for strengthening a "unified military strategic space" in the CIS and protecting Russia's major interests there. It warned that a third state's military-political presence in the CIS, or actions among the CIS states such as creation of an economic or religious bloc of Central Asian states, could negatively affect Russia's interests. In the case of Central Asia, this would occur if ethnic Russians were forced to flee the region. On a somewhat more liberal note that showed its compromise quality, the concept recognized that intraregional cooperation could have positive results and that Russia should react to each effort individually. The primacy of relations with the CIS was strengthened after the December 1993 Russian legislative elections, in which nationalist factions expanded their power base.

For the conservatives, Russian dominance was necessary to secure southern borders and to ensure continued access to the waterways, ports, and natural resources of the newly independent states. Some conservatives asserted that Russia's military security required a line of defense outside Russia's own borders and along the borders of the former Soviet Union (and even, according to some, including a "neutral" Central Europe) (see The Geopolitical Context, ch. 9). A related position called for Russia to counter efforts by countries such as Turkey and Iran to gain influence in the new states.

Some Western observers suggested that the characteristic positions of Russian conservatives and liberals regarding the near abroad differed only in the degree of hegemony they demanded that Russia have over the CIS states. These observers also saw Russia engaging in a two-sided foreign policy that distinguished policy toward the near abroad from policy toward the rest of the world (see The Near Abroad, this ch.).

The 1993 concept and a new military doctrine were to be parts of an all-inclusive Russian national security concept. In April 1996, the Yeltsin government announced a draft national security concept. That document included the seemingly progressive renunciation of strategic and military parity with the United States, reaffirmation of collective security within the CIS, and support for reductions in nuclear arsenals and domestic military reforms. Ratification of the new concept was subject to the political events of mid-1996, including the presidential election.

The State of the Federation Speeches

In February 1994, Yeltsin outlined Russia's foreign policy in his first state of the federation address to the Russian parliament, as the 1993 constitution required. Yeltsin's address to the more nationalistic legislative body that had just been elected called for a more assertive Russian foreign policy. However, Yeltsin showed the still inchoate and even contradictory character of Russian foreign policy by making several references to conciliatory, Western-oriented policies.

Yeltsin noted that as a great country, Russia had its own foreign policy priorities to pursue, including prevention of cold or hot global war by preventing the proliferation of weapons of mass destruction. By mentioning the possibility of global war, he supported the view of the Russian military and other conservative and hard-line groups that the United States and the West remain a threat. Yeltsin voiced support for the Partnership for Peace (PfP—see Glossary) program of the North Atlantic Treaty Organization (NATO—see Glossary) and opposition to the expansion of NATO to include Central European states without including Russia (see Western Europe, this ch.). On international economic matters, Yeltsin called for quick removal of obstacles to trade with the West and for making the CIS into an economic union with a common market as well as a common security system and guarantees on human rights. As a warning to those calling for reconstituting the empire, he stated that such integration should not damage Russia by depleting the nation's material and financial resources.

Yeltsin's February 1995 state of the federation address did not repeat the contradictory and sometimes harsh tone of the 1994 speech. Yeltsin broadly depicted a cooperative and conciliatory Russian foreign policy, but he offered few details on policy toward specific countries or regions. Yeltsin outlined Russia's cooperation with the Group of Seven (G–7; see Glossary) of top world economic powers, the Organization for Security and Cooperation in Europe (OSCE—see Glossary), the UN, and NATO; the need for Russia to adhere to arms control agreements; and reductions in Russian armed forces. Despite his broadly conciliatory attitude toward the West and his general support of world cooperation, Yeltsin still objected to NATO enlargement as a threat to European security.

Some political analysts in the West suggested that the 1995 speech was an attempt to reassure the world of Russia's peaceful foreign policy in the wake of its widely censured attempt to suppress separatism in the Republic of Chechnya in December 1994 (see Movements Toward Sovereignty, ch. 4). Later in 1995, arguing that the West was wrong to fear Moscow's intentions toward Central Europe, Yeltsin announced that in 1995

Russian foreign policy would be nonconfrontational and would follow the principle of "real partnership in all directions" with the United States, Europe, China, India, Japan, and Latin America. The priorities of this stance would be enhanced interaction with the CIS states and partnership with the United States on the basis of a "balance of interests."

The February 1996 state of the federation speech occurred just after the convocation of the Federal Assembly (parliament) following the December legislative elections and a few months before the June 1996 presidential election. The legislative elections brought substantial gains for the Communist Party of the Russian Federation (Kommunisticheskaya partiya Rossiyskoy Federatsii—KPRF) and losses for reformists, which indicated deep discontent with the Yeltsin administration. Under these conditions, Yeltsin gave foreign policy only brief mention in his February speech. He noted that there had been problems in defining Russia's foreign policy priorities and in matching policy to execution. He vaguely promised a more realistic and pragmatic policy that would support Russia's national interests. Yeltsin singled out NATO enlargement, efforts against Russian interests in the CIS, conflict in the former Yugoslavia, and controversies over the Conventional Forces in Europe Treaty (CFE Treaty—see Glossary) and the Anti-Ballistic MissileTreaty (ABM Treaty—see Glossary) as persisting problems of Russia's foreign policy.

Despite these problems, Yeltsin emphasized that his foreign policy had scored several major achievements, including moves toward further integration of the CIS. Repeating statements from the 1995 speech, he noted that Russia's strategic arms control and security agreements ensured that the country faced no real military or nuclear threat. He argued that such security gains made Russia's signing of the second Strategic Arms Reduction Treaty (START II—see Glossary) advisable. He praised United States and Russian cooperation in extending the Nuclear Nonproliferation Treaty (NPT—see Glossary), and he noted the international prestige that Russia had gained through participation in meetings of the G–7, membership in the Council of Europe (see Glossary), and new ties with China and the states of the Association of Southeast Asian Nations (ASEAN) and the Persian Gulf.

The Foreign Policy Mechanism

In the Soviet system, the predominant foreign policy actor

was the general secretary of the CPSU, who also was the preeminent figure in the party's Politburo (the highest executive body of the government). By virtue of this position, the general secretary also was the country's recognized foreign representative. Other Politburo members with major foreign policy responsibility were the ministers of foreign affairs and defense (always members of the Politburo), the chairman of the Committee for State Security (Komitet gosudarstvennoy bezopasnosti—KGB; see Glossary), and the chief of the CPSU's International Department. The minister of foreign economic relations had foreign policy responsibility in commercial relations, and other members of the Council of Ministers provided input when their specific areas involved foreign affairs.

In 1988 constitutional revisions gave the Supreme Soviet, the Soviet Union's national parliament, new powers to oversee foreign policy and some input in policy formulation. The centralization of foreign policy decision making in the Politburo, together with the long tenure of its members, contributed to the Soviet Union's ability to plan and guide foreign policy over long periods with a constancy lacking in pluralistic political systems.

When a large part of the Soviet Union's foreign policy functions devolved to Russia in 1992, the Soviet pattern of centralizing foreign policy continued. The Russian constitution of 1993 gives the executive branch the chief role in making foreign policy, with the legislative branch occupying a distinctly subsidiary role. In the years since 1993, President Yeltsin has formed various organizations in the executive branch to assist him in formulating foreign policy. The mechanism of policy making has remained unwieldy, however, and the increasingly nationalistic parliament has used every power it commands to influence policy making.

The President

Under the provisions of the 1993 constitution, the president exercises leadership in forming foreign policy, represents Russia in international relations, conducts talks and signs international treaties, forms and heads the Security Council, approves military doctrine, delivers annual messages to the parliament on foreign policy, appoints and recalls diplomatic representatives (after consultation with committees or commissions of the parliament), and accepts credentials and letters of recall from foreign diplomats.

Between 1992 and 1996, there were indications that Yeltsin made important foreign policy decisions with little or no consultation with other officials of his administration or with the legislative branch. In that period, the size of the presidential apparatus steadily increased until it reportedly numbered several thousand staffers, including a Security Council staff of hundreds (see The Executive Branch, ch. 7). At the end of 1993, Yeltsin appointed a national security adviser who established his own staff, and during 1995 the Presidential Security Service, under the direction of Aleksandr Korzhakov, apparently also assumed some responsibility for foreign policy analysis. According to some observers, the vast size of the presidential apparatus exacerbated the confused and unwieldy formulation and implementation of foreign policy. In the early 1990s, the Ministry of Foreign Affairs came directly under presidential control, which further enhanced presidential power.

The Security Council

The function of the Russian Security Council is somewhat similar to that of the Defense Council that Nikita S. Khrushchev (in office 1953–64) created. Khrushchev's successor, Leonid I. Brezhnev (in office 1964–82), had retained the Defense Council as a consultative body on foreign policy and defense security, and this role was codified in the 1977 Soviet constitution. Gorbachev replaced the Defense Council in 1990, first by the Presidential Council and then by the Security Council.

After its statutory establishment in mid-1992, the Russian Security Council became part of Yeltsin's presidential apparatus. To distinguish his Security Council from earlier councils, Yeltsin presented the new body as an open organization that would obey the constitution and other laws and would work closely with executive and legislative bodies. He said the new council was based partly on that of the United States National Security Council. By statute, the Security Council is a consultative rather than decision-making body. It has the authority to prepare decisions for the president on military policy, protection of civil rights, internal and external security, and foreign policy issues, and it has the power to conduct basic research, long-range planning, and coordination of other executive-branch efforts in the foreign policy realm.

The Security Council's founding statute stipulates that voting members include the president, the vice president, the prime minister, the first deputy chairman of the Supreme Soviet, and the secretary of the council. It also includes nonvoting members from the Government (Russia's cabinet), including the ministers or chiefs of defense, internal affairs, foreign affairs, security, foreign intelligence, justice, and others. Other officials and foreign policy experts, including the chairman of the Supreme Soviet, also are invited to participate in council sessions. By statute the Security Council is to meet at least once a month. The 1993 constitution makes formation of the council the prerogative of the president, who is to be its chairman. In February 1994, Yeltsin reapportioned the membership of the council, giving additional influence to defense, internal affairs, justice, civil defense, security, foreign intelligence, and foreign affairs bureaucracies. Another adjustment in mid-1994 included the heads of both chambers of the new Federal Assembly and the head of the Federal Border Service. In 1995 Yeltsin added the minister of atomic energy to the council. After the election of a heavily antireformist parliament in December 1995, Yeltsin announced that the speakers of the two chambers of the Federal Assembly would be excluded from membership in the Security Council.

Some Russian commentators complained that the methods of the Security Council under its first secretary, Yuriy Skokov, were authoritarian, secretive, and antireformist. In early 1993, a major rift occurred between the Security Council and Yeltsin. Skokov led the council in opposing Yeltsin's attempt to declare a so-called special rule for the executive branch as a means of circumventing an executive-legislative deadlock and forcing legislative elections. After Yeltsin won this power struggle against the parliament, he felt strong enough to replace Skokov as secretary of the council. He named Oleg Lobov as secretary in September 1993, and Lobov served until Aleksandr Lebed' replaced him in June 1996.

The Security Council reportedly has played an important role in several vital foreign policy decisions. In September 1992, after an outcry from the Security Council over possible concessions to Japan on the issue of possession of the Kuril Islands, Yeltsin canceled a planned visit to Japan (see Japan, this ch.). In 1993 the Security Council's Interdepartmental Foreign Policy Commission (IFPC) reworked Foreign Minister Kozyrev's foreign policy concept to make it more conservative. The IFPC also appeared to be influential in Russian troop withdrawal policy in the Baltic states, which concluded in mid-1994.

The Security Council's agenda also reportedly included deliberations on United States-Russian relations, nuclear arms
reduction, ethnic relations within Russia, crime fighting, and
relations with the former Soviet republics. On many issues,
however, the council apparently failed to conciliate opposing
positions of the ministries of defense and foreign affairs, and
the council's overall influence appeared to wane after Skokov's
dismissal. In December 1994, the council rubber-stamped
Yeltsin's decision to send Russian security forces into Chechnya, and it invariably approved his policies there during 1995
and early 1996. Major questions remained about the quality of
debate in the council because military and police authorities
may not have furnished Yeltsin with complete information on
operations in Chechnya during this period. The council likely
had become moribund as a consultative body before Lebed'
attempted to revitalize its role in 1996.

The Security Council contains various subdepartments and
committees. Most significant to foreign policy formation is the
IFPC, which was created in December 1992. The IFPC analyzes
and forecasts information on foreign policy for the president.
Creation of the IFPC coincided with increased opposition to
Kozyrev's conduct of foreign policy and to Yeltsin's pro-Western
policies. In 1993 the IFPC attempted to block Kozyrev's pro-
Western foreign policies and urged a more "imperial" foreign
policy toward the near abroad. After 1993, however, the IFPC
appeared more amenable to the foreign ministry's policies.

The Parliament

During the first two years of Russia's independence, the Russian parliament's foreign policy powers were a matter of contention with the executive branch. This discord was part of a
broader legislative-executive branch standoff that culminated
in Yeltsin's forced takeover of the legislative building—the so-
called White House—in early October 1993 and his rule by
decree until December. In 1992–93 the parliament still derived
its power from the 1978 constitution of the Russian Republic
and numerous amendments to that document. Its foreign policy prerogatives included the right to ratify or abrogate international treaties, to confirm or recall diplomats serving abroad,
to approve or reject the deployment of armed forces to areas of
conflict abroad, and to approve the general direction of foreign policy.

In this period, the parliament increasingly attempted to widen its foreign policy prerogatives in opposition to official policies. These efforts included attempts to influence Russia's votes in the UN Security Council on economic and military sanctions against the former Yugoslavia, an open letter decrying Yeltsin's planned September 1992 visit to Japan, a July 1993 resolution declaring the Crimean city of Sevastopol' a Russian port although it is located in Ukrainian territory, and denunciation of United States aerial bombing of Iraq in 1993. Kozyrev tried to work with the International Affairs Committee of the Supreme Soviet and its successor, the State Duma, on several of those issues, but legislative criticism became increasingly strident in the period before Yeltsin forcibly dissolved the parliament in September 1993.

The 1993 constitution substantially reduced the parliament's foreign policy powers. The State Duma retained broad responsibility for adopting laws on foreign policy, but the constitution stipulated no specific foreign policy duties for the legislative branch. The constitution gave the Federation Council, the upper house of parliament, the responsibility for deciding on the use of troops abroad and reviewing State Duma ratification and denunciation of international treaties and Duma decisions on war and peace. In January 1994, the newly elected parliament established committees dealing with foreign policy issues, including a Committee on Geopolitics with a member of hard-liner Vladimir Zhirinovskiy's Liberal-Democratic Party of Russia as chairman. Vladimir Lukin returned from his post as ambassador to the United States to head the Duma's International Affairs Committee, which worked in 1994 with Kozyrev and Yeltsin to forge a more conservative consensus on foreign policy issues.

After remaining relatively quiescent on foreign policy matters in 1994, the parliament stepped up its criticism of Government policy in 1995. Four State Duma committees investigated Ministry of Foreign Affairs policies toward the near abroad, Asia, and the West, timing their queries to enhance electoral prospects for anti-Yeltsin deputies in the December legislative elections. In September 1995, the State Duma called for Russia to unilaterally lift UN-approved economic sanctions against Serbia; then it demanded that Yeltsin condemn NATO air strikes against Bosnian Serb targets and convened a special session to debate Russian policy toward the former Yugoslavia. In that session, ultranationalist and communist deputies called for

Kozyrev's resignation and for a wholesale redirection of foreign policy.

After the legislative elections of 1995, more deputies called for the parliament to take a more active role in foreign policy oversight. The reformist Yabloko coalition managed to gain the chairmanship of the International Affairs Committee in the State Duma, somewhat mitigating the anti-Government and anti-Western tone of legislative proceedings. However, many of the State Duma's nonbinding resolutions complicated foreign policy by arousing protests from foreign governments. In March 1996, the State Duma passed nonbinding resolutions abrogating the dissolution of the Soviet Union, which brought condemnation from most CIS member states as a threat to their sovereignty and independence. In 1996 the Duma also passed a resolution calling for elimination of international economic sanctions against Libya.

The Government (Cabinet)

According to the 1993 constitution, the chairman of the Government, the prime minister, defines basic policy guidelines, and the Government enacts the nation's foreign policy according to those guidelines. After referendum approval of the 1993 constitution, Prime Minister Viktor Chernomyrdin, whom Yeltsin had appointed in December 1992, began to play a more prominent role in meeting with foreign officials, particularly CIS leaders. The prime minister focused primarily on economic and governmental relations, however, and made few foreign policy pronouncements.

The Ministry of Foreign Affairs

The Ministry of Foreign Affairs was a central battleground of foreign policy formation from October 1990 until January 1996, when Andrey Kozyrev led it. In the two years before the dissolution of the Soviet Union, Russia's Ministry of Foreign Affairs under Kozyrev had played an important role in challenging the supremacy of Soviet foreign policy. At the end of 1991, Kozyrev's ministry formally absorbed the functions and many of the personnel of the defunct Soviet Ministry of Foreign Affairs. At that point, budgetary constraints forced the closure of three dozen former Soviet embassies and consulates and the release of more than 2,000 personnel.

After some uncertainty about the role of the ministry, Yeltsin decreed in 1992 that it should ensure a unified policy line in

Russian relations with foreign states and coordinate the foreign policy activities of other government agencies. At the end of 1992, increasing criticism of policy led Yeltsin to subordinate the role of the ministry to the supervision of the IFPC.

Beginning in 1992, Kozyrev and his ministry became the targets of increasingly forceful attacks from Russia's nationalist factions, who found any hint of pro-Western policy a pretext to call for Kozyrev's ouster. On several occasions, Yeltsin also criticized his foreign minister in public. Remarkably, Kozyrev retained his position until January 1996, when Yeltsin replaced him during a wave of nationalist appointments.

In December 1992, Kozyrev delivered what came to be called his shock diplomacy speech at a meeting of the Conference on Security and Cooperation in Europe (CSCE—see Glossary). In the speech, he outlined what he termed corrections to Russian foreign policy in a list of priorities that ultranationalists advocated. The corrections included a shift in policy away from the West and toward Asia; admonitions against NATO involvement in the Baltic states or other areas of the near abroad; a call for lifting UN economic sanctions against Serbia; and a demand that the near abroad rejoin Russia in a new federation or confederation. Western foreign ministries expressed shock, and Kozyrev retracted the speech by describing it as a rhetorical warning of what might happen if ultranationalists came to dictate Russian foreign policy. Although some Russian and Western observers said the speech was irresponsible, others saw it as an attempt to discredit ultranationalist views (and prevent the creation of the IFPC, then under consideration) by dramatizing the potential impact of extremist views.

In March 1995, Yeltsin criticized Kozyrev for his actions on several policy fronts and assumed control of the Ministry of Foreign Affairs with the authority to appoint all deputy foreign ministers. At the same time, Yeltsin enhanced the ministry's powers by making it responsible for coordinating and controlling all governmental foreign policy actions. Perhaps to head off mounting electoral criticism of foreign policy during 1995, as well as to enhance coordination efforts, Yeltsin also established a governmental commission on foreign policy. Ostensibly, the commission was to evaluate the ministry's conduct of foreign policy and to determine policy coordination needs between the presidential apparatus and government agencies having foreign policy responsibilities. Then, after intensified NATO bombardment of Bosnian Serb military targets in September 1995, Yeltsin reiterated his dissatisfaction with the ministry and the need for personnel and policy changes.

In December 1995, Yeltsin created yet another advisory group, the Council on Foreign Policy, to present him with proposals for coordinating the foreign policy activities of various government bodies and to inform him of their activities. Members of the council were to be the ministers of foreign affairs, defense, foreign trade, and finance; the heads of the foreign intelligence, security, and border guard services; and Yeltsin's foreign policy adviser. Scheduled to meet monthly, the council had projected functions virtually indistinguishable from those of the Security Council.

In January 1996, Yeltsin announced Kozyrev's resignation, which had long been expected in view of the harsh criticism of Russian foreign policy. Western analysts explained that the powerful reactionary forces in the State Duma had been poised to name their own candidate to head the Ministry of Foreign Affairs, so Yeltsin forestalled their move by dismissing Kozyrev and naming the more moderate Yevgeniy Primakov, an Arabist who had been KGB chief of espionage in 1991. Analysts viewed Primakov as a pragmatist with no strong views toward the West and predicted he would serve only until the winner of the upcoming presidential election replaced him. They expected Primakov to follow Yeltsin's lead in foreign policy by making no new gestures of friendship toward the West during the presidential election year. Although Primakov began his tenure by reassuring the United States that Russia would remain true to its international commitments, he also declared that Russia was and remains a great power and that his primary goal was to reintegrate the former Soviet republics, especially the Baltic states and Ukraine. These statements blunted the nationalist factions' complaints that Yeltsin was a puppet of Western interests.

The Ministry of Defense

In the Soviet era, the Ministry of Defense and its General Staff officers played a central role in the formation of national security policy because of their monopoly of defense information. After 1991 many senior officers in the armed forces continued to view military coercion as the main instrument for preventing the other side from gaining in foreign policy disputes (see Military Doctrine, ch. 9). In the early 1990s, most of the military establishment appeared to back both an assertive stance in the near abroad, where the Soviet military had exercised substantial influence through its military districts and played a role in local politics, and a less conciliatory relationship with the West. Some reformist elements of the military, mainly junior officers, rejected these views, and local military leaders sometimes seemed to act independently of their ministry in such areas of the near abroad as Moldova and Abkhazia, Georgia's breakaway autonomous republic. More often, the military leadership was united on actions having foreign policy repercussions, such as their advocacy of violating CFE Treaty limitations on military equipment deployed in the Caucasus region.

Regional Policies

The geographical extent of Russia's foreign policy interests is considerably less than that of the Soviet Union, which sought support and bases of operation wherever they might be available in the world. Nevertheless, most of the Soviet Union's primary zones of interest—Central and Western Europe, the Far East, the Mediterranean and Black Sea regions, and the United States—are priorities for Russia in the 1990s. To that list has been added the near abroad, which has become a zone of insecurity and the subject of constant debate.

The Near Abroad

Many Russians use the term "near abroad" (*blizhneye zarubezhiye*) to refer to the fourteen other former Soviet republics that had declared their independence by the time the Soviet Union broke up at the end of 1991. Leaders and elites in those republics objected that the term implied limitations on the sovereignty or status of the new states. Since independence, Russian policy makers have tried both to restore old bilateral connections and to create new relationships wherever possible. Throughout the first half of the 1990s, inconsistency and reverses characterized these diplomatic efforts because no firm principles underlay them. However, Russia maintained strong influence with all but the Baltic states, so the nationalists' hope of reclaiming part of the lost empire stayed alive.

Particularly perplexing for Western observers were apparent contradictions between Yeltsin government policies and the Russian military forces' actions in certain of the newly independent states (NIS) of the former Soviet Union. An example was

Russian military support of Abkhazian rebels against the Georgian government in 1993 at the same time that the Yeltsin government was promoting a cease-fire in the region. Some Western observers explained those contradictions as partly a result of differing bureaucratic interests and turfs, with the military seeking to continue its traditional influence and presence in the near abroad against the meddling of the Ministry of Foreign Affairs. If Russia's overall policy goal were to emasculate Georgia and force it farther into the Russian sphere of influence, ran the argument, then military and diplomatic actions would have been more compatible.

However, beginning in 1993 a greater degree of concordance appeared between the actions of the military and the government. Yeltsin and Kozyrev stressed that Russia ensured regional stability and acted in accordance with international standards in offering Russian diplomatic and military "peacekeeping" services to help end conflicts in the NIS. They also emphasized, however, that Russia had vital interests in using diplomatic or military means to protect the rights of the more than 25 million ethnic Russians residing in the near abroad. Accordingly, Russia pressured the NIS to enact legal protections such as dual citizenship for ethnic Russians. At the same time, Russia provided some aid to ease the internal economic distress that stimulated the emigration of ethnic Russians from the new states.

The new states signed friendship treaties and other agreements with Russia pledging them to protect ethnic Russian residents from harm and to respect their human and cultural rights. Because the borders among the states were open (except for Russia's borders with the Transcaucasus states, which were wholly or partly closed in 1994–96 during the Chechnya conflict), Russia's leaders asserted that Russia had important interests in ensuring the security of NIS borders with other states, such as Tajikistan's border with Afghanistan. In some cases, Russian troops served as so-called peacekeepers in conflict areas at the request of host governments such as Tajikistan and Georgia. In April 1994, at the request of the Ministry of Defense, Yeltsin decreed that Russia would seek military bases throughout most of the NIS.

Some analysts in the NIS and the West warned that Russia was showing a desire either to reconstitute its traditional empire or at least to include the NIS within an exclusive sphere of influence. They speculated that its arrangement with the near abroad might take the form of a collective security pact, similar to the former Warsaw Pact (see Glossary), that would counter NATO. Western analysts concluded that Russia's political and military elites adopted a more assertive foreign policy after the election of large numbers of ultranationalists and communists to the parliament in December 1993. They observed this trend toward assertiveness again during campaigns for the legislative elections of December 1995 and in the rhetoric of the 1996 presidential election campaign.

However, the Yeltsin government took considerable diplomatic actions to end NIS conflicts, and it stated that the financial burdens and human loss involved in burgeoning regional peacekeeping efforts precluded continuing such operations. Opinion polls showed that although some Russians supported a greater role in the near abroad, particularly in safeguarding ethnic Russians, the majority did not want Russia to assume new economic and defense burdens, particularly in Central Asia. Even in the State Duma, many members expressed doubt about the wisdom of even the peacekeeping efforts already under way in Tajikistan and Georgia.

Russian peacekeeping efforts in the NIS began with ad hoc agreements. For example, in August 1993 Russia formally invoked a Collective Security Agreement, signed by members of the CIS and ratified by the Russian parliament, to justify those efforts in Tajikistan. Avowing in the UN and the CSCE that its diplomatic and military efforts in the NIS supported regional stability, Russia requested international approval and financial support for its efforts. Kozyrev called for the deployment of UN and CSCE observers and the involvement of the international diplomatic community in solving the conflict in Georgia. In March 1994, Kozyrev asked the UN to recognize the CIS as an observer international organization and asked the European Union (EU—see Glossary) and the CSCE to recognize the CIS as a regional organization. Acknowledgment from these organizations would implicitly endorse the regional peacekeeping actions of the CIS.

At the December 1993 CIS meeting of heads of state, held after the Russian elections, Yeltsin's calls for strengthening military and economic cooperation within the CIS met with greater approval than they had previously. Since then the CIS states have been far from unanimous in supporting closer CIS integration, however: Armenia, Tajikistan, and Belarus have been most amenable; Azerbaijan, Georgia, Kazakstan, Kyrgyzstan, and Uzbekistan have maneuvered to maintain independence while seeking support in some areas; and Ukraine, Moldova, and Turkmenistan have been most opposed (see The Commonwealth of Independent States, ch. 9).

In September 1995, Yeltsin again maneuvered toward a more conservative CIS policy by repeating the Russian nationalists' concerns with border security and the treatment of ethnic Russians. In a program stressing regional integration, including a "defensive alliance," Yeltsin stipulated that the CIS should consist of countries "friendly toward Russia" and that Russia should be "a leading power" in the CIS, while reiterating the call for UN and OSCE participation in CIS peacekeeping actions. Among CIS regional problems of concern to Russia were relations between China and Kazakstan, the effect of ethnic separatism in China's Xinjiang Uygur Autonomous Region on neighboring nations of Central Asia, ethnic problems in Russian regions bordering Transcaucasia and Mongolia, and emigration of ethnic Russians from Central Asia.

Moldova

In the Moldavian Soviet Socialist Republic, ethnic minority Russians had proclaimed the autonomous Dnestr Moldavian Republic, or Transnistria, in September 1990. By late 1992, forces of the Russian 14th Army had enabled these Russians to consolidate control over most of the Dnestr region. Russia's actions chilled its relations with the now-independent Moldova, whose legislature had not ratified the 1991 CIS agreement. The pressure of a Russian trade blockade contributed to the victory of anticommunist candidates in Moldova's February 1994 legislative elections. In April 1994, the new legislature ratified Moldova's membership in the CIS, bringing the last of the non-Baltic Soviet republics into the organization. In October 1994, Russia and Moldova agreed on the withdrawal of the 14th Army, pending settlement of the political status of Transnistria. The agreement was jeopardized immediately, however, when Russia unexpectedly declared that the State Duma had to ratify the agreement, an outcome that had not occurred as of mid-1996.

Georgia

In Georgia, Russian mercenaries, allegedly bolstered by Russian military support, fought alongside separatist forces from Georgia's Abkhazian Autonomous Republic, who finally defeated Georgian forces in September 1993. In October Georgia was forced to end its strong opposition to membership in the CIS by becoming a full member and signing a series of security cooperation agreements. That step prompted Russia to send military peacekeepers to support government forces, which saved Georgia's president Eduard Shevardnadze from large-scale insurrection and further fragmentation of the country. The terms of the so-called rescue included a Georgian-Russian friendship treaty calling for the establishment of Russian military bases in Georgia. In June 1994, Abkhazia and Georgia agreed to the interpositioning of Russian peacekeepers between Abkhazia and the rest of Georgia to enforce a cease-fire. In September 1995, a Russian-Georgian treaty established twenty-year Russian leases of three bases. The Russian forces continued to share cease-fire enforcement in Georgia's breakaway South Ossetian Autonomous Oblast, where they had been since 1992, because no treaty had ended that conflict. The UN military observer group deployed in Abkhazia reported cooperative relations with the Russian peacekeepers.

Central Asia

In Tajikistan, oppositionist forces ousted the procommunist government in September 1992. Strong circumstantial evidence indicates that Russian forces assisted in the routing of the Tajikistani coalition government three months later. In 1993 several agreements formalized Russian military assistance. That year the new Tajikistani government deployed about 24,000 CIS peacekeeping troops from Russia, Uzbekistan, Kazakstan, and Kyrgyzstan (the majority of them Russian) along Tajikistani borders and at strategic sites. In late 1993, Tajikistan agreed to Russia's conditions on joining the ruble zone (see Glossary), including giving Russia control over monetary and fiscal policy, in return for subsidies. Tajikistan and Russia signed a cease-fire agreement in September 1994, but Tajikistani settlement talks, held under UN supervision with close Russian participation, remained inconclusive as of mid-1996. A small team of temporary UN military observers deployed in Tajikistan after the cease-fire agreement reported cooperative relations with CIS troops.

In Kazakstan in the mid-1990s, ethnic tensions increased between the Kazaks and the large minority population of Slavs (Russians, Ukrainians, and Belarusians) located primarily in northern areas of Kazakstan. The two groups represented an approximately equal share of the population, and Kazak president Nursultan Nazarbayev did a skillful job of balancing ethnic needs. He addressed many ethnic Russians' concerns while pushing language and other policies that were in the interests of the Kazak population. He resisted Russia's pressure to grant ethnic Russians dual citizenship; the legislature elected in 1995 contained a majority of ethnic Kazaks. In 1993 Kazakstan and Uzbekistan introduced their own national currencies rather than accept Russia's onerous conditions for membership in the ruble zone. Kazakstan also defied Russian pressure on its vital fuel industry by seeking new pipeline routes that Russia could not control. Nevertheless, for all five Central Asian republics, cooperation with Russia remains an essential element of economic and military policy.

In 1995 Yeltsin achieved a customs union with Belarus that later included Kazakstan and Kyrgyzstan. In March 1996, a new treaty among the four countries strengthened the terms of their economic integration. That treaty was part of Yeltsin's presidential campaign effort to show that he advocated gradual and voluntary integration among CIS members, in contrast to the threatening gestures of the State Duma and the Communist Party of the Russian Federation. However, an April 1996 agreement between Russia and Belarus to set a timetable for closely coordinating their governments and foreign policies brought opposition from Kazakstan, Turkmenistan, and Uzbekistan, which saw the agreement as a danger to their national sovereignty.

Other Former Soviet Republics

Although a strong body of opinion in Belarus supported the April 1996 bilateral agreement that would bring closer integration with Russia, independence-minded Belarusians in Minsk staged large-scale protests, and the policy encountered substantial opposition in Belarus's parliament and among reform factions in Russia. Nuclear weapons in Belarus, which reportedly were under tight Russian control after 1991, were scheduled for transfer to Russia by the end of 1996.

The last Russian troops left Estonia and Latvia in 1994, leaving significant populations of Russians behind. Russian officials criticized citizenship and other laws allegedly discriminating against those groups in the Baltic republics, and some Russian enclaves in the Baltic states made separatist threats. Border disputes with Estonia and Lativa remained unresolved and heated in mid-1996.

Azerbaijan, which anticipated substantial economic rewards from Western development of its Caspian Sea oil, resisted Russian offers to station peacekeeping troops in its war-torn Nagorno-Karabakh region. Azerbaijan's president Heydar Aliyev was a former member of the Soviet Politburo and came to office in a Russian-supported coup in 1993. But Aliyev has proven more independent than Russian policy makers expected. He has accused Russia (with some justification) of supporting Armenia against Azerbaijan in the Nagorno-Karabakh conflict. In 1994 Russia demanded and received a 10 percent interest in a Western-dominated oil consortium that is to develop rich offshore Caspian Sea deposits for Azerbaijan. Russia called for construction of a new export pipeline that would terminate at the Russian Black Sea port of Novorossiysk and allow Russia to collect transit fees and control the flow. In 1995–96 Russia objected to a territorial delineation of Caspian Sea resources to pressure Azerbaijan for concessions on oil revenue sharing and political and security matters. Azerbaijan decided on dual routes for oil shipments, one of which would bypass Russian territory by crossing Georgia to reach the Black Sea.

Many Western experts believe that Russia's relationship with Ukraine was the truest test of its willingness to accept the independence of the former Soviet republics. After regaining its independence at the end of 1991, Ukraine argued with Russia over the division of the Black Sea Fleet and the disposition of the Crimean Peninsula, which Nikita Khrushchev had "awarded" to the Ukrainian Soviet Socialist Republic in 1954 to mark the 300th anniversary of the union of Ukraine and Russia. After the end of the Soviet Union, the ethnic Russians who had come to dominate the Crimean Peninsula lobbied for autonomy from Ukraine or reunification with Russia. Ukrainian-Russian relations improved after the election of Ukraine's president Leonid Kuchma in July 1994. Russia did not support Crimean separatism, and both countries moved toward a peaceful settlement on dividing the Black Sea Fleet (see Naval Forces, ch. 9). The United States-Russian-Ukrainian Trilateral Nuclear Statement signed in early 1994 resolved many disputes over compensation for the transfer of nuclear weapons from Ukraine to Russia, and Ukraine transferred its last nuclear weapon to Russia in June 1996.

The United States

Relations with the United States have been a central concern of Soviet and Russian foreign policy since World War II. The United States gained unique stature in the Soviet Union when it emerged from World War II as the ultimate guarantor of European security against attack from the east and the top military power in the NATO alliance. A crucial factor of Soviet-United States relations was the mutual nuclear threat that arose in the 1950s as the Soviet Union developed first a nuclear capability and then a nuclear strategy. The nuclear threat and the underlying potential of "mutually assured destruction" created a chilling presence for the rest of the world. A high point in Soviet-United States relations was the Anti-Ballistic Missile Treaty (ABM Treaty) that resulted from the Strategic Arms Limitation Talks (SALT) of 1972. This agreement was an early achievement of the détente, or easing of tensions, that prevailed between the superpowers through most of the 1970s until the December 1979 Soviet invasion of Afghanistan.

The early 1980s were a time of tense relations and confrontations. The Soviet occupation of Afghanistan brought trade and cultural embargoes from the United States and highly visible gestures such as the United States boycott of the 1980 Summer Olympics in Moscow. In Europe the superpowers publicly traded threats and took actions such as the deployment of advanced nuclear weapons while they exchanged compromise positions at the negotiating table. Several events of 1983—the downing of a South Korean civilian airliner by the Soviet air force, the United States invasion of the Caribbean island of Grenada to evict a Marxist regime, and the exit of the Soviet delegation from arms control talks—kept bilateral tensions high.

By the mid-1980s, the Soviet Union had resumed talks on intermediate-range nuclear forces and strategic arms reduction. During that period, Soviet leadership underwent a major shift from Leonid I. Brezhnev, who died in November 1982, to Mikhail S. Gorbachev, who became general secretary in March 1985. The accession of Gorbachev ultimately ended a period of strident Soviet propaganda against United States president Ronald W. Reagan, whom Russia blamed for prolonging Cold War tensions because of his staunchly anticommunist positions.

In 1985 Reagan and Gorbachev began a series of annual summit meetings that yielded cultural exchange agreements, the Intermediate-Range Nuclear Forces Treaty (INF Treaty—

see Glossary) in 1987, and less tangible benefits. The sight of the "cold warrior" Reagan consorting with his Russian opposite number combined with the instant popularity that Gorbachev gained in the United States to again warm relations. In the mid- and late 1980s, the Soviet Union also stepped up media access and contacts. Soviet spokesmen began appearing regularly on United States television, and United States journalists received unprecedented access to everyday life in the Soviet Union.

In the early 1990s, relations with the United States lost none of their significance for Russia. Russia viewed summitry with the United States as the mark of its continued status as a great power and nuclear superpower. Presidents Gorbachev and George H.W. Bush declared a United States-Soviet strategic partnership at the summit of July 1991, decisively marking the end of the Cold War. President Bush declared that United States-Soviet cooperation during the Persian Gulf crisis of 1990–91 had laid the groundwork for a partnership in resolving bilateral and world problems. For Russia, the closer relations of the early 1990s included a broad range of activities, including tourism and educational exchanges, the study of United States institutions and processes to adapt them for a new "Union of Sovereign States" (one proposed title for a new, nonideological Soviet Union), and the beginning of United States aid to Russia.

During this period, the Soviet Union and subsequently Russia supported the United States on several international issues. In the UN Security Council, the Soviet Union and Russia supported sanctions and operations against Iraq before, during, and after the Iraqi invasion of Kuwait in 1990; called on the Democratic People's Republic of Korea (North Korea) to abide by safeguards of the International Atomic Energy Agency (IAEA); supported sending UN observers to conflict-ridden Georgia and Tajikistan; and supported UN economic sanctions against Serbia. The Soviet Union cosponsored Middle East peace talks that opened in October 1991.

In its cooperation with the United States on strategic arms control, Russia declared that it was the successor to the Soviet Union in assuming the obligations of START, which had been signed in July 1991. The Supreme Soviet ratified this treaty in November 1992. Presidents Bush and Yeltsin signed the second Strategic Arms Reduction Treaty (START II) in January 1993. The United States ratified that treaty in January 1996, but the much more problematic ratification by the new, nationalist-dominated State Duma was left until after the midyear presidential election. In September 1993, Russia acceded to the Missile Technology Control Regime, reaffirming an earlier decision not to transfer sensitive missile technology to India.

However, Soviet and Russian parliaments often opposed policies that they deemed helpful to the United States. The Supreme Soviet, which was less supportive than the Gorbachev government had been of international actions against Iraq, condemned United States air strikes in 1993. The Supreme Soviet approved START I in November 1992 with some conditions and after some delay, but then successive parliaments conducted hearings and debates on START II, without ratifying the treaty, from 1993 through mid-1996 (see Nuclear Arms Issues, ch. 9).

Beginning in 1993, the Russian Ministry of Foreign Affairs issued statements critical of United States actions and policies. Some United States observers interpreted them as part of a more assertive Russian foreign policy that insisted on protecting nebulous Russian vital interests. Other observers saw such statements primarily as rhetoric designed to mollify hard-line critics of Russian foreign policy in the parliament and elsewhere. Events corroborating the former interpretation included Russia's opposition to NATO membership for Central European and Baltic states, Russian military moves in Georgia that raised questions of its intentions in the near abroad, and Russia's insistence on selling nuclear reactor technology to Iran, as well as doubts about Russia's adherence to chemical and biological weapons bans, the Conventional Forces in Europe Treaty (CFE Treaty), and other arms control pacts. Another blow to United States-Russian relations came in 1994 with the United States arrest of Aldrich Ames, a longtime Soviet and Russian spy.

These events led some in the United States to question Russia's commitment to bilateral cooperation and the soundness of continued United States aid for Russia. Nevertheless, many elements of bilateral cooperation, including most United States aid programs, continued in 1995. From its high point in September 1993, when the United States Congress approved US$2.5 billion in aid to Russia and the NIS, the amount had declined to less than US$600 million for 1996. Only about one-third of the 1996 NIS appropriation was earmarked for Russia. In 1995 Congress placed several conditions on providing aid to

Russia, such as requiring that Russia reduce assistance to Cuba. The United States also censured Russian behavior such as nuclear energy agreements with Iran (see Latin America; The Middle East, this ch.).

The Yeltsin-Bush Summits

Before the dissolution of the Soviet Union, President Bush met with Boris Yeltsin in 1990, when Yeltsin was chairman of the Russian Supreme Soviet, and again in July 1991, immediately after Yeltsin's election as president of Russia. After the demise of the Soviet Union, Yeltsin met with Bush at a full-scale summit meeting in Washington in June 1992. The two leaders then agreed on many of the START II terms, and a joint session of the United States Congress enthusiastically received Yeltsin. According to some observers, that summit and Yeltsin's speech to Congress were the high points of Russia's conciliatory, pro-Western foreign policy orientation. At Bush's final summit with Yeltsin in January 1993, the leaders signed the landmark START II agreement.

The Yeltsin-Clinton Summits

The administration of William J. Clinton, which took office in January 1993, advocated more concerted United States efforts to aid Russian and NIS transitions to democracy and market economies. The justification of that policy was that these transitions served United States security and human rights interests and would provide markets for United States products. The April 1993 Vancouver summit, the first formal meeting between Yeltsin and Clinton, furthered United States-Russian cooperation on many bilateral issues. The resulting Vancouver Declaration pledged the two sides to uphold "a dynamic and effective United States-Russian partnership." The joint communiqué noted Yeltsin's pledge to continue reform efforts such as privatization.

The major summit initiative was finalization of a United States aid package of US$1.6 billion. On bilateral and international security issues, the two sides called for strengthening the Nuclear Nonproliferation Treaty (NPT) and urging North Korea not to carry out its threat to withdraw from the NPT. The sides also agreed to work for implementation of the START treaties.

An important by-product of the Vancouver meeting was the Gore-Chernomyrdin Commission, which initially was a vehicle for Vice President Albert Gore and Prime Minister Viktor Chernomyrdin to work out the details of bilateral agreements on space, energy, and technology. Between 1993 and early 1996, the two men met six times, each time with an expanded agenda. By 1996 the commission was a forum for establishing joint endeavors on topics ranging from the sale of Siberian timber to delivery of diphtheria vaccine to rural Russia. The United States also used the relationship to send messages to Yeltsin on urgent diplomatic topics such as Bosnia and Chechnya. In 1996 a similar commission brought Chernomyrdin into regular consultation with French foreign minister Alain Juppé.

Whereas the Vancouver summit had highlighted economic aid to Russia, the Moscow summit of January 1994 emphasized issues of arms control and nonproliferation. The summit included a hastily arranged meeting of the leaders of the United States, Russia, and Ukraine that produced Ukraine's commitment to give up all nuclear weapons on its territory and sign the NPT. The meeting's Trilateral Nuclear Statement also committed Russia and the United States to provide Soviet-era "nuclear powers" Belarus, Kazakstan, and Ukraine with security guarantees in exchange for giving up the uranium in the nuclear weapons located on their territory. Presidents Clinton and Yeltsin also pledged that, beginning in May 1994, strategic ballistic missiles no longer would be aimed at any country. This agreement marked the superpowers' first cessation of the nuclear operations that had been based on Cold War presumptions of mutual enmity.

A potential stumbling block to the success of the 1994 summit was Russia's objection to proposals for early admission of some Central European states into NATO (see Western Europe, this ch.; The NATO Issue, ch. 9). Nevertheless, the summit communiqué affirmed that the new European security order must include all nations as equal partners. The role of Russia in its near abroad was also an important point of discussion at the summit. Yeltsin sought to reassure the West that Russia's border policy was aimed only at stability, not neo-imperialist goals. Yeltsin repeated his call for peacekeeping assistance from the UN, CSCE, and other international organizations and complained about the international community's restrained response to Russian appeals for mediation in the conflict regions of Georgia, Azerbaijan, and Tajikistan.

United States aid played a less prominent role in the Clinton-Yeltsin summit in Washington in September 1994. Instead, both sides emphasized the growth of future bilateral trade and investment. International policy differences were more visible in the Washington meeting than they had been previously, but both sides stressed the nonconfrontational nature of the "working partnership" in resolving differences. The two presidents signed a framework agreement termed the Partnership for Economic Progress (PFEP), which outlined principles and objectives for the development of trade and economic cooperation and for United States business investment in Russia. They also planned a Commercial Partnership Program to help guide Russia toward better bilateral commercial relations. United States business leaders warned Yeltsin, however, that private investment in Russia could not increase appreciably under the still capricious and complex Russian laws, taxes, import duties, and governmental red tape.

A major initiative at the summit was agreement that once Moscow and Washington had ratified START II, the two sides would quickly remove warheads from missiles whose launchers would be eliminated under START II. Other initiatives covered the storage and security of nuclear materials and continued moratoriums on nuclear weapons tests.

The conflict in Bosnia remained an issue of contention. Yeltsin refused to support a UN Security Council resolution lifting the arms embargo against Bosnia's Muslim-led government. The United States also voiced concern about Russian peacekeeping activities in former Soviet republics, although Russia insisted that its actions respected the sovereignty of the new states. Russian recalcitrance on arms sales to Iran, classified by the West as a terrorist state, also was a source of conflict. While agreeing that no new arms contracts would be signed with Iran, Yeltsin insisted that existing commitments would be upheld.

Three issues dominated the Clinton-Yeltsin summit meeting held in Moscow in May 1995—NATO enlargement, Russia's sale of nuclear reactors to Iran, and the Chechnya conflict. In spite of their differences on key issues, Clinton and Yeltsin pledged to continue a cooperative relationship.

The two leaders referred the matter of nuclear sales to Iran to the Gore-Chernomyrdin Commission, which subsequently crafted an agreement on two Russian concessions on the transfer issue. On the subject of European security, the two sides underscored the importance of ongoing integration and of joint participation in international bodies, including Russia's membership in NATO's Partnership for Peace (PfP). Discussions of NATO enlargement remained inconclusive.

At the May 1995 summit, President Clinton expressed his expectation that Russia would meet all conditions of the CFE Treaty, which was due to come into full force in November 1995. Meeting this deadline would require withdrawing several hundred tanks and other weapons from the North Caucasus region of Russia, including many in Chechnya. At the review conference in May 1996, Clinton offered to support modifications to the CFE Treaty to meet Russia's "legitimate security interests." Clinton reiterated United States concerns about human rights abuses in Chechnya and called for a permanent cease-fire. Yeltsin responded by calling Russia's Chechnya campaign a battle against terrorism rather than a conventional military action.

The summit meeting of October 1995, held in Hyde Park, New York, continued the previous emphasis on the most contentious issues of bilateral relations. These included Russian nuclear sales to Cuba and Iran, objections to expansion of NATO in Central Europe and to United States plans to build a ballistic missile defense system, and Russia's noncompliance with the CFE Treaty. The dominant question of this summit, which yielded no agreements, was the form of Russia's participation in NATO-commanded international peacekeeping forces to be sent into Bosnia. Clinton and Yeltsin referred most of the contentious issues to lower levels for detailed discussion and emerged from the summit emphasizing the continued strength of Russian-United States cooperation.

The Moscow summit of April 1996 took place during presidential campaigns in both countries. It also followed directly the G–7 meeting on nuclear safety and security in Moscow. As in Hyde Park, the two leaders emphasized the positive aspects of their partnership and announced progress in negotiations over the CFE and ABM treaties, but without citing any details. Yeltsin briefed Clinton on his progress toward ratification of the START II agreement, and Clinton criticized Russia's fears of NATO enlargement as completely unfounded. For Yeltsin, the meeting was an opportunity to demonstrate to the electorate that the leader of the United States respected him, but he also felt constrained to demonstrate that he was independent of coercion by Clinton.

Western Europe

The Soviet Union's relations with Western Europe following World War II were colored heavily by Soviet relations with Eastern Europe and by the Warsaw Pact forces arrayed in Europe against NATO forces. The Soviet influence over Eastern Europe, punctuated by the 1956 invasion of Hungary and the 1968 invasion of Czechoslovakia and by a constant buildup of conventional and nuclear forces, prompted West European NATO member nations to reinforce their defenses and discouraged direct relations between those nations and the Soviet Union.

The Soviet Union's policy toward Western Europe had five basic goals: preventing rearmament and nuclearization of the Federal Republic of Germany (West Germany); preventing the political, economic, or military integration of Western Europe; obtaining West European endorsement of the existing territorial division of the continent; splitting the NATO alliance by encouraging anti-Americanism on various issues; and creating nuclear-free zones by encouraging European peace groups and leftist movements. The more general aim was to make Western Europe as similar as possible to the Soviet Union's highly advanced northwestern neighbor, Finland: a neutral buffer zone whose political reactions could be anticipated under any circumstances, and which would refrain from commitments to Western nations. In the early 1980s, a conflict in Western Europe over NATO and Warsaw Pact nuclear installations accelerated Soviet efforts to neutralize NATO's European contingent. The Soviet Union tried to foster a European détente separate from one with the United States. The effort was defeated because West European governments were determined to uphold and modernize NATO, and Soviet-sponsored peace groups failed to arouse public opinion against NATO participation.

The Soviet-era division of Europe into two distinct military alliances continues to influence Russia's policy toward Western Europe. NATO remains an active presence in Western Europe, and Russia sees a persistent threat that NATO will embrace the former Warsaw Pact allies and leave Russia without its European buffer zone. Because of this perceived threat, sharpened in the rhetoric of Russian nationalist factions, Russia has been reluctant to accommodate West European nations on a number of issues, even as it has hastened to bolster relations in other areas such as commerce.

Even before the breakup of the Soviet Union, Yeltsin pursued closer relations with Western Europe on behalf of the Russian Republic. In his first foreign trip after the failure of the August 1991 coup had substantially improved his stature as president of the Russian Republic, Yeltsin visited Germany to seek safeguards for Germans residing in Russia. After 1991 Russia's relations with Western Europe achieved a level of integration and comity that the Soviet Union had aspired to but had never reached. The draft foreign policy concept of January 1993 called for Russian foreign policy to consolidate the emerging partnership with the states of Western Europe, but it also emphasized that Russia's vital interests might cause disagreement on some issues. Russia's major goals included gaining West European aid and markets, recognition of Russia's interests in Central Europe and the CIS, and regional cooperation in combating organized crime and nuclear smuggling. Germany emerged as the largest European aid donor to Russia and its largest trade and investment partner.

In June 1994, Yeltsin and the leaders of the European Union (EU) signed an agreement on partnership and cooperation. Pending the ratification of the agreement by the member states, a provisional economic accord was drawn up in early 1995 extending most-favored-nation status to Russia and reducing many import quotas. Because of Western disapproval over the war in Chechnya, the EU did not sign the agreement until July 1995, following a cease-fire in Chechnya.

The Council of Europe also sidelined a Russian application for membership as a sign of disapproval of events in Chechnya, and in July 1995 the council issued a report detailing Russian (as well as some Chechen) human rights abuses in Chechnya. After the conclusion of the cease-fire, Russian officials requested reconsideration of Russia's application. The council granted Russia full membership in January 1996. European authorities explained that admitting Russia into Europe's foremost body on human rights, democracy, and the rule of law would promote democratic trends in Russia more effectively than the isolation that would result if membership were denied. A substantial body of European opinion continued to oppose admission, however, especially when Russian army attacks on Chechen civilians continued and Russia failed to impose a required moratorium on capital punishment (see Chechnya, ch. 9; The Criminal Justice System, ch. 10).

In February 1996, the Council of Europe and the EU announced an aid package to help Russia meet the legal and human rights requirements of membership in the council. Tensions in Russia's relations with the West continued, however, with its refusal in April 1996 to provide arms sales data. These data are necessary for establishment of a military technology export control regime to replace the Coordinating Committee for Multilateral Export Controls (CoCom), which NATO used during the Soviet era to monitor world arms shipments.

The CFE Treaty, which the Soviet Union signed in 1990, aimed at stabilizing and limiting the nonnuclear forces of all European nations. Signed in the context of the NATO-Warsaw Pact division of Europe, the treaty remained a basis for reduction of tensions in Europe after the Warsaw Pact and the Soviet Union dissolved.

Although the Russian military accepted the CFE Treaty, in the ensuing years it increasingly insisted that the signatories allow modification of force limits on Europe's flanks, which included the still substantial garrison in Kaliningrad Oblast on the Baltic and the troublesome Caucasus region (see The Geopolitical Context, ch. 9). In the early 1990s, Russia shifted much weaponry to the southern flank area to stabilize its North Caucasus republics, particularly breakaway Chechnya, as well as the independent but conflict-plagued Caucasus states of Armenia, Azerbaijan, and Georgia. Although NATO proposed some alterations in Russia's flank limits in September 1995, Russia still was not in compliance when the treaty came into full force in November 1995. Russia met the treaty's overall arms reduction targets, however. Russia called for further modifications of the treaty's troop disposition requirements to be put on the agenda of a planned May 1996 review conference. After intense negotiations, the conferees finally agreed to allow Russia to retain additional equipment in the southern flank area for three years.

NATO

The January 1993 draft foreign policy concept of the Ministry of Foreign Affairs called for increasing ties with NATO through the North Atlantic Cooperation Council and other means, including military liaison, joint maneuvers, and exchange visits. Russia objected to full NATO membership for Poland and other Central European states, so the United States proposed establishment of NATO's Partnership for Peace (PfP) in the fall of 1993. The PfP was to be an ancillary of NATO, consisting entirely of the former Warsaw Pact states and former Soviet republics. By the end of 1995, twenty–seven states—the entire complement of those two groups—had joined. Yeltsin supported Russia's membership in the PfP in his "state of the federation" address to the Russian parliament in February 1994, but he opposed the future inclusion in NATO of Central European states as unacceptably excluding Russia from participation in European affairs.

In response to NATO air strikes on Bosnian Serb forces in April 1994, Yeltsin hinted that Russia might delay signing the PfP agreement. Instead, Kozyrev announced shortly thereafter that the Russian ministries of foreign affairs and defense had decided that Russia should have a special status in the PfP "to protect it from hostile acts by NATO." In May 1994, the Russian Security Council called unsuccessfully for NATO to agree to a list of special privileges for Russia. The Russian delegation walked out of the December 1994 signing ceremonies for membership in the PfP before finally joining in June 1995.

At the Budapest meeting of CSCE heads of state in December 1994, Russia called for the CSCE to transform itself into the major security organization in Europe. The CSCE rejected Russia's proposal, but it did agree to change its name to the Organization for Security and Cooperation in Europe (OSCE) to reflect its status as a permanent organization. The West viewed Russia's overture as seeking a new forum from which to gain influence over NATO and other Western organizations. Through 1995 Russian spokesmen continued their criticism of NATO, including its air strikes in Bosnia, and called for an alternative European security structure. Nevertheless, Yeltsin vetoed a State Duma resolution canceling Russia's PfP membership.

In late 1995, Russia agreed to join NATO's efforts to enforce the Dayton Peace Accords, formally signed in December as the Peace Agreement on Bosnia-Herzegovina, to end the conflict in Bosnia. In January 1996, some 1,600 Russian troops arrived in northern Bosnia to work closely with United States forces as part of the Bosnian Peace Implementation Force (IFOR). In the first six months of that arrangement, little controversy arose over command roles or goals.

Central Europe

Soviet influence in Eastern Europe began with Soviet occupation of territories during World War II. By 1949 communist regimes had been put into place in all the occupied states: Bulgaria, Czechoslovakia, the German Democratic Republic (East Germany), Hungary, Poland, and Romania. Under the leadership of Josip Broz Tito, Yugoslavia maintained an independent position as a communist state that Soviet leaders first vilified but ultimately recognized in 1955. Domination of the East European countries belonging to the Warsaw Pact and the Council for Mutual Economic Assistance (known as Comecon—see Glossary) remained a fundamental priority of Soviet foreign policy through the disintegration of both organizations in 1991. Soviet leaders used the continued existence of socialist regimes in Eastern Europe as part of the ideological justification of socialism at home because it fulfilled the Marxist-Leninist recipe of the rule of the multinational proletariat. Because of that logic, a threat to Eastern Europe became a threat to the Soviet Union itself.

In the 1950s, the Soviet military used force to restrain mass expressions of resistance to conventional, Soviet-backed regimes in East Germany (1953), Poland (1956), and Hungary (1956). After the 1968 Warsaw Pact invasion of Czechoslovakia quelled political liberalization in that country, the irreversibility of communist control in East European countries was formulated in what became known as the Brezhnev Doctrine, which for the next twenty years was the foundation of Soviet policy toward the region. Soviet policy makers determined that occupation forces were the only sure guarantee of continued communist rule in Eastern Europe and that some limited local control over domestic policy was necessary to avoid future resistance. When Polish workers pushed their demands for independent trade unions and the right to strike in 1980–81, the implicit threat of invasion by Soviet forces led Polish police and security forces to quell disturbances and a new, military prime minister, General Wojciech Jaruzelski, to declare martial law.

In the mid-1980s, Gorbachev's internal liberalization was paralleled by his doctrine of "many roads to socialism," which called for cooperation rather than uniformity among East European nations. That call coincided with the implicit revocation in 1988 of the Brezhnev Doctrine as Soviet military doctrine recognized the need to conserve resources (see Soviet Doctrine, ch. 9). Gorbachev's internal reform programs of *glas-*

nost (see Glossary) and *perestroika* (see Glossary) received varying degrees of support and imitation among East European leaders. Regimes in Bulgaria, Hungary, and Poland showed substantial support, but those in Czechoslovakia, East Germany, and Romania refused to adopt the type of far-reaching domestic reforms that Gorbachev introduced at home (see The Gorbachev Era, ch. 2). Nevertheless, by the late 1980s the nature of Soviet influence had shifted unmistakably away from coercion toward political and economic instruments of influence. The last stage of Soviet relations with the region, 1989–91, was fundamentally different. By 1990 all the East European member states of the Warsaw Pact and Comecon had rejected their communist regimes and were straining toward the West. Although Soviet policy makers struggled to keep the two multinational organizations alive as instruments of influence, events had rendered them moribund before their formal demise in 1991. Now the world redesignated Eastern Europe as Central Europe, and the great western buffer zone disappeared.

Immediately after the collapse of the Warsaw Pact and Comecon and the breakup of the Soviet Union in 1991, relations with Central Europe were a relatively low priority of Russian foreign policy. This situation began to change during 1992, when many Russian reformists argued that closer ties with the new Central European democracies would bolster Russia's own commitment to democratization. Closer commercial ties also would make Central Europe's relatively inexpensive goods more readily available and afford better opportunities to make valuable connections with Western Europe as the former Warsaw Pact states moved closer to full integration into Europe.

Russia's January 1993 draft foreign policy concept stressed the importance of Central Europe. The concept proclaimed that the region "falls within the historical sphere of our interests" because it abuts "the belt of sovereign states"—Ukraine, Belarus, Moldova, Lithuania, Latvia, and Estonia—of great interest to Russia. The concept warned against attempts by the West to push Russia out of Central Europe and to make the region into a buffer zone that would isolate Russia from Western Europe. Russia would counter such movements by reestablishing good trade and other relations with the Central European states.

The NATO Issue

The draft concept did not present NATO involvement in Central Europe as inherently threatening to Russian interests. Later in 1993, however, Yeltsin reversed course under the political exigency of his upcoming confrontation with the State Duma. The new position was that former members of the Warsaw Pact could join NATO only if Russia also were included. This opposition then spurred the United States proposal of the Partnership for Peace.

The military doctrine that Yeltsin decreed in November 1993 was not directed clearly at NATO. Calling for a neutral Central Europe, the doctrine warned that Russia would interpret as a threat the expansion of any alliance in Europe to the detriment of Russia's interests or the introduction of foreign troops in states adjacent to the Russian Federation. Throughout 1995 and the first half of 1996, Russian military officials continued to demand that the Central European states remain neutral. During the Moscow visit of Poland's president Alexander Kwasniewski in April 1996, Yeltsin hailed warmer ties, but he noted that the NATO issue remained the single obstacle over which the two sides disagreed.

Russia's Role in the Former Yugoslavia

In Russia's debate over its national interests and in Yeltsin's power struggle with hard-liners, a major issue was the appropriate attitude toward Serbia, a long-time ally whose aggression against several other republics of the former Socialist Federal Republic of Yugoslavia, most notably Bosnia and Herzegovina, had made it an international pariah. The key question was how to cooperate with Western efforts to end the crisis in the former Yugoslavia while preserving Russia's traditional support of Serbia.

After the Serbian government expressed support for the August 1991 coup in Moscow, the Yeltsin government of the Russian Republic condemned the Serbian attacks of late 1991 on Croatia, one of the two initial breakaway republics from the Yugoslav federation. Russia supported efforts in the UN to compel Serbia to accept a negotiated settlement of the conflict with Croatia. This relatively low-key involvement shifted to a more active policy in 1993.

The 1993 foreign policy concept's language on the former Yugoslavia was rather neutral; it simply called for Russia to cooperate with the UN, the CSCE, and other parties in peace-making efforts and to use its influence in the former Yugoslavia to encourage a peaceful settlement. As it began to speak more specifically for Serbian interests later in 1993, Russia hoped at the same time to maintain its image with the West as a useful mediator of a thoroughly frustrating conflict. However, this approach caused some tensions with the United States and its Western allies, who had hoped for straightforward Russian support of UN-sanctioned military actions against Serbian aggression. Russian hard-liners, meanwhile, urged that Russia give priority to defying what they called a "Western drive for hegemony" over the former Yugoslavia and to otherwise protecting Russian and Serbian geopolitical interests.

Hard-liners in Russia and Serbia espoused a so-called pan-Slavic solidarity that emphasizes ethnic, religious, and historical ties. Its adherents shared a frustration at diminished geopolitical dominance (in Serbia's case, the loss of influence over other parts of the former Yugoslavia, and in Russia's case the loss of control over the near abroad). Perceived threats to Serbs and Russians now outside the redrawn borders of their respective states aggravated this frustration. However, the rocky, thirty-five-year relationship between the Soviet Union and Tito's Yugoslavia disproved the natural affinity of the two nations.

Russia launched a more assertive phase of involvement in the former Yugoslavia when it opposed NATO air strikes against Bosnian Serb forces around Sarajevo in 1994 and 1995. Russia argued that there should be no air strikes until peace negotiations had been exhausted. Russia also demanded a larger role as a superpower in decision making on UN, NATO, and other international actions involving the former Yugoslavia.

In August 1995, Yeltsin and the Russian parliament harshly criticized intensified NATO air strikes on Bosnian Serb military targets. When mediation efforts finally led to a cease-fire in Bosnia in October 1995, Russia agreed to provide troops for a NATO-sponsored peacekeeping force. After some rearrangement of lines of command to avoid direct NATO command of Russian forces, Russian troops joined the peacekeepers in January 1996. Although it cooperated with IFOR, Russia asserted its views on other aspects of the Bosnia situation. In February 1996, Russia withdrew unilaterally from UN-imposed economic sanctions on Bosnian Serbs, arguing that the Serbs had met the conditions for withdrawing the sanctions.

China

Relations between China and the Soviet Union were cool and distrustful from the mid-1950s until the demise of the Soviet Union. Joseph V. Stalin (in office 1927–53) fostered an alliance when communists took over mainland China in 1949. When Khrushchev announced his de-Stalinization policy in 1956, Chinese leader Mao Zedong sharply disapproved, and the alliance was weakened. In 1959 and 1960, the Sino-Soviet rift came to full world attention with Khrushchev's renunciation of an agreement to provide nuclear technology to China, the Soviet withdrawal of all economic advisers, and mutual accusations of ideological impurity. Leonid Brezhnev attempted to improve relations, but serious border clashes and Brezhnev's proposal of an Asian collective security system that would contain China were new sources of hostility. In the 1970s, China began to improve relations with the West to counter Soviet political and military pressure in Asia. After Mao's death in 1976, the Soviet Union again sought to improve relations with China. But polemics were renewed in 1977, and tension between two Southeast Asian client states, Cambodia and Vietnam, further damaged relations. In 1979 China invaded Vietnam to defend Cambodia from the Vietnamese incursion of 1978. The Soviet Union condemned the invasion and increased arms shipments to Vietnam. Competing goals in Southeast Asia remained a key issue for nearly a decade.

A new set of bilateral negotiations began in 1979, but the Chinese ended talks shortly after the Soviet Union invaded Afghanistan in late 1979. Thereafter, China added withdrawal of Soviet troops from Afghanistan to its conditions for renewing the two nations' 1950 friendship treaty. Talks on the Sino-Soviet border situation finally resumed in late 1982, but relations remained static until Gorbachev began making conciliatory gestures in 1986 and 1987. In 1988 two major obstacles were removed when the Soviet Union committed itself to removing troops from Afghanistan, and Vietnam did likewise for Cambodia. The Sino-Soviet summit meeting of June 1989 was the first since the Khrushchev regime.

Russia's foreign policy toward China generally has had two goals: to preserve a counterweight against United States influence in the Pacific and to prevent Chinese regional hegemony and a Sino-Japanese alliance that could exclude Russia. This balancing act appeared in Russia's 1993 foreign policy concept in its call for weighing the benefits of increased Russian arms sales to China against the danger of re-creating a Cold War arms race in which the respective proxies would be Taiwan and China. Accordingly, the concept endorsed neighborly and substantive relations with China while ensuring that "third countries," such as the United States or Japan, would not be able to use China as an ally against Russia.

In the early 1990s, relations got a boost from China's interest in renewed weapons imports from Russia and other forms of military cooperation. In 1992 an exchange of visits by high defense officials established defense ties and included the signing of a major arms technology agreement with a reported value of US$1.8 billion. In 1993 another series of defense exchange visits yielded a five-year defense cooperation agreement (see Foreign Arms Sales; China, ch. 9). A strategic partnership, signed in early 1996, significantly strengthened ties.

In December 1992, Yeltsin went to China and signed a nonaggression declaration that theoretically ended what each called the other's search for regional hegemony in Asia. Another treaty included Russian aid in building a nuclear power plant, the first such provision since Sino-Soviet relations cooled in the late 1950s. Chinese party chairman Jiang Zemin visited Moscow in September 1994 and concluded a protocol that resolved some border disputes and generally strengthened bilateral ties. During Yeltsin's visit to China in April 1996, both sides described their relationship as evolving into a "strategic partnership," which included substantially increased arms sales. At the April meeting, new agreements made progress toward delineating and demilitarizing the two countries' 3,645 kilometers of common border. Although border security and illegal Chinese immigration into the Russian Far East were controversial issues for Russian regional officials, Yeltsin demanded regional compliance with the agreements. Russia has respected China's claim that Taiwan is part of its territory, although Russia's trade with Taiwan increased to nearly US$3 billion in 1995 and Russia planned to open trade offices on the island in 1996.

In 1994–96 China emerged as a major market for Russian arms, having bought several dozen Su–27 fighter aircraft and several Kilo-class attack submarines. Russia also had a positive trade balance in the sale of raw materials, metals, and machinery to China. A series of high-level state visits occurred in 1994 and 1995. Both countries pursued closer ties, in each case partly to counterbalance their cooling relations with the

United States. In March 1996, Russia announced that it would grant China a loan of US$2 billion to supply Russian nuclear reactors for power generation in northeast China, and further cooperation was proposed in uranium mining and processing, fusion research, and nuclear arms dismantlement.

Japan

Historians identify the crushing victory of Japan over Russia in the Russo-Japanese War of 1904–05 as the beginning of those countries' poor relations. After World War I, Japan took Vladivostok and held the key port for four years, initially as a member of the Allied interventionist forces that occupied parts of Russia after the new Bolshevik (see Glossary) government proclaimed neutrality in 1917. At the end of World War II, Stalin broke the neutrality pact that had existed throughout the war in order to occupy vast areas of East Asia formerly held by Japan. His action resulted in the incorporation of the entire Kuril Islands chain and the southern half of Sakhalin Island into the Soviet Union, and it created an issue that blocked the signing of a peace treaty and forging closer relations. In the Gorbachev era, relations thawed somewhat as high officials exchanged visits and the Soviet Union reduced its Far East nuclear forces and troops, but fundamental differences remained unchanged when the Soviet Union dissolved.

Since World War II, twin concerns have dominated Japanese relations with the former Soviet Union: the East-West Cold War and the so-called Northern Territories—the four southernmost Kuril islands—that the Soviet Union occupied under the terms of the Yalta Conference in 1945 and continued to occupy on grounds of national security. The dissolution of the Soviet Union initially raised Japanese expectations of a favorable resolution of the islands dispute and Russian hopes of significant Japanese economic aid and investment in return. But the return of the islands to Japan remained politically inadvisable for Soviet and Russian leaders throughout the first half of the 1990s.

Just before he became de facto president of Russia in 1990, Yeltsin had advanced a bold, five-point plan to deal with the territorial issue. After initially criticizing the plan, the Gorbachev government incorporated several of Yeltsin's recommendations into its foreign policy position. The plan envisioned several steps leading to a full peace treaty, without a firm Russian commitment to return the islands, and in 1992 the Russian Federation continued the discussions that the Gorbachev regime had initiated.

However, Japan refused to increase commercial activity with Russia until the countries resolved the territorial issue (by which Japan meant that Russia would recognize its sovereignty) and signed a peace treaty. Russia offered only to return two islands after a peace treaty was signed. In the meantime, Yeltsin's efforts to improve bilateral relations faced increased domestic criticism from hard-line legislators, regional officials in Russia's Far East, and elements within the military establishment. In 1992 this criticism culminated in Yeltsin's Security Council forcing an embarrassing, last-minute cancellation of a presidential trip to Japan. Russia's January 1993 foreign policy concept approached the problem only obliquely. It made an improved role in Asian geopolitics a top general priority and improved relations with Japan a primary specific goal in that process.

In 1993–96 Russo-Japanese relations showed signs of improvement, although there were also repeated setbacks as both sides proposed and then withdrew conditions. After postponing a second visit, Yeltsin finally made an official visit to Japan in October 1993. The resulting bilateral Tokyo Declaration represented some movement on both sides, but Russia's dumping of nuclear waste in the Sea of Japan and the issue of Japanese fishing rights off the Kuril Islands marred relations in the ensuing years. In 1995 the two sides came close to agreements on both issues—including Japanese aid to build sorely needed nuclear waste processing facilities in Russia's Maritime (Primorskiy) Territory—but the terms of the treatment plant remained mired in controversy, and continued Japanese violations stymied the fishing agreement in 1995 (see Environmental Conditions, ch. 3).

After two years of talks, in January 1996 Russia reached an agreement with Japanese and United States firms to build a liquid nuclear waste treatment ship with financing from Russia, Japan, and the United States. Negotiations over fishing rights remained deadlocked after a fifth round of talks ended in February 1996, and Russian border troops continued to fire on Japanese fishing vessels. The Russians protested a Japanese proposal to extend a 200-mile economic exclusion zone around its coastlines, in line with Japan's imminent ratification of the UN Convention on the Law of the Sea prescribing the limits of national coastline authority. Because of the proximity of the two countries, such a zone would include substantial Russian coastal waters. Meanwhile, the Kuril Islands issue remained unresolved in the first half of 1996, although at the Moscow G–7 meeting the two sides agreed to resume talks.

Other Asian States

The four major goals of Soviet policy in Asia were defense of the Soviet Union's eastern borders, including areas disputed with China, Japan, and Mongolia; maintenance of a set of alliances with key nations along the Asian periphery; improved relations with Western-oriented, relatively advanced states in order to obtain assistance in developing Siberia; and as much isolation as possible of China, South Korea, and the United States. In pursuit of these goals, the main instrument was the large Soviet military presence in Asia, which backed foreign policy assertions that the Soviet Union was an Asian power. In the late 1980s, Gorbachev sought to update this approach by improving relations with China, India, and Japan.

According to the 1993 draft foreign policy concept, Russia aimed to correct the imbalance in the former Soviet Union's East-West relations by paying greater attention to ties with Asian states. This view reflected the debate in Russian foreign policy between the westward-looking so-called Atlanticists and the so-called Eurasianists who would focus on relations with the near abroad and the wealthiest Asian states.

Reflecting the Eurasian alternative, the January 1993 concept called for a flexible policy of mutually beneficial relations with all the states of Asia, thus fostering good relations by reducing Russian military forces and cooperating with the United States and other regional powers to bolster security and regional stability. Such cooperation would include joint prevention of undesirable and unstable behavior, including organized crime and drug dealing. By following such a policy, Russia would come to be seen as an "honest prospective partner" in the region.

Some conservatives argued that the breakup of the Soviet Union pushed Russia geopolitically toward Asia because the great bulk of Russia's territory and resources are in its eastern regions and because the most European territories of the Soviet Union—Belarus, the Baltic states, and Ukraine—now were gone. Russian territory directly abuts three Asian powers: China, Japan, and North Korea. The security of the large populations of Russians remaining in Central Asia, which has an extensive border with China, were a continuing concern; thus, events such as changes in Chinese-Kazakstani relations have focused added Russian attention on Asia. Russia's relations with Mongolia, an adjoining state that moved decisively out of the Soviet sphere of influence in 1991, have been affected by separatism in areas of Russia bordering Mongolia.

Russia's presence and influence in Asia generally declined in the early 1990s. Elements of that movement were shifts of ethnic Russian populations away from areas near the Russo-Chinese border, growing anti-Russian sentiment in Vietnam, loss of Russian influence over an increasingly unpredictable North Korea, and a rapidly expanding, uncontrolled Chinese economic and even demographic influence in Russia's Far East. Russia soon took a series of measures to stem the erosion of its influence, including efforts to maintain and rebuild military ties with Vietnam and increased arms sales to China and Malaysia. In 1993 and 1995, Russia protested the failure of the Asia-Pacific Economic Conference (APEC) to offer it membership, and it characterized the decision as a national insult.

Analysts interpreted the replacement of Kozyrev with Middle East specialist Primakov in early 1996 as marking a further tilt of Russian foreign policy toward the Eurasian emphasis. Early in his term, Primakov noted that his priorities would include reinforcing ties with the former Soviet republics and with such countries as China, Japan, and the Middle Eastern states. At the same time, Russia announced a new trade policy that called for increased commercial links with China, Pakistan, India, and South Korea, among other Asian nations. Yeltsin reaffirmed the new emphasis in his 1996 state of the federation speech. Economic interests played a large part in this change. In 1995 exports to Asian countries had increased to US$20 billion, more than one-quarter of Russia's total trade that year. Many Russian analysts observed that economically sound and technologically developed Asian states could provide markets, technology, and investments at advantageous terms.

Soviet policy in Southeast Asia, aimed at limiting the influence of China and eliminating the influence of the United States, was not especially successful in the 1970s. In 1978 support for Vietnam's invasion of Cambodia eliminated the pro-Chinese government of Cambodia, but it also pushed the member states of the pro-Western Association of Southeast Asian Nations (ASEAN) to cooperate more closely among themselves and with the United States. In the late 1980s, Russia established bilateral ties with ASEAN states as part of Gorbachev's revised Third World policies, which included improved relations with Asian nations of all economic descriptions.

In the early 1990s, Russia's efforts to improve relations with Vietnam met significant obstacles. In October 1993, the two sides discussed extending Russian use of the port at Cam Ranh Bay beyond its expiration date in the year 2005. Vietnam called for rental payments for use of the base, but the two countries reached no agreement. During Kozyrev's July 1995 visit to Vietnam, the two sides discussed enhancing bilateral and regional cooperation, which had reached a low level. Stumbling blocks to improved relations included Vietnam's repayment of its large debt to Russia, Russia's desire to repatriate many of the 50,000 to 80,000 Vietnamese guest workers stranded in Russia after the collapse of the Soviet Union, and the status of Cam Ranh Bay. Vietnam also requested that Russia aid its army in modernizing itself as a counterweight to China, which remains a regional threat.

In the Soviet period, India was among the Third World states that responded the most positively to Soviet overtures, and the closeness of Indian-Soviet relations was a source of tension between China and the Soviet Union. In turn, the Soviet Union saw India as an important means of containing Chinese expansionism. Despite occasional declines, relations with India remained close through the end of the Gorbachev era, and India profited from abundant military and other foreign aid.

On a visit to India in January 1993, Yeltsin stressed that continued good relations were pivotal to Russia's balanced foreign relations, including its pro-Eastern policy. Although Russian trade with India had plummeted in the early 1990s, commercial relations recovered somewhat in 1994–95 following the establishment of an Indian-Russian Joint Commission. Much of the trade was linked to Indian repayment of past debts.

In March 1996, Primakov became the first Russian foreign minister to visit India. At that time, he termed India a priority partner, and he signed an agreement reestablishing the Soviet-era hot line communications link between New Delhi and Moscow. Primakov stressed that both Russia and India were seeking closer relations with China and that those new ties would not threaten the closer Russian-Indian ties.

Relations with communist North Korea and capitalist South Korea, defined clearly by the dichotomy of the Cold War, changed noticeably in the early 1990s. The January 1993 foreign policy concept endorsed the goal of a peaceful Korean unification to reduce regional instability on Russia's borders. Although the concept called for full ties with South Korea, which it described as sharing Russia's "basic values of world civilization," the concept also urged the maintenance of some levers of containment over North Korea to prevent that country from developing nuclear arms.

The Soviet Union's treaty ties with North Korea included the friendship, cooperation, and mutual assistance treaty of 1961. After the collapse of the Soviet Union, Kozyrev indicated that many of the Soviet friendship treaties would be reevaluated, but at that time Russia did not renounce the pact with North Korea. In August 1995, Russia forwarded a new draft "friendly relations" treaty to North Korea that excluded a crucial provision calling for mutual military assistance in the case of attack. In April 1996, a Russian government delegation traveled to P'yongyang to discuss that proposal and to convince North Korea to halt bellicose moves along its border with South Korea.

North Korea's inconsistent positions on the issue of nuclear technology have been a major concern for Russia. The Russian Ministry of Foreign Affairs criticized North Korea's March 1993 announcement that it would withdraw from the Nuclear Nonproliferation Treaty (NPT), and Russia subsequently supported the international community in urging North Korea to adhere to the NPT as a nonnuclear weapons power and to accept international inspections of its nuclear facilities. To ease the tension caused by the potential of nuclear weapons in the two Koreas, Russia called an international conference to declare the Korean Peninsula a nuclear-free zone. In October 1994, Russia endorsed a United States-North Korean agreement on halting North Korean nuclear proliferation while urging that Russian reactors be supplied to North Korea under the agreement. Moscow criticized the decision to supply South Korean reactors instead, and the new disagreement became another sore point in United States-Russian relations.

Other issues of conflict between Russia and North Korea were allegations of human rights violations against North Korean guest workers in Siberian forests and North Korea's unpaid debt to Russia of more than US$3 billion. In 1995 Russian conservatives urged renewal of arms sales and other ties with North Korea as a means of encouraging it to repay the debt.

On his 1992 visit to South Korea, Yeltsin signed the Treaty on Principles of Relations, which called for relations to be based on "common ideals of freedom, democracy, respect for human rights, and the principles of a market economy." This treaty placed Russia in the unique position of having treaty ties with both North and South Korea, each based on fundamentally different principles. Russia and South Korea reportedly also discussed joint projects in natural gas exploitation and industrial development. In 1995 the two countries signed an agreement that alleviated a sore point in relations by authorizing Russia to partially repay its debt to South Korea in goods. Russian arms transfers have included T–80 tanks and BMP–3 armored fighting vehicles. South Korea is assisting in the development of an industrial park in the Russian city of Nakhodka, a port on the Sea of Japan that Russia has declared a free economic zone.

The Third World

The Cold War affected the relations the United States and the Soviet Union had with Third World states. Both superpowers wooed Third World allies, many of which used the Cold War to extract favorable aid as the price of closer relations. The Soviet Union endeavored to construct socialism in the Third World to demonstrate that Marxism-Leninism would someday triumph worldwide. Many of its so-called client states were proclaimed as "socialist oriented" or following the path of "noncapitalist development," and the Soviet Union signed friendship treaties and other security and aid agreements with them. Some Third World states, however, involved themselves in the influential Nonaligned Movement, which began in 1955 and represented more than half the world's population. Most of those countries formally eschewed major security and other relations with the superpowers, with conspicuous exceptions such as Cuba. At some stages of its existence, however, the Nonaligned Movement appeared to have a pro-Soviet bias.

The collapse of the Soviet Union broke most of Russia's ties with Third World states. The Soviet ideological mission of fostering socialism also ceased. Russia was unable to continue economic subsidies to client regimes, including the Soviet-installed regime in Afghanistan that collapsed in 1992. Russia continued to play a reduced role in some of the regional peace negotiation efforts it had inherited from the Soviet Union, notably in the Middle East and in Cambodia.

Relations with Africa received a relatively low priority, and in 1992 Russia closed nine embassies and four consulates on that continent. Relations with some African states already had worsened in late 1991 when Yeltsin ordered the end of all foreign aid and demanded immediate repayment of outstanding debts. Most African states responded that their debts with the former Soviet Union should be forgiven or reduced because they had been largely military outlays resulting from a moribund superpower rivalry.

The January 1993 draft foreign policy concept made no mention of Russian support for former Soviet client states in Africa or elsewhere. Instead, the concept emphasized the use of diplomatic leverage to induce payment of debts by those states. Beginning in mid-1994, a shift began toward increased economic ties with more economically developed African states such as South Africa and Nigeria.

The Middle East

The Middle East was among the most important Third World regions for Soviet foreign policy and national security. The Soviet Union shared boundaries with Middle Eastern states Iran and Turkey, and some of those states' ethnic, religious, and language groups also were represented on the Soviet side of the border. The region's oil resources and shipping lanes were of significant interest to the Soviet Union and to the West. After World War II, the main Soviet goal in the region was to minimize the influence of the United States. Toward that end, the Soviet Union gave large-scale support to a group of radical Arab states that were united by their quest to eliminate Israel and to oust all vestiges of Western influence in the region. At various times, the strategy also included extensive economic assistance to NATO member Turkey, unsuccessful attempts at negotiation of the Iran-Iraq War in the mid-1980s (during a period of strained relations with both countries), and, in the late 1980s, pursuit of closer relations with moderate states of the region such as Bahrain, Egypt, Jordan, Kuwait, and Saudi Arabia as well as United States ally Israel. In 1987 the Soviet Union protected Kuwaiti shipping in the Persian Gulf against Iranian attack, and it established consular relations with Israel. At the same time, the Soviet Union continued ties with radical regimes in Libya, Syria, and the People's Democratic Republic of Yemen (South Yemen).

In the last years of the Soviet Union, influence with Libya, Iraq, the Palestine Liberation Organization (PLO), and Kuwait ebbed, and the Soviet Union played a peripheral role in the Persian Gulf War of 1991. Despite its friendship treaty with Iraq, the Soviet Union supported the United States-led international effort to reverse Iraq's occupation of Kuwait. After the war, the Soviet Union found itself marginalized by United States dominance in the region. The Soviet Union played a minor but significant role as co-coordinator with the United States of peace talks between Israel and the Arab states that began in January 1992.

The independence of the five former Soviet Central Asian republics put a geographical barrier between Russia and the states of the Middle East. Some Russian democrats and some ultranationalists believed that the Soviet Union's involvement with Islamic states such as Afghanistan and the Central Asian republics had drained resources and harmed Russia's economic and political development and stability. This sentiment was a major factor in the original formulation of the CIS, which included only the Slavic republics in that new organization and added the Central Asian and Caucasus states only at the insistence of Kazakstan's president Nursultan Nazarbayev.

Beginning in 1993, however, Russian policy toward the Middle East and the Persian Gulf became more assertive in selected areas. In late 1992, Russia endeavored, with limited success, to prevent Iran from supporting the Islamic elements of a coalition government in Tajikistan, then under siege by antireformist Tajikistani elements. On other issues, Iran and Russia pursued similar interests in constraining anti-Russian and anti-Iranian political currents in Azerbaijan, and Iran used relations with Russia to counteract United States-led international economic and political ostracism.

A major factor in renewed Russian interest in the region was the prospect of arms sales and other trade, which were the goals of Chernomyrdin's visit to Saudi Arabia and other Persian Gulf states in November 1994. In December 1994, Russia signed a trade agreement with Egypt with the stated purpose of resuming Egypt's Soviet-era position as the most important trade partner in the Middle East. Russia moved to reestablish its earlier lucrative arms sales ties with Iran, selling that country fighter aircraft, tanks, submarines, fighter-bombers, and other arms. Kuwait, the United Arab Emirates, and Algeria also made arms purchases in the early 1990s, as did Egypt and Syria. However, the level of Russian arms sales remained low compared with the previous decades of high Soviet visibility in the region. In 1996 Russia continued to observe international bans on arms sales to Libya and Iraq.

Ultranationalists and other deputies in the Russian parliament called for rebuilding ties with Iraq and condemned United States air strikes against that country in January and June 1993. Among Russia's overtures for better relations was an appeal in the UN Security Council for easing international economic sanctions on Iraq, but in late 1995 these efforts were set back by revelations that Iraq was seeking to develop a nuclear weapons program. The apparently poor performance of Russian equipment during the Persian Gulf War discouraged many Middle Eastern states from buying Russian arms. Another negative effect on Russia's ties with the Middle East was Russia's aggression against Chechen Muslims and its stance favoring Serbia against Muslim Bosnia.

A series of Russian contracts to build nuclear power plants and to share nuclear technology with Iran became a major international issue and a source of particular friction with the United States. The initial 1993 contract was not fulfilled; a new contract, worth a reported US$800 million, called for construction of a nuclear reactor on the Persian Gulf. In September 1995, Moscow announced a further contract to build two additional, smaller reactors. Although the United States strongly protested what it viewed as potential nuclear proliferation to a terrorist state, Russia responded that international law permitted such deals and that the reactors would be under full safeguards of the International Atomic Energy Agency.

Russian diplomats encouraged Arab participation in the Arab-Israeli peace talks that began in 1992, and Russians participated in talks between Israel and the PLO on the issue of PLO self-rule in Israeli-occupied territories. Among other reasons, Russia supported the peace process as a means of reducing the threat of the spread of Islamic fundamentalism.

Russian foreign minister Primakov launched shuttle diplomacy in the Middle East in April 1996 in an attempt to end fighting in southern Lebanon and to increase Russia's diplomatic role in the region. However, Russia's condemnation of Israeli attacks against militant Arab Hezbollah guerrillas in southern Lebanon led Israel to respond that it preferred the more evenhanded diplomatic approach of the United States. Russia subsequently was excluded from a multilateral force agreed upon by Israel, Lebanon, and Syria to monitor a United States-brokered cease-fire in Lebanon.

Latin America

In the Soviet period, the main reasons for involvement in Latin America were not historical, cultural, or economic, but related to strategic competition with the United States. Accordingly, the Soviet Union endeavored to foster leftist insurgencies and other distractions to interfere with United States foreign policy in the region.

The main bases of Soviet involvement in Latin America were Cuba and Nicaragua, but the Soviet Union also attempted some involvement in Peru and Grenada. The Soviet Union placed military and intelligence facilities in Cuba to spy on the United States. It also supported Cuba as an attractive and successful model of Latin American socialism that would induce other countries to move into the same sphere and become export bases for ideology. In 1962 Khrushchev attempted to redress Soviet strategic nuclear inferiority by surreptitiously placing intermediate-range nuclear missiles in Cuba. The resulting crisis brought the United States and the Soviet Union to the brink of war. Although tensions over Cuba subsided considerably in the decades that followed, Cuba remained an important Soviet outpost until the Gorbachev regime began substantially cutting aid in the late 1980s. The other potential outpost of communism in Latin America, Nicaragua, was lost when a free election rejected the procommunist Sandinista Party in 1990. Meanwhile, Soviet purchases of grain and other goods from Latin America slumped severely in the decade before the breakup of the Soviet Union and thereafter because of the Soviet Union's inability to pay in hard currency (see Glossary).

The January 1993 draft foreign policy concept viewed relations with Latin America as particularly important for Russia's economic development. Russia saw the Latin American countries, particularly Argentina, Brazil, and Mexico, as a source of low-price food and other goods for the Russian market, as a source of mutually beneficial technological cooperation, and as a market for arms. The 1993 concept called for establishing and consolidating ties with regional organizations such as the Organization of American States, in which Russia is a permanent observer. The concept was vague about relations with Cuba, Nicaragua, El Salvador, and Guatemala, and it avoided mention of Soviet-era support for Marxist-Leninist ideological movements in those states.

Some Russian analysts argued for revival of the mutually profitable pre-Soviet trade ties that had exchanged goods from Siberia for goods from Latin America. These analysts advocated obtaining Latin America's trade products—coffee, cocoa, sugar, fruit, footwear, and oil—in exchange for Siberian timber, coal, fish, and furs. Some also argued that Russia's trade in the entire Pacific Basin should intensify to compensate for the loss of ports on the Baltic and Black seas.

In the first post-Soviet years, the Russian government received criticism from nationalist factions for declining trade and lax diplomacy with Latin America. In 1993 commercial activity recovered somewhat as Brazil and Russia concluded a trade agreement that was worth about US$2 billion and included arms purchases by Brazil. In 1994 Vladimir Shumeyko, speaker of the Federation Council, Russia's upper legislative chamber, toured Argentina, Brazil, Chile, Ecuador, and Venezuela. Many Russians urged restored ties with Cuba, Nicaragua, and Peru in order to persuade those states to pay back Soviet-era loans. Some of the many Latin American students who had benefited from the Soviet Union's large student-exchange program also began to seek new entrepreneurial and cultural contacts with Russia on behalf of their native countries. In 1994 Russia cooperated with the United States by supporting a United States-led international intervention force in Haiti.

In early 1996, Foreign Minister Primakov traveled to Cuba and other Latin American states to indicate Russia's determination to expand ties in the region. In March 1996, Russia and Colombia announced an agreement on the supply of Russian small arms and ammunition. Seeking to restore ties with Nicaragua, Russia agreed in April 1996 to cancel the bulk of that nation's debt (US$3.4 billion) to the former Soviet Union.

The Soviet-era status of Cuba deteriorated seriously late in the Gorbachev regime. Ties between the communist parties of the two countries were severed, economic subsidies were suspended, and, in late 1991, Gorbachev announced the pullout of the Soviet military brigade from Cuba. The Soviet Union announced that "mutual benefit" and world prices would dictate future economic relations and that Cuba no longer would enjoy the special status it had had until that time. The end of subsidies was a severe blow to the Cuban economy. In November 1992, a Russian-Cuban trade agreement endeavored to restore some trade ties with a sugar-for-oil barter arrangement, but it did not include subsidies for Cuba. During 1992 the Russian government also failed to defend Cuba against increased commercial sanctions based on international accusations of human rights violations. Some Russian hard-liners criticized the Ministry of Foreign Affairs' treatment of Cuba, and that policy was reversed partially between 1993 and 1995. First Deputy Prime Minister Oleg Soskovets committed Russia to a credit of US$350 million and a sugar-for-oil barter agreement in 1993, and he made a high-level visit to strengthen bilateral ties in 1995.

Renewed Russian connections in Cuba have been of significant concern in the United States. Russia has argued that barter arrangements with Cuba do not violate provisions of the United States trade embargo on Cuba, which sets severe penalties for United States trading partners that deal with Cuba. In 1995 the United States voiced concern over Russian plans to assist Cuba in completing a nuclear power reactor. In February 1996, the United States tightened economic sanctions against Cuba in response to the shooting down of two United States civilian airplanes in international airspace. At that time, Yeltsin criticized the United States for overreacting, and he reaffirmed his intention of reestablishing traditional ties with Cuba.

Foreign Policy Prospects

In the 1990s, a number of sometimes contradictory factors have driven Russian foreign policy. The most formidable and unchanging factor is the country's immense geographical span, which gives Russia natural interests in three vastly different regions—Europe, the Pacific, and the vast, largely Muslim stretch of the Middle East and Central Asia. Russia's recent history gives it particular geopolitical motivation to perpetuate relations with the fourteen nations that emerged along its periphery when the Soviet Union dissolved. Recent history also has motivated efforts to maintain an influence over some states of the Third World in which the Soviet Union had a substantial foothold.

The process of focusing priorities among a number of possibilities has proved to be unusually complex in an era when ideology and bilateral rivalry no longer dictate responses. The main recurring disagreement in post-Soviet foreign policy pits advocates of stronger ties with the capitalist world, especially

Western Europe, against advocates of some form of reconstituted union in which Russia would be the dominant force, politically and economically. The first option truly could take Russia in a new direction. The second option offers the security of returning to a familiar role, but it also threatens to burden Russia with client states that it no longer can afford.

Between 1992 and mid-1996, the Yeltsin administration wavered from one side to the other, emitting contradictory signals as it tried to maintain as many options as possible. At the same time, however, Russia moved into Western organizations such as the Council of Europe, and treaty arrangements such as START I, which gave it stronger connections with, and obligations to, the West than it had ever had in the Soviet era. In this process, Russia showed consistently that it wished to be taken seriously as a diplomatic power upon which the world could rely, not merely as a plaintiff for its own national causes.

Meanwhile, in the mid-1990s, increasingly strong political forces in Russia have blocked further movement toward the West by arguing that Russia cannot recapture superpower status as a second-rate partner of rich capitalist states. The centerpiece of this position is opposition to NATO expansion eastward, which has been the pretext for nationalists to block other international commitments such as the START II disarmament agreement. At the same time, Russia has maintained substantial influence in parts of the former Soviet Union, taking advantage of destabilizing ethnic struggles in the new nations of the Caucasus and Central Asia to play a dual role as peace negotiator and military guarantor of security. Finally, Russia's closer ties with China, a country that still is the object of substantial suspicion in the West, have increasingly alarmed Western policy makers.

The replacement of Foreign Minister Andrey Kozyrev by Yevgeniy Primakov in January 1996 was an indication that Russia might be more concerned with restoring power than with conforming to international standards, although its Great Power infrastructure continued to crumble and Primakov proved to be more pragmatic than dogmatic in his initial policy statements. After Yeltsin's reelection in mid-1996, the president's illness obscured the locus of power in all areas of governance, including foreign policy. Western observers wondered whether a nation in acute economic distress, with a disastrously inefficient military and few dependable allies around the world, might still be willing to make the sort of pragmatic concessions that Yeltsin and Kozyrev practiced in the first years of Russia's post-Soviet existence.

*   *   *

Because Russian foreign policy is in a period of formation and flux, most scholarly publications are articles or edited works, but some useful monographs have appeared. Noteworthy among the latter are Suzanne Crow's *The Making of Foreign Policy in Russia under Yeltsin*; Gerard Holden's *Russia after the Cold War: History and the Nation in Post-Soviet Security Politics*; and John George Stoessinger's *Nations at Dawn—China, Russia, and America*. Useful compilations of articles are *Damage Limitation or Crisis?: Russia and the Outside World*, edited by Robert D. Blackwill and Sergei A. Karaganov; *The Making of Foreign Policy in Russia and the New States of Eurasia*, edited by Adeed and Karen Dawisha; *Central Asia and the Caucasus after the Soviet Union: Domestic and International Dynamics* and *Russia and the Third World in the Post-Soviet Era*, both edited by Mohiaddin Mesbahi; *Rethinking Russia's National Interests*, edited by Stephen Sestanovich; and *Russian Foreign Policy since 1990*, edited by Peter Shearman. For more current coverage of foreign policy developments, the Foreign Broadcast Information Service's *Daily Report: Central Eurasia* digests and translates items from the Russian press, the Jamestown Foundation's *Prism* and *Monitor* publications offer short articles, and the Open Media Research Institute's biweekly *Transition* provide longer articles on domestic and foreign policy issues. (For further information and complete citations, see Bibliography.)

Chapter 9. The Armed Forces

Tsar Saltan approaches three sisters, who are wistfully talking about what each would do if the tsar were to marry her (design from lacquer box made in village of Palekh).

IN THE SOVIET ERA, THE ARMED FORCES were the most stable institution in the nation, exercising strong influence over general national security policy as well as over specific issues of military doctrine. However, the last regime of the Soviet Union, that of Mikhail S. Gorbachev (in office 1985–91), saw unprecedented debate over military issues, including a movement away from the primarily offensive concerns (which always had been cloaked in declarations of their necessity for an effective national defense) to a more defensive position in military doctrine. It is now known that discussion of such a change began in the Soviet Union as early as the 1970s but only became manifest between 1987 and 1989. Ultimately, the change was dictated by policy makers' recognition of grave shortcomings in the Soviet Union's political, economic, and technological positions versus the West. After long discussion, in 1993 Russia finally produced a military doctrine that nominally reflected the new military thinking. But that doctrine was only the first step in a long and painful process of reassessing the needs and capabilities of Russia's armed forces under a completely new set of global and domestic circumstances.

When the Soviet Union collapsed at the end of 1991, the former Russian Republic, henceforth known as the Russian Federation, inherited about 85 percent of the union's overall military establishment, including manpower, defense industries, and equipment. However, Russia inherited only about 60 percent of the union's economic capacity—the resources needed for future support of that military machine. Moreover, the military power that remained was a fragmentary mixture of elements from the former Soviet military structure rather than an organized whole. Many of the priorities in the Soviet Union's national security doctrine—such as the capability to launch amphibious invasions in support of client states on the other side of the world—had no logical priority in the new Russian state. Requiring substantial reshaping of their capabilities according to economic resources, the Russian armed forces in the 1990s have received budget allocations sufficient to maintain a force numbering less than half the 1.5 million personnel on duty in mid-1996. Beginning in 1994, the campaign fought in Chechnya illustrated clearly that Russian forces were poorly coordinated and not combat ready.

The decline of the Russian armed forces—and the shocking shrinkage of the territory they had occupied until the beginning of the 1990s—was a blow to national pride. Nationalist politicians urged a new military buildup that would return Russia to the superpower status of the Cold War years. Particularly in the election year of 1996, national security policy became entwined in political rhetoric, and, as with other urgent issues in Russia, constructive solutions were delayed until the nature of the next presidential regime could be clarified. In the mid-1990s, individual steps such as arms agreements and an apparent shift of strategic emphasis from the West toward China continued, but overall public and state support for the armed forces languished.

At the same time, the Russian military retained a strong role in the formation of a new national foreign policy, especially policy relating to the recently independent former Soviet states, referred to in Russia as the "near abroad." Military occupation under various guises continued in the Caucasus, Moldova, and Central Asia, as well as the separatist Republic of Chechnya, and in 1996 strong nationalist factions exerted pressure to increase the Russian presence in order to tighten Russia's links with the other former republics of the Soviet Union.

Historical Background

Modern Russian military history begins with Peter the Great, who established the Imperial Russian Army (see Peter the Great and the Russian Empire, ch. 1). That force, conceived by Peter along the Western lines that he had studied, won its first great battle against the Swedish army of Charles XII at Poltava in 1709. The first great Russian naval victory, at the Hango Peninsula on the Baltic Sea in 1714, also came at the expense of the Swedes; Peter had modernized the Russian navy with the same diligence he applied to the army. The victories over Sweden made Russia the dominant power in the Baltic region.

For the first time, under Peter the armed forces were staffed by recruits from the peasantry, whose twenty-five-year obligation made them professional soldiers and sailors devoted to service because they had been liberated from serfdom—together with all their offspring—in the bargain. Officers were nobles called to an equally rigorous lifetime service. Under Peter, Russia had the largest standing army in Europe, and elements of the military system he introduced lasted until 1917.

Under Catherine II (the Great; r. 1762–96), the Russian Empire expanded to the west, the south, and the east, and wars were fought with the Ottoman Empire (1768–74 and 1787–92) and Poland (1794–95) (see Imperial Expansion and Maturation: Catherine II, ch. 1). The greatest Russian military leader of Catherine's time was Aleksandr Suvorov, who fought in the second Russo-Turkish War and the Polish campaign, then led a Russian and Austrian army against the revolutionary French in northern Italy in 1799. In the first decades of the nineteenth century, Russian armies continued a long series of wars against the Ottoman Empire. They also met Napoleon's French forces at several points in Europe; the most famous encounter was the legendary defeat of Napoleon's 1812 invasion force by the Russians under Mikhail Kutuzov. That victory established the pattern of scorched-earth retreat that left Napoleon and succeeding invaders without material support, and it brought a Russian army to Paris in triumphant occupation.

Under Tsar Nicholas I (r. 1825– 55), Russia became known as the "gendarme of Europe," an archconservative defender of monarchies against the forces of liberation that had begun to sweep Europe in the previous century. In 1831 Nicholas quelled a Polish rebellion against his own empire, and in 1849 Russia sent 100,000 troops to suppress an uprising by Hungarian patriots against the Austrian Empire. The Crimean War (1853–56), the fruit of Europe's complex system of alliances and a series of diplomatic misunderstandings, centered on the British and French siege of the Russian port of Sevastopol', which was well defended for nearly a year before surrendering. However, the Russian defeat in that campaign revealed that Russian command and supply systems had fallen behind those of Western Europe in the first half of the nineteenth century.

In the second half of the century, Russia waged a series of military campaigns to conquer the khanates of Central Asia, extending the empire and providing a domestic supply of cotton. With relatively little military resistance, the entire region had been incorporated into the empire by 1885. Russia's next military campaign, however, was not so reassuring. The Russo-Japanese War of 1904–05 brought stunning defeats on land and at sea, capped by the naval Battle of Tsushima in which the Russian Baltic Fleet was decimated (see Imperialism in Asia and the Russo-Japanese War, ch. 1). Like the Crimean War, the Russo-Japanese War was a signal that Russia's war machine was not keeping pace with the modern world. Ten years later,

World War I would confirm that evaluation, as an inept defense administration and poorly equipped troops suffered heavy losses to the Germans.

Despite those failures, it was growing dissatisfaction on the home front that ultimately undermined Russia's military effort in World War I. Under the direct command of the tsar, the army actually performed quite well in 1916, but by 1917 the war effort had crippled civilian society and readied Russia for the overthrow of the tsar. As the home front faltered in its moral and material support of the military, the results of 1916 were reversed. The Provisional Government that followed the tsar in 1917 was determined to continue the war; that policy was a major factor in the success of the Bolshevik Revolution in toppling the Provisional Government only eight months after it took power.

The imperial army and navy disintegrated after the Bolshevik Revolution of 1917. Although the Bolsheviks quickly signed a peace treaty with Germany, there was soon a need for a military force to defend the new state against the anticommunist Whites in what became a bloody, three-year civil war. In April 1918, the Red Army was established when the Soviet government announced compulsory military service for peasants and workers. The army's chief organizer was Leon Trotsky, the new nation's first commissar of war (1918–24); Trotsky's initial officer cadre was made up of about 50,000 former tsarist officers. Trotsky was able to mold his peasant and worker recruits into an effective force that eventually prevailed over five separate White armies, with the benefit of access to Russia's industrial heartland and concentrated lines of supply and communications. Under Trotsky, political officers were attached to all military units to ensure the loyalty of all individuals—a practice that persisted throughout the Soviet era.

When the Civil War ended in 1921, General Mikhail Tukhachevskiy led an extensive program of reorganization and equipment modernization; he also established several military schools. In the first fifteen years of the Red Army, communist party membership increased rapidly among the enlisted ranks and, especially, among the officer corps. By the mid-1930s, training schools and academies had turned out a generation of young officers and noncommissioned officers with strong political indoctrination, thus ensuring the ideological loyalty of the entire armed forces. Beginning in 1931, Tukhachevskiy began a large-scale rearmament program based on the industrial development of the five-year plans (see Glossary), and the armed forces and their supplies of equipment were enlarged greatly as the shadow of war began falling over Europe in the mid-1930s.

In 1937 the purges instigated by Joseph V. Stalin (in office 1927–53) reached the army. Tukhachevskiy, now first deputy commissar of war, was executed for treason together with seven top generals. As many as 30,000 other officers were imprisoned or dismissed, leaving the Red Army without experienced commanders at the end of the 1930s. The first campaign that revealed this weakness was the so-called Winter War against Finland (1939–40), in which an estimated 100,000 troops of the Red Army died while defeating a small Finnish army.

Although the Nazi invasion of 1941 drove far into the Russian interior to threaten Leningrad and Moscow, a new generation of officers gradually asserted themselves as the Germans were driven from Russian territory in 1943 and 1944 after the climactic Battle of Stalingrad. A crucial event in that turnaround was Stalin's removal of political officers having parallel command authority, allowing his top officers to exercise military judgment independent of ideological concerns.

The most important Russian military leader of World War II was Marshal Georgiy Zhukov, who was instrumental at four key points of Soviet resistance: the siege of Leningrad; the defense of Moscow, the first point at which the German advance was stopped; the Battle of Stalingrad (February 1943); and the Battle of Kursk (July 1943), in which the last strong German counteroffensive was defeated. Zhukov also commanded the final push against the German armies across Belorussia, Ukraine, and Poland. In April 1945, Zhukov led the Red Army's final assault on Berlin that ended what Russians called the Great Patriotic War.

By the end of World War II, the Soviet armed forces had swelled to about 11.4 million officers and soldiers, and the military had suffered about 7 million deaths. At that point, this force was recognized as the most powerful military in the world. In 1946 the Red Army was redesignated as the Soviet army, and by 1950 demobilization had reduced the total active armed forces to about 3 million troops. From the late 1940s to the late 1960s, the Soviet armed forces focused on adapting to the changed nature of warfare in the era of nuclear arms and on achieving parity with the United States in strategic nuclear weapons. Conventional military power showed its continued importance, however, when the Soviet Union used its troops to invade Hungary in 1956 and Czechoslovakia in 1968 to keep those countries within the Soviet alliance system.

In the 1970s, the Soviet Union began to modernize its conventional warfare and power projection capabilities. At the same time, it became more involved than ever before in regional conflicts and local wars. The Soviet Union sent arms and military advisers to a variety of Third World allies in Africa, Asia, and the Middle East. Soviet generals planned military operations against rebels in Angola and Ethiopia. However, Soviet troops saw little combat in such assignments until the invasion of Afghanistan in December 1979. There, they fought a counterinsurgency campaign against Afghan rebels for nearly eight and one-half years. An estimated 15,000 Soviet soldiers had been killed and 35,000 wounded in the conflict by the time Soviet forces began to withdraw from Afghanistan in May 1988. By early 1989, all of the roughly 110,000 Soviet troops who had been deployed had left Afghanistan.

After incurring the heavy blow of failure in the Afghanistan campaign, the Soviet armed forces faced an even larger, albeit nonviolent setback as the Soviet sphere of influence in Europe began to crumble in 1989. It disappeared entirely by 1991, when the Warsaw Pact (see Glossary) alliance dissolved. As a result, by 1994 all Soviet/Russian troops had been withdrawn from territory west of Ukraine and Belarus, as well as from the three Baltic states, which achieved independence in 1991. Together with the end of the Soviet Union as a state, the events of that period set the military on a bewildering search for a new identity and a new doctrine.

Military Doctrine

In Russia military doctrine is the official formulation of concepts on the nature of present and future war and the nation's potential role, given existing or anticipated geopolitical conditions. In the late 1980s, the military doctrine of the Soviet Union underwent a dramatic change toward defensive readiness before the dissolution of the union. After inheriting the unfinished transition of that period, Russia struggled to develop a suitable new set of concepts in the 1990s. The first step, the doctrine of 1993, was considered a temporary document leading to a full statement of goals and circumstances to be formulated around 2000.

Soldier on guard at World War II memorial, Volgograd (formerly Stalingrad) Courtesy Carolou Marquet

Soviet Doctrine

The Soviet Union's first military doctrine was based on the teachings of Vladimir I. Lenin about defense of the socialist homeland and on the military theories of Civil War general Mikhail Frunze. Starting in the early 1920s, doctrine underwent a series of changes in response to geopolitical and economic conditions. After World War II, Stalin introduced the concept of two mutually irreconcilable international coalitions—the capitalist and the socialist—that inevitably would come into armed conflict. In the 1950s, the Soviet acquisition of nuclear weapons added a new dimension to Stalin's postwar concept of a massive, combined-arms struggle on the fields of Europe. Soviet leader Nikita S. Khrushchev (in office 1953–64) saw adequate nuclear deterrence as a guarantee that socialism would be able to advance in peace toward its inevitable triumph. Based on that theory, he shifted support from conventional forces to a new military group, the nuclear-armed strategic rocket forces. However, in this period the Soviet military establishment argued for the use of nuclear weapons in fighting, rather than preventing, a war—including the initiation of nuclear attack. In the 1960s, that idea was refined with the addition of small-scale nuclear strikes and a renewed emphasis on conventional warfare. By 1970 the doctrine envisioned two major possibilities: an entirely conventional war or a nuclear war fought between the Soviet Union and the United States solely in Western and Central Europe.

In the 1970s and the 1980s, military thinkers continued to question the military efficacy of nuclear weapons, although official doctrine assumed that the Soviet Union could win a nuclear war. In this period, the concept of a nonnuclear, high-technology global war, advanced by Chief of the General Staff Marshal Nikolay Ogarkov, attracted substantial support. By the late 1980s, military doctrine had begun to evolve toward a defensive concept of "reasonable sufficiency" of military force to ensure national security but not to initiate offensive operations. At the behest of the Soviet Union, in 1987 the Warsaw Pact officially adopted a defense-oriented military doctrine and called for reductions in conventional arms in Europe.

The Doctrine of 1993

Although it is verbose and highly theoretical, the 1993 military doctrine contains important indicators of policy under various scenarios. It is the statement of the military policy of the Russian government, arrived at after long and intense debate among all interested parties, whose input reflects their relative political power. Russian military doctrine is roughly the equivalent of a formal statement of the military policy of a presidential administration in the United States.

The official Russian definition of military doctrine is "a nation's officially accepted system of scientifically founded views on the nature of modern wars and the use of armed forces in them, and also on the requirement arising from these views regarding the country and its armed forces being made ready for war." Military doctrine answers these five basic questions for the Russian armed forces: Who is the enemy in a probable war? What is the probable character of a war, and what will be its aims and tasks? What forces will be necessary to fulfill these tasks, and what direction will military development follow? How should preparation for war be carried out? What will be the means of warfare?

The demise of the Soviet Union made the formulation of a new military doctrine to replace that of the Gorbachev regime an obvious necessity. However, urgent political questions delayed the onset of deliberation on a new doctrine until May 1992. From that time, completion of the doctrine required seventeen months, much of which was filled with acrimonious debate. In November 1993, the final version was approved by the Russian Federation's Security Council and signed by President Boris N. Yeltsin as Decree Number 1833 (see The Security Council, ch. 8).

Although the full doctrine text had not been published as of mid-1996, detailed accounts have been released to the public. According to these summaries, the document includes three main sections, entitled political principles, military principles, and military-technical and economic principles.

The introduction to the 1993 military doctrine defines the document as an interim policy covering the period of transition from the Soviet Union to the establishment of Russian statehood and the emergence of a new form of international relations. The interim period is defined as continuing from the time of adoption to 2000.

From 1993 until 1996, the primary goal was to restructure and reduce the armed forces as units were withdrawn from locations outside Russia. The remaining four years would be devoted to conversion from a purely conscript personnel base to a mixed (conscript and voluntary) system, together with the creation of a new military infrastructure.

Political Principles

The first main section of the doctrine describes the Russian Federation's attitude toward armed conflicts, and how the armed forces and security troops are to be used in them. It defines what the Russian Federation perceives as the military danger to it, the sociopolitical principles supporting military security, and national policy for ensuring military security. The underlying goal of the principles is to maintain domestic and international political stability on the borders while the Russian Federation is consolidating itself. In describing this goal, the doctrine makes no reference to defending an ideology or the gains of previous years, as was standard practice in all Soviet military doctrines.

Peace on the borders, especially in and among the newly independent republics of the former Soviet Union, is part of the defensive strategy. The only departure from this self-interested approach is a stated willingness to participate in international peacekeeping efforts. In 1996 Russian participation in the Bosnian Peace Implementation Force (IFOR) was justified by this clause in the military doctrine.

The military doctrine retains no vestige of the international activism that pervaded its Marxist-Leninist (see Glossary) antecedents. Resolution of internal Russian economic, political, and social problems is the principal order of business. The only formal international obligations that are recognized are formal treaty obligations of the Commonwealth of Independent States (CIS—see Glossary); the Conference on Security and Cooperation in Europe (CSCE), since 1995 known as the Organization for Security and Cooperation in Europe (OSCE—see Glossary); and those resulting from membership in the United Nations (UN). The document does not refer to the Conventional Forces in Europe Treaty (CFE Treaty—see Glossary), which in the 1990s is a key constraint on Russia's deployment of military forces in certain areas.

The paramount goal of this interim doctrine is to protect Russia from attack in the weakened condition in which it has found itself in the 1990s. The principal threats to the Russian Federation are defined as wars and armed conflicts on the Russian borders, the potential employment of weapons of mass destruction against the Russian Federation or on its borders, the buildup of armed forces along Russian borders, or physical attacks on Russian installations or territories. The term "installations" refers to Soviet-era bases in the newly independent former Soviet republics that continue to be garrisoned by Russian troops. (The last Russian troops in Central Europe left Germany in August 1994.)

Military Principles

The interim Russian military doctrine sets the primary objective for the armed forces as the prevention, early termination, and containment of military conflict through employment of peacetime standing forces. The principal areas of concern are the territory and property of the Russian Federation, the areas contiguous to its borders, and the threat of nuclear attack by a foreign power.

Military operations in Chechnya are justified under the paragraph on protection of the territory and property of the Russian Federation. Justification for a continued Russian military presence in the former Central Asian republics derives from the paragraph on protection of areas contiguous to Russian borders, as well as provisions of the CIS treaty (see The Geopolitical Context, this ch.).

Russia reserves the right of first use of weapons of mass destruction, which remain a primary concern of policy makers in the age of nuclear disarmament. This reservation, which is in apparent violation of the terms of the Nuclear Nonproliferation Treaty (NPT—see Glossary), has been retained nevertheless in response to Russia's uncertainty as to the intentions of the three neighboring states—Belarus, Kazakstan, and Ukraine—that were left with nuclear weapons after the dissolution of the Soviet Union. However, the last nuclear weapons in Kazakstan were destroyed in 1995, the last nuclear weapons left Ukraine in mid-1996, and the last nuclear weapons were scheduled to leave Belarus by the end of 1996—seemingly eliminating this rationale. Suspicion of the nuclear intentions of the United States and the North Atlantic Treaty Organization (NATO—see Glossary) is the remaining foundation for the first-use provision of the doctrine.

Military-Technical and Economic Principles

The military doctrine's treatment of the military-technical and economic foundations of the armed forces—the process of providing and maintaining modern military hardware—is the aspect that shows the greatest gap between policy and reality. The doctrine describes a policy of preserving a military-industrial base capable of manufacturing modern military equipment in quantity. It also describes a ten- to fifteen-year research, development, testing, and evaluation cycle for new weapons. In the mid-1990s, only a very fragmentary commitment to those goals was visible in Russia's assignment of spending priorities (see Structure and Conditions, this ch.). At the very least, defense policy has delayed until after the turn of the century a large share of the acquisition costs and demands on the national industrial base that such a commitment would involve. At that point, a new military doctrine probably will address the issue of technological and economic support.

The Doctrine of the Future

The concluding section of the military doctrine contains an assurance of the defensive and peaceful intentions of the Russian Federation and of its intention to adhere strictly to the UN Charter and the tenets of international law. However, the conclusion also states that this document will be supplemented, adjusted, and improved as Russian statehood is established and as a new system of international relations is formed.

Assumedly, the nature of such changes would depend on Russia's success in achieving another primary goal: preserving the basis of military power inherited from the Soviet Union and setting the stage for making the Russian Federation a major military power after the turn of the century. The view of the future contained in the doctrine is projected against specific time lines. The new Russian armed forces and the basis for their military power are projected to be in place by 2000, when a new, and presumably more assertive, military doctrine is promised. Serious consideration of the content of a more permanent doctrine was not expected to begin until a new government was in place after the 1996 presidential election.

Meanwhile, early in 1996 the government-supported Institute for Defense Studies produced a set of "conceptual theses" on Russia's national security against external threats. Although not a formal outline for a new military doctrine, experts saw the theses as an important indication of current military thought.

The 1996 report lists four major threats to Russia's national security: interference in its internal affairs by the United States and its allies; political and economic penetration of Azerbaijan by Turkey and its Western allies; expansion of NATO into Central Europe, the Baltic states, and ultimately Ukraine; and unilateral disarmament of Russia through forced treaties, modification of the existing Anti-Ballistic Missile Treaty (ABM Treaty—see Glossary), degradation of existing Russian strategic weapons systems and research and development centers, or obstructions to the integration of the CIS.

Among "recommended strategies" to neutralize such threats, the report lists refusing to work with the International Monetary Fund (IMF—see Glossary) and the World Bank (see Glossary), preventing Western access to Caspian Sea oil, establishing a military alliance of CIS members to block NATO expansion (and invading the Baltic states if they try to join NATO), and deploying tactical nuclear weapons in the Caucasus, Baltic, or Far North regions. The report also recommends enlarging Russia's stockpile of strategic nuclear weapons when the limits of phase one of the Strategic Arms Reduction Treaty (START—see Glossary) end in 2009. The particular concern with NATO expansion drives several of these proposals, and comments made in 1996 by top military officials confirm that a set of active responses has been prepared for such an eventuality (see The NATO Issue, this ch.). However, experts see both the Institute for Defense Studies report and supporting statements by military authorities as part of a pattern of pressure applied to potential new NATO states to discourage them from pursuing membership.

In June 1996, the office of the president's national security adviser, Yuriy Baturin, released a draft statement on national security policy goals for the period 1996–2000 that indicated a less aggressive approach to the next military doctrine. The document's authors recognized that Russia faces no external threat, stressing instead that Russia's chief national security need is to strengthen the Russian state economically and politically rather than to maintain military parity with the West. Because the United States no longer is interested in manipulating European geopolitics, according to the document, it is now safe to make concessions—including arms reduction treaties—in the search for balanced and cooperative relations (see The United States, ch. 8). The NATO expansion issue was recognized as the chief obstacle to achieving such relations in 1996. Although the draft policy statement was generally pro-Western, it assigned the highest value to relations with the CIS rather than the West. Experts saw the draft as an attempt to counter the nationalist faction that continues to emphasize military power as the most important element of national security and whose position was forcefully stated in the report of the Institute for Defense Studies.

The Geopolitical Context

According to the Ministry of Defense, between 1991 and 1995 the Soviet Union and then Russia withdrew about 730,000 troops from eleven countries: Azerbaijan, Cuba, the Czech Republic, Estonia, Germany, Hungary, Latvia, Lithuania, Mongolia, Poland, and Slovakia. Including military families, about 1.2 million people were involved in this shift. Besides the troops, all the paraphernalia of fifteen army directorates, forty-nine combined-arms divisions, seventy brigades, seventy-two aviation regiments, and twenty-four helicopter regiments also were moved from foreign posts.

The unprecedented speed with which Russia's direct military influence shrank had a strong effect on the national psyche. Beginning in 1993, Russia's foreign policy increasingly reflected the views of influential nationalist and communist elements of the government. Those elements sought political support by reviving the memories of Soviet world power, promising an end to the "subservient" role being played by Russia on the world political stage of the 1990s. Inevitably, Russia's real-world application of its military doctrine is an implicit and explicit element in expanding influence in the directions dictated by a revised foreign policy program. (The 1996 Institute for Defense Studies report indicates that viewpoint.) Given severe funding limitations, however, that expansion seemed to have limited possibilities in mid-1996.

Chechnya

The Republic of Chechnya, located on the north slope of the Caucasus Mountains within 100 kilometers of the Caspian Sea, is strategically vital to Russia for two reasons. First, access routes to both the Black Sea and the Caspian Sea go from the center of the federation through Chechnya. Second, vital Russian oil and gas pipeline connections with Kazakstan and Azerbaijan also run through Chechnya. The declaration of full independence issued in 1993 by the Chechen government of Dzhokar Dudayev led to civil war in that republic, and several Russian-backed attempts to overthrow Dudayev failed in 1993 and 1994. After a decision of unclear origin in the Yeltsin administration, three divisions of Russian armor, pro-Russian Chechen infantry, and internal security troops—a force including units detailed from the regular armed forces—invaded Chechnya in December 1994. The objective was a quick victory leading to pacification and reestablishment of a pro-Russian government. The result, however, was a long series of military operations bungled by the Russians and stymied by the traditionally rugged guerrilla forces of the Chechen separatists. Although Russian forces leveled the Chechen capital city of Groznyy and other population centers during a long and bloody campaign of urban warfare, Chechen forces held extensive territory elsewhere in the republic through 1995 and into 1996. Two major hostage-taking incidents—one at Budennovsk in southern Russia in June 1995 and one at the Dagestani border town of Pervomayskoye in January 1996—led to the embarrassment of unsuccessful military missions to release the prisoners. The Pervomayskoye incident led to the complete destruction of the town and numerous civilian casualties.

As the campaign's failures and substantial casualties were being well documented by Russia's independent news media (an estimated 1,500 Russian troops and 25,000 civilians had died by April 1995, and the total killed was estimated as high as

40,000 one year later), public opinion in Russia turned strongly against continued occupation. However, fearing that capitulation to a separatist government in one ethnic republic would set a precedent for other independence-minded regions, in 1995 President Yeltsin wavered between full support of Chechnya operations and condemnation of the supposed incompetence of Defense Minister Pavel Grachev and his generals (see Movements Toward Sovereignty, ch. 4). Yeltsin fired several top generals, including Deputy Minister of Defense Boris Gromov, who were critical of the war.

In 1995 and early 1996, Chechen forces fought from mountain enclaves, into which they had been driven by Russian forces with superior firepower and air support. The Chechens used various opportunities to attack targets outside their enclaves, including the Budennovsk raid of June 1995. On several occasions, Russian forces continued bombardments of Chechen strongholds after Yeltsin had announced a cease-fire. In May 1996, Chechen leader Zelimkhan Yandarbiyev signed a cease-fire with Yeltsin in Moscow, followed by full armistice protocols negotiated by the OSCE in the Ingush city of Nazran. The protocols set August 30 for withdrawal of "temporary" Russian forces (plans already existed for permanent stationing of two brigades), contingent on parallel disarmament of Chechen forces. At the end of June, Russian forces began a partial withdrawal, but fighting continued in some regions, and negotiations stalled amid mutual recriminations. In July Russian forces began a new assault on villages described as harboring guerrilla forces, and Russia again seemed to lack a unified policy toward Chechnya.

Russian military and political actions immediately before and after the protocols indicated little respect for their terms. The Russian-supported regime in Groznyy signed a draft political status on Chechnya without consulting the rebels, and the Russian Ministry of Defense reaffirmed its plan to keep troops in Chechnya indefinitely. Those circumstances indicated strongly that peace negotiations were a short-term strategy to reduce the Chechnya obstacle to Yeltsin's reelection in the summer of 1996.

Because of the poor performance of regular troops in Chechnya, Russia had been forced to use elite naval infantry and airborne assault units—the former gathered from fifty units of the Baltic Fleet and more than 100 ships or units of the

Pacific Fleet. Airborne units from two divisions were used to end the Pervomayskoye hostage crisis in January 1996.

According to Russian and Western experts, the many serious command errors made in the Chechnya campaign were at least partly the result of a fragmented command system in which the lack of direct coordination deprived commanders of the ability to make timely decisions. A major cause of this problem was the lack of field training among all levels of the officer corps (see Training, this ch.).

The Chechnya crisis was the most visible indication of the division in Russia's government over the application of military doctrine, and of a disintegration process that even Boris Yeltsin had recognized in 1994. With numerous declarations of sovereignty having emerged from ethnic republics and regions in 1991 and 1992, the 1993 military doctrine had stipulated that the military could be used against separatist groups within the federation, providing a theoretical justification for the Chechnya action. Many military authorities argued that such a campaign was foolhardy, given military budget cuts that made proper training and equipping of troops impossible. Nevertheless, the "war party" of officials and advisers surrounding Yeltsin failed to foresee the media storm that resulted from a bloody military struggle within the federation. In 1995 and early 1996, Grachev's inability to obtain a favorable outcome and continued disarray in top command echelons indicated that he had lost control of the military establishment.

The Commonwealth of Independent States

In the mid-1990s, an increasingly prominent component of Russian foreign policy was recovery of military and economic influence in as many Commonwealth of Independent States (CIS) nations as possible. Along Russia's southern borders, postindependence instability offered a series of opportunities to retain a military presence in the name of "peacekeeping" among warring factions or nations, some of whose hostility could be traced back to actions taken by Russian forces. Variations of this theme occurred in Georgia, Armenia, Azerbaijan, Moldova, and Tajikistan.

Georgia

The course of events along Russia's southwestern frontiers has given Georgia increased military significance since 1991. A critical event was Russia's recognition of Ukrainian sovereignty in Crimea, formerly Russia's only basing area for its Black Sea Fleet. The drive of the Abkhazian Autonomous Republic for independence from Georgia provided Russia with an opportunity to bargain for access to Black Sea ports in Georgia. Reportedly organized by Russian intelligence agencies and heavily supported by Moscow, a mercenary force of North Caucasus Muslim troops threatened to occupy large portions of Georgia in the early fall of 1993. At this desperate point, the Georgian government offered Russia extended basing privileges in return for the protection of Russian "peacekeeping" forces. Ironically, the Russian-supported mercenaries fighting for Abkhazia formed the Confederation of Mountain Peoples of the North Caucasus, which declared its intention of destabilizing Russia's Muslim North Caucasus republics. Therefore, continued access to Georgian territory acquired the additional purpose of encircling potentially separatist enclaves—which is exactly what Russia did in 1994 in preparing to enter Chechnya.

The 1995 basing agreement that resulted from the Georgian capitulation of 1993 permits the presence of three Russian bases—in Tbilisi, Poti, and Batumi—with tanks, armored personnel carriers, and heavy artillery. However, other Russian forces in Georgia also were identified in 1995 after they took part in bombardments in Chechnya. The troops in Georgia, designated strictly for control of domestic conflicts such as the one in Chechnya, also constitute a violation of the CFE Treaty, to which Russia has sought a special adjustment.

In mid-1996 there were an estimated 1,700 Russian troops on peacekeeping duty between Georgian and Abkhazian lines in northwestern Georgia, including one airborne regiment and two motorized rifle battalions. The three main Russian bases housed about 8,500 troops with 110 main battle tanks, 510 armored combat vehicles, and 238 artillery pieces.

Armenia

Armenia's continued desperate position, locked between Muslim states Azerbaijan, Iran, and Turkey and still reeling from the long blockade inflicted by Azerbaijan and Turkey in the Nagorno-Karabakh conflict, provides ample justification for heavy reliance on Russia for national security. For Russia, Armenia's position on the eastern border of Turkey is a prime location for preventing Russia's traditional enemy from expanding its influence to the north and east. A new unified

CIS defense system being created by Russian military planners in 1996 has included the long-term basing of Russian troops on Armenian soil and joint Armenian-Russian exercises on Armenian territory. Russia has lent substantial nonmilitary aid to Armenia in the Nagorno-Karabakh conflict, but Russia does not see supporting a complete victory by Armenia over Azerbaijan as strategically advantageous. In mid-1996 Russia had an estimated 4,300 troops at a single base in Armenia, with eighty main battle tanks, 190 armored personnel carriers, and 100 artillery pieces. Russian border troops also assisted in patrolling Armenia's border with Turkey.

Azerbaijan

Azerbaijan, whose location adjacent to the rich oil resources of the Caspian Sea makes it strategically more vital to Russia than Armenia, is the only one of the three Caucasus states to refuse any deployment of Russian troops on its soil. Russia fears the increasing influence of Turkey in Azerbaijan, which, according to national security planners, is a likely bridge for Turkish influence into Central Asia and Russia's Muslim republics to the north and east of Azerbaijan. Because of these factors, Russia has exerted substantial diplomatic and economic pressure on Azerbaijan to reappraise its independent policy. However, former Soviet Politburo member Heydar Aliyev, now president of Azerbaijan, has proven much more independent than Russia expected when it assisted him in becoming head of state in 1993.

Moldova

The Russian (formerly Soviet) 14th Army has been based on Moldovan (formerly Moldavian) territory since 1956. In September 1990, Slavs on the east bank of the Nistru (Dnestr) River in the Moldavian Republic declared an independent Dnestr Moldavian Republic, or Transnistria. After armed conflict began between forces of the new republic and Moldovan troops in the spring of 1992, part of the 14th Army became a peacekeeping force following an agreement between Russia and the government of newly independent Moldova. The original Russian force included six battalions (2,400 troops), which occupied a security zone together with troops of Moldova and Transnistria. Subsequently, Transnistrian units began replacing units of the 14th Army, taking advantage of what observers called a decided bias by the army in favor of its fellow Slavs.

By the end of 1994, about 3,500 Transnistrian troops were in the security zone with the tacit approval of the Russian forces, enabling the separatists to consolidate their state. At the same time, Russia violated the agreement with Moldova by withdrawing all but 630 of its peacekeepers, citing the Russian military's funding problems. However, in 1996 the bulk of the 14th Army remained in Moldova, subject to the outcome of long-inconclusive negotiations, under the title Operational Group of Russian Forces in Moldova. (A bilateral 1994 agreement to withdraw the 14th Army entirely never was ratified by the State Duma, the lower house of Russia's parliament.) In mid-1996 some 6,400 Russian troops of the 14th Army and two "peacekeeping" battalions remained. Russia has opposed participation by the OSCE in the withdrawal negotiations. Some experts have described Moldova as a potential staging point for Russian operations in Central Europe.

In 1994 Moldova also was the scene of a divisive struggle in the military command. In midyear Minister of Defense Grachev attempted to remove the popular General Aleksandr Lebed' from command of the 14th Army after Lebed' voiced increasingly sharp criticism of the Yeltsin administration. But Yeltsin refused to remove Lebed', magnifying the open struggle between two top military commanders and polarizing the military. Lebed' resigned his command in May 1995 to begin a political career.

Central Asia

Large numbers of Soviet military forces were located in the five Central Asian republics when the Soviet Union dissolved officially at the end of 1991. All the newly independent states took measures to gain control over the Soviet units they inherited, establishing a variety of agencies and ministries to define the gradual process of localization. In the mid-1990s, as support grew in Russia for recapturing in some form the lost territories of the former Soviet Union, attention focused on the five Central Asian republics, which still had substantial economic and military ties with the Russian Federation. When the Soviet Union dissolved at the end of 1991, the main military force in Tajikistan was the 201st Motorized Rifle Division, whose position and resources the Russian Federation inherited. Although nominally neutral in the civil war that broke out in Tajikistan in the fall of 1992, the 201st Division, together with substantial forces from neighboring Uzbekistan, played a significant role in the recapture of the capital city, Dushanbe, by former communist forces. As the civil war continued in more remote regions of Tajikistan during the next three years, the 201st Division remained the dominant military force, joining with Russian border troops and a multinational group of "peacekeeping" troops (dominated by Russian and Uzbekistani forces and including troops from Kazakstan and Kyrgyzstan) to patrol the porous border between Tajikistan and Afghanistan.

The openly avowed purpose of the continued occupation was to protect Russia's strategic interests. Those interests were defined as preventing radical Islamic politicization and the shipment of narcotics, both designated as serious menaces to Russia itself. Meanwhile, Tajikistan formed a small army of its own, of which about three-quarters of the officer corps were Russians in mid-1996. Tajikistan, having no air force, relied exclusively on Russian air power. In mid-1996 the preponderance of the estimated 16,500 troops guarding Tajikistan's borders belonged to Russia's Federal Border Service. Border troops received artillery and armor support from the 201st Division, whose strength was estimated in 1996 as at least 12,000 troops.

Russia has kept more limited forces in the other Central Asian republics. Turkmenistan consistently has refused to join multilateral CIS military groupings, but Russia maintains joint command of the three motorized rifle divisions in the Turkmenistani army. Under a 1993 bilateral military cooperation treaty, some 2,000 Russian officers serve in Turkmenistan on contract, and border forces (about 5,000 in 1995) are under joint Russian and Turkmenistani command. Altogether, about 11,000 Russian troops remained in Turkmenistan in mid-1996. Uzbekistan has full command of its armed forces, although the air force is dominated by ethnic Russians and Russia provides extensive assistance in training, border patrols, and air defense. Kazakstan, which has the largest standing army (about 25,000 in 1996) of the Central Asian republics, had replaced most of the Russians in its command positions with Kazaks by 1995—mainly because a large part of the Russian officer corps transferred elsewhere in the early 1990s. No complete Russian units are stationed in Kazakstan, but an estimated 6,000 troops from the former Soviet 40th Army remained there in training positions in 1996, including about 1,500 at the Baykonur space launch center, which Russia leases from Kazakstan.

In Kyrgyzstan, which has developed little military capability of its own, Russian units guard the border with China. But maintaining military influence in Kyrgyzstan has not been a high priority of Russian military planners; a 1994 bilateral agreement improves incentives for Russian officers to remain in the Kyrgyzstan's army on a contract basis through 1999, but, as in Kazakstan, the Russian exodus has continued. President Askar Akayev of Kyrgyzstan lobbied for a larger Russian military presence to improve his country's security situation, but no action had been taken as of mid-1996.

Kaliningrad

In the immediate postwar period, the Soviet Union established a formidable, closed enclave in the former East Prussia, including a large naval port at Kaliningrad (formerly Königsberg). When the Soviet Union collapsed, the independence of Estonia, Latvia, and Lithuania deprived the new Russian state of major ports on the Baltic Sea, and 15,000-square-kilometer Kaliningrad Oblast between Poland and Lithuania was cut off from Russia. When Russia insisted on maintaining Kaliningrad as a heavily armed garrison, it aroused considerable international criticism, especially from Poland. Königsberg was awarded to the Soviet Union under the Potsdam Accord in 1945, but the Russian Federation holds no legal title to the enclave.

When Russia withdrew all its former Warsaw Pact forces from Poland and the Baltic states during 1992–94, some air, naval, and ground forces were relocated to Kaliningrad, ostensibly because of housing shortages elsewhere in Russia. In mid-1996 the official military garrison was estimated at 24,000 ground troops of the 11th Guards Combined Arms Army, including one tank division and three motorized rifle divisions, three artillery brigades, surface-to-surface and surface-to-air missiles, and attack helicopters. The Baltic Fleet, which has its headquarters at Kaliningrad, includes three cruisers, two destroyers, eighteen frigates, sixty-five patrol boats, and 195 combat aircraft, together with one brigade of naval infantry and two regiments of coastal defense artillery. Western experts estimate that the total Kaliningrad garrison includes as many as 200,000 military personnel, compared with the official Russian figure of 100,000.

In 1993 the population of the enclave was about 900,000, of whom about 700,000 were Russians. There is strong sentiment in favor of autonomy among the civilian population, and international pressure continues to advocate reducing the garrison to a level of "reasonable sufficiency," far below its current size. Many Russian military authorities agree with this idea because maintaining the Kaliningrad force is extremely expensive. However, a large-scale deemphasis of the military would be difficult because the entire oblast has been structured to meet the needs of the armed forces. In addition, Russian nationalists argue that Kaliningrad is a vital outpost at a time when Russia is menaced by possible Polish or even Lithuanian membership in NATO.

China

In 1995 and 1996, Russia and China moved closer on economic and military issues, after many years of insecurity along the two countries' long common frontier. On the Russian side, the move was prompted by a new general emphasis on relations with Asia that also includes the Korean Peninsula and Southeast Asia; on the Chinese side, there was concern about the stability of the Central Asian republics and the possible spread of separatist sentiments together with politicized Islam, especially in the predominantly Muslim Xinjiang Uygur Autonomous Region, which borders Kyrgyzstan, Tajikistan, and Kazakstan. With Russia sharing those concerns, in April 1996 Beijing and Moscow announced a "strategic partnership" that was hailed as a watershed agreement and was accompanied by combined blasts at Western attempts to dominate lesser countries. China voiced support for Russia's Chechnya operation, and Russia backed China's claims of hegemony in Taiwan and Tibet.

New military agreements provide for long-term military and technical cooperation, including Russian aid to Chinese arms industries, modernization of weapons already sold to China, and the sale of new weapons to China at advantageous prices. Among the reported terms of the April 1996 agreement is the sharing of space technology by Russia's State Space Agency, the sale of diesel submarines and S–300 air defense missile complexes, and production in China of Su–27 jet fighters.

In the April 1996 talks, the two sides pledged to observe earlier border demarcation agreements, and Russia ceded some disputed pieces of land. The issue of reducing military forces and defining the border was the subject of ongoing talks in 1996.

Display of naval power on Naval Forces Day, July 1991, Vladivostok
Courtesy Michael E. Samojeden
Sailors on Naval Forces Day, July 1991, Vladivostok
Courtesy Michael E. Samojeden

The NATO Issue

The Russian military has unanimously opposed any expansion of NATO in Central Europe or the former Soviet Union since the idea first appeared in the early 1990s, and virtually all political factions are in agreement. Russia worries that such expansion would leave it in a strategically untenable position, despite NATO's claims of the purely defensive character of its alliance. In the mid-1990s, Russian fears have been fanned by the increasingly influential anti-Western factions in the State Duma and by the increased urgency with which Central European and Baltic states have sought NATO membership.

Russian military thinkers see NATO expansion as moving the world's most powerful military force to the very border of the former Soviet Union (or even past the border, were Ukraine and the Baltic states to join). Contrary to Western claims, Russians see no potential for improvement in Russia's security in this process, except in the unlikely inclusion of Russia as a full NATO member. In 1994 Russia was offered, and eventually accepted, membership in the NATO Partnership for Peace (PfP—see Glossary), into which all former Soviet republics and former Warsaw Pact members were admitted by the end of 1995 (see NATO, ch. 8).

In the period 1994–96, top-level Russian national security representatives put forward a variety of threats and proposals on the subject of NATO expansion. Extreme nationalist factions used the issue to back their argument that the United States is leading an international plot against Russia. In 1995 a set of perceived NATO deceptions of Russian negotiators in Bosnia and Herzegovina was used as evidence of NATO's untrustworthiness. Russia counterproposed that NATO transform itself into a strictly political alliance that would become part of a new pan-European security system on the model of the OSCE. Meanwhile, Russia has exerted strong pressure on the states most imminently eligible for NATO membership, especially Poland, Hungary, and the Baltic states, including threats that nuclear war might break out in Central Europe if Russia needed to defend itself against NATO forces that had moved into the region. In 1995 Russian national security representatives promised that NATO expansion would suspend Russian compliance with the CFE Treaty and make impossible Russian ratification of part two of the Strategic Arms Reduction Treaty (START II)—two cornerstones of disarmament in the view of Western policy makers. Meanwhile, the "NATO threat" was a rationale for maintaining a large garrison at the western outpost in Kaliningrad.

Nuclear Arms Issues

In the 1990s, Russia's status as a nuclear power raised two major issues. First, the deactivation of nuclear weapons in Russia and elsewhere in the former Soviet Union caused a series of problems that affected primarily the civilian population. Second, the rate and conditions for reduction of Russia's nuclear arsenal were matters of heated debate among military and civilian policy makers in the mid-1990s.

During five decades of the Cold War, the Soviet Union stockpiled an estimated 40,000 nuclear warheads, which were located from the Far East to the Ukrainian Republic on the western border. Besides the Russian Republic, three other Soviet republics—Belorussia, Kazakstan, and Ukraine—had nuclear weapons on their soil. In the early 1990s, Russia and the United States agreed that, to prevent proliferation of nuclear weapons and materials, the three other republics should relinquish their entire stockpiles to Russia or destroy them. Although the final cleanup of nuclear materials promises to last into the next century, by the end of 1994 the three former Soviet republics had signed START I and the NPT as nonnuclear states. (Ukraine required additional security assurances and financial aid from the United States as a condition of its participation.)

Experts estimated that disposal of all deactivated nuclear warheads would require at least ten years because Russian facilities can only dismantle 2,000 warheads per year. Another complication is the disposition of an estimated 100,000 now-superfluous employees of nuclear weapons installations who had access to nuclear technology; failure to find suitable employment for such individuals might cause them to sell their highly valuable knowledge abroad. And the total number of displaced employees of nuclear installations is estimated to be much larger.

The presence of nuclear material in Russia has caused other problems. Between 1990 and 1994, the number of documented cases of smuggling of nuclear materials out of Russia went from zero to 124, mainly because of lax security at nuclear sites (see Crime, ch. 10). Although most cases of nuclear smuggling have involved civilians, in 1994 naval officers stole three uranium fuel rods from a submarine in Murmansk—and in the mid-

1990s the fast-deteriorating living standards of Russia's military made such incidents more likely (see Troop Support Elements, this ch.). The Ministry of Defense has voiced concern that terrorists might take advantage of security lapses to seize a nuclear weapon; in 1995 a Chechen guerrilla leader threatened to use nuclear terrorism against Russia's civilian population. In a deal signed in 1992, the United States agreed to buy 500 tons of weapons-grade uranium, mainly to ensure that such material did not move into unscrupulous hands. In December 1994, Russia and the United States agreed to inform each other of dangerous incidents involving nuclear materials, and the United States has provided assistance in upgrading Russia's nuclear security procedures.

A second problem related to Russia's nuclear arms is the radiation pollution that has resulted from the discarding of nuclear materials into the ground and the sea. The naval forces have continued the Soviet-era practice of dumping nuclear materials overboard in the Sea of Japan and the Kara Sea, provoking strong reactions from neighboring countries. In mid-1996 at least fifty of Russia's decommissioned nuclear submarines were standing with fuel rods intact along the Arctic coast, awaiting dismantlement (see Environmental Conditions, ch. 3).

The geopolitical and diplomatic aspects of the nuclear situation are equally problematic. Russia ratified START I in November 1992. That treaty limited the United States and Russia to 1,600 strategic nuclear delivery vehicles (bombers, submarines, and intercontinental ballistic missiles—ICBMs) and 6,000 nuclear warheads each. (The actual number was between 7,000 and 9,000 because of the treaty's counting rules.) The treaty also set a limit of 4,900 ballistic missile warheads and 1,100 warheads mounted on mobile ICBMs. The number and configuration of bombers also was prescribed.

In January 1993, United States president George H.W. Bush and President Yeltsin signed START II. That treaty, which is based on the limitations of START I, would eliminate heavy ICBMs and ICBMs with multiple warheads, and the total number of warheads would be reduced from the nominal START I level of 6,000 to an actual figure between 3,000 and 3,500. START II calls for two phases of reduction, the first of which would begin in 2000. At the end of the second phase, new reductions would be complete in all three delivery modes: land-based ICBM, submarine, and bomber.

In March 1993, the Supreme Soviet (later in 1993 renamed the State Duma) began discussion of START II. The debate over ratification of the treaty continued sporadically for three years and showed no signs of reaching a resolution as of mid-1996. Opponents of the treaty described it as another Western effort to penetrate Russia's national security; treaty backers, including Yeltsin, argued that maintaining the nuclear force at START I levels was financially impossible for Russia, so the much lower START II level matches Russia's capabilities while holding the United States far below its potential. In any case, most of the 2,500 warheads that START II would eliminate were outmoded and scheduled for retirement by the mid-1990s. According to Western experts, in 1996 Russia had the financial resources to deploy only about 500 single-warhead ICBMs, although more than 900 were permitted under START I at that point (see Strategic Rocket Forces, this ch.). Also, Russia's failure to ratify START II encouraged the United States to deploy an anti-ballistic missile (ABM) system that would negate much of Russia's nuclear potential. The matchup of potential United States ABM capabilities with existing Russian nuclear strike capabilities became a key consideration in the START II ratification debate.

Nevertheless, beginning in 1995 the question of NATO expansion overshadowed other aspects of the START II debate; the more anti-Western State Duma that was seated in January 1996 made the impending expansion of NATO a primary argument against START II ratification. Some Russian treaty supporters concurred that the treaty should not be ratified unless NATO expansion plans were shelved.

The Defense Industry

The Russian Federation inherited the largest and most productive share of the former Soviet defense industry, employing as many as 9 million workers in 1,125 to 1,500 research, design, and production facilities. Those installations are concentrated in particular regions, whose economies tend to be heavily dependent on the industry; in the Republic of Udmurtia, for example, more than two-thirds of workers and industrial capacity were attached to defense in some way in the early 1990s. Moscow has large plants for air force and missile components, and St. Petersburg specializes in naval design and production as well as infantry weapons.

Structure and Conditions

Russia's military-industrial complex (MIC) is coordinated by the State Committee for the Defense Industry (Gosudarstvennyy komitet po oboronnoy promyshlennosti—Goskomoboronprom). In 1996 this agency included about 2,000 production enterprises and 920 research organizations with a directly employed work force of about 5 million. However, a 1996 estimate identified about 35 million Russians as receiving their income from enterprises linked in some way to Goskomoboronprom. The research organizations are the heart of Russian military research and development. They take new weapons and military matériel projects from concept to prototype, then hand them off to the production enterprises. Production enterprises do prototype construction, production runs, and modifications.

Zinoviy Pak was appointed director of Goskomoboronprom in January 1996. Prior to his promotion, Pak managed a large defense enterprise in Moscow. His predecessor, Viktor Glukhikh, was dismissed by President Yeltsin for mismanagement—a move that made Glukhikh the scapegoat for a multitude of problems that beset the defense industry in the first half of the 1990s.

The Russian MIC includes an industrial base that is wholly owned by the Russian military. In the Soviet era, defense industries were created solely to arm the Soviet Union, and as such they had the highest national priority in the allocation of technology and talent. The complex regularly consumed 20 percent of the gross national product (GNP—see Glossary) and 15 percent of the industrial labor force. In the drive for privatization after the fall of communism, Russian planners initially believed that this, the best supplied and most efficient of Russian industries, could be converted easily to production for the civilian market and thereafter would become an engine of economic growth. Such optimism obscured the complex's total lack of a civilian market for its products and its inexperience in developing and selling goods in a competitive marketplace. Beginning in the late Gorbachev era, planners mistakenly expected to achieve conversion by a Soviet-style centralized program and without additional funding to support the lengthy, stagewise conversion process.

Although MIC conversion received much publicity and billions of dollars in Western aid after 1992, government funding for that program decreased steadily in the mid-1990s, and only a small percentage of allotted funds actually were spent for conversion. No funds were authorized for conversion in the 1995 budget. Some defense industries have mounted successful conversion and restructuring programs, however. Russia's leading aviation firm, the Mikoyan-Gurevich (MiG) Aviation-Scientific Production Complex, has formed joint ventures with the Moscow Aircraft Production Association (MAPO) and enterprises in Germany, India, and Malaysia. The Sukhoy Holding Corporation has been formed to combine formerly separate design, development, and production operations for high-performance aircraft; Sukhoy has branched out into production of business and commuter aircraft, which accounted for about half its sales in 1995. The MiG and Yakovlev design bureaus also began developing commercial aircraft in the early 1990s.

Given its intrinsic shortcomings, the MIC became a major liability rather than a boon to the Russian economy as the initial momentum of conversion dissipated. In December 1995, the complex's average basic wage rate fell to two-thirds the average for industries in the nonmilitary sector.

Shortly after assuming the Goskomoboronprom directorship, Pak admitted that the defense industry could not survive unless it were reconfigured. He proposed a smaller military and a smaller defense industry—a course whose wisdom was reflected in statistics on recent performance. In 1995 defense industrial production fell by 21 percent compared with 1994, when production in turn was 25 percent lower than 1993. In January 1996, orders were 25 percent below the level for January 1995, and in the first half of 1996 the Ministry of Defense had not completed payment for its 1994 and 1995 deliveries from defense plants. Hardest hit were the shipbuilding, radio, electronics, and ammunition industries. The reason for such a steady decline is that the MIC had only a single customer, the Ministry of Defense, which had an ever-shrinking budget allocation for repairing and modernizing old equipment, buying new matériel, and funding research for future models. Because few enterprises of the MIC had been privatized (a situation that ensured that complete state control would continue), government subsidies kept many alive through the mid-1990s.

Between 1991 and 1994, annual production of main battle tanks dropped from 900 to forty, of infantry fighting vehicles from 3,000 to 400, of fighter aircraft from 225 to fifty, and of helicopters from 350 to 100. Those statistics partly reflect the intentional reduction of forces that began in the late Gorbachev era before the dissolution of the Warsaw Pact in 1991, but they also indicate the overall deterioration of the industry.

In the first half of 1996, the only fully active production program was that for the SS–25 intercontinental ballistic missile (ICBM). Some other enterprises were producing relatively small batches of armored vehicles, most of which were for export. The great majority of the production facilities, including most of the aircraft and shipbuilding installations, were dormant.

The Defense Budget

The 1996 defense budget of the Russian Federation, ratified by the State Duma in December 1995, allotted 78.9 trillion rubles (about US$19 billion—see Glossary for value of the ruble), of which about 16 percent, or 12.6 trillion rubles (about US$3.0 billion), was allocated to acquisitions, and 7.3 percent, or 5.8 trillion rubles (about US$1.4 billion), was earmarked for research and development (R&D). Russia's 1995 budget had allocated 10.2 percent to R&D and 21.2 percent to acquisitions. By comparison, the 1996 United States budget for the Department of Defense totaled US$249 billion, of which US$39 billion (15.7 percent) was designated for acquisitions and US$34 billion (13.7 percent) for R&D. In February 1996, the Security Council allocated between 50 and 54 trillion rubles (US$10 to US$11 billion) to fund additional state orders from the MIC, including money for accelerated R&D and production of advanced weapons systems. This supplementary, targeted allocation represented a significant increase over the allocations for 1994 (US$2 billion) and 1995 (about US$3.4 billion), indicating a possible redirection of resources to R&D even as the military operating budget remained flat.

New Weaponry Acquisitions

Despite the general crisis besetting the defense industry, examples of highly advanced military technology continued to emerge from Russia's defense plants in the mid-1990s. The T–90 main battle tank, the most modern tank in the army arsenal, went into low-level production in 1993, based on a prototype designated as the T–88. The T–90 was developed by the Kartsev-Venediktov Design Bureau at the Vagonka Works in Nizhniy Tagil. Initially seen as an entirely new design, the production model is in fact based on the T–72BM, with some added features from the T–80 series. The T–90 features a new generation of armor on its hull and turret. Two variants, the T–90S and T–90E, have been identified as possible export models. Plans called for all earlier models to be replaced with T–90s by the end of 1997, subject to funding availability. By mid-1996 some 107 T–90s had gone into service in the Far Eastern Military District.

In the mid-1990s, the first priority for the air forces was the Su–T–60S multirole bomber, which had been designed to replace the Tu–22M and the Su–24 (see Force Structure, this ch.). The Su–T–60S is a long-range supersonic tactical/operational nuclear-capable bomber with built-in stealth technology developed by the Sukhoy Design Bureau. Although its development was officially secret, the Su–T–60S was reported to be in the prototype stage and ready for flight testing in mid-1996.

The second priority for the air forces was the Su–27IB tactical fighter-bomber being built for the Frontal Aviation Command. A naval aviation version was designated the Su–32FN. This side-by-side, two-seat aircraft was in serial production in the mid-1990s at the Sukhoy Chkalov Aircraft Plant in Novosibirsk. In its bomber mode, the Su–27IB was expected to be armed with the AA–11 Archer short-range air-to-air missile, and in its fighter mode with the AA–12 Adder mid-range, air-to-air, fire-and-forget missile.

Russia's submarine technology developed faster in the mid-1990s than Western experts had expected, as the fleet underwent reduction from its 1986 total of 186 vessels to ninety-nine. According to one intelligence estimate, more than half of the 1996 fleet was capable of moving undetected into Western sealanes. In mid-1996 the navy scheduled four submarines for production, including one upgraded addition to its existing fleet of Akula-class vessels and three of the new Severodvinsk class, which were expected to go into service in 2000. The Severodvinsk is a state-of-the art submarine that allegedly is so quiet that it eliminates the United States technical lead in this area, and it is armed with the new 650mm Shkval rocket that travels at 200 knots underwater.

The new modification of the SS–25 ICBM, the Topol M–2, is a three-stage, solid-fuel rocket designed to carry a single warhead. Scheduled to go into production in 1996, the Topol M–2 is a permitted modernization under START I terms; it can be deployed in a fixed silo or made mobile. Because it is earmarked for the elite strategic rocket forces as a replacement for missiles being destroyed under START I, the Topol is a high-priority project protected from cutbacks in the acquisitions budget.

Information about the funding of Russia's defense R&D programs remains hard to obtain because many such programs are secret. The official budget allocation of US$1.4 billion, even with the addition of the Security Council's supplemental funding in February 1996, seems extremely modest in an era of rapid technological advances. Most of the acquisition programs of the mid-1990s do not have known R&D follow-on programs; instead, they are products of R&D programs started in the early 1980s.

The MiG–MAPO 1.42 R&D program has been advertised as the Russian response to the United States Air Force's F–22 advanced tactical fighter (ATF) program. The MiG–MAPO 1.42, a single-seat, multirole stealth fighter, is projected to reach operational capability between 2005 and 2008. The air force R&D funds also reportedly have been shifted to a high-priority program to field highly accurate precision-guided munitions (PGM) in response to the United States success with that type of weapon in the Persian Gulf War of 1991. A shift of funds to the PGM program may further delay the MiG–MAPO 1.42 program.

Beginning in 1993, the defense industry had an influential spokesman at Yeltsin's side to lobby for improved support. First Deputy Prime Minister Oleg Soskovets, long a top metallurgy industry executive in the Soviet era, was a forceful proponent of bolstering the existing complex with minimum privatization or conversion to civilian production. However, Soskovets, who was chiefly responsible for increasing Russia's defense budget by 3 trillion rubles in 1996, was dismissed unexpectedly in June 1996 when Yeltsin ousted most of the hard-liners from his inner circle in preparation for the second round of that year's presidential election.

Foreign Arms Sales

In the first half of 1996, defense planners appeared to favor delaying privatization and civilianization and letting the MIC do what it does best: make weapons. Instead of depending upon Russia's armed forces as the customer, Soskovets intensified his pursuit of the international arms market in an attempt to improve the industry's earnings. Russia offered military hardware both for sale as a means to raise capital and in barter arrangements to repay international debts. In April 1996, the

State Corporation for Export and Import of Armaments (Rosvooruzheniye) reported fifty-one countries as current customers, with the largest sales totals involving China, India, Syria, and the United Arab Emirates (UAE). Together with lesser customers Algeria, Cuba, Kuwait, Malaysia, Turkey, and Vietnam, those countries accounted for 75 percent of arms sales in early 1996. Arms exports were being produced at more than 500 enterprises in Russia and more than 1,200 enterprises in ten other CIS nations having production-sharing agreements with Russia.

Arms sales and military technology transfers to China expanded rapidly in the mid-1990s, although many defense authorities had strong reservations about sharing advanced technology with such an unpredictable neighbor. For China, Russia is a source of sophisticated, reasonably priced armaments unavailable from the West. For Russia, China is another source of hard currency (see Glossary). Among China's key purchases in recent years were Su–27 fighter-bombers, MiG–31 fighters, heavy transport aircraft, T–72 tanks, and S–300 antiaircraft missile launchers. In 1994 and 1995 agreements, China bought a total of ten Kilo-class diesel submarines, the first four of which cost US$1 billion altogether. Russia received repeated warnings from the United States about the dangers of enhancing China's military capabilities. Such a warning came in May 1996 against the sale of technology for SS–18 ICBMs, which China had requested ostensibly for its space program.

Russia has agreed to repay part of its trade debt to Finland with its modern SA–11 air defense missile system in a deal worth US$400 million. The SA–11 is an army-level, mobile, low- to medium-altitude, surface-to-air missile system that went into serial production in 1979. The SA–11 can successfully engage any aircraft at altitudes from fifteen to 22,000 meters at a range of up to 35,000 meters using its tracking and engagement radar system. It has an on-board identification friend-or-foe (IFF) system and an electronic countermeasures suite. Experts predicted that Finland would employ the SA–11 as its national air defense system. The SA–11 also is in service in India, Poland, Syria, the Federal Republic of Yugoslavia (Montenegro and Serbia), and several former Soviet republics.

In yet another debt reduction arrangement, Russia is furnishing Hungary 200 BTR–80 wheeled armored personnel carriers (APCs) as replacements for the thirty-year-old Hungarian-manufactured FUG APC. The BTR–80 is a modern, lightly armored vehicle with a diesel power plant. It is manufactured at the Gorkiy Automobile Factory in Nizhniy Novgorod and has been in service since the early 1980s. The BTR–80 is a lightly armored amphibious vehicle with a collective chemical-biological-radiological (CBR) protective system. Operated by a crew of three, the vehicle can carry a squad of seven infantry troops.

In the mid-1990s, the Russian defense industry was anticipating the end of the arms embargo against Serbia as an opportunity to generate hundreds of millions of dollars in sales. Russia's long association with the Serbs has established a traditional Russian arms market in the Federal Republic of Yugoslavia (Montenegro and Serbia). However, in the aftermath of an extremely expensive economic embargo, it is not clear that the Ministry of Defense of Yugoslavia has the funds to purchase large quantities of Russian military matériel.

Russia is aggressively promoting its combat aircraft in the East Asian arms market. Russia and India signed a defense agreement in November 1994 during a state visit by Prime Minister Viktor Chernomyrdin. This agreement marked the end of the strained relations that had resulted from India's loss of access to generous Soviet credit terms and low prices when cash-strapped Russia demanded hard currency (see Glossary) after the fall of the Soviet Union (see Other Asian States, ch. 8). During a related visit to India in March 1995, First Deputy Minister of Defense Andrey Kokoshin made a sale of ten MiG–29 aircraft for US$200 million. At the time, Kokoshin asserted that this and future defense deals with India would save several hundred thousand jobs in the Russian defense sector.

India and Russia have a tradition of cooperation in armaments that began in the 1960s; in the mid-1990s, India needed new equipment from Russia to modernize its armed forces in view of ongoing arms imports by traditional enemy Pakistan and persistent suspicion of neighboring China. In early 1996, India and Russia signed a treaty of military technical cooperation, estimated to be worth US$3.5 billion through the expiration date of 2003. Among key purchases are Russian technology for armored vehicles, artillery, and naval systems in addition to aircraft. In early 1996, experts estimated that as much as 70 percent of India's armaments had been purchased from Russia.

In early 1996, MIC chairman Pak astounded the United States Army by marketing the Russian SA–12 surface-to-air missile system in the UAE in direct competition with the United

States Army's Patriot system. He directed Rosvooruzheniye to offer the UAE the highest-quality Russian strategic air defense system, the SA–12 Gladiator, as an alternative to the Patriot at half the cost. The offer also included forgiveness of some of Russia's debt to the UAE.

Prospects for the Defense Industry

As the defense budget faces annual threats of receiving a smaller share of a shrinking GNP, experts predict that either the defense industry will collapse under its own weight in the near future or that the national budget will reallocate so much money to civilian programs that the industry simply will wither away.

The collapse theory is based on the fact that the two sources of funds in the military budget appropriations that support the defense industry—acquisitions and R&D—are shrinking at a rate faster than the industry can absorb. Although Pak claimed in early 1996 that defense orders constituted only 15 to 20 percent of the MIC's current orders, the civilian economy was not healthy enough to absorb the industry's new products, and most of the converted industries were not producing items with high market appeal. Therefore, Pak's Goskomoboronprom has emphasized dual-use technology that would bridge the gap between the two production sectors.

The fund reallocation theory is based on the premise that the real threats to Russian national security are domestic problems such as regionalism, terrorism, corruption, and crime. A hungry and disillusioned population existing on the edge of economic catastrophe since 1991 does not favor spending scarce funds on a military for which it perceives no immediate need.

The real long-term threat to the Russian defense industry is the reduced R&D funding allotment in the Russian military budget. In the opinion of Western experts, foreign sales will not provide the long-term security required to revive the R&D programs of Russia's military laboratories. In turn, the absence of an aggressive research program for new technology will cause foreign markets to dry up. In June 1996, President Yeltsin named Aleksandr Lebed', an outspoken advocate of smaller, better-equipped armed forces, to chair the Security Council. That move was expected to end arbitrary funding of inefficient MIC enterprises, but its meaning for future R&D was not clear.

The Soviet Union produced an excellent array of military equipment that has been distributed around the world. However, modernization has not continued under the Russian Federation, and the poor performance of Soviet equipment against United States equipment in Operation Desert Storm reduced the eagerness of international arms purchasers. Another problem is repair and replacement. The Russian record on resupply to foreign defense ministries has not been good, and the well-documented prospect of further deterioration in the Russian MIC does not build customer confidence.

From the onset of his tenure as director of Goskomoboronprom, Zinoviy Pak proved to be an imaginative and aggressive marketer of Russian military hardware. He energized the moribund Rosvooruzheniye to the point that it even was placing sophisticated advertisements in Western commercial publications aimed at United States and NATO armed forces. Pak also entered Russian dual-use technology, applied in such products as sports airplanes and high-speed passenger boats, in numerous international exhibitions. In March 1996, Soskovets reported that Russia's 1995 arms sales abroad exceeded US$3 billion, an increase of 80 percent over 1994 and 60 percent more than sales to the Russian military. About 75 percent of foreign payments for weapons were made in cash. By mid-1996 new sales of about US$7 billion already had been identified, and the predicted 1996 income was US$3.5 billion.

Force Structure

The Armed Forces of the Russian Federation are organized into six services subordinate to the Ministry of Defense. In 1996 approximately 1.5 million personnel were serving, including about 160,000 women. The services are the ground forces, the naval forces, the air forces, the air defense forces, the strategic rocket forces, and the airborne troops (see fig. 13). There were plans to reduce the number of armed services to three by combining the air forces, air defense forces, and strategic rocket forces into a single space force, but this change had not been approved officially by mid-1996. Another proposed change, aimed at improving cost and operational efficiency, would establish a regional command structure that would encompass ground, air, and naval forces in a particular region. Altogether, the 1996 state budget authorized funding of 1,470,000 military personnel and 600,000 civilian support personnel.

Command Structure

The armed forces chain of command prescribed in the military doctrine clearly establishes central government control of the military. The president of the Russian Federation is the commander in chief. The Government (called a council of ministers or cabinet in other countries) is responsible for maintaining the armed forces at the appropriate level of readiness. Direct leadership of the armed forces is vested in the Ministry of Defense; the General Staff exercises operational control.

Executive authority over the military lies in the office of the president of the Russian Federation. The State Duma exercises legislative authority through the Government. The minister of defense exercises operational authority, and the General Staff implements instructions and orders. This structure, which has a superficial similarity to the division of power in the United States military establishment, does not imply military subordination to civilian authority in the Western sense, however. The historical tradition of military command is considerably different in Russia. The tsars were educated as officers, and they regularly wore military uniforms and carried military rank. Stalin always wore a military uniform, and he assumed the title generalissimo. Even General Secretary Leonid I. Brezhnev (in office 1964–82) appointed himself general of the army, and he encouraged portraits of himself in full uniform.

By tradition dating back to the tsars, the minister of defense normally is a uniformed officer. The State Duma also seats a large number of deputies who are active-duty military officers—another tradition that began in the Russian imperial era. These combinations of military and civilian authority ensure that military concerns are considered at the highest levels of the Russian government. They also demonstrate that strict subordination of the military to civilian authority in the Western sense is neither a tradition nor a concern in Russia.

The minister of defense is the nominal commander of all the armed forces, serving under the president of the Russian Federation. In this capacity, the minister exercises day-to-day authority over the armed forces. President Yeltsin appointed General of the Army Pavel Grachev to the post in May 1992. Grachev's decision to side with Yeltsin in the president's October 1993 confrontation with parliament deprived a rebellious State Duma of an opportunity to overturn the president's authority. At least partly for that reason, Yeltsin retained his defense minister despite intense criticism of Grachev's manage-

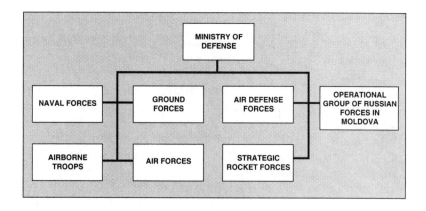

Figure 13. Organization of the Ministry of Defense, 1996

ment of the Chechnya campaign and the Russian military establishment in general. Finally, victory in the first round of the 1996 presidential election spurred Yeltsin to dismiss Grachev; General Igor' Rodionov, who had commanded troops in the controversial occupation of Tbilisi in 1989 but had a reputation as a soldier of integrity who was sympathetic to reform, was appointed minister of defense in July 1996.

The Ministry of Defense is managed by a collegium of three first deputy ministers, six deputy ministers, and a chief military inspector, who together form the principal staff and advisory board of the minister of defense. The executive body of the Ministry of Defense is the General Staff. It is commanded by the chief of the General Staff. In keeping with the Soviet practice of permitting senior officers to hold civilian positions, in 1996 the chief of staff also was a first deputy minister of defense.

Contrary to the United States tradition of military authority derived strictly from the civilian sector, Russian General Staff officers exercise command authority in their own right. In 1996 the General Staff included fifteen main directorates and an undetermined number of operating agencies. The staff is organized by functions, with each directorate and operating agency overseeing a functional area, generally indicated by the organization's title (see table 28, Appendix).

The most secret of the General Staff directorates is the Main Intelligence Directorate (Glavnoye razvedochnoye upravleniye—GRU), which has been an important and closely guarded element of national security since its establishment in the 1920s. The GRU system delivers detailed information on the capabilities of Russia's most likely military adversaries to the General Staff and to political leaders. The organization is divided into five operational directorates, each covering a designated geographical area. The first four cover Europe, Asia, the Western Hemisphere and Britain, and the Middle East and Africa, respectively. In the Soviet era, the fifth directorate coordinated military intelligence activities, but in the 1990s that agency has been assigned to provide intelligence from the other former Soviet republics. Headquartered in Moscow, the GRU has an estimated 2,500 personnel, including area and technical specialists and field offices abroad. Each military district and fleet also has its own intelligence directorate.

Ground Forces

The commander in chief of the ground forces, who in 1996 was Colonel General Valeriy Patrikeyev (appointed in September 1992), has two first deputy commanders, three deputy commanders, and a Main Staff. The first deputies have general responsibilities, and the deputies have specified functional responsibility for armaments, aviation, and combat training, respectively. The executive agency for the commander in chief is the Main Staff of the Ground Forces.

The Ground Forces of the Russian Federation are estimated to number approximately 670,000 officers and enlisted personnel. Of that number, about 170,000 are contract volunteer enlistees and warrant officers, and about 210,000 are conscripts. Presumably, the remaining 290,000 are commissioned officers. These figures indicate that 43 percent of ground forces personnel are officers, an extraordinarily high percentage that reflects the Soviet and Russian tradition of giving little authority to the enlisted ranks, as well as the vestiges of the much larger military cadre inherited from the Soviet army. Much of this bulge is made up of senior field-grade officers and generals who no longer are needed in a smaller military but who are too young to retire. In the mid-1990s, this situation was one of the most difficult personnel problems facing the ground forces command.

The ground forces are organized into eight military districts, one independent army, and two groups of forces (see fig. 14; fig. 15). Although the districts are ground forces commands, they may include forces from the other services, in which case

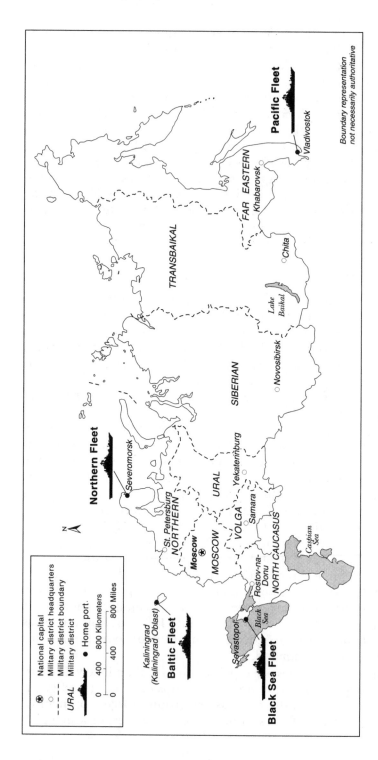

Figure 14. Military Districts and Fleets, 1996

they also serve as regional commands. In February 1996, four of Russia's eight independent airborne brigades were placed under ground forces command, with one each going to the North Caucasus, Siberian, Transbaikal, and Far Eastern districts. At the same time, two of five airborne divisions, stationed at Pskov and Novorossiysk, were assigned for special joint operations to the Northern and Siberian districts, respectively. These shifts, which outside observers interpreted as the end of plans to form a mobile force for rapid insertion in trouble areas, reflected a shortage of the airlift capacity needed to support independent operations by such troops, as well as a possible fear of coup activity in independent elite military units.

Altogether, in 1996 the ground forces included sixty-nine divisions: seventeen armored, forty-seven motorized infantry, and five airborne. Included in their armaments were 19,000 main battle tanks, 20,000 artillery pieces, 600 surface-to-surface missiles with nuclear capability, and about 2,600 attack and transport helicopters.

Among the specially designated units, the Operational Group of Russian Forces in Moldova (also known as the Group of Russian Forces in the Dnestr Region) is part of the ground forces, but operationally the group is directly subordinate to the Ministry of Defense. This command arrangement probably derives more from political than military concerns. The second force group, the Group of Russian Forces in the Transcaucasus, stationed in Armenia and Georgia, is operationally subordinate to the ground forces command (see The Commonwealth of Independent States, this ch.). The Northwest Group of Forces is an administrative title given to ground forces headquarters in Kaliningrad, whose troops are under the command of the 11th Independent Army. That army, in turn, is operationally subordinate to the ground forces.

The eight military districts are the Northern, Moscow, Volga, North Caucasus, Ural, Siberian, Transbaikal, and Far Eastern. The Northern Military District is the successor to the Soviet-era Leningrad Military District, although the old name still was in use in 1995, and reports in 1996 indicated that it might be reinstated officially. The district includes the 6th Combined Arms Army, the 30th Army Corps, the 56th District Training Center, and several smaller units. One air army also is stationed in the district, but it appears to be subordinate to the Air Force High Command. The airborne division stationed at Pskov, formerly

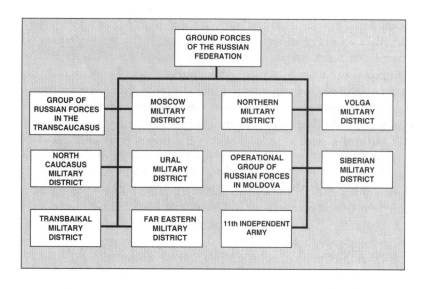

Figure 15. Organization of the Ground Forces, 1996

operationally subordinate to the Ministry of Defense, was reassigned for special combined duty in 1996.

The Moscow Military District is an anomaly in the command structure because it includes the national capital. It has special significance because of its proximity to the western border with Belarus and Ukraine, traditionally the routes followed by invaders from the west. The district's official troop strength includes the 1st and 22d combined arms armies and the 20th Army Corps. However, CFE Treaty data indicate that operational control of these forces is vested in the Ministry of Defense rather than the ground forces or the district commanders. Other forces within the Moscow district include the Moscow Air Defense District, one airborne brigade, and one brigade of special forces (*spetsnaz*) troops. The Moscow Air Defense District has boundaries coterminous with those of the Moscow Military District, but it is under the command of the air defense forces. The special forces brigade is directly subordinate to the Ministry of Defense.

The Volga Military District, headquartered at Samara, is an interior district that includes the 2d Combined Arms Army, together with an airborne division that is operationally subordinate to the Ministry of Defense. The 2d Combined Arms Army is an understrength unit consisting of the 16th and 90th Tank

Divisions. Also in the Volga district are the 27th Motorized Rifle Division and the 469th District Training Center, which are directly subordinate to the district commander.

The North Caucasus Military District, headquartered at Rostov-na-Donu, faces the former Soviet republics of Georgia, Armenia, and Azerbaijan. It is defended by the 58th Combined Arms Army and the 8th and 67th Army Corps. However, these are not robust forces. The 8th Army Corps and the 58th Army each include only one motorized rifle division, and the 67th Army Corps has only reserve forces with no heavy equipment. The weakness of these units has helped motivate Russian proposals to renegotiate CFE Treaty limitations to allow additional forces along Russia's southern flank.

The Ural Military District lies south of the Northern district and east of the Ural Mountains, with the Siberian district to its east. The Ural district, whose headquarters is at Yekaterinburg, includes two tank divisions and two motorized rifle divisions. The Siberian Military District lies in the center of Asiatic Russia, with its headquarters in Novosibirsk. Its ground forces are organized into one corps of four motorized rifle divisions and one artillery regiment.

The Transbaikal Military District is headquartered in Chita. The district comprises three combined arms armies totaling four tank divisions and six motorized rifle divisions. One tank division and one motorized rifle division are headquartered at district training centers that are believed to be directly subordinate to the district headquarters. One artillery division and two machine gun-artillery divisions deployed on the Chinese border also have district training-center status.

The Far Eastern Military District, headquartered in Khabarovsk, includes four combined arms armies and one army corps. Among them, those units have three tank divisions and thirteen motorized rifle divisions, of which one tank division and two motorized rifle divisions have headquarters that serve as district training centers. One artillery division and five machine gun-artillery divisions are directly subordinate to the district headquarters.

Naval Forces

The naval forces include about 200,000 sailors and marines, about 20 percent of whom are conscripts, and 500,000 reserves. Of the active-duty personnel, about 30,000 are in naval aviation and 24,000 in coastal defense forces. The primary missions of the naval forces are to provide strategic nuclear deterrence from the nuclear submarine fleet and to defend the sea-lanes approaching the Russian coast. The naval forces include shore-based troops, naval aviation units, four fleets, and one flotilla (see fig. 16). The shore-based forces and naval aviation forces are operationally subordinate to the fleets. The strategic naval forces, comprising forty-five nuclear submarines and 13,000 personnel, are operationally subordinate to the Ministry of Defense and logistically supported by the fleets in whose ports they are based. Some 138 other submarines are in service, although in the mid-1990s a major reduction of the nonstrategic submarine force was in progress (see table 29, Appendix).

In the mid-1990s, Russia's naval aviation force was almost entirely shore based, after having achieved substantial sea-based strike capability in the Soviet era. In 1996 only the steam-powered aircraft carrier *Admiral Kuznetsov,* assigned to the Northern Fleet, conducted active flight operations at sea. Two new nuclear-powered carriers were scrapped before completion, indicating abandonment of that program, and older aircraft-carrying cruisers were sold to the Republic of Korea (South Korea) for scrap. However, in 1996 the nuclear-powered cruiser *Petr Velikiy* (Peter the Great) was scheduled for launching at St. Petersburg after eight years under construction; assigned to the Pacific Fleet, the 28,000-ton vessel is armed with guided missiles believed to be designed to destroy enemy aircraft carriers. Experts rated the *Petr Velikiy* the most powerful cruiser in the world.

Each of Russia's four fleets has a subordinate, land-based naval air force. The Caspian Flotilla has no naval air arm. The naval shore-based troops consist of naval infantry and coastal defense forces. The naval infantry forces include one infantry division subordinate to the Pacific Fleet and four naval infantry brigades—one in the Baltic Fleet, one in the Black Sea Fleet, and two in the Northern Fleet. The coastal defense forces are a combination of infantry regiments, brigades, and divisions with air defense missile regiments. Amphibious landings are a low priority; according to intelligence estimates, only 2,500 marines and 100 tanks could be put ashore by Russia's thirteen amphibious ships. According to a Russian source, in 1996 most ships were at a relatively low readiness level, with most units remaining close to home port.

The Northern Fleet is headquartered at Severomorsk, at the top of the Kola Peninsula near Murmansk, with additional home ports at Kola, Motovskiy, Gremikha, and Ura Guba. The mission of the Northern Fleet is to defend Russia's far north-western Arctic region surrounding the Kola Peninsula. The fleet provides home ports for thirty-seven nuclear submarines, twenty-two other submarines, forty-seven principal surface combatants, and ten coastal and smaller ships. The naval aviation contingent includes a complement of twenty Su–39 fixed-wing aircraft and ten antisubmarine warfare helicopters on board the *Admiral Kuznetsov*, which heads the air defense of the Barents Sea. Shore-based naval aviation includes 200 combat aircraft and sixty-four helicopters. The Northern Fleet has two naval infantry brigades, one coastal defense regiment, and an air defense missile regiment.

The Baltic Fleet is headquartered in Kaliningrad, where it is defended by a naval infantry brigade. From this rather exposed location, the fleet controls naval bases at Kronshtadt and Baltiysk. Operational forces include nine submarines, twenty-three principal surface combatants, and approximately sixty-five smaller vessels. The air arm of the Baltic Fleet includes five regiments of combat aircraft and a number of other fixed-wing aircraft and helicopters.

Headquartered at Sevastopol', with an additional home port in Odessa, the Black Sea Fleet became an object of contention between Russia and Ukraine when the latter republic achieved independence after the dissolution of the Soviet Union. Although Ukraine has no use for a blue-water navy and cannot afford to maintain one, it has been reluctant to surrender its share of the fleet, both of whose home ports are in Ukraine, to a larger neighbor with a tradition of domination. A long international squabble ended temporarily when a June 1995 summit meeting arrived at a formula for disposition of the Black Sea Fleet's assets: the ships of the fleet were to be divided equally between the two nations, but Russia eventually would buy back approximately 60 percent of Ukraine's share. The Russian portion of the Black Sea Fleet continued to be based in Sevastopol', with separate Russian and Ukrainian ports designated on the coast. All ships were to be under dual command until the agreement took effect in 1998. However, substantial nationalist opinion on the Russian side opposed this solution.

The Black Sea Fleet comprises fourteen submarines, thirty-one capital ships of the line, and forty-one coastal ships. The *Moskva*, Russia's first seagoing aircraft cruiser, is assigned to the Black Sea Fleet. It is an antisubmarine warfare helicopter car-

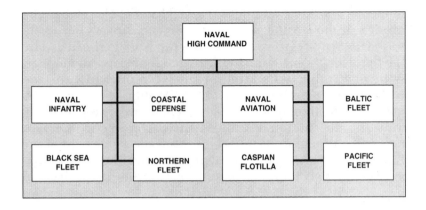

Figure 16. Organization of the Naval Forces, 1996

rier with a complement of eighteen KA–25 helicopters. The land component of the Black Sea Fleet comprises one naval infantry brigade, a coastal defense division, and a surface-to-air missile (SAM) regiment. It is not known how these assets will be distributed between Russia and Ukraine. The naval aviation component of the fleet includes an inventory of nearly 8,000 aircraft of all types. Its strike power is concentrated in a bomber regiment and a mixed fighter and ground-attack regiment.

The Caspian Flotilla is a small force for coastal defense and waterways patrol consisting of two frigates, twelve patrol boats, and about fifty other small craft based in Astrakhan'. Command and equipment are shared with Azerbaijan and Kazakstan, other former Soviet republics on the Caspian littoral.

The Pacific Fleet and the Northern Fleet are rated as the two most powerful Russian naval forces. Pacific Fleet headquarters is in Vladivostok, with additional home ports in Petropavlovsk-Kamchatskiy, Magadan, and Sovetskaya Gavan'. The Pacific Fleet includes eighteen nuclear submarines that are operationally subordinate to the Ministry of Defense and based at Pavlovsk and Rybachiy. The blue-water striking power of the Pacific Fleet lies in thirty-four nonnuclear submarines and forty-nine principal surface combatants.

The air power of the Pacific Fleet consists of the 250 combat aircraft and helicopters of the Pacific Fleet Air Force, all of which are land-based. Its most powerful strike force is two bomber regiments stationed at Alekseyevka. Each regiment consists of thirty supersonic Tu–26 Backfire aircraft. The land power of the Pacific Fleet consists of one naval infantry division and a coastal defense division. The naval infantry division includes more than half of the total manpower in the Russian naval infantry. Following the pattern established elsewhere in the naval infantry, in the mid-1990s the Pacific Fleet infantry is expected to be reorganized into brigades in the near future.

Air Forces

The air forces include about 130,000 troops, of which 40,000 are conscripts. According to CFE Treaty figures, at the end of 1994 Russia's air forces, including air defense, possessed a total of 3,283 combat aircraft. The air forces are organized into four commands under the Air Force High Command (see fig. 17). These commands are the Long-Range Aviation Command, the Frontal Aviation Command, the Military Transport Aviation Command, and the Reserve and Cadre Training Command. The usual command configuration includes a division of three regiments, each with three squadrons of aircraft, plus independent regiments. Like units of the ground forces, most air force units are deployed according to military district.

The air force contingent of the Far Eastern Military District consists of 124 Su–24 Fencer bombers of the long-range aviation force, and 245 ground-attack and fighter aircraft of the Su–17, Su–24, Su–25, Su–27, and MiG–29 classes in frontal aviation. The Transbaikal Military District hosts an air army comprising 185 combat aircraft. The long-range contingent in that district consists of eighty Su–24 bombers. The frontal aviation portion includes thirty MiG–29 and seventy-five Su–17 and Su–24 ground-attack and dual-role aircraft.

The Siberian Military District has no frontal or long-range assets. It deploys only 239 L–39 jet training aircraft of the Reserve and Cadre Training Command. The Ural Military District is supported by one regiment of thirty Su–24 fighter-bombers of the Frontal Aviation Command. The North Caucasus Military District's air assets are organized as an air army that includes a long-range bomber division of eighty-five Su–24 bombers, together with two frontal aviation divisions, a ground-attack division of 110 Su–25 fighter-bombers, and a fighter division of 110 MiG–29 fighters. The North Caucasus Military District air army also has a reconnaissance regiment consisting of thirty-five Su–24 aircraft.

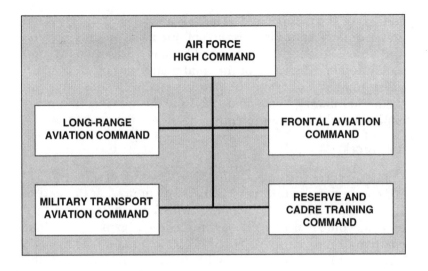

Figure 17. Organization of the Air Forces, 1996

Two training centers of the Reserve and Cadre Training Command are located in the North Caucasus district. They base five training regiments equipped with 500 operational and training aircraft of various types. Two more fighter training regiments deploying a combination of ninety-four combat aircraft are stationed in the Volga Military District. The Moscow Military District is supported by an air army that consists of a bomber division of ninety Su–24 aircraft of the Long-Range Aviation Command, a fighter division of 145 Su–27 and MiG–29 aircraft, a ground-attack regiment of forty Su–25 fighters, and a reconnaissance regiment of fifty-five Su–24 and MiG–25 aircraft. The Moscow Military District also hosts two training regiments of the Reserve and Cadre Training Command.

The Northern Military District is supported by an air army consisting of a bomber division under the Long-Range Aviation Command and a fighter division and a reconnaissance regiment under the Frontal Aviation Command. The bomber division is equipped with eighty Su–24 bombers, the fighter division with ninety-five Su–27 and MiG–29 aircraft.

In addition to the allocations made by district, forty-six aircraft officially belong to the Long-Range Aviation Command but are under the control of Ukraine. Their operational readiness is suspect. A composite regiment of transport aircraft and helicopters from the Military Transport Aviation Command is stationed at Kaliningrad.

The Military Transport Aviation Command is organized into three divisions, each comprising three regiments of thirty aircraft. In addition, there are a few independent aviation transport regiments, including one stationed in Kaliningrad. Overall, the independent training regiments deploy about 350 aircraft of the Il–76 Kandid, An–12, An–22, and An–124 types.

Strategic aviation is an intercontinental nuclear strike force that includes about 15,000 personnel. In concert with the strategic rocket forces, it provides the Russian Federation's strategic nuclear threat. Organizationally, strategic aviation falls under the Long-Range Aviation Command of the air forces, but it is under the operational control of the Ministry of Defense. Bases are located in the Far Eastern, Moscow, and Northern military districts. According to the reckoning of START I, strategic aviation aircraft can deliver a total of 1,506 nuclear warheads, including bombs, cruise missiles, and air-to-surface missiles. The Far Eastern force deploys 107 Tu–95 Bear bombers of the G and H models and twenty Tu–160 Blackjack bombers.

The Bear is a long-range subsonic turboprop bomber modeled after the United States B–29 of World War II vintage. Although still serviceable, it is an obsolete combat aircraft by modern military standards. Its operational range would carry it over the United States, however. The Blackjack is a modern, high-performance aircraft that has a shorter range than the Bear. The Blackjack can reach long-range targets in the United States with the aid of midair refueling. For this purpose, the strategic bomber force has forty tanker aircraft in its inventory.

The Northern and Moscow military districts each house a heavy bomber regiment of twenty modern Tu–22M high-performance jet bombers. The Tu–22M has less range than the older Tu–95 models, but it is better suited to modern air warfare. According to experts, the Bears are located in Asia because they match China's obsolete air defenses, and the more modern aircraft are in Europe to be matched against the more formidable West European defenses.

Air Defense Forces

The air defense forces, charged with defense against enemy air attack, have a total of about 200,000 troops, of whom 60,000 are conscripts. The air defense forces include missile, air force, and radio-technical units and an air defense army. There also are two independent air defense corps (see fig. 18). The missile forces are equipped with approximately 2,500 launchers deployed in about 250 different sites around the country. Air defense forces have particular responsibility for defending administrative and industrial centers; for instance, they surround Moscow with about 100 missile launchers. The air force troop contingent consists of about 850 combat aircraft, including 100 MiG–23, 425 MiG–31, and 325 Su–27 aircraft.

The air defense forces also operate twenty Il–76 aircraft configured for airborne early warning and command and control. The air force troops operate their own training program from one training center that includes four regiments equipped with more than 380 MiG–23 and L–39 aircraft.

The missile troops are equipped with about 150 SA–2 Guideline, 100 SA–3 Goa, 500 SA–5 Gammon, and 1,750 SA–10 Grumble missile launchers. A program to replace all of the older systems with the SA–10, well under way by 1996, has been considered by experts to be one of the most successful reequipment programs of the post-Soviet armed forces. Seven of the military districts have at least one aviation air defense regiment each; two districts, Moscow and the Far Eastern, have specially designated air defense districts.

The borders of the Moscow Air Defense District are the same as those of the Moscow Military District. The Far Eastern Air Defense District combines the territory of the Far Eastern Military District and the Transbaikal Military District. Presumably, the boundaries of the other military districts are the same for air defense as for other defense designations.

Strategic Rocket Forces

In the Soviet era, the strategic rocket forces (SRF) were established as the elite service of the nation's military because they have the vital mission of operating long- and medium-range missiles with nuclear warheads. They remained so in the mid-1990s. In 1996 the SRF had about 100,000 troops, of which about half were conscripts; the SRF has the highest proportion of well-educated officers among the armed services. The SRF also is the only service with an active force modernization program.

Russia's report for the CFE Treaty indicated the existence of ten SRF missile bases within the European scope of the treaty, including sites at Plesetsk (north of Moscow), Kapustin Yar (near Volgograd), Vladimir (east of Moscow), Vypolzovo (northwest of Moscow), Yoshkar Ola (in the Republic of Mari El), Kozel'sk (southwest of Moscow), Tatishchevo (north of Volgograd), Teykovo (northeast of Moscow), and Surovatikha (south of Nizhniy Novgorod). Indicating the priority given air defense of the European sector, Russia listed only four additional missile bases outside the CFE Treaty reporting area, at Nizhniy Tagil, Irkutsk, Novosibirsk, and Kansk. There is a training regiment at the missile test facility near Plesetsk and another at the Kapustin Yar test facility. Russia has continued the reduction in strategic missile inventory required under START I, although at a pace slower than the United States would like. By mid-1996 all nuclear warheads on former Soviet SRF missiles in Kazakstan and Ukraine had been returned to Russia or destroyed, and all missiles were scheduled to leave Belarus by the end of 1996 (see Nuclear Arms Issues, this ch.).

The Russian SRF missile inventory not only is shrinking in response to treaty requirements but also is changing in character. The new SS–25 Topol is the only system suited to Russian strategic requirements and acceptable under the requirements of START I, so rocket production efforts will concentrate on this model for the foreseeable future.

The Topol is fielded in SRF regiments comprising three battalions totaling nine launch vehicles. In 1996 forty such regiments were operational. Several older operational ICBM systems also remained in the field. These included an SS–17 regiment of ten silos, six SS–18 silo fields totaling 222 missiles with multiple warheads, four SS–19 silo fields totaling 250 missiles with multiple warheads, and ninety-two SS–24 missiles of which thirty-six are mounted on trains. All except the SS–24 were being phased out in favor of the SS–25 Topol. Two remaining SS–25 regiments without warheads were scheduled for redeployment from Belarus to the Perm' region in 1996.

Airborne Troops

The airborne troops comprise five airborne divisions and eight air assault brigades. They were designated as a separate service in 1991, at which time the air assault brigades were reassigned from ground forces units and military districts to Airborne Troop Headquarters, with direct responsibility to the Ministry of Defense. The justification for this reorganization was that airborne troops could not respond as quickly to an emergency under ground forces command as they could as a

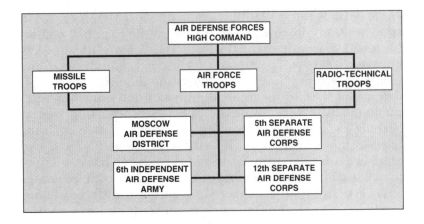

Figure 18. Organization of the Air Defense Forces, 1996

separate command. Experts believe that the decision to reorganize came mainly in response to internal politics rather than military necessity; at that time, the Russian national leadership did not want airborne troops under the control of the General Staff or the ground forces. In early 1996, four of the eight independent airborne brigades and two of the five airborne divisions were placed under the command of their respective district commanders, and the remaining three divisions became part of the strategic reserve. The command adjustments constituted a return to the pre-1991 arrangement.

The reason given for the transfer of authority was that the military districts already controlled the helicopter, fixed-wing, and other resources needed to support the air assault brigades, and that historically air assault brigades were created to operate in an operational-tactical role attached to a high-level headquarters. They were never intended to be a strategic asset. In the case of the Novorossiysk Division engaged in Chechnya, a chain of command running back to Moscow allegedly proved unworkable. However, the reassignment of the airborne units brought interservice charges that the move was an attempt to rein in a service branch perceived as having a dangerous combination of independence and mobility. The chief of the General Staff, General Mikhail Kolesnikov, characterized the decision as purely operational.

The mission of the airborne forces is to make possible a quick response to national emergencies. The airborne troops are considered an elite force because they are individually selected from volunteers based on physical fitness, intelligence, and loyalty. By traditional military standards, the airborne troops are not a powerful force. Each division is assigned about 6,000 lightly armed troops with lightly armored vehicles. Their value is that they have special training and have operational and strategic mobility provided by long-range aircraft. Their parachute assault capability means that they can be deployed anywhere within airlift range in a matter of hours without the need for an air base in friendly hands. However, resupply and support by heavy ground troop formations are necessary in a matter of days because the airborne troops lack the self-sustaining combat and logistical power of regular ground forces.

All of the airborne divisions are based in European Russia. One division is based in the Northern Military District, two in the Moscow Military District, and one each in the Volga and North Caucasus districts. The division in the North Caucasus Military District has taken part in the Chechnya conflict.

The eight airborne assault brigades are smaller than divisions, and they lack the armor and artillery assets that give conventional divisions ground mobility and firepower. Once the airborne brigades are on the ground, they can move no faster than walking speed. Their role is primarily focused on helicopter operations, but they also are trained for parachute assault from fixed-wing aircraft.

Performance

In the 1990s, the direction of change in the Russian armed forces is toward a smaller and more defense-oriented force almost entirely deployed within the borders of Russia. As of mid-1996, that change was occurring faster than military or civilian leaders could manage. The result was a large armed force with too many officers and not enough enlisted personnel, one unable to provide adequate training, and, according to Russian and Western experts, deficient in purpose and direction. The military leadership remained in the hands of holdovers from the Soviet regime who had failed to adjust to new political and military realities. The force's one strength lay in the sheer numbers of its personnel and the size of its equipment inventory.

The performance of Russia's armed forces in the Chechnya conflict provided a glimpse of the capabilities of Russian ground and air forces. The image is not an impressive one, particularly if evidence on training and force morale is considered.

Troop Support Elements

The social implications of Russia's troop support effort in the mid-1990s are staggering. In the United States, a lack of military housing means that military families have to find homes or apartments in the civilian community. Because that option does not exist in Russia, a military family without military housing is literally homeless. Families of field-grade officers subsist in tents or packing crates salvaged from troop redeployments from Central Europe. In other cases, homeless military families have been sheltered for years at a time in gymnasiums or warehouses set up like emergency shelters. At the end of 1994, an estimated 280,000 military personnel and family members were homeless. Many units live in permanent field conditions under canvas. In 1995 only 2,500 of 5,000 rated pilots in flight-status jobs had apartments. The elite strategic rocket forces (SRF) have not fared much better than the other branches of the armed forces. In 1995 the SRF commander in chief, General Igor' Sergeyev, stated that only fourteen of forty-two apartment blocks needed in 1994 to house his troops and their families had been constructed, leaving 11,000 of his troops unhoused; one year later, 4,000 of his troops still were without housing. In 1996 the overall housing situation worsened.

The impact on military preparedness is immense. The daily lives of officers and enlisted personnel are consumed with providing the means of survival for themselves and their families. This marginal existence provides fertile ground for illegal activities such as trading military property for means of sustenance, or engaging in illicit acts to obtain money earned, but not received, in pay (see Crime in the Military, this ch.). There is little energy, time, funds, matériel, or even motivation to conduct individual or small-unit training.

Soldiers often wait two to four months to be paid, and often only partial pay is issued. According to a complex financial system, Russian commercial banks have responsibility for issuing funds from the Ministry of Defense's budget account to individuals, but the system has proved extremely cumbersome, and substantial amounts of money have simply disappeared or have been long delayed while being processed. The pay level also is unsatisfactory. In early 1996, a Russian pilot holding the rank

MiG–29K Fulcrum naval variant armed with missiles, on display at 1992 Moscow Air Show

of major was paid approximately 1.5 million rubles per month, or about US$300. By comparison, a NATO pilot of equivalent rank earned US$6,000 per month.

Force readiness also depends on equipment maintenance and resupply. In 1995 aviation units received only 39 percent of the required fuel, reducing annual flight time by a factor of 3.5. In 1994 the Ministry of Defense purchased only thirty of the 300 aircraft listed as being required, and only one aircraft was purchased in 1995. General Petr Deynekin, air forces commander in chief, has estimated that, at that rate of acquisition and maintenance, the air forces would have no flyable aircraft by 2005.

The naval forces are in approximately the same state of readiness as the air forces. Only one ship, the aircraft carrier *Admiral Kuznetsov,* had as much as five months of time at sea in

1994. Other naval sea time training was described as "infrequent." In 1995 nearly 95 percent of the ready naval vessels remained at dockside because of shortages of fuel, ammunition, and crews, and a backlog of repairs. Fuel shortages have caused the Pacific Fleet to cancel visits by single ships to Asian ports, and electricity was cut off to a nuclear submarine base in the Kola Peninsula, nearly causing a serious nuclear accident, because the base could not pay its bills. The Black Sea Fleet was embarrassed when a cruiser in the Mediterranean in 1996 ran out of water and had to request emergency resupply from the United States Navy. The once-proud aircraft carrier *Admiral Gorshkov,* the last of the Kiev class in service, was in drydock in 1996 for repair after a serious fire, and there were proposals to sell the ship for scrap or to the Indian navy.

Naval logistics had reached a crisis state by the mid-1990s. In 1996 fuel allocations were reduced by 65 percent from 1995, and rations were cut by 60 percent. Similar cuts were made in funds for maintenance, parts, tools, and batteries. The result was that fleet readiness was reduced by an estimated 30 percent for coastal forces and 50 percent for the blue-water navy.

Russia's four Kirov-class nuclear cruisers have fallen into disuse because they require large crews and are expensive to operate. Of the ships in that category, the *Ushakov* had been at dockside in its home port, Murmansk, for nearly five years in 1996 because of a lack of spare parts. The *Petr Velikiy* began sea trials in 1996 after a delay of three years. The *Lazarev* was scheduled to be refueled in 1996, but scrapping also was considered. Conventionally powered ships also have experienced maintenance difficulties. The Slava-class *Marshal Ustinov* was in drydock in St. Petersburg for two years for refurbishing, but it was expected to be scrapped for lack of parts and funds.

The air defense forces also have found it difficult to maintain readiness. In February 1996, the commander in chief, General Viktor Prudnikov, admitted that inadequate funding and poor matériel and technical support had lowered his branch's standard of combat readiness. Russia's missile forces receive no systematic daily training, and there is no firing-range practice. Air defense pilots get little flight time, and no funds are available for maintenance or aircraft parts. An estimated 50 percent of Russia's border is unprotected by radar because equipment of the radio-technical forces is inoperable. As of 1996, the air defense forces had not had funds for new

AS–14 Kedge air-to-surface missile on display at 1992
Moscow Air Show

orders for two years, and no improvement was expected in the near future.

The readiness condition of the ground forces is comparable to that of the other branches. In 1994 General Vladimir Semenov, commander in chief of the ground forces, admitted that the ground forces lacked the capacity to perform their assigned tasks. The council reported that more than a third of the helicopters cannot fly and that even emergency supplies (war stocks) had been partially consumed. General Semenov has reported that ground forces units are drastically under-staffed; motorized rifle regiments, the heart of ground combat power, are said to be understaffed by 60 percent. Semenov has concluded that Russian ground combat units lack adequate personnel to participate in military actions and that full staff-ing of units would take a prohibitively long time.

Crime in the Military

By the mid-1990s, both organized and random crime had penetrated Russia's military, as they had penetrated many other parts of society. As the military reorganizes, personnel are faced with strong temptations to engage in criminal activity, particularly when valuable state property is available for sale and when the professional prospects and social prestige of military service are sinking. Military and security personnel also offer criminal organizations a useful set of skills.

Petty criminal activity and systematic abuses by the officer corps have long been acknowledged aspects of the Soviet military system. As early as the late 1980s, authorities noticed escalating rates of weapons and munitions theft, narcotics trafficking, and diversion of various types of military resources. But the fragmentation of military authority and organization that began with the dissolution of the Soviet Union multiplied the opportunities for such activities. Drug use afflicted the military on a large scale during the nine-year occupation of Afghanistan, and the general increase in drug use in civilian society brought more users into the armed forces in the 1980s and 1990s. Episodes of random violence also increased. In 1989 fifty-nine officers were killed in attacks unrelated to military action. As morale dropped, cases of severe hazing of new recruits (*dedovshchina*—a tradition that began under Peter the Great) increased until, in 1994, an estimated 2,500 soldiers died and another 480 committed suicide as a direct result of hazing.

The illegal sale of weapons of all sizes became pervasive in the 1990s. Already in the late 1980s, Soviet troops in Europe were selling large numbers of individual weapons; as withdrawal from Europe progressed in the early 1990s, the sale of heavy equipment, including armored vehicles and jet fighters, also was reported. The largest force group in the region, the Western Group of Forces stationed in Germany, was the most active in this area, according to a series of investigations in the early and mid-1990s. Underground sales were reported inside Russia as well, with large numbers of weapons moving to civilian criminal organizations.

In late 1993, President Yeltsin formed the State Corporation for Export and Import of Armaments (Rosvooruzheniye) to consolidate and control arms sales under a single agency, but after that time the state still realized only a small part of the huge hard-currency profits from arms sales, while a number of top Rosvooruzheniye officials, with ties to a complex web of financial enterprises in Russia and abroad, flourished as sales continued to go undocumented. The agency acquired the nickname "Ros-vor," meaning "Russian thief," as the controversial activities of its officers were publicized and public confidence dropped. Shortly after creating Rosvooruzheniye, the government approved direct arms sales activities by weapons manufacturers, further complicating the effort to monitor sales. Another state agency, the State Armament and Military Equipment Sales Company (Voyentekh), was established in 1992 to sell used equipment and arms overseas, with the proceeds to finance housing for troops. According to frequent allegations, that program also is riddled with corruption, most of its profits have not reached the housing fund, and much equipment has gone to the criminal world. Among the beneficiaries of such uncontrolled movement have been the Chechen guerrillas, who apparently were able to buy Russian arms even after the beginning of hostilities in late 1994.

Training

According to Russian and Western reports, inadequate funding and bad organization have caused all of the armed forces to suffer from extremely poor training. Although numerous top military leaders criticized this situation, little progress has been made in the mid-1990s.

Military Schools

In 1996 the Ministry of Defense administered a multilevel system of military training institutions, none of which had full enrollment in the mid-1990s. The system included eight military academies and one military university, offering university-level training and education in military and related fields. There were specialized academies for artillery, chemical defense, air defense, air engineering, space engineering, and medicine. The Military University in Moscow specialized in jurisprudence and journalism. In addition, there were about seventy institutions of higher education (*vysshiye uchebnyye zavedeniya*—VUZy; sing., VUZ) for military studies, most of which fell under one of the main force groups and were further specialized according to subject (for example, the Kazan' Higher Artillery Command-Engineer School and the Ufa Higher Military Aviation School for Pilots).

Field Training

Nominally, the Russian armed forces operate on the same six-month training cycle that was observed by the Soviet armed forces. Each cycle begins with induction of draftees and basic individual training, proceeds to unit training at the levels of squad through division, and terminates with an army-level exercise. In 1994 General Semenov reported that the ground forces had not conducted any divisional exercises for the previous two years. As early as 1989, a reduction in Russia's military training activity became obvious in CSCE reports of major training exercises. This means that by 1996 the armed forces had passed through more than ten cycles without conducting any serious training.

Considering the Russian military five-year personnel assignment cycle, the training hiatus means that there was one, and part of another, military generation in each rank with a serious training deficiency, or no training at all in their nominal assignments. There were platoon and company commanders with no field experience. Few battalion, regimental, and division commanders had practical experience in commanding troops in the field at their present or preceding level.

The air forces of the Russian Federation are the most technologically sensitive of the armed forces. Modern high-performance aircraft demand skilled crews to operate and maintain them. However, in 1995 General Deynekin reported receiving only 30 percent of required funding for fuel, equipment, and parts in 1995—a shortfall that cut pilot flight time in operational squadrons to thirty to forty hours per year, approximately three hours per month in the cockpit. By contrast, the United States standard for pilot proficiency is 180 to 260 hours per year.

Reform Plans

In 1996 Aleksey Arbatov, deputy chairman of the State Duma Defense Committee, stated that the armed forces must be reduced by at least 500,000 personnel, a force reduction of one-third, with a simultaneous increase in the annual military budget of about US$20 billion—more than twice its level at the time.

The official plan for armed forces reorganization was put forth in a presidential decree of August 1995. Reforms would occur in two stages, which were outlined only vaguely. The first stage, to last from 1996 to 2000, would include reorganization of the civilian economy to provide better overall budgetary support, stabilize the defense industry, and revamp the territorial divisions of the national defense system to match a new concept of strategic deployment. The second stage, 2001 to 2005, would address the international role of the Russian armed forces, ending with the creation of the "army of the year 2005."

The first phase was defined by five goals. First, a "rational" level of strategic nuclear forces would remain in place on land, sea, and air to defend against a global nuclear or conventional war. The level of such forces would be influenced by whether other powers had developed ABM defenses. Second, further downsizing was possible, depending on the leadership's estimation of optimal size given world conditions. Third, organizational structure would be changed only after comprehensive research, with numerous ground forces units to be combined and maintained at cadre strength. Fourth, procurement would be centralized, spending priorities strictly observed, and expenditures carefully monitored. Fifth, the command and control system would be improved in all operational-strategic groupings, optimizing control to ensure maximum combat readiness. There would be a clear definition of the respective functions of the Ministry of Defense, the General Staff, and the main directorates. The newly created State Commission for Military Organization and Development and the General Staff were to direct the fifth phase.

After issuing the reform decree, President Yeltsin periodically criticized the military (most notably Minister of Defense Grachev) for what he described as a complete lack of progress toward the stated goals. According to Western experts, this was a justified criticism, given the disorder and internal friction that prevented the military establishment from reaching consensus on any policy.

Military service became particularly unpopular in Russia in the mid-1990s. Under conditions of intense political and social uncertainty, the traditional appeal to Russian patriotism no longer resonated among Russia's youth (see Social Stratification, ch. 5). The percentage of draft-age youth who entered the armed forces dropped from 32 percent in 1994 to 20 percent in 1995. The Law on Military Service stipulates twenty-one grounds for draft exemption, but in many cases eligible individuals simply refuse to report; in July 1996, a report in the daily *Pravda* referred to a "daily boycott of the draft." In the first half of 1995, about 3,000 conscripts deserted, and in all of 1995 between 50,000 and 70,000 inductees refused to report. According to a 1996 Russian report, such personnel deficiencies meant that only about ten of Russia's sixty-nine ground forces divisions were prepared for combat. The armed forces responded to manpower shortages by extending the normal two-year period of active-duty service of those already in uniform; only about 19,000 of the approximately 230,000 troops scheduled for discharge in December 1994 were released on time.

The two most compelling reasons for the failure of conscription are the unfavorable living conditions and pay of soldiers (less than US$1 per month at 1995 exchange rates) and the well-publicized and extremely unpopular Chechnya operation. The Russian tradition of hazing in the ranks, which became more violent and was much more widely reported in the 1990s, also has contributed to society's antipathy toward military service (see Crime in the Military, this ch.). By 1996 the approval rating of the military as a social institution had slipped to as little as 20 percent, far below the approval ratings achieved in the Soviet era.

Although by 1996 Russia's armed forces were less than one-third the size they reached at their Cold War peak in the mid-1980s, there still was a need for large numbers of personnel who were appropriately matched to their assigned duties and who could be motivated to serve conscientiously. The issue of gradually replacing Russia's ineffectual conscription system with a volunteer force has brought heated discussion in the defense establishment. The semiannual draft, which has set about 200,000 as its regular quota, has been an abysmal failure in the post-Soviet era because of evasion and desertion. During evaluation of an initial, experimental contract plan, in May 1996 Yeltsin unexpectedly proposed the filling of all personnel slots in the armed forces with contract personnel by 2000. In 1996 some units already were more than half staffed by contract personnel, and an estimated 300,000 individuals, about 20 percent of the total nominal active force, were serving under contract. At that time, more than half of new contractees were women.

But the main obstacle to achieving Yeltsin's goal is funding. To attract competent contract volunteers, pay and benefits must be higher than those offered to conscripts. Already in early 1996, a reported 50,000 contract personnel had broken their contracts because of low pay and poor housing, and many commanders expressed dissatisfaction with the work of those who remained. In mid-1996 a final decision on the use of volunteers awaited discussion in the State Duma and a possible challenge in the Constitutional Court.

Prospects for the Military

In the mid-1990s, Russia's military establishment included a number of influential holdovers from the Soviet era, together with incomplete plans for reform. That inauspicious combination of elements was not reconciled because there was little agreement among military or civilian policy makers on the appropriate speed and direction of change, and because economic conditions offered no flexibility for experimentation.

To the extent that the Chechnya conflict of 1994–96 was a fair test of combat capability, Russia's armed forces were far from fighting form, even by their own evaluation. As they received pessimistic assessments of the current and future situation, Russian policy makers faced a complex of other adjustments. In 1996 the shapers of policy on international relations and national security could not agree on Russia's status in the post-Soviet world (see Foreign Policy Prospects, ch. 8). Utilization of the military's very limited financial resources would require a consensus on the areas of the world most vital to national security. For example, would a second Chechnya-type uprising within the Russian Federation merit the kind of effort expended on the first one? What sort of response should the seemingly inevitable expansion of NATO elicit? Should Russia seek a permanent military presence in other CIS nations, to bolster national security? In answering such questions, military policy makers confront a national psyche still damaged by the dissolution of the Warsaw Pact and the Soviet Union itself. They also are tempted to divert attention from fundamental problems by renewing campaigns against old enemies.

No redirection of national security priorities could have meaning without a strong commitment to reorganize the military establishment that was inherited from the Soviet era. Only a leaner force could recapture the Soviet-era reservoir of skill, pride, and dedication that was dissipated in the first half of the 1990s. Through 1996 the budgetary strategy was to finance selected high-technology R&D projects and MIC enterprises capable of satisfying foreign arms customers (together with internal security "armies" such as that of the Ministry of Internal Affairs), while literally starving conventional troops and neglecting maintenance budgets. With the formation of a new government in mid-1996, the voices of reform became louder, but consensus on the basic requirements had grown no closer.

*   *   *

The *Russian CFE Data Exchange,* supplied in concurrence with the terms of the CFE Treaty, provides current and accurate information on the organization, deployment, equipment, and staffing of Russia's armed forces in the European sector covered by the treaty. Translations of Russian military periodicals and press releases in the military affairs section of the Foreign Broadcast Information Service's *Daily Report: Central Eurasia* are an invaluable primary source of current material. The best recent monograph on the Russian armed forces is Richard F. Staar's *The New Military in Russia,* which evaluates recent policy shifts and prospective changes of doctrine. *Jane's Defence Weekly* and *Jane's Intelligence Review* provide articles on specific issues of military policy. The annual *The Military Balance* contains detailed listings of force strength, weaponry, and deployment, and the annual *World Defence Almanac* addresses the same information with background on treaties such as START I and START II. The journals *Military Technology* and *Defense News* articles on the Russian defense industry and arms trade. A study by Graham H. Turbiville, Jr., "Mafia in Uniform: The Criminalization of the Russian Armed Forces," is a detailed report on post-Soviet criminal activity in the military. (For further information and complete citations, see Bibliography.)

Chapter 10. Internal Security

Sadko, a Russian folk hero, sings at the shore of Lake Il'men' near Novgorod (design from lacquer box made in village of Kholuy).

RUSSIA'S INTERNAL SECURITY APPARATUS underwent fundamental changes beginning in 1992, after the Soviet Union dissolved and what had been the Russian Soviet Federated Socialist Republic (RSFSR) was reconstituted as the Russian Federation. These changes, initiated by the government of Russian Federation president Boris N. Yeltsin, were part of a more general transition experienced by Russia's political system. The state security apparatus was restructured in the period after 1991, when the functions of the Committee for State Security (Komitet gosudarstvennoy bezopasnosti—KGB) were distributed among several agencies. In that period, the interactions among those agencies and the future course of internal security policy became key issues for the Russian government. As the debate proceeded and the Yeltsin government's hold on power became weaker in the mid-1990s, some aspects of the Soviet-era internal security system remained in place, and some earlier reforms were reversed. Because Yeltsin was perceived to use the security system to bolster presidential power, serious questions arose about Russia's acceptance of the rule of law.

In the same period, Russia suffered an escalating crime wave that threatened an already insecure society with a variety of physical and economic dangers. In the massive economic transformation of the 1990s, organized-crime organizations pervaded Russia's economic system and fostered corruption among state officials. White-collar crime, already common in the Soviet period, continued to flourish. The incidence of random crimes of violence and theft also continued to increase in the mid-1990s. Meanwhile, Russia's police were handicapped in their efforts to slow the crime rate by a lack of expertise, funding, and support from the judicial system. In response to public outrage at this situation, the Yeltsin government increased the powers of internal security agencies, endangering the protections theoretically enjoyed by private citizens in post-Soviet Russia.

Internal Security Before 1991

The KGB had been an integral feature of the Soviet state since it was established by Nikita S. Khrushchev (in office

1953–64) in 1954 to replace the People's Commissariat for Internal Affairs (Narodnyy komissariat vnutrennikh del— NKVD), which during its twenty-year existence had conducted the worst of the Stalinist purges. Between 1954 and 1991, the KGB acquired vast monetary and technical resources, a corps of active personnel numbering more than 500,000, and huge archival files containing political information of the highest sensitivity. The KGB often was characterized as a state within a state. The organization was a rigidly hierarchical structure whose chairman was appointed by the Politburo, the supreme executive body of the Communist Party of the Soviet Union (CPSU—see Glossary). Key decisions were made by the KGB Collegium, a collective leadership including the agency's top leaders and selected republic and departmental chiefs. The various KGB directorates had responsibilities ranging from suppressing political dissent to guarding borders to conducting propaganda campaigns abroad. At the end of the Soviet period, the KGB had five chief directorates, three smaller directorates, and numerous administrative and technical support departments.

In contrast to the United States government, which assigns the functions of domestic counterintelligence and foreign intelligence to separate agencies, the Federal Bureau of Investigation (FBI) and the Central Intelligence Agency (CIA), respectively, the Soviet system combined these functions in a single organization. This practice grew out of the ideology of Soviet governance, which made little distinction between external and domestic political threats, claiming that the latter were always foreign inspired. According to that rationale, the same investigative techniques were appropriate for both foreign espionage agents and Soviet citizens who came under official suspicion. For example, the KGB's Seventh Chief Directorate, whose task was to provide personnel and equipment for surveillance operations, was responsible for surveillance of both foreigners and Soviet citizens.

The KGB's branches in the fourteen non-Russian republics duplicated the structure and operations of the unionwide organization centered in Moscow; KGB offices existed in every subnational jurisdiction and city of the Soviet Union. The KGB's primary internal function was surveillance of the Soviet citizenry, using a vast intelligence apparatus to ensure loyalty to the regime and to suppress all expressions of political opposition. This apparatus served as the eyes and ears of the party

Uniformed members of KGB at the Kremlin, Moscow, 1985
Courtesy Charles Trew

leadership, supplying information on all aspects of Soviet society to the Politburo.

The First Chief Directorate was responsible for KGB operations abroad. It was divided into three subdirectorates, responsible respectively for deep-cover espionage agents, collection of scientific and technological intelligence, and infiltration of foreign security operations and surveillance of Soviet citizens abroad. Segmented into eleven geographical regions, the First Chief Directorate placed intelligence-gathering officers in legal positions in embassies and elsewhere abroad. Such activities increased markedly after détente with the West in 1972 permitted many more Soviet officials to take positions in Western and Third World countries. In the 1970s and 1980s, as many as 50 percent of such officials were estimated to be conducting espionage.

The KGB Security Troops, which numbered about 40,000 in 1990, provided the KGB with coercive potential. Although Soviet sources did not specify the functions of these special troops, Western analysts believed that one of their main tasks was to guard the top leaders in the Kremlin, as well as key government and party buildings and officials at the major subnational levels. Such troops presumably were commanded by the Ninth Directorate of the KGB.

The Security Troops also included several units of signal personnel, who reportedly were responsible for installation, maintenance, and operation of secret communications facilities for leading party and government bodies, including the Ministry of Defense. Other special KGB troops performed counterterrorist and counterintelligence operations. Such troops were employed, together with the Internal Troops of the Ministry of Internal Affairs (Ministerstvo vnutrennikh del—MVD), to suppress public protests and disperse demonstrations. Special KGB troops also were trained for sabotage and diversionary missions abroad.

The Internal Troops were a component of the armed forces but were subordinate to the MVD. Numbering about 260,000 in 1990, the Internal Troops were mostly conscripts with a two-year service obligation. Candidates were accepted from both the active military and civilian society. Four schools trained the Internal Troops' officer corps.

The Internal Troops supported MVD missions by aiding the regular police in crowd control in large cities and by guarding strategically significant sites such as large industrial enterprises, railroad stations, and large stockpiles of food and matériel. A critical mission was the prevention of internal disorder that might endanger a regime's political stability. Likely working in concert with KGB Security Troops, the Internal Troops played a direct role in suppressing anti-Soviet demonstrations in the non-Russian republics and strikes by Russian and other workers. Most units of the Internal Troops were composed solely of infantry with no heavy armaments; only one operational division was present in Moscow in 1990. In this configuration, the Internal Troops also might have been assigned rear-echelon security missions in case of war; they performed this duty in World War II.

Regular police forces, called the militia, which were the direct responsibility of the MVD, also played an important role in preserving internal order and fighting corruption; regional and local jurisdictions had no police powers. The Procuracy was the chief investigatory and prosecutorial agency for nonpolitical crimes, with a hierarchical organization that provided procurators (state prosecutors) at all levels of government. Although the new Russian government made several changes in the laws and organization of criminal justice after 1991, the overall system of internal security retained many of the characteristics of its Soviet predecessor.

Successor Agencies to the KGB

By early 1991, the powerful KGB organization was being dismantled. The development of the post-Soviet internal security apparatus took place in a highly volatile political environment, with President Yeltsin threatened by political opposition, economic crises, outbreaks of ethnic conflict, and sharply escalating crime. Under these circumstances, Yeltsin and his advisers had to rely on state security and internal police agencies for support in devising and implementing internal security strategies.

The KGB was dissolved officially in December 1991, a few weeks before the Soviet Union itself. Foreign observers saw the end of the KGB as a sign that democracy would prevail in the newly created Russian Federation. But President Yeltsin did not completely eliminate the security apparatus. Instead, he dispersed the functions of the former KGB among several different agencies, most of which performed tasks similar to those of the various KGB directorates.

In 1992 Yeltsin never made a clear statement of his plans for the security services, except for occasional claims that the new services would be very different from the KGB. Nevertheless, early in 1992 certain trends already could be discerned. Generally speaking, Yeltsin had three main aims for the internal security services. Above all, he wanted to use the services to support him in his battles with high-level political opponents. Second, he wanted the security apparatus to counter broader domestic threats—ethnic separatism, terrorism, labor unrest, drug trafficking, and organized crime. Third, he intended that the security apparatus carry out counterintelligence against foreign spies operating in Russia.

After the creation of fifteen new states from the republics of the former Soviet Union, the territorial branches of the former KGB were transferred to the control of the new governments of these states, each of which made reforms deemed appropriate to the political and national security needs of the regime in power. The Russian Federation, however, which as the RSFSR had housed KGB central operations in Moscow, inherited the bulk of the KGB's resources and personnel. As early as January 1992, five separate security agencies had emerged in Russia to take the place of the KGB. Four of them were concerned with internal security; the fifth was the Foreign Intelligence Service, which replaced the KGB's First Chief Directorate.

Ministry of Security (MB)

Within Russia the largest KGB successor agency was the Ministry of Security (Ministerstvo bezopasnosti—MB), which numbered some 137,000 employees and was designated a counterintelligence agency. The Ministry of Security inherited the tasks of several KGB directorates and chief directorates: the Second Chief Directorate (counterintelligence against foreigners), the Third Chief Directorate (military counterintelligence), the Fourth Directorate (transportation security), the Fifth Chief Directorate (domestic political security), the Sixth Directorate (activities against economic crime and official corruption), and the Seventh Directorate (surveillance activities).

In July 1992, Yeltsin signed—and Russia's Supreme Soviet (parliament) ratified—a law concerning the governance of the Ministry of Security. The law gave Yeltsin sweeping authority over security operations and aroused concern among Russian democrats. They worried because the new law so closely resembled the one on the KGB that had been enacted by the Soviet government just fourteen months earlier. The law conferred essentially the same mission and powers on the Ministry of Security that the earlier law had granted to the KGB, in some cases almost verbatim. The main difference was that in the past the KGB had been controlled by the leadership of the CPSU, whereas the 1992 law gave Yeltsin, as president, control of the Ministry of Security. The Russian parliament was granted some theoretical oversight functions, but they never were exercised in practice.

Yeltsin's first minister of security, former MVD chief Viktor Barannikov, left most of the organization's former KGB officials in place. In the spring of 1993, when an uneasy truce between Yeltsin and the Russian parliament was broken and the Supreme Soviet voted to deprive Yeltsin of his extraordinary presidential powers, Yeltsin called upon Barannikov and the Ministry of Security for support as the president declared the imposition of "special rule" giving him veto power over parliamentary legislation until new elections were held. However, Barannikov declined to involve his ministry in the political confrontation between the executive and legislative branches, urging that a compromise be found. When the Ministry of Defense

Parade on last Soviet "May Day," on Dzerzhinskiy Square with KGB building in background, 1991
Courtesy Michael E. Samojeden

also failed to support his position, Yeltsin backed down from his confrontational stance.

The split between Yeltsin and Barannikov was exacerbated by Barannikov's response to the government corruption issue in 1992–93. Bribe taking and behind-the-scenes deals, which had been accepted practices for Soviet officials, were traditions that died hard, especially in the absence of laws and regulations prohibiting officials from abusing their positions. When privatization of state property began, the scale of corruption increased dramatically. The overlap between government-controlled economic enterprises and private entrepreneurial ventures created vast opportunities for illegal economic activity at the highest levels.

Beginning in 1992, the Ministry of Security became involved in the war against organized crime and official corruption. Before long, however, the campaign turned into an exchange of accusations of corruption among Russia's political leaders, with the Ministry of Security in the middle. Yeltsin wanted to use the corruption campaign as a political weapon in fighting his opponents, but his own entourage was soon hit with charges of covering up crimes—a tactic of Yeltsin's enemies to which Barannikov lent at least passive support. Barannikov's failures to support Yeltsin led to the security minister's dismissal in mid-1993.

Barannikov's replacement, Nikolay Golushko, did not last long in his job. After Yeltsin's threat to dissolve the Russian parliament in September 1993, which ended in bloodshed on the streets of Moscow, the president realized that Golushko was also unwilling to use the forces of the Ministry of Security to back up the president. In this case, Yeltsin not only dismissed his minister of security but also disbanded the ministry and replaced it with a new agency, the Federal Counterintelligence Service (Federal'naya sluzhba kontrarazvedki—FSK).

Federal Counterintelligence Service (FSK)

The law creating the FSK, signed in January 1994, gave the president sole control of the agency, eliminating the theoretical monitoring role granted to the parliament and the judiciary in the 1992 law on the Ministry of Security. The original outline of the FSK's powers eliminated the criminal investigative powers of the Ministry of Security, retaining only powers of inquiry. But the final statute was ambiguous on this issue, assigning to the FSK the task of "carrying out technical-operational measures, [and] criminological and other expert assessments and investigations." The statute also stipulated that the FSK was to "develop and implement measures to combat smuggling and corruption." Such language apparently assigned a key role to the successor of the Ministry of Security in the intensifying struggle against economic crime and official corruption.

According to its enabling statute, the FSK had eighteen directorates, or departments, plus a secretariat and a public relations center. Because some of the Ministry of Security's functions were dispersed to other security agencies, the initial FSK staff numbered about 75,000, a substantial reduction from the 135,000 people who had been working for the Ministry of Security in 1992. The reduction process began to reverse itself within a few months, however, as the FSK regained the criminal investigation functions of the Ministry of Security. By July 1994, the FSK reported a staff of 100,000.

Golushko's replacement as minister of security was his former first deputy, Sergey Stepashin, who had served as head of the Parliamentary Commission on Defense and Security during 1992–93. Stepashin's arrival coincided with the establishment of a new economic counterintelligence directorate in the FSK and development of new laws to improve the FSK's ability to fight corruption. Stepashin announced measures against underground markets and "shadow capital," phenomena of the transition period that had been defended as stimuli for the national economy. He also defended the FSK against critics who accused the agency of persecuting private entrepreneurs.

In addition to fighting crime and corruption, the FSK played a prominent role in dealing with ethnic problems. One worry for the agency was the possibility of terrorist acts by dissident non-Russian nationalities within the Russian Federation. Approximately 20 percent of Russia's population is non-Russian, including more than 100 nationalities concentrated in Russia's thirty-two ethnically designated territorial units. Tension over unresolved ethnic and economic issues had been mounting steadily since 1990, as non-Russian minorities became increasingly belligerent in their demands for autonomy from Moscow (see Ethnic Composition, ch. 4). The FSK was responsible for cooperating with other agencies of the Yeltsin government in monitoring ethnic issues, suppressing separatist unrest, and preventing violent conflict or terrorism. In keeping with this mandate, FSK troops joined MVD forces in backing Russian regular armed forces in the occupation of Chechnya (see Security Operations in Chechnya, this ch.). Russian security elements also have been active in Georgia, where they have assisted regular forces in containing the independence drive of Abkhazian troops and policing a two-year ceasefire that showed no sign of evolving into a permanent settlement as of mid-1996.

Federal Security Service (FSB)

The FSK was replaced by the Federal Security Service (Federal'naya sluzhba bezopasnosti—FSB) in April 1995. The new Law on Organs of the Federal Security Service outlined the FSB's mission in detail. The FSB regained a number of the functions that had been eliminated in earlier post-KGB reorganizations. Investigative authority was fully restored by the law, although the FSK had already been conducting criminal investigations on the basis of a presidential decree issued months before. Russia's fourteen investigative detention prisons and several special troop detachments also returned to the control of the security service.

The 1995 law authorizes security police to enter private residences if "there is sufficient reason to suppose that a crime is being or has been perpetrated there . . . or if pursuing persons suspected of committing a crime." In such cases, related laws require the officer in charge only to inform the procurator within twenty-four hours after entering a residence. Like the FSK statute, the new law gave the president direction of the activities of the security service, which has the status of a federal executive organ. Article 23 of the law stipulated that the president, the Federal Assembly (parliament), and the judicial organs monitor the security service. But the only right given deputies of the State Duma (the assembly's more powerful lower house) in this regard was a vague stipulation that deputies could obtain information regarding the activity of FSB organs in accordance with procedures laid down by legislation. The imprecision of actual oversight functions was compounded by the security law's provision that unpublished "normative acts" would govern much of the FSB's operations.

The law gave the FSB the right to conduct intelligence operations both within the country and abroad for the purpose of "enhancing the economic, scientific-technical and defense potential" of Russia. Although FSB intelligence operations abroad are to be carried out in collaboration with the Foreign Intelligence Service, the specifics of the collaboration were not spelled out. The liberal press reacted with great skepticism to the new law's potential for human rights violations and for reincarnation of the KGB.

Although the FSB is more powerful than its predecessor, FSB chief Stepashin operated under a political cloud because of his support for the botched Chechnya invasion. In July 1995, pressured by the State Duma and members of his administration, Yeltsin replaced Stepashin with the head of the Main Guard Directorate, General Mikhail Barsukov (see Main Guard Directorate (GUO), this ch.). Barsukov was closely linked to the director of Yeltsin's personal bodyguard organization (the Presidential Security Service), Aleksandr Korzhakov, who had acquired powerful political influence in the Kremlin.

Federal Agency for Government Communications and Information (FAPSI)

The KGB's Eighth Chief Directorate, which oversaw government communications and cipher systems, and another technical directorate, the sixteenth, were combined as the Federal

Agency for Government Communications and Information (Federal'noye agentstvo pravitel'stvennykh svyazi i informatsii—FAPSI), of which the former head of the Eighth Chief Directorate, Aleksandr Starovoytov, was named director. FAPSI has unlimited technical capabilities for monitoring communications and gathering intelligence. When the Law on Federal Organs of Government Communications and Information was published in February 1993, Russia's liberal press protested loudly. The newspaper *Nezavisimaya gazeta* called it the "law of Big Brother," pointing out that it not only gives the executive organs of government a monopoly over government communications and information but permits unwarranted interference in the communications networks of private banks and firms.

The communications and information law authorized FAPSI to issue licenses for the export and import of information technology, as well as for the telecommunications of all private financial institutions. Equipped with a body of special communications troops (authorized by the 1996 budget to number 54,000), FAPSI was given the right to monitor encoded communications of both government agencies and nonstate enterprises. This means that the agency can penetrate all private information systems. The law stipulated little parliamentary supervision of FAPSI aside from a vague statement that agency officials were to give reports to the legislative branch. The president, by contrast, was given specific power to monitor the execution of basic tasks assigned to FAPSI and to "sanction their operations."

Some of the functions of FAPSI overlap those of the FSB. The FSB's enabling law mandated that it detect signals from radio-electronic transmitters, carry out cipher work within its own agency, and protect coded information in other state organizations and even private enterprises. No specific boundary between the ciphering and communications functions of the two agencies was delineated in their enabling legislation, and there was even speculation that FAPSI would be merged into the FSB. A presidential decree of April 1995 defined agency responsibilities in the area of telecommunications licensing.

A critical area of overlap—and competition—is protection of data of crucial economic and strategic significance. By mid-1995 FAPSI director Starovoytov was pushing for a larger role for FAPSI in this area. He began issuing warnings about the intensified threat to secret economic data (including that of the Russian Central Bank) from Western special services, which he said required his agency to take more stringent security measures.

Main Guard Directorate (GUO)

In mid-1992 the KGB's Ninth Directorate, charged with guarding government leaders and key buildings and installations, became the Main Guard Directorate (Glavnoye upravleniye okhraneniya—GUO), which until July 1995 was headed by Mikhail Barsukov. When Barsukov moved to the FSB, he was replaced as chief of the GUO by his deputy, General Yuriy Krapivin. Until mid-1996 the GUO included an autonomous subdivision, the Presidential Security Service, headed by Aleksandr Korzhakov. Beginning in 1991, both the GUO and Korzhakov's service grew steadily. By late 1994, the GUO staff reportedly had increased from 8,000 to more than 20,000 persons assigned to guard the offices, automobiles, apartments, and dachas of Russia's highest leaders, together with a variety of secret "objects of state importance."

The tasks and missions of the GUO are described in the Law on State Protection of Government Bodies and Their Officials, passed in April 1993. As of mid-1996, the agency had the same status as a state committee, but in fact the general statutes describing the government and the office of the presidency made no provision for such a structure (see The Constitution and Government Structure, ch. 7). The GUO's legal authorization to engage in investigative operations gives its officers the power to undertake invasive activities such as shadowing citizens and tapping telephones. The GUO was reported to have an unlimited budget, which it used to acquire sophisticated Western listening devices for use in Kremlin offices.

Shortly after the creation of the GUO, Yeltsin included in it the elite Alpha Group, a crack antiterrorist unit of 500 personnel (200 in Moscow, 300 elsewhere in Russia) that had been involved in operations in Afghanistan, Azerbaijan, and Lithuania. The Alpha Group had played a decisive role in the coup of August 1991 by refusing the coup leaders' orders to storm the parliament building, in spite of the group's subordination to the KGB, whose chief, Vladimir Kryuchkov, was a coup leader. In the following years, the Alpha Group gained a national reputation and became connected with figures in legitimate business, organized crime, and politics. In early 1996, Alpha Group veterans headed an estimated thirty-five commercial enterprises in Moscow.

In June 1995, the Alpha Group was sent to break the Buden-novsk hostage crisis when Chechen rebels seized a hospital in southern Russia. Yeltsin disavowed responsibility for the attack's subsequent failure, and two months later he trans-ferred the Alpha Group back to the jurisdiction of the FSB. In 1995, under the leadership of Sergey Goncharov, the Alpha vet-erans' association became politically active, strongly opposing Yeltsin loyalists in the December parliamentary elections (see The Elections of 1995, ch. 7). This antigovernment activity by former members of Yeltsin's security force raised questions about the loyalty of active security agencies. Following the 1995 elections, Goncharov's group continued to advocate restora-tion of Russia's military influence among the former Soviet republics that make up its "near abroad," as well as harsh mea-sures against domestic organized crime.

By December 1993, Korzhakov's Presidential Security Ser-vice had become independent of the GUO, placing Korzhakov in a position subordinate only to Yeltsin. From the time of his appointment, Korzhakov was at Yeltsin's side constantly, becom-ing the most indispensable member of the presidential security force. Besides overseeing about 4,000 guards, Korzhakov came to supervise all the services in support of the president's opera-tions. These included communications, presidential aircraft, and the secret bunker to be occupied in case war broke out. This prominent role led to speculation about Korzhakov's influence on policy matters outside the area of security, and his infrequent policy statements were closely analyzed by the news media. In June 1996, Yeltsin dismissed Korzhakov, together with FSB chief Barsukov and First Deputy Prime Minister Oleg Soskovets, eliminating some of the most influential govern-ment figures of the anti-Western political faction prior to the second round of the presidential election.

Federal Border Service and Border Security

The fourth agency to emerge from the dismantled KGB was the national border troops command, which formerly had been administered as the KGB's Border Troops Directorate. By the mid-1990s, both the subordination and the size of this organization had undergone considerable change. For the Russian Federation, national border security issues have been much different from those of the Soviet Union; for this reason, and because of depleted resources to support security opera-tions, border policy has become an especially important part of

Russia's overall relations with other members of the Commonwealth of Independent States (CIS—see Glossary).

Border Security Agencies

In 1989 the Border Troops' personnel strength was estimated at 230,000. Although under the operational authority of the KGB, border troops were conscripted as part of the biannual callup of the Ministry of Defense, and troop induction and discharge were regulated by the 1967 Law on Universal Military Service applicable to all the armed forces of the Soviet Union.

In the 1980s, the duties of the Border Troops included repulsing armed incursions into Soviet territory; preventing illegal crossings of the border or the transport of subversive or dangerous materials; monitoring the observance of established procedures at border crossings and of navigation procedures in Soviet territorial waters; and assisting state agencies in the preservation of natural resources and in environmental protection. In carrying out these duties, border troops were authorized to examine documents and possessions of persons crossing the borders and to confiscate articles; to conduct inquiries in cases of violation of the state border; and to arrest, search, and interrogate individuals suspected of border violations.

In the Soviet system, the border soldier was expected to defend both the physical border and the state ideology. The second of those assignments involved detecting and confiscating subversive literature and preventing, by violent means if necessary, the escape of citizens across the border.

In 1992 the Committee for the Protection of State Borders, an agency subordinate to the Ministry of Security, succeeded the KGB's Border Troops Directorate in administering frontier control. Although the personnel level had been reduced to about 180,000, the basic structure of the agency and the border configuration remained substantially the same as they had been in the late Soviet period. Viktor Shlyakhtin, the first post-Soviet chief of the border troops, was dismissed in July 1993 after more than twenty Russian border guards were killed in an attack on their post along the Afghanistan-Tajikistan border. Yeltsin replaced Shlyakhtin with General Andrey Nikolayev, who had been first deputy chief of the General Staff of the armed forces. This appointment was a sharp departure from the usual practice of naming a career border troops officer to the top post.

In late 1993, Yeltsin established the Federal Border Service to administer frontier control and gave that agency the status of a federal ministry under direct presidential control. The FSK (and then its successor, the FSB) retained operational responsibility for counterintelligence along the borders, however. In 1995 Nikolayev announced an ambitious program for building up and improving the border service in the years 1996–2000. The 1996 federal budget authorized a total troop strength of 210,000, which would be a significant increase from the 135,000 troops on duty in 1994. In 1996 the Federal Border Service oversaw six border districts and three special groups of border troops in the Arctic, Kaliningrad, and Moscow, as well as an independent border control detachment operating at Russia's major airports.

Given the agency's ambitious personnel requirements, staffing and financing the new border posts became problematic in the mid-1990s. Although Nikolayev warned parliament that his resources were insufficient, the Federal Border Service's 1995 budget was only 70 percent of the amount requested. Equipment was hopelessly outdated and in need of repair. According to estimates, in 1995 some 40 percent of the signaling and communications systems along the border had surpassed their service lives.

Post-Soviet Border Policy

In the 1990s, Russia lacked the secure buffer zone of Soviet republics and subservient East European countries that had provided border security in the Soviet era. The status of Russia's borders with neighbors Azerbaijan, Estonia, Georgia, Latvia, and Ukraine has required the presence of a substantial force of armed troops. In Azerbaijan, Georgia, and Tajikistan, ethnic conflict has caused chronic instability near Russia's borders in the first half-decade of independence. In early 1996, the FSB reported that 13,500 kilometers of the national borders were not defined by internationally recognized treaties. After negotiations with Estonia failed in 1996, Russia unilaterally defined its border with that state, requiring the presence of border forces until disputes can be resolved. The border between Latvia and Russia also remained in dispute as of mid-1996.

After the Soviet Union was dissolved, it soon became clear that Russia did not have the resources to establish a fully equipped border regime along its boundaries within the CIS.

In 1993 Russia stated openly that its top priority was to guard the outside borders of the CIS (hence most of what had been the international borders of the Soviet Union) rather than the borders that Russia now shared with CIS countries (see The Near Abroad, ch. 8). Such a policy reestablished the border republics as a buffer zone against potential invasion from China or the Islamic states of Central Asia. The other CIS states do not have the resources to secure their outer boundaries, a situation that led in the early and mid-1990s to the mutually acceptable deployment of Russian border forces in each of the five Central Asian republics. In Kyrgyzstan a few thousand troops were stationed along the Chinese border. Certain outer boundaries of the CIS, such as the Tajikistani border with Afghanistan, required extra troop strength because of constant armed conflict. In 1994 Russia doubled its Tajikistan border force to about 15,000 troops.

One goal of this policy was to preserve the capability for quick action in case of border conflict and to protect Russia's "internal" frontiers from the smuggling of people and contraband, including arms. The second goal, most visible in Georgia and Tajikistan, was "peacekeeping" in pursuit of Moscow's foreign policy priorities within the border country. In pursuit of the second goal, in the mid-1990s border forces increasingly were used as an extension of Russia's military power in the CIS.

The revised view of border security naturally brought with it an effort at reintegration of the former Soviet republics. Russia began to advocate "transparent borders" with the coterminous CIS states—Azerbaijan, Belarus, Georgia, Kazakstan, and Ukraine. This meant that borders would remain open for the unrestricted passage of people and goods. Strict border regimes would be established only in zones of acute conflict, such as the North Caucasus. The April 1993 Law on the State Border of the Russian Federation reflected this policy by abolishing the specially designated border districts of the Soviet system, leaving only border strips five kilometers wide. The law stipulated the goal of establishing a reduced and simplified border regime with all CIS states.

Security Operations in Chechnya

The internal instability of the Soviet government during 1990–91 invited expressions of separatism in many of Russia's distinct ethnic enclaves, as well as in ethnically Russian districts in the Soviet Far East. The most volatile and troublesome area within the new Russian Federation was the North Caucasus, where the predominantly Muslim former Chechen-Ingush Autonomous Republic is located. A crisis had been building there for some time (see Movements Toward Sovereignty, ch. 4). In October 1991, a Chechen nationalist movement headed by former Soviet air force general Dzhokar Dudayev overthrew the existing government and installed Dudayev as president. Shortly thereafter, the Chechen Supreme Soviet declared Chechnya a sovereign republic.

Yeltsin responded by deploying Ministry of Internal Affairs (MVD) troops in the region, but the Russian Supreme Soviet declared the action invalid and ordered him to settle the conflict peaceably. The perceived indecision by the Russian government encouraged Chechen nationalists to pursue complete political independence and Russian recognition of that status. The Yeltsin administration was equally adamant in its refusal to negotiate until Chechnya redesignated itself part of the Russian Federation. Violence erupted in Chechnya on numerous occasions during 1993–94, and Russian security forces became fully involved in the conflict. In July 1994, a group of hostages taken by Chechen guerrillas near Pyatigorsk in Russian territory perished during an unsuccessful rescue operation by the MVD. The FSK armed Chechen opposition forces, which launched several unsuccessful attacks against the Dudayev government in the fall of 1994. When Russian conventional forces finally invaded Chechnya in December, they received substantial support from troops of the FSK, its successor the FSB, and the MVD. The FSB and MVD remained part of an uneasy occupation force through mid-1996 (see Chechnya, ch. 9).

Crime

The liberalizing changes of the post-Soviet era brought new types of crime, many of them associated with economic activities that had not existed until 1992. As the opportunities for legal commercial initiatives expanded rapidly, so did the opportunities to defraud Russian citizens inexperienced in economic matters and to take advantage of Russia's complete lack of laws covering many types of crime, including the organized extraction of protection money from economic enterprises.

Crime in the Soviet Era

Because the Soviet Union did not publish comprehensive

crime statistics, comparison of its crime rates with those of other countries is difficult. According to Western experts, robberies, murders, and other violent crimes were much less prevalent than in the United States because of the Soviet Union's larger police presence, strict gun controls, and relatively low incidence of drug abuse. By contrast, white-collar economic crime permeated the Soviet system. Bribery and covert payments for goods and services were universal, mainly because of the paucity of goods and services on the open market. Theft of state property was practiced routinely by employees, as were various forms of petty theft. In the last years of the Soviet Union, the government of Mikhail S. Gorbachev (in office 1985–91) made a concerted effort to curtail such white-collar crime. Revelations of corruption scandals involving high-level party employees appeared regularly in the Soviet news media, and many arrests and prosecutions resulted from such discoveries.

The Crime Wave of the 1990s

In the first half of the 1990s, crime statistics moved sharply and uniformly upward. From 1991 to 1992, the number of officially reported crimes and the overall crime rate each showed a 27 percent increase; the crime rate nearly doubled between 1985 and 1992. By the early 1990s, theft, burglary, and other acts against property accounted for about two-thirds of all crime in Russia. Of particular concern to citizens, however, was the rapid growth of violent crime, including gruesome homicides.

Crime Statistics

Moscow's 1995 statistics included 93,560 crimes, of which 18,500 were white-collar crimes—an increase of 8.3 percent over 1994. Among white-collar crimes, swindling increased 67.2 percent, and extortion 37.5 percent, in 1995. Among the conventional crimes reported, murder and attempted murder increased 1.5 percent, rape 6.5 percent, burglaries 6.6 percent, burglaries accompanied by violence 20.8 percent, and serious crimes by teenagers 2.2 percent. The rate of crime-solving by the Moscow militia (police) rose in 1995 from 57.7 percent to 64.9 percent, but that statistic was bolstered substantially by success in solving minor crimes; the projected rate of solving burglaries was 18.8 percent, of murders 42.2 percent, and of crimes involving use of a firearm, 31.4 percent. Moscow and St.

Petersburg were the centers of automobile theft, which increased dramatically through the first half of the 1990s. In Moscow an estimated fifty cars were stolen per day, with the estimated yearly total for Russia between 100,000 and 150,000. In the first quarter of 1994, Russia averaged eighty-four murders a day. Many of those crimes were contract killings attributed to criminal organizations. In 1994 murder victims included three deputies of the State Duma, one journalist, a priest, the head of a union, several local officials, and more than thirty businesspeople and bankers. Most of those crimes went unsolved.

The 1995 national crime total exceeded 1.3 million, including 30,600 murders. Crime experts predicted that the murder total would reach 50,000 in 1996. In 1995 some 248 regular militia officers were killed in the line of duty.

Confiscation of firearms, possession of which has been identified as another grave social problem, increased substantially in 1995, according to the Moscow militia's Regional Organized Crime Directorate. About 3 million firearms were registered in 1995, but the number of unregistered guns was assumed to far exceed that figure. Military weapons are stolen frequently and sold to gangsters; in 1993 nearly 60,000 cases of such theft were reported, involving machine guns, hand grenades, and explosives, among other weapons (see Crime in the Military, ch. 9). The ready availability of firearms has made the work of the poorly armed militia more dangerous.

Organized Crime

By early 1994, crime was second only to the national economy as a domestic issue in Russia. In January 1994, a report prepared for President Yeltsin by the Analytical Center for Social and Economic Policies was published in the national daily newspaper *Izvestiya.* According to the center, between 70 and 80 percent of private enterprises and commercial banks were forced to pay protection fees to criminal organizations, which in Russia received the generic label *mafiya.* Unlike organized crime in other countries, which controls only such criminal activities as drug trafficking and gambling, and specific types of legitimate enterprise such as municipal trash collection, the Russian crime organizations have gained strong influence in a wide variety of economic activities. In addition, beginning with the collapse of the Soviet Union and the weakening of border controls, Russia has been drawn into the network of international organized crime. In this way, Russia has become a major conduit for the movement of drugs, contraband, and laundered money between Europe and Asia. In 1995 an estimated 150 criminal organizations with transnational links were operating in Russia.

Among the main targets of organized crime are businesses and banks in Russia's newly privatized economy and foreigners—both individual and corporate—in possession of luxury goods or the hard currency (see Glossary) to purchase them. Many of Russia's *mafiya* figures began their "careers" in the black market during the communist era. They are now able to operate overtly and are increasingly brazen. Many current and former government officials and businesspeople have been identified as belonging to the *mafiya* network.

The 1994 report to the president described collusion between criminal gangs and local law enforcement officials, which made controlling crime especially difficult. The enforcement problem, which became acute in 1993, was exacerbated by overtaxation, confusing regulations, and the absence of an effective judicial system. By 1993 criminal groups had moved into commercial ventures, using racketeering, kidnapping, and murder to intimidate competition. In 1994 an MVD official estimated that there were 5,700 criminal gangs in Russia, with a membership of approximately 100,000.

In March 1995, Vladislav List'ev, a prominent television journalist, was assassinated. List'ev had been a supporter of efforts to stop corruption in state television, where large amounts of advertising revenues were being extorted by organized crime. A Russian news agency reported that, between 1992 and mid-1995, there had been eighty-three attempts—forty-six of which were successful—to kill bankers and businesspeople. In 1996 contract killings remained a regular occurrence, especially in Moscow.

Nuclear Security

Neither civilian nor military nuclear facilities have adequate security. Thefts of nuclear materials from Russia gained international attention in 1993 and 1994. In 1995 the FSB reported investigations of thirty such incidents. Such thefts assumedly were intended to supply smuggling operations into Iran and Germany, among other destinations. Although the Russian government took nominal steps to improve nuclear security early in 1995, the minister of internal affairs reported that 80 percent of nuclear enterprises lacked checkpoints. Western experts pointed to the potential for organized criminals to obtain weapons-grade nuclear materials, and in 1996 new reports described lax security at nuclear installations.

Terrorism

Security police reported that between 1991 and 1993 the incidence of terrorist bombings rose from fifty to 350. The methods used by organized criminals in Russia caused experts to include Russia as a likely location in their identification of a new wave of world terrorism in the 1990s. Besides organized crime, a second factor potentially contributing to terrorism is the extreme instability of economic and social conditions: high unemployment and job insecurity, friction among ethnic groups and between urban populations and job-seeking migrants into their cities, and a general decline in the standard of living. The vulnerability of Russia's isolated transport and pipeline systems and the proximity of hazardous-materials centers to cities further increase the prospect of terrorist activities. In 1995 terrorist acts and two major instances of hostage taking by Chechen separatists promoted fears that vulnerable citizens and locations in other parts of Russia might be targeted by separatist groups. In December 1995, an international conference on terrorism in Ottawa categorized the Budennovsk hostage incident of June 1995—in which Chechen guerrillas captured more than 1,000 hostages 120 kilometers inside Russian territory—with the Oklahoma City bombing and Middle Eastern terrorist acts as examples of flagrant international terrorism.

Narcotics

In the mid-1990s, narcotics addiction and sales play a growing role in the disruption of Russian society. This trend has been promoted by an adverse economic situation, a general lack of high-level control over the use and movement of narcotic substances, and the continued laxity of border controls. Between 1993 and 1995, the annual amount of seized drugs increased from thirty-five to ninety tons; experts believe that Russia has the largest per capita drug market of all the former Soviet republics.

According to the Russian government's Center for the Study of Drug Addiction, in early 1996 at least 500,000 Russians were dependent on illegal drugs. With use increasing at an estimated rate of 50 percent per year, the total number of users was estimated at 2 million in 1995. Drug traffickers, supplied mainly with opium from Central Asia and heroin from Iran, Pakistan, and Afghanistan, have targeted Russia as a market and as a conduit to Western markets. In the early 1990s, cocaine use appeared among affluent young Russians, and beginning in 1993 the interception of cocaine shipments in St. Petersburg indicated that South American producers had entered the Russian market. Criminal organizations are believed to control most trafficking and distribution in Russia. Some local Russian distributors are closely linked with criminal groups in Central Asia, the Caucasus, and Ukraine. Russian soldiers and officers in Afghanistan and later in Central Asia became active in smuggling the narcotics easily available in those countries into Russia. Reportedly, members of the Russian 201st Motorized Infantry Division, stationed in Tajikistan, have established a profitable enterprise that is tacitly accepted by Russian and Tajikistani authorities. The Moscow State Institute of International Relations has reported the existence of a regular smuggling route going fromTajikistan to Russia's Black Sea port of Rostov-na-Donu via Turkmenistan, and from there to Western Europe. One explanation of the Russian attack on Chechnya, published in the independent newspaper *Nezavisimaya gazeta,* was that it was a reprisal against Chechen president Dzhokar Dudayev for demanding more protection money for narcotics shipments through Chechnya to Rostov-na-Donu.

Narcotics production in Russia also is rising. In 1993 the government seized 215 laboratories, many of them small-scale amphetamine producers who used stolen government equipment. Newly privatized chemical laboratories are more difficult to monitor than were Soviet-era state facilities. Opium poppies and marijuana are grown in southern Russia, although cultivation is illegal. In 1995 an MVD official estimated that about 1 million hectares of wild cannabis was growing and easily available in Siberia; opium cultivation also is believed to be increasing.

The laundering of drug money is encouraged by Russia's lax monetary regulations and controls. Some local banks are controlled by criminal groups that use them to launder profits from illegal activities, including drug sales. According to one 1995 estimate, as many as 25 percent of Moscow's commercial banks are part of this operation. Legislation against money laundering was proposed but had not been passed as of mid-1996.

In 1994 the Yeltsin administration formed an interministerial counternarcotics committee, involving twenty-four agencies, to coordinate drug policy. In 1995 a three-year antidrug program was approved to support interdiction and drug treatment facilities. The program also was intended to criminalize drug use, extend sentences for drug trafficking, and establish a pharmaceuticals-monitoring process. In 1995 the full-time staff of the anti-drug-trafficking department of the MVD increased from about 3,500 to 4,000. The State Customs Committee increased its drug control staff by 350 and added fifty field offices, and the Federal Border Service created an antidrug force. The Moscow City Council instituted drug education programs in some city schools in 1993, and several private organizations have sponsored national programs to curb demand. The government has not aggressively addressed the rehabilitation of drug addicts or the reduction of demand, however; in 1995 an estimated 90 percent of Russia's drug addicts went untreated (see Health Conditions, ch. 5).

The Russian government has signed a number of international conventions on narcotics (responsibility for some of which it inherited from the Soviet Union), including the 1988 United Nations Convention on Narcotic Drugs. Russia will not be in full compliance with the convention, however, until it has stricter controls on production and distribution and tougher criminal penalties for possession of drugs. The United States government has offered Russia advice and training courses on various aspects of narcotics control. A mutual legal-assistance agreement with the United States went into effect in early 1996, and the Federal Border Service has memorandums of understanding on narcotics cooperation with the United States Coast Guard and with Kyrgyzstan and Tajikistan.

The Criminal Justice System

The Federal Security Service (FSB) has a staff of several thousand responsible for investigating crimes of national and international scope such as terrorism, smuggling, treason, violations of secrecy laws, and large-scale economic crime and corruption—an area of jurisdiction similar to that of the United States Federal Bureau of Investigation (FBI). Several other state organizations also have designated criminal investigatory responsibilities.

Ministry of Internal Affairs (MVD)

Unlike the successor agencies to the KGB, the Ministry of Internal Affairs (Ministerstvo vnutrennikh del—MVD) did not undergo extensive reorganization after 1991. The MVD carries out regular police functions, including maintenance of public order and criminal investigation. It also has responsibility for fire fighting and prevention, traffic control, automobile registration, transportation security, issuance of visas and passports, and administration of labor camps and most prisons.

In 1996 the MVD was estimated to have 540,000 personnel, including the regular militia (police force) and MVD special troops but not including the ministry's Internal Troops. The MVD operates at both the central and local levels. The central system is administered from the ministry office in Moscow. As of mid-1996, the minister of internal affairs was General Anatoliy Kulikov. He replaced Viktor Yerin, who was dismissed in response to State Duma demands after the MVD mishandled the 1995 Budennovsk hostage crisis.

MVD agencies exist at all levels from the national to the municipal. MVD agencies at lower operational levels conduct preliminary investigations of crimes. They also perform the ministry's policing, motor vehicle inspection, and fire and traffic control duties. MVD salaries are generally lower than those paid in other agencies of the criminal justice system. Reportedly, staffers are poorly trained and equipped, and corruption is widespread.

Until 1990 Russia's regular militia was under the direct supervision of the Ministry of Internal Affairs of the Soviet Union. At that time, the Russian Republic established its own MVD, which assumed control of the republic's militia. In the late 1980s, the Gorbachev regime had attempted to improve training, tighten discipline, and decentralize the administration of the militia throughout the Soviet Union so that it might respond better to local needs and deal more effectively with drug trafficking and organized crime. Some progress was made toward these objectives despite strong opposition from conservative elements in the CPSU leadership. However, after 1990 the redirection of MVD resources to the Internal Troops and to the MVD's new local riot squads undercut militia reform. In the August 1991 coup against the Gorbachev government, most Russian police remained inactive, although some in Moscow joined the Yeltsin forces that õpposed the overthrow of the government.

Police watch demonstration in Red Square, Moscow, March 1992.
Courtesy Mike Albin

In early 1996, a reorganization plan was proposed for the MVD, with the aim of more effective crime prevention. The plan called for increasing the police force by as many as 90,000, but funding was not available for such expansion. Meanwhile, the MVD recruited several thousand former military personnel, whose experience reduced the need for police training. At the end of 1995, the MVD reported debts of US$717 million, including US$272 million in overdue wages. In February 1996, guards at a jail and a battalion of police escorts went on a hunger strike; at that point, some of the MVD's Internal Troops had not been paid for three months. Minister of Internal Affairs Kulikov described the ministry's 1996 state budget allocation of US$5.2 billion as wholly inadequate to fulfill its missions. Participation in the Chechnya campaign added enormously to ministry expenditures.

The MVD's militia is used for ordinary policing functions such as law enforcement on the streets, crowd control, and traffic control. As part of a trend toward decentralization, some municipalities, including Moscow, have formed their own militias, which cooperate with their MVD counterpart. Although a new law on self-government supports such local law enforcement agencies, the Yeltsin administration attempted to head off further moves toward independence by strictly limiting local powers. The regular militia does not carry guns or other weapons except in emergency situations, such as the parliamentary crisis of 1993, when it was called upon to fight antigovernment crowds in the streets of Moscow.

The militia is divided into local public security units and criminal police. The security units run local police stations, temporary detention centers, and the State Traffic Inspectorate. They deal with crimes outside the jurisdiction of the criminal police and are charged with routine maintenance of public order. The criminal police are divided into organizations responsible for combating particular types of crime. The Main Directorate for Organized Crime (Glavnoye upravleniye organizovannogo prestupleniya—GUOP) works with other agencies such as the MVD's specialized rapid-response detachments; in 1995 special GUOP units were established to deal with contract killings and other violent crimes against individuals. The Federal Tax Police Service deals primarily with tax evasion and similar crimes. In an attempt to improve Russia's notoriously inefficient tax collection operation, the Federal Tax Police Service received authority in 1995 to carry out preliminary criminal investigations independently. The 1996 budget authorized a staff of 38,000 for this agency.

Throughout the first half of the 1990s, Russia's militia functioned with minimal arms, equipment, and support from the national legal system. The inadequacy of the force became particularly apparent in the wave of organized crime that began sweeping over Russia after the collapse of the Soviet Union. Many highly qualified individuals have moved from the militia into better-paying jobs in the field of private security, which has expanded to meet the demand of companies needing protection from organized crime. Frequent bribe taking among the remaining members of the militia has damaged the force's public credibility. Numerous revelations of participation by militia personnel in murders, prostitution rings, information peddling, and tolerance of criminal acts have created a general public perception that all police are at least taking bribes. Bribery of police officers to avoid arrest for traffic violations and petty crimes is a routine and expected occurrence.

In a 1995 poll of the public, only 5 percent of respondents expressed confidence in the ability of the militia to deal with crime in their city. Human rights organizations have accused the Moscow militia of racism in singling out non-Slavic individuals (especially immigrants from Russia's Caucasus republics), physical attacks, unjustified detention, and other rights violations. In 1995 Kulikov conducted a high-profile "Clean Hands Campaign" to purge the MVD police forces of corrupt elements. In its first year, this limited operation caught several highly placed MVD officials collecting bribes, indicating a high level of corruption throughout the agency. According to experts, the main causes of corruption are insufficient funding to train and equip personnel and pay them adequate wages, poor work discipline, lack of accountability, and fear of reprisals from organized criminals.

The Special Forces Police Detachment (Otryad militsii osobogo naznacheniya—OMON), commonly known as the Black Berets, is a highly trained elite branch of the public security force of the MVD militia. Established in 1987, OMON is assigned to emergency situations such as hostage crises, widespread public disturbances, and terrorist threats. In the Soviet period, OMON forces also were used to quell unrest in rebellious republics. In the 1990s, OMON units have been stationed at transportation hubs and population centers. The Moscow contingent, reportedly 2,000 strong, receives support from the mayor's office and the city's internal affairs office as well as from the MVD budget. OMON units have the best and most up-to-date weapons and combat equipment available, and they enjoy a reputation for courage and effectiveness.

The MVD's Internal Troops, estimated to number 260,000 to 280,000 in mid-1996, are better equipped and trained than the regular militia. The size of the force, which is staffed by both conscripts and volunteers, has grown steadily through the mid-1990s, although the troop commander has reported serious shortages of officers. Critics have noted that the Internal Troops have more divisions in a combat-ready state than do the regular armed forces (see Force Structure, ch. 9).

According to the Law on Internal Troops, issued in October 1992, the functions of the Internal Troops are to ensure public order; guard key state installations, including nuclear power plants; guard prisons and labor camps (a function that was to end in 1996); and contribute to the territorial defense of the nation. It was under the last mandate that Internal Troops were deployed in large numbers after the December 1994 invasion of Chechnya. In November 1995, MVD troops in Chechnya totaled about 23,500. This force included unknown proportions of Internal Troops, specialized rapid-response troops, and special military detachments. Internal Troops are equipped with guns and combat equipment to deal with serious crimes, terrorism, and other extraordinary threats to public order. In 1995 the crime rate among Internal Troops personnel doubled. A contributing factor was a steep increase in desertions that coincided with service in Chechnya, where the Internal Troops were routinely used for street patrols in 1995.

The Procuracy

In the Soviet criminal justice system, the Procuracy was the most powerful institution dealing with nonpolitical crimes. Since 1991 the agency has retained its dual responsibility for the administration of judicial oversight and for criminal investigations—which means, essentially, that prosecution of crimes and findings of guilt or innocence are overseen by the same office. As it was under the Soviet system, the Procuracy in the 1990s is a unified, centralized agency with branches in all subnational jurisdictions, including cities. The chief of the agency is the procurator general, who is appointed by the president with the approval of the State Duma. (Under the Soviet system, the Supreme Soviet appointed the procurator general.)

Proposed reforms of the notoriously corrupt and inefficient Procuracy had not yet been enacted by the Russian government as of mid-1996, so the agency continued to function in much the same way as it did in the Soviet period. Experts did not believe that a new law on the Procuracy, proposed in 1995 and 1996, would establish a reliable oversight system over security-agency and regular police operations. In the meantime, procurators continued to arrest citizens without constitutionally mandated arrest warrants, and the general surveillance departments of the Procuracy continued to spy on law-abiding groups and individuals.

In 1995 about 28,000 procurators were active at some level in the Russian Federation. Appointed to five-year terms, procurators must have a postgraduate education in jurisprudence. The Procuracy employs a large number of investigators who carry out preliminary investigations in what are called specific areas of competence. Special investigators are designated for cases identified as "essentially important" by state authorities. The Procuracy also has several institutions for research and education attached to it.

Criminal Law Reform in the 1990s

In the mid-1990s, several efforts were made to pass a Criminal Code of the Russian Federation to replace the inadequate and antiquated Criminal Code of the RSFSR, which was passed in the 1960s and had remained the fundamental law of the land, with numerous amendments, since that time. In December 1995, Yeltsin, heeding MVD objections to certain articles, vetoed a code that had been developed by his own State Law Directorate and passed by parliament. No amended code was expected until after the presidential election of July 1996. Meanwhile, Russia lacked laws on organized crime and corruption under which *mafiya* and economic crimes could be prosecuted.

In the absence of a comprehensive overhaul of the Criminal Code, Yeltsin responded to the growing problem of crime by enacting measures that broadly expanded police powers. In June 1994, he issued a presidential decree, Urgent Measures to Implement the Program to Step Up the Fight Against Crime. The decree included major steps to increase the efficiency of the law enforcement agencies, including material incentives for the staff and better equipment and resources. The decree also called for an increase of 52,000 in the strength of the MVD Internal Troops and for greater coordination in the operations of the Federal Counterintelligence Service (FSK), the MVD, and other law enforcement bodies. Control over the issuing of entry visas and the private acquisition of photocopiers was to be tightened. The decree also mandated the preparation of laws broadening police rights to conduct searches and to carry weapons.

Yeltsin's anticrime decree had the stated purpose of preserving the security of the society and the state; however, the system of urgent measures it introduced had the effect of reducing the rights of individuals accused of committing crimes. Under the new guidelines, individuals suspected of serious offenses could be detained up to thirty days without being formally charged. During that time, suspects could be interrogated and their financial affairs examined. The secrecy regulations of banks and commercial enterprises would not protect suspects in such cases. Intelligence service representatives have the authority to enter any premises without a warrant, to examine private documents, and to search automobiles, their drivers, and their passengers. Human rights activists protested the decree as a violation of the 1993 constitution's protection of individuals from arbitrary police power (see Civil Rights, ch. 7). Already in 1992, Yeltsin had expanded the infamous Article 70, a Soviet-era device used to silence political dissent, which criminalized any form of public demand for change in the constitutional system, as well as the formation of any assemblage calling for such measures.

Meanwhile, the Russian police immediately began acting on their broad mandate to fight crime. In the summer of 1994, the Moscow MVD carried out a citywide operation called Hurricane that employed about 20,000 crack troops and resulted in 759 arrests. A short time later, the FSK reported that its operatives had arrested members of a right-wing terrorist group, the so-called Werewolf Legion, who were planning to bomb Moscow cinemas. Although crime continued to rise after Yeltsin's decree, the rate of crime solving improved from its 1993 level of 51 percent to 65 percent in 1995, assumedly because of expanded police powers.

Although the Russian parliament opposed many of Yeltsin's policies, the majority of deputies were even more inclined than Yeltsin to expand police authority at the expense of individual rights. In July 1995, the State Duma passed the new Law on Operational-Investigative Activity, which had been introduced by the Yeltsin administration to replace Article 70. The law widened the list of agencies entitled to conduct investigations, at the same time broadening the powers of all investigatory agencies beyond those stipulated in the earlier law.

The 1995 draft Criminal Code included an article specifically prohibiting "conspiracy with the aim of seizing power and forcibly changing the constitutional form of government," an activity subject to a sentence of up to life imprisonment. The new law opened the concept of conspiracy to broad interpretation by state authorities, varying from a meeting held by the leadership of an opposition party to a simple telephone conversation between two citizens.

The draft code also broadened the law on violations of civil rights on the basis of nationality or race, which carries a maximum sentence of five years. As in the case of conspiracy and political statutes, the ambiguity of the nationality and race law opened the door for serious abuses of individual rights. Prosecutors and judges were granted wide latitude in deciding what constitute "acts directed at incitement of social, national, racial, or religious hostility or discord." Such a charge could be leveled easily in a society with a huge variety of ethnic and religious groups, particularly groups with existing claims of autonomy or traditions of hostility toward one another (see Ethnic Composition, ch. 4).

Many legal experts considered the new draft Criminal Code, which is a synthesis of presidential and State Duma proposals, to be a significant improvement over the old code. But, unlike Western states, Russia does not have a tradition of respect for legal rights or a well-established, balanced system of justice to interpret and administer the laws. Many of the laws adopted in the early 1990s concern crimes whose investigation is delegated to the security police, which have a history of human rights abuses and were not placed under effective oversight by the reforms of the early 1990s. Thus, in the atmosphere of relative political pluralism and freedom of expression in the first years of the Yeltsin administration, security agents still sometimes take advantage of the law to employ KGB-style tactics.

Despite a lack of sympathy for personal liberty, in the early 1990s the Yeltsin administration made some reforms in the legal system to protect the rights of the individual. In June 1992, the Code of Criminal Procedure was amended to give a detainee the right to legal counsel immediately, rather than, as in the past, only after initial questioning. A detainee's right to demand a judicial review of the legality and grounds for detention also was recognized. In practice, however, these changes often have been offset by other laws intended to protect the state at the expense of the individual. The clearest example is Yeltsin's sweeping anticrime decree of 1992, but other instances have followed. In March 1995, Yeltsin issued a decree against fascist organizations and practices, which gave the security police broad new authority to arrest and investigate suspects. Under the 1995 draft Criminal Code, a person under arrest could not appeal to the courts to protest his or her confinement, but only to the procurator. The president also could appoint a special prosecutor to bring "highly placed individuals" to justice, thus undermining the principle of independent judges. The new code also extended the maximum period of internment of suspects without formal charges from three to seven days, although the counsel for the defense could not become acquainted with the materials of the criminal case until after the preliminary investigation had been completed.

Secrecy Laws

The passage of a new secrecy law in 1993 indicated that the

Yeltsin government was not prepared to abjure the protection of state secrets as a rationale for controlling the activities of Russian citizens. The secrecy law of 1993, harshly criticized by human rights activists, set forth in detail the procedure for labeling and protecting information whose dispersal would constitute a danger to the state. The concept of secrecy was given a broad interpretation. The law prescribed secret classifications for information on foreign policy, economics, national defense, intelligence, and counterintelligence. However, a more specific description of the classification process, including which specific types of information were to be classified as secret and which agencies and departments were authorized to classify information, was to be made public at a later date.

In general, the security police under Yeltsin do not use secrecy laws to prosecute individuals, but there have been exceptions. In October 1992, officers from the Ministry of Security arrested two chemical scientists, Vil' Mirzayanov and Lev Fedorov, for having written an article on current Russian chemical weapons research in a widely circulated daily newspaper. The article's revelation was embarrassing to the Yeltsin government because Russia had claimed it was no longer conducting such research. Although Mirzayanov was brought to trial in early 1994, public and international protest caused the Yeltsin government to release him two months later. In a landmark decision, the procurator's office awarded Mirzayanov about US$15,500 in damages for having been illegally detained.

How the System Works

According to Russian criminal procedure, officers of the MVD, the Federal Security Service (FSB), or the Procuracy can arrest an individual on suspicion of having committed a crime. Ordinary crimes, including murder, come under the jurisdiction of the MVD; the FSB and the Procuracy are authorized to deal with crimes such as terrorism, treason, smuggling, and large-scale economic malfeasance. The accused has the right to obtain an attorney immediately after the arrest, and, in most cases, the accused must be charged officially within seventy-two hours of the arrest. In some circumstances, the period of confinement without charge can be extended. Once the case is investigated, it is assigned to a court for trial. Trials are public, with the exception of proceedings involving government secrets.

Sevastopol' District Court, Moscow
Courtesy Michael E. Samojeden

In August 1995, the State Duma passed a law giving judges and jurors protection against illegal influence on the process of trying a case. To the extent that it actually is practiced, the new law is a significant barrier to the Soviet-era practice of judges consulting with political officials before rendering verdicts. The protection of jurors became a concern in 1995 as jury trials, outlawed since 1918, returned on an experimental basis in nine subnational jurisdictions. Between January and September 1995, some 300 jury trials were held in those areas. Although another sixteen jurisdictions applied to begin holding jury trials, in mid-1996 the State Duma had not passed enabling legislation. In 1996 the court system convicted some 99.5 percent of criminal defendants, although only 80 percent were convicted in jury trials—about the same percentage as in Western courts. Expansion of the jury system faced strong opposition among Russia's police and prosecutors because the conviction rate is much lower and investigative procedures are held to much higher standards under such a system. Meanwhile, the advent of trial by jury and a nominally independent judiciary exposed a serious problem: in 1995 there were only about 20,000 private attorneys and about 28,000 public prosecutors in all of Russia, and most judges who had functioned under the old system had never developed genuine juridical skills. By the mid-1990s, a number of younger judges were actively promoting the jury system.

In the mid-1990s, claims of illegal detention received somewhat more recognition in the Russian legal system than they had previously. An estimated 13,000 individuals won their release by court order in 1994—about 20 percent of the total number who claimed illegal detention that year. In general, the criminal justice system is more protective of individual rights than it was in the Soviet period, although the Mirzayanov case demonstrated that substantial obstacles to Western-style jurisprudence remain in Russia's legal system.

Capital punishment is reserved for grave crimes such as murder and terrorism; it cannot be inflicted on a woman or on an individual less than eighteen years old. In 1995 four offenses—terrorist acts, terrorist acts against a representative of a foreign state, sabotage, and counterfeiting—were removed from the list of capital crimes. In March 1991, Yeltsin formed a thirteen-member Pardons Commission of volunteer advisers for the specific purpose of considering reductions of death sentences. According to one member of that commission, between 1991 and 1994 the incidence of capital punishment (inflicted in Russia by firing squad) dropped sharply; in 1994 only four executions were carried out, and 124 death sentences were commuted. In 1995, however, the political pressure generated by Russia's crime wave changed the totals to eighty-six executions and only six commutations. After Yeltsin repeatedly ignored its clemency recommendations in 1995, the Pardons Commission reportedly ceased functioning in early 1996, despite the protests of Russian and international human rights organizations. Russia's membership in the Council of Europe (see Glossary), which became official in January 1996, requires an immediate moratorium on executions, plus complete elimination of the death penalty from the Criminal Code within three years. Russia's execution rate rose in the first months of 1996 before declining sharply.

Prisons

In the 1980s, the Soviet Union had few conventional prisons. About 99 percent of convicted criminals served their sentences in labor camps. These were supervised by the Main Directorate for Corrective Labor Camps (Glavnoye upravleniye ispravitel'no-trudovykh lagerey—Gulag), which was administered by the MVD. The camps had four regimes of ascending severity. In the strict-regime camps, inmates worked at the most difficult jobs, usually outdoors, and received meager rations. Jobs were progressively less demanding and rations better in the three classifications of camps with more clement regimes. The system of corrective labor was viewed by Soviet authorities as successful because of the low rate of recividism. However, in the opinion of former inmates and Western observers, prisons and labor camps were notorious for their harsh conditions, arbitrary and sadistic treatment of prisoners, and flagrant abuses of human rights. In 1989 new legislation, emphasizing rehabilitation rather than punishment, was drafted to "humanize" the Gulag system. Nevertheless, few changes occurred in the conditions of most prisoners before the end of the Soviet period in 1991.

In the post-Soviet period, all prisons and labor camps except for fourteen detention prisons fell under the jurisdiction of the MVD. In the early and mid-1990s, the growth of crime led to a rapid rise in the number of prisoners. Because of overcrowding and the failure to build new prison facilities, conditions in prisons deteriorated steadily after 1991, and some incidents of Soviet-style arbitrary punishment continued to be reported. In 1994 a Moscow prison designed to hold 8,500 inmates was housing well over 17,000 shortly after its completion. Many prisons are unfit for habitation because of insufficient sanitation systems. In 1995 *Nezavisimaya gazeta* reported that the capacity of isolation wards in Moscow and St. Petersburg prisons had been exceeded by two to two-and-one-half times. Observers claimed that some prisons stopped providing food to prisoners for months at a time, relying instead on rations sent from outside. The lack of funding also led to a crisis in medical care for prisoners. In 1995 Yeltsin's Human Rights Commission condemned the prison system for continuing to allow violations of prisoners' rights. The report cited lack of expert supervision as the main reason that such practices, which often included beatings, were not reported and punished.

In 1995 conditions in the penal system had deteriorated to the point that the State Duma began calling for a transfer of prison administration from the MVD to the Ministry of Justice. According to Western experts, however, the MVD's Chief Directorate for Enforcement of Punishment has been prevented from improving the situation by funding limitations, personnel problems, and lack of legislative support, rather than by internal shortcomings.

By the mid-1990s, Russian penal legislation resembled that enacted in Western countries, although the conditions of detention did not. Post-Soviet legislation has abolished arbitrary or inhumane practices such as bans on visitors and mail, head shaving, and physical abuse. Also, prison officials now are required to protect prisoners who have received threats, and freedom of religious practice is guaranteed. Prisoners are rewarded for good behavior by being temporarily released outside the prison; in 1993 the MVD reported a 97 percent rate of return after such releases. However, the penalty for violent escape has increased to eight additional years' detention. In 1996 the function of guarding prisons was to pass completely from the MVD to local prison administrations, and a complete restructuring was announced for that year.

Although conditions in the labor camps are harsh, those in pretrial detention centers are even worse. According to the Society for the Guardianship of Penitentiary Institutions, the government's inability to implement a functional system of release on bail meant that by the end of 1994 some 233,500 persons—more than 20 percent of the entire prison population—were incarcerated in pretrial detention centers, sometimes for a period longer than the nominal punishment for the crime of which they were accused.

In 1994 the total prison population was estimated at slightly more than 1 million people, of whom about 600,000 were held in labor camps. Of the latter number, about 21,600 were said to be women and about 19,000 to be adolescents. Among the entire prison population in 1994, about half were incarcerated for violent crimes, 60 percent were repeat offenders, and more than 15 percent were alcoholics or drug addicts.

As in the Soviet period, corrective-labor institutions have made a significant contribution to the national economy. In the early 1990s, industrial output in the camps reached an estimated US$100 million, and forest-based camps added about US$27 million, chiefly from the production of commercial lumber, railroad ties, and summer cabins. Because the camps supply their products to conventional state enterprises, however, they have suffered from the decline in that phase of Russia's economy; an estimated 200,000 convicts were without work in the camps in early 1994 (see Economic Conditions in Mid-1996, ch. 6). In 1995 the chief of the Directorate for Supervision of the Legality of Prison Punishment reported that the population of labor camps exceeded the capacity of those facilities by an average of 50 percent.

Outlook

In the mid-1990s, the Russian government maintained a precarious balance between the newly discovered rights of citizens and the government's perceived need for security from domestic criticism and threats to its power. Between 1992 and 1996, the record of the Yeltsin administration was decidedly mixed. Reforms gradually appeared in prison administration, the rights of those accused of crimes, and the introduction of trial by jury, but beginning in 1993 legislation and executive decrees increasingly had the objective of strengthening the arbitrary powers of government over its citizens in the name of national security. The Procuracy maintains much of the independence it had in the Soviet period; although the role of judges and defense attorneys nominally is greater in the post-Soviet system, Russia suffers a severe shortage of individuals experienced in the workings of a Western-style legal system.

The national security establishment, generally smaller and less competent than the pervasive KGB monolith of the Soviet period, has undergone reorganization and internal power struggles in the 1990s, and in some instances it has been made the scapegoat for setbacks such as the Chechnya invasion. Agencies such as the regular militia (police) and the Federal Border Service have not been able to deal effectively with increased crime, smuggling, and illegal immigration; lack of funding is an important reason for this failure. More specialized national security agencies such as the FSB maintain special investigative prerogatives beyond the purview of normal law enforcement.

As average Russian citizens have gained marginally greater freedom from the fear of arbitrary government intrusion, they have been plagued with a crime wave whose intensity has mounted every year since 1991. All types of illegal activity—common street theft, drug-related crime, murder, white-collar financial crime, and extortion by organized criminals—have flourished. Although the government has announced studies and special programs, Russian society continues to present an inviting target to criminals in the absence of effective law enforcement and the presence of rampant corruption.

*   *   *

The status and development of Russia's internal security agencies and crime situation are described in numerous periodical articles and a few substantive monographs. In *The KGB: Police and Politics in the Soviet Union,* Amy Knight describes the structure and influence of the KGB in its final stage before the end of the Soviet Union. The post-Soviet position of internal security agencies is described by J. Michael Waller in *Secret Empire: The KGB in Russia Today.* In *Comrade Criminal: Russia's New Mafia,* Stephen Handelman investigates Russia's organized criminal element and official corruption, against the backdrop of social conditions and government attitudes prevalent in the 1990s. The 1996 *International Narcotics Control Strategy Report* of the United States Department of State's Bureau of International Narcotics Matters provides a summary of narcotics activity and government prevention measures in Russia. Penny Morvant's article "War on Organized Crime and Corruption" describes Russia's crime wave and government attempts to combat it; two articles in the *RFE/RL Research Report,* Christopher J. Ulrich's "The Growth of Crime in Russia and the Baltic Region" and Julia Wishnevsky's "Corruption Allegations Undermine Russia's Leaders," approach the same topics from different perspectives. Numerous articles in the *Christian Science Monitor,* the Foreign Broadcast Information Service's *Daily Report: Central Eurasia,* and the Moscow daily newspapers *Nezavisimaya gazeta* and *Izvestiya* include current information on Russia's criminal justice and prison systems and on the crime problem. (For further information and complete citations, see Bibliography.)

Appendix

Table 1. Metric Conversion Coefficients and Factors

When you know	Multiply by	To find
Millimeters..........................	0.04	inches
Centimeters.........................	0.39	inches
Meters.............................	3.3	feet
Kilometers	0.62	miles
Hectares $(10,000^2)$	2.47	acres
Square kilometers	0.39	square miles
Cubic meters	35.3	cubic feet
Liters	0.26	gallons
Kilograms..........................	2.2	pounds
Metric tons.........................	0.98	long tons
....	1.1	short tons
....	2,204	pounds
Degrees Celsius (Centigrade)..........	1.8 and add 32	degrees Fahrenheit

Table 2. Rulers of Muscovy and the Russian Empire, 1462–1917

Period	Ruler
Rurik Dynasty	
1462–1505	Ivan III (the Great)
1505–33	Vasiliy III
1533–84	Ivan IV (the Terrible)
1584–98	Fedor I
Time of Troubles	
1598–1605	Boris Godunov
1605	Fedor II
1605–06	First False Dmitriy
1606–10	Vasiliy Shuyskiy
1610–13	Second False Dmitriy
Romanov Dynasty	
1613–45	Mikhail Romanov
1645–76	Aleksey
1676–82	Fedor III
1682–89	Sofia (regent)
1682–96	Ivan V (co-tsar)
1682–1725	Peter I (the Great)
1725–27	Catherine I
1727–30	Peter II
1730–40	Anna
1740–41	Ivan VI
1741–62	Elizabeth
1762	Peter III
1762–96	Catherine II (the Great)
1796–1801	Paul I
1801–25	Alexander I
1825–55	Nicholas I
1855–81	Alexander II
1881–94	Alexander III
1894–1917	Nicholas II

Source: Based on information from Marc Raeff, "History of Russia/Union of Soviet Socialist Republics," *Academic American Encyclopedia*, 16, Danbury, Connecticut, 1986, 358.

Table 3. Populated Places in European Russia Irradiated by Chernobyl' and Other Industrial Accidents[1]

Jurisdiction	Populated Places by Degree of Irradiation[2]			Total
	0–1	1–5	5–15	
Belgorod Oblast...............	318	232	0	550
Bryansk Oblast[3]...............	1,183	479	264	1,926
Kaluga Oblast..................	262	281	69	612
Kursk Oblast	915	201	0	1,116
Leningrad Oblast...............	68	87	0	155
Lipetsk Oblast	123	92	0	215
Moscow Oblast.................	9	0	0	9
Nizhniy Novgorod Oblast........	137	0	0	137
Orel Oblast	683	876	15	1,574
Penza Oblast	57	23	0	80
Republic of Bashkortostan	16	0	0	16
Republic of Chuvashia	34	0	0	34
Republic of Mari El.............	25	0	0	25
Republic of Mordovia	290	48	0	338
Rostov Oblast..................	2	0	0	2
Ryazan' Oblast.................	246	293	0	539
Smolensk Oblast	89	0	0	89
Tambov Oblast.................	116	7	0	123
Tula Oblast....................	1,072	1,150	144	2,366
Ul'yanovsk Oblast	101	8	0	109
Volgograd Oblast...............	2	3	0	5
Voronezh Oblast	758	214	0	972
TOTAL......................	6,506	3,994	492	10,992

[1] Includes results of 1986 accident at Chernobyl' Nuclear Power Station in Ukraine and three nuclear accidents at Mayak nuclear weapons plant in Chelyabinsk.
[2] In curies per square kilometer.
[3] Bryansk Oblast also has ninety-three populated places with more than fifteen curies per square kilometer.

Source: Based on information from Russia, Committee on Land Resources and Utilization, *Zemlya Rossii 1995: Problemy, tsifry, kommentarii*, Moscow, 1996, 35–36.

Table 4. Area, Population, and Capitals of the Soviet Republics, 1989 Census

Republic	Area of Republic[1] (in square kilometers)	Population of Republic[1]	Capital	Population of Capital[2]
Russia..........	17,075,400	145,311,000	Moscow	8,815,000
Kazakstan.......	2,717,300	16,244,000	Alma-Ata	1,108,000
Ukraine	603,700	51,201,000	Kiev	2,544,000
Turkmenistan ...	488,100	3,361,000	Ashkhabad	382,000
Uzbekistan......	447,400	19,026,000	Tashkent	2,124,000
Belorussia	207,600	10,078,000	Minsk	1,543,000
Kyrgyzstan	198,500	4,143,000	Frunze	632,000
Tajikistan	143,100	4,807,000	Dushanbe	582,000
Azerbaijan	86,600	6,811,000	Baku	1,115,000
Georgia	69,700	5,266,000	Tbilisi	1,194,000
Lithuania.......	65,200	3,641,000	Vilnius	566,000
Latvia..........	64,500	2,647,000	Riga	900,000
Estonia.........	45,100	1,556,000	Tallin	478,000
Moldavia	33,700	4,185,000	Kishinev	663,000
Armenia........	29,800	3,412,000	Yerevan	1,168,000
TOTAL	22,403,000[3]	286,717,000[4]		24,008,000

[1] Estimated.
[2] Estimated. Each republic's capital is also the largest city in the republic.
[3] Includes the area of the White Sea and the Sea of Azov.
[4] Soviet citizens outside the Soviet Union are included.

Source: Based on information from *Izvestiya* [Moscow], April 29, 1989, 1–2.

Table 5. *Largest Nature Reserves and National Parks, 1992*

Name and Location	Year Established	Area[1]	Number of Protected Species		
			Animals	Birds	Plants
Putoran Reserve, Krasnoyarsk Territory	1988	1,887	38	142	650
Ust'-Lena Reserve, Republic of Sakha.	1986	1,433	32	99	523
Taymyr Reserve, Krasnoyarsk Territory	1979	1,349	16	85	714
Tunka Park, Republic of Buryatia	1991	1,184	47	200	100
Kronotskiy Reserve, Kamchatka Oblast.	1967	1,142	42	217	810
Central Siberian Reserve, Krasnoyarsk Territory.	1931	972	45	241	545
Magadan Reserve, Magaden Oblast.	1982	884	46	135	300
Altay Reserve, Republic of Gorno-Altay.	1932	881	67	320	1,454
Dzhugdzhur Reserve, Khabarovsk Territory	1990	860	29	69	480
Olekminsk Reserve, Republic of Sakha.	1984	847	40	180	450
Wrangel Island Reserve, Magadan Oblast	1976	796	15	151	438
Pechero-Il'ich Reserve, Republic of Komi	1930	722	46	215	702
Baikal-Lena Reserve, Irkutsk Oblast.	1986	660	48	171	679
Verkhnetazov Reserve, Tyumen' Oblast.	1986	631	25	55	291
Yugan Reserve, Tyumen' Oblast.	1982	623	24	180	739

[1] In thousands of hectares.

Source: Based on information from *Novaya Rossiya '94: Informatsionno-statisticheskiy al'manakh*, Moscow, 1994, 95–96.

Table 6. *Per Capita Annual Consumption of Selected Foods, 1991–94*
(in kilograms unless otherwise specified)

Food	1991	1992	1993	1994
Meat and meat products.	63	55	54	53
Milk and milk products	347	281	294	278
Eggs (units)	288	263	250	234
Fish and fish products	16	12	12	10
Sugar and confections	38	30	31	31
Vegetables	86	77	71	65
Fruits	35	32	29	n.a.[1]
Potatoes	112	118	127	122

[1] n.a.—not available.

Source: Based on information from Organisation for Economic Co-operation and
Development, *OECD Economic Surveys: The Russian Federation 1995*, Paris, 1995,
124.

Table 7. *Population by Age and Sex, 1992*

Age-Group	Males	Females	Total
0–1	861,576	818,432	1,680,008
1–4	4,351,791	4,159,567	8,511,358
5–9	6,168,816	5,957,872	12,126,688
10–14	5,578,416	5,418,283	10,996,699
15–19	5,274,609	5,142,603	10,417,212
20–24	4,960,535	4,648,853	9,609,388
25–29	5,274,783	5,146,580	10,421,363
30–34	6,498,819	6,414,389	12,913,208
35–39	6,172,658	6,217,575	12,390,233
40–44	5,403,038	5,563,779	10,966,817
45–49	2,839,814	3,041,791	5,881,605
50–54	4,518,016	5,270,041	9,788,057
55–59	3,576,791	4,410,415	7,987,206
60–64	3,580,852	4,957,475	8,538,327
65–69	2,194,867	4,362,140	6,557,007
70–74	966,641	2,476,577	3,443,218
75–79	727,427	2,254,410	2,981,837
80–84	432,457	1,602,017	2,034,474
85 and over	180,568	884,901	1,065,469
TOTAL	69,562,474	78,747,700	148,310,174

Source: Based on information from United Nations, Department for Economic and
Social Information and Policy Analysis, *Demographic Yearbook, 1993*, New York,
1995, 214–15.

Table 8. Major Ethnic Groups, Selected Years, 1959–89
(in thousands of people)

Ethnic Group	1959	1970	1979	1989
Russians	97,863	107,748	113,522	119,866
Tatars	4,075	4,758	5,011	5,522
Ukrainians	3,359	3,346	3,658	4,368
Chuvash	1,436	1,637	1,690	1,774
Dagestanis[1].............	797	1,152	1,402	1,749
Bashkirs	954	1,181	1,291	1,345
Belorussians.............	844	964	1,052	1,206
Mordovians	1,211	1,177	1,111	1,074
Chechens	261	572	712	899
Germans................	820	762	791	842
Udmurts................	616	678	686	715
Mari	498	581	600	644
Kazaks..................	383	478	518	636
Jews....................	875	808	701	537
Armenians	256	299	365	532
Buryats.................	252	313	350	417
Ossetians	248	313	352	402
Kabardins...............	201	277	319	386
Yakuts..................	233	295	327	380
Komi...................	283	315	320	336
Azerbaijanis	71	96	152	336
Ingush	56	137	166	215
Tuvinians	100	139	165	206
Moldavians..............	62	88	102	173
Kalmyks	101	131	140	166
Roma	72	98	121	153
Karachay................	71	107	126	150
Georgians...............	58	69	89	131
Karelians	164	141	133	125
Adyghs	79	98	107	123
Khakass.................	56	65	69	79
Balkars	35	53	59	69
Altays	45	55	59	69
Cherkess................	29	38	45	51

[1] Category based on about thirty nationalities.

Source: Based on information from *Novaya Rossiya '94: Informatsionno-statisticheskiy al'manakh*, Moscow, 1994, 110.

Table 9. Ethnic Composition of Autonomous Republics, 1989
(in percentages)

Republic	Russians	Titular Nationality		Other Major Group	
Adygea...................	68	Adyghs	22	Ukrainians	3
Bashkortostan	39	Bashkirs	22	Tatars	28
Buryatia..................	70	Buryats	24	—[1]	
Chechnya and Ingushetia[2]....	23	Chechens	53	—	
....		Ingush	13	—	
Chuvashia	27	Chuvash	68	Tatars	3
Dagestan	9	Dagestanis[3]	80	Azerbaijanis	4
Gorno-Altay (Altay)	60	Altays	31	—	
Kabardino-Balkaria..........	32	Kabardins	48	—	
....		Balkars	9	—	
Kalmykia	38	Kalmyks	45	Dagestanis	6
Karachayevo-Cherkessia	42	Karachay	31	—	
....		Cherkess	10	—	
Karelia	74	Karelians	10	Belorussians	7
Khakassia.................	80	Khakass	11	—	
Komi	58	Komi	23	—	
Mari El..................	48	Mari	45	Tatars	6
Mordovia.................	61	Mordovians	33	Tatars	5
North Ossetia (Alania)	30	Ossetians	53	Ingush	5
Sakha (Yakutia).............	50	Yakuts	33	Ukrainians	7
Tatarstan	43	Tatars	49	Chuvash	4
Tyva (Tuva)	32	Tuvinians	64	—	
Udmurtia.................	59	Udmurts	31	Tatars	7

[1] —indicates no other major group present.
[2] Republics of Chechnya and Ingushetia were united until 1992.
[3] Category includes about thirty nationalities.

Table 10. *Ethnically Designated Jurisdictions, 1996*

Jurisdiction	Area[1]	Capital	Population[2]
Republics			
Adygea........................	7,600	Maykop	450,400
Bashkortostan	143,600	Ufa	4,000,000
Buryatia.......................	351,300	Ulan-Ude	1,050,000
Chechnya (Chechnya-Ichkeria)	19,300	Groznyy	n.a.[3]
Chuvashia	18,000	Cheboksary	1,361,000
Dagestan	50,300	Makhachkala	2,067,000
Gorno-Altay	92,600	Gorno-Altaysk	200,000
Ingushetia	19,300	Nazran	254,100
Kabardino-Balkaria..............	12,500	Nalchik	800,000
Kalmykia	75,900	Elista	350,000
Karachayevo-Cherkessia	14,100	Cherkessk	422,000
Karelia........................	172,400	Petrozavodsk	800,000
Khakassia......................	61,900	Abakan	600,000
Komi	415,900	Syktyvkar	1,227,900
Mari El........................	23,300	Yoshkar Ola	754,000
Mordovia......................	26,200	Saransk	964,000
North Ossetia	8,000	Vladikavkaz	660,000
Sakha	3,100,000	Yakutsk	1,077,000
Tatarstan	68,000	Kazan'	3,800,000
Tyva	170,500	Kyzyl	314,000
Udmurtia......................	42,100	Izhevsk	1,500,000
Autonomous oblast			
Birobidzhan (Yevreyskaya autonom-naya oblast')	36,000	Birobidzhan	218,000
Autonomous regions (*okruga*)			
Aga Buryat.....................	19,000	Aga	77,000
Chukchi.......................	737,700	Anadyr	156,000
Evenk.........................	767,600	Tura	25,000
Khanty-Mansi...................	523,100	Khanty-Mansiysk	1,301,000
Koryak........................	301,500	Palana	39,000
Nenets	176,700	Naryan-Mar	55,000
Permyak.......................	32,900	Kudymkar	160,000
Taymyr (Dolgan-Nenets)	862,100	Dudinka	55,000
Ust'-Orda Buryat................	22,400	Ust'-Ordynskiy	137,000
Yamalo-Nenets..................	750,300	Salekhard	495,000

[1] In square kilometers.
[2] 1995 estimates for all republics except Karachayevo-Cherkessia (1990) and Buryatia, Karelia, Komi, and Sakha (1994); 1990 estimates for autonomous oblast and all autonomous regions.
[3] n.a.—not available.

Source: Based on information from *Eastern Europe and the Commonwealth of Independent States 1997*, London, 1996, 666–76, 691–94.

Table 11. Indicators of Living Standards, 1991–94

Indicator	1991	1992	1993	1994
Life expectancy, males (in years)	63.5	62.0	58.9	57.3
Life expectancy, females (in years)	74.3	73.8	71.9	71.1
Daily caloric intake	2,527	2,438	2,552	2,427
Percentage of consumer expenditure on food	38.4	47.1	46.3	46.8
Automobiles per 1,000 persons	63.5	68.5	75.7	84.4
Telephones per 1,000 persons	164.0	167.0	172.0	176.0

Source: Based on information from Organisation for Economic Co-operation and
Development, *OECD Economic Surveys: The Russian Federation 1995*, Paris, 1995,
123.

Table 12. Students in Primary and Secondary Schools, Selected Years, 1986–93
(in millions of students)

	1986	1991	1992	1993
Grades 1 to 4				
Urban	4.6	5.3	5.3	5.3
Rural	2.0	2.3	2.4	2.5
Total grades 1 to 4	6.6	7.6	7.7	7.8
Grades 5 to 9				
Urban	7.0	7.5	7.5	7.5
Rural	2.8	2.8	2.8	2.9
Total grades 5 to 9	9.8	10.3	10.3	10.4
Grades 10 to 11 (or 12)				
Urban	1.2	1.4	1.4	1.3
Rural	0.7	0.6	0.6	0.6
Total grades 10 to 11 (or 12)	1.9	2.0	2.0	1.9
Schools for the mentally or physically handicapped	0.3	0.4	0.4	0.4
TOTAL	18.6	20.3	20.4	20.5

Source: Based on information from *Novaya Rossiya '94: Informatsionno-statisticheskiy
al'manakh*, Moscow, 1994, 557.

Table 13. Education Statistics for the Autonomous Republics, 1994

Republic	Number of General Schools	Number of General School Students	Vocational Schools	Higher Schools
Adygea	169	63,500	10	1
Bashkortostan	3,264	606,300	157	9
Buryatia	602	190,600	44	4
Chechnya and Ingushetia[1]	554	250,700	22	3
Chuvashia....................	715	210,100	35	3
Dagestan.....................	1,589	395,000	29	5
Gorno-Altay	135	36,700	4	1
Kabardino-Balkaria	249	131,300	19	3
Kalmykia.....................	250	56,300	12	1
Karachayevo-Cherkessia	186	71,600	8	2
Karelia	336	116,400	21	3
Khakassia	281	93,900	12	1
Komi........................	591	196,200	12	1
Mari El	435	120,500	34	3
Mordovia	823	132,800	42	2
North Ossetia.................	210	105,900	17	4
Sakha	711	197,900	33	2
Tatarstan.....................	2,422	525,100	118	15
Tyva........................	163	61,200	11	1
Udmurtia	882	252,700	45	5

[1] Combined figures for Chechnya and Ingushetia.

Source: Based on information from Russian Business Agency et al., *Russia 1994–95: Business, Social, Economic Analytic Profile*, 2 and 3, Moscow, 1994.

Table 14. Incidence of Selected Diseases, 1990–94
(rate per 1,000 persons)

Disease	1990	1991	1992	1993	1994
Infectious diseases.	34.9	33.4	34.9	38.6	44.2
Cancer	5.5	5.8	5.9	6.1	6.5
Endocrinological diseases	3.6	4.0	4.2	4.5	5.2
Blood diseases	1.3	1.6	1.9	2.2	2.4
Diseases of the nervous system. . . .	45.8	47.6	50.6	54.3	56.5
Circulatory diseases	11.2	11.0	11.5	11.8	12.9
Respiratory diseases	336.2	351.9	289.7	309.2	283.2
Diseases of the digestive organs. . .	27.2	28.6	31.2	32.3	33.2
Diseases of the urinary tract.	19.6	20.1	22.3	24.1	26.9
Skin diseases	35.0	35.0	35.7	39.9	45.6
Bone and muscle diseases	24.8	25.5	25.6	25.9	26.9

Source: Based on information from Organisation for Economic Co-operation and
Development, *OECD Economic Surveys: The Russian Federation 1995*, Paris, 1995,
129.

Table 15. Land Utilization, 1993 and 1994
(in millions of hectares)

	1993	1994
Agricultural (enterprise and individual ownership)	656.6	667.7
Under municipal or village jurisdiction	38.0	38.6
Designated for industry, transportation, or other nonagricultural purpose	17.8	17.6
Protected lands	26.7	27.3
Owned by timber companies	843.3	838.6
Water resources.	19.0	19.4
Lands held in reserve	108.3	100.6
TOTAL	1,709.7	1,709.8

Source: Based on information from Russia, Committee on Land Resources and Utilization, *Zemlya Rossii: Problemy, tsifry, kommentarii, 1995*, Moscow, 1996, 5.

Table 16. Revenue Sources of Subnational Jurisdictions, 1992, 1993, and 1994
(in millions of United States dollars) [1]

Source	1992	1993	1994
Transfers from national and other government levels	1,419	4,686	7,345
Percentage of total transfers	(86.0)	(99.0)	(98.0)
Profit taxes...............................	4,150	12,110	10,560
Percentage of total profit taxes	(58.5)	(67.4)	(64.9)
Value-added taxes (VAT)....................	2,290	4,309	5,023
Percentage of total VAT	(24.9)	(35.7)	(35.0)
Excise taxes	500	941	990
Percentage of total excise taxes	(52.5)	(49.4)	(40.0)
Sales taxes	21	n.a.[2]	n.a.
Percentage of total sales taxes	(100.0)	(n.a.)	(n.a.)
Personal income taxes......................	1,943	4,700	5,799
Percentage of total personal income taxes....	(100.0)	(100.0)	(99.3)
Property taxes	247	585	1,611
Percentage of total property taxes...........	(100.0)	(100.0)	(100.0)
Foreign economic activity...................	36	97	58
Percentage of total foreign economic activity...............................	(2.1)	(4.5)	(0.8)
Natural resource use payments	496	639	681
Percentage of total natural resource use payments.............................	(100.0)	(70.6)	(84.3)
Land taxes	243	293	517
Percentage of total land taxes	(76.1)	(86.8)	(93.3)
Government duties	n.a.	109	60
Percentage of total government duties	(n.a.)	(71.5)	(61.7)
Privatization revenues......................	196	271	n.a.
Percentage of total privatization revenues	(69.7)	(79.2)	(84.5)
Other tax and nontax revenue................	392	187	n.a.
Percentage of total other revenue...........	(n.a.)	(n.a.)	(n.a.)
TOTAL[3]	11,887	30,722	36,619

[1] Exchange rate used in calculations: 1992, 222 rubles per US$1; 1993, 933 rubles per US$1; 1994, 3,000 rubles per US$1.
[2] n.a.—not available.
[3] Figures do not add to totals because of "n.a." figures.

Source: Based on information from World Bank, *Russian Federation: Toward Medium-Term Viability*, Washington, 1996, 44.

Table 17. Labor Force Employment Indicators, 1995 and 1996
(in percentage of workforce unless otherwise indicated)

Date	Unemployment[1]	Underemployment		Vacancies
		Short-Time	On administrative leave	(in thousands)
1995				
January	7.3	2.8	1.6	311
February	7.4	2.9	1.5	316
March	7.5	3.1	1.7	329
April	7.7	2.8	1.4	368
May	7.7	2.6	1.6	405
June	7.7	2.7	1.3	445
July	7.8	2.5	1.3	454
August	7.8	2.5	1.3	460
September	7.9	2.6	1.3	446
October	8.1	2.5	1.3	404
November	8.1	2.7	1.1	352
December	8.2	n.a.[2]	n.a.	309
1996				
January	8.3	n.a.	n.a.	294
February	8.4	n.a.	n.a.	287
March	8.5	n.a.	n.a.	286

[1] As estimated by United Nations International Labour Organisation.
[2] n.a.—not available.

Source: Based on information from Economist Intelligence Unit, *Country Report: Russia, 2d Quarter 1996,* London, 1996, 27.

Table 18. Production Trends in Selected Branches of Heavy Industry, 1992–96
(January 1990=100)

Date	All Industry	Ferrous Metallurgy	Chemical and Petrochemical	Machine Building and Metalworking
1992				
January	81	73	80	81
July................	70	65	69	75
1993				
January	70	66	67	79
July................	62	58	58	66
1994				
January	51	47	40	37
July................	50	52	41	37
1995				
January	50	54	49	37
July................	50	55	48	34
1996				
January	46	53	44	31
April...............	45	54	43	32

Source: Based on information from Foreign Broadcast Information Service, *Daily Report: Central Eurasia Economic Review,* September 3, 1996, 50.

Table 19. Modes of Public Transportation, Selected Years, 1985–92
(in millions of passengers)

Mode	1985	1990	1991	1992
International				
Bus.....................	0.2	0.1	0.3	1.5
Air	3.4	4.4	3.6	3.5
Boat....................	n.a.[1]	n.a.	0.1	0.2
Intercity				
Bus.....................	702	705	790	520
Railroad.................	236	261	274	245
Air	69.9	86.4	82.4	59.1
Inland waterway..........	20.8	20.6	17.1	7.9
Suburban				
Bus.....................	5,498	5,052	5,153	4,531
Railroad.................	2,799	2,882	2,421	2,127
Inland waterway..........	30.5	26.5	36.8	21.2
Municipal				
Bus.....................	19,818	22,869	21,359	19,739
Taxi	680	557	526	266
Trolley..................	5,314	6,020	8,005	8,619
Tramway	5,997	6,000	7,619	8,071
Subway..................	3,319	3,659	3,229	3,567

[1] n.a.—not available.

Source: Based on information from *Novaya Rossiya '94: Informatsionno-statisticheskiy al'manakh*, Moscow, 1994, 481.

Table 20. Modes of Transportation of Selected Products, Selected Years, 1985–92
(in millions of tons)

Product and Mode	1985	1990	1991	1992
Coal				
Railroad......................	371.6	387.4	341.0	321.4
Inland waterway	16.8	14.6	12.7	10.8
Truck........................	22.0	23.3	n.a.[1]	n.a.
Sea	9.8	16.2	11.7	10.4
Coke				
Railroad......................	16.0	12.2	10.1	10.9
Truck........................	0.1	0.1	0	0
Petroleum products				
Railroad......................	265.9	246.7	234.9	212.0
Inland waterway	38.8	33.0	31.0	20.5
Truck........................	27.4	28.3	n.a.	n.a
Sea	51.3	53.4	33.9	38.3
Iron and manganese ore				
Railroad......................	110.3	113.0	96.4	89.8
Inland waterway	3.1	2.3	1.4	1.1
Truck........................	1.4	4.5	n.a.	n.a.
Sea	3.7	4.1	2.4	2.8
Ferrous metals				
Railroad......................	158.0	142.1	118.6	94.5
Inland waterway	3.4	2.5	2.5	2.1
Truck........................	n.a.	30.8	n.a.	n.a.
Sea	0	3.0	2.2	3.1
Chemical and mineral fertilizers				
Railroad......................	79.6	76.4	69.1	51.7
Inland waterway	4.4	5.0	4.2	3.6
Truck........................	5.5	3.7	n.a.	n.a.
Sea	4.3	2.8	1.3	1.3
Timber				
Railroad......................	137.5	131.7	116.3	97.2
Inland waterway	67.5	49.7	37.5	27.5
Truck........................	19.7	15.0	n.a.	n.a.
Sea	13.2	11.3	7.1	4.7
Grains				
Railroad......................	79.3	81.5	69.9	63.2
Inland waterway	5.6	5.9	5.3	6.3
Trucks	59.6	60.5	n.a.	n.a.

[1] n.a.—not available.

Source: Based on information from *Novaya Rossiya '94: Informatsionno-statisticheskiy al'manakh*, Moscow, 1994, 479.

Table 21. *Major Import Partners, 1992, 1993, and 1994*
(in millions of United States dollars)

Country	1992	1993	1994
Germany	6,725	5,142	5,597
Ukraine	n.a.[1]	n.a.	4,473
Belarus	n.a.	n.a.	2,088
United States	2,885	2,304	2,053
Kazakstan	n.a.	n.a.	2,016
Finland	1,223	724	1,618
Netherlands	368	431	1,603
Italy	3,052	1,106	1,510
Japan	1,680	1,367	1,004
Poland	1,230	529	1,001

[1] n.a.—not available.

Source: Based on information from Economist Intelligence Unit, *Country Report: Russia, 2d Quarter 1996*, London, 1996, 35.

Table 22. *Major Export Partners, 1992, 1993, and 1994*
(in millions of United States dollars)

Country	1992	1993	1994
Ukraine	n.a.[1]	n.a.	6,602
Germany	5,873	5,074	5,296
Switzerland	865	1,726	3,748
United States	694	1,998	3,694
Britain	2,287	3,353	3,640
Belarus	n.a.	n.a.	3,112
China	2,737	3,068	2,833
Italy	2,951	2,629	2,729
Netherlands	2,277	979	2,389
Kazakstan	n.a.	n.a.	2,288
Japan	1,569	2,005	2,165
Finland	1,564	1,364	2,028

[1] n.a.—not available.

Source: Based on information from Economist Intelligence Unit, *Country Report: Russia, 2d Quarter 1996*, London, 1996, 35.

Table 23. Trade with the United States by Selected Products, 1995 and 1996

(in thousands of United States dollars)

Product	1995	1996
Exports		
Unwrought aluminum	782,865	588,247
Precious metals and related items	425,348	533,856
Milled steel products	462,252	461,297
Base metals and chemicals	411,749	397,519
Uranium and plutonium	277,010	228,484
Fertilizers	208,080	169,609
Frozen fish	58,869	90,755
Petroleum products	52,129	81,686
Crude petroleum	68,055	79,698
Shellfish	73,015	77,166
Ferroalloys	132,250	74,168
Inorganic chemicals	70,282	62,897
Other	1,097,975	682,437
Total exports	4,019,879	3,527,819
Imports		
Poultry	606,622	912,705
Cigarettes	69,874	360,792
Construction and mining equipment	191,755	174,395
Miscellaneous animals and meats	103,902	140,429
Vehicles and vehicle chassis	88,452	95,100
Commercial and pleasure vessels	9,326	93,323
Automatic data processing machines	113,947	92,847
Medical goods	59,488	65,392
Telephone and telegraph equipment	53,538	59,044
Scientific and industrial instruments	37,537	50,579
Cereals	63,289	46,211
Edible preparations	33,471	44,456
Other	1,322,536	1,125,329
Total imports	2,753,737	3,260,602

Source: Based on official statistics of the United States Department of Commerce.

Table 24. Presidential Election Second-Round Results by Autonomous Republic, 1996

Republic	Boris Yeltsin	Gennadiy Zyuganov	Against Both Candidates	Absentee	Voided
Adygea	76,146	133,665	7,575	12,595	118,457
Bashkortostan . . .	1,170,774	990,148	83,484	81,180	535,815
Buryatia	192,933	210,791	16,036	26,454	26,448
Chechnya	275,455	80,877	15,184	33,541	122,438
Chuvashia	205,959	405,129	21,614	27,596	313,864
Dagestan	471,231	401,069	7,423	26,446	249,200
Gorno-Altay	40,026	48,057	3,527	5,805	35,166
Ingushetia	75,768	14,738	3,136	1,973	19,681
Kabardino-Balkaria	259,313	135,287	7,952	16,739	95,083
Kalmykia	103,515	39,354	2,919	14,642	53,731
Karachayevo-Cherkessia	109,747	101,379	5,286	12,510	73,749
Karelia	251,205	100,104	25,025	17,669	96,990
Khakassia	116,729	116,644	11,842	11,030	96,086
Komi	308,250	134,224	31,577	15,955	301,146
Mari El	154,301	199,872	19,628	26,479	171,064
Mordovia	238,441	249,451	16,328	29,106	167,499
North Ossetia . . .	133,748	164,308	7,317	11,630	98,451
Sakha	274,570	126,888	17,293	30,581	62,849
Tatarstan	1,253,121	658,782	74,178	73,109	569,118
Tyva	73,113	37,227	2,423	11,474	33,625
Udmurtia	392,551	302,649	40,302	29,756	279,947
RUSSIA	40,208,384	30,113,306	3,604,550	3,615,336	31,013,641

Source: Based on information from *Rossiyskaya gazeta* [Moscow], July 16, 1996, translated in Foreign Broadcast Information Service, *Daily Report: Central Eurasia*, July 31, 1996, 1–3.

Table 25. Funding of Government Functions by Jurisdiction, 1994

Function	Federal	Republic, Oblast, or Territory	*Rayon*
Defense	100 percent, except military housing	—[1]	Military housing
Internal security....	100 percent	—	—
Foreign economic relations........	100 percent	—	—
Education.........	All expenses of universities and research institutes	All technical and vocational schools	Wages and maintenance of primary and secondary schools
Health[2].	Medical research institutes	Tertiary, veterans', and specialized hospitals	Secondary hospitals
Public transportation.	—	Interjurisdictional highways, air, and railroad facilities (former federal)	Some facilities such as subways
Libraries..........	Special libraries such as Lenin Library	Special services	Most services
Housing	A portion of construction	A portion of construction	A portion of construction; maintenance
Price subsidies	A portion of food and medicine	—	Fuels, mass transportation, basic foods, and medicines
Welfare payments ..	A portion	A portion	Program management
Environment	National issues	Regional functions such as forest preservation	—

[1] — no jurisdictional responsibility.
[2] Towns and villages are responsible for paramedical personnel.

Source: Based on information from World Bank, *Russian Federation: Toward Medium-Term Viability,* Washington, 1996, 40–41.

Table 26. Political Parties and Groups Receiving Highest Vote Count in State Duma Elections, 1995

Full Name of Party or Group	National Vote Count
Communist Party of the Russian Federation (KPRF)[1]	15,432,963
Liberal-Democratic Party of Russia (LDPR)[2]	7,737,431
Our Home Is Russia All-Russian Political Movement (NDR)[3]	7,009,291
Yabloko Public Association...................................	4,767,384
Women of Russia Political Movement...........................	3,188,813
Communist Workers of Russia for the Soviet Union	3,137,406
Congress of Russian Communities Public Political Movement (KRO)[4]	2,980,137
Party of Workers' Self-Government...........................	2,756,954
Russia's Democratic Choice-United Democrats (DVR-OD)[5]	2,674,084
Agrarian Party of Russia.....................................	2,613,127
Derzhava (State Power) Social-Patriotic Movement................	1,781,233
Forward, Russia! Public Political Movement.....................	1,343,428
Power to the People!	1,112,873
Republican Party of the Russian Federation (RPRF-Pamfilova-Gurov-Vladimir Lysenko)[6].................................	1,106,812
Trade Unions and Industrialists of Russia-Union of Labor	1,076,072
Votes against all federal tickets................................	1,918,151

[1] KPRF—Kommunisticheskaya partiya Rossiyskoy Federatisii.
[2] LDPR—Liberal'no-demokraticheskaya partiya Rossii.
[3] NDR—Nash dom Rossiya.
[4] KRO—Kongress russkikh obshchin.
[5] DVR-OD—Demokraticheskiy vybor Rossii-Ob"yedinennoye dvizheniye.
[6] RPRF—Respublikanskaya partiya Rossiyskoy Federatsii.

Source: Based on information from *Rossiyskaya gazet*a [Moscow], January 24, 1996, translated in Foreign Broadcast Information Service, *Daily Report: Central Eurasia: Russia, Results of December 1995 State Duma Elections,* April 24, 1996, 20–21.

Table 27. Major Periodicals, 1995–96

Newspaper	Type	Date Established	Circulation
Argumenty i fakty	Weekly, independent	1992	3,200,000
Izvestiya	Daily, independent since 1991	1917	604,765
Kommersant Daily	Daily, focuses on business, youth	1990	104,400
Komsomol'skaya pravda . .	Daily, lacks former strong ideology	1925	1,547,000
Krasnaya zvezda	Daily, conservative, mainly military	1924	107,350
Literaturnaya gazeta	Weekly, liberal, cultural coverage	1929	280,000
Megapolis ekspres	Weekly, international, neoconservative	1990	400,000
Moskovskiye novosti	Weekly, independent, antiestablishment	1930	167,367
Moskovskaya pravda	Daily	1918	377,000
Nezavisimaya gazeta	Daily, independent, owned by banker Boris Berezovskiy	1990	50,400
Ogonek	Weekly, independent, owned by banker Boris Berezovskiy	1899	100,000
Pravda	Independent, pro-communist	1912	210,000
Rossiyskaya gazeta	Daily, source of official documents, very pro-government	1990	500,000
Rossiyskiye vesti	Weekly, highest-quality government voice	1991	131,000
Segodnya	Daily, political and business emphasis	1993	100,000
Sovetskaya Rossiya	Daily, communist and nationalist views	1956	250,000
Trud	Daily, trade union paper	1921	800,000

Source: Based on information from Richard F. Staar, *The New Military in Russia: Ten Myths That Shape the Image*, Annapolis, 1996, 229–32; and Foreign Broadcast Information Service, *Daily Report: Central Russia, Pre-Election Survey of Major Russian Media*, December 5, 1995, 9–19.

Table 28. Main Directorates of the Armed Forces General Staff, 1994

Directorate	Function
Armaments	Liaison with military industrial complex
Armor	Staff supervision of maintenance and modernization of combat vehicles
Artillery	Staff supervision of maintenance and modernization of weapons
Billeting and Maintenance	Maintenance and operation of military real estate
Cadres	Management of careers of professional military officers and warrant officers
Construction	Supervision of funding and resources for new military construction
Construction Industry of Ministry of Defense	Supervision of classified construction projects
Education	Education and training of cadres and specialists
Foreign Relations	Direction of foreign assistance programs and military attachés
Intelligence	Successor to Soviet Main Intelligence Directorate (GRU); collection of strategic, technical, and tactical information for armed forces[1]
Military Counterintelligence	Oversight of military security matters
Motor Vehicles	Supervision of maintenance and modernization of wheeled vehicles
Organization-Mobilization	Development and dissemination of mobilization plans for national emergencies
Personnel Work	Successor to Soviet political office, for management of enlisted personnel
Trade	Management of foreign military sales

[1] GRU—Glavnoye razvedyvatel'noye upravleniye.

Source: Based on information from Joint Publications Research Service, *JPRS Report: Central Eurasia Military Affairs: Directory of Military Organizations and Personnel,* Washington, 1994, 32–53.

Table 29. Strategic Nuclear Forces, 1995

Type	Number in Inventory	Description
Submarines		
Typhoon	6	20 Sturgeon SS–N–20 missiles
Delta–IV....................	7	16 Skiff SS–N–23 missiles each
Delta–III	13	16 Stingray SS–N–18 missiles each
Delta–II	4	16 Sawfly SS–N–8 missiles each
Delta–I.....................	15	12 Sawfly SS–N–8 missiles each
Total	45	684 missiles
Intercontinental ballistic missiles		
SS–17 Spanker (RS–16)	10	All MIRV, all in Russia[1]
SS–18 Satan (RS–20)	222	10 MIRV, 174 in Russia, remainder without warheads in Kazakstan
SS–19 Stiletto (RS–18)	250	6 MIRV, 160 in Russia, 90 in Ukraine
SS–24 Scalpel (RS–22)	92	10 MIRV, 46 in Russia, 46 in Ukraine; in Russia, 10 in silos, 36 on rails
SS–25 Sickle (RS–12M)	354	Mobile, single-warhead, at 10 bases; 336 in Russia, 18 in Belarus

[1] MIRV—multiple-warhead independently targeted reentry vehicle.

Source: Based on information from *The Military Balance, 1995–1996*, London, 1995, 113–14.

Bibliography

Chapter 1

Auty, Robert, and Dmitry Obolensky, eds. *An Introduction to Russian History, 1: Companion to Russian Studies.* Cambridge: Cambridge University Press, 1976.

Avrich, Paul. *Russian Rebels, 1600–1800.* New York: Schocken, 1972.

Baron, Samuel Haskell. *Plekhanov: The Father of Russian Marxism.* Stanford: Stanford University Press, 1963.

Billington, James H. *The Icon and the Axe: An Interpretive History of Russian Culture.* New York: Knopf, 1966.

Blackwell, William L. *The Beginnings of Russian Industrialization, 1800–1860.* Princeton: Princeton University Press, 1968.

Blum, Jerome. *Lord and Peasant in Russia from the Ninth to the Nineteenth Century.* Princeton: Princeton University Press, 1961.

Cherniavsky, Michael. *Tsar and People: Studies in Russian Myths.* New York: Random House, 1969.

Chew, Allen F. *An Atlas of Russian History: Eleven Centuries of Changing Borders.* New Haven: Yale University Press, 1970.

Crummey, Robert O. *The Formation of Muscovy, 1304–1613.* London: Longman, 1987.

Curtiss, John Shelton. *The Russian Army under Nicholas I, 1825–1855.* Durham: Duke University Press, 1965.

De Madariagha, Isabel. *Russia in the Age of Catherine the Great.* New Haven: Yale University Press, 1981.

Dmytryshyn, Basil. *A History of Russia.* Englewood Cliffs, New Jersey: Prentice-Hall, 1977.

Emmons, Terrance. *The Russian Landed Gentry and the Peasant Emancipation of 1861.* London: Cambridge University Press, 1968.

Fedotov, Georgii Petrovich. *The Russian Religious Mind.* 2 vols. Cambridge: Harvard University Press, 1946–66.

Fennell, John Lister Illingsworth. *Ivan the Great of Moscow.* London: Macmillan, 1961.

Florinsky, Michael T. *Russia: A History and Interpretation.* 2 vols. New York: Macmillan, 1953.

Gershchenkron, Alexander. *Europe in the Russian Mirror: Four Lectures on Economic History.* London: Cambridge University Press, 1970.

Geyer, Dietrich. *Russian Imperialism: The Interaction of Domestic and Foreign Policy, 1860–1914.* Trans., Bruce Little. New Haven: Yale University Press, 1987.

Grekov, Boris Dmitreevich. *Kievan Rus.* Trans., Y. Sdobnikov. Moscow: Foreign Languages, 1959.

Gurko, Vladimir Iosifovich. *Features and Figures of the Past: Government and Opinion in the Reign of Nicholas II.* Stanford: Stanford University Press, 1939.

Hittle, J.M. *The Service City: State and Townsmen in Russia, 1600–1800.* Cambridge: Harvard University Press, 1979.

Hosking, Geoffrey A. *The Russian Constitutional Experiment: Government and Duma, 1907–1914.* Cambridge: Cambridge University Press, 1973.

Hrushevsky, Mykhailo. *A History of the Ukraine.* Trans. and condensed, O.J. Fredericksen. New Haven: Yale University Press, 1941.

Jelavich, Barbara. *A Century of Russian Foreign Policy 1814–1914.* Philadelphia: Lippincott, 1964.

Keep, John L.H. *The Rise of Social Democracy in Russia.* Oxford: Clarendon, 1963.

Kliuchevsky, Vasily. *A Course in Russian History, 3: The Seventeenth Century.* Trans., N. Duddington. Chicago: University of Chicago Press, 1968.

Kliuchevsky, Vasily. *A Course in Russian History, 4: Peter the Great.* Trans., Liliana Archibald. New York: Knopf, 1959.

Kliuchevsky, Vasily. *The Course of Russian History.* 5 vols. Trans., C.J. Hogarth. New York: Dutton, 1911–31.

Kohut, Zenon E. *Russian Centralism and Ukrainian Autonomy: Imperial Absorption of the Hetmanate, 1760s–1830s.* Cambridge: Harvard Ukrainian Research Institute and Harvard University Press, 1988.

Lang, David Marshall. *A Modern History of Soviet Georgia.* New York: Grove Press, 1962.

Lawrence, John. *A History of Russia.* London: George Allen and Unwin, 1969.

Liashchenko, P.I. *A History of the National Economy of Russia to the 1917 Revolution.* Trans., L.M. Herman. New York: Macmillan, 1949. Reprint. New York: Octagon, 1970.

Lincoln, Bruce D. *Nicholas I: Emperor and Autocrat of all the Russians.* Bloomington: Indiana University Press, 1978.

MacKenzie, David, and Michael W. Curran. *A History of Russia and the Soviet Union.* Chicago: Dorsey Press, 1987.

Malia, Martin Edward. *Alexander Herzen and the Birth of Russian Socialism, 1812–1855.* Cambridge: Harvard University Press, 1961.

Malozemoff, Andrew. *Russian Far Eastern Policy, 1881–1904.* Berkeley: University of California Press, 1958. Reprint. New York: Octagon, 1977.

Masaryk, Tomás Garrigue. *The Spirit of Russia: Studies in History, Literature, and Philosophy.* 3 vols. Trans., Eden and Cedar Paul. New York: Macmillan, 1961–67.

Miliukov, Pavel Nikolaevich. *Outlines of Russian Culture.* Ed., Michael Karpovich; trans., Eleanor Davis and Valentine Ughert. Philadelphia: University of Pennsylvania Press, 1942.

Nichols, Robert L., and Theofanis George Stavrous, eds. *Russian Orthodoxy under the Old Regime.* Minneapolis: University of Minnesota Press, 1978.

Norretranders, Bjarne. *The Shaping of Czardom under Ivan Groznnyi.* Copenhagen: 1964. Reprint. London: Variorum, 1971.

Oberländer, Edwin ed., *Russia Enters the Twentieth Century.* New York: Schocken, 1971.

Orlovsky, Daniel T. *The Limits of Reforms: The Ministry of Internal Affairs in Imperial Russia, 1807–1881.* Cambridge: Harvard University Press, 1981.

Pares, Bernard. *The Fall of the Russian Monarchy: A Study of Evidence.* New York: Knopf, 1939.

Pelenski, Jaroslav. *Russia and Kazan: Conquest and Imperial Ideology, 1438–1560s.* The Hague: Mouton, 1974.

Pierce, Richard A. *Russian Central Asia, 1867–1917: A Study in Colonial Rule.* Berkeley: University of California Press, 1960.

Pintner, Walter McKenzie, and Don Karl Rowney, eds. *Russian Officialdom: The Bureaucratization of Russian Society from the Seventeenth to the Twentieth Century.* Chapel Hill: University of North Carolina Press, 1980.

Pipes, Richard. *Russia under the Old Regime.* New York: Scribner's, 1974.

Platonov, Sergei Fedorovich. *The Time of Troubles: A Historical Study of the Internal Crisis and Social Struggle in Sixteenth and Seventeenth Century Muscovy.* Trans., J.T. Alexander. Lawrence: University Press of Kansas, 1970.

Raeff, Marc. "History of Russia/Union of Soviet Socialist Republics." Page 358 in *Academic American Encyclopedia,* 16. Danbury, Connecticut: Grolier, 1986.

Raeff, Marc. *Michael Speransky: Statesman of Imperial Russia, 1772–1839.* The Hague: Martinus Nijhoff, 1969.

Raeff, Marc. *Russian Intellectual History: An Anthology.* New York: Humanities Press, 1978.

Riasanovsky, Nicholas. *A History of Russia.* 4th ed. New York: Oxford University Press, 1984.

Rieber, Alfred J. *Merchants and Entrepreneurs in Imperial Russia.* Chapel Hill: University of North Carolina Press, 1982.

Rieber, Alfred J. *Nicholas I and Official Nationality in Russia, 1825–1855.* Berkeley: University of California Press, 1959.

Robinson, Geroid Tanquary. *Rural Russia under the Old Regime.* Berkeley: University of California Press, 1967.

Rogger, Hans. *National Consciousness in Eighteenth-Century Russia.* Cambridge: Harvard University Press, 1960.

Rogger, Hans. *Russia in the Age of Modernization and Reform, 1881–1917.* London: Longman, 1987.

Rurad, C.A. *Fighting Words: Imperial Censorship and the Russian Press, 1804–1906.* Toronto: University of Toronto Press, 1982.

Schwartz, Solomon H. *The Russian Revolution of 1905: The Workers' Movement and the Formation of Bolshevism and Menshevism.* Chicago: University Press, 1967.

Seton-Watson, Hugh. *The Russian Empire, 1801–1917.* Oxford: Clarendon, 1967.

Smith, Clarence J. *The Russian Struggle for World Power, 1914–1917: A Study of Russian Foreign Policy During World War I.* New York: Philosophical Society, 1946.

Stites, Richard. *The Women's Liberation Movement in Russia: Feminism, Nihilism, and Bolshevism, 1890–1930.* Princeton: Princeton University Press, 1978.

Subtelny, Orest. *Ukraine: A History.* Toronto: University of Toronto Press, 1988.

Sumner, Benedict Humphrey. *Russia and the Balkans, 1870–1880.* Oxford: Clarendon, 1947.

Thaden, Edward C. *Conservative Nationalism in Nineteenth-Century Russia.* Seattle: University of Washington Press, 1964.

Thaden, Edward C., ed. *Russification of the Baltic Provinces and Finland, 1855–1914.* Princeton: Princeton University Press, 1981.

Treadgold, Donald W. *The West in Russia and China: Religious and Secular Thought in Modern Times.* 2 vols. Cambridge: Cambridge University Press, 1973.

Venturi, Franco. *Roots of Revolution: A History of the Populist and Socialist Movements in Nineteenth-Century Russia.* Trans., Francis Haskill. New York: Knopf, 1960.

Vernadsky, George. *The Mongols and Russia.* New Haven: Yale University Press, 1954.

Von Laue, Theodore. *Sergei Witte and the Industrialization of Russia.* New York: Columbia University Press, 1963.

Walicki, Andrzej. *A History of Russian Thought from the Enlightenment to Marxism.* Stanford: Stanford University Press, 1979.

Wortman, Richard. *The Development of a Russian Legal Consciousness.* Chicago: University of Chicago Press, 1976.

Zaionchkovsky, Peter Andreevich. *The Russian Autocracy under Alexander III.* Trans., David R. Jones. Gulf Breeze, Florida: Academic International Press, 1976.

Zenkovsky, Serge A. *Pan-Turkism and Islam in Russia.* Cambridge: Harvard University Press, 1960.

Chapter 2

Antonov-Ovseyenko, Anton. *The Time of Stalin.* New York: Harper and Row, 1981.

Armstrong, John A. "Nationalism in the Former Soviet Empire," *Problems of Communism,* 41, January–April 1992, 121–35.

Aslund, Anders. *Gorbachev's Struggle for Economic Reform.* 2d ed. Ithaca: Cornell University Press, 1991.

Barner-Barry, Carol, and Cynthia A. Hody. *The Politics of Change: The Transformation of the Former Soviet Union.* New York: St. Martin's Press, 1995.

Bialer, Seweryn. *Stalin's Successors: Leadership, Stability, and Change in the Soviet Union.* Cambridge: Cambridge University Press, 1980.

Black, Cyril E., ed. *The Transformation of Russian Society.* Cambridge: Harvard University Press, 1960.

Blaney, John, and Michael Gfoeller. "Lessons from the Failure of Perestroyka," *Political Science Quarterly,* 108, Fall 1993, 481–96.

Bradley, J.F.N. *Civil War in Russia, 1917–1920.* London: Batsford, 1975.

Brown, Archie. *The Gorbachev Factor in Soviet Politics.* 2d ed. Oxford: Oxford University Press, 1992.

Brown, Archie. "The Soviet Succession: From Andropov to Chernenko," *World Today,* 40, April 1984, 134–41.

Brown, Archie, and Michael Kaser, eds. *The Soviet Union since the Fall of Khrushchev.* New York: Macmillan, 1978.

Burant, Stephen R. "The Influence of Russian Tradition on the Political Style of the Soviet Elite," *Political Science Quarterly,* 102, No. 2, Summer 1987, 273–93.

Burdzhalov, E.N. *Russia's Second Revolution: The February 1917 Uprising in Petrograd.* Bloomington: Indiana University Press, 1987.

Carrère d'Encausse, Hélène. *The End of the Soviet Empire.* New York: Basic Books, 1993.

Chamberlin, William H. *The Russian Revolution, 1917–1921.* 2 vols. New York: Macmillan, 1972.

Checkel, Jeffrey. "Gorbachev's 'New Political Thinking' and the Formation of Soviet Foreign Policy," *Radio Liberty Research Report* [Munich], RL 429/88, September 23, 1988.

Cohen, Stephen F. *Rethinking the Soviet Experience: Politics and History since 1917.* New York: Oxford University Press, 1985.

Conquest, Robert. *The Great Terror: Stalin's Purge of the Thirties.* New York: Macmillan, 1968.

Conquest, Robert. *Harvest of Sorrow.* New York: Oxford University Press, 1986.

Cook, Linda J. "Brezhnev's 'Social Contract' and Gorbachev's Reforms," *Soviet Studies,* 44, No. 1, 1992, 37–56.

Daniels, Robert V. "The Chernenko Comeback," *New Leader,* 67, February 20, 1984, 3–5.

Daniels, Robert V. *Red October: The Bolshevik Revolution of 1917.* Boston: Beacon Press, 1984.

Daniels, Robert V. *Russia: The Roots of Confrontation.* Cambridge: Harvard University Press, 1985.

Dunlop, John B. *The Rise of Russia and the Fall of the Soviet Empire.* Princeton: Princeton University Press, 1993.

Dyker, David A., ed. *The Soviet Union under Gorbachev: Prospects for Reform.* London: Croom Helm, 1987.

Elliot, Iain. "Andropov Scrutinized," *Survey,* 28, Spring 1984, 61–69.

Evans, Alfred, Jr. "Gorbachev's Unfinished Revolution," *Problems of Communism,* 40, January–April 1991, 133–43.

Fitzpatrick, Sheila. *The Russian Revolution.* New York: Oxford University Press, 1982.

Florinsky, Michael T. *The End of the Russian Empire.* New York: Fertig, 1973.

Gelman, Harry. *The Brezhnev Politburo and the Decline of Détente.* Ithaca: Cornell University Press, 1985.

Goldman, Marshall I. "Economic Problems in the Soviet Union,"*Current History,* 82, October 1983, 322–25.

Gorbachev, Mikhail. *The August Coup.* London: Harper Collins, 1991.

Haimson, Leopold H. "The Parties and the State: The Evolution of Political Attitudes." Pages 110–44 in Cyril E. Black, ed., *The Transformation of Russian Society.* Cambridge: Harvard University Press, 1960.

Halstead, John. "Chernenko in Office," *International Perspectives,* May–June 1984, 19–21.

Hanson, Philip. *From Stagnation to Catastroika: Commentaries on the Soviet Economy, 1983–1991.* New York: Praeger, 1992.

Hardt, John P., and Donna Gold. "Andropov's Economic Future," *Orbis,* 27, No. 2, Spring 1983, 11–28.

Hasegawa, Tsuyoshi. *The February Revolution: Petrograd, 1917.* Seattle: University of Washington Press, 1981.

Hazan, Baruch. "Infighting in the Kremlin: Andropov vs. Chernenko," *Crossroads,* No. 11, 1984, 55–74.

Heller, Michel. "Andropov: A Retrospective View," *Survey,* 28, Spring 1984, 45–60.

Heller, Mikhail, and Aleksandr Nekrich. *Utopia in Power.* New York: Summit Books, 1986.

Hill, Ronald J., and Jan Ake Dellenbrant, eds. *Gorbachev and Perestroyka.* Aldershot, United Kingdom: Edward Elgar, 1989.

Hosking, Geoffrey A. *The First Socialist Society.* London: Fontana Press/Collins, 1985.

Hough, Jerry. "Andropov's First Year," *Problems of Communism,* 32, November–December 1983, 49–64.

Hough, Jerry. "Soviet Politics under Andropov," *Current History,* 82, October 1983, 330–33.

Hudson, George E., ed. *Soviet National Security Policy under Perestroyka.* Boston: Unwin Hyman, 1990.

Kanet, Roger E., Deborah Nutter Miner, and Tamara J. Reslar, eds. *The Soviet Union and International Politics.* Cambridge: Cambridge University Press, 1992.

Kelley, Donald R. *Soviet Politics from Brezhnev to Gorbachev.* New York: Praeger, 1987.

Khrushchev, Nikita S. *Khrushchev Remembers.* Ed. and trans., Strobe Talbott. Boston: Little, Brown, 1970.

Knight, Amy. "Andropov: Myths and Realities," *Survey,* 28, Spring 1984, 22–44.

Kontorovich, Vladimir. "The Economic Fallacy," *National Interest,* No. 31, Spring 1993.

Kramer, Mark. "Soviet Foreign Policy after the Cold War," *Current History,* 90, October 1991, 317–22.

Lerner, Lawrence W., and Donald W. Treadgold, eds. *Gorbachev and the Soviet Future.* Boulder, Colorado: Westview Press, 1988.

Lewin, Moshe. *Russian Peasants and Soviet Power.* Evanston: Northwestern University Press, 1968.

Linden, Carl A. *Khrushchev and the Soviet Leadership, 1957–1964.* Baltimore: Johns Hopkins Press, 1966.

MacKenzie, David, and Michael W. Curran. *A History of Russia and the Soviet Union.* Chicago: Dorsey Press, 1987.

Malia, Martin. *The Soviet Tragedy: A History of Socialism in Russia, 1917–1991.* New York: Free Press, 1994.

McCauley, Martin. *The Soviet Union 1917–1991.* 2d ed. London: Longman, 1993.

Medvedev, Roy A. *Khrushchev.* Garden City, New York: Anchor Press, 1983.

Medvedev, Roy A. *Let History Judge.* New York: Knopf, 1971.

Medvedev, Zhores A. *Andropov.* New York: Norton, 1983.

Meissner, Boris. "Soviet Policy: From Chernenko to Gorbachev," *Aussenpolitik* [Bonn], 36, No. 4, April 1985, 357–75.

Miller, Robert F., John H. Miller, and Thomas Henry Rigby. *Gorbachev at the Helm: A New Era in Soviet Politics?* London: Croom Helm, 1987.

"Moscow, August 1991: The Coup de Grace," *Problems of Communism*, 40, November–December 1991, 1–62.

Nahaylo, Bohdan, and Viktor Swoboda. *Soviet Disunion: A History of the Nationalities Problem in the USSR*. London: Hamish Hamilton, 1990.

Nichol, James P. *Diplomacy in the Former Soviet Republics*. Westport, Connecticut: Praeger, 1995.

Nichol, James P. *Perestroyka of the Soviet Ministry of Foreign Affairs*. Amherst: Program in Soviet and East European Studies, University of Massachusetts, 1988.

Nichol, James P. *Stalin's Crimes Against the Non-Russian Nations: The 1987–1990 Revelations and Debate*. Carl Beck Papers, Center for Russian and East European Studies, University of Pittsburgh, December 1991.

Olcott, Martha Brill. "The Slide into Disunion," *Current History*, 90, October 1991, 338–44.

Pares, Bernard. *The Fall of the Russian Monarchy: A Study of Evidence*. New York: Knopf, 1939.

Pipes, Richard. *The Formation of the Soviet Union*. Cambridge: Harvard University Press, 1954.

Ponton, Geoffrey. *The Soviet Era: Soviet Politics from Lenin to Yeltsin*. Oxford, United Kingdom: Blackwell, 1994.

Rabinowich, Alexander. *The Bolsheviks Come to Power*. New York: Norton, 1976.

Remington, Thomas. *Building Socialism in Bolshevik Russia*. Pittsburgh: University of Pittsburgh Press, 1984.

Remnick, David. *Lenin's Tomb: The Last Days of the Soviet Empire*. New York: Vintage, 1994.

Riasanovsky, Nicholas. *A History of Russia*. 4th ed. New York: Oxford University Press, 1984.

Robinson, Neil. "Gorbachev and the Place of the Party in Soviet Reform, 1985–91," *Soviet Studies*, 44, No. 3, 1992, 423–43.

Schapiro, Leonard B. *The Communist Party of the Soviet Union*. New York: Vintage Books, 1960.

Schapiro, Leondard B. *The Russian Revolutions of 1917.* New York: Basic Books, 1984.

Schull, Joseph. "Self-Destruction of Soviet Ideology," *Harriman Institute Forum,* 4, No. 7, July 1991.

Simes, Dmitri. "Gorbachev's Time of Troubles," *Foreign Policy,* No. 102, Spring 1991, 97–117.

Simis, Konstantin. "Andropov's Anticorruption Campaign," *Washington Quarterly,* 6, Summer 1983, 111–21.

Smith, Graham. *The Nationalities Question in the Soviet Union.* London: Longman, 1990.

Tatu, Michel. *Mikhail Gorbachev: The Origins of Perestroyka.* Boulder, Colorado: East European Monographs, 1991.

Teague, Elizabeth, and Vera Tolz. "CPSU R.I.P.," *Report on the USSR,* 3, No. 47, 1991, 1–8.

Treadgold, Donald W. *Twentieth Century Russia.* Boulder, Colorado: Westview Press, 1987.

Tucker, Robert C. *Stalin as Revolutionary, 1879–1929.* New York: Norton, 1977.

Tucker, Robert C., ed. *Stalinism: Essays in Historical Interpretation.* New York: Norton, 1977.

Ulam, Adam B. *Expansion and Coexistence: Soviet Foreign Policy, 1917–1973.* 2d ed. New York: Praeger, 1974.

Ulam, Adam B. *A History of Soviet Russia.* New York: Praeger, 1976.

Ulam, Adam B. "Looking at the Past: The Unraveling of the Soviet Union," *Current History,* 91, October 1992, 339–46.

Ulam, Adam B. *Stalin: The Man and His Era.* New York: Viking Press, 1973.

Urban, Michael E. "From Chernenko to Gorbachev: A Repolitization of Official Soviet Discourse," *Soviet Union/Union Soviétique,* 13, No. 2, 1986, 131–61.

Wallace, William W. *Gorbachev and the Revolution in Soviet Foreign Policy.* Aldershot, United Kingdom: Dartmouth, 1992.

Wessell, Nils H. "Arms Control and 'Active Measures,'" *Orbis,* 27, No. 2, Spring 1983, 5–11.

White, Stephen. *Gorbachev in Power.* 3d ed. Cambridge: Cambridge University Press, 1992.

Yeltsin, Boris. *The Struggle for Russia.* New York: Random House, 1994.

Zacek, Jane Shapiro, ed. *The Gorbachev Generation.* New York: Paragon House, 1988.

Zemtsov, Ilya. "Yuriy Andropov: Consolidation of Power," *Crossroads,* No. 11, 1984, 1–17.

Zlotnik, Marc. "Chernenko Succeeds," *Problems of Communism,* 33, March–April 1984, 17–31.

Zlotnik, Marc. "Chernenko's Platform," *Problems of Communism,* 31, November–December 1982, 70–75.

(Various issues of the following periodicals also were used in the preparation of this chapter: *Izvestiya* [Moscow]; and *Radio Liberty Research Bulletin* [Munich]).

Chapter 3

Bellona Foundation. *Sources of Radioactive Contamination in Murmansk and Arkhangelsk Counties.* Oslo: 1994.

Blaney, John W. "Environmental and Health Crises in the Former Soviet Union." Pages 134–42 in John W. Blaney, ed., *The Successor States to the USSR.* Washington: Congressional Quarterly, 1995.

Blaney, John W., ed. *The Successor States to the USSR.* Washington: Congressional Quarterly, 1995.

Bodrova, Valentina. "Reproductive Behaviour of Russia's Population in the Transition Period," *Berichte des Bundesinstituts für ostwissenschaftliche und internationale Studien* [Cologne], 15, 1995.

Cole, John. *Geography of the USSR.* Baltimore: Penguin Books, 1967.

The Europa World Year-Book 1994, 2. London: Europa, 1994.

The Europa World Year-Book 1995, 2. London: Europa, 1995.

Feshbach, Murray. *Ecological Disaster: Cleaning Up the Hidden Legacy of the Soviet Regime.* New York: Twentieth Century Fund, 1995.

Feshbach, Murray. *Environmental and Health Atlas of Russia.* Moscow: PAIMS, 1995.

Feshbach, Murray, and Alfred Friendly, Jr. *Ecocide in the USSR: Health and Nature under Siege.* New York: Basic Books, 1992.

Goldman, Marshall I. *Ecology and Economics: Controlling Pollution in the '70s.* Englewood Cliffs, New Jersey: Prentice-Hall, 1972.

Goldman, Marshall I. *The Spoils of Progress: Environmental Pollution in the Soviet Union.* Cambridge: MIT Press, 1972.

Gundarov, Igor' Alekseevich. *Pochemu umirayut v Rossii, kak nam vyzhit'?* (Why Are People Dying in Russia, and How Are We to Survive?) Moscow: Media sfera, 1995.

Heleniak, Tim. "The Projected Population of Russia in 2005," *Post-Soviet Geography,* 35, No. 10, October 1995, 608–14.

Hooson, David. *The Soviet Union: People and Regions.* Belmont, California: Wadsworth, 1968.

Institut gumanitarno-politicheskikh issledovaniy. *Ocherki rossiyskoy politiki* (Essays on Russian Politics). Moscow: 1994.

Israel. Central Bureau of Statistics. *Immigrant Population from Former USSR 1993: Demographic Trends.* Jerusalem: 1995.

Jacobs, Margot. "USSR Faces Mounting Refugee Problem," *Report on the USSR* [Munich], 2, No. 37, September 20, 1990, 14–18.

Jones, Anthony, Walter D. Connor, and David E. Powell, eds. *Soviet Social Problems.* Boulder, Colorado: Westview Press, 1991.

Klatt, Martin. "Russians in the 'Near Abroad,'" *RFE/RL Research Report* [Munich], 3, No. 32, August 19, 1994, 3–44.

Kozlov, Viktor. "Social and Geographical Analysis of the Flow and Territorial Distribution of Refugees and Migrants in Russia." Pages 39–59 in Klaus Segbers and Stephan De Spiegeleire, eds., *Post-Soviet Puzzles: Mapping the Political Economy of the Former Soviet Union.* Baden-Baden: Nomos, 1995.

Kuz'min, A.T. *Sem'ya na Urale: Demograficheskiye aspekty vybora zhiznennogo puti* (The Family in the Urals: Demographic Aspects of Lifestyle Choices). Yekaterinburg: UIF Nauka, 1993.

Loescher, Gil. "Forced Migration Within and from the Former USSR: The Policy Changes Ahead," *Rand DRU–564–FF,* 1993.

Lydolph, Paul E. *Geography of the U.S.S.R.* New York: John Wiley and Sons, 1964.

Marnie, Sheila, and Wendy Slater. "Russia's Refugees," *RFE/RL Research Report* [Munich], 2, No. 37, September 17, 1993, 46–53.

Morvant, Penny. "Alarm over Falling Life Expectancy," *Transition* [Prague], 1, No. 21, October 20, 1995, 40–45.

National Geographic Society. *National Geographic Atlas of the World.* 6th ed. Washington: 1992.

Novaya Rossiya '94: Informatsionno-statisticheskiy al'manakh. Moscow: Vsya Moskva, 1994.

Organisation for Economic Co-operation and Development. *OECD Economic Surveys: The Russian Federation 1995.* Paris:1995.

Peterson, D.J. *Troubled Lands: The Legacy of Soviet Environmental Destruction.* Boulder, Colorado: Westview Press, 1993.

Pisareva, Vera. "Ekologicheskaya problematika v rossiyskoy politike" (Ecological Problems in Russian Politics). Pages 53–62 in Institut gumanitarno-politicheskikh issledovaniy. *Ocherki rossiyskoy politiki* (Essays on Russian Politics). Moscow: 1994.

Popper, Steven W. "A Note on the Emigration of Russia's Technical Elite," *Rand Reprints,* No. 304, 1994.

Population Reference Bureau. *1995 Population Data Sheet.* Washington: 1995.

"Report on the State of the Environment in the Russian Federation in 1993." Foreign Broadcast Information Service, *JPRS Report: Environmental Issues,* April 17, 1995.

Rowland, Richard H. "Declining Towns in the Former USSR," *Post-Soviet Geography,* 35, No. 6, June 1994, 352–65.

Russia. Committee on Land Resources and Utilization. *Zemlya Rossii 1995: Problemy, tsifry, kommentarii.* Moscow: 1996.

Russia and Eurasia: Facts and Figures Annual 1994. Ed., Theodore W. Karasik. Gulf Breeze, Florida: Academic International Press, 1994.

Russian Regions Today: Atlas of the New Federation. Washington: International Center, 1994.

"Russia's Wildlife Faces Grave Danger," *World Wildlife Fund Focus,* 17, No. 5, September–October 1995, 1.

Segbers, Klaus, and Stephan De Spiegeleire, eds. *Post-Soviet Puzzles: Mapping the Political Economy of the Former Soviet Union.* Baden-Baden: Nomos, 1995.

Slater, Wendy. "The Problem of Immigration into Russia," *RFE/RL Research Report* [Munich], 3, No. 26, July 1, 1994, 39–44.

The Statesman's Year-Book 1993-1994. Ed., Brian Hunter. New York: St. Martin's Press, 1993.

The Statesman's Year-Book 1994–1995. Ed., Brian Hunter. New York: St. Martin's Press, 1994.

The Statesman's Year-Book 1995–1996. Ed., Brian Hunter. New York: St. Martin's Press, 1995.

Union of Soviet Socialist Republics. Gosudarstvennyy komitet po statistike. *Demograficheskiy yezegodnik SSSR 1990* (DemographicYearbook of the USSR 1990). Moscow: Finansy i statistika, 1990.

Union of Soviet Socialist Republics. Gosudarstvennyy komitet po statistike. Informatsionno-izdatel'skiy tsentr. *Natsional'nyy sostav naseleniya SSSR* (The National Composition of the Population of the USSR). Moscow: Finansy i statistika, 1990.

United Nations. Department for Economic and Social Information and Policy Analysis. *Demographic Yearbook 1993.* New York: 1995.

United States. Central Intelligence Agency. *USSR: Demographic Trends and Ethnic Balance in the Non-Russian Republics.* Washington: 1990.

United States. Central Intelligence Agency. *The World Factbook 1995.* Washington: 1995.

Velkoff, Victoria A., and Kevin Kinsella. *Aging in Eastern Europe and the Former Soviet Union.* Washington: Department of Commerce, Bureau of the Census, 1993.

Wolfson, Zeyev. *The Geography of Survival.* London: M.E. Sharpe, 1994.

World Bank. *Environmental Action Program for Central and Eastern Europe.* Washington: 1993.

World Bank. *Statistical Handbook 1995: States of the Former USSR.* Washington: 1995.

"The Year of Chernobyl: Some Environmental and Social Aspects of the Disaster," *Environmental Policy Review,* 1, No. 6, June 1987, 1–11.

(Various issues of the following periodicals also were used in the preparation of this chapter: *Christian Science Monitor;* Foreign Broadcast Information Service, *Daily Report: Central Eurasia; Izvestiya* [Moscow]; *New York Times;* and *Washington Post.*)

Chapter 4

Akiner, Shirin. *Islamic Peoples of the Soviet Union.* 2d ed. London: Routledge and Kegan Paul, 1986.

Bennigsen, Alexandre, Marie Broxup, and S. Enders Wimbush. *Muslims of the Soviet Empire: A Guide.* Bloomington: Indiana University Press, 1992.

Billington, James H. "The Case for Orthodoxy," *New Republic*, 210, No. 22, May 30, 1994, 24–27.

Billington, James H. *The Icon and the Axe: An Interpretive History of Russian Culture.* New York: Knopf, 1966.

Birch, Julian. "Ossetia: A Caucasian Bosnia in Microcosm," *Central Asian Survey*, 14, No. 1, 1995, 43–74.

Bourdeaux, Michael. "Glasnost and the Gospel: The Emergence of Religious Pluralism." Pages 113–28 in Michael Bourdeaux, ed., *The Politics of Religion in Russia and the New States of Eurasia.* Armonk, New York: M.E. Sharpe, 1995.

Bourdeaux, Michael, ed. *The Politics of Religion in Russia and the New States of Eurasia.* Armonk, New York: M.E. Sharpe, 1995.

Brown, Edward J. *Russian Literature since the Revolution.* 2d ed. London: Collier-Macmillan, 1969.

Bruk, Solomon Il'ich. *Ethnodemographic Processes: The World Population at the Threshold of the 21st Century.* Moscow: Nauka, 1986.

Buttino, Marco. *In a Collapsing Empire: Underdevelopment, Ethnic Conflicts, and Nationalism in the Soviet Union.* Milan: Feltrinelli Editore, 1993.

Chaplin, Vsevolod. "The Church and Politics in Contemporary Russia." Pages 95–112 in Michael Bourdeaux, ed., *The Politics of Religion in Russia and the New States of Eurasia.* Armonk, New York: M.E. Sharpe, 1995.

Chinyaeva, Elena. "The Fate of Soviet Mass Culture in Russia," *Transition* [Prague], 2, No. 6, March 22, 1996, 22–25.

Chinyaeva, Elena. "Russian Orthodox Church Forges a New Role," *Transition* [Prague], 2, No. 7, April 5, 1996, 10–15.

Dannreuther, Roland. "Creating New States in Central Asia," *Adelphi Papers*, No. 288, March 1994.

Dawisha, Karen, and Bruce Parrott. *Russia and the New States of Eurasia: The Politics of Upheaval.* Cambridge: Cambridge University Press, 1995.

Dunlop, John B. "The Russian Orthodox Church as an 'Empire-Saving' Institution." Pages 15–40 in Michael Bourdeaux, ed., *The Politics of Religion in Russia and the New States of Eurasia.* Armonk, New York: M.E. Sharpe, 1995.

Eastern Europe and the Commonwealth of Independent States 1997.
London: Europa, 1996.

Fuller, Elizabeth. "Chechen Politics: A Murky Prospect, *Transition* [Prague], 1, No. 6, March 15, 1995, 11–13.

Gibson, James L. "Understandings of Anti-Semitism in Russia: An Analysis of the Politics of Anti-Jewish Attitudes, *Slavic Review,* 53, No. 3, Fall 1994, 796–835.

Griffiths, Stephen Iwan. "Nationalism and Ethnic Conflict: Threats to European Security," *SIPRI Research Reports* [Stockholm], No. 5, 1993.

Gulevsky, Alexander, and Yuri Simchenko. *Administrative Units of Peoples of the Russian North: Economy and Social Development in the Last Decade of the 20th Century.* Moscow: Rossiyskaya akademiya nauk, Institut etnologii i antropologii, 1994.

Guroff, Gregory, and Alexander Guroff. "The Paradox of Russian National Identity." Pages 78–100 in Roman Szporluk, ed., *National Identity and Ethnicity in Russia and the New States of Eurasia.* Armonk, New York: M.E. Sharpe, 1994.

Hanbury-Tennison, Robin. "Native Peoples of Russia's Far East," *Asian Affairs,* 25, June 1994, 131–38.

Harris, Chauncey D. "The New Russian Minorities: A Statistical Overview," *Post-Soviet Geography,* 34, No. 1, January 1994, 1–27.

Heleniak, Tim. "The Projected Population of Russia in 2005," *Post-Soviet Geography,* 35, No. 10, October 1995, 608–14.

Henze, Paul B. "Ethnic Dynamics and Dilemmas of the Russian Republic," *Studies in Conflict and Terrorism,* 17, January–March 1994, 61–86.

Hughes, Robert P., and Irina Paperno, eds. *Russian Culture in Modern Times.* Berkeley: University of California Press, 1994.

Israel. Central Bureau of Statistics. *Immigrant Population from Former USSR 1993: Demographic Trends.* Jerusalem: 1995.

Kaiser, Robert J. "Ethnoterritorial Conflict in the Former Soviet Union." Pages 59–73 in United States, Central Intelligence Agency, *The Challenge of Ethnic Conflict to National and International Order in the 1990s: Geographic Perspectives.* Washington: 1995.

Kaiser, Robert J. *The Geography of Nationalism in Russia and the USSR.* Princeton: Princeton University Press, 1994.

Katz, Zev, ed. *Handbook of Major Soviet Nationalities*. New York: Free Press, 1975.

Kolosov, Vladimir Aleksandrovich. *Ethno-Territorial Conflicts and Boundaries in the Former Soviet Union*. Durham, United Kingdom: University of Durham, 1992.

Krag, Helen, and Lars Funch. *The North Caucasus: Minorities at a Crossroads*. Brixton, United Kingdom: Minority Rights Group, 1994.

Lemon, Alaina. "In Russia, a Community Divided," *Transition* [Prague], 1, No. 7, March 29, 1995, 12–18.

Mickiewicz, Ellen. "Ethnic Differentiation and Political Communication." Pages 24–38 in Anthony Jones, Walter D. Connor, and David E. Powell, eds., *Soviet Social Problems*. Boulder, Colorado: Westview Press, 1991.

Nahaylo, Bohdan, and Viktor Swoboda. *Soviet Disunion: A History of the Nationalities Problem in the USSR*. London: Hamish Hamilton, 1990.

Neroznak, V.P., ed. *Krasnaya kniga yazykov narodov Rossii: Entsiklopedicheskiy slovar'-spravochnik* (The Red Book of Languages of the Peoples of Russia: An Encyclopedic Dictionary and Directory). Moscow: Akademiya, 1994.

Novaya Rossiya '94: Informatsionno-statisticheskiy al'manakh. Moscow: Vsya Moskva, 1994.

Organisation for Economic Co-operation and Development. *OECD Economic Surveys: The Russian Federation 1995*. Paris: 1995.

Pospielovskiy, Dimitry V. "The Russian Orthodox Church in the Postcommunist CIS." Pages 41–74 in Michael Bourdeaux, ed., *The Politics of Religion in Russia and the New States of Eurasia*. Armonk, New York: M.E. Sharpe, 1995.

Russia and Eurasia: Facts and Figures Annual 1994. Ed., Theodore W. Karasik. Gulf Breeze, Florida: Academic International Press, 1994.

"Russia and Islam: Is Russia Threatened by Islamic Resurgence?" *Central Asia Brief* [Markfield, United Kingdom], 11, No. 3, March 1995, 11–14.

"Russian Aggression Strengthens Muslim Identity in Chechnya," *Central Asia Brief* [Markfield, United Kingdom], 11, No. 3, March 1995, 3–9.

Russian Regions Today: Atlas of the New Federation. Washington: International Center, 1994.

Ryan, Michael, comp. *Social Trends in Contemporary Russia: A Statistical Source Book.* New York: St. Martin's Press, 1993.

Saikal, Amin, and William Maley, eds. *Russia in Search of Its Future.* Cambridge: Cambridge University Press, 1995.

Sakwa, Richard. *Russian Politics and Society.* New York: Routledge, 1993.

Sawczak, Peter. "Reconstruction, Deconstruction, and the Restoration of Literature in Russia." Pages 178–89 in Amin Saikal and William Maley, eds., *Russia in Search of Its Future.* Cambridge: Cambridge University Press, 1995.

Segel, Harold B., ed. *The Literature of Eighteenth-Century Russia: A History and Anthology.* New York: E.P. Dutton, 1967.

Serebriany, Sergei. "Culture in Russia and Russian Culture." Pages 158–77 in Amin Saikal and William Maley, eds., *Russia in Search of Its Future.* Cambridge: Cambridge University Press, 1995.

Slonim, Marc. *The Epic of Russian Literature from Its Roots Through Tolstoy.* New York: Oxford University Press, 1964.

Smeets, Rieks. "Circassia," *Central Asian Survey,* 14, No. 1, 1995, 107–25.

Szporluk, Roman, ed. *National Identity and Ethnicity in Russia and the New States of Eurasia.* Armonk, New York: M.E. Sharpe, 1994.

Teague, Elizabeth. "Center-Periphery Relations in the Russian Federation." Pages 21–57 in Roman Szporluk, ed., *National Identity and Ethnicity in Russia and the New States of Eurasia.* Armonk, New York: M.E. Sharpe, 1994.

Teague, Elizabeth. "Russia and Tatarstan Sign Power-Sharing Treaty," *RFE/RL Research Report* [Munich], 3, No. 14, April 8, 1994, 19–27.

Union of Soviet Socialist Republics. Gosudarstvennyy komitet po statistike. *Natsional'nyy sostav naseleniya SSSR* (The National Composition of the Population of the USSR). Moscow: Finansy i statistika, 1990.

United States. Central Intelligence Agency. *The Challenge of Ethnic Conflict to National and International Order in the 1990s: Geographic Perspectives.* Washington: 1995.

United States. Central Intelligence Agency. *USSR: Demographic Trends and Ethnic Balance in the Non-Russian Republics.* Washington: 1990.

United States. Central Intelligence Agency. *The World Factbook 1995.* Washington: 1995.

World Bank. *Statistical Handbook 1994: States of the Former USSR.* Washington: 1995.

Zenkovsky, Serge A., ed. *Medieval Russia's Epics, Chronicles, and Tales.* New York: E.P. Dutton, 1963.

Zhukovskaya, Natalya L. "Religion and Ethnicity in Eastern Russia, Republic of Buryatiya: A Panorama of the 1990s, *Central Asian Survey,* 14, No. 1, 1995, 25–42.

Chapter 5

Acton, Edward. *Russia: The Tsarist and Soviet Legacy.* 2d ed. London: Longman, 1995.

Balzer, Harley. "Plans to Reform Russian Higher Education." Pages 27–46 in Anthony Jones, ed., *Education and Society in the New Russia.* Armonk, New York: M.E. Sharpe, 1993.

Belyanko, O.Ye., and L.B. Trushina. *Russkiye s pervogo vzglyada: chto prinyato i chto ne prinyato u russkikh* (The Russians at First Glance: What Is Acceptable and Not Acceptable for the Russians). Moscow: Russkiy yazyk kursy, 1994.

Bodrova, Valentina. "Reproductive Behaviour of Russia's Population in the Transition Period," *Berichte des Bundesinstituts für ostwissenschaftliche und internationale Studien* [Cologne], 15, 1995.

Bodrova, Valentina. "The Russian Family in Flux, *Transition* [Prague], 1, No. 16, September 8, 1995, 10–11.

Bremer, Ian, and Ray Taras, eds. *Nations and Politics in the Soviet Successor States.* Cambridge: Cambridge University Press, 1993.

Buckley, Mary. *Redefining Russian Society and Polity.* Boulder, Colorado: Westview Press, 1993.

Center for International Health Information. *Russia: USAID Health Profile.* Arlington, Virginia: 1992.

Davis, Christopher M. "Health Care Crisis: The Former Soviet Union," *RFE/RL Research Report* [Munich], 2, No. 40, October 8, 1993, 38.

Dawisha, Karen, and Bruce Parrott. *Russia and the New States of Eurasia: The Politics of Upheaval.* Cambridge: Cambridge University Press, 1994.

Delpla, Jacques, and Charles Wyplosz. "The Increase in Death and Disease under Katastroika," *Cambridge Journal of Economics* [Cambridge], No. 18, 1994, 329–55.

The Europa World Year-Book 1994, 2. London: Europa, 1994.

The Europa World Year-Book 1995, 2. London: Europa, 1995.

"The Feministki Are Coming," *Economist* [London], 336, No. 7927, August 12, 1995, 44–45.

Feshbach, Murray, ed. *Environmental and Health Atlas of Russia.* Moscow: Paims, 1995.

Fong, Monica S. *The Role of Women in Rebuilding the Russian Economy.* Washington: World Bank, 1993.

Friedgut, Theodore, and Jeffrey Hahn, eds. *Local Power and Post-Soviet Politics.* Armonk, New York: M.E. Sharpe, 1994.

Gerhart, Genevra. *The Russian's World: Life and Language.* New York: Harcourt Brace Jovanovich, 1974.

Guermanovich, Alexei. "Drugs Join Alcohol as Bane to Russian Society," *Christian Science Monitor,* 87, No. 218, October 5, 1995, 1.

Heritage Foundation. *Crime and Corruption in Eurasia: A Threat to Democracy and International Security.* Washington: 1995.

Jones, Anthony. "The Educational Legacy of the Soviet Period." Pages 3–21 in Anthony Jones, ed., *Education and Society in the New Russia.* Armonk, New York: M.E. Sharpe, 1993.

Jones, Anthony, ed. *Education and Society in the New Russia.* Armonk, New York: M.E. Sharpe, 1993.

Kerr, Stephen T. "Diversification in Russian Education." Pages 47–73 in Anthony Jones, ed., *Education and Society in the New Russia.* Armonk, New York: M.E. Sharpe, 1993.

Kon, Igor. *The Sexual Revolution in Russia: From the Age of the Tsars to Today.* Trans., James Riordan. New York: Free Press, 1995.

Kuz'min, A.T. *Sem'ya na Urale: Demograficheskiye aspekty vybora zhiznennogo puti* (The Family in the Urals: Demographic Aspects of Lifestyle Choices). Yekaterinburg: UIF Nauka, 1993.

Leighton, Marian. *Almanac of Russian Politics: Members of the Federal Assembly of the Russian Federation.* Washington: International Republican Institute, 1995.

Mezentseva, Elena. *The System of Gender Protection for Women.* Moscow: Center for Gender Studies, 1992.

Mezentseva, Elena. *Women and Social Policy.* Moscow: Center for Gender Studies, 1992.

Morvant, Penny. "Alarm over Falling Life Expectancy," *Transition* [Prague], 1, No. 21, October 20, 1995, 40–45.

Morvant, Penny. "Bearing the 'Double Burden' in Russia," *Transition* [Prague], 1, No. 18, September 8, 1995, 4–9.

Morvant, Penny. "Compromise Reached on New AIDS Legislation," *Transition* [Prague], 1, No. 11, May 26, 1995.

Nizsky, Vadim. "The Russian Needle," *New Times,* September 1994, 60–61.

Non-Military Aspects of International Security. Paris: UNESCO and Presses Universitaires de France, 1995.

Novaya Rossiya '94: Informatsionno-statisticheskiy al'manakh. Moscow: Vsya Moskva, 1994.

Organisation for Economic Co-operation and Development. *OECD Economic Surveys: The Russian Federation 1995.* Paris: 1995.

Pilkington, Hilary. *Russia's Youth and Its Culture: A Nation's Constructors and Constructed.* London: Routledge, 1994.

Puffer, Sheila M. "Education for Management in a New Economy. Pages 171–85 in Anthony Jones, ed., *Education and Society in the New Russia.* Armonk, New York: M.E. Sharpe, 1993.

Rancour-Laferriere, Daniel. *The Slave Soul of Russia: Moral Masochism and the Cult of Suffering.* New York: New York University Press, 1995.

Rhodes, Mark. "Religious Believers in Russia," *RFE/RL Research Report* [Munich], 1, No. 14, April 3, 1992, 60–64.

Richmond, Yale. *From Nyet to Da: Understanding the Russians.* Yarmouth, Maine: Intercultural Press, 1992.

Russia. Committee on Land Resources and Utilization. *Zemlya Rossii 1995: Problemy, tsifry, kommentarii.* Moscow: 1996.

Russia and Eurasia: Facts and Figures Annual 1994. Ed., Theodore W. Karasik. Gulf Breeze, Florida: Academic International Press, 1994.

Russian Business Agency et al. *Russia 1994–95: Business, Social, Economic Analytical Profile, 2–3.* Ed., Yuri V. Volkov. Moscow: Russian Business Agency, 1994

Ryan, Michael, comp. *Social Trends in Contemporary Russia: A Statistical Source Book.* New York: St. Martin's Press, 1993.

Shlapentokh, Vladimir. "Early Feudalism—The Best Parallel for Contemporary Russia," *Europe-Asia Studies,* 48, No. 3, 1996, 393–411.

Smith, Julia. *Housing Reform in Russia: Slow but Certain.* Washington: Woodrow Wilson Center, 1995.

Solomon, Andrew. "Young Russia's Defiant Decadence," *New York Times Magazine,* July 18, 1993, 16–23.

The Statesman's Year-Book 1993–1994. Ed., Brian Hunter. New York: St. Martin's Press, 1993.

The Statesman's Year-Book 1994–1995. Ed., Brian Hunter. New York: St. Martin's Press, 1994.

The Statesman's Year-Book 1995–1996. Ed., Brian Hunter. New York: St. Martin's Press, 1995.

Tolz, Vera. "Thorny Road Toward Federalism in Russia," *RFE/RL Research Report* [Munich], 2, No. 48, December 3, 1993, 1–8.

United States. Central Intelligence Agency. *The World Factbook 1994.* Washington: 1994.

United States. Central Intelligence Agency. *The World Factbook 1995.* Washington: 1995.

Vovchenko, Olga. *The Status of Women in Russia.* Moscow: Center for Social Protection of Children and Families and Demographic Policy, 1992.

World Bank. *Poverty in Russia: An Assessment.* Washington: 1995.

World Bank. *Russia, Housing Reform and Privatization: Strategy and Transition Issues.* Washington: 1995.

World Bank. *Russia: Social Protection During Transition and Beyond.* Washington: 1995.

World Bank. *Statistical Handbook 1995: States of the Former USSR.* Washington: 1995.

(Various issues of the following periodicals also were used in the preparation of this chapter: *Christian Science Monitor;* Foreign Broadcast Information Service, *Daily Report: Central Eurasia;* Jamestown Foundation, *Monitor; New York Times; Prism;* and *Washington Post.*)

Chapter 6

Aslund, Anders. *How Russia Became a Market Economy.* Washington: Brookings Institution, 1995.

Aslund, Anders, ed. *Economic Transformation in Russia.* London: Pinter, 1994.

Boycko, Maksim, Andrei Schleifer, and Robert W. Vishny. *Privatizing Russia.* Cambridge: MIT Press, 1995.

Brown, A.N., Barry W. Ickes, and Randi Ryterman. *The Myth of Monopoly: A New View of Industrial Structure in Russia.* Washington: World Bank, 1993.

Campbell, Robert W., ed. *The Postcommunist Economic Transformation: Essays in Honor of Gregory Grossman.* Oxford: Westview Press, 1994.

Campbell, Robert W., ed. "The Russian Telecommunications Sector: A Status Report," *PlanEcon Report,* 11, Nos. 26–27, September 14, 1995.

Cooper, William. "Russia: Economic Conditions and the Prospects for Reform." *CRS Report for Congress,* No. 94–406E, 1994.

Economist Intelligence Unit. *Country Report: Russia, 1st Quarter 1996.* London: 1996.

Economist Intelligence Unit. *Country Report: Russia, 2d Quarter 1996.* London: 1996.

Ericson, Richard E. "The Russian Economy since Independence." Pages 37–77 in Gail W. Lapidus, ed., *The New Russia: Troubled Transformation.* Boulder, Colorado: Westview Press, 1995.

The Europa World Year Book 1994, 2. London: Europa, 1994.

The Europa World Year Book 1995, 2. London: Europa, 1995.

Feshbach, Murray, and Alfred Friendly, Jr. *Ecocide in the USSR: Health and Nature under Siege.* New York: Basic Books, 1992.

Fortescue, Stephen. "Privatisation of Large-Scale Russian Industry." Pages 85–100 in Amin Saikal and William Maley, eds., *Russia in Search of Its Future.* Cambridge: Cambridge University Press, 1995.

Frenkl, William G., and Michael Y. Sukhman. "New Foreign Investment Regimes of Russia and the Other Republics of the Former U.S.S.R.: A Legislative Analysis and Historical

Perspective," *Boston College International Comparative Law Review,* 16, Summer 1993, 321–423.

Gavrilenkov, Evgeny, and Vincent Koen. "How Large Was the Output Collapse in Russia?" International Monetary Fund Research Department Working Paper 94/154. Washington: 1994.

Granville, Brigitte, and Judith Shapiro. "Russian Inflation: A Statistical Pandora's Box," *Royal Institute of International Affairs Discussion Paper* [London], No. 53, 1994.

Grossman, Gregory. "The Second Economy in the USSR," *Problems of Communism,* 26, September 5, 1977, 25–40.

Grossman, Gregory. *Soviet Statistics of Physical Output of Industrial Commodities.* Princeton: Princeton University Press, 1960.

Hanson, Philip. "Structural Change in the Russian Economy," *Transition* [Prague], 2, No. 2, January 26, 1996, 18–21.

Hewett, Edward A. *Open for Business: Russia's Return to the Global Economy.* Washington: Brookings Institution, 1992.

Hewett, Edward A. *Reforming the Soviet Economy.* Washington: Brookings Institution, 1988.

Holt, Jane. *Transport Strategies for the Russian Federation.* Washington: World Bank, 1993.

Interflo. *Special Statistical Supplement: U.S. Trade with the Former Soviet Republics.* Maplewood, New Jersey: 1994.

International Monetary Fund. *Economic Review: Russian Federation 1993.* Washington: 1993.

International Monetary Fund. *Economic Review: Russian Federation 1994.* Washington: 1994.

International Monetary Fund. *Economic Review: Russian Federation 1995.* Washington: 1995.

International Monetary Fund, World Bank, Organisation for Economic Co-operation and Development, and European Bank for Reconstruction and Development. *A Study of the Soviet Economy.* Washington: World Bank, 1991.

Koen, Vincent, and Steven Philips. "Price Liberalization in Russia: Behavior of Prices, Household Incomes, and Consumption During the First Year," International Monetary Fund, *Occasional Paper,* No. 104, 1993.

Kontorovich, Vladimir. "Imperial Legacy and the Transformation of the Russian Economy," *Transition* [Prague], 2, No. 17, August 23, 1996, 22–25.

Kurtzweg, Laura. "Trends in Soviet Gross National Product." Pages 126–65 in United States, 1st Session, 100th Congress, Joint Economic Committee. *Gorbachev's Economic Plans.* Washington: GPO, 1987.

Lapidus, Gail W., ed. *The New Russia: Troubled Transformation.* Boulder, Colorado: Westview Press, 1995.

Lazear, Edward, ed. *Lessons of Economic Reform in Eastern Europe and the Former Soviet Union.* Stanford: Hoover Institution Press, 1995.

Lemon, Alaina. "Making Ends Meet in Moscow," *Transition* [Prague], 2, No. 9, May 3, 1996, 48–51.

Liefert, William, David Sedik, and Christian Foster. "Progress in Agricultural Reform," *Transition* [Prague], 1, No. 16, September 8, 1995, 50–52.

Maley, William. "The Shape of the Russian Macroeconomy." Pages 48–65 in Amin Saikal and William Maley, eds., *Russia in Search of Its Future.* Cambridge: Cambridge University Press, 1995.

Michalopoulos, Constantine, and David Tarr, eds. *Trade in the New Independent States.* (World Bank Studies of Economies in Transformation, No. 13.) Washington: World Bank, 1994.

Millar, James R. "From Utopian Socialism to Utopian Capitalism: The Failure of Revolution and Reform in Post-Soviet Russia," *Problems of Post-Communism,* May–June 1995, 7–14.

Miller, Robert F. "Reforming Russian Agriculture: Privatisation in Comparative Perspective." Pages 66–84 in Amin Saikal and William Maley, eds., *Russia in Search of Its Future.* Cambridge: Cambridge University Press, 1995.

Morvant, Penny, and Peter Rutland. "Russian Workers Face the Market," *Transition,* 2, No. 13, June 28, 1996, 6–15.

Novaya Rossiya '94: Informatsionno-statisticheskiy al'manakh. Moscow: Vsya Moskva, 1994.

Nove, Alec. *The Soviet Economic System.* London: George Allen and Unwin, 1990.

Organisation for Economic Co-operation and Development. *Agricultural Policies, Market and Trade in the Central and Eastern European Countries, Selected New Independent States of the Former Soviet Union, Mongolia, and China: Monitoring and Outlook for 1995.* Paris: 1995.

Organisation for Economic Co-operation and Development. *OECD Economic Surveys: The Russian Federation 1995*. Paris: 1995.

Organisation for Economic Co-operation and Development. International Energy Agency. *Energy Policies of the Russian Federation: 1995 Survey*. Paris: 1995.

Osakowe, Christopher. "Navigating the Minefields of Russian Joint Venture Law and Tax Regulations: A Procedural Compass," *Vanderbilt Journal of Transnational Law*, 25, February 1993, 799–879.

PlanEcon. *Review and Outlook for the Former Soviet Republics*. Washington: 1996.

Russia. Committee on Land Resources and Utilization. *Zemlya Rossii 1995: Problemy, tsifry, kommentarii*. Moscow: 1996.

Russian Business Agency et al. *Russia 1994–95: Business, Social, Economic Analytical Profile, 2–3*. Ed., Yuri V. Volkov. Moscow: Russian Business Agency, 1994.

Russian Union of Industrialists and Entrepreneurs. Expert Institute. *Russia's Regions in Transition*. Moscow: 1994.

Rutland, Peter. "Firms Trapped Between the Past and the Future," *Transition* [Prague], 2, No. 6, March 22, 1996, 26–32.

Rutland, Peter. "Russia's Energy Empire under Strain," *Transition* [Prague], 2, No. 9, May 3, 1996, 6–11.

Rutland, Peter. "Russia's Natural Gas Leviathan," *Transition* [Prague], 2, No. 9, May 3, 1996, 12–13.

Sachs, Jeffrey. "Prospects for Monetary Stabilization in Russia." Pages 32–58 in Anders Aslund, ed., *Economic Transformation in Russia*. London: Pinter, 1994.

Saikal, Amin, and William Maley, eds. *Russia in Search of Its Future*. Cambridge: Cambridge University Press, 1995.

The Statesman's Year-Book 1993–1994. Ed., Brian Hunter. New York: St. Martin's Press, 1993.

The Statesman's Year-Book 1994–1995. Ed., Brian Hunter. New York: St. Martin's Press, 1994.

The Statesman's Year-Book 1995–1996. Ed., Brian Hunter. New York: St. Martin's Press, 1995.

Strong, John, and John R. Meyer. *Moving to Market: Restructuring Transport in the Former Soviet Union*. Cambridge: Harvard Institute for International Development, 1995.

United States. Central Intelligence Agency. *Handbook of International Economic Statistics 1995*. Washington: 1995.

United States. Central Intelligence Agency. *Russia: An Economic Profile*. Washington: 1994.

United States. Central Intelligence Agency. *The World Factbook 1994*. Washington: 1994.

United States. Central Intelligence Agency. *The World Factbook 1995*. Washington: 1995.

United States. Department of Agriculture. *International Agriculture and Trade Reports: Former USSR*. Washington: 1995.

United States-Russia Business Council. *A U.S.-Russia Business Council Mid-year Report*. Washington: 1995.

Van Atta, Don. "Yeltsin Decree Finally Ends 'Second Serfdom' in Russia," *RFE/RL Research Report* [Munich], 2, No. 46, November 19, 1993, 33–39.

Wallich, Christine. *Fiscal Decentralisation, Intergovernmental Relations in Russia*. (World Bank Studies of Economies in Transformation, No. 6.) Washington: World Bank, 1992.

Wallich, Christine, ed. *Russia and the Challenge of Fiscal Federalism*. Washington: World Bank, 1994.

WEFA Group. *Eurasia Economic Outlook, February 1996*. Eddystone, Pennsylvania: 1996.

Werner, Klaus. "Russia's Foreign Trade and the Economic Reforms," *Intereconomics*, 28, May–June 1993, 144–52.

Wertman, Patricia. "Rescheduling Russia's Debt: A Status Report," *CRS Report for Congress*, No. 95–856 E, 1995.

Wertman, Patricia. "Russian Economic Reform and the IMF: Mission Impossible?" *CRS Issue Brief*, No. 92128, 1994.

Wertman, Patricia. "Russia's Other Debt Problem: Enterprise Debt and Why It's Important," *CRS Report for Congress*, 93–255E, 1993.

White, Stephen. *After Gorbachev*. Cambridge: Cambridge University Press, 1993.

World Bank. *Food and Agricultural Policy Reforms in the Former U.S.S.R.* Washington: 1992.

World Bank. *Russia: Joining the World Economy*. Washington: 1993.

World Bank. *Russian Federation: Toward Medium-Term Viability*. Washington: 1996.

World Bank. *Statistical Handbook 1995: States of the Former USSR.* Washington: 1995.

World Bank and Russia, Gosudarstvennyy komitet po statistike. *Russian Federation: Report on the National Accounts.* Washington: World Bank, 1995.

Yergin, Daniel, and Thane Gustafson. *Russia 2010 and What It Means for the World.* New York: Random House, 1993.

(Various issues of the following periodicals also were used in the preparation of this chapter: *Christian Science Monitor;* Foreign Broadcast Information Service, *Daily Report: Central Eurasia* and *Daily Report: Central Eurasia Economic Review;* Jamestown Foundation, *Monitor; New York Times; Prism;* and *Washington Post.*)

Chapter 7

Afanasyev, Yuri. "Russian Reform Is Dead: Back to Central Planning," *Foreign Affairs,* 73, No. 2, March–April 1994, 21–26.

Amnesty International. *Amnesty International Report 1995.* New York: 1995.

Aslund, Anders. "Russia's Success Story," *Foreign Affairs,* 73, No. 5, September–October 1994, 58–71.

Barner-Barry, Carol, and Cynthia A. Hody. *The Politics of Change: The Transformation of the Former Soviet Union.* New York: St. Martin's Press, 1995.

Belin, Laura. "Wrestling Political and Financial Repression," *Transition* [Prague], 1, No. 18, October 6, 1995, 59–63.

Brown, Archie. "Political Leadership in Post-Communist Russia." Pages 28–46 in Amin Saikal and William Maley, eds., *Russia in Search of Its Future.* Cambridge: Cambridge University Press, 1995.

Busygina-Thaenert, Irina. "Russia: Difficulties in Establishing a Federation," *Aussenpolitik* [Bonn], No. 3, 1995, 253–70.

Clark, Susan L., and David R. Graham. "The Russian Federation's Fight for Survival," *Orbis,* 39, No. 3, Summer 1995, 329–51.

Colton, Timothy J., and Robert Legvold, eds. *After the Soviet Union: From Empire to Nation.* New York: Norton, 1992.

Colton, Timothy J., and Robert C. Tucker, eds. *Patterns in Post-Soviet Leadership.* Boulder, Colorado: Westview Press, 1995.

Davidova, Alla. "Russia's No. 1 Manager," *Prism*, 2, No. 11, Pt. 4, May 31, 1996.

Dawisha, Karen, and Bruce Parrott. *Russia and the New States of Eurasia: The Politics of Upheaval.* Cambridge: Cambridge University Press, 1995.

Fish, M. Steven. *Democracy from Scratch: Opposition and Regime in the New Russian Revolution.* Princeton: Princeton University Press, 1995.

Friedgut, Theodore H., and Jeffrey W. Hahn, eds. *Local Power and Post-Soviet Politics.* Armonk, New York: M.E. Sharpe, 1994.

Goldman, Stuart. "Russia's New Parliament," *CRS Report for Congress*, 94–844F, October 31, 1994.

Gualtieri, Dominic. "Russia's New 'War of Laws,'" *RFE/RL Research Report* [Munich], 2, No. 35, September 3, 1993, 10–15.

Hahn, Jeffrey W., ed. *Democratization in Russia: The Development of Legislative Institutions.* Armonk, New York: M.E. Sharpe, 1996.

Henze, Paul B. "Ethnic Dynamics and Dilemmas of the Russian Republic," *Studies in Conflict and Terrorism*, 17, January–March 1994, 61–86.

Holden, Gerard. *Russia after the Cold War: History and the Nation in Post-Soviet Security Politics.* Boulder, Colorado: Westview Press, 1994.

"How Many Other Chechnyas?" *Economist* [London], 334, No. 33, January 14, 1995, 43–45.

Ingwerson, Marshall. "In Term No. 2, Yeltsin Struggles to Patch Up a Torn Democracy," *Christian Science Monitor*, 88, No. 180, August 12, 1996, 1.

Kirkow, Peter. "Regional Warlordism in Russia: The Case of Primorskiy Krai," *Europe-Asia Studies*, 47, September 1995, 923–47.

Lynch, Allen. "Politics Without Government," *Transition* [Prague], 1, No. 1, February 15, 1995, 2–4.

Malik, Hafeez. "Tatarstan's Treaty with Russia: Autonomy or Independence," *Journal of South Asian and Middle Eastern Studies*, 18, Winter 1994, 1–36.

McFaul, Michael. "Why Russia's Politics Matters," *Foreign Affairs*, 74, No. 1, January–February 1995, 87–99.

McFaul, Michael, et al. "Russia Symposium: Is Russian Democracy Doomed?" *Journal of Democracy*, 5, April 1994, 4–41.

Millar, James R. "From Utopian Socialism to Utopian Capitalism: The Failure of Revolution and Reform in Post-Soviet Russia," *Problems of Post-Communism*, May–June 1995, 7–14.

Moses, Joel. "Soviet Provincial Politics in an Era of Transition and Revolution, 1989–1991," *Soviet Studies*, 44, No. 3, 1992, 479–509.

Nichol, James P. "The Russian Federation: Will It Hold Together?" *CRS Report for Congress*, 92–752F, October 6, 1992.

Nichol, James P. "Russian Legislative Elections and Constitutional Referendum: Outcome and Implications for U.S. Interests," *CRS Report for Congress*, 93–456F, January 7, 1994.

Nichol, James P. "Russia's Civil-Military Relations," *CRS Report for Congress*, 94–631F, July 28, 1994.

Nichol, James P. "Russia's Constitutional Crisis," *CRS Issue Brief*, IB93052, March–June, 1993.

Nichol, James P. "Russia's December 1995 Legislative Elections: Outcome and Implications for U.S. Interests," *CRS Report for Congress*, 96–17F, January 4, 1996.

Nichol, James P. "Russia's Future: Issues and Options for U.S. Policy," *CRS Report for Congress*, 95–1128F, November 15, 1995.

Nichol, James P. "Russia's Presidential Election: Outcome and Implications for U.S. Interests," *CRS Report for Congress*, 96–620F, July 12, 1996.

Nichol, James P. "Russia's Upcoming Presidential Election: Implications for Russia and U.S. Interests," *CRS Report for Congress*, 96–457F, May 20, 1996.

Nichol, James P. "Russia's Violent Showdown: A Chronology of Events, September 21–October 4, 1993," *CRS Report for Congress*, 93–879F, October 5, 1993.

Nichol, James P. "Yeltsin and the Russian Congress of People's Deputies: Outcome and Implications for U.S. Interests," *CRS Report for Congress*, 92–988F, December 30, 1992.

Nogee, Joseph L., and R. Judson Mitchell. *Russian Politics: The Struggle for a New Order.* Boston: Allyn and Bacon, 1996.

Orttung, Robert. "Chechnya: A Painful Price," *Transition* [Prague], 1, No. 3, March 15, 1995, 3–10.

Rahr, Alexander. "The Implications of Russia's Parliamentary Elections," *RFE/Rl Research Report* [Munich], 3, No. 1, January 7, 1994, 32–37.

Rahr, Alexander. "Russia's Future: With or Without Yeltsin," *RFE/RL Research Report* [Munich], 3, No. 17, April 29, 1994, 1–7.

Reese, Andrew. "Democracy in Russia: The December Elections," *Russian Political Review,* December 7, 1993, 1–6.

Russia. President. *Draft Constitution of the Russian Federation Submitted by the Russian Federation President for Nationwide Vote.* Translated in Foreign Broadcast Information Service, *Daily Report: Central Eurasia,* FBIS-SOV–93–216, November 10, 1993, 19–37.

"Russia in Crisis," *The World & I,* 10, May 1995, 22–41.

"Russian Democracy: The Missing Pieces," *Economist* [London], 332, No. 7878, September 3, 1994, 53–54.

Saikal, Amin, and William Maley, eds. *Russia in Search of Its Future.* Cambridge: Cambridge University Press, 1995.

Sakwa, Richard. *Russian Politics and Society.* New York: Routledge, 1993.

Sharlet, Robert. "The New Russian Constitution and Its Political Impact," *Problems of Post-Communism,* January–February 1995, 3–7.

Sharlet, Robert. "The Prospects for Federalism in Russian Constitutional Politics," *Publius,* 24, Spring 1994, 115–27.

Slater, Wendy. "Russia: The Return of Authoritarian Government?" *RFE/RL Research Report* [Munich], 3, No. 1, January 7, 1994, 22–31.

Slater, Wendy, and Vera Tolz. "Yeltsin Wins in Moscow but May Lose to the Regions," *RFE/RL Research Report* [Munich], 2, No. 40, October 8, 1993, 1–7.

Slider, Darrell. "Political Tendencies in Russia's Regions: Evidence from the 1993 Parliamentary Elections," *Slavic Review,* 53, No. 3, Fall 1994, 711–32.

Smith, M.A. *Consolidating the Russian State.* London: Ministry of Defence, 1996.

Solnick, Steven L. "The Breakdown of Hierarchies in the Soviet Union and China: A Neo-institutional Perspective," *World Politics,* 48, January 1996, 209–38.

Staar, Richard F. *The New Military in Russia: Ten Myths That Shape the Image.* Annapolis: Naval Institute Press, 1996.

The Statesman's Year-Book 1993–1994. Ed., Brian Hunter. New York: St. Martin's Press, 1993.

The Statesman's Year-Book 1994–1995. Ed., Brian Hunter. New York: St. Martin's Press, 1994.

The Statesman's Year-Book 1995–1996. Ed., Brian Hunter. New York: St. Martin's Press, 1995.

Teague, Elizabeth. "Russia and Tatarstan Sign Power-Sharing Treaty," *RFE/RL Research Report* [Munich], 3, No. 14, April 1, 1994, 19–27.

Teague, Elizabeth. "Russia's Local Elections Begin," *RFE/RL Research Report* [Munich], 3, No. 7, February 18, 1994, 1–4.

Tolz, Vera. "Problems of Building Democratic Institutions in Russia," *RFE/RL Research Report* [Munich], 3, No. 10, March 4, 1994, 1–7.

Tolz, Vera. "The Shifting Sands of Stabilization," *Transition* [Prague], 1, No. 1, February 15, 1995, 5–8.

Tolz, Vera. "Thorny Road Toward Federalism in Russia," *RFE/RL Research Report* [Munich], 3, No. 48, December 3, 1993, 1–8.

United States. Central Intelligence Agency. *The World Factbook 1994.* Washington: 1994.

United States. Central Intelligence Agency. *The World Factbook 1995.* Washington: 1995.

United States. Congress. Commission on Security and Cooperation in Europe. *Human Rights and Democratization in the Newly Independent States of the Former Soviet Union.* Washington: GPO, 1993.

United States. Department of State. *Country Reports on Human Rights Practices for 1995.* Washington: GPO, 1995.

Urban, Michael. "The Politics of Identity in Russia's Postcommunist Transition: The Nation Against Itself," *Slavic Review,* 53, No. 3, Fall 1994, 733–65.

Voorhees, James C. "Russian Federalism and Reform," *Demokratizatsiya,* 2, Fall 1994, 549–64.

Walker, Edward W. "Federalism Russian Style: The Federation Provisions in Russia's New Constitution," *Problems of Post-Communism,* July–August 1995, 3–12.

Warhola, James W. *Politicized Ethnicity in the Russian Federation: Dilemmas of State Formation.* Lewiston, Maine: Edwin Mellen Press, 1996.

Wedgwood Benn, David. "The Russian Media in Post-Soviet Conditions," *Europe-Asia Studies,* 48, No. 3, 1996, 471–79.

White, Stephen. *After Gorbachev.* Cambridge: Cambridge University Press, 1993.

"Who Runs Russia?" *Economist* [London], 331, No. 7869, June 25, 1994, 47–48.

World Bank. *Russian Federation: Toward Medium-Term Viability.* Washington: 1996.

World Radio TV Handbook 1996. Ed., Andrew G. Sennitt. Amsterdam: Billboard, 1996.

Yasmann, Victor. "Security Services Reorganized: All Power to the Russian President?" *RFE/RL Research Report* [Munich], 3, No. 6, February 11, 1994, 7–14.

Yeltsin, Boris. *The Stuggle for Russia.* New York: Random House, Times Books, 1994.

Yergin, Daniel, and Thane Gustafson. *Russia 2010.* 2d ed. New York: Vintage Books, 1995.

Zelikow, Philip. "Beyond Boris Yeltsin: Following America's Enduring Interests," *Foreign Affairs,* 73, No. 1, January–February 1994, 44–55.

(Various issues of the following periodicals also were used in the preparation of this chapter: *Christian Science Monitor;* Foreign Broadcast Information Service, *Daily Report: Central Eurasia;* Jamestown Foundation, *Monitor* and *Prism; New York Times; Transition* [Prague]; and *Washington Post.*)

Chapter 8

Adams, Jan S. *A Foreign Policy in Transition: Moscow's Retreat from Central America and the Caribbean, 1985–1992.* Durham: Duke University Press, 1992.

Adams, Jan S. "Who Will Make Russia's Foreign Policy in 1994?" *RFE/RL Research Report* [Munich], 3, No. 6, February 11, 1994, 36–40.

Alexandrovna, Olga. "Divergent Russian Foreign Policy Concepts," *Aussenpolitik* [Bonn], No. 4, 1993, 363–72.

Allison, Roy. "Russian Peacekeeping: Capabilities and Doctrine," *Jane's Intelligence Review* [Coulsdon, United Kingdom], 6, December 1994, 544–47.

Arbatov, Alexei G. "Russia's Foreign Policy Alternatives," *International Security*, 18, Fall 1993, 5–43.

Blackwill, Robert D., and Sergei A. Karaganov, eds. *Damage Limitation or Crisis?: Russia and the Outside World.* Washington: Brassey's, 1994.

Blank, Stephen. *Challenging the New World Order: The Arms Transfer Policies of the Russian Republic.* Carlisle Barracks, Pennsylvania: U.S. Army War College Strategic Studies Institute, 1993.

Blank, Stephen. *The New Russia in the New Asia.* Carlisle Barracks, Pennsylvania: U.S. Army War College Strategic Studies Institute, 1994.

Blank, Stephen. "Russia's Real Drive to the South," *Orbis*, 39, No. 3, Summer 1995, 369–86.

Bogaturov, Alexei D. "Russia in Northeast Asia," *Korea and World Affairs*, 17, Summer 1993, 298–315.

Brusstar, James H. "Russian Vital Interests and Western Security," *Orbis*, 38, No. 4, Fall 1994, 607–19.

Brusstar, James H., and Ellen Jones. "Great Power Restorationists Make Gains in the Russian Duma," *Institute for National Strategic Studies Strategic Forum*, No. 65, March 1996.

Brusstar, James H., and Ellen Jones. *The Russian Military's Role in Politics.* (McNair Paper No. 34). Washington: National Defense University Institute for National Strategic Studies, 1995.

Brutents, Karen. "Russia and the East," *International Affairs* [Moscow], 70, January–February 1994, 40–44.

Brzezinski, Zbigniew. "The Premature Partnership," *Foreign Affairs*, 73, No. 2, March–April 1994, 67–82.

Cohen, Ariel. "The Empire That Would," *The World and I*, 10, May 1995, 30–35.

Crow, Suzanne. "Ambartsumov's Influence on Russian Foreign Policy," *RFE/RL Research Report* [Munich], 2, No. 18, May 7, 1993, 1–8.

Crow, Suzanne. *The Making of Foreign Policy in Russia under Yeltsin.* Munich: RFE/RL Research Institute, 1993.

Crow, Suzanne. "Russia Asserts Its Strategic Agenda," *RFE/RL Research Report* [Munich], 2, No. 50, December 17, 1993, 1–8.

Crow, Suzanne. "Why Has Russian Foreign Policy Changed?" *RFE/RL Research Report* [Munich], 3, No. 18, May 7, 1994, 1–6.

Dannreuther, Roland. "Russia, Central America, and the Persian Gulf," *Survival,* 35, Winter 1993–94, 92–112.

Dawisha, Adeed, and Karen Dawisha, eds. *The Making of Foreign Policy in Russia and the New States of Eurasia.* Armonk, New York: M.E. Sharpe, 1995.

Dawisha, Karen, and Bruce Parrott. "Foreign Policy Priorities and Institutions: Russia." Pages 198–207 in Karen Dawisha and Bruce Parrott, *Russia and the New States of Eurasia.* Cambridge: Cambridge University Press, 1994.

Dawisha, Karen, and Bruce Parrott. *Russia and the New States of Eurasia: The Politics of Upheaval.* Cambridge: Cambridge University Press, 1994.

Dick, Charles. "The Military Doctrine of the Russian Federation," *Jane's Intelligence Review* [Coulsdon, United Kingdom], 6, January 1994, 1–12.

Ellison, Herbert J. "Toward a New Realism," *The World & I,* 10, May 1995, 36–41.

Foye, Stephen. "Russo-Japanese Relations: Still Traveling a Rocky Road" *RFE/RL Research Report* [Munich], 2, No. 44, November 5, 1993, 27–34.

Fuller, Elizabeth. "Russian Strategy in the Transcaucasus since the Demise of the USSR," *Berichte des Bundesinstituts für ostwissenschaftliche und internationale Studien* [Cologne], 40, 1994.

Goldberg, David H., and Paul Marantz, eds. *The Decline of the Soviet Union and the Transformation of the Middle East.* Boulder, Colorado: Westview Press, 1994.

Halbach, Uwe, and Heinrich Tiller. "Russia and Its Southern Flank," *Aussenpolitik* [Bonn], 45, No. 2, 1994, 156–65.

Hee Lee, Chang. *Global Change and the Korean Peninsula.* Washington: Institute for Foreign Policy Analysis, 1993.

Hermann, Richard K. "Russian Policy in the Middle East: Strategic Change and Tactical Contradictions," *Middle East Journal,* 48, Summer 1994, 455–74.

Holden, Gerard. *Russia after the Cold War: History and the Nation in Post-Soviet Security Politics.* Boulder, Colorado: Westview Press, 1994.

Holmes, Leslie. "Russia's Relations with the Former External Empire." Pages 123–41 in Amin Saikal and William Maley, eds., *Russia in Search of Its Future*. Cambridge: Cambridge University Press, 1995.

Hudson, George E. "Russia's Search for Identity in the Post-Cold-War World," *Mershon International Studies Review*, 38, October 1994, 235–40.

Jackson, William D. "Imperial Temptations: Ethnics Abroad," *Orbis*, 38, No. 1, Winter 1994, 1–17.

Johnson, Teresa Pelton, and Steven E. Miller, eds. *Russian Security after the Cold War: Seven Views from Moscow*. Washington: Brassey's, 1994.

Jones, Ellen, and James H. Brusstar. "Moscow's Emerging Security Decisionmaking System: The Role of the Security Council," *Journal of Slavic Military Studies*, 6, September 1993, 345–74.

Jonson, Lena. "The Foreign Policy Debate in Russia: In Search of a National Interest," *Nationalities Papers*, No. 1, Spring 1994, 175–93.

Kasatkin, Anatoliy. "Priorities and Other Components of Foreign Policy," *International Affairs* [Moscow], No. 12, 1994, 79–86.

Kim, Won Bae. "Sino-Russian Relations and Chinese Workers in the Russian Far East," *Asian Survey*, 34, December 1994, 1064–76.

Kortunov, Sergei, and Andrey Kortunov. "From 'Moralism' to 'Pragmatics': New Dimensions or Russian Foreign Policy," *Comparative Strategy*, 13, 1994, 261–76.

Kozyrev, Andrei. "The Lagging Partnership," *Foreign Affairs*, 73, No. 3, May–June 1994, 59–71.

Kozyrev, Andrei. "Partnership or Cold Peace?" *Foreign Policy*, No. 99, Summer 1995, 3–14.

Kullberg, Judith S. *The End of New Thinking?: Elite Ideologies and the Future of Russian Foreign Policy*. Columbus: Mershon Center, Ohio State University, 1993.

Lepingwell, John W. "The Russian Military and Security Policy in the 'Near Abroad,'" *Survival*, 36, Autumn 1994, 70–92.

Lough, Jean. "The Place of the 'Near Abroad' in Russian Foreign Policy," *RFE/RL Research Report* [Munich], 2, No. 10, March 12, 1993, 21–29.

Lugar, Richard G. "Assessing the Soviet Union and Eastern Europe in the 1990s," *Problems of Communism*, 41, January–April 1992, 76–80.

Lynch, Allen. "Postcommunist Political Dynamics: Ex Uno Plura," *RFE/RL Research Report* [Munich], 3, No. 1, January 7, 1994, 1–8.

Maksudov, Sergei, and William Taubman. "Russian-Soviet Nationality Policy and Foreign Policy." Pages 15–43 in Michael Mandelbaum, ed., *The Rise of Nations in the Soviet Union.* New York: Council on Foreign Relations Press, 1991.

Mandelbaum, Michael, ed. *The Rise of Nations in the Soviet Union.* New York: Council on Foreign Relations Press, 1991.

Mesbahi, Mohiaddin, ed. *Central Asia and the Caucasus after the Soviet Union: Domestic and International Dynamics.* Gainesville: University Press of Florida, 1994.

Mesbahi, Mohiaddin, ed. *Russia and the Third World in the Post-Soviet Era.* Gainesville: University Press of Florida, 1994.

Meyer, Peggy Falkenheim. "Moscow's Relations with Tokyo: Domestic Obstacles to a Territorial Agreement," *Asian Survey*, 33, October 1993, 953–67.

Mitchell, Nina. "Loose Cannon? The Russian Military in the Near Abroad," *Harvard International Review*, 16, Summer 1994, 40–41.

Nevers, Renee de. "Russia's Strategic Renovation," *Adelphi Papers*, No. 289, 1994.

Nichol, James P. *Diplomacy in the Former Soviet Republics.* Westport, Connecticut: Praeger, 1995.

Olcott, Martha Brill. "Sovereignty and the 'Near Abroad,'" *Orbis*, 39, Summer 1995, 353–67.

Polsky, Yury. "Russia's Policy Toward Israel," *Journal of South Asian and Middle Eastern Studies*, 27, Fall 1994, 19–35.

Pushkov, Alexei K. "Letter from Eurasia: Russia and America—the Honeymoon's Over," *Foreign Policy*, No. 93, Winter 1993, 76–90.

Rahr, Alexander. "New Faces and Old Priorities," *Transition* [Prague], 1, No. 1, February 15, 1995, 9–11.

Saikal, Amin. "Russia and Central Asia." Pages 142–56 in Amin Saikal and William Maley, eds., *Russia in Search of Its Future.* Cambridge: Cambridge University Press, 1995.

Saikal, Amin, and William Maley. "From Soviet to Russian Foreign Policy." Pages 102–22 in Amin Saikal and William Maley, eds., *Russia in Search of Its Future.* Cambridge: Cambridge University Press, 1995.

Saikal, Amin, and William Maley, eds. *Russia in Search of Its Future.* Cambridge: Cambridge University Press, 1995.

Sestanovich, Stephen. "Andrei the Giant," *New Republic,* 210, April 11, 1994, 24–27.

Sestanovich, Stephen, ed. *Rethinking Russia's National Interests.* Washington: Center for Strategic and International Studies, 1994.

Shearman, Peter, ed. *Russian Foreign Policy since 1990.* Boulder, Colorado: Westview Press, 1995.

Slagle, James H. "New Russian Military Doctrine: Sign of the Times," *Parameters,* 24, Spring 1994, 88–89.

Smith, Mark. *Pax Russica: Russia's Monroe Doctrine.* London: Royal United Services Institute for Defence Studies, 1993.

Stoessinger, John George. *Nations at Dawn—China, Russia, and America.* New York: McGraw-Hill, 1994.

Sudarev, Vladimir P. "Russia and Latin America," *Hemisphere,* 5, Winter–Spring 1993, 12–14.

Szporluk, Roman. "Belarus, Ukraine, and the Russian Question: A Comment," *Post-Soviet Affairs,* 9, October–December 1993, 366–74.

Szporluk, Roman. "Soviet Domestic Foreign Policy: Universal Ideology and National Tradition," *Nationalities Papers,* 22, Spring 1994, 195–207.

Teague, Elizabeth. "North-South Divide: Yeltsin and Russia's Provincial Leaders," *RFE/RL Research Report* [Munich], 2, No. 47, November 26, 1993, 7–23.

Timmermann, Heinz. "Russian Foreign Policy under Yeltsin: Priority for Integration into the 'Community of Civilized States,'" *Journal of Communist Studies,* 8, December 1992, 163–85.

Tolz, Vera. "Thorny Road Toward Federalism in Russia," *RFE/RL Research Report* [Munich], 2, No. 48, December 3, 1993, 1–8.

Tyurdenev, Vladimir. "Latin America and Russia," *International Affairs* [Moscow], No. 11, 1994, 31–37.

Valkenier, Elizabeth Kridl. "Russian Policies in Central Asia: Change or Continuity?" *SAIS Review,* 14, Summer–Fall 1994, 15–28.

Webber, Mark. "The Emergence of the Foreign Policy of the Russian Federation," *Communist and Post-Communist Studies,* 26, September 1993, 243–63.

Werner, Klaus. "Russia's Foreign Trade and the Economic Reforms," *Intereconomics,* 28, May–June 1993, 144–52.

Wittag, Gerhard. "Moscow's Perception of NATO's Role," *Aussenpolitik* [Bonn], No. 2, 1994, 123–33.

Yassman, Victor. "Five Different Perceptions on the Future of Russian Foreign Policy," *Demokratizatsiya,* No. 4, 1993, 84–95.

Zelikow, Philip. "Beyond Boris Yeltsin," *Foreign Affairs,* 73, No. 1, January–February 1994, 44–55.

(Various issues of the following periodicals also were used in the preparation of this chapter: *Christian Science Monitor;* Foreign Broadcast Information Service, *Daily Report: Central Eurasia;* Jamestown Foundation, *Monitor; New York Times; Prism;* and *Washington Post.*)

Chapter 9

Ahmedullah, Mohammed. "Renewing Indo-Russian Defence Cooperation," *Military Technology,* 22, No. 3, March 1996, 38–48.

Almquist, Peter. "Arms Producers Struggle to Survive as Defense Orders Shrink," *RFE/RL Research Report* [Munich], 2, No. 25, June 18, 1993, 33–41.

Benson, Sumner. "Will Moscow Use High-Tech to Remilitarize?" *Orbis,* 39, No. 3, Summer 1995, 403–16.

Billington, James H. *The Icon and the Axe: An Interpretive History of Russian Culture.* New York: Knopf, 1966.

Blank, Stephen. *Challenging the New World Order: The Arms Transfer Policies of the Russian Republic.* Carlisle Barracks, Pennsylvania: U.S. Army War College Strategic Studies Institute, 1993.

Bukharin, Oleg A. "Meeting the Challenges of Dismantlement," *Transition* [Prague], 1, No. 21, November 17, 1995, 30–33.

Clarke, Douglas L. "A Hollow Russian Military Force in Asia?" *Transition* [Prague], 1, No. 17, September 22, 1995, 24–27.

Clarke, Douglas L. "Rusting Fleet Renews Debate on Navy's Mission," *RFE/RL Research Report* [Munich], 2, No. 25, June 18, 1993, 25–32.

Cullin, Tony, and Christopher Foss, eds. *Jane's Land Based Air Defence 1993–94.* Coulsdon, United Kingdom: Jane's Information Group, 1993.

Dick, Charles. "The Military Doctrine of the Russian Federation," *Jane's Intelligence Review* [Coulsdon, United Kingdom], 6, January 1994, 1–12.

Dunlop, John B. "Russia: Confronting a Loss of Empire," *Political Science Quarterly,* 109, Winter 1993–94, 603–63.

Ford, Peter. "Young Russians Want Out of Their Own Brutal Army," *Christian Science Monitor,* 87, August 8, 1995, 1.

Foye, Stephen. "Civilian and Military Leaders in Russia's 'New' Political Arena," *RFE/RL Research Report* [Munich], 3, No. 15, April 15, 1994, 1–6.

Foye, Stephen. "A Hardened Stance on Foreign Policy," *Transition* [Prague], 1, No. 9, June 9, 1995, 36–40.

Foye, Stephen. "The Soviet Legacy," *RFE/RL Research Report* [Munich], 2, No. 25, June 18, 1993, 1–8.

Fuller, Elizabeth. "Stopping the Shooting Is Only Half the Battle," *Transition* [Prague], 2, No. 1, January 12, 1996, 22–24.

Glantz, David M. *Soviet and Commonwealth Military Doctrine in Revolutionary Times.* Ft. Leavenworth, Kansas: Foreign MilitaryStudies Office, 1992.

"Glasnost" Public Foundation. Public Investigation Commission. Round Table VI. *The War in Chechnya: Necessity of Holding an International Tribunal.* Moscow: 1995.

Glogan, Tim. "Russia to Pay Debt with SA–11 Missile Systems," *Jane's Defence Weekly* [Coulsdon, United Kingdom], 25, December 16, 1995, 9.

Grechko, Aleksandr. *The Armed Forces of the Soviet Union.* Moscow: Progress, 1977.

Gribincea, Mihai. "Rejecting a New Role for the Former 14th Russian Army," *Transition* [Prague], 2, No. 6, March 22, 1996, 38–40.

Handler, Joshua. "The Future of Russia's Strategic Forces," *Jane's Intelligence Review* [Coulsdon, United Kingdom], 7, April 1995, 162–65.

Heilbrunn, Jacob. "The Big East: A New Russian Empire," *New Republic,* 214, May 27, 1996, 22–24.

Heinrich, Andreas, and Heiko Pleines. "Russia's 'Nuclear Flea Market' Tempts Smugglers," *Transition* [Prague], 1, No. 21, 1995, 9–11.

Herspring, Dale R. "The Russian Military: Three Years On," *Communist and Post-Communist Studies,* 28, No. 2, June 1995, 163–82.

Hoff, Magdalene, and Heinz Tammerman. "Kaliningrad: Russia's Future Gateway to Europe?" *RFE/RL Research Report* [Munich], 2, No. 36, September 10, 1993.

Holcomb, James F. *Russian Military Doctrine.* Camberley, United Kingdom: Soviet Studies Research Centre, 1992.

Ingwerson, Marshall. "Russia's Army: A Loose Cannon in Power Transfer," *Christian Science Monitor,* 88, 138, June 12, 1996, 1.

Ionescu, Dan. "Russia's Long Arm and the Dniester Impasse," *Transition* [Prague], 1, No. 19, 1995, 14–15.

Joint Publications Research Service. *JPRS Report: Central Eurasia Military Affairs: Directory of Military Organizations and Personnel.* Washington: 1994.

Katz, Mark N. "Nationalism and the Legacy of Empire," *Current History,* 94, October 1995, 328–36.

Kogan, Yevgeni. "Russian Defence Conversion and Arms Exportation," *Peace Research Institute Frankfurt Reports* [Frankfurt-am-Main], No. 41, 1995.

Konovalov, Aleksandr. "Will Yeltsin Sacrifice His Defense Minister?" *Prism,* 2, No. 9, Pt. 3, May 3, 1996.

Lepingwell, John W.R. "Is the Military Disintegrating from Within?" *RFE/RL Research Report* [Munich], 2, No. 25, June 18, 1993, 9–16.

Lepingwell, John W.R. "Restructuring the Russian Military," *RFE/RL Research Report* [Munich], 2, No. 25, June 18, 1993, 17–24.

Lunev, Stanislav. "Future Changes in Russian Military Policy," *Prism,* 2, No. 3, Pt. 2, February 9, 1996, 1–5.

Lunev, Stanislav. "Russian Military Policy in the Transcaucasus," *Prism,* 2, No. 8, Pt. 4, April 19, 1996.

Mackenzie-Wallace, Donald F. *Russia on the Eve of War and Revolution.* New York: Random House, 1961.

Marshall-Hasdell, Dennis J. *Russian Airpower in Chechnya.* Camberly, United Kingdom: Conflict Studies Research Centre, 1996.

Mihalka, Michael. "Continued Resistance to NATO Expansion," *Transition* [Prague], 1, No. 14, August 11, 1995, 36–41.

The Military Balance, 1993–1994. London: Brassey's, 1993.

The Military Balance, 1994–1995. London: Brassey's, 1994.

The Military Balance, 1995–1996. London: Brassey's, 1995.

Orr, Michael. *The Russian Army and the War in Tajikistan.* Camberly, United Kingdom: Conflict Studies Research Centre, 1996.

Orttung, Robert. "Chechnya: A Painful Price," *Transition* [Prague], 1, No. 3, March 15, 1995, 3–10.

Oznobishchev, Sergei. "Russia Now Has Its Own 'National Security Policy,'" *Prism,* 2, No. 12, Pt. 3, June 14, 1996, 1–5.

Parrish, Scott. "Nuclear Arms: A Soviet Legacy," *Transition* [Prague], 1, No. 21, November 17, 1995, 6–8.

Parrish, Scott. "A Turning Point in the Chechen Conflict," *Transition* [Prague], 1, No. 15, July 28, 1995, 42–50.

Petersen, Phillip A., and Shane C. Petersen. "The Kaliningrad Garrison State," *Jane's Intelligence Review* [Coulsdon, United Kingdom], 5, February 1993, 59–62.

Plater-Zyberk, Henry. *Russia's Future Security: The Zhirinovskiy Factor.* Camberley, United Kingdom: Conflict Studies Research Centre, 1994.

Rutland, Peter, and Ustina Markus. "Russia as a Pacific Power," *Transition* [Prague], 1, No. 16, September 8, 1995, 4–7.

Slagle, James H. "New Russian Military Doctrine: Sign of the Times," *Parameters,* 24, Spring 1994, 88–89.

Socor, Vladimir. "The Fourteenth Army in Moldova: There to Stay?" *RFE/RL Research Report* [Munich], 2, No. 25, June 18, 1993, 42–49.

Staar, Richard F. "Beyond the Unipolar Moment: Moscow's Plans to Restore Its Power," *Orbis,* 40, No. 3, Summer 1996, 375–89.

Staar, Richard F. *The New Military in Russia: Ten Myths That Shape the Image.* Annapolis: Naval Institute Press, 1996.

Stockholm International Peace Research Center. *SIPRI Yearbook 1995: Armaments, Disarmament, and International Security.* New York: Oxford University Press, 1995.

Thomas, Timothy. "Fault Lines and Factions in the Russian Army," *Orbis*, 39, No. 4, Fall 1995, 531–48.

Turbiville, Graham H., Jr. *Mafia in Uniform: The Criminalization of the Russian Armed Forces*. Washington: Foreign Military Studies Office, 1996.

"World Defence Almanac 1995–96," *Military Technology* [Bonn], 20, No. 1, 1996.

World Directory of Defense Authorities. Bethesda, Maryland: Worldwide Government Directories, 1996.

(Various issues of the following periodicals also were used in the preparation of this chapter: *Defense News*; Foreign Broadcast Information Service, *Daily Report: Central Eurasia* and *Daily Report: Central Eurasia Military Affairs*; *Komsomol'skaya pravda* [Moscow]; *Krasnaya zvezda* [Moscow]; and *Washington Post*.)

Chapter 10

Albats, Yevgeniia. *The State Within a State: The KGB and Its Hold on Russia Today*. New York: Farrah, Strauss, Giroux, 1994.

"Crime and Corruption in Russia." Briefing on the Commission on Security and Cooperation in Europe. Washington: June 1994.

Fuller, Elizabeth. "Chechen Politics: A Murky Prospect," *Transition* [Prague], 1, No. 6, March 15, 1995, 11–13.

"Groping Ahead," *Economist* [London], 336, No. 7930, September 2, 1995, 42–48.

Handelman, Stephen. *Comrade Criminal: Russia's New Mafia*. New Haven: Yale University Press, 1994.

Handelman, Stephen. "The Russian 'Mafiya,'" *Foreign Affairs*, 73, No. 2, March-April 1994, 83–96.

Heritage Foundation. *Crime and Corruption in Eurasia: A Threat to Democracy and International Security*. Washington: 1995.

Ingwerson, Marshall. "Russia's Juries Give Police an O.J.-Style Rap," *Christian Science Monitor*, 88, No. 103, April 23, 1996.

Knight, Amy. *The KGB: Police and Politics in the Soviet Union*. Boston: Allen and Unwin, 1988.

Knight, Amy. "Russian Security Services under Yeltsin," *Post-Soviet Affairs*, 9, No. 1, 1993, 40–65.

Morvant, Penny. "Corruption Hampers War on Crime in Russia," *Transition* [Prague], 2, No. 6, March 8, 1996, 23–27.

Morvant, Penny. "War on Organized Crime and Corruption," *Transition* [Prague], 1, No. 4, February 15, 1995, 32–36.

"The Rise of Russia's Crime Commissars," *World Press Review*, 41, June 1994, 13–14.

Sterling, Claire. *Thieves' World. The Threat of the New Global Network of Organized Crime.* New York: Simon and Schuster, 1994.

Tolz, Vera, "The Moscow Crisis and the Future of Democracy in Russia," *RFE/RL Research Report* [Munich], 2, No. 42, October 22, 1993, 1–9.

Ulrich, Christopher J. "The Growth of Crime in Russia and the Baltic Region," *RFE/FL Research Report* [Munich], 3, No. 23, June 10, 1994, 24–32.

Ulrich, Christopher J. *The Price of Freedom: The Criminal Threat in Russia, Eastern Europe, and the Baltic Region.* Washington: Research Institute for the Study of Conflict and Terrorism, 1994.

United States. 104th Congress, 1st Session. Commission on Security and Cooperation in Europe. *Crisis in Chechnya.* Hearings Held January 19 and 27, 1995. Washington: GPO, 1995.

United States. Department of State. *Country Reports on Human Rights Practices for 1995.* Washington: GPO, 1995.

United States. Department of State. Bureau of International Narcotics Matters. *International Narcotics Control Strategy Report March 1996.* Washington: GPO, 1996.

Waller, J. Michael. *Secret Empire: The KGB in Russia Today.* Boulder, Colorado: Westview Press, 1994.

Wishnevsky, Julia. "Corruption Allegations Undermine Russia's Leaders," *RFE/RL Research Report* [Munich], 2, No. 37, September 17, 1993, 16–22.

Wishnevsky, Julia. "Manipulation, Mayhem, and Murder," *Transition* [Prague], 1, No. 6, February 15, 1995, 37–40.

Woff, Richard. "The Border Troops of the Russian Federation," *Jane's Intelligence Review* [Coulsdon, United Kingdom], 7, No. 2, February 1995, 70–73.

Zhdanov, Vladimir, and James Hughes. "Russia's 'Alpha Group' Changes with the Times," *Transition* [Prague], 2, No. 6, March 8, 1996, 28–31.

Zimmerman, Tim, and Alan Cooperman. "The Russian Connection," *U.S. News and World Report*, October 23, 1995, 56–67.

(Various issues of the following periodicals also were used in the preparation of this chapter: Foreign Broadcast Information Service, *Daily Report: Central Eurasia; Izvestiya* [Moscow]; *Keesings Record of World Events* [London]; *Komsomol'skaya Pravda* [Moscow]; *Moskovskiye Novosti* [Moscow]; *Nezavisimaya gazeta* [Moscow]; *Pravda* [Moscow]; and *Rossiyskaya gazeta* [Moscow]).

Glossary

Academy of Sciences (Akademiya nauk)—Russia's most prestigious scholarly institute, established in 1725 by Peter the Great. The Academy of Sciences has historically carried out long-range research and developed new technology. The Academy of Sciences of the Soviet Union conducted basic research in the physical, natural, mathematical, and social sciences. In 1991 Russia established its own academy for the first time in the Soviet era.

Anti-Ballistic Missile Treaty (ABM Treaty)—A 1972 agreement limiting deployment of United States and Soviet anti-ballistic missile (ABM) systems. A protocol signed in 1974 limited each party to a single ABM system deployment area. In 1996 the United States and Russia negotiated to modify the terms of the treaty in order to permit testing of technology against non-intercontinental delivery systems.

balance of payments—A record of receipts from and payments to the rest of the world by a country's government and its residents. The balance of payments includes the international financial transactions of a country for commodities, services, capital transactions, and gold movements.

balance of trade—A record of a country's trade in goods with the rest of the world. The balance of trade differs from the balance of payments (*q.v.*) because the latter includes transactions for services and the former does not. When the exports of merchandise exceed imports, a country is said to have a balance of trade surplus or to have a favorable balance of trade. When the imports of merchandise exceed exports, a country is said to have a balance of trade deficit or to have an unfavorable balance of trade.

Bank for International Standards (BIS)—Established in 1930 to assist national central banks in managing and investing monetary reserves and to promote international cooperation among those banks.

Bolshevik—Originally referring to a member of the majority (*bol'shinstvo*), a name adopted by the radical members of the Russian Social Democratic Labor Party in 1903. In March 1918, the Bolsheviks formed the Russian Communist Party (Bolshevik). That Party was the precursor of the Communist Party of the Soviet Union (CPSU—*q.v.*).

boyar—Between the tenth and seventeenth centuries, a member of the upper level of the nobility and state administration in Kievan Rus' and Muscovy. Abolished as a class by Peter the Great.

Brezhnev Doctrine—The Soviet Union's declared right to intervene in the internal affairs of another socialist state if the leading role of that state's communist party was threatened. Formulated as justification for the Soviet Union's invasion of Czechoslovakia in August 1968. Mikhail S. Gorbachev implicitly abandoned the Brezhnev Doctrine in 1989.

chernozem—Literally, black earth. A type of rich, black soil indigenous to large parts of Ukraine and southwestern Russia.

collective farm (*kollektivnoye khozyaystvo—kolkhoz*)—In the Soviet agricultural system, an agricultural "cooperative" where peasants, under the direction of party-approved plans and leaders, were paid wages based in part on the success of their harvest. Still in existence in the 1990s.

Commonwealth of Independent States (CIS)—Created on December 21, 1991, when eleven heads of state signed the Alma-Ata Declaration, expanding membership of the all-Slavic CIS established at Minsk two weeks earlier by Belarus, Russia, and Ukraine. The eight other members were Armenia, Azerbaijan, Kazakstan, Kyrgyzstan, Moldova, Tajikistan, Turkmenistan, and Uzbekistan. The CIS aims to coordinate intracommonwealth relations and oversee common interests of its members in economics, foreign policy, and defense matters. In October 1993, Georgia became the twelfth member of the CIS. Efforts to strengthen CIS authority and interaction generally have not been successful.

communism/communist—A doctrine based on revolutionary Marxist socialism (*q.v.*) and Marxism-Leninism (*q.v.*). As the official ideology of the Soviet Union, it provided for a system of authoritarian government in which the CPSU (*q.v.*) alone controlled state-owned means of production. Communism nominally sought to establish a society in which the state would wither away and goods and services would be distributed equitably.

Communist Party of the Soviet Union (CPSU)—The official name of the communist party in the Soviet Union after 1952. Originally the Bolshevik (*q.v.*) faction of the Russian

Social Democratic Labor Party, the party was named the Russian Communist Party (Bolshevik) from March 1918 to December 1925, then the All-Union Communist Party (Bolshevik) from December 1925 to October 1952. After the August 1991 Moscow coup, Russian president Boris N. Yeltsin banned the party in Russia and ordered its property turned over to the government.

Conference on Security and Cooperation in Europe (CSCE)— *See* Organization for Security and Cooperation in Europe.

Congress of People's Deputies—Established in 1988 by constitutional amendment, the highest organ of legislative and executive authority in the Soviet Union. As such, it elected the Supreme Soviet, the Soviet Union's standing legislative body. The Congress of People's Deputies elected in March–April 1989 consisted of 2,250 deputies. The congress ceased to exist with the demise of the Soviet Union.

Conventional Forces in Europe Treaty (CFE Treaty)—An agreement signed in November 1990 by the members of the North Atlantic Treaty Organization (NATO—*q.v.*) and the Warsaw Pact (*q.v.*) states. The CFE Treaty sets ceilings from the Atlantic to the Urals on armaments essential for conducting a surprise attack and initiating large-scale offensive operations. The treaty includes a strict system of inspection and information exchange. The CFE Treaty entered into force in November 1992.

Cossacks—Originally an amalgamation of runaway peasants, fugitive slaves, escaped convicts, and derelict soldiers, primarily Ukrainian and Russian, settling frontier areas along the Don, Dnepr, and Volga rivers. They supported themselves by brigandry, hunting, fishing, and cattle raising. Later the Cossacks organized military formations for their own defense and as mercenaries. The latter groups were renowned as horsemen and were absorbed as special units in the Russian army.

Council for Mutual Economic Assistance (Comecon; also CEMA or CMEA)—A multilateral economic alliance created in January 1949, ostensibly to promote economic development of member states and to provide a counterweight to the United States-sponsored Marshall Plan. Shortly before its demise in January 1991, organization members included Bulgaria, Cuba, Czechoslovakia, the German Democratic Republic (East Germany), Hungary, Mongolia, Poland, Romania, the Soviet Union, and

Vietnam.

Council of Europe—Founded in 1949, an organization overseeing intergovernmental cooperation in designated areas such as environmental planning, finance, sports, crime, migration, and legal matters. In 1995 the council had thirty-five members. Russia achieved membership in January 1996.

Cyrillic—An alphabet based on Greek characters that was created in the ninth century for translating Eastern Orthodox religious texts into Old Church Slavonic (*q.v.*). Named for Cyril, the leader of the first religious mission from Byzantium to the Slavic people, the alphabet is used in Russia, Belarus, Bulgaria, Ukraine, and Yugoslavia. The Central Asian republics, Moldova, and Azerbaijan used a modified Cyrillic alphabet in the Soviet period.

demokratizatsiya (democratization)—Campaign initiated in the late 1980s by Mikhail S. Gorbachev to expand the participation of a variety of interest groups in political processes.

duma (pl., *dumy*)—An advisory council to the princes of Kievan Rus' and the tsars of the Russian Empire.

Duma (In full, Gosudarstvennaya duma—State Assembly)—Lower chamber of the legislature of Russia, established by Nicholas II after the Revolution of 1905, and functioning until 1917. Unlike advisory bodies such as the boyar (*q.v.*) *dumy* of the Kievan Rus' period and city *dumy* of the nineteenth and early twentieth centuries, the Duma originally was to be a national representative body with the power to approve legislation. The first two Dumy (1905–07) were quickly dissolved because they opposed tsarist policies; the next two (1907–17) were more conservative and served full five-year terms.

East Slavs—A subdivision of Slavic peoples including Russians, Ukrainians, and Belarusians.

European Union (EU)—Successor organization to the European Community. Began official operation in November 1993 to promote the economic unification of Europe, leading to a single monetary system and closer cooperation in matters of justice and foreign and security policies. In 1995 members were Austria, Belgium, Britain, Denmark, Finland, France, Germany, Greece, Ireland, Italy, Luxembourg, the Netherlands, Portugal, Spain, and Sweden.

five-year plan—A comprehensive plan that set the middle-range economic goals in the Soviet Union. Once the Soviet regime stipulated plan figures, all levels of the economy, from individual enterprises to the national level, were obligated to meet those goals. Such plans were followed from 1928 until 1991.

General Agreement on Tariffs and Trade (GATT)—An integrated set of bilateral trade agreements among more than 100 contracting nations. Originally drawn up in 1947 to abolish quotas and reduce tariffs among members. The Soviet Union eschewed joining GATT until 1987, when it applied for membership. It achieved observer status in 1990. In January 1995, GATT became the World Trade Organization (WTO—*q.v.*).

general secretary—The title of the head of the Communist party Secretariat, who presided over the Politburo and was the Soviet Union's de facto supreme leader. From 1953 until 1966, the title was changed to first secretary.

glasnost—Russian term for public discussion of issues and accessibility of information to the public. Devised by Soviet leader Mikhail S. Gorbachev to provoke public discussion, challenge government and party bureaucrats, and mobilize support for his policies through the media.

Golden Horde—A federative Mongol state that extended from western Siberia to the Carpathian Mountains from the mid-thirteenth century to the end of the fifteenth century. Generally, it exacted tribute and controlled external relations but allowed local authorities to decide internal affairs.

Great Terror—A period from about 1936 to 1938 of intense repression in the Soviet Union when millions were imprisoned, deported, and executed by Stalin's secret police for spurious political or economic crimes. The Great Terror affected all of Soviet society, including the highest levels of the party, government, and military.

gross domestic product (GDP)—A measure of the total value of goods and services produced by the domestic economy during a given period, usually one year. Obtained by adding the value contributed by each sector of the economy in the form of profits, compensation to employees, and depreciation (consumption of capital). Only domestic production is included, not income arising from investments and possessions owned abroad.

gross national product (GNP)—The total market value of final goods and services produced by an economy during a year. Obtained by adding the gross domestic product (GDP— *q.v.*) and the income received from abroad by residents and subtracting payments remitted abroad to nonresidents. Real GNP is the value of GNP when inflation has been taken into account.

Group of Seven (G–7)—Formed in September 1985 to facilitate cooperation among the seven major noncommunist economic powers: Britain, Canada, France, Germany, Italy, Japan, and the United States. Russia took part in numerous G–7 meetings, and when Japan ended its opposition, Russia achieved full membership in the renamed G–8 in 1997.

hard currency—Currency freely convertible and traded on international currency markets.

Intermediate-Range Nuclear Force Treaty (INF Treaty)—A bilateral treaty signed in Washington in December 1987, eliminating United States and Soviet land-based missiles with ranges between 500 and 5,500 kilometers. Most of the Soviet missiles were deployed inside the Soviet Union; all of the United States missiles were in Belgium, Italy, the Federal Republic of Germany (West Germany), and Britain.

internal passport (*propiska*)—Government-issued document presented to officials on demand, identifying citizens and their authorized residence. Used in both the Russian Empire (*q.v.*) and the Soviet Union to restrict the movement of people. More limited use continued in some parts of Russia in the 1990s.

International Monetary Fund (IMF)—Established along with the World Bank (*q.v.*) in 1945, the IMF has regulatory surveillance and financial functions that apply to its more than 150 member countries. The IMF is responsible for stabilizing international exchange rates and payments. Its main function is to provide loans to its members (including industrialized and developing countries) when they experience balance of payments (*q.v.*) difficulties. These loans frequently have conditions that require substantial internal economic adjustments by the recipients, most of which are developing countries.

KGB (Komitet gosudarstvennoy bezopasnosti)—Committee for State Security. The predominant Soviet agency for espionage and internal security since 1954. After the dissolution of the Soviet Union, Russia inherited the central agency in Moscow. Governments of other former Soviet republics took over KGB property on their territory.

kolkhoz—*See* collective farm.

kray (territory)—Term for six widely dispersed administrative subdivisions whose boundaries are laid out primarily for ease of administration. Two include subdivisions based on nationality groups—one autonomous oblast (*q.v.*) and two autonomous regions (*okruga*—*q.v.*).

kremlin (*kreml'*)—Central citadel in many medieval Russian towns, usually located at a strategic spot along a river. Moscow's Kremlin is the seat and symbol of the Russian government.

Lisbon Protocol—Agreement that implemented the first phase of the Strategic Arms Reduction Treaty (START—*q.v.*) after the collapse of the Soviet Union. The protocol is an amendment to the START agreement by which Russia, Ukraine, Belarus, and Kazakstan undertook the Soviet Union's obligations under START I.

Marshall Plan—A plan announced in June 1947 by United States secretary of state George Marshall for the reconstruction of Europe after World War II. The plan was extended to all European countries, but the Soviet Union refused the offer and forbade the East European countries to accept aid under the Marshall Plan. As a counterweight, the Soviet Union created the Council for Mutual Economic Assistance (Comecon—*q.v.*).

Marxism/Marxist—The economic, political, and social theories of Karl Marx, a nineteenth-century German philosopher and socialist, especially his concept of socialism (*q.v.*).

Marxism-Leninism/Marxist-Leninist—The ideology of communism (*q.v.*) developed by Karl Marx and refined and adapted to social and economic conditions in Russia by Vladimir I. Lenin. Marxism-Leninism was the guiding ideology for the Soviet Union and its satellites.

Menshevik—A member of a wing of the Russian Social Democratic Labor Party that existed until 1917. Unlike the Bolsheviks (*q.v.*), the Mensheviks believed in the gradual achievement of socialism (*q.v.*) by parliamentary methods. The term Menshevik is derived from the word *men'shinstvo* (minority).

near abroad (*blizhneye zarubezh'ye*)—Collective Russian term for the other fourteen newly independent states of the former Soviet Union. Frequently used in policy discussions about Russia's continued domination of certain of those states, especially in Central Asia and the Caucasus.

New Economic Policy (Novaya ekonomicheskaya politika— NEP)—Instituted in 1921, it let peasants sell produce on an open market and permitted private ownership of small enterprises. Cultural restrictions also were relaxed during this period. NEP declined with the introduction of collectivization and was officially ended by Joseph V. Stalin in December 1929.

nomenklatura—The communist party's system of appointing reliable party members to key government positions and other important organizations. Also refers to the individuals as a social group.

North Atlantic Treaty Organization (NATO)—Founded in 1949, NATO served as the primary collective defense alliance in the containment of Soviet expansionism. Its military and administrative structure remain intact. The question of expanding NATO to include former Warsaw Pact (*q.v.*) members and successor states to the Soviet Union became a key issue in Russian foreign policy in the mid-1990s. In 1994 the alliance introduced a program for the former Soviet republics and the former Warsaw Pact countries called Partnership for Peace (*q.v.*).

Nuclear Nonpoliferation Treaty (NPT; full title Treaty on the Nonproliferation of Nuclear Weapons)—Went into effect in 1970 to prevent the spread of nuclear weapons and promote the peaceful uses of nuclear energy over a period of twenty-five years. In May 1995, it was extended indefinitely. Only thirteen countries have not joined the NPT.

oblast—A major territorial and administrative subdivision in the newly independent states. Russia has forty-nine such divisions, which approximate provinces.

okrug (pl., *okruga*)—An autonomous territorial and administrative subdivision of a territory (*kray*—*q.v.*) or oblast (*q.v.*) in the Russian Federation that grants a degree of administrative autonomy to a nationality; most are in remote, sparsely populated areas. In 1997 the Russian Federation had ten such jurisdictions.

Old Believers—A sect of the Russian Orthodox Church that rejected the liturgical reforms made by Patriarch Nikon in the mid-seventeenth century.

Old Church Slavonic (also known as Old Church Slavic)—The first Slavic literary language, which influenced the development of the modern Slavic languages, including literary Russian. Used in liturgies of the Slavic Orthodox churches. After the twelfth century, known as Church Slavonic.

Organisation for Economic Co-operation and Development (OECD)—Founded by Western nations in 1961 to stimulate economic progress and world trade. It also coordinated economic aid to less developed countries. In late 1996, twenty-eight nations were members, and Russia had been invited to join at an unspecified date.

Organization for Security and Cooperation in Europe (OSCE)—Established as the Conference on Security and Cooperation in Europe (CSCE) in July 1972 by Canada, the United States, and all of the European states except Albania. In August 1975, these states signed the Helsinki Accords, confirming existing, post-World War II boundaries and obligating signatories to respect basic principles of human rights. Subsequently the CSCE held sessions and consultations on European security issues. The Charter of Paris (1990) established the CSCE as a permanent organization. In 1992 new CSCE roles in conflict prevention and management were defined, potentially making the CSCE the center of a Europe-based collective security system—a role advocated by Russia in the mid-1990s. The CSCE became the OSCE in January 1995. As of 1996, fifty-three nations were members.

Partnership for Peace (PfP)—An initiative by NATO (*q.v.*) for the former Warsaw Pact (*q.v.*) member countries and the former Soviet republics, including Russia, to expand political and military cooperation and promote democratic principles in those countries. PfP aims to facilitate transparency in defense planning and budgeting, ensure democratic control of defense forces, maintain readiness to contribute to United Nations and OSCE (*q.v.*) operations, and develop cooperative military relations with NATO for peacekeeping, search-and-rescue, and humanitarian operations. All former Soviet and Warsaw Pact states were members by 1996, and many had conducted joint military exercises with NATO forces.

patriarch—Head of an independent Orthodox Church, such as the Russian Orthodox Church or one of the Uniate (*q.v.*) churches.

perestroika—Literally, rebuilding. Mikhail Gorbachev's campaign to revitalize the communist party, the Soviet economy, and Soviet society by reforming economic, political, and social mechanisms.

permafrost—Permanently frozen condition of soil except for surface soils that thaw when air temperatures rise above freezing. Thawing and refreezing cause instability of the soil, which greatly complicates the construction and maintenance of roads, railroads, and buildings. Permafrost covers roughly the northern one-third of the Russian Federation.

rayon—A low-level territorial and administrative subdivision for rural and municipal administration. A rural *rayon* is a county-sized district in a territory (*kray—q.v.*), oblast (*q.v.*), republic (*q.v.*), region (*okrug—q.v.*), or autonomous oblast. A city *rayon* is similar to a borough in some large cities in the United States.

republic—A territorial and administrative subdivision of the Russian Federation created to grant a degree of administrative autonomy to some large minority groups. In 1996 the Russian Federation had twenty-one republics (before 1992 called autonomous republics), including the war-torn Republic of Chechnya.

ruble—The monetary unit of the Soviet Union and the Russian Federation; divided into 100 kopeks. The exchange rate as of July 1997 was 5,790 rubles per US$1. Historically, the ruble has not been considered hard currency (*q.v.*). It became convertible on the international market in June 1996.

ruble zone—Name given the group of newly independent states that continued to use the Soviet, then Russian, ruble as the primary currency for financial transactions after the collapse of the Soviet Union. The ruble zone existed from December 1991 until July 1993, when the Russian Central Bank withdrew all ruble notes issued before January 1993.

Russian Empire—Successor state to Muscovy. Formally proclaimed by Tsar Peter the Great in 1721 and significantly expanded during the reign of Catherine II, becoming a major multinational state. The empire's political structure collapsed with the revolution of February 1917, but most of its territory was included in the Soviet Union, which was established in 1922.

Russian Soviet Federated Socialist Republic (Rossiyskaya

Sovetskaya Federativnaya Sotsialisticheskaya Respublika—
RSFSR). Official name of the largest of the fifteen union
republics of the Soviet Union. Inhabited predominantly by
Russians, the RSFSR comprised approximately 75 percent
of the area of the Soviet Union, about 62 percent of its
population, and more than 60 percent of its economic output.

serf—Peasant legally bound to the land. Serfs were emanci-
pated by Tsar Alexander II in 1861.

Slavophiles—Members of the Russian intelligentsia in the mid-
nineteenth century who advocated the preservation of
Slavic, and specifically Russian, culture rather than opening Russian society and institutions to the influences of
West European culture. Philosophically opposed to Westernizers (*q.v.*).

socialism/socialist—According to Marxism-Leninism (*q.v.*), the
first phase of communism (*q.v.*). A transition from capitalism in which the means of production are state owned and
whose guiding principle is "from each according to his
abilities, to each according to his work." Soviet socialism
bore scant resemblance to the democratic socialism that
some West European countries adopted in the twentieth
century.

sovkhoz—*See* state farm.

state farm (*sovetskoye khozyaystvo*—*sovkhoz*)—A government-
owned and government-managed agricultural enterprise
where workers are paid salaries. Still in existence in 1997.

Strategic Arms Reduction Treaty (START)—Name of two treaties. START I, signed in July 1991 by the Soviet Union and
the United States, significantly reduced limits for the two
parties' intercontinental ballistic missiles (ICBMs) and
their associated launchers and warheads; submarine-
launched ballistic missile launchers and warheads; and
heavy bombers and their armaments, including long-range
nuclear air-launched cruise missiles. START II, signed in
January 1993 by Russia and the United States but still
unratified by Russia in mid-1997, further reduced strategic
offensive arms of both sides by eliminating all ICBMs with
multiple-warhead independently targeted reentry vehicles
(MIRVs) and reducing the overall total of warheads for
each side to between 3,000 and 3,500. In 1997 an important part of Russia's debate over future military and foreign policy.

taiga—The extensive, sub-Arctic evergreen forest of the Soviet Union. The taiga, the largest of the five primary natural zones, lies south of the tundra (*q.v.*).

territory—*See kray.*

tundra—The treeless plain within the Arctic Circle that has low-growing vegetation and permanently frozen subsoil (permafrost—*q.v.*). The northernmost of the five primary natural zones of the Soviet Union.

Uniate—A branch of the Roman Catholic Church that preserves the Eastern Rite (Orthodox) liturgy and discipline but recognizes papal authority.

Union of Soviet Socialist Republics (USSR)—Successor state to the Russian Empire. Officially founded by Vladimir I. Lenin, head of the Russian Communist Party (Bolshevik), in 1922. Dissolved on December 25, 1991.

value-added tax (VAT)—A tax applied to the additional value created at a given stage of production and calculated as a percentage of the difference between the product value at that stage and the cost of all materials and services purchased or introduced as inputs.

Warsaw Pact—Political-military alliance founded by the Soviet Union in 1955 as a counterweight to NATO (*q.v.*). Members included Bulgaria, Czechoslovakia, the German Democratic Republic (East Germany), Hungary, Poland, Romania, and the Soviet Union. Served as the Soviet Union's primary mechanism for keeping political and military control over Eastern Europe. Disbanded in March 1991.

Westernizers—Russian intellectuals in the mid-nineteenth century who emphasized Russia's cultural ties with the West as a vital element in the country's modernization and development. Opposed by the Slavophiles (*q.v.*).

White armies—Various noncommunist military forces that attempted to overthrow the Bolshevik (*q.v.*) regime during the Civil War (1918–21). Operating with no unified command, no clear political goal, and no supplies from the Russian heartland, they were defeated piecemeal by the Red Army.

World Bank—Name used to designate a group of four affiliated international institutions that provide advice on long-term finance and policy issues to developing countries: the International Bank for Reconstruction and Development (IBRD), the International Development Association

(IDA), the International Finance Corporation (IFC), and the Multilateral Investment Guarantee Agency (MIGA). The IBRD, established in 1945, has the primary purpose of providing loans to developing countries for productive projects. The IDA, a legally separate loan fund administered by the staff of the IBRD, was set up in 1960 to furnish credits to the poorest developing countries on much easier terms than those of conventional IBRD loans. The IFC, founded in 1956, supplements the activities of the IBRD through loans and assistance designed specifically to encourage the growth of productive private enterprises in the less developed countries. The president and certain senior officers of the IBRD hold the same positions in the IFC. The MIGA, which began operating in June 1988, insures private foreign investment in developing countries against such noncommercial risks as expropriation, civil strife, and inconvertibility. The four institutions are owned by the governments of the countries that subscribe their capital. To participate in the World Bank group, member states must first belong to the International Monetary Fund (IMF—*q.v.*).

World Trade Organization (WTO)—The legal and institutional foundation of the multilateral trading system and successor to the General Agreement on Tariffs and Trade (GATT—*q.v.*) as of January 1, 1995. The WTO acts as a forum for multinational trade negotiations, administers dispute settlements, reviews the trade policies of member nations, and works with organizations such as the International Monetary Fund (*q.v.*) and the World Bank (*q.v.*) in developing coherent global economic policies. The WTO also covers new commercial activities beyond the jurisdiction of GATT, such as intellectual property rights, services, and investment. Russia sought membership in 1996, but it had not been accepted as of mid-1997.

Yalta Conference—Meeting of Josph V. Stalin, Winston Churchill, and Franklin D. Roosevelt in February 1945 that redrew post-World War II national borders and established spheres of influence in Europe.

Index

Prudnikov, Viktor, 544
Prussia (*see also* Germany): and partition
of Poland, 25; in Quadruple Alliance,
30; relations with, 37, 38
Pskov, 12
Pskov Oblast: population growth, 157
publishing: private, 227–28; samizdat,
226, 227
Pugachev, Emel'yan, 26
Pugachev Uprising, 26
Pugo, Boris, 117
purges: cultural, 82; in Eastern Europe,
84; of Jews, 218; by KGB, lix, 556; of
party, 82; of Politburo, 67; under Sta-
lin, 56, 70–71, 72–74, 82, 84, 493
Pushkin, Aleksandr, 32, 224–25
Putoran Mountains, 131
Pyatigorsk: hostage crisis in, 571

Quaker missionaries, 210
The Quiet Don (Sholokhov), 226
Qizilqum Desert: expansion of, 144
Ququon (Kokand) Khanate: annexed, 38

Rabin, Oskar, 234
Rachmaninov, Sergey, 229
radio, 371–72; programming, 371, 424–
25; sets, number of, 372, 424; in Soviet
system, 423; transmission operations,
371
Radishchev, Aleksandr, 27, 224
Rahmonov, Imomali, xciv
railroads, 359–60; construction, 44, 48;
debts to, cv; development, 34, 36, 41,
42; network, 34, 359; reform, cv
Rapallo, Treaty of (1922), 69
Rasputin, 51; assassinated, 51
Rastrelli, Bartolomeo, 232-33
Razin, Stenka, 18
RCB. *See* Russian Central Bank
Reagan, Ronald W., 99–100; summit
meetings with Gorbachev, 102–3, 454–
55
reconstruction, 81–82
Red Army, 492; casualties in, 493; in Civil
War, 62; communists in, 492; purges
in, 493; terror by, 64–65; under
Trotsky, 62
Red Terror, 64–65
reform: under Alexander II, 34–37;

under Catherine II, 26–27; demands
for, 4–5; under Gorbachev, 57, 102,
109–12; under Khrushchev, 85–86,
90–91; under Nicholas II, 5; under
Peter the Great, 21–23; in Poland, 25;
resistance to, 47–48, 388; under
Stolypin, 46–47; under Yeltsin, liv,
lxxvi, 388
refugees (*see also* immigration; migration): from Chechnya, lxxxi, 200; geographic distribution, 166–67, 200;
illegal, 162; laws on, 163; number, 162,
164; origins, 162; registration, 163;
resentment toward, 165; support for,
163
Regent, Tat'yana, 255
religion (*see also under individual sects*),
lxiv–lxv, 202–20; animist, 186; under
Bolsheviks, 206–7; under Brezhnev,
98; censorship of, 37; and foreign policy, 220; freedom of, 172, 202–3, 211,
420; under Gorbachev, 208; influences
on, 171; under Khrushchev, 207; in
Kievan Rus', 7, 173; persecution of, 37,
75, 206, 212; practice, 98, 171; restrictions on, cvi–cvii, 211; revival, xcvi,
207–8; under Stalin, 75
Repin, Il'ya, 233
Republican Party, 255
reservoirs, 133–34, 145
Revolution of 1905, 4–5, 44–45; origins,
45
revolutionary movements, 40–41; under
Alexander II, 30, 40; Decembrist, 30–
31; Jews in, 217
Rimskiy-Korsakov, Nikolay, 228
The Rite of Spring (Stravinskiy), 229, 231
rivers: geographic distribution of, 133; in
Siberia, 129; transportation on, 363
roads, 359; maintenance, 359; network,
359
Rodionov, Igor', lviii, lix, lxxix, cii, 526
Rodionov, Petr, cvi
Roma (Gypsies), 193–94; discrimination
against, 193–94; occupations, 193; origins, 192–93; population, 192; Russka,
193; Vlach, 193
Roman Catholic Church, lxv; and ecu-
menism, 211
Roman Catholicism: missionaries, 210
Roman Catholics: in Russian Federation,
213; in Russian Empire, 28

183; in Khakassia, 190; in Komi, 184; as majority ethnic group, liv, 153, 171, 176, 386, 408, 453; in Mari El, 186; in Mordovia, 186; nationalism of, 113, 115–16; in near abroad, 124, 433, 435, 448, 451, 452, 453, 508, 509; in North Ossetia, 182; origins, 9, 174; in Russian Federation, 124, 153; in Sakha, 190; in Tatarstan, 187; in Tyva, 191; in Udmurtia, 188

Russian People's Friendship University, 265

Russian People's Republican party, lxxx

Russian Poland. *See* Poland, Kingdom of

Russian Public Television (ORT), 371, 425

Russian Republic: borders, 63, 64; declaration of sovereignty, 116, 386–87; nationality issues in, 115–16; distribution of power in, 409–10; in Soviet Union, 55, 66; Virgin Lands campaign in, 90–91

Russian River Fleet, 363

Russian Social Democratic Labor Party (*see also* Bolsheviks; Mensheviks; Russian Communist Party [Bolshevik]), 42; factions of, 43, 59; party congresses, 43; in Petrograd Soviet, 59

Russian State Insurance Company (Rosgosstrakh): privatized, 317

Russian State Television, 371; privatized, 371

Russian Telecommunications (Rostelekom), lxix–lxx, 368

Russian Women's Party, 255

Russia-United States International Space Station, lxxiv

Russification, 116; and language, 221; of nationalities, 37; origins, 26; by religion, 207; resistance to, 4

Russia's Choice party (*see also* Russia's Democratic Choice), 149, 416

Russia's Democratic Choice party (*see also* Russia's Choice), 150, 419; in 1995 elections, 419

Russo-Japanese War (1904–05), 4, 43–44, 471, 491

Rutskoy, Aleksandr, lxxxiv, 417; as president, 390

Rutul people, 179

Ryazan', 12

Rybinsk Reservoir, 133

Rybkin, Ivan, lxxx, 417

Rybkin bloc, 417

Ryzhkov, Nikolay, 106

Sadko (Rimskiy-Korsakov), 228

Sagalayev, Eduard, 425

St. Basil's Cathedral, 232

St. Petersburg (*see also* Leningrad), 126; architecture, 232–33; birthrate, 268; climate, 135; construction of, 23; crime, 572–73; defense industry, 515; HIV infection rate, 274; industry, 34, 354; pollution in, lxii, 139; population, 154, 160; power sharing by, 411; status, 409; subway system, 364

St. Petersburg Maritime Port, 363; privatized, 317

St. Petersburg nuclear reactor, 337

St. Petersburg State University, 265

St. Petersburg Television, 371

Sakha, Republic of (Yakutia), 126, 175, 190; area, 190; economy, 190; ethnic groups, 190; natural resources, lxii, 190, 197; population, 157, 190; sovereignty, lv, 197, 414

Sakhalin Island: ceded to Japan, 44, 471; Koreans in, 192

Sakharov, Andrey: in Interregional Group, 110

salinization, 138

SALT. *See* Strategic Arms Limitation Talks

Saltykov-Shchedrin, Mikhail, 225

Salvation Army: homeless services, 293; missionaries, 210

Samara: pollution in, 139; population, 154; subway system, 364

samizdat, 226, 227

Samsonov, Viktor, cii

San Stefano, Treaty of (1878), 39

Saratov: immigration to, 165

Saudi Arabia: relations with, 105, 478; visits to, 479

Savings Bank (Sberbank), 340; branches, 344; reorganized, 343

Sayan Aluminum, 352

Sayan Mountains, 130

Sberbank. *See* Savings Bank

Scheherezade (Rimskiy-Korsakov), 228

Schnittke, Alfred, 230

schools: business, 265–66; curricula, 36,

Contributors

William Baxter is an analyst of Central Eurasian military affairs for BDM Federal, Inc.

William Cooper is a specialist in international trade and finance for the Congressional Research Service, Library of Congress.

Glenn E. Curtis is senior research analyst for Central Eurasia and Central Europe in the Federal Research Division, Library of Congress.

David M. Goldfrank is professor of history at Georgetown University.

Amy W. Knight has published several monographs on the internal security organizations of the Soviet Union and Russia.

Zenon E. Kohut is director of the Canadian Institute for Ukrainian Studies at the University of Alberta.

Marian Leighton is an independent researcher on Soviet and Russian affairs.

David McClave is an independent researcher on Soviet and Russian affairs.

James P. Nichol is a specialist in Central Eurasia for the Congressional Research Service, Library of Congress.

Thomas Skallerup is a former research analyst in Soviet affairs in the Federal Research Division, Library of Congress.

Published Country Studies

(Area Handbook Series)

550–65	Afghanistan	550–36	Dominican Republic
550–98	Albania		and Haiti
550–44	Algeria	550–52	Ecuador
550–59	Angola	550–43	Egypt
550–73	Argentina	550–150	El Salvador
550–111	Armenia, Azerbaijan, and Georgia	550-113	Estonia, Latvia, and Lithuania
550–169	Australia	550–28	Ethiopia
550–176	Austria	550–167	Finland
550–175	Bangladesh	550–173	Germany
550–112	Belarus and Moldova	550–153	Ghana
550–170	Belgium	550–87	Greece
550–66	Bolivia	550–78	Guatemala
550–20	Brazil	550–174	Guinea
550–168	Bulgaria	550–82	Guyana and Belize
550–61	Burma	550–151	Honduras
550–50	Cambodia	550–165	Hungary
550–166	Cameroon	550–21	India
550–159	Chad	550–154	Indian Ocean
550–77	Chile	550–39	Indonesia
550–60	China	550–68	Iran
550–26	Colombia	550–31	Iraq
550–33	Commonwealth Caribbean, Islands of the	550–25	Israel
		550–182	Italy
550–91	Congo	550–30	Japan
550–90	Costa Rica	550–34	Jordan
550–69	Côte d'Ivoire (Ivory Coast)	550–114	Kazakstan, Kyrgyzstan, Tajikistan, Turkmenistan, and Uzbekistan
550–152	Cuba		
550–22	Cyprus	550–56	Kenya
550–158	Czechoslovakia	550–81	Korea, North

550–41	Korea, South	550–37	Rwanda and Burundi
550–58	Laos	550–51	Saudi Arabia
550–24	Lebanon	550–70	Senegal
550–38	Liberia	550–180	Sierra Leone
550–85	Libya	550–184	Singapore
550–172	Malawi	550–86	Somalia
550–45	Malaysia	550–93	South Africa
550–161	Mauritania	550–95	Soviet Union
550–79	Mexico	550–179	Spain
550–76	Mongolia	550–96	Sri Lanka
550–49	Morocco	550–27	Sudan
550–64	Mozambique	550–47	Syria
550–35	Nepal and Bhutan	550–62	Tanzania
550–88	Nicaragua	550–53	Thailand
550–157	Nigeria	550–89	Tunisia
550–94	Oceania	550–80	Turkey
550–48	Pakistan	550–74	Uganda
550–46	Panama	550–97	Uruguay
550–156	Paraguay	550–71	Venezuela
550–185	Persian Gulf States	550–32	Vietnam
550–42	Peru	550–183	Yemens, The
550–72	Philippines	550–99	Yugoslavia
550–162	Poland	550–67	Zaire
550–181	Portugal	550–75	Zambia
550–160	Romania	550–171	Zimbabwe
550–115	Russia